PRAISE FOR

The Owner's Manual for the Brain

66 *A WONDERFUL COMBINATION OF COFFEE-TABLE BOOK,* engaging and informative reading experience, and handy reference. It provides fascinating insight into the workings of the brain and their implications. Howard, like Carl Sagan, may be thought of as a popularizer who presents real science in an engaging and entertaining way. 99

Booklist

66 *I WAS SURPRISED TO FIND* that what had started at ten at night as a quick scan ended about three the following morning. Simply put, this is good stuff. Complex subject matter is presented in a simple, straightforward, graphically appealing manner. And all of it is organized to help you deal not only with your role in business, but also your roles as spouse, parent, child, and friend. 99

Working Smart newsletter

66 *EDUCATES WITHOUT PAIN!* A virtual cornucopia of practical suggestions guaranteed to maximize our potential—a valuable tool for leaders at all levels. 99

Rick Bradley
Senior Vice President, Learning & Organization Effectiveness
Bank of America, Charlotte, North Carolina

66 *IF YOU WORK WITH PEOPLE IN ANY CAPACITY*—as a leader, a trainer, a teacher, or simply as a fellow passenger through life—this book will bring you invaluable insight and information. It's all in here: how we're wired, how we react, what makes us motivated, stressed, or inspired. As an add-on bonus . . . this is serious research written in a highly readable and enjoyable format! 99

Cris Wildermuth, M.Ed.
International Consultant—North, Central, and South America

" *A SCIENTIFICALLY SOUND, WELL-WRITTEN, AND ENTERTAINING REVIEW* of the many central nervous system influences that affect the way we feel and function. As a practicing physician, I believe that this book will provide my patients with extremely useful information that will help them lead happier and more productive lives. **"**

David Lefkowitz III, M.D.

" *NICELY ORGANIZED AND HIGHLY USEFUL COMPENDIUM* . . . with suggestions for the reader's personal and professional life. It's rare to find a useful book that's this entertaining and engaging. **"**

The Rotarian

" *COMPREHENSIVE, PRACTICAL, AND READER-FRIENDLY.* I have been using *The Owner's Manual for the Brain* in my psychotherapy, coaching and training practices, as part of the bibliotherapy for patients and clients—and also in my own personal life. It's an excellent source. **"**

Jose Renato M. Salles
Psychotherapist, Executive Coach and Organization Consultant
Sao Paulo, Brazil

" *A VARIETY OF IDEAS AND PERSPECTIVES* and some excellent reading lists for the general reader. **"**

Library Journal

" *AN OUTSTANDING AND VERY USER-FRIENDLY RESOURCE* packed with up-to-the-minute information. Whether you're a professional who needs easily accessible, current research on how we use our brains or an intellectually curious person who wants to browse, there's something here for you. **"**

Janice M. Gamache, Ed.D.
Executive Coach, Alexandria, Virginia

> *MY COPY OF* THE OWNER'S MANUAL FOR THE BRAIN is dog-eared and dilapidated from continual use, marked and scribbled in from front to back. It accompanies me on every flight around the world, and to every meeting. It is on my desk whenever I design a change program or training for a company, write an article, or prepare for a presentation. It provides helpful arguments and solutions that are very useful for a consultant or coach.

Rob Geurtsen
Partner, Paragon Consulting
Amsterdam, Santa Cruz, Vail

> *A SUCCINCT, RESEARCH-BASED BOOK* essential for corporate leaders.

Shirley Lim
President, Research Communications International
Singapore

> *COMBINES AND INTERPRETS RESEARCH ON THE BRAIN* and its functioning in a very understandable fashion even for the lay reader—a very difficult task pulled off amazingly well. It will be a useful tool for people in many professions and with many frames of reference.

Richard Coop, Ph.D.
Sports Psychologist
The University of North Carolina at Chapel Hill
Author of *Mind over Golf*

> *PIERCE HOWARD CONVEYS THIS COMPLICATED SUBJECT IN PLAIN ENGLISH* so that 21st century managers can use the findings to acquire and leverage the best human capital—and help employees have the maximum opportunity to be successful in their assignments.

Jim Blasingame
Award-winning host of *The Small Business Advocate Show*
Author of *Three Minutes to Success*

❝ *CHOCK-FULL OF EVERYDAY APPLICATIONS OF BRAIN RESEARCH.* Well organized and presented, the book gives short summaries of the current state of knowledge in each area followed by numerous illustrations and practical tips. **❞**

Brain/Mind Bulletin

❝ *IT'S A JOY TO READ THIS BOOK*—like embarking on an exciting adventure. As a trainer and HR professional, it is helpful to know how to apply mind-brain research in the workplace. **❞**

Abdulrahman Al-Essa
Career Development Trainer
SABIC (Saudi Basic Industries Company), Saudi Arabia

❝ *IT HELPS INTRODUCE US TO OURSELVES.* Drawing upon the latest research on our own mental processes, Dr. Howard presents practical applications to help us develop our own potential as well as the potential of those with whom we live and work. **❞**

Stephen M. Stevick
Executive Director
The Sierra Club Foundation

❝ *A MUST-READ FOR EVERY MANAGER, TRAINER, AND PERSON* curious about the final frontier! An invaluable tool—full of practical features, insightful uses, and surprising benefits. **❞**

Chip R. Bell, Ph.D.
Coauthor (with Bilijack R. Bell) of *Magnetic Service*

❝ *THIS IS A TERRIFIC BOOK!* Not only is *The Owner's Manual for the Brain* one of the most practical, down-to-earth applications of research this reviewer has read, but it is so interesting. **❞**

Training and Development Journal

❝ *THE SUCCESSOR TO MAXWELL MATZ! The Owner's Manual for the Brain* can be a key to unlocking the rich and exciting potential of your mind. **❞**

Ty Boyd
Motivational Speaker

THE
Owner's Manual
FOR
TheBrain

Everyday Applications from Mind-Brain Research

THIRD EDITION

Pierce J. Howard, Ph.D.

Bard Press
AUSTIN

The Owner's Manual for the Brain
Everyday Applications from Mind-Brain Research

Bard Press
5275 McCormick Mtn. Dr.
Austin, Texas 78734
512-266-2112 voice
512-266-2749 fax
ray@bardpress.com
www.bardpress.com

ISBN 1-885167-64-4 paperback
ISBN 1-885167-65-2 cloth

Library of Congress Cataloging-in-Publication Data

Howard, Pierce J.
    The owner's manual for the brain : everyday applications from mind-brain research / Pierce J. Howard. — 3rd.
        p.   cm.
    Includes bibliographical references and index.
    ISBN 1-885167-65-2 (cloth) — ISBN 1-885167-64-4 (pbk.)
    1. Brain. 2. Neuropsychology. I. Title.
QP376.H76 2006
6.12.8'2–dc22   2006040778

The author may be contacted through

*Cent*ACS Center for Applied Cognitive Studies
1100 Harding Place
Charlotte, North Carolina 28204
704-331-0926 voice
704-331-9408 fax
info@centacs.com or www.centacs.com

A BARD PRESS BOOK

MANAGING EDITOR: JEFF MORRIS
PROOFREADERS: STEVE CARRELL, DEBORAH COSTENBADER
INDEXER: LINDA WEBSTER
ILLUSTRATORS: JEANNE BAREFOOT, JEFF MORRIS
TEXT DESIGNER: SUZANNE PUSTEJOVSKY
COVER DESIGNER: GARY HESPENHEIDE, SUZANNE PUSTEJOVSKY
COMPOSER: JEFF MORRIS

Printings:	First Edition	Second Edition	Third Edition
	May 1994	*November 1999*	*March 2006*
	May 1995	*August 2000*	
	November 1996	*June 2001*	
	November 1997	*January 2003*	
		August 2004	

Contents

Part One. Forming a Foundation: The Context for Using Your Owner's Manual

Part Five. Illness and Injury:
What We Know about Brain Repair

15 Brain-Related Disorders: Some Big Picture Stuff

16 Structural Disorders: Bats in Your Belfry

17 Insults and Injuries: A Blow-by-Blow Account

18 Degenerative Conditions: Slowly Falling Apart

Part Six. Learning: The Brain as Student

Part Ten. Closing with a Prayer:
A Peek at States of Consciousness

Quick Content Guide

Although everyone will find each chapter in this book relevant to his or her life in some way, those who fill special roles may find certain chapters of particular interest. Parts Three and Four deal with subjects like sleep, music, and sex, which affect everybody every day; therefore, we suggest that all readers, regardless of their roles, would benefit from the materials in these chapters.

Below are listed several role categories and the additional chapters that may be of special interest to people in these roles.

Doctors, lawyers, and others in professional practice	21, 23, 26-28, 31-32, 35-37
Human resource professionals	All
Managers	27-37
Mental health professionals	All
Negotiators	27-29, 33, 35
Parents	All
Religious professionals	15, 21-22, 29-30, 33-38
Research-and-development professionals	27-31, 36-37
Salespeople	30-33, 36-37
Students	5, 21-28, 34-37
Teachers, trainers, and coaches	5, 21-29, 33-37

> **" There are two ways of spreading light: to be the candle or the mirror that reflects it. "**
>
> —Edith Wharton

Preface

Why this book?

Tomes about the mind and brain pepper the shelves of airport kiosks and bookstores from Phoenix to Philly. The available books about the brain can be divided into two categories: research reports and practical applications. Neurobiology texts belong in the first category, and how-to books (*How to Increase Your Memory, How to Be More Creative*) belong in the second.

This book serves to create an explicit overlap between these two categories. Research books generally decline to identify the everyday applicability of their findings—indeed, that is not their purpose. Practical books usually avoid the explicit connection between a piece of advice and its basis in research. This book is meant to yoke the two together as a team by saying, "Here's what we know about memory storage in the brain, and here's how that knowledge can help us improve our recall of information." When I presented at Eric Jensen's brain conference in San Diego, he had listed speakers

in three categories: researchers, practitioners, and interpreters. The last is what I am—an interpreter, one who follows the research and interprets as needed to the practitioners.

Why me? I'm not an academic who must publish or perish, and I'm not a natural writer possessed with an irresistible urge to put pen to paper (or, more aptly, fingertips to keyboard). So why did I write this book? A story will explain.

All my life I had viewed myself as something of a dilettante, with a wide variety of interests. That changed in the spring of 1988, when I read *The Universe Within,* by Morton Hunt. Hunt, a science popularizer, introduced the English-reading world to cognitive science, the interdisciplinary approach to understanding the workings of the mind-brain. Each chapter of his book summarized research in an area that had been of interest to me: problem solving, creativity, learning theory, and so on. Voilà! I was no longer a dilettante, but a cognitive scientist. I began to read everything I could find dealing with this new field (which is described in chapter 1), and I found that the extensive scientific literature on brain research provided me with a basis for my applied interests.

In December 1988, I began serving a term on the program committee of the local chapter of the American Society for Training and Development (ASTD). The committee asked for program suggestions for monthly meetings in 1989, so I suggested that we bring in a speaker on the subject of cognitive science. After hearing my justification, they agreed that the chapter would benefit from such a program and asked me to find a speaker. I was

> "It is like the man who claimed to be selling Abraham Lincoln's ax—he explained that over the years the head had to be replaced twice and the handle three times."
>
> —Stephen Pinker,
> *The Language Instinct*

able to find speakers who were expensive and practical in their approach or speakers who were inexpensive and theoretical in their approach, but I had to report that I was unable to find anyone we could afford who was willing to present an application-oriented program to our group. I argued, and they agreed, that the more theoretical speakers would be hooted out of the hall. As a result, they asked, "Pierce, why don't you do a program?" I agreed.

I presented the program—entitled "Brain Update"—in August 1989. After an encouraging reception, I presented the program in two other cities and then at the regional meeting in Gatlinburg, Tennessee, in the fall of 1990. After each of the four presentations, people

came up to me and asked, "What have you written? Your content is fascinating, but we'd like something written to consider in more depth." Responding to this encouragement as evidence of a genuine need, my wife and partner, Jane, and I decided that I should cut back on my consulting duties and write a book. That was in August 1991. I started writing and reading to fill in the gaps, closing in on fulfilling my commitment to provide you with written documentation of what I enjoyed talking about from the front of the classroom. The result was the first edition of *The Owner's Manual for the Brain,* published in 1994; five years later came the second edition. With this third edition, as with the second, I have found that some, but not all, of the previous edition has been replaced. Much has been added. Like Abe Lincoln's ax, the form remains the same.

How is this book unique? First, it stands with one foot in the research camp and the other in practice. Second, it reflects my 30-plus years of experience as a management consultant. (I cannot apologize for the fact that this book reflects the part of the world with which I am familiar.) Third, I have included only brain research findings that have widespread practical applications. Findings that are interesting but not generally useful have not been included. Fourth, for the most part, the structure is aimed at those using the research, not the researchers themselves.

The basic structure of the book employs what I like to refer to as the "So what?" format. The typical response to reported research findings is "So what?" For example, research shows that the level of the hormone melatonin is directly related to the quality of our sleep. You may say, "So what?" Well, this book is designed with that question in mind. Every piece of research reported is followed by one or more specific suggestions for its application. Here is an example of what you will find.

TOPIC 9.5	**Sleep and Exercise**

Exercising tends to elicit cortical alertness, which is not what you want when going to sleep. Exercise relaxes you after experiencing stress, but good aerobic exercise generally puts your nervous system in a state of moderate arousal. In this condition, you are ideally suited for mental tasks. In order to sleep soon after a workout, you would need to consume carbohydrates and dairy products.

Applications

1 Exercise no later than several hours before bedtime.

2 If you must exercise just before retiring for the evening (I know a television sports announcer who exercises after a night game because he's so keyed up), try reading a relatively unemotional book in bed rather than an exciting one (for example, Plato rather than Dan Brown) to help you get to sleep.

The book is organized around these topics (except for chapters 1, 2, 3, and 39). The numerical identifier refers to the chapter number and the sequence within that chapter. Although most of the application ideas are mine, several of my readers have suggested additional ideas. I have indicated their authorship following the suggestion. I look forward to including suggestions from other readers in subsequent editions of this book.

In its most general sense, this book is for people who want to use their heads. More specifically, it is for lifelong learners, professionals who value keeping up with or ahead of the game, people developers, human resource professionals, leaders, consultants (internal and external), supervisors of teachers, training managers, educators of teachers, adult education professionals, train-the-trainer professionals, curriculum writers, curriculum designers, industrial and organizational psychologists, writers, and research-and-development professionals. I could summarize this list by reducing it to five types of readers: lifelong learners, educators, consultants, managers, and psychologists. You will gain insights into improving your personal effectiveness without having to wade through the tedium of academic detail (I've done that for you) or the fluff of wordy popularizers (I've cut away the padding).

This book *is not*

- A biology or medical text

- A psychology text

- An in-depth treatment of specific research findings

- A collection of esoteric findings that are interesting but not useful

- An in-depth treatment of general subjects (I report only the brain research findings that are relevant to the subject)

- A reference work for research scientists

This book *is*

- Application-oriented
- A reflection of my experiences as a management consultant
- Composed of findings that have practical applications
- A reference work for consumers
- Centered on the what and the why: what brain research suggests we could do for personal improvement and why we should do it

The book is designed to be something of an encyclopedia or resource book of application ideas. I suspect that a few people will read it from cover to cover, with most of you preferring to browse according to which sections are of the most current interest to you. Where the understanding of a chapter or topic is particularly dependent on material covered elsewhere in the book, I have attempted to indicate that fact. In order to group the chapters for the convenience of most readers, I have divided the book into ten parts.

Part One serves as an introduction to the field of cognitive science. Chapter 1 provides an overview both of the field of cognitive science and of the book itself; Chapter 2 reviews some of the basics of brain functions, including current research on the nature-nurture controversy; Chapter 3 reviews major brain research technology. If you have a strong or recent background in cognitive science, you may choose to skim or skip these first three chapters. Part Two explores brain development

and characteristics during the three age ranges of greatest interest—early childhood (Chapter 4), adolescence (Chapter 5), and aging (Chapter 6). Part Three will probably prove to be of the greatest interest for most people, covering findings related to diet, drugs, sleep, exercise, humor, and music. Part Four covers matters of sex, gender, love, and relationships. Part Five discusses illness and injury, including some of the more commonly known mental disorders. Part Six is designed for the teacher in us all; it discusses how we learn and remember, facilitate learning, and develop language, with a special chapter on giftedness. Part Seven shows ways to maximize our creativity and problem-solving ability. Part Eight covers workplace design (including the five senses) and dealing with change; it should be of particular interest if you are a people manager. Part Nine is the most ambitious, as we begin here to take a look at the total person, moving from personality traits and mental abilities, through the emotions and stress, and finally to motivation and happiness. This section will be particularly useful if you are interested in personal growth, personnel selection, parenting, or similarities and differences in personal styles at work and at home. Part Ten, as it were, closes the book with a "prayer" by taking a stab at defining the nature of consciousness, an effort that cannot be undertaken without familiarity with the material leading up to it.

My main purpose in writing this book is to help you discover ways to improve. By giving specific suggestions along with their research justifications, I hope to pique your interest in opportunities for personal improvement. Because the scope is so inclusive, some of you may be frustrated by finding insufficient information on these pages that helps you immediately implement an idea. To solve this problem, I would like to suggest several resources that could be helpful in leading you to further information or skill mastery:

- Talk with your public library's reference staff.

- Consult the continuing education department of a school of higher education near you.

- Consult officers in your local chapters of the ASTD or the National Society for Performance and Instruction (directories are available in your library).

- Write the authors of books mentioned in a specific topic.

- Explore the Internet resources listed at the end of this book, and conduct your own Internet keyword searches.

- Read the materials listed at the end of each chapter and in the resources at the end of the book that relate to ideas in which you are interested.

If, in your search to improve your skills, you seek out workshops on a particular subject mentioned in this book, be sure to evaluate the content of the workshop before attending. For example, don't just go to a "motivation" workshop; find out whose theories or work the session is based on. Many workshops today use outmoded information. But that's a subject for another book.

I acknowledge debts to many in writing this book. To my hosts and the locales they provided me for inspiration: Bill and Deanna Culp by the water in Beaufort, South Carolina; Robert and Carolyn Shaw by the water in Highlands, North Carolina; Bob Snyder by the water at Topsail Motel in South Topsail Beach, North Carolina; our daughter Hilary and son-in-law Jy by the skyscrapers in Manhattan; and several other B&Bs, hotels, and motels where I've written while Jane worked with clients. To my readers, who've provided helpful suggestions and criticism: Mark Ardis, Rick Bradley, Susan Close, Bill Davis, Richard Furr, Janice Gamache, Vicki Halsey, Eric Jensen, John Kello, Shirley Lim, Deb Morris, Marselino Pangan, Dillon Robertson, Captain Eurydice Stanley (U.S. Army), and Malu Velazquez. To the readers whom my publisher recruited: Montgomery Scott Bard, Sandra Hirsh, Gary John, Ann McGee-Cooper, Luis Picard-Ami, John Shamley, Patricia Valdez, and Claire Ellen Weinstein. To Chip Bell, who has encouraged me to write and who introduced me to Ray Bard. To Ray Bard, my publisher, for his wise counsel and constant support. To Helen Hyams, editor of the first two editions, who taught me respect for the editing process. To Jeff Morris for editing with humor, authority, and sensitivity to both me and the reader. To my daughters, Allegra and Hilary, whose excitement in the process fuels me to return to the keyboard. To Jane, my wife and partner, for bearing the brunt of the emotional cost associated with writing a book. To the staff at *Cent*ACS, who make the daily trek from home to office a time of joy and support. And to Liam, Rowan, and Stella Rose, our grandchildren, who give more to me by keeping me youthful than I can ever give them as they grow—I love you guys and gal!

The Author

Pierce J. Howard is director of research of the Center for Applied Cognitive Studies (*Cent*ACS), a research and dissemination firm headquartered in Charlotte, North Carolina. His wife, Jane, is managing director at *Cent*ACS. Together, they develop both public and organizational programs based on the most current research in cognitive science. These programs include workshops, breakfast seminars, speeches, retreats, a website (www.centacs.com), custom-designed programs, and publications. Their special focus is on the Five-Factor Model of personality, for which they offer certification training and a wide range of support materials, software, services, advanced training programs, and annual learning conferences.

For the last 25 years, Dr. Howard has also been an organization development consultant. His motivation and, hence, his own professional development stem from a deep-seated desire to help others learn how to overcome their obstacles. He has attended numerous workshops and professional meet-ings, read extensively in the field, conducted computer database searches, and created hundreds of workshop designs in an unrelenting effort to find the best ways to help people solve problems, make decisions, create new approaches, and understand themselves and others—in effect, to take responsibility for their own growth and development both as individuals and as members of teams and organizations. Dr. Howard's skill and interest in debunking myths and finding the most effective ways to help others learn has served him well in the business community.

Dr. Howard grew up in Kinston, North Carolina. He received his B.A. degree in 1963 from Davidson College and his M.A. degree in 1967 from East Carolina University, both in English. In 1972, he received his Ph.D. degree in education with a special emphasis in curriculum and research from the University of North Carolina at Chapel Hill. His college years were interrupted by a three-year tour with the U.S. Army in Germany, where he served as an intelligence specialist.

In addition to his writing, research, and dissemination responsibilities, Dr. Howard serves as Adjunct Professor of Psychology at the University of North Carolina at Charlotte. His professional affiliations include membership in the American Psychological Association, the International Society for the Study of Individual Differences, and the Organization Development Network. In 1992, the Charlotte Area ASTD Chapter recognized him with its Excellence in Service to the Profession Award. He has written and published numerous workbooks, tests, and other materials for clients. The first edition of this book, *The Owner's Manual for the Brain,* was published in 1994. In 2001, Pierce and Jane Howard published *The Owner's Manual for Personality at Work* (Bard Press). For relaxation, they enjoy walking, cooking, chamber music, choral singing, reading, and camping. Their older daughter, Hilary, is a journalist and actress in New York, and their younger daughter, Allegra, is a medical risk specialist in Charlotte. Together, they have provided the authors with three grandchildren as a sure way to remain young at heart (and mind).

Part One

Forming a Foundation

*The Context
for Using
Your
Owner's
Manual*

Part One. Forming a Foundation
The Context for Using Your Owner's Manual

1

Getting Started

A Framework for Exploring Mind-Brain Concepts

World War II started something. The pain and tragedy of head injuries catapulted brain research into the foreground of scientific and pseudoscientific investigation. From the popular claims of split-brain research to the profound findings of neurotransmitter studies, discoveries by increasing numbers of researchers and readers have focused on learning how the brain works.

66 *Few minds wear out; more rust out.* **99**
—Christian Nestell Bovee

This explosion of research has given birth to a new field of knowledge: *cognitive science,* also known as brain science. One feature that makes this field unique is its interdisciplinary nature—it is made up of more than one traditional field of study. The research has been conducted by investigators from seven broad fields, although some subdivisions of these fields are more germane to cognitive science than others; for example, psychopharmacology is more germane than social psychology. The fields are

1. Biology
2. Chemistry
3. Psychology
4. Information science
5. Philosophy
6. Anthropology
7. Linguistics

Prior to World War II, communication among scholars in these fields was minimal. But the momentum increased noticeably soon after the war ended. Most people seem to date the beginning of cognitive science as a formal interdisciplinary field of study from September 1948 (Gardner, 1985), when scientists assembled at the Hixon Symposium, titled "Cerebral Mechanisms of Behavior," at the California Institute of Technology. Presenters included John von Neumann and Karl Lashley, representing mathematics and psychology. Many regard this meeting as the death knell for the behaviorism of B. F. Skinner, Ivan Petrovich Pavlov, Edward Lee Thorndike, and John B. Watson, which had held sway until then. No more would strict stimulus-response explanations of human behavior be ascendant. With the rise of cognitive science came the doctrine that human behavior consisted of more than conditioned responses, that the human mind was indeed able to create, to choose, to reflect—in short, to explore the universe between stimulus and response. Stephen Covey (1990, p. 69) suggests that between stimulus and response, man has the freedom to choose. Or, as Richard Restak (1991, p. 50) observes, we are moving from Socrates's "know thyself" to Kierkegaard's "choose thyself." In a recent resounding affirmation of Kierkegaard's dictum, filmmakers have given us the award-winning *What the Bleep Do We Know?*—an intense plea for self-determination of the world's citizens (check their website at www.whatthebleep.com for study groups and so forth).

Emerging from over 30 years in the relative obscurity of academia, cognitive science had its coming-out with the publication in 1982 of Morton Hunt's *The Universe Within: A New Science Explores the Human Mind.* His highly readable volume introduced many to this new field. Drawing from examples in areas such as problem solving, creativity, decision science, epistemology, moral development, personality theory, artificial intelligence, logic, linguistics, learning theory, and memory, he showed how cognitive science has brought previously isolated fields together into one common alliance committed to describing how the mind works. He related how this alliance of scholars is collaborating to describe the mind's functioning from both the detailed, microscopic, bottom-up perspective, as in cellular neurobiology, and the big-picture, global, top-down perspective, as in discussions of primary personality traits. The excitement of this multipronged scientific movement lies in the moment when the bottom-up, or *molecular,* studies become recognized as equivalent to the top-down, or *molar,* studies.

An example of such a "meeting at the middle" can be found in Hans Eysenck's *The Biological Basis of Personality* (1967), in which he begins to establish the relationship between the reticular activating system (RAS) in the brain (a molecular structure) and the personality traits of extraversion and neuroticism (molar behaviors). Paul MacLean (1990) describes the bottom-up perspective as "objective" and the top-down approach as "subjective." For an excellent and timely discussion of this molecular-molar relationship, see Cacioppo and Berntson (1992).

The Mind-Brain Dichotomy

As we slip into the content proper of this book, you will notice that the terms *brain* and *mind* are used interchangeably. IBMer E. Baird Smith has a comedy routine in which he asks, "Is your mind a part of your brain, or is your brain all in your mind?" In the 19th century, English scholar Thomas Hewitt Key played with this semantic difficulty by asking, "What is mind? No matter. What is matter? Never mind." This semantic puzzle needs attention! Dealing with the historical debate between mind and brain is beyond the purpose of this book. Understandable treatments are available in Gardner (1985) and Hunt (1982). In the seventeenth century, René Descartes argued for *dualism,* with "mind" a kind of software and "brain" a kind of hardware; he apparently developed this idea as a result of a rift with the church authorities, who allowed him to continue his work so long as he stuck to the body and let the church take care of the mind and spirit. Later, behaviorists like Skinner argued for *monism* (nothing exists other than cells), whereas current thinking argues for an *interactionist* approach, which describes the intimate, sensitive way in which mind (ideas and images) and body (cells, chemicals, and electricity) directly and immediately influence each other. As a simple example, we know that a joyful disposition (mind and spirit) can increase the number of "helper cells" in the immune system (brain and body) and, conversely, that a reduction in the number of helper cells can dampen a joyful disposition. We also know that using our memory and skills tends to preserve nerve cells ("use it or lose it") and that, conversely, losing nerve cells over time interferes with memory and skills.

To say "use your mind" or "use your brain" is to say the same thing. It is like saying "use your computer" versus "use your word processing program." The features of one influence the features of the other. Ira Black (1991, p. 8) argues that our mental software and hardware are one and the same when he speaks of the "essential unity of structure and function." When the computer is turned off, the word-processing program cannot function. Yet just because the computer is turned on, that doesn't mean the program is being used, or being used to capacity. When the brain is dead, the mind cannot function. Yet just because the brain is alive doesn't mean the mind is being used, or being used to capacity. In a sense, then, the best definition of mind is that it is the state that occurs when the brain is alive and at work. Richard M. Restak, who wrote the books and television series *The Brain* (1984), *The Mind* (1988), and *Receptors* (1994), despaired of a crisp, clear definition that could distinguish between the two, concluding, "Mind is the astounding interplay of 100 billion neurons. And more" (1988, p. 31; *Note:* More recent research puts this number at 23 billion, not 100). J. A. Hobson (1988, p. 230), in *The Dreaming Brain,* writes, "I believe that when we have truly adequate descriptions of brain and mind, dualism and all of its dilemmas will disappear. We will speak of the brain-mind as a unity, or invent some new word to describe it." To talk of the brain is to refer to the more molecular aspects of a phenomenon, while to talk of the mind is to refer to the more molar aspects.

Cognitive and *cognition* are our only words that refer to both brain and mind, and the public finds them smacking of the ivory tower. We do need a new word that the public will accept—perhaps something like *processor* or *reactor, main,* or *brind.* Candace Pert, discoverer of the endorphin receptor, refers to the *bodymind,* thus enlarging the discussion. She teaches that the brain and nervous system are so widely represented throughout the body with mutual receptors that it does not make sense to speak of them separately. Meanwhile, a good discussion of the nature of the mind and various states of consciousness is available in Daniel Dennett's *Kinds of Minds* (1996).

Human or Animal: What's the Difference?

Humorists, philosophers, scientists, theologians—all have made stabs at defining the difference between humans and animals. Consider:

> *No animal admires another animal.*
> —**Blaise Pascal**

> *Man is the only animal that blushes. Or needs to.*
> —**Mark Twain**

> *The desire to take medicine is perhaps the greatest feature which distinguishes man from animals.*
> —**Sir William Osler**

The parade of quotes could quickly become tiring. I will, however, summarize both the popular and scientific efforts to describe this difference by one top-down and one bottom-up observation. The top-down observation: humans can learn to write, whereas animals can't. The bottom-up observation: humans have a proportionately greater area of uncommitted *cerebral cortex,* or cortex in which unused synapses are available to be committed to new learning (see fig. 1.1). The cerebral cortex (see chapter 2 and appendix A) is the part of the brain that houses the rational functions, such as problem solving, planning, and creativity. The comparison between a rat's brain and a human brain is dramatic. All but a sliver of the rat's brain is "committed" to motor, auditory, somatosensory, olfactory, and visual functions—that is, survival activities. These committed, or dedicated, areas can't be used for any other function, such as memory or problem solving, in much the same way that a word-processing machine can't be used for other computing functions. In contrast, well over half of the human brain is uncommitted and thus available for forming new synapses and networks in the service of creativity, problem solving, analysis, memory—in short, of civilization itself. In other words, we have a greater capacity for learning. (See the discussion of synapses in chapter 2.)

Since the publication of the first edition of this book in 1994, a flurry of books on the subject of evolutionary psychology have appeared. These books are based on 20 years of assimilation of E. O. Wilson's monumental *Sociobiology,* which was published in 1975. Wilson's text has provided the major source of data for new Darwinists who are committed to the notion that a single human nature is deeply rooted in our primate ancestors and that this single human nature satisfactorily explains both the diversity and the commonality among us. This flurry of books includes J. Diamond, *The Third Chimpanzee: The Evolution and Future of the Human Animal* (1992) and *Guns, Germs, and Steel: The Fates of Human Societies* (1997a); J. L. Elman and others, *Rethinking Innateness: A Connectionist Perspective on Development* (1996); R. Wrangham and D. Peterson, *Demonic Males: Apes and the Origins of Human Violence* (1996); and R. Wright, *The Moral Animal: The New Science of Evolutionary Psychology* (1994). The net impact of these works is not so much to change the way we understand the mind-brain, but rather to deepen our understanding of how we got to be who we are. Specific points made by these new Darwinists will appear throughout this edition. Michael Gazzaniga (1998, p. 59) sums up these arguments as follows:

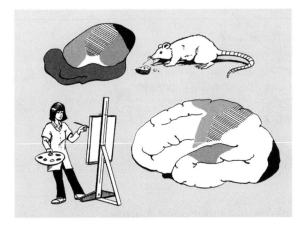

Figure 1.1. Cortical Commitment
A comparison of committed (shaded) and uncommitted (unshaded) regions of the cerebral cortex in rat (top) and human (bottom).

> No scientist seriously questions whether we are the product of natural selection. We are a finely honed machine that has amazing capacities for learning and inventiveness. . . . The ability to learn and think comes with our brains. The knowledge we acquire with these devices results form interactions with our culture. But the devices come with the brain, just as the brakes come with the car.

What Is the Mind-Brain?

Metaphors abound to explain the physical process that governs our behavior. Some explain it as a power plant, emphasizing the electrochemical ionic transfers that culminate in the nervous system's capacity to supply enough power to illuminate a 25-watt light bulb. Others explain it as a computer and use the analogy of RAM and ROM, bits and bytes, and memory and storage to describe the brain's capacity to store 2.8×10^{20} bits of information. Still others see the brain as a library that can store 10 million thousand-page books. And some see the brain as a mini-government that administers a vast array of bodily functions, from breathing and blood flow to meditation and stock market analysis.

May I have the envelope, please? The winner is—all of these and more. The closer we get to understanding the structure and function of the mind-brain, the more anomalies slip through the cracks of our descriptions. Should our goal be to have complete understanding? Probably. To settle for a lesser goal may blind us to new insights: if we are not expecting large gains in scientific progress, we are less likely to experience them. However, to the degree that we can humbly marvel in wonderment at the vast unexplained mystery of mind, brain, and behavior, we are more likely to live in peace with ourselves and our neighbors. With admitted imperfection of the self comes the humility necessary for developing satisfying relationships.

The Core Principles of Cognitive Science

When we reflect on the vast mind-brain literature, we see several patterns emerge. These patterns may best be described as the core principles of cognitive science—the concepts essential to making sense out of the thousands of pieces of research available to us. As an aid to browsing through this book, I will state here what I see as the core principles.

Nativism. The principle of nativism holds that we inherit our behavior and that our environment can either nurture it to develop naturally or distort it by withholding nurturance (food, shelter, warmth, touch, affection, attention, and so on).

Unity. The principle of unity holds that the body and the mind are one and the same, and that a change in one results in a change in the other.

Connectivity. The principle of connectivity holds that the establishment of new connections between prior learnings is the essence of growth and development and that the condition of the connection points, like the condition of the gap in a spark plug, determines how well we function.

Interconnectivity. The principle of interconnectivity holds that each identifiable element in our vast storehouse of experiences and learnings is connected to each of the other elements, some more strongly or closely and others more loosely or distantly (thus, to remember a name, we silently say the alphabet until the name pops out).

Control. The principle of control holds that the health of the human (and animal) organism is a function of the degree to which the individual feels in control of his or her situation, with less perceived control resulting in poorer health and performance and greater perceived control resulting in better health and performance.

The Nature-Nurture Debate: The Pendulum Swings

In the first edition of this book (1994), I made a moderately strong statement about nature having drawn even with nurture in their power to account for the causes of individual differences. In the 10 years since that time, the overwhelming accumulation of research supporting the genetic basis of individual differences renders that statement overly cautious. William Wright, in his excellent summary of behavioral genetics research, *Born That Way* (1998), concludes that genetics is the hands-down dominant determinant of who we are. Although the statistical concordance rates suggest that genetics, or nature, accounts for more than 50 percent of individual differences, the remainder is not necessarily accounted for by the environment.

> "A devil, a born devil, on whose nature Nurture can never stick, on whom my pains, Humanely taken, all, all lost, quite lost. . . ."
>
> —Prospero, of Caliban, in William Shakespeare's *The Tempest*

Environmental influences come in two forms: shared and nonshared. Shared influence includes the example of my mother having played the piano for all seven of us kids, whereas nonshared influence includes the example of my mother being 45 when I was born (and no longer a tennis player, with all that entailed). Wright cites research that conclusively identifies nonshared influence as second in influence after genetics, with shared influence accounting for almost nothing. And Judith Rich Harris, in her paradigm-challenging book *The Nurture Assumption* (1998), points out that this nonshared influence comes primarily from the peer group, not the home. Harris contends, with convincing evidence, that the primary source of nurture-type influence on personality comes from the peer group and not the family. She calls her view Group Socialization Theory. Its axioms run something like this:

1. Peer group influence is greatest between ages 8 and 25.

2. During this period, a person self-categorizes according to the many groups she belongs to: girl, musical, athletic, scholarly, violent, and so on.

3. In any given period of the youth's history, one peer group is salient, for whatever reason.

4. A young person attempts to minimize differences between himself and others in the salient peer group (assimilation).

5. He develops according to the peer group's needs and what he brings to the group: leadership, comic, drone, peacemaker, and so on (differentiation).

6. The individual feels some hostility toward other groups and tends to maximize the contrast between self and these non-salient groups.

7. It is from the salient peer group that one takes one's rules of conduct.

8. When an individual, for whatever reason or circumstance, switches to a new salient peer group, she takes on the rules of that new group.

Harris further describes the "social module" of the brain, which apparently has two modes, one for relationships and one for groups. The relationship mode supports long-term relationships; the group mode switches easily when one group increases in salience. In fact, one can gain a new peer group simply by the power of suggestion. Call a child a loser, for example, and he then belongs to a new peer group of losers. To this extent, we can exert influence on young people by the degree to which we can reinforce membership in and identity with desirable peer groups.

Rounding out the influence pattern is what has come to be known as the phenomenon of genetics choosing environment (rather than the old-school paradigm of environment shaping behavior). Examples of this include my having chosen to spend relatively more time with my mother, because my high-openness genes found more expression there than with the low-openness profile of my father. I could have chosen to go fishing with him, but that was not my cup of tea; I preferred experiencing arts and crafts and music and literature and travel and games and cooking with my mother. For several other ways that genes and environment interact, consider the information in table 1.1.

Furthermore, Wright and others (for example, Loehlin, 1992) have documented the phenomenon of the "certain transitoriness of environmental effects" (Loehlin, 1992, p. 84), which says that as we age, we tend to become more like the genetic blueprint with which we started life. In one study, identical twins reared in the same home were measured in similarity of behavior at high school graduation, and again some dozen years later, in an attempt to determine whether monozygotic twins increased, decreased, or experienced no change in similarity after leaving their common nest. The result: they were more

Table 1.1. Three Kinds of Genotype-Environment Interaction

Kind	Definition	Example
Passive	Child's nature is a natural fit with his or her environment	1. Musical child born to musical home
		2. Ambitious child born to ambitious parents
Evocative	Others respond to child's nature	1. School sees musical talent, encourages, provides instrument
		2. N+ child encounters a "Boys don't cry" culture*
Active	Child seeks environment that suits nature	1. Musical child asks to go to summer musical camp
		2. Job-person fit, where an E+ goes into a sales role*

Based on Plomin, DeFries, McClearn, and Rutter (1997), p. 256.
* N+ and E+ are trait identifiers; see chapter 33.

similar. Apparently, family and community accentuated supposed differences in the twins, but once they were out on their own, they could eschew unnatural behaviors and become truer to their common genetic makeup. As Columbia University's Nathan Brody once commented in a speech, "Change is the process of becoming more like who we are." Loehlin points out that it is this transitoriness of environmental effects on personality that accounts for the variations in test-retest scores with personality instruments. Firmly rooted gene-based behaviors are constant, while episodic, environmentally influenced behaviors are more likely to come and go.

Consider the following cases, which show evidence of the heritability of behavior in organisms as simple as bees and as complex as humans.

Honeybees

"Foul brood" is an infectious disease of honeybees that afflicts larvae in the cells of their honeycomb. Certain hygienic strains of bees fight the disease by locating cells that have the disease, opening the wax cap, removing the larvae, and moving them out of the hive. W. C. Rothenbuhler (Dawkins, 1989) discovered that the behavior of the hygienic bees was governed by two distinct genes—one gene for uncapping the cell and a second gene for dragging out and disposing of the diseased larvae. Unless both genes were present in a worker bee, the hygienic behavior didn't happen. If a bee possessed only the uncapping gene, it would gleefully fill its day uncapping the disease-containing cells but would not remove the afflicted larvae. Alone, without any of the uncapping bees around, bees with the removal gene would do nothing. However, if Rothenbuhler himself removed the wax caps, the removal bees would gladly spend their days dragging diseased larvae out of the hive. (This reminds me of a friend who loved to wash dishes: when our Boy Scout troop went camping, I would always cook, and he would always wash. He didn't cook, and I didn't wash.)

Twins

Neubauer and Neubauer (1990, pp. 20–21) relate two striking examples of this persistence of genetic material:

1. Two monozygotic twin girls were separated at birth and placed in homes far apart. About four years later, researchers interviewed the adoptive parents of each girl. The parents of Shauna said, "She is a terrible eater—won't cooperate,

stubborn, strong-willed. I can't get her to eat anything unless I put cinnamon on it." The parents of Ellen said, "Ellen is a lovely child—cooperative and outgoing." The researcher probed, asking, "How are her eating habits?" The response was: "Fantastic—she eats anything I put before her, as long as I put cinnamon on it!" (p. 20).

2. Two monozygotic twin boys were separated at birth and placed in homes far apart. They were interviewed 27 years later. Both had turned out to be obsessive-compulsive neatniks, scrubbing their separate homes frequently and constantly picking up and making things neat and clean. When they were asked to explain their compulsion for neatness, one attributed it to his reaction to an adoptive parent who was a slob, while the other attributed it to his upbringing by an adoptive parent who was a neatnik!

Most researchers currently studying this nature-nurture relationship are calling it a 50-50 ratio, attributing half the variation in behavior to genetics and half to environmental influence. For example, if your IQ is 20 points above the mean, or about 120, then roughly 10 of the points are attributable to genetic influence and the other 10 to environmental influence. The general conclusion of most behavioral genetics researchers, however, is that environmental influence serves as an enhancer or preventer of genetic predispositions and, therefore, that environment can't create dispositions for which no genetic basis exists. This current research is a confirmation of the ancient saw that you can't make a silk purse from a sow's ear.

> "There are an infinite number of causes for everything."
>
> —Leda Cosmides

Just how do twin studies lead us to this conclusion? Monozygotic twins, who develop from a single egg, have identical genetic coding. Some sets of twins are separated at birth; for example, they may be given up for adoption, with one twin moving to California, the other to Georgia. Other pairs grow up together. To the degree that environmental influences shape behavior, identical twins reared together would be expected to be more alike than those reared apart. That, however, is not the case; the similarity between identical twins does not increase if they are reared together. Separated identical twins show strong similarities, even in their religious feelings and vocational preferences.

However, we must beware of the temptation to think of specific traits or behaviors as purely innate. Elman states, "There is virtually no interesting aspect of development that is strictly 'genetic,' at least in the sense that it is exclusively a product of information contained within the genes" (Elman and others, 1996, p. xii). There is no sociability gene, no fat gene, no rape gene. But there are genes that will interact with the complex landscape of environment and inheritance to explain all manner of things. Quartz and Sejnowski (2002, p. 128) paint a clear portrait of this truth in this manner:

> But doesn't the fact that we are all born some particular way sound depressingly deterministic? No, because being born *some* way doesn't amount to being forever destined to remain that way. Genes help determine your height at birth, but your environment—for example, what you eat as you mature—also has an important influence. The average European today is eight inches taller than the typical European 150 years ago, a change that is attributed to environmental factors. So it is with temperament.

I can't emphasize enough, however, that, although at times we seem to have discovered causes of certain behaviors, in truth the picture is far more complex. Even though brain chemicals control our genes' manufacture of proteins (e.g., turn them on or off, speed them up, slow them down), outside events can also influence this process. Consider the simple and lowly prairie vole. Quartz and Sejnowski (2002, pp. 44–45) relate that the female prairie vole has no pre-established age for arriving at puberty. Instead, she must wait until she gets a whiff of the urine of an unrelated male, which sends her brain chemicals into overdrive, resulting in her becoming fully ready to mate within 24 hours, attaching herself to the first unrelated male, and bonding with him for life, with no attraction to any other. Now, if such a thing as a whiff of urine can alter the female prairie vole's behavior for a lifetime, how many other such apparently innocent occurrences influence human behavior to varying degrees of magnitude?

Conclusions Regarding Nature and Nurture

According to Pinker (1994, p. 357), "It is not so easy to show that a trait is a product of selection. The trait has to be hereditary. It has to enhance the probability of reproduction of the organism, relative to organisms without the trait, in an environment like the one its ancestors lived in." So to the degree that all traits are hereditary, they are adaptive; they are helpful to survival. Every trait, then, whether it be anger or reliability, solitude or defiance, has its survival value.

It is important to acknowledge the inherited component of individual differences. However, we need to avoid simplistic thinking. Here's one interesting and little-considered fact about twins that constitutes an exception to their rule of being identical in all things: because identical twins compete more for resources in the womb than do fraternal twins, the identicals exhibit more differences in birth weight. For example, identicals share the same sack within the placenta and must share finite resources, whereas fraternals have their own individual sacks and are more likely to consume similar amounts of nutrients (Plomin, DeFries, McClearn, and Rutter, 1997, p. 73).

This does not mean that we must disavow the efficacy of environmental nurture, however. Wrangham and Peterson (1996, p. 106) underscore this point when they lament Margaret Mead's falsification of Samoan data in favor of her favorite theory: cultural determinism, the doctrine that culture, not inheritance, is the basis of behavior. They write, "Cultural determinism . . . leads us to hope . . . but it can also bring us to oversimplify necessarily complex problems and to avoid examining hard realities. It can lead to denial, and the regressive creation of a mythical Arcadia." John Watson (1925) wrote, "Give me a dozen healthy infants, well-formed, and my own specified world to bring them up in, and I'll guarantee to take any one at random and train him to become any type of specialist I might select—doctor, lawyer, artist, merchant-chief, and yes, even beggar-man and thief, regardless of his talents, penchants, tendencies, and abilities, vocations, and race of his ancestors" (cited in Pinker, 1994, pp. 406–407). But today we know better. We owe our behavior to both our genes and our upbringing. They are inextricably interdependent, the weft and the warp of personality.

SUGGESTED RESOURCES

Dennett, D. C. (1996). *Kinds of Minds: Toward an Understanding of Consciousness.* New York: Basic Books.

Gardner, H. (1985). *The Mind's New Science: A History of the Cognitive Revolution.* New York: Basic Books.

Hunt, M. (1982). *The Universe Within: A New Science Explores the Human Mind.* New York: Simon & Schuster.

Neubauer, P. B., and A. Neubauer (1990). *Nature's Thumbprint: The New Genetics of Personality.* Reading, Mass.: Addison-Wesley.

Pinker, S. (1997). *How the Mind Works.* New York: Norton.

Restak, R. M. (1984). *The Brain.* New York: Bantam.

Restak, R. M. (1988). *The Mind.* New York: Bantam.

Restak, R. M. (1991). *The Brain Has a Mind of Its Own.* New York: Harmony.

Restak, R. M. (1994). *Receptors.* New York: Bantam.

Wright, R. (1994). *The Moral Animal: The New Science of Evolutionary Psychology.* New York: Vintage Books.

Wright, W. (1998). *Born That Way: Genes, Behavior, Personality.* New York: Knopf.

Website.

National Center for Biotechnology Information (Human Genome Project Information): www.ncbi.nlm.nih.gov

2

Brain Basics

A Refresher Course in Hardware and Hormones

> **66 We need education in the obvious more than investigation of the obscure. 99**
>
> —Attributed to
> Oliver Wendell Holmes Jr.

*O*nce upon a time there were only lizards and other such reptilian creatures. The *lizard brain* was simple, geared only to the maintenance of survival functions: respiration, digestion, circulation, and reproduction. Over evolutionary time, the leopard and other such mammalian creatures emerged. Extending out from the lizard brain stem, the *leopard brain* (now called the *limbic system*) added to animals' behavioral repertoire the capacity for emotion and coordination of movement. This second phase of brain evolution yielded the well-known *general adaptation syndrome* (GAS), or fight-or-flight response (Selye, 1952). The evolutionary advantages of this syndrome are attested to by the disappearance of many reptilian species. The third phase of evolution was the *learning brain*—the cerebral cortex (see appendix A). This third and most recent phase of brain evolution provided the ability to solve problems, use language and numbers, develop memory, and be creative. MacLean (1990) refers to the three stages of brain evolution as *protoreptilian, paleomammalian* (early mammal), and *neomammalian* (late mammal). Figure 2.1 contrasts the three brain stages.

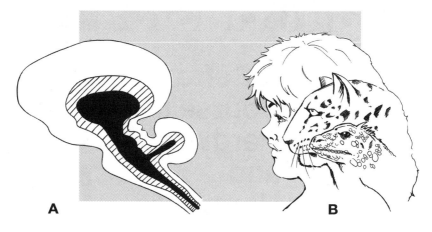

Figure 2.1. Two Views of the Evolution of the Brain
(A) The dark area represents the earliest appearance of the brain, the lizard or reptilian brain; the shaded area, the leopard or early mammalian brain; the light area, the learning or late mammalian brain. (B) Alternate illustration of these levels of brain development.

The millions of years of brain development from lizard to leopard to learner are repeated in each human embryo during the nine months in the womb. Thus, the development of an individual embryo (ontogeny) retraces (recapitulates) the evolutionary path of its ancestors (phylogeny). Scientists summarize this complex concept with those three words: "Ontogeny recapitulates phylogeny." The consequences of poisoning the brain with drugs or alcohol during pregnancy can be seen in infants whose development was arrested or thwarted at the lizard or leopard level. More complete yet highly readable treatments of brain development and function are available in Hunt (1982), Restak

(1984, 1988, 1994), and Greenfield (1996); a detailed encyclopedia of information is available in Gregory (1987).

Because this book is concerned with the day-to-day applications of brain science, I will not attempt to provide a complete physical description of the brain and all of its functions. However, for readers who would like to see where the various parts of the brain mentioned in this book are located, I have provided several illustrations in appendix A (such readers might wish to make a tab to that appendix for ready reference). It is not really important for you to know, for example, what the hypothalamus is or even what it does. I will dwell only on the physical aspects that you should understand in order to apply the ideas presented here to everyday life. Two such physical aspects are the *reticular activating system* and the *synaptic gap*.

Two Key Features of the Brain: RAS and the Gap

A kind of "toggle switch" controls whether the leopard brain or the learning brain is currently in charge. This toggle, the reticular activating system (RAS), is located in an area beginning in the upper brain stem and continuing into the lower reaches of the cerebral cortex (see figure 2.2). RAS switching appears to occur at one of two times: when we become emotionally charged up or when we relax. When we become emotionally charged, as in the fight-or-flight response, the RAS shuts down the cerebral cortex, or learning brain. For all practical purposes, when the cortex is shut down, we proceed on "automatic pilot," where instinct and training take over. When the limbic system, or leopard brain, is shut down as a result of general bodily relaxation and removal of threat, the RAS switches the cortex back on and allows creativity and logic to return to center stage. The RAS

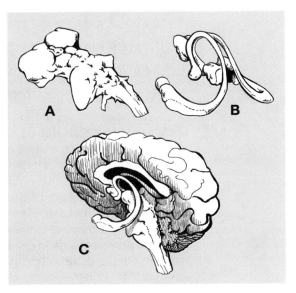

Figure 2.2. Control Elements in the Brain.
The reticular activating system (A) serves as a kind of toggle switch to allow either (B) the limbic system or (C) the cerebral cortex (shown with the RAS and limbic systems) to be in control of the brain at any one time.

is a large, diffuse neural process, and its effective functioning is important to both our personal survival and our ability to enjoy life.

Martin Moore-Ede, surgeon, physiologist, educator, researcher, consultant, and writer, talks about the nine "switches" that foster cortical alertness when activated (Moore-Ede, 1993):

1. A sense of danger, interest, or opportunity

2. Muscular activity

3. Time of day on the circadian clock

4. Sleep bank balance

5. Ingested nutrients and chemicals

6. Environmental light

7. Environmental temperature and humidity

8. Environmental sound

9. Environmental aroma

I would add to his list the following:

10. Recency of stressful episodes

11. Recency of aerobic exercise

12. Environmental negative ions

13. Degree of one's self-perception as being in control

If you are responsible for the overall effectiveness of a place of work, you might take this as a checklist for evaluating the degree to which that workplace fosters mental alertness. The overall effect of these switches is to influence our levels of alertness, described in figure 2.3.

Another key feature of the brain is the *synapse*. The synapse is the point at which neurons, or nerve cells, connect with one another; its effective functioning is vital to our quality of life. A typical nerve cell is composed of a main cell body (with nucleus) and two branches, one outgoing and the other incoming, that serve as communication links with other nerve cells. The outgoing branch is called the *axon,* the incoming branch the *dendrite.* The axon and the dendrite both have many connector points, so that a neuron can receive many messages through its dendritic terminals and send different messages through its axonic terminals. The space where the axon of one neuron

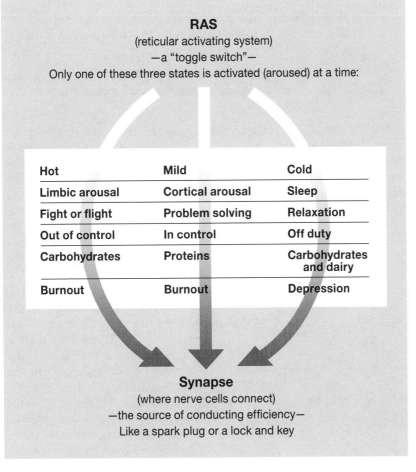

RAS
(reticular activating system)
—a "toggle switch"—
Only one of these three states is activated (aroused) at a time:

Hot	Mild	Cold
Limbic arousal	Cortical arousal	Sleep
Fight or flight	Problem solving	Relaxation
Out of control	In control	Off duty
Carbohydrates	Proteins	Carbohydrates and dairy
Burnout	Burnout	Depression

Synapse
(where nerve cells connect)
—the source of conducting efficiency—
Like a spark plug or a lock and key

Figure 2.3. The Brain Process at a Glance

establishes a connection with the dendrite of another neuron is the synapse, or synaptic gap (see figure 2.4).

Dr. Gabrielle M. de Courten-Myers, professor of neuropathology at the University of Cincinnati, worked with a team at the University of Lausanne in Switzerland to count the number of cells in the brain. The team studied brain slices from 11 cadavers over several years. Their findings:

- The typical human brain has about 23 billion cells, not the 100 billion previously asserted.

- Males averaged 2 billion more neurons than female brains, and the difference held proportionately in both hemispheres, unlike current thought that asserts that males and females have an equal number of cells.

- Females have more *neuropil*—the fibrillar substance comprising dendrites, axons, and synapses that facilitates interneuron communication.

What should we make of these findings? First, the differences in male and female brains is not negligible. Second, the difference does not necessitate differences in intelligence. Third, the difference could explain why more women have Alzheimer's disease, as well as why men do better at spatial reasoning. Studies are underway to determine the significance of these findings—but, for the moment, I must retract my statement in the first and second editions of this book that the typical brain comprises 100 billion neurons.

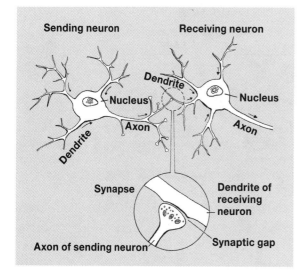

Figure 2.4. Basic Neuronal Structure
The lower enlarged area shows the synapse in some detail; the upper area shows how it fits into the overall neuronal structure.

Within each synapse, hundreds of receptors on the dendritic side wait for the proper chemical to be exuded from its dedicated axon. These chemicals are *ligands* or, as Candace Pert calls them, "informational substances"; they comprise three groups of chemicals: neurotransmitters, steroids, and peptides. These informational substances move from axon to dendritic receptor in a "lock-and-key" manner, in which one type of receptor and that type alone can admit its dedicated ligand. A given synaptic gap can contain multiple types of receptors, but each individual receptor can only admit its unique ligand. Only an endorphin can attach to an endorphin receptor, for example; dopamine would bounce off it.

Although synapses are extremely important, they represent only 2 percent of the total number of receptor sites in the body, with various kinds of receptors distributed far and wide, from the immune system to the gut, from the heart muscles to the gonads. In addition to synaptic transmission, ligands travel through intercellular space using blood and cerebrospinal fluid as a medium. This process is called *chemotaxis* (literally, "the chemical ferries itself"). Chemotaxis is the capacity of a cell that has a certain kind of receptor to detect, as if by radar, the presence of its ligands at some remote location within what Pert calls the bodymind. So, in addition to synaptic transmission, which is a direct form of intercellular connection, cells can connect, or communicate, by remote travel. The difference between synaptic transmission and chemotaxis is really one of distance. In the former, the ligand travels only microns, while in the latter the ligand travels inches, feet, or even meters.

Just as the condition of the gap in an automotive spark plug is important to effective operation of a car, the receptors must be clean and in good condition for our nerves to work properly. You can clean the gap of a spark plug with a wire brush, and you can also clean the synaptic gap. Normal maintenance of the synapse is accomplished by the presence of *calpain,* a compound derived from calcium. Calpain acts as a kind of cleanser, dissolving protein buildup at the synaptic gap like a miniature PacPerson (remember the PacMan video game of the early 1980s in which a moving circular head gobbled a diet of dots?). The dietary sources of the cleanser calpain are dairy products and leafy green vegetables. Too little calcium in the diet results in protein buildup at the synapse, with resulting loss of mental performance (for example, memory) as the buildup interferes with the ability of neural messengers to "jump" the synapse. On the other hand, if there is too much calcium in the diet, the excess calpain itself begins to interfere with neural transmissions. One drastic solution to remove protein from the synaptic gap is electric shock. Studies have shown that for aged patients with severe memory loss, improvements in memory lasted up to six months following shock treatment. Additional suggestions for caring for the synaptic gap appear in table 2.1.

In a sense, RAS switching is the major determinant of our primary strategies from situation to situation (proactive-cortical vs. reactive-limbic), whereas the conditions of the synaptic gap and ligand receptors generally determine the effectiveness of the tactics we employ (memory, logic, creativity, movement, coordination, perception, and so on). The consequences of ineffective RAS switching are devastating. Recent studies have revealed tumors in the brains of some criminals. These tumors are hypothesized to have prevented RAS switching from the limbic system to the cortex, thus maintaining a level of rage behavior. In 1980, in Sacramento, California, a man turned himself in to authorities after repeated violent outbursts. His physician discovered

Table 2.1. The Care and Feeding of Synapses

Sources	Work Examples
Environmental richness	Posters; sculpture; paintings; variation in paint, drapes, wallpaper; puzzles; games (mental and physical)
Diet	Follow National Research Council's Recommended Daily Allowances; do *not* eliminate fats, and avoid extremes of calcium (see chapter 7)
Snacks	For mentation: proteins and complex carbohydrates For relaxation: simple carbohydrates and fats
Exercise	Aerobic exercise 4–5 times per week
Atmosphere (such as ions)	Encourage fresh air for invigoration, not simple carbohydrates or caffeine; use air purifiers
Breaks	Encourage breaks after each learning episode (at least every 1½ hours)
Habits	Make new learning the organizational norm: skills, games, tapes, languages, names and faces; openly acknowledge and reward suggestions for improvement and new learning

that a tumor was causing pressure in a way that sustained limbic arousal. After surgical removal of the tumor, the pattern of rage disappeared. Apparently, the tumor had caused this man's RAS to lock up. Experimental efforts (Restak, 1984) to create the same type of uncontrollable rage have been carried out by implanting electrodes into the brains of bulls and cats. Activation of an electrode is the equivalent of constant pressure from a tumor. By simply turning a switch on or off, experimenters have turned rage and aggression on and off. An implanted cat in the middle of attacking a mouse would instantly turn friendly when the experimenter turned off the switch.

Neurotransmitters: The Alphabet of Personality

So, we are born with 23 billion brain cells, or neurons. But it is not the number of neurons itself that determines our mental characteristics; it is how they are connected. Each cell reaches out to other cells through its axon (it "acts-on" other cells), with endpoints of the axon pairing up with receiving points on the dendrites ("end-right") of neighboring cells. Each neuron is connected to hundreds of other neurons by anywhere from 1,000 to 10,000 synapses. Edelman (1992) estimates that it would take some 32 million years to count synapses in the cerebral cortex alone.

Learning is defined as the establishment of new neural networks composed of synaptic connections and their associated chemotaxic patterns. Gary Lynch of the University of California, Irvine, is one researcher who has confirmed that new synapses appear after learning. It is the density of the brain, as measured by the number of synapses, that distinguishes greater from lesser mental capacity. Ira Black (1991) defines knowledge as the "pattern of connectivity" between neurons, and learning as modifications to this pattern of connectivity. Only 10 years ago, it was thought that learning consisted solely of the formation of new synapses. Today we regard the synapse as the structural center but acknowledge the vast intercellular movement through blood and cerebrospinal fluid as a coequal player in the learning process. The number of synapses and their condition, the circulatory system, and the cerebrospinal fluid form the stage upon which our electrochemical language plays out its drama. The alphabet of its physiological language is composed of over two hundred ligands.

The ligands are secreted by nerve cells, immune cells, and other cells that affect the formation, maintenance, activity, and longevity of synapses, neurons, and various organs. They are like the letters of the alphabet, with their "words" corresponding to behaviors. As words are composed of letters, with individual letters having predictable phonetic effects and groups of letters having predictable semantic effects, so behaviors are composed of ligand activity, with individual informational substances having predictable physiological effects and groups of them having predictable behavioral effects.

The ligands create two broad categories of effect: *excitation* (or *activation*) and *inhibition.* For example, one neurotransmitter will activate sleep and another will inhibit it. Drinking milk will trigger the release of *melatonin,* the neurotransmitter that activates sleep (and, along with the neurotransmitter *serotonin,* depression), but eating chocolate, which contains caffeine, will interfere with sleep. Still other chemicals serve as neuromodulators, affecting the intensity of excitation or inhibition. Intensity of transmission is measured by the *action potential,* an electrical charge with wave properties (see figure 2.5). In the figure, Jane has a lower threshold for tasting salt (that is,

Figure 2.5. The Action Potential

she doesn't need as much for the same effect) compared to Janet. The *potential* for a "too much salt" response is not *activated* unless Jane's threshold is crossed.

The nature of the action potential is a key to understanding individual differences. Neurons don't even fire (react to a stimulus), for example, if the stimulus is too weak to cross the response threshold. The threshold for activation of a particular neuron is determined by a complex interplay of one's genetic code, physical condition (tired, pained, alert), and environment (noisy, light, cold, stimulating). Thus, although ligands constitute a kind of alphabet, other factors affect the nature of neural communication, in much the same way that volume, pitch, and speed affect how our spoken words are understood. I once counseled a young female manager who felt that she was being passed over unjustly for promotion to a field management position. Her manager declined her requests, saying that she was too valuable to be promoted. Her manner was so contrite that I speculated to her that her manager had most likely not heard her pleas for promotion; her voice and emotional level had not crossed his "threshold" for acknowledgment. She practiced a more forceful presentation, delivered it to her manager, and was promoted within days!

Neurons average about three informational substances apiece: some may contain channels for only two, while others may have channels for five. Because each ligand can exist in a continuum of states—

weak, medium, and strong—the types of information transmitted in one synapse can range from a dozen to a thousand. I have often thought of the human personality not as a computer but rather as something of a giant equalizer (see chapter 33), the contraption stereo buffs use to modulate and transmit sound from their records, tapes, and CDs. Surely you've seen those electrical units with their levers and gauges hooked up to a stereo system. Well, the levers of the equalizer are analogous to the informational substances: one affects the quality of sound, the other the quality of behavior. A little less serotonin and more testosterone, a little less of the endorphins, the body's own tranquilizer—now we've got a real Bengal tiger on our hands! Add more serotonin—ah, now we're purring.

But this process is complex. Don't let my effort to simplify it obscure the vast interconnectedness of cells, chemicals, and systems. Black (1991, p. 37) writes: "Consideration of synaptic transmission has illustrated that the synapse is hardly a simple digital switch, enslaved to a few, simple physiological variables. Quite the opposite occurs. Synaptic communication is a remarkably flexible and changing process, subject to modification by intraneuronal, extraneuronal, local microenvironmental and even distant regulatory mechanisms."

Black goes on to describe the range of complexity of a single neuron. My summary of his description follows:

- Circuits of neurons are electrochemically coded.

- The circuits of a single neuron may use from two to five transmitters, or coded signal types.

- One transmitter may respond to stimuli independent of other transmitters.

- Each transmitter has multiple states (from two or three discrete states to a continuous state).

- So, for example, four transmitter types with three states each (weak, medium, and strong) would possess the potential for 81 distinct neuronal states.

- The number of neuronal states for a typical neuron may range from just under 100 to the thousands.

- Multiplying these numbers by 10^{11} neurons gives you some idea of the complexity of the system.

Following are some of the informational substances that appear frequently in the literature:

Norepinephrine (also called noradrenaline). This serves as a kind of "printer" that fixes information into long-term memory and helps establish new synapses associated with memory. Rats deprived of norepinephrine can still learn but can't remember. The release of norepinephrine as a result of sympathetic arousal in the fight-or-flight response explains why we so vividly remember information related to moments of shock, fright, or anger.

Calpain. This neurotransmitter serves as a cleanser when it is released by calcium into the synaptic gap.

Dopamine. Dopamine's performance is multifaceted, with various researchers arguing for rival primary roles. LeDoux (2002) suggests that all are correct, that dopamine simply wears many hats, including:

- The basis of reward
- Notification that something novel has occurred
- Switching of attention
- Curiosity-type behaviors (poking around, and so forth) (p. 246)

Too much dopamine is one of the causes of schizophrenia, whereas too little dopamine is associated with Parkinson's symptoms. Higher levels of dopamine are also associated with creativity, the ability to imagine visual scenes in one's head, and the tendency to ask "what if . . ." questions.

Endorphins. Literally, this is the "morphine within" the brain, serving as a tranquilizer and analgesic. It is released in the presence of pain, relaxation exercises, vigorous exercise, and hot chili peppers. Frank Etscorn, of the New Mexico Institute of Mining and Technology, injected endorphin blockers into the bloodstreams of jalapeño pepper eaters. The result was sheer agony. Hot chili peppers are not enjoyable without endorphin release.

Serotonin. Low levels are associated with depression, while increased levels are associated with sleep and relaxation. Serotonin is an amine that is metabolized from the amino acid tryptophan, which is produced in the pancreas by the hydrolyzing action of the enzyme trypsin on proteins. Serotonin constricts blood vessels and contracts smooth muscles; it and norepinephrine are both associated with the RAS switching mechanism: extreme levels prevent flexible switching.

Serotonin is being closely observed in research on depression. While serotonin levels appear to be consistently related to depression, it cannot act alone in influencing depression. (In a 1983 UCLA study, a higher-than-average level of serotonin was found in dominant male vervet monkeys and in officers of college fraternities!)

GABA. GABA (gamma aminobutyric acid) is an inhibitor. When low levels of GABA are found in combination with low levels of serotonin, we have a recipe for violence and aggression. High levels of serotonin and GABA are associated with passive behavior. Franklin (1987) reported that levels of GABA drop while a person is watching violence in action, thus setting the stage for possible increased personal aggression.

Glutamate. Glutamate is the primary excitatory neurotransmitter. As a mnemonic, associate glutamate with a "glutton" for action, or the "gluteus maximus" buttocks muscles, signifying action.

Acetylcholine. Acetylcholine is a neurotransmitter metabolized from dietary fat (fat → lecithin → choline + cholinacetyltransferase → acetylcholine). It is absolutely essential to the health of the neuronal membrane: the cell wall becomes brittle without it. It is also necessary for activating REM (rapid eye movement) sleep, the stage of sleep in which we dream. That is why a minimum level of fat is necessary in our diet (see chapter 7).

The Two Sides of the Brain

Volumes of research have documented the specialization of function in the two hemispheres of the brain, and this topic has captured the imagination of the reading public. Yet the practical, day-to-day implications are few. In addition, many of the findings are exaggerated, with fantastic conclusions drawn from scant data. We do know that the "left brain" (in right-handed individuals, at least) is the seat of language, logic, interpretation, and arithmetic, whereas the "right brain" is the seat of geometry, nonverbal processes, visual pattern recognition (faces, lines), auditory discrimination, and spatial skills. The left brain is used more when examining details, the right when considering the big picture. We know that the left hemisphere

> Note: When you see cross references to other sections of this book, you may benefit from taking time now to read them; they provide information that will deepen your understanding of the current material.

governs activity on the right side of the body and the right hemisphere governs activity on the left side. We know that people of all
ages inwardly exhibit measurable left-brain activity when they out-
wardly engage in approach behaviors, cheerfulness, and other such
positive emotions. Avoidance behaviors and negative emotions, on
the other hand, are associated with activity in the right brain (Fox,
1991). Further, we know (Geary, 1998, pp. 265–268) that with respect
to language, males use most areas of the left hemisphere. In other
words, scans show diffused patterns throughout the left hemisphere
during language use. On the other hand, females show more concentrated focal points of brain activation, and in both hemispheres. With
respect to spatial skills, males use the right hemisphere, females use
both. Many excellent summaries of this research are available (for example, Gazzaniga, 1985).

Although an abundance of literature is available on hemisphericity,
the primary applications of its findings relate to medical and pharmaceutical research-and-development departments. Those of us out on
the street can get little more than interesting poetry. A few everyday applications are available. For example, there is some evidence that talking, in and of itself, promotes positive emotions. If you know people who
need cheering up, find ways to engage them in conversation, either actively or passively: go to a movie or carry on a conversation with a sick
friend. There also is some evidence that artistic activity serves as a ve-
hicle to express negative emotions. So if you know people who need to
deal openly with negative emotions or experiences, try artistic, nonverbal modes of expression. However, to make a big deal, for example, out
of "teaching to the right brain" makes appealing to one's creativity sound
like something new. Hemisphere research has only confirmed that we
have a more creative side and a more linear side.

Brain Waves and Conscious States

The nervous system transmits electrical signals. One way of describing the level of electrical activity is by categorizing the frequency of
the "waves" that are generated in an electroencephalograph:

Beta waves. Above 11 cycles per second (Hz); associated with the
wakeful alertness known as attention and arousal.

Alpha waves. About 9–11 Hz; associated with resting quietly and meditating with the eyes closed; alpha waves typically move back up to beta waves when eyes reopen.

Theta waves. About 4–8 Hz; associated with light sleep.

Delta waves. Under 4 Hz; associated with deep sleep.

References to these four kinds of brain waves will appear throughout this work. An acronym for remembering the sequence is "Brains are thinking daily"—BATD.

SUGGESTED RESOURCES

Dennett, D. C. (1996). *Kinds of Minds: Toward an Understanding of Consciousness.* New York: Basic Books.

Greenfield, S. A. (1996). *The Human Brain: A Guided Tour.* New York: BasicBooks.

Gregory, R. L. (Ed.). (1987). *The Oxford Companion to the Mind.* New York: Oxford University Press.

MacLean, P. D. (1990). *The Triune Brain in Evolution.* New York: Plenum.

Pinker, S. (1997). *How the Mind Works.* New York: Norton.

Restak, R. M. (1994). *The Modular Brain.* New York: Scribner.

3

Tools of the Trade

Brain Imaging Technology and Other Research Methods

> **66 You cannot solve a problem with the same consciousness that created it. 99**
> —Albert Einstein

*T*wo popular resources enable current researchers to make progress in understanding the brain: imaging technology and animals. In this chapter, I will take a brief look at the options currently available and their unique capabilities. The imaging options will appear in roughly chronological order. I will then summarize the reasons for using animals to form conclusions about humans.

Closing out the chapter, I will review the basic features of scientific method as they relate to brain research.

Computerized Axial Tomography (CAT)

Provides a 3-D, structural image of the brain

Computerized axial tomography scanning (also called CAT, or CT, scanning) was invented simultaneously in 1972 by Godfrey Newbold Hounsfield of EMI Central Research Laboratories and Allan McLeod Cormack of Tufts University, who shared a Nobel Prize in medicine in 1979. The word *tomography* comes from the Greek *tomos*, meaning "slice"; the word *tome* claims the same root. Tomography produces cross-sectional pictures of the brain that are like books, or tomes. When placed beside each other, they provide a complete 3-D image of the brain. The word *axial* refers to the scan's ability to rotate about the body's natural line of symmetry, the spine, as it captures the multiple X-ray pictures in order to produce an image of the entire human brain. CAT scans have decreased the need for more invasive surgeries to be performed on patients, because they fully accomplish the same goals of standard exploratory surgical procedures, only without the debilitating pain and lengthy recuperation. Since CAT scans combine X-ray technology and computer-imaging techniques, they are more detailed and thorough than X-ray images alone. You can see illustrations of the CAT machine at www.nerad.com/ct-scan.htm and of its output at www.radiologyinfo.org.

Strengths: Can be used to verify the presence of tumors, blood clots, skull fractures, cysts, infections, and changes in the body's anatomy due to trauma; to measure bone density in evaluating osteoporosis; and for early detection of lung cancer.

Weaknesses: Cannot precisely capture bodily movement, such as heartbeat.

Positron-Emission Tomography (PET)

Measures the level of brain activity

Close on the heels of CAT, UCLA's Michael Phelps invented the PET scanner in 1973. *Positron-emission tomography* (PET) catches the level of activity of specific areas of the brain at specific times. In contrast to CAT, PET is used to determine the chemical function of an organ or tissue, namely the brain, rather than its physical structure. The mechanism consists of injecting very low level radioactive particles (such as the short-lived isotopes of carbon, nitrogen, oxygen, and fluorine) from a tracing solution directly into the brain's blood flow. The PET scanner monitors the emissions of these radionuclides as they flow through the brain. When the particles flow into a given area of the brain, it becomes more active, uses more blood, and therefore registers stronger signals on the scanner. However, the PET process has two significant drawbacks: first, because it uses radioactive material, it cannot be performed repeatedly on the same person; second, it is slow. The process takes one minute to capture the picture and nine more minutes for the radioactive particles to disperse within the brain's blood flow. PET scans cannot be repeated rapidly enough to give a smooth depiction of a process or function. You will find illustrations of the PET machine at www.lymphomainfo.net/tests/pet.html and of its output at www.alzheimers.org/unraveling/07.htm.

Strengths: Used to detect and monitor cancerous growths, malignant tumors, and blocked or narrowed blood vessels; to manage epilepsy by determining the precise region of the brain responsible for the condition; for diagnosing Alzheimer's disease.

Weaknesses: Radioactive particles remain in the body for several days after the scan. Very expensive. Image is not as clear as with CAT and MRI scans. Trained readers are required to analyze results. Difficult to distinguish between inflammation and tumor growth.

Single-Photon Emission-Computed Tomography (SPECT)

Measures the level of brain activity

Single-photon emission-computed tomography (SPECT) is a process similar to PET in that it uses radioactive particles, provides information regarding blood flow to tissue, and has been in use since the early 1970s. It is cheaper and easier to use than PET, but provides less detail. Like PET scans, SPECT scans use radionuclides to determine the amount of blood flow in a given area of tissue. A camera rotates around the patient once the radionuclides have been absorbed into the body, detecting these particles in the body's tissue as it revolves. The radionuclides are absorbed by healthy tissue at a different rate than diseased or damaged tissue. The varying rates of absorption are indicated by differing colors of the SPECT scan, allowing doctors to locate possible areas of cancer or tumor growth. To see pictures of the

SPECT machine, go to amenclinics.com/bp/atlas/ch1.php; for output examples, see amenclinics.com/bp/atlas/ch2.php.

Strengths: Used to detect and monitor cancerous growths, malignant tumors, and blocked or narrowed blood vessels, or to manage epilepsy by determining the precise region of the brain responsible for the condition. Three-dimensionsal; shows contours. Not as expensive as standard PET scans.

Weaknesses: Radioactive particles remain in the body for several days after the scan. Image not as clear as with PET scans. Difficult to distinguish between inflammation and tumor growth; thus, a structurally based scan such as a CAT or MRI will also be required.

Magnetic Resonance Imaging (MRI)

Provides a 3-D, structural image of the brain

Magnetic resonance imaging (MRI) uses a machine in the shape of a huge tube that envelops the subject's whole body. Even with earplugs, the mighty racket is hard to tune out. Regarded as the safest of the brain-imaging techniques, MRI has been around since the early 1980s, and its popularity is steadily growing. Basically, it provides a real-time image of blood flow patterns, revealing what parts of the brain are active during particular tasks. (Illustrations of the MRI machine can be found at www.radiologyinfo.org ; see examples of MRI scan results at faculty.washington.edu/chudler/neurok.htm.)

Researchers are able to view the way brain areas switch on and off as the subject performs different tasks. In place of conventional radiation technology, MRI uses a complex interaction of radio waves and magnetic fields. Low-frequency radio waves (somewhat lower than FM radio waves) activate protons in brain tissue. Water molecules in different parts of the body respond differently to the presence of this wave-field. The resulting 3 mm slices, or images, picked up by the superconducting electromagnet come together to form a 3-D portrait that tells the operator where surges in blood occur in relation to specific mental processes.

In 1991, Ken Kwong and Jack Belliveau of the Imaging Laboratory at Boston's Massachusetts General Hospital showed that MRI technology could be used to do more than take "still" pictures. *Functional MRI* (fMRI) was born; in fMRI, a series of pictures taken close in time actually portray a process, like a "moving" picture. The PET process is ineffective in taking such time-series shots because of its slowness: PET takes one minute to take the picture and nine minutes for the radioactive particles to dissipate. Thus, with PET, the steps of a function can be described only once every 10 minutes. With fMRI, a single shot takes 2–6 seconds, and it can be repeated within seconds. The difference between portraying a process with PET and with fMRI is like the difference between using a 35-mm still camera and a 16-mm movie camera.

Because it is both safe and noninvasive, fMRI can be used on any subject who can handle the noise, the confinement, and the length of the session (up to one hour). Through 1997, the largest MRI machines were rated at 4–4.2 teslas (units of magnetic field strength). In 1998, Ohio State University and the University of Minnesota each acquired machines rated at 7–8 teslas, a 20-fold increase in resolution, or clarity. Plans are under way for two 10-tesla machines to be installed, one on each coast of the U.S. These larger-capacity imagers will permit giant steps in fields of research ranging from dyslexia to depression. But they don't come cheap. Researchers in early 1998 were charged an average of $439 per hour for using the fMRI setup; the machine itself costs around $2 million. With the large price tag comes a good deal of flexibility: the fMRI machine can be programmed to perform a variety of analyses, including

- Classic structural scans

- Blood oxygen level scans

- Diffusion-weighted scans to detect the water level in damaged cells (used for stroke diagnosis)

- Perfusion-weighted scans to detect capillary blood flow

- Spectroscopy, for detecting levels of specific brain chemicals

Interpreting the output of a two-hour fMRI session is a mammoth undertaking. Approximately half a gigabyte of information is produced, enough to nearly fill a standard data CD. The actual changes in blood flow that are measured are not huge swings; they typically represent around a 2–4 percent change. Multiple imaging technologies can be used together to provide complementary perspectives for better diagnosis and understanding.

Strengths: Nontoxic (involves neither radioactive substances nor X-rays); provides detailed images in multiple perspectives; painless;

noninvasive; no preparation other than removing metal objects; no dietary restrictions preceding procedure.

Weaknesses: Expensive; patients with metallic objects such as pacemakers cannot undergo the procedure; must lie still for substantial period; claustrophobia can be a problem.

Positron-Emission Tomography/Computerized Tomography (PET/CT)

Combines the functional information of PET with the structural information of CAT

Named "Invention of the Year" in 2000 by *Time* magazine, PET/CT scans combine the strengths of both PET and CAT scans in one machine. Although a PET scan can detect the presence of a potentially cancerous area of the body, it cannot by itself discern the exact position. A CAT scan is needed to determine detailed information about the location, size, and shape of the growth. However, if the two scans are combined into one PET/CT scan, doctors can pinpoint the exact location, level, and extent of abnormal cell activity. Combining these two scans in one machine saves the patient time and money. See illustrations of the PET/CT machine at www.harthosp.org/cancer/PETCT.htm and of its output at interactive.snm.org.

Strengths: Used to detect cancerous growths and lesions, as well as the exact positioning and shape of each. More cost-efficient than CAT and PET scans performed individually. Quantity of radiation is low. Noninvasive.

Weaknesses: No known drawbacks.

Other Imaging Options

Optical Scanning: Currently under development, optical scanning is a device that attempts to use near infrared light to measure photons emerging through the skull. If successful, this technique could be used in the early detection of brain tumors.

Proton Echo-Planar Spectroscopic Imaging (PEPSI): Permits one to trace the activities of specific brain chemicals in real time. PEPSI was created by Todd Richards, neurophysicist in the radiology department at the University of Washington in Seattle, and colleagues. It is 32 times faster than fMRI, capturing similar information in far less time.

Magnetoencephalography (MEG): Records the magnetic fields produced by actively firing neurons. The MEG system is able to follow the exact time sequence of firing events.

The Use of Animals in Human Research

Both ethical and scientific questions surround the use of animals in human research. The benefits that humans derive from animal-based research continue to outweigh, in the eyes of most, concerns about the animals. The American Psychological Association (1992), along with other professional scientific associations, has established detailed ethical guidelines for the humane treatment of animal (as well as human) subjects. Professional researchers who do not adhere to these ethical guidelines are subject to disciplinary action.

Without animal research, the only way to test the effectiveness of pharmaceutical and surgical procedures would be with humans, or not at all. Without animals, experiments designed to identify the causes of human disorders would have to be done on humans, or not at all. Among the reasons neuroscientists feel comfortable using animals to test hypotheses about the human brain are the following:

- In rats, cats, dogs, monkeys, and humans, the brain consists of nerve cells and glial cells.

- They have equal numbers of neurons in their cortical columns.

- Neurons in all five have axons and dendrites.

- Synaptic complexity accounts for differences in individual behaviors.

- All five communicate through the synapse.

- Neurotransmitters are similar in all five.

- Neurons all receive, store, and transmit impulses.

- Hormonal relationships are similar.

- The brains of all five are immature at birth.

- Brain development differs by sex for all five.

- Most of what we know about the human nervous system originated in animal research.

The Scientific Method: A Warning

Many of us tend to react to the reported results of scientific research as isolated fragments of absolute truth that identify predictable cause-and-effect relationships. The misery that can accompany such gullibility comes chiefly from two kinds of scientific report formats: the *correlation* and the *comparison of means.*

Correlation

Correlations are reported in statements such as "The more melatonin, the better you sleep" or "Melatonin is positively correlated with sleep" or "Melatonin and sleep are positively related" or "Melatonin and wakefulness are negatively related." We misunderstand these statements, because they don't actually say that melatonin *causes* good sleep, just that good sleep is more common among people who have more melatonin. The correlation doesn't mention, and may not take into account, other influences that might disrupt this relationship, such as daylight, other hormones, body weight, high stress levels, age, the source of the melatonin (animal vs. laboratory), the environment (lab, airplane, bedroom, hotel) where the sleep was measured, or the recent consumption of a big meal, alcoholic or caffeinated beverages, or artificial sweeteners. It also doesn't specify whether the quality of the sleep was self-reported or measured by an objective observer. All we know is that for some people, more melatonin means better sleep; however, this may not be true for me or for you.

Recommendation: Approach such conclusions with a cautious, experimental spirit. For example, to see if melatonin works for you, try a cup of warm milk, which triggers melatonin production, before bedtime to see if you sleep better. If you don't, look for an influence that might prevent the melatonin from "working," assuming that it actually works. For example, don't drink alcohol or caffeine or eat chocolate close to bedtime.

Comparison of Means

Be wary when comparisons of means are reported in statements such as "Males score higher on mathematics achievement tests; females score higher on language achievement tests." It is easy to misinterpret this type of statement, because it doesn't say how much higher each sex scores. The gender difference in math achievement scores is extremely small and of little or no practical significance. The comparison also doesn't say which subtests are involved and whether the differences are true for all subtests. It doesn't say at what time of day the tests were administered; some evidence suggests that males' lower testosterone levels in the afternoon influence their achievement and females' lower estrogen-progesterone levels during the 7 to 14 days following ovulation influence theirs. In fact, if half the females in the sample took the tests during the two weeks following ovulation, which is a reasonable assumption, this could more than account for their lowered scores. In addition, we don't know whether the differences hold for all possible cultural groups—socioeconomic, ethnic, educational, and international. And the comparison doesn't say whether the range of scores of one group was similar to that of the other group. One group might score somewhat higher but with a very narrow range of scores, while the second group might score somewhat lower but with a wide range of scores. In searching for the tallest person, for example, you would be more likely to find the tallest person in the second group (lower average height but with a wide range of heights) than in the first group (higher average height but a narrower range).

Recommendation: Realize that differences in average scores are differences in groups, not differences between individuals. Any individual may outscore or underscore members of another group, except in the rare circumstance in which the ranges of scores do not overlap. The value of knowing about group differences is that it explains variations on some basis other than intentional derelictions of duty! For example, males tend to have better day vision, females better night vision, and this difference, where it is true, tends to increase with age. Here's how it applies to me: I typically do the laundry chores in our home, but if I do laundry in the evening, Jane sorts the socks. Acknowledging that this difference applies to us keeps her from accusing me of shirking!

The Caveat Box

As a way of reminding you of the pitfalls of inappropriate reactions to scientific research results, I have come up with the Caveat Box. In the first edition, this message appeared throughout the book as a reminder to take statements with a grain of salt. We made the point emphatically! In this edition, we will show it only this one time.

I hope you will view it both as a personal disclaimer—hey, I'm just passing on research reports—and as a consumer warning: life is not

Warning to Reader: Swallowing everything in this book hook, line, and sinker could be hazardous to your health.

Regarding the (unspecified) measurements shown in the three boxes below, one might state that Group B averages higher than Group A. However, this statement does not, by itself, give you much information.

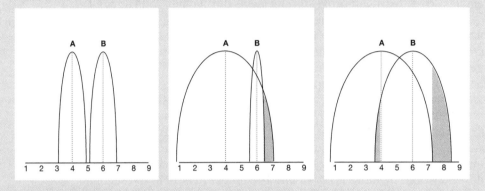

Why is this information incomplete?

- In all three examples, the average for Group A is 4 and the average for Group B is 6.
- In the left-hand box, however, *everyone* in Group B scored higher than anyone in Group A. This is very unusual.
- In the middle box, everyone in Group B scored higher than the Group A average, but a substantial number in Group A outscored Group B altogether (shaded area).
- In the right-hand box, most of those in Group B outscored the average of Group A, but only a fraction of them outscored the highest scorers in Group A (right shaded area), and a few scored below the average of Group A (left shaded area). Beware!

Why might a research finding not apply to you?

- Experiments conducted in laboratories don't always apply to the everyday world.
- You may exhibit a particular feature that the research didn't account for, such as living in an unusual climate, having unusual dietary or exercise patterns, or being subject to environmental influences of which you may or may not be aware, such as gases or X-rays.
- Your genetic code may render you resistant to the finding.
- You may be affected by medication, illness, stress, or other factors.
- Cultural differences may affect the findings.
- The statistics may be incompletely or misleadingly represented.
- The researchers may have made one of two basic errors:

    1. Saying that relationships or differences are present when in fact they are not.

    2. Saying that relationships or differences are absent when in fact they are present.

Figure 3.6. Why Statistics May Be Misleading

drawn in black and white, nor should our judgments be. A demonstration of the problems involved in accepting statistics without question is given in figure 3.6. Helpful hints for detecting misleading presentations in statistical graphs and charts are also found in Darrell Huff, *How to Lie with Statistics* (1954), a classic still available in paperback.

SUGGESTED RESOURCES

American Psychological Association (December 2002). "Ethical Principles of Psychologists and Code of Conduct." *American Psychologist* 57(12), 1060–1073. Available at www.apa.org/ethics.

Bremner, J. D. (2005). *The Brain Imaging Handbook.* New York: W. W. Norton.

Carter, R. (1998). *Mapping the Mind.* Berkeley: University of California Press.

Huff, D. (1954). *How to Lie with Statistics.* New York: Norton.

Shute, N. (1998, March 30). "The Ten-Minute Test for Strokes: New Breakthroughs in What MRIs Can See." *U.S. News & World Report,* pp. 69–72.

Part Two

From the Cradle to the Grave . . .

. . . *with a Turbulent Stop at Adolescence*

Part Two. From the Cradle to the Grave

. . . with a Turbulent Stop at Adolescence

4

Starting Well

Windows of Opportunity

"Reckless youth makes rueful age. "

—Variously attributed to
Sir Thomas More,
Ben Franklin,
and an obscure
French wastrel

Traditional theories of child development, such as those of Jean Piaget, have emphasized stages, or steps. Accordingly, a child might be described as entering the "concrete operations stage." The mountain range of research data generated in child development centers around the world has wreaked havoc on this linear stage model, however, and a new, nonlinear model is emerging. Robert Siegler, psychology professor at Carnegie-Mellon University, has called it the "wave" model, implying that children might begin using a particular task or scheme earlier than was once thought and that at any given point in his or her development, a child might use as many as seven strategies that were formerly thought to appear at different stages. In any specific period of development, according to Siegler (1996), only one or two strategies typically predominate.

| TOPIC 4.1 | The Pregnant Brain: An Up-Front Note to Moms and Dads |

I sometimes teach a module called "Gender Implications of Brain Research" for a local Women in Management seminar. On several occasions, women have asked me to explain their apparent (no, not apparent—real!) absent-mindedness and forget-fulness during late pregnancy and in the postpartum period (during which memory maladies are sometimes joined by depression). Until now, my answer has been a combination of "We don't know" and "It's probably due to being awash in a sea of hormones." New findings from London's Royal Postgraduate Medical School, reported in the July 17, 1997, *Montreal Gazette,* help to clarify this. Anita Holdcroft, an anes-thetist with the research team, has reported that brain shrinkage of 3–5 percent during pregnancy is normal. Compare that with shrinkage of around 10 percent in Alzheimer's patients. Six months after deliv-ery, all the women's brains had returned to normal size. The shrink-age was found in all areas of the brain except for the pituitary, which in fact increased (this increase is related to the hormone bath). This finding helps to explain my students' concerns, as well as the find-ing of a research team at the University of Southern California. There, researchers administered cognitive functioning tests and found that 70 percent of the women in the ninth month of pregnancy exhibited dif-ficulty in learning new information, with an average that was 15–20 per-cent worse than after delivery.

Application

❶ When you experience an increase in absent-mindedness or some other decrease in mental effectiveness during late maternity and the early postpartum period, be amused at yourself and don't take it seriously.

Know that your body is allocating resources elsewhere, and that everything will probably be back to normal within six months after delivery.

TOPIC 4.2   Effects of Various Agents on the Embryo

During the first four months of pregnancy, brain cells in the embryo migrate from their original position to their ultimate destinations by way of *glial cells,* a type of supportive tissue. Alcohol appears to extend these migrations (the cells travel too far), whereas radiation appears to shorten them (they don't travel far enough). As a result, cells end up in the wrong location. The consequence is unpredictable malformation and dysfunction in the newborn infant. Heavier alcohol consumption during pregnancy may lead to mental retardation and abnormal physical development, whereas smaller amounts result in more subtle consequences. David Earnest led a Texas A&M University team that discovered that high doses of alcohol during the last trimester of pregnancy (actually, its equivalent period in rats) resulted in symptoms of advanced aging in the offspring (*Houston Chronicle,* October 27, 1997, p. A5). The symptoms were those of a disrupted circadian rhythm, in which the rats' sleep was severely disturbed and erratic. Sleep disturbances are the second leading cause of institutionalization of seniors. Fetal alcohol syndrome, which was not discovered until 1973, is associated with a plethora of problems in adulthood: 90 percent of those born with this syndrome later have mental health problems, 60 percent have trouble with the law, 50 percent are involuntarily confined, and 50 percent are accused of inappropriate sexual behavior.

The effects of cocaine on the embryo are well documented in most daily newspapers, with lower birth weights, newborn withdrawal, smaller head sizes, and developmental delays among the consequences. Marijuana use during pregnancy appears to be associated with lower birth weights. Pregnant women who consume multivitamins in excess have children with a 25 percent greater incidence of spinal-column defects, which is attributed to an excess of vitamin A. Recommended: only one multivitamin a day (and keep vitamins below 10,000 IU daily). Prescription drugs can also have damaging effects on the embryo; double- and triple-check a prescribed drug before exposing an embryo to it. The effects of nicotine are mentioned in topic 8.7.

Trauma experienced soon after delivery is associated with future heightened response to pain and stress. A team from Queen Charlotte's and Chelsea Hospital in London, England, reported (in *The Lancet*, January 2000) that infants delivered with forceps show greater reaction to routine inoculations and are harder to soothe. In contrast, infants delivered by caesarean section show the least reaction to such pain, and babies born naturally show an in-between, moderate reaction to pain.

On the positive side, research shows that adequate folic acid ("folate") in the diet of women of childbearing age is associated with a 50 percent reduction in risk of neural tube defects (such as spina bifida) in their future offspring. Folate promotes the formation of red blood cells as well as positively influencing genetic development at the cellular level. Since the Centers for Disease Control (CDC) and March of Dimes joined in a campaign to promote folic acid Recommended Daily Allowances in 1998, the number of women taking the RDA has risen to 40 percent in 2004, while the number of neural tube defects has dropped around 25 percent. Most people who eat a balanced diet get their RDA of folate naturally, from vegetables, fruits, grains, nuts, and a variety of other food sources.

Applications

1 Make no assumptions about what is safe to consume while pregnant. Instead, consult your obstetrician. If you are not sure of the advice you are given, consult a neuropharmacologist; if you are still not sure, do your own library and Internet research.

2 The first four months of pregnancy are especially critical. If you think there's a chance you are pregnant, assume you are and consume accordingly.

3 Pregnancy is a good time for mommy and daddy alike to have a nine-month moratorium on alcohol, tobacco, caffeine, and other drugs. Find benign but acceptable substitutes, such as exotic juices, herbal teas and other flavorful but decaffeinated beverages, Postum, flavored/sparkling-flavored or sparkling waters (but *not* those containing aspartame—look for sucralose instead), exercise, and snacks.

4 According to the National Institute on Drug Abuse, 25 percent of the 4 million babies born annually in the United States have been exposed to some legal or illegal drug and have thereby been placed at risk. Don't let your baby, or the baby of someone close to you, be one of these statistics.

⑤ Women of childbearing age should take 400 micrograms daily of folic acid.

⑥ Do not accept forceps delivery of your infant unless no more benign alternative is available.

TOPIC 4.3   Prenatal Learning and Development

Increasing research (Lecanuet, 1995) points to the fetal environment as crucial in the formation of personality, tastes, and even ability. Garlic in the amniotic fluid, for example, appears to predispose a child to accept garlic later in breast milk. Gestating infants learn to prefer their mother's voice patterns and heartbeat and recognize them after birth in contrast to those of strangers. The fetus can also learn to habituate to a stimulus (pay less attention to it over time), a precursor of later ability. The heart rate of the mother varies with the heart rate of the fetus: the mother's heart starts beating faster, then the baby's follows suit. Stress for the mother equates to stress for the fetus: higher cortisol in the mother is accompanied by higher cortisol in the fetus (see explanation of the role of cortisol in stress at topic 36.1.)

Anja Huizink, a researcher at Utrecht University and the Erasmus Medical Center, reports on increasing evidence that intense stress (such as that during the Nazi invasion of the Netherlands) experienced by the mother during the first two trimesters of pregnancy is associated with increased risk for various kinds of psychopathology, but especially schizophrenia (see *Psychological Bulletin*, January 2004). Speaking at the Society of Behavioral Medicine in San Diego (reported in *USA Today*, March 8, 1999), Pathik Wadhwa (University of Kentucky College of Medicine, Lexington) emphasized that the uterus is an environment in which stress affects the development of the fetus. In one study of 156 fetuses, those whose mothers wanted the baby, had high self-esteem, and received plenty of support had the calmest heart rate, whereas those whose mothers felt anxiety, received little support, and had high levels of stress hormones had significantly higher heart rates (linked to later heart disease and diabetes). In another study of 513 expectant mothers, stress level was associated with retarded fetal growth, lower birth weight, and increased likelihood of premature delivery. These effects are detectable as early as the second trimester. Reducing stress during pregnancy can eliminate these problems.

Christine Dunkel-Schetter and her associates at UCLA have conducted a variety of studies concerning stress and maternity. Among their findings (summarized in the *APA Monitor,* October 1999):

1. Expectant mothers experiencing high stress are up to four times more likely to deliver prematurely.

2. Their babies are more likely to have lower birth weight.

3. They show elevated levels of corticotropin-releasing hormone (CRH) as early as 18 weeks after conception.

4. It appears that stress per se does not influence length of gestation and birth weight, but rather the mother's response to stressors. More optimistic expectant mothers who have positive expectations and feel a sense of control during their pregnancy do not appear to be adversely affected by high stress.

Applications

❶ Don't underestimate the value of the nine months of pregnancy as a time to begin providing the optimum environment for your child. Introduce different tastes, your favorite music, dance steps, and other experiences you enjoy.

❷ Pregnancy is a crucial time in your life to marshal whatever resources are available to you in order to minimize significant, sustained sources of stress. The more your network can help you during pregnancy, the less you'll have to call on them over the duration of your child's lifetime.

❸ Pregnancy is the time to use all of the stress reduction techniques at your disposal: meditation, relaxation methods, and so forth (see topic 36.1 for a list of stress-reduction strategies).

TOPIC 4.4   Temperament and the Prediction of Adult Personality

The term *temperament* refers to neurological processes that are (1) inherited and (2) observable as behaviors from infancy—even, in some cases, in the womb. Here are some examples of temperament:

- *Activity.* The number of times the infant moves his or her head, arms, hands, legs, or feet per unit of time

- *Adaptability (anger).* How quickly an infant adjusts to changes, such as the disappearance of a parent

- *Approach/withdrawal.* The tendency to examine a novel object or person (vs. backing away)

- *Attentiveness/persistence.* How long an infant persists in focusing his or her attention on a particular object or person

- *Rhythmicity.* The regularity or irregularity with which an infant defecates, urinates, gets hungry, and goes to sleep

- *Sensory sensitivity.* How much sensory stimulation (light, heat, touch, smell, noise) an infant is comfortable being around

These infant behaviors, known as the temperament of the child, foreshadow later adult personality. Although temperament is inherited, adult personality is based on inheritance plus what is learned from the environment. But what is learned must form around the core of these inherited neurological processes (Halverson, Kohnstamm, and Martin, 1994).

Adult personality (see chapter 33 for a more complete treatment) is currently described in terms of the "Big Five" traits, and each of these traits has at its core one or more of the infant temperaments:

- The adult trait of *Need for Stability* concerns one's capacity for dealing with stress: rhythmicity predicts it.

- The adult trait of *Extraversion* concerns one's capacity for sensory stimulation: activity level and sensory sensitivity predict it. Very active infants who are comfortable with lots of stimulation tend to become more extraverted.

- The adult trait of *Originality* concerns one's breadth of interests: approach/withdrawal predicts it. Infants who approach and examine tend to be more innovative and creative.

- The adult trait of *Accommodation* concerns one's tendency to submit to or defy others: adaptability predicts it. Infants who get angry when a parent departs tend to become challenging and egocentric as adults.

- The adult trait of *Consolidation* concerns the degree to which one is self-disciplined and focused on goals: attentiveness/persistence predicts it. Infants who spend longer periods of time focused on a single object or person tend to be more ambitious and self-disciplined as adults.

Applications

❶ *Accept.* Although these infant precursors of adult personality are not 100 percent predictive, they are strong indicators. Begin at a child's earliest age to appreciate her individuality. Understand that trying to suppress or change her inherited neurological processes can result in unhealthy development. Rather than wishing a child were more still (that is, less active), celebrate her activity level and don't expect her to be a retiring introvert as an adult.

❷ *Build.* Identify activities that build on a child's temperament rather that fight against it. For example, for a child who naturally likes to focus on one toy for an extended period, don't keep introducing new toys or activities. Wait until he loses interest in the current activity. This encourages focus rather than trying to force variety. Focus and variety are two different elements of temperament; watch for them separately, and celebrate whichever you find (or even both!).

TOPIC 4.5   Breastfeeding

After reviewing some 20 published studies on breastfeeding, James W. Anderson, professor of medicine and clinical nutrition at the University of Kentucky in Lexington, reported (in *American Journal of Clinical Nutrition,* October 1999) that suckled infants average 3–5 points higher on IQ than formula-fed babies. What's more, the longer the infant is breastfed, the greater the gain in IQ (up to nine months, at which point the effect appears to end). Anderson attributes this edge to the presence of DHA (docosahexaenoic acid) and AA (arachidonic acid) in breast milk and not in formula sold in the U.S. DHA and AA are long-chain polyunsaturated fatty acids associated with neural growth.

A debate rages concerning the wisdom of adding DHA to infant formula. Common in Asia and Europe (and approved by the World Health Organization), the practice has been banned by the FDA in the U.S. DHA is found in mothers' breast milk and is associated with improved vision and cognitive functioning of infants. Adding synthetic DHA to infant formula would make it more like breast milk, but authorities are uncertain of its safety and effectiveness. Some suspect that the decision is a political one, due to the added expense of producing formula with DHA.

It is instructive to note that research results are easily confounded by pesky rival explanations. In the case of breastfeeding and IQ, as the University of Kentucky points out, the increased IQ could be attributed to the enhanced bonding between mother and nursing infant, in comparison to supposedly inferior bonding when bottle fed.

Incidentally, in December 1997 the American Academy of Pediatrics changed its minimum recommended period of breastfeeding from 6 months to 12 months.

Applications

1 If you are the mother of a newborn, do what you need to do to breastfeed your baby as long as you can. A commitment to breastfeed until the child is nine months old is optimum for the child. Anything beyond that is really more a matter of the mother's personal preference or lifestyle.

2 Many states have laws that make public breastfeeding a crime. Florida struck down its statute in March 1993. Help your state do the same if it has such a law.

TOPIC 4.6   The Critical Early Years (Ages 1–3)

A growing body of research suggests that the first three years of life are critical to brain development. During this period, the infant has twice as many neurons *and* twice as many synapses as adults.

Dr. Frances Campbell, chief investigator for the Abecedarian Project, reported in October 1999 (at www.fpg.unc.edu/~abc) on the results of a 21-year study of the effects of high-quality child care on later development. In 1972, the University of North Carolina–Chapel Hill's Frank Porter Graham Child Development Center accepted applications from 111 low-income infants' families. The newborns were randomly assigned to treatment (high-quality care) or nontreatment (standard care, including staying at home). Twenty-one years later, the treatment group excelled (over the nontreatment group) in reading skills, college attendance, and job retention. Moreover, the treatment group had their first child on average at age 19, compared with 17 for the nontreatment group.

In a related study conducted by the Graham center, researchers evaluated 89 African American children in 27 different U.S. day care centers representing the full spectrum of quality, from high to low. Two-thirds of these six-month-old to four-year-old children were from low-income families. The reported (in *Child Development,* March–April 2000) results showed the children in higher-quality child care to be about 12 points higher in IQ and about 2½ months advanced in language skills.

William Staso, a school psychologist in Orcutt, California, in his book *What Stimulation Your Baby Needs to Become Smart* (1995), recommends addressing seven critical periods:

1. *Month 1:* Eliminate background distraction (radio, television, washing machine) so your baby is optimally relaxed and attentive to your talking, singing, or other foreground activity.

2. *Months 1–3:* For proper neural articulation, emphasize contrasts (light vs. dark colors, low vs. high pitch, simple vs. complex timbre, rough vs. smooth textures). Parenthetically, it is interesting to note that children whose fathers were actively involved in the first six months of their care scored higher on subsequent measures of intellectual and motor development.

3. *Months 3–5:* For visual development, use pictures of baby's real-world objects (spoons, cups, wagons) as part of play activity.

4. *Months 6–7:* Emphasize cause and effect (turn the knob and the door opens), locations of various objects ("Where's the kitty? There she is!"), and functions of environmental objects ("What does the ball do? Bounce! See!").

5. *Months 7–8:* Emphasize sound as a signal of impending events (running water signals a bath, car in the driveway signals "Mommy's back!").

6. *Months 9–12:* Explore motor and sensory skills and how they combine (turn the faucet and feel the water). Twelve-month-olds can remember behaviors they have observed for 30 seconds for up to one week. By around 12 months of age, infants typically learn one or two new behaviors daily simply by observing people in their environment.

7. *Months 13–18:* Explore objects in the environment; this is the time to make the environment especially diverse and rich. Explore sequences and relationships (build towers of diverse shapes, make trains of different sizes—bigger, smaller, bigger, smaller, and so on). Hayne finds that 18-month-olds can remember observed behaviors for up to one month.

Recent research has established parental nurture, specifically touching and stroking, as essential not only for healthy development in animals and humans but also for normal neuronal growth. Mark Smith, of the DuPont Merck Research Laboratories, Wilmington, Delaware, found that laboratory animal infants deprived of maternal care lost brain cells at twice the rate of those who were left with their moms. Stroking stimulates the production of chemicals that inhibit the stress hormones—including cortisol—that kill neurons. In fact, Ron de Kloet, a neurobiologist at the University of Leiden in the Netherlands, reported at the October 1997 New Orleans meeting of the Society for Neuroscience that even substitute parenting helps to avoid the chemical damage resulting from maternal deprivation. By stroking newborn mice who were deprived of their mothers with a moist brush (simulating mom's licking) for one minute three times a day (sound like a prescription?), researchers were able to eliminate most of the neuronal damage that typically results from maternal deprivation. Mary Carlson of Harvard Medical School studied two- to three-year-old Romanian infants raised in orphanages or sent to poor-quality day care centers. She found that the orphans had abnormally high and lasting levels of cortisol, and that the day care children had abnormally high cortisol levels on weekdays; however, when they returned home for the weekend, their levels returned to normal (*Los Angeles Times,* October 28, 1997, p. 1A). High levels of cortisol are associated both with the destruction of brain cells and with learning and memory problems.

Craig Ramey, a psychologist at the University of Alabama in Birmingham, cites evidence that disadvantaged children benefit from a rich educational curriculum and a loving environment. Infants enrolled in such educational programs five days a week had IQs 15 points higher than those of similar children who were not helped; the difference was first observed at the age of two. In a 1975 study of 180 high-risk children, Byron Egeland of the University of Minnesota's Institute of Child Development found that children with a strong attachment to their mothers at age one were significantly less likely to exhibit behavior problems and more likely to have stable relationships later in life. He further found that infants who were neglected by their mothers ended up just as prone to violence as infants who were severely abused physically. Moreover, neglect resulted not only in aggression but in a large and permanent drop in IQ. Egeland's research has given birth to the "Attachment Theory" and an accompanying movement to secure strong bonds between infants and their mothers early on.

John Bruer, a philosopher by training and president of the research-sponsoring James S. McDonnell Foundation in St. Louis, Missouri (see more at www.jsmf.org), takes on the folks who claim that parents must flood their infants with education and stimulation during the first three years of life, at the end of which the capacity for learning supposedly slams shut. He identifies (1999) three arguments of these "critical periods" advocates: during the first three years of life, (1) an abundance of synapses are available, (2) critical periods come and go for learning specific skills, knowledge, and behaviors, and (3) enriched environments are crucial for taking advantage of (1) and (2). Bruer systematically takes these arguments apart and down, showing that (1) an abundance of uncommitted synapses are available for learning throughout the lifespan—far more than we can ever employ, (2) the "critical periods" (e.g., visual perception and language development) can be satisfactorily met through a normal upbringing, and (3) the "enriched environment" argument is basically a "slippery slope" in which impoverished environments are shown to be inferior to enriched ones (the evidence shows that environments somewhere in between are fine for learning and development). Bruer also argues for the pervasive influence of genetics, so that parenting becomes a job of recognizing a child's strengths and encouraging them.

Applications

❶ Support early childhood interventions such as Head Start and an expanded Family and Medical Leave Act.

2 Expect and work toward the highest quality in day care programs. The U.S. Department of Defense has been cited for exemplary quality in its day care programs.

3 Make a poster of the seven periods identified above by Dr. Staso. Use it as an aid in remembering what to emphasize in your play with your (and others') infants.

4 Ensure that the infants in your life receive touches and stroking from birth and throughout every day of their lives.

5 If you (as a nurse, aide, teacher, social worker) are around infants and have an idle moment, pick them up and hold or stroke them. In a recent trip to visit a friend in a hospital, I saw two nurses at their station who were holding babies from the nursery, cooing, stroking, cradling, singing—laughing—generally giving pleasure and enjoying it. I don't know if they knew the research, but they were certainly engaged in behavior that the research strongly encourages.

6 For more details, obtain a copy of the Carnegie Corporation of New York's 1994 report, *The Early Brain,* by visiting its website at **www.carnegie.org**.

7 In accordance with John Bruer's findings, don't be too hung up on making the absolutely right move at the absolutely right time with your infant. Enjoy her, love her, live as full a life as you can with her, listen to and respond to her. But don't fret if you don't introduce just the right toy on just the right day of just the right month! It's like prayer: pray, but act as though the prayer will be unanswered. Trust your child to be resilient, but why not introduce her on occasion to something an "expert" says is timely?

| TOPIC 4.7 | **Prematurity—A Whine Before Its Time . . .** |

Marilyn Stern and colleagues at the University of Albany reported (in *APA Monitor,* October 1999) on a phenomenon called "prematurity stereotyping." According to their findings, when told falsely that full-term five- to seven-month-old infants were prematurely delivered, mothers (of other children), nurses, college students, and medical students alike not only talked about the infant in a more negative manner, they behaved negatively toward them. This preemie stereotyping involved describing the infants as weaker, less sociable, and less mature. The "handlers" held them and touched them less, and they interacted with them less than with babies identified as full term. When allowed to select toys for infants identified as "premature," these handlers picked more "immature" toys. Premature children whose mothers scored high on Stern's "Prematurity Stereotyping" scale showed less cognitive development than premature infants whose mothers were less prone to stereotyping.

Dr. Heidelise Als of Harvard University reports that premature babies tend to develop reading problems when exposed at birth to bright, noisy, busy environments that interrupt necessary brain development of communication networks. Altering the birth environment to more closely resemble that of the womb—i.e., dark, quiet, and calm—allows brain development to proceed apace. This alleviates later reading problems.

Applications

❶ Maternity clinics should identify pessimistic expectant mothers and train them in Seligman's "learned optimism," which involves a positive explanatory style (explained at some length at topic 37.5).

❷ Maternity clinics should educate parents on the negative effects of stereotyping premature infants. This is closely related to the optimism training.

❸ If you are involved around premature deliveries, make your associates aware of the need to keep premature babies in a dark, quiet, calm, womb-like environment through the approximate length of their normal term.

TOPIC 4.8   Irreversible Damage (Age Eight)

Generally, studies point to eight years of age as the point after which brain damage is irreversible at the worst, difficult to overcome at best. Although neurons can be replaced, the current evidence is that replacement is slow and meager. In young children, however, other parts of the brain can pick up functions lost due to brain damage. The story is frequently told of a five-year-old who lost one entire hemisphere; this individual is now in her 50s and possesses an above-average IQ. After the age of eight, such recovery appears to be impossible.

On the other hand, loss of brain function is different from loss of brain cells. If the cells remain and only function is lost, growing evidence of the brain's plasticity suggests that dramatic recoveries are possible. Richard Restak (1997, pp. 50–51) tells the story of a 78-year-old woman who suffered worsening mental function for four years. When she was finally diagnosed with an obstructed cerebrospinal flow, doctors inserted a shunt and, to their surprise, found that she experienced significant recovery of mental function.

Applications

❶ Every time you put your children in an automobile, buckle them up with seat belts and car seats.

❷ Have high expectations for children younger than eight years of age who are recovering from brain damage.

❸ Be prepared for the possibility of permanent loss of function from brain damage that occurs after age eight.

❹ For a thorough review of neuroplasticity issues and the prospects for remapping the brain, read J. M. Schwartz and S. Begley (2002), *The Mind and the Brain: Neuroplasticity and the Power of Mental Force.*

TOPIC 4.9   Adverse Conditions and the Resilient Child

In a special issue of the *American Psychologist*, Ann Masten and Douglas Coatsworth (1998, pp. 205–220) conclude that two factors are associated most with the tendency of some children in unfavorable, adverse environments to emerge with competence in meeting the developmental tasks of growing up, from language development and self-control to the ability to form close friendships and succeed in both academic and extracurricular performance. The first factor is the child's relationships with *prosocial* (as opposed to antisocial) adults, whether they are within the immediate family or outside the family. The second factor is the possession of good intellectual functioning, including problem-solving ability, language comprehension and vocabulary, and logical-mathematical ability. Apparently a lack of sufficient brainpower reduces some children's ability to be clever in resisting and escaping antisocial influences.

Applications

❶ Focus on the schoolwork of at-risk children and help them develop the cognitive skills that foster quick thinking, patience in problem solving, and creative, out-of-the-box solutions so they can take the time to understand the causes of problems and generate multiple possible solutions.

❷ Focus on the social development of at-risk children, helping them build long-term relationships with adults who are making positive contributions to society, whether they are teachers, coaches, Big Brothers and Big Sisters, internship sponsors, career mentors, family members, neighbors, public safety officers, employers, co-workers, club advisers, social workers, or the members or staff of religious organizations.

TOPIC 4.10   Memory in Early Childhood (Infancy to Ages 7–10)

The formation of memory involves both storage and recall. Infants appear to have an unusually high incidence of failure to store new memories. According to a panel of early childhood researchers at the April 1995 meeting of the Society for Research in Child Development (reported in the *APA Monitor,* June 1995, pp. 1 ff.), the storage failure rate begins to decline around age seven and reaches a normal rate around age ten. However, under the proper circumstances, children can store memories permanently starting at the age of two. The panel described the proper circumstances as events having to do with the personal values, goals, and pleasures of the two-year-old.

Application

❶ If you would like your two-year-old or older child to especially remember a particular experience, you must periodically assist the child in recalling the event. Practice is crucial for memory formation (see more on memory in chapter 23, especially at topic 23.4).

TOPIC 4.11 **Infants and Sleep**

Dr. Jodi Mindell is associate director of the Sleep Disorders Center at Children's Hospital of Philadelphia, where she specializes in treating sleep problems of infants, children, and adolescents. Some of her findings:

1. Once infants are capable of falling asleep on their own (i.e., without an adult rocking or otherwise soothing them into sleep), they are also capable of sleeping through the night.

2. Many sleep problems stem from irregular going-to-bed times, inconsistent bedtime routines, parents staying in the room after laying the child down, and excessive reliance on being "rocked" to sleep in a moving car. Eliminating these behaviors can eliminate associated sleep problems.

3. Other sleep problems are addressed with medications or surgery (e.g., for tonsils).

4. For other information, check Dr. Mindell's contributions to the Baby Center website at www.babycenter.com/refcap/baby/babysleep/7526.html. Also, get her two books:

   a. *Sleeping Through the Night* (1997)

   b. Mindell, J. A., and J. A. Owens, *A Clinical Guide to Pediatric Sleep* (2003)

Applications

 Begin expecting your infant to sleep through the night when he begins to fall asleep spontaneously—i.e., without your rocking, lullabying, etc.—during the day.

❷ Establish a regular bedtime for your infant.

❸ Do not fall into the habit of allowing your child to fall asleep in the car at night as a way to induce sleep.

4 Read Dr. Mindell's books for other ideas, and follow her work through her website.

SUGGESTED RESOURCES

Alkon, D. L. (1992). *Memory's Voice: Deciphering the Brain-Mind Code.* New York: HarperCollins.

Bruer, J. T. (1999). *The Myth of the First Three Years.* New York: The Free Press.

Caplan, T., and F. Caplan (1982). *The Second Twelve Months of Life.* New York: Bantam Books.

Caplan, T., and F. Caplan (1984). *The Early Childhood Years: The Two- to Six-Year-Old.* New York: Bantam Books.

Caplan, T., and F. Caplan (1995). *The First Twelve Months of Life* (rev. ed.). New York: Bantam Books.

Eisenberg, A., H. E. Murkoff, and S. E. Hathaway (1996). *What to Expect: The Toddler Years.* New York: Workman Publishing.

Halverson, C. F., Jr., G. A. Kohnstamm, and R. P. Martin (Eds.). (1994). *The Developing Structure of Temperament and Personality from Infancy to Adulthood.* Hillsdale, N.J.: Erlbaum.

Leach, P. (1997). *Your Baby and Child: From Birth to Age Five* (rev. ed.). New York: Knopf.

Lecanuet, J. P. (1995). *Fetal Development: A Psychobiological Perspective.* Hillsdale, N.J.: Erlbaum.

Nathanielsz, P. W. (1999). *Life in the Womb: The Origin of Health and Disease.* Ithaca, N.Y.: Promethean Press.

Sears, W., and M. Sears (1993). *The Baby Book.* New York: Little, Brown.

Shelov, S. P. (1998). *Caring for Your Baby and Young Child* (rev. ed.). New York: Bantam Books.

5

The Tumultuous Teens

Understanding the Adolescent Brain

Most of this book is about what we might refer to as the "normal" times of life, when no major brain and body changes are taking place. This section, however, addresses the three periods when such major changes occur: birth and early childhood, adolescence, and aging. Adolescence, the period from puberty to early adulthood, is a complex period characterized by major brain growth, hormonal changes, physical changes, emotional changes, and social changes. The teen years have been likened to a railroad switching yard with far more miles of track than any one train needs in order to maneuver from one siding to another. The teen's brain, as we shall see, is very much like that—and it is precisely this excess capacity that accounts for the volatility of emotions and relationships during these years.

TOPIC 5.1   The Pre-Puberty Neuronal Explosion

Dr. Jay Giedd, chief of brain imaging, child psychiatry section, National Institute of Mental Health, has studied the brains of 1,800 teenagers since 1990 (see feature in *Time,* May 10, 2004). Challenging the traditional notion that the brain fully matures by puberty, Giedd places the point of maturity closer to age 25. Explaining typical adolescent emotional outbursts and risk-taking behavior, Giedd points to (1) raging hormones and (2) late development of the decision-making part of the brain. Also, in an 8- to 10-year longitudinal study examining the development of the brain in 13 children ages 4–21, lead researcher Dr. Nitin Gogtay (NIMH, Bethesda, Maryland) used brain-mapping technology to make periodic scans, ultimately combining them into a presentation showing 17 years of brain development in only a few seconds. The results show that the prefrontal cortex is the last to mature, typically between ages 18 and 21; this explains in part why teenagers find it difficult to reason, plan, and make decisions.

The brain undergoes two episodes of major growth and subsequent pruning back of excess cells, one during the second trimester of gestation, the other in late adolescence. These two "tidal waves" (i.e., rise and fall, growth and pruning) are qualitatively different. The first involves birth and subsequent pruning of new cells; the second involves growth and subsequent pruning of new synapses. Sometime between the ages of 6 and 12, the growth spurt of synaptic elaboration begins, reaching highest density ("bushiness") for girls around age 11, for boys around age 12½. (Note, however, that brain growth and puberty are independent—the brain will continue its growth spurt even if puberty is delayed.) This profusion of "gray matter" is far more than can be used and represents raw material for learning. Between the peak density around puberty and around age 25 (somewhat later for boys), the gray matter dies out (i.e., the excess is "pruned") at a rate of about 0.7 percent annually. While excess capacity is being shed, the "white matter"—the myelin sheath that protects the axon—continually thickens, thus increasing the safety, permanence, and speed of the axon's transmission. Thus we simultaneously lose capacity and gain efficiency, and although we gain in speed of transmission, we lose in ease of learning and recovery from trauma.

With all this capacity, and with its relentless dying off, the rate of loss is inversely proportional to what we learn with it. The more we learn—languages, musical instruments, athletic skills, history—the less dies off. And the more we practice what we learn—practice the violin, recite the poetry, speak the French—the thicker grows the myelin sheath. That is why London cabbies have such large hippocampi: the myelin sheaths on their neural connections associated with memory for London streets thickens daily with practice. Learning saves gray matter, while practice thickens white matter. It seems that gray matter appears on our stage and remains only if used, if we learn new roles with it, stalking off our stage forever if ignored.

In both growth spurts, the process begins in the rear of the brain (the part that connects us to the world through the five senses), moving through the middle part (the part that coordinates movement and sensation), finally reaching the *prefrontal cortex*—the executive part of the brain that governs decision making and planning (see appendix A). Hence, it is not just hormones that affect teenage emotionality and unpredictability: the management function is the last to develop. The typical teenager walks around with excess capacity, hormones urging him on to learn with that capacity ("Explore!"), yet lacking the capacity he will later develop for sound decision making. Compounding this tendency are the elevated levels of dopamine circulating in the teen's body, with the associated increase in "What if I. . . ?" behavior characterized by curiosity, fantasizing, and risk-taking. The capacity for acting responsibly is the last to develop. And, of course, this is an individual difference variable—some begin with more "executive function" than others.

This combination—excess capacity, maturity of the sensory cortex, flooding of sex hormones, elevation of dopamine, and late development of the maturity module—is a recipe for excitement seeking, like a race car without brakes. But a word of warning for teenagers: late maturation of the maturity module doesn't mean you must wait to practice maturity! Just as you practice your violin daily to thicken your myelin sheath in order to develop effective violin movements, so must you be expected to practice daily your management skills—prioritizing, scheduling, follow-through, evaluating alternatives, considering consequences. Develop the habit early of talking to yourself with phrases such as "Do I really want this on my résumé?" Reinforce mature actions and attitudes with wall posters, notes, parental and teacher reminders. This will prepare your brain for a time when such managerial behavior will come more naturally.

One key to managing adolescents is to remember that short-term motivation is linked to the pleasure-pain centers, whereas long-term motivation is linked to the prefrontal cortex, which is not yet mature. Thus, linking an undesirable behavior (skipping class) to a short-term consequence (you don't get your favorite breakfast made for you) should be more effective than linking it to a long-term consequence (you won't get into the college of your choice).

All this explains the influence of the salient peer group. In the absence of self-management maturity modules, young people from 8 to 25 allow the salient peer group to structure their time. (See more below at topic 5.6.)

Applications

❶ The American Bar Association has urged all states to ban the death penalty for adolescents because of their reduced capacity for self-management. Your state should comply. (In 2005 the U.S. Supreme Court ruled that sentencing anyone under the age of 18 to death is cruel and unusual punishment and therefore unconstitutional.)

❷ Teenagers should never be tried as adults.

❸ Twenty-five is a good target age for considering a young person sufficiently mature for adult responsibilities. (This happens to be the minimum age at which you can rent a car!)

❹ Lavish praise and affection on your adolescent. The research shows no ill effects, so long as you don't embarrass her around her friends.

❺ Don't back off just because your child is older. Remain a part of his activities and get to know his friends.

❻ Provide discipline and structure, but be appropriately flexible. Be fair but firm, kind but strict. Relax the rules when maturity is exhibited, then tighten up again when you see backsliding.

7 Teenage independence is normal and should not be viewed as disrespectful. Provide structure, but don't get too much into the details.

8 Have good reasons for your rules. Teens' capacity for reasoning will outgrow the old "because I said so" rationale.

9 For more ideas (and rationale) for parenting teens, see Laurence Steinberg's *The Ten Basic Principles of Good Parenting* (2004).

10 Remember the Big Three of parenting a teen: love, structure, and patience.

11 Remember the Big Three of being a teen: explore (but accept limits), be independent (but accept love), and practice what you're good at (so you'll have something to show for all your exploration).

12 Be creative and use your computer graphic capabilities (or your own natural artistic skill) to make posters, t-shirt transfers, and other external reminders that take the burden off both the parent and teenager of remembering deadlines, obligations, and so forth.

TOPIC 5.2   Processing Instructions with Emotion

Deborah Yurgen-Todd, director of neuropsychology and cognitive neuroimaging at McLean Psychiatric Hospital, Belmont, Massachusetts, has found that teenagers process emotions and instructions differently from adults (*U.S. News & World Report*, August 9, 1999, pp. 45–54). Functional MRI images that compared young people ages 9–17 with 20- to 40-year-old adults revealed that the young people processed emotions, instructions, and procedures much more consistently in the *amygdala* (the seat of emotions), whereas adults processed the same activities more consistently in the *frontal lobe* (the seat of rationality). In addition to processing these activities in an emotion-ridden manner—as if normal conversation were being passed through an emotional filter—the young people found it more difficult to identify these emotions accurately to other people. Part of the explanation for these phenomena relates to the continuing development of white matter necessary for complete communication. The frontal area of the brain does not appear to be fully mature until the late 20s (some say 25, others 28, still others 30). Boys' brains typically mature later—by a couple of years—than girls' brains.

Applications

1 When young people respond emotionally, understand that the storm is natural and not to be taken personally. Let it pass like a summer shower, and get on with life.

2 Teach your young people over time to identify the emotions of others in their lives. Accurately identifying emotions is a development-related skill.

3 When young people follow directions imperfectly, understand that internally the directions had to pass through a tempest-tossed sea. Supplement the original instructions or directions with spoken or written reminders or crutches—and be kind. Expect incomplete reception of your original message. Don't be blameful; be patient. And be glad when they've grown out of it!

4 Use your teenager's outbursts as an opportunity to practice and expand your sense of humor: "Isn't that just like a teenager!?" Receive the tempest with a chuckle, not a groan. However, your smile should probably be internal; overt delight in a teen's outburst could be perceived as discounting or mocking.

TOPIC 5.3   Memory vs. Musing as a Basis for Decision Making

When they need to make a decision, adults rely on quickly accessible images associated with the situation. For example, when feeling the car begin to fishtail on an icy road, the adult, who has probably had many such previous experiences, doesn't have to reason about what to do. Instead, she quickly reviews visual memories of her past responses to this situation and selects the most promising one. Teenagers, on the other hand, simply because they've not lived long enough, do not have a repertoire of responses, nor the established emotional link to the response that is most satisfying. As a result, the teenager is more likely to attempt to reason through the situation. This takes longer and can lead to disastrous results if a quick response is necessary.

Antonio Damasio has demonstrated that the amygdala is involved in decision making. Given the alternatives, the amygdala provides an emotional push to select the alternative that feels right. If the individual lacks experience in the context of the specific decision, it becomes very difficult, if not downright paralyzing, to make a decision. No alternative emerges as the gut-supported right one.

Applications

❶ Teens should defer to more experienced persons in situations where quick decision making is required. However, teens also need the experience in order to build up their internal encyclopedia of memories for future use. The compromise: the teen drives but has a more experienced partner in the front seat with permission to intervene when necessary.

❷ Find ways to get teens to acquire more experience in risky decision making by means of exposure to situations that have a safety net of some sort. For example, get a wintry driving simulation that the teen can play with on the computer.

TOPIC 5.4   **Teenage Circadian Rhythm and School Start Time**

Mary Carskadon, sleep physiologist at Brown University's Bradley Hospital sleep lab, finds that teenagers need approximately 9¼ hours of sleep nightly, but most get only 7 hours or so (Martin, 1999). Teenagers need the extra sleep in order to produce the hormones necessary for growth. Also, before puberty, melatonin production in kids tends to shut down around 7:17 A.M.; puberty delays the shutdown to around 8:34 A.M. The typical teenager in class at 8:00 A.M. is still producing melatonin and fighting the urge to sleep.

In a study of 3,120 Rhode Island school children, Amy Wolfson, psychology professor at the College of the Holy Cross, Worcester, Massachusetts, found significant correlation between amount of sleep and grades: the less sleep, the lower the grades (Martin, 1999). In Edina, Minnesota (a suburb of Minneapolis), school start time was moved in 1996 from 7:20 to 8:30 A.M. Before this switch, the top 10 percent of the graduating seniors scored 580–720 on the SAT, but by three years after the switch, the range for the top 10 percent had jumped to 600–760. The Minneapolis school system has followed Edina's lead. Start time for the seven high schools in the district was changed from 7:15 to 8:40 A.M., dismissal time from 1:45 to 3:20 P.M. Kyla Wahlstrom, Associate Director of the Center for Applied Research and Educational Improvement (CAREI) at the University of Minnesota, conducted the study. The data for Minneapolis, which came out in December 2000, are even more impressive. Grades improved (although the difference was not statistically significant because of severe difficulties in analyzing the data), attendance improved, the dropout rate fell, teenagers' sleep increased, classroom performance improved, fewer mood swings were evident, and morale improved. Wahlstrom recommends an ideal start time of 8:30 A.M. (or later) for children who have reached puberty; if a more definite age is desired, she would peg it at 14.

Applications

❶ For teenagers (or anyone) who must wake early each morning, keep the lights low in the evening; encourage a reasonably early bedtime; then, at wakeup time, throw open the curtains and turn on all the lights. Have them do something active, preferably outdoors, like walking the dog.

❷ Most sleep researchers agree that the best school start time for teenagers is 8:30 A.M. or later. Follow the results of school start time changes in high schools around the country that have dared to move their start time to 8:30 A.M.: Minneapolis, Pike County (Kentucky), and Arlington County (Virginia) are three examples.

❸ Politically and logistically, changing school start time is rife with complications, not the least of which is what to do about bus fleets. One estimate was that the fleet must be tripled as a consequence of no longer being able to use the same buses for older students (who have gone to school earlier) as for younger students (who have gone to school later). A possible solution is to switch, with elementary students starting earlier, high schoolers later.

❹ Because sleep deprivation interferes more with divergent thinking tasks than with convergent ones, place extra importance on teenagers' getting nine hours of sleep before essay-question tests or other tests that involve recall and complex associations. Performance on simpler recall tests, such as standard multiple-choice, seem to suffer less from sleep deprivation.

⑤ Check periodically for updated information on CAREI's website at www.education.umn.edu/CAREI.

| **TOPIC 5.5** | **Self-Destructive Behavior: Alcohol, Pregnancy, Drugs** |

Roughly one-third of high school seniors have engaged in binge drinking (five or more drinks in one episode). Those who begin drinking alcohol before age 15 are four times more likely to become alcoholics than those who begin at age 21 (*Prevention,* March 2004, p. 165). That's not all. Early drinking does permanent brain damage. When one experiences 100 drinking events between the ages of 15 and 17, the results include a reduction in the number of ways one approaches a problem (i.e., restricted range of problem solving strategies), decreased attention, and decreased memory. Moreover, in research with adolescent rats, Duke University researchers found that the brain actually shrinks, especially the *hippocampus* (the seat of memory) (*Prevention,* March 2004, p. 199).

Least at risk for alcohol problems are teenagers who experience strong attachment with their parents, and whose parents have clear and firm policies on alcohol use. Most at risk are these three categories of adolescents:

- Parents who are non-nurturing or who abuse drugs themselves.

- Peer groups that use drugs and alcohol.

- Kids in transition, as from middle school to high school, one school to another, or high school to work or college.

Applications

(*Note:* These applications are based on a March 2004 story in *Prevention* magazine on the teenage brain and the relative immaturity of the prefrontal cortex. The authors recommended these 12 guidelines to address the problem.)

1 Be accessible to talk about anything.

2 Eat dinner together. Studies from Columbia University's Center on Addiction and Substance Abuse reveal that teenagers who eat dinner with their family two times a week or less are twice as likely to abuse drugs or alcohol as teens who eat dinner with their family six or seven times a week.

3 Do whatever you can to help teens get 9–9½ hours of undisturbed sleep each night. The average is 7, and that is just not enough.

4 Permit thrill-seeking, but make it safe. Rock climbing yes, speeding cars no. Trying to keep the lid on a teen's urge to explore her wild side is unnatural. Encourage safe approaches to scuba, biking, skiing, skateboarding, surfing, and other adventuring.

5 Encourage after-school activities. Those spending one to four hours a week in extracurricular activities are less than half as likely to use drugs or become pregnant as others. Exercise is particularly effective, whether in organized sports or self-directed.

6 Talk with teens about the risks of drinking. See above.

7 Encourage after-school jobs.

8 Avoid giving them too much spending money. The highest risk group for smoking, drugs, and alcohol is girls with more than $50 a week.

9 Use your soapbox. Have open, honest conversations about sex, drugs, alcohol, speeding. Don't let objectionable material on television or movies go unanswered.

10 Use teenagers' vanity as a lever. Talk about the effect of smoking on skin, teeth, and body odor. Remind them that prom dresses don't come in "maternity" sizes.

11 Respect their privacy, but know when to snoop. Trust them—don't read their mail and journals—but when evidence (depression, declining grades, shady or elusive new friends) hits you in the face, it is time to check things out.

12 Understand that everything matters to a teenager.

TOPIC 5.6   Harris on the Role of the Salient Peer Group

Judith Rich Harris (see discussion of her views in the context of the nature-nurture debate in chapter 1) has established the principle of the *salient peer group*. According to this paradigm-changing theory, it is the salient peer group, not the parents, who have the most profound influence on shaping personality development from age 8–25. During these 17 years, an individual has many peer groups: neighborhood, home room at school, football team, jazz band, dance club, "best friends," religious classes and fellowships, gangs, sports "pickup" groups, and so forth. Anyone can have several dozen peer groups (for example, each class and organization at school).

So what is the salient peer group? Let us say that, as a 15-year-old, I had 20-odd peer groups: band, church choir, six classes at school, home room, Senior Hi-Y Club, Latin Club, basketball team, annual staff, Sunday School class, neighborhood friends, and others. What Harris discovered is that, at any given time in my life as an 8- to 25-year-old, *one* of these many peer groups would be *salient*—that is, of special importance to me. It would be that salient peer group that formed my primary source of *peer pressure,* which Harris defines as my urge to minimize differences between myself and others in the group. It is not the other group members' putting pressure on me to be like them, but my putting pressure on myself to be like the others. They wear baggy pants, I wear baggy pants. They take advanced and challenging courses, I become the budding Rhodes scholar. They smoke cigarettes, I light up. And so forth. "Be like Mike" says it all. But remember that this peer pressure is internally, not externally, imposed. Mike isn't asking you to be like him—you're pressuring yourself to be like him, to minimize differences between yourself and Mike.

When I was 15, my salient peer group was clearly the youth fellowship of my church that met on Sunday evenings. It was the focal point of my life. Highest priority. Perfect attendance. Went to all the district and state meetings, to summer camp. In fact, that group probably was my salient peer group for four years. Before that, it was my Boy Scout troop; afterwards, it was a small group of friends at undergraduate school who were all nonconformists. In fact, as I recall these various peer groups, I can feel the power they had over me at the time that caused me to want to be like them. The power of the salient peer group is a complex interaction between one's personal abilities, traits, and needs with the features of the group itself. If you're a leader, and the group needs a leader, then that could be the basis. If you need recognition (e.g., not getting any at home), and this group provides such recognition, then. . . . Here's the problem: if the group is toxic—leading you down the path to perdition—you are likely to follow it, and your parents' wringing of hands won't change the dynamics. The only solution is to eliminate the individual's access to that peer group. Harris tells of a New England girl who was into drugs, sex, and so forth, all because of a toxic peer group. The only solution the parents felt they could employ was to move—and move they did, to the Southwest. A radical solution, but the girl ended up with a more positive peer group and returned to honor roll and socially responsible patterns.

Applications

1 Read Judith Rich Harris's *The Nurture Assumption* (1998) for more discussion of the rationale behind this issue and for many suggestions on how to approach it.

2 Discuss with your child the pull of the peer group so that he is at least aware of the dynamics going on. Get him to identify his many peer groups, which group is currently salient, and which might be salient in his best interests. Offer to do whatever it takes to switch to a less toxic, more positive peer group.

3 If your child is in a toxic peer group, do not hesitate to employ tough love and do whatever it takes to deny access to the peer group. We know of a family who told their daughter that she would get no more allowance so long as she associated with a particular group of girls. The daughter hated her parents for that and refused to communicate for about a month. However, after cooling off, she thanked her parents, saying she knew she was in a downward spiral and felt helpless to rescue herself.

TOPIC 5.7   A Win-Win Approach to Discipline

For effective discipline, I am a big fan of the Dreikurs method of "logical consequences" (Dreikurs and Gray, 1993). Read his *Logical Consequences* (or his earlier *Discipline Without Tears*) for the full treatment. In brief, he encourages the parent to have a chat with a child after an event or behavior that needs to be addressed; in other words, the child needs to experience some consequence for having done what she did. Dreikurs's approach builds on the assumption that, deep down, the child knows as well as the parent that the event or behavior should not go unaddressed. The focus of the conversation should be on what some possible logical consequences might be. Initially the focus is not on choosing a punishment but rather on simply brainstorming or listing a number of possible logical (making sense in terms of the event or behavior itself) consequences. For example, the logical consequences of drinking beer at a party without chaperones and throwing up might be

- Cleaning up the mess
- Cleaning the family bathroom for the next month
- Reading the "Big Blue Book," *Alcoholics Anonymous,* by Ernest Kurtz
- Going to a teen drinking support group
- Attending individual or family counseling sessions
- Volunteer work at a homeless shelter or rehab program
- Writing a research paper on effects of teen drinking
- Conducting field research on the extent of drinking at the teen's school
- Reading biographies or novels about characters with drinking problems (e.g., a biography of the poet Dylan Thomas)

Once the two of you have developed such a list, then you decide together on the one that makes the most sense as a consequence of the event. This approach is based on the research-proven principle that participation in identifying and choosing a strategy makes it more likely that the strategy will have the desired effect. (See more at topics 30.5 and 30.6.)

Applications

❶ Read one or more of Dreikurs's books.

❷ Resist imposing punishment; rather, take time to discuss the event, mutually suggesting logical consequences (it is important that the parent not make *all* the suggestions!—be patient and encourage the child to suggest some) and selecting one that makes sense to both child and parent(s).

TOPIC 5.8   Depression During the Teens

Although depression by itself increases the likelihood of suicide, many of the current drugs for teenage depression also seem to increase the chances of suicide. The least risky appears to be Prozac, which, according to a study of 400 youth reported in the *Journal of the American Medical Association,* is most effective when taken in combination with cognitive-behavioral therapy (*Time,* August 30, 2004). However, in all countries that have prescribed *selective serotonin reuptake inhibitor* (SSRI) antidepressants for teenage depression since the mid-1990s, teenage suicides have dropped about one-third. The greatest danger is doing nothing; the optimum approach is Prozac with cognitive-behavioral therapy. Remember, one of the primary benefits of such drugs is that they facilitate behavior change.

Applications

1 Teenagers with bipolar disorder on antidepressants alone are especially susceptible to suicidal thoughts. Add talk therapy, especially cognitive behavior therapy, if possible.

2 Maintain communication with your teenager.

3 Do not let the warning labels on antidepressants cause you to allow depression to go untreated. Remember that antidepressants should be used in combination with cognitive behavior therapy.

4 Adolescents in the early stages of recovery from depression are, ironically, more susceptible to suicidal thoughts. Pay particular attention to your teenagers' changes in behavior upon beginning a new prescription, or upon a change in level of dosage, and discuss such changes immediately with your child's physician. Here are some specific changes to look for:

- Increased fidgeting and impulsiveness
- Thoughts about dying or suicide

- Suicide attempts
- Increased anxiety
- Increased agitation/restlessness
- Panic attacks
- Increased levels of activity, including increased talking
- Increased anger, aggression, violence
- Increased irritability
- Increased sleep difficulties
- In general, any significant changes in behavior or mood

SUGGESTED RESOURCES

Brownlee, S. (August 9, 1999). "Behavior Can Be Baffling When Young Minds Are Taking Shape." *U.S. News & World Report*, pp. 45–54.

Steinberg, L. S. (2004). *The Ten Basic Principles of Good Parenting.* New York: Simon & Schuster.

Steinberg, L. S., and R. Lerner (2004). *Handbook of Adolescent Psychology* (2nd ed.). New York: Wiley.

Steinberg, L. S., N. D. Reyome, and C. A. Bjornsen (2005). *Adolescence* (7th ed.). New York: McGraw-Hill.

6

Finishing Well

Use It
or Lose It

Although not all of us will be blessed with the opportunity to experience the perspective of old age, certainly all of us have an interest in knowing what research in cognitive science has discovered about the effect of aging on mental structure and ability. This chapter focuses on findings that can help us to age with maximum effectiveness and to better understand those who are preceding us into the Golden Years.

“Do not go gentle into that good night.”

—Dylan Thomas

First, one note. Much of what we know about adult development is coming out of the Baltimore Longitudinal Study of Aging, in which 2,400 volunteers of all ages travel annually (at their own expense) to Johns Hopkins Bayview Medical Center for three days of examination. Begun in 1958, it is the longest-running study of its kind. In the first 20 years, only white men were studied, with women and African Americans added to the study in 1978. African Americans are still underrepresented at 13 percent (compared with the target of 20 percent). The study continues to recruit volunteers in specific age, race, and sex categories. If you are interested in joining, call 800-225-2572. Among their findings: personality doesn't change essentially from age 30 on, vocabulary continues to grow into later life, problem-solving and reasoning skills continue into old age, and people age at different rates.

Parallel to the Baltimore study (which emphasizes personality), the Seattle Longitudinal Study emphasizes mental ability over the life span. The director is Warner Schaie (a professor at Pennsylvania State University). Here are some of their major findings (Schaie, 1996, pp. 12–15):

1. "There is no uniform pattern of age-related changes across all intellectual abilities." Different abilities decline at different times for different sexes for different reasons.

2. The primary factors that prevent decline in mental ability are

   (a) absence of cardiovascular and other chronic diseases;

   (b) a favorable environment mediated by high socioeconomic status;

   (c) involvement in a complex and intellectually stimulating environment;

   (d) flexible personality style at midlife;

   (e) maintenance of high levels of perceptual processing speed.

3. "Observed decline in many community-dwelling older people might well be a function of disuse and is clearly reversible for many. Indeed, cognitive training resulted in approximately two-thirds of the experimental subjects showing significant improvement, and about 40 percent of those who had declined significantly over 14 years were returned to their predecline level."

Another adult development study just beginning to bear fruit is the Nun Study, which was initiated by graduate student David Snowdon in 1986. His study, housed at the Sanders-Brown Center on Aging at the

University of Kentucky, involved nuns from School Sisters convents in Mankato, Minnesota, and six other cities, beginning with 3,926 Notre Dame sisters born between 1886 and 1916, most of whom had joined the order in their 20s. Results from this study are of particular interest because of the nuns' similar lifestyles. Autopsies are beginning to reveal new knowledge, particularly about Alzheimer's disease.

One promising line of research was reported by Marsel Mesulam, then of Harvard Medical School, now a psychiatry professor at Northwestern University. While at Harvard, Mesulam and other researchers identified a chemical, *acetylcholinesterase,* that is present at higher levels in people over 90 who have better mental abilities. The Harvard researchers have isolated a kind of cell in the brain that makes this chemical; it is hoped that, in time, drugs will be able to regulate acetylcholinesterase. In addition, researchers at Scripps Research Institute, La Jolla, California, have identified (in *Science,* March 2000) 61 genes that appear to control the speed of aging. These genes appear to slow down over time, leading to fragile bones, stiff joints, gum disease, and other maladies. Researchers are looking for drugs that target these genes and prevent their slowdown. In effect, they are working on "perpetual youth" drugs.

On another front, Barbara Sherwin, researcher at McGill University in Montreal, has reported (in *New Scientist,* July 31, 1999) that estrogen levels have a direct effect on women's memory. Sherwin studied 100 women who experienced sharp drops in estrogen level after their ovaries and uterus had been surgically removed. Half received HRT (hormone replacement therapy) and half received a placebo. The results: women with restored estrogen levels performed on memory tests as well as their presurgery performance, while the placebo women performed significantly lower than presurgical levels.

TOPIC 6.1 General Effects of Aging

We are born with roughly 23 billion neurons. By making new synapses (establishing connections between neurons), the brain increases its mass threefold until the early 20s. Conventional wisdom has held that we lose some 100,000 neurons daily. This is not the case; individual rates of brain cell loss vary widely. Proportionately more are lost in the frontal and temporal cortex, especially the motor cortex, which contains the long axons from the spine necessary for balance (see appendix A). Alcohol consumption increases the daily destruction proportional to the quantity consumed (around 60,000 neurons per day for a heavy drinker or alcoholic). Sickness, medication, and untold other assailants can also increase the rate of neuronal loss. The average person loses about 10 percent of his brain weight in a lifetime. This loss in brain weight used to be interpreted as the result of deceased neurons, but today it is interpreted as the result of shrunken neurons. Men lose more mass than women, and men lose more in the left hemisphere, which controls language, than in the right, which controls visual-spatial skills. Females experience about a two-ounce drop in brain mass around menopause, whereas males experience their accelerated loss beginning somewhere around age 60.

Experts caution that we should take extra care of our brains, for, unlike other organs and body systems, neurons have not been thought to divide and duplicate or replace themselves. However, in October 1998, Fred Gage, a professor at the Salk Institute for Biological Studies in La Jolla, California, along with Swedish researchers, reported the first observed regenerated brain cells in humans. Marian Diamond, a professor of integrative biology with the University of California, Berkeley, has found a higher proportion of *glial cells* (structural cells, also called "helper" cells, which provide nutrition for other neurons), in enriched-environment rats, and also in the preserved brain of our most famous physicist. Albert Einstein's brain, protected and maintained by Princeton University scientists in 1955 when he died at age 75, shows a clearly higher ratio of glial cells to normal neurons when compared with the brains of 11 men of average intelligence. In the meantime, why not play it safe and encourage everyone to keep body and mind active? Certainly this is a modest proposal.

As a general rule, aging itself does not have a large impact on deterioration of brain function. Mary N. Haan, director of the University of California, Davis, Center for Aging and Health, reported (in *Journal of the American Medical Association,* July 7, 1999) that a 10-year longitudinal study of more than 5,000 community-dwelling senior citizens revealed no significant cognitive decline for 70 percent of the group. Seniors with the ApoE4 gene (associated with Alzheimer's) and either atherosclerosis or diabetes were eight times more likely than others to show significant cognitive decline. In a large-scale French study of elder citizens (reported in *Neurology,* December 1999), persons of retirement age were found to be twice as likely to suffer a decrease in mental ability if they had untreated high blood pressure. In fact, the study suggested that antihypertensive medications have a beneficial effect on mental ability during the aging process. Although debate continues to rage on this issue, following are a dozen of what are accepted to be the most significant assailants on neurons:

- Medication
- Chronic disease (especially heart disease)
- Extended grief over personal loss
- Alcohol
- Absence of a stimulating partner
- Unfavorable living environment
- Inflexible personality style
- Sedentary lifestyle
- High blood pressure, especially in middle age
- Lack of stimulation
- Low educational level and lack of curiosity or desire to learn
- Malnutrition
- Depression

The lesson of all this is: *Use it or lose it!* As neurologist David Krech says, "They who live by their wit die with their wit." Dean Keith Simonton, who teaches psychology at the University of California, Davis, has studied the creative careers of composers, writers, and artists. He found that their creativity does not diminish with age, but the kind of creative energy sometimes changes. Igor Stravinsky, for example, switched in later life from a more traditional tonality to the "12-tone row," or writing music "in series." Thomas Edison, Johann Wolfgang von Goethe, Victor Hugo, Claude Monet, and Titian did some of their best work in their 70s and 80s. George Bernard Shaw, Pablo Picasso, Arthur Rubinstein, Albert Schweitzer, and Pablo Casals were still productive in their 90s. Also:

- David Ray of Franklin, Tennessee, learned to read at 99.
- Armand Hammer actively headed Occidental Petroleum at 91.
- At 92, Paul Spangler completed his 14th marathon.
- At 91, Hulda Crooks climbed Mount Whitney (the highest mountain in the continental United States).

- George Burns performed in Proctor's Theater, Schenectady, New York, first at age 31 and again 63 years later at age 94.

- Kathrine Everett was still practicing law in North Carolina at age 96.

- The classical pianist Mieczyslaw Horszowski recorded a new album at the age of 99.

- Martha Graham still choreographed in her 90s.

- Photographer Imogen Cunningham worked in her 90s.

- Grandma Moses retired from crocheting around age 70 (because of arthritis) and started a new career in painting.

At age 76, my mother-in-law moved to North Carolina from Alabama. A longtime church organist, she found a new service niche. She was in high demand for after-dinner music and music therapy classes at her retirement home, and she played frequently in the musical interlude just before her church's Sunday morning service. Seven years later and 83, she moved to a nursing home, where she still tried on her better days to entertain her friends and fellow residents on an electronic keyboard and was known to experiment with some unfamiliar rhythms and timbres provided by Sony. She was well respected for her talent.

The more we use our brains as we age, the higher our performance level stays and the higher is our ratio of synapses to neurons—that is, our brains stay denser the more we use them. *Nerve growth factor* (NGF) is one of many trophic, or nutritional, agents that stimulate and support growth of the myelin sheath—the coating of the neural fiber—and of new synapses. NGF is released as a result of neural transmission itself. Exercise also produces extra NGF (see topic 10.2). In other words, by using our nervous system, we grow it.

Applications

1 Make it a personal goal to continually learn something new. Once you've mastered it to the point where it is routine, it's time to learn something new. Linus Pauling, winner of two Nobel prizes (chemistry in 1954, peace in 1962) was asked, "What does one do after one wins the Nobel prize?" Pauling quipped, "One changes fields!" Never stop learning. Never stop setting goals.

② Disuse breeds disuse. Use what you know and have. Fight idleness and boredom with all your energy. If you can't think of anything to do, remember that there are plenty of organizations looking for volunteers. You can be helpful either from the confines of your own home (by telephoning, addressing, sewing, mending), in an an office park, or at the hospital.

③ Establish and maintain a balanced diet. (See chapter 7.)

④ Exercise caution when changing physical positions after age 50. Be especially careful when using ladders or stools to gain height; most people's sense of balance just isn't what it used to be. Leave the shower, tub, and car with a little more caution. And be sure to exercise regularly.

⑤ Assume that you will retain your full mental powers forever. Just because we slow down doesn't mean we have to stop! We will always have a contribution to make!

TOPIC 6.2   Old Age and Mental Ability

There are two clear trends associated with the aging of the brain:

1. Between ages 20 and 60, reaction time doubles—we slow down.

2. The ratio of synapses to neurons increases for people who continue using their brains and decreases for those who stop (see figure 6.1). Learning means new synapses, and new synapses mean higher density, which counterbalances the normal brain weight loss. Accordingly, performance continues to improve with age among those who use their brains, while it declines among those whose brains retire when they retire from their jobs.

Quartz and Sejnowski (2002) report that "nuns [in the Nun Study] who are more educated and perform stimulating work, such as teaching, tend to age more successfully than those who have less education and perform mundane tasks. They also live an average of four years longer" (p. 241). Further (p. 243):

The dendrites of those who lived in a complex environment— had a college degree, a stimulating job, and were mentally active throughout their life—were a full 40 percent more complex than those of high school dropouts. They were also more complex than those of university graduates who had not been mentally active after college. . . . It turns out that it is never too late to engage the brain in a stimulating environment. Sherry Willis and Warner Schaie demonstrated in the Seattle Longitudinal Study that reengagement in later life can boost mental performance even in people whose mental performance has already significantly declined. They studied a group of two hundred people over the age of sixty-five, half of whom had significantly declined in mental performance over the previous fourteen years. Through training, most improved significantly. Among those who had declined, a full 40 percent were able to regain their performance levels of fourteen years earlier. Seven years later, they were still significantly ahead of those with similar levels seven years earlier.

A pattern of avoiding new situations and new learning as we age takes its toll. Schaie has found that middle-aged folks who are set in their ways exhibit far greater decreases in mental performance in their gray years than aging seniors who continue to experiment, to learn, to explore, to take on new challenges. Schaie encourages seniors to seek therapeutic assistance if needed to achieve greater mental flexibility.

Renee Solomon and Monte Peterson, two experts in social interventions for older adults, suggest that "flexibility and adaptability are critical personality dimensions of successful aging. . . . Older persons who lack optimism, humor, and relatedness find it difficult to be flexible and adaptable and may well be a risk for emotional collapse."

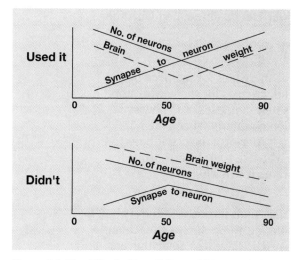

Figure 6.1. The Effect of Inactivity and Disuse on the Brain

In a Harvard Medical School study of over 1,000 physicians, Dean Whitla and Sandra Weintraub found that the 10 physicians over age 65 with the highest scores on a standard cognitive skills test were still actively working as physicians, whereas the 10 physicians with the lowest performance scores were no longer working. The working and nonworking physicians showed similar patterns of medication and illness, so the difference in performance cannot be attributed to those factors. In other words, their physical health and mental health scores were independent. I know that "Use it or lose it" sounds like an oversimplification, but. . . .

Many reports show mental abilities declining in old age, but these reports typically fail to control for degree of brain use. Apparently the nonusers are bringing down the scores of the users! Researcher C. Edward Coffey, Henry Ford Health System, Detroit, has documented that well-educated seniors (age 65–90), in spite of significant brain shrinkage (as measured by MRI), continue to perform well with no signs of memory or reasoning loss. Less educated seniors, however, do show memory and reasoning decline. Referencing the Seattle Longitudinal Study, Warner Schaie, Director of the Pennsylvania State University Gerontology Center, finds that measurable loss in mental performance (for example, loss in spatial reasoning) can be reversed with training, except for performance loss caused by brain damage from drug use, disease, or trauma.

In a project funded by the University of California, Los Angeles Task Force on Psychoneuroimmunology, George Solomon and John Morley found that age does not uniformly affect the immune system (Cousins, 1989). Older healthy people show immune levels of white blood cells, lymphocytes, granulocytes, and so on that are somewhat higher than those of comparable younger people. In addition, older adults with "hardy" attitudes (those who maintain their commitment, positive emotion, self-control, and exercise) show an even higher level of immune cells as well as endorphins.

Applications

❶ Plan for retirement. Don't become a television addict without hobbies or interests.

❷ Beware, as you age, of depending on speedy performance in order to feel good about yourself. If you feel that you are overextending yourself, begin to move toward activities that are compatible with slower reaction times. You might move from driving cars and riding motorcycles to walking, riding bicycles or tricycles, and taking buses. Move from power tools to hand tools, from debate to dialogue, from reading stories to storytelling. Card and board games that tolerate varying speeds of individual play are often successful as intergenerational activities. Take greater pride in the quality of your accomplishments rather than your speed.

❸ As you age, maintain high expectations for yourself, keep developing your sense of humor, take control of stress, and continue to exercise and eat right.

❹ In the face of disease, "accept the diagnosis but defy the verdict," as Norman Cousins says (Cousins, 1989). Examples of recovery from "terminal" illnesses are numerous and increasing. The limits of the mind's ability to positively influence health are unknown.

❺ Lawrence Katz, Duke University neurobiologist, and coauthor Manning Rubin (1999) propose a series of exercises they dub "neurobics." Each of the exercises below is designed to form new associations among previously unassociated parts of the brain, thereby bringing new resources to one's consciousness. A kind of mental jogging, these neurobic exercises result in the formation of new synapses and the rejuvenation of already established synapses. The result: countering the tendency toward decline in memory and general ability that some experience during aging.

1. Make different smells available from morning to morning.

2. Occasionally use your unaccustomed hand to brush your teeth.

3. Switch what you normally wear (pins, wristwatch, pocket contents, hair part, etc.) on the left side to the right side, and vice versa.

4. Take a different route to a frequently destination, such as work.

5. Try picking out the right coins (and other objects) without looking.

6. Turn things literally upside down, such as a picture in your office.

7. Chat with people whom you (and others) tend to overlook (e.g., store clerks).

8. If you're not an artist, try painting or drawing a picture. If you are an artist, try doing it with your feet.

9. Try searching for foods in the wild.

10. If you exercise indoors, try switching occasionally to outdoors, and vice versa.

11. Master some new piece of technology from time to time. This could range from something as simple as a new wine bottle opener to a digital camera.

12. Try eating and preparing ethnic foods you've never experienced.

13. Acquire a new hobby.

TOPIC 6.3   Control, Social Capital, and Optimism

The principles elaborated later (in chapter 36) concerning the effect of control on stress apply equally to seniors. Specifically, Judith Rodin of Yale University (Keeton, 1992) has demonstrated that nursing home residents age 65 to 90 who are allowed to take a direct planning and decision-making role in their programming (1) live longer, (2) are sick less, (3) are happier, (4) are more alert, and (5) have less of the stress hormone cortisol.

Psychology professors Christopher Peterson of the University of Michigan and Martin Seligman of the University of Pennsylvania (see topic 37.5) found that baseball players who were more optimistic at age 25 lived significantly longer. Depression is thought to be common among the elderly and may well be the cause of many of their medical problems. In 1999, 10 medical centers around the country began a long-term control study on 200 patients each, using the antidepressant Celexa (citalopram) and a placebo.

Now, there is control, and then there is control. Having some control over one's destiny is one thing, but being a control freak is another. Michael Babyak, an assistant clinical professor of medical psychology at Duke University, in a 22-year longitudinal study of 750 white, middle-class men, found that men who always need to be in control (monopolizing conversations, frequently interrupting, having a compulsive need to be number one, etc.) tend to die younger than men whose social behavior is calmer and more accepting of the ascendancy of others. Robert Sapolsky (1997, pp. 161–173) describes two different male primate behaviors in the gray years. Some tend to leave the tribe in which they had held a fixed place in the hierarchy and join new groups, alone and friendless, but not picked on any more, just ignored. Others stay with their tribe, having something the deserters don't—friends (to be specific, female friends). These latter males at an early age tend to avoid the hierarchy battles and establish relationships (not necessarily sexual) with females. As a result, these friendly males do not suffer the scornful picking that the first group does.

Quartz & Sejnowski (2002) suggest that "the parent that cares for the offspring typically lives longer than the mate, regardless of gender"

(p. 179). This is based on the work of John Allman at Caltech on both animals and humans. He mentions that epidemiologists Lisa Berkman and S. Leonard Syme, in a nine-year study of 7,000 adults in California, found that people with fewer social ties were up to three times as likely to die of all causes than people with more contacts (p. 180).

In another vein, William Strawbridge of the California Public Health Foundation, in a study of 5,000 people over 28 years old, found that people who attended religious services had a 36 percent lower death rate. Harold Koenig, family physician with Duke University Medical Center, followed 4,000 senior citizens in the Durham, North Carolina area for six years and found that those who reported little or no religious meditation (e.g., Bible reading, prayer) ran a 50 percent greater risk of dying than those who reported at least two episodes of religious meditation monthly (*Journal of Gerontology,* July 2000). However, reporting in the June 1997 *American Journal of Public Health,* Strawbridge qualified his findings, cautioning that the lower rate could be related to improved health practices, higher social contacts, and more stable marriages, each of which is associated with, but not limited to, religious participation.

This and similar findings relate to a recent term, "social capital," which is the capability of an individual's social contacts to assist in realizing common goals. Other examples of social capital include participation in volunteer organizations and trust in civic government, both of which are associated with lower mortality rates.

Applications

❶ If you are responsible for the care of older adults, do everything you can to include them in planning, decision making, and problem solving. Share responsibility and control with them. If you are on the staff of a community for older adults, establish committees, consult with the residents, and empower them by responding to their ideas, requests, and needs.

❷ If you are an older adult, whether you are living alone or in a community, stay involved in planning your life; if you live in a community for older adults, establish committees, create suggestion boxes, ask those charged with your care to consider your ideas, and pool your resources for trips and other big-ticket items, such as lawyers, entertainment, transportation, or equipment.

❸ Establish friendships early on, regardless of sex; nurture them; enter old age with a support system.

TOPIC 6.4   Diet and Aging

Evidence points toward significant effects of restricted diets on longevity: the less you eat, the longer you live. Roderick Bronson and Ruth Lipman of the Human Nutrition Research Center at Tufts University in Boston report that reducing patients' normal food intake by 40 percent yields a 20 percent longer life span. Their report (Raloff, 1991) argues that diet restriction (1) limits *deoxyribonucleic acid* (DNA) damage, (2) increases enzyme-mediated repair of DNA, and (3) reduces expression of *proto-oncogenes* (cancer-causing genes). Richard Weindruch of the Institute on Aging at the University of Wisconsin–Madison recommends eating 1 gram of protein and 0.5 gram of fat for each kilogram (2.2 pounds) of body weight. In the 1930s, Clive McCay of Cornell University found that rats with diets of 35 percent fewer calories lived 35 percent longer. However, although excessive consumption clearly affects longevity, current research reveals that people naturally gain weight as they age. The new weight charts, such as the one devised by Reubin Andres, clinical director at the National Institute on Aging, allow for considerably more weight than the traditional charts developed by Metropolitan Life Insurance Company.

Restak (1997) cautions about generalizing animal research results to humans. He does, however, find promise in a line of research by Denham Harman of the University of Nebraska Medical School. Harman worked with *free radicals,* molecules containing one unpaired electron. Such molecules are unstable, grabbing at available electrons like starving creatures and indiscriminately foraging. In this situation, a negative outcome would be that free radicals could consume available electrons in the *mitochondria* of the cell nuclei and destroy DNA, with the effect of accelerated aging. On the other hand, a positive outcome could be that free radicals are bound by the available electrons in *antioxidants* such as vitamin C and beta-carotene. Restak warns that people should not rely on pills as a source of antioxidants, preferring that they consume them in their natural form by eating fresh fruits and vegetables.

Kristine Yaffe at the University of San Francisco studied 8,000 women over age 64. The six-year study (reported in *Journal of the American Geriatrics Society,* October 1999) found a high correlation between incidence of osteoporosis and level of intellectual functioning. As bone density decreases, so does mental performance; women with higher bone density outperformed those with lower bone density by an average of 8 percent.

Applications

❶ If living longer is more important to you than eating a lot, consider cutting back your consumption by about one-third. For more information, contact the Human Nutrition Research Center, Tufts University, Boston, Massachusetts 02111; phone: 617-556-3000. Be aware, however, of the Mayo Clinic finding (Minninger, 1984) that a diet of less than 2,100 calories daily—unless it is personally monitored by a physician—typically results in less than ideal mental functioning.

❷ To keep free radicals from chomping down on you, provide anti-oxidants to keep them at bay. Feed them, or they'll feed on you. Sample recommendation for one day's worth of feeding free radicals: 6 ounces of cranberry juice, 2 cups of broccoli, 2 cups of strawberries, 2 cups of orange juice, or a kiwi fruit.

TOPIC 6.5   Exercise and Aging

According to research reported in Folkins and Sime (1981), exercise programs can at least arrest and often reverse many of the degenerative physical effects of aging in older patients. One explanation of this phenomenon is that exercise promotes increased absorption of oxygen. William Greenough, a neuroscientist at the University of Illinois, identified an increase in capillaries around neurons in the brain as a result of aerobic exercise. Carl Cotman, a neurology professor at the Institute for Brain, Aging and Dementia at the University of California, Irvine, found that aerobic exercise produces an increase in *neurotrophins.* Neurotrophins are nerve growth agents—"fertilizer" for nerve cells.

Arthur Kramer, a psychology professor with the University of Illinois' Beckman Institute, established that aerobic exercise (a 45-minute water aerobics class, three times a week for 10 weeks) in 63- to 82-year-olds results in improved, faster reaction times. He avers that declines in reaction time are generally more attributable to declines in fitness than to aging. Aerobic exercise is best. In a study conducted by researchers at the Salt Lake City Veterans Administration Hospital, three out-of-shape groups were followed: one was put on a walking regimen, another lifted weights, and the third carried on business as usual with no exercise of any kind. The walkers showed much higher scores on eight tests of mental ability, the weight lifters showed a little improvement, and the others showed no improvement. Researchers at the University of Illinois (at Urbana-Champaign) worked with 124 sedentary seniors (age 60–75), comparing aerobic and anaerobic exercise programs for their effect on mental processes, including planning, scheduling, inhibition, and working memory. The walkers showed significant improvement in all categories (*BrainWork,* August 2004). They cited Harry Truman (88) and John Glenn (83 in 2004) as power walkers. Anaerobic exercise (stretching, weightlifting, etc.) was not accompanied by the same improvements.

Applications

❶ Keep walking, briskly. Or, swimming—lap it up!

❷ Inquire about organized and medically supervised exercise programs for seniors and join up. Senior centers have taken the lead in this area.

❸ Don't stop exercising because you think you're too old. There's an aerobic exercise that's safe and beneficial for you.

❹ Ensure that you and all your family members get aerobic exercise for 30 to 45 minutes at least five days per week.

TOPIC 6.6   Combining Diet and Exercise

In a study reported in Merzbacher (1979), individuals with cardiovascular disease and an average age of 60 were placed on the Pritikin diet, which includes more complex carbohydrates and fewer proteins and fats, and were assigned six to ten miles per day of jogging or walking. After completing this 26-day program, subjects scored higher on intelligence tests and had measurably improved their circulatory systems.

Application

 Don't just exercise; eat right.

TOPIC 6.7   Night Vision

The quality of our night vision decreases with age. At 63, I am aware of poorer perception when driving at night. It is getting harder to see the curbs of the road onto which I want to turn when lighting is suboptimal. Also, men tend to have better day vision (note that more women wear sun-protective glasses), and women tend to have better night vision (Moir and Jessel, 1991).

Manley West, a University of West Indies pharmacology professor, researched the rumor that marijuana improved night vision. He found that a nonpsychoactive ingredient in marijuana, *canasil,* caused a significant improvement in night vision. At the time of this writing, canasil, which is the same ingredient in marijuana that relieves glaucoma, is not yet available in the United States.

Applications

❶ As you age, take extra precautions when you drive at night, especially if you are a man. Allow extra distance between you and vehicles in front of you, drive more slowly, and take more breaks. Let a younger person or a woman drive when possible. Don't let your male ego interfere with safe driving options.

❷ All other things being equal (driving skill, physical condition, road familiarity, and so on), a woman will be a safer driver at night because of generally superior night vision. During the day, men will tend to be safer because they are less subject to fatigue from the sun. Women will generally desire or require more breaks to avoid eye fatigue during the day, with men requiring more during the night.

❸ Understand that these differences exist, and don't assume that people who are different from you are weak, malingering, or inferior.

TOPIC 6.8   Memory and Aging

Although the memory processes slow down as we age, the accuracy of our memories improves. When he administered recall-and-recognition tests to youths and seniors in church fellowship halls, Paul Foos, of the psychology department at the University of North Carolina at Charlotte, found that the seniors, with an average age of 65, consistently beat the youths. As we age, the number of items we can associate to a particular memory chunk dramatically increases. So although we may take longer, we are more likely to remember things accurately. In fact, there is some evidence that the rich associative network of seniors is one factor in the slow-down of their memory processes.

My 82-year-old brother-in-law and I were riding through eastern North Carolina in 1993 to a family reunion. Making small talk, I referred to a basketball player from our hometown of Kinston who had recently signed to play basketball at the University of North Carolina; I called him Shackleford. My brother-in-law commented that I didn't have the name right. I agreed. We both started searching our minds for the correct name. He won the race. I asked him how he'd remembered. He said that he got an image in his mind of a furniture store in Goldsboro (on his route for many trips from Chapel Hill to Kinston) called Stackhouse Furniture, flipped from that image to one of a retired professor friend in California named Stackhouse, and came up with "Stackhouse," the right name. (Alas! How memory is fickle. After reading this passage, my brother-in-law corrected me: his friend Stackhouse was not a professor, but a businessman, and the Goldsboro store was not a furniture store, but a lumber business!) My effort to describe this process is captured in Kim Allman's illustration in figure 6.2. Apparently, my brother-in-law's network of isolated memories connected in something like the following manner to give him the right answer (try following along in the figure):

1. He heard "Shackleford," a relatively new auditory memory gained around age 70, based on a well-known Kinston athlete who attended North Carolina State University, not the University of North Carolina at Chapel Hill.

2. He associated the name Shackleford to basketball and Kinston.

3. He unconsciously and instantaneously relived his frequent trips from Chapel Hill to Kinston to visit his parents and his in-laws.

4. A prominent building halfway between the two towns, Stackhouse Furniture (correction: Lumberyard), popped up ever so briefly into his consciousness.

5. This submerged memory of the furniture (lumber) store, firmly entrenched from about the age of 17, connected to

another strong memory of his longstanding friendship, from about the age of 48 on, with a California professor (correction: businessman) named Stackhouse.

6. By the time he envisioned his California friend, he became conscious that the name "Stackhouse" was the one he was looking for.

I hope that at age 82 my memory processes will be as abundant and effective as my brother-in-law's.

In a recent line of research using PET scans to compare the brain activity of youths vs. seniors, Daniel Schacter, a psychologist at Harvard University, has found equal levels of hippocampal activity when both youths and seniors are engaged in the process of remembering something easily. However, when they are "searching" for a memory, the youths show greater activity in the frontal area. Apparently, in a significant number of seniors, the "search engine" becomes sluggish, while the memories lie in wait for a rise to consciousness.

Working with a large sample of older Swedish people, David Bunce, psychologist at the University of London, and others found (*Neuropsychology,* Vol. 18, No. 2) three factors associated with poor memory performance in seniors:

- possessing the gene for Alzheimer's (ApoE4)

- low levels of vitamin B-12 and folate

- absence of cues or hints to assist in recall

When any one of these three factors was missing, memory performance in seniors improved markedly.

Applications

❶ Slow is okay. You'll get there.

❷ Don't push seniors to remember more quickly; the frustration of being pushed will interfere with the effort to remember. Give people the time they need.

❸ Try the "I knew it all the time" test. Harvard University psychiatry and neurology professor Marilyn Albert suggests that when your memory fails you and you subsequently recall, or are reminded of, what you tried

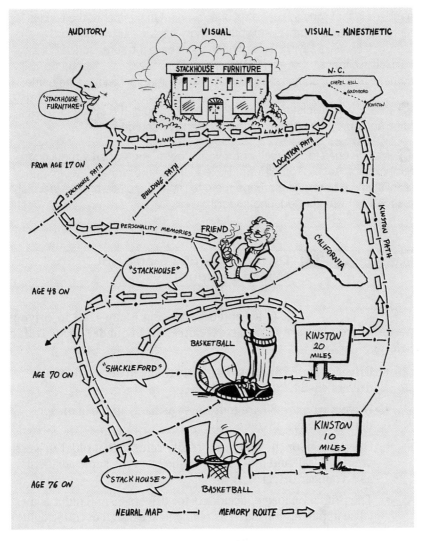

Figure 6.2. My Brother-in-Law's Memory Process

to remember originally, you should have the feeling: "Yes—I knew that all along." A more appropriate time to worry about your memory is when you recall or are reminded of a memory and it does not feel familiar to you.

❹ When finding a familiar word or term inaccessible to your memory, try silently saying the alphabet, once through, twice through, etc. What happens is that you say the vowel or consonant that matches the first letter of your familiar word. Soon your memory bank will allow the word to surface. In fact, while saying the alphabet, you'll have the sensation of "Okay, I think it is either a 'k' or an 'r'." And in a matter of seconds, "kangaroo" will come to mind. Or something like that. This is a form of "priming the pump."

❺ Check your levels of vitamin B-12 and folic acid. If they are low, determine an appropriate dietary or supplementary source.

❻ Provide cues for yourself or for your elder friends when struggling to remember a name or other term. Have them try the alphabet technique (application 4 above), encourage them to recall the place or time in which the memory was formed, and so forth.

TOPIC 6.9	Driving over 65 (Years, Not Miles Per Hour!)

It is accepted that aging is not kind to driving performance. Here are some facts (Source: AAA Foundation for Traffic Safety):

- Drivers over 65 are twice as likely to die in an accident as drivers 45–64.

- Drivers who are 85 are four times as likely to die in an accident as drivers 45–64.

- One reason for the higher mortality rates is that older drivers are more frail and more likely to die from the same accident as a younger driver.

- The primary cause of accidents for drivers 65 and older is a lapse in perception (such as failing to see a sign or traffic light).

- Fifty-nine percent of drivers 75 and older in accidents report such a lapse. Incidentally, this is the same percentage as that for 15-year-old drivers!

- Sixty-seven percent of drivers 85 and older in accidents report such a lapse.

- Drivers 65 and older are 25 percent more likely to have an accident of any kind than a middle-aged driver.

- Older drivers are more likely to have accidents while attempting a left turn, a maneuver that often requires quick judgment of the speed and distance of oncoming traffic.

Applications

1 As you age, use caution when making a left turn. Don't take a chance on the accuracy of your perception as to the speed and distance of oncoming traffic. Wait for oncoming traffic to pass before you turn. Wait until there's no doubt as to your safety in turning.

2 Where possible, figure out routes that do not involve making left turns in heavy traffic. Find a way to limit entry into heavy traffic to right turns only.

3 Anticipate where signs *should* be! Be paranoid about the location of stop signs.

4 As you age, don't let your ego (see description of the "low A" personality in topic 33.2) lead you into high-risk driving behaviors. Act your age, and learn to exercise appropriate caution. Let others drive when possible. Let your ego learn to be fed by achievements other than driving.

TOPIC 6.10 | **Sex and Longevity**

Based on a study of 918 men between the ages of 45 and 59, research epidemiologists George Davey Smith of the University of Bristol and Stephen Frankel of Queen's University, Belfast, Northern Ireland, reported in the December 1997 *British Medical Journal* that there appears to be a rather strong relationship between rate of sexual orgasm and length of life. The men were followed up 10 years later and analyzed on the basis of three groups: those who had two or more orgasms per week, fewer than one per month, or a number between these two extremes. The death rate for the least sexually active men was twice as high as that for the most active, whereas the death rate for the intermediate group was 1.6 times that of the most active group. Although some have criticized the methodology of the study, following its implications could not be harmful in and of itself, certainly! On the other hand, we need to be alert for studies that confirm or challenge these findings, as well as for studies that include women.

Application

❶ Rest assured that frequent orgasms do not appear to affect mortality adversely. However, if you have less frequent sexual activity and wish to hedge your bets longevity-wise, don't go looking for more mates or browbeat your partner into reluctantly increasing his or her frequency: simply take things in hand.

TOPIC 6.11   Sleep and Aging

The senior adult's sleep episodes (which can include more than one sleep cycle) are 20 percent shorter than those of younger people (6 vs. 7½ hours), and the total time awake during the night between initially going to sleep and getting up for good in the morning progresses gradually from around 1 percent in infancy to around 6 percent in seniors.

Applications

❶ Although some shortening of sleep requirements and some increase in sleep-time wakefulness are normal in senior adults, drastic changes are not. Look for pharmaceuticals, diet, illness, or lack of exercise as probable culprits.

❷ Understand that you probably will not sleep as long and as continuously at age 75 as you did at 25. Build a nap into your schedule, and simply get up and do something constructive if you cannot sleep.

❸ It's okay to "wake up" throughout the night. Don't worry about it. Everyone wakes up between cycles; as we age, we just tend to be more aware of it. See more about sleep cycles at topic 9.1.

A Final Word on Aging Gracefully

In his book *Older and Wiser* (1997, pp. 228–244), Richard Restak lists "30 steps you can take to enhance your brain in the mature years."

I have reviewed his list, added to and subtracted from it, combined items, and modified them. Here's my revision of Restak's list:

1. Stop smoking.

2. Do weight-bearing exercises daily.

3. Don't rely on any particular food, drug, or chemical to promote longevity.

4. Maintain normal levels of blood pressure, blood sugar, and cholesterol.

5. Avoid a sedentary lifestyle; don't stop being active just because you are slower.

6. Prefer standing exercises to sitting exercises.

7. Walk at least four hours a week.

8. Practice balancing daily when standing for long stretches (for example, while in a line, or singing a hymn, or standing at a party) by standing on one leg for as long as possible, then the other, and so on, alternating, just barely lifting the other foot off the floor. Try to do it without people noticing what you're up to.

9. Reduce stress, or change (reframe) your attitude toward stressors.

10. Indulge your curiosity to the max.

11. Enjoy your coffee and other caffeine-drink energizers (but don't exceed the proper dosage—see topic 8.3).

12. Nap.

13. Don't fret about the possibility of memory loss; work on developing and improving your memory with books and gadgets (such as palm-held computers).

> **"To add life to years, not just years to life."**
> —Motto of the Gerontological Society of America

14. Don't worry about becoming senile.

15. Keep working—gainfully or not—at something you enjoy for as long as possible.

16. Minimize spare time.

17. Avoid excessive use of alcohol.

18. Keep challenging your mental abilities, from doing crossword puzzles to learning new skills and knowledge.

19. Keep a diary in some form that you enjoy. For example, work on your autobiography as a legacy for your children, relatives, or associates. Leave a copy to your library—they like to keep these as a form of local history.

20. Avoid social isolation. Engage in many diverse kinds of activities with other people: if you get "retired" from your church choir, start a choir for seniors; if you live alone, get a pet.

21. Remain active on the Internet. Use it as a support group, information source, and means of communication with family and friends. Start and maintain a family web page. My oldest sister at age 88 has just this year acquired her first computer. She never learned to type except by "hunt and peck," but we're exchanging e-mails now to our mutual satisfaction.

22. Continue to stimulate your five senses with art, food, people, and nature in its abundance.

23. Accept the fact that your ability to concentrate will shorten (to about 15 minutes), and take 3- to 5-minute breaks between 15-minute concentration periods.

24. Enjoy games as a way to nurture your ability to concentrate.

25. Accept being a slower organism and avoid activities that rely on speed of response: replace speed with wisdom.

26. Maintain—even increase—your sense of humor.

27. Maintain your friendships and develop new ones.

28. Prefer a diet with a moderate caloric intake, with a predominance of fresh fruits and vegetables.

29. Women after menopause should consult with their physician regarding the risks and advantages of taking estrogen supplements.

30. Take melatonin as a sleep aid (see particularly topic 9.10).

31. Follow the research on dehydroepiandrosterone (DHEA), and begin taking it when the studies consistently point to its safety and effectiveness in promoting physical and mental

vitality; if you're already in your 70s, you might consider taking it now. Ask your physician.

If you consider 31 steps too intimidating, try these guidelines from the California Human Population Laboratory's study conducted in the 1970s (Hobson, 1994, p. 188). People who followed six out of these seven recommendations lived longer and in better health: (1) Sleep. (2) Exercise. (3) Eat breakfast. (4) Don't snack. (5) Watch your weight. (6) Do not smoke. (7) Use alcohol moderately.

Perhaps you are content with the way things are. If so, you might, just to amuse yourself, try taking the online life expectancy quiz at www.livingto100.com. This quiz is maintained by the Paul Beeson website, www.beeson.org, center of activity for the Beeson scholars, who are devoted to research for the purpose of improving quality of life, especially as it relates to aging.

SUGGESTED RESOURCES

Fossel, M. (1996). *Reversing Human Aging.* New York: Morrow.

Friedan, B. (1993). *The Fountain of Age.* New York: Simon & Schuster.

Keeton, K. (1992). *Longevity: The Science of Staying Young.* New York: Viking Penguin.

Medina, J. J. (1996). *The Clock of Ages.* Cambridge: Cambridge University Press.

Restak, R. M. (1997). *Older and Wiser.* New York: Simon & Schuster.

Ricklefs, R. E., and C. E. Finch (1995). *Aging: A Natural History.* New York: Scientific American Library.

Schaie, K. W. (1994, April). "The Course of Adult Intellectual Development." *American Psychologist,* 49(4), 304–313.

Schaie, K. W. (1996). *Intellectual Development in Adulthood: The Seattle Longitudinal Study.* New York: Cambridge University Press.

Schaie, K. W., and S. L. Willis (1996). *Adult Development and Aging* (4th ed.). New York: Addison-Wesley.

Part Three

Wellness

*Getting
the Most
out of
Every Day*

Part Three. Wellness
Getting the Most out of Every Day

7

Nourishment

Food for the Body, Fuel for the Brain

66 *The best doctors in the world are Doctor Diet, Doctor Quiet, and Doctor Merryman.* **99**

—*Jonathan Swift*

As recently as World War II, scientists as well as the general public considered diet to have little or no influence on mental functioning. Research over the last 40 years, however, has revealed a close relationship between diet and the brain—so much so, in fact, that trendy brain bars are popping up that specialize in juices and foods considered to improve mentation, or mental activity. It is becoming clearer that our brain influences what and how we eat, and that what and how we eat influences our brain. This chapter identifies various specific findings in this arena of the food-brain connection.

| TOPIC 7.1 | **Appetite Control** |

   Two primary chemical actors head the complex cast of characters in the tense drama of appetite control: chemicals that trigger hunger and chemicals that trigger satiety. If these are in good order, much of the rest of one's chemical makeup will have a minimal effect on appetite and weight control. Significant discoveries have come on the scene in the last five years, and huge pharmaceutical product development research efforts currently focus on finding acceptable exogenous (externally administered) ways to optimize a person's hunger-satiety balance. Current estimates based on twin studies consider the genetic influence on weight to be extremely high—around 60–70 percent. Combined with the meager 5 percent success rate of diets, this paints a bleak picture for the role of self-control in weight management. Authorities suggest that we'd be better off changing the environment than trying to change the individual. Do we hear a movement afoot to abolish faux food? The environmentalists formed the Sierra Club. How about the Fiber Club for the nutritionists?

Chemicals That Signal Hunger

Sarah Leibowitz, a neurobiologist at Rockefeller University in New York City, has identified the area of the brain in which this drama plays out: the *paraventricular nucleus* (PVN) of the hypothalamus (see appendix A). Chemical players that trigger appetite include *galanin* (discovered by Leibowitz, this is a neuropeptide that craves fat), *norepinephrine, neuropeptide Y,* and *cortisol.* In addition, a research team led by Masashi Yanigasawa at the Howard Hughes Medical Institute at the University of Texas Southwestern Medical Center in Dallas reported the discovery of two hormones that send a hunger message (*Cell,* February 20, 1998). Yanigasawa calls these hormones *orexin-A* and *orexin-B.* The orexins have their own receptor network in the hunger section of the hypothalamus and have been found to send an extremely strong hunger signal in mice. Development is under way for use with humans as both a stimulant and a suppressant of appetite.

Another hormone related to weight is *ghrelin*: it makes people hungry, slows metabolism, and slows the ability to burn fat. It is highest before meals, lowest just after. Unfortunately, those who lose significant amounts of weight tend to produce more ghrelin, so it apparently serves evolutionarily as a defense against starvation. Persons injected with ghrelin report feeling hungrier and, if exposed to a buffet with a large quantity and variety of food, will eat 30 percent more than they typically would consume.

University of California, Irvine, College of Medicine researchers have identified the receptor for *melanin-concentrating hormone* (MCH), a key ingredient in the appetite control process. Earlier research discovered that MCH influences how often and how much rats and humans eat: the more of the hormone, the stronger the appetite. The Irvine research team, headed by pharmacology professor Olivier Civelli and senior pharmacology researchers Hans-Peter Nothacker and Yumiko Saito, located the receptors that bind with MCH in the hypothalamus, olfactory area, and the nucleus accumbens, all involved in one way or another in smell, taste, and feeding urges. Research is under way to clarify these processes and how they might be brought under control for the benefit of the masses desiring and needing to be less massive.

Sarah Leibowitz has identified the chemical sources of urges for specific food groups, as well as the time of day during which the urges are strongest (Collin, 1992, p. 74). A summary is shown in table 7.1.

Table 7.1. The Chemistry of Food Urges

Food Group	Chemical Basis of Desire	When Desire Is Strongest
Carbohydrates	Turned on by norepinephrine, neuropeptide Y, cortisol; turned off by serotonin	On waking and early morning; desire decreases as the day goes on
Protein	Turned on by serotonin, opiates; turned off by neuropeptide Y, norepinephrine, dopamine, galanin	Alternates with carbohydrates in morning; rises gradually toward middle of day; peaks at dinner and evening
Fat	Turned on by galanin, opiates, aldosterone; turned off by dopamine	Desire for fat increases during middle of day and predominates in evening

Source: Adapted from Fran Collin (May 1992), "Sarah Leibowitz (Interview)," *Omni*, 14(8), p. 74.

At a spring 1998 meeting of the Society of Behavioral Medicine in New Orleans, Yale University researchers reported that high levels of cortisol are associated with high cravings for fatty snacks. When given a choice, high-cortisol snackers head for the nachos, low-cortisol snackers for lower-fat snacks. Cortisol levels are increased by stressful experiences.

Chemicals That Signal Satiety

Chemical players that shut down appetite include *enterostatin* (produced by the stomach and pancreas in response to the ingestion of fat), *serotonin, dopamine, cholecystokinin* (CCK), and *leptin* (from the Greek *leptos,* "thin"), a protein produced by the newly discovered "obesity gene" on chromosome 6. After you've eaten, cholecystokinin is released in the intestines to tell the brain you're full. Leptin tells the body whether to burn fat you're eating or store it as fat. GlaxoSmithKline is developing a synthetic version of cholecystokinin, with exciting early results. Regeneron is developing a synthetic version of leptin to tell the body that it has enough stored fat and it's time to burn all calories. Houston's M. D. Anderson Cancer Center has developed a chemical that melts fat cells in mice by attacking the proteins in blood vessels that feed their fat cells. In Paris, Sanofi has developed rimonabant, which should complete its human testing by the time this book is published. Rimonabant makes one feel full, reduces triclycerides, increases good cholesterol, and restores sensitivity to insulin.

Food is more than physical nourishment—it forms the basis of bonding between mother and child and, according to recent research, between friends. Eating sets off two (at least) processes: *oxytocin* and cholecystokinin are released to brain. We've known for a while that oxytocin was released during maternal nursing (and during sexual orgasm in both sexes, and in nest building, and in uterine contraction during childbirth, and in response to massage), thus helping to cement the bond between mother and child. But we now know that nursing and eating in general not only set off oxytocin, but also cholecystokinin, the latter of which sends a message from the intestine to the brain that says, "Food has now gotten where it needed to! Thanks, system, you're working just fine." But Kerstin Uvnas-Moberg of Sweden's Karolinska Institute has discovered that when oxytocin and cholecystokinin are blocked, a suckling lamb will not bond with its mother. Both messengers must be active for bonding to take place.

Thus we understand why business partners, sales reps and their prospects, and friends in general like to "do lunch." Therefrom comes bonding, and the cooperative, pleasurable mood with which it is associated. If food be the music of bonding, munch on, together. One's associates shall be known by one's table mates.

David York, of the Pennington Biomedical Research Center at Louisiana State University, learned that *enterostatin* shuts off the pleasure system of the brain (see topic 35.6), which is activated in ecstasy as a response to fat consumption. Fat loses its appeal when enterostatin levels are sufficiently high. Low galanin levels are associated with low fat intake and high galanin levels with high fat intake, *unless* enterostatin levels are also high, when fat intake will be limited (because fat satiety is reached quicker). If enterostatin levels are low, then fat satiety will be delayed, *unless* galanin is also low, when little fat will be ingested. More recently, Stephen Bloom, an endocrinologist at the Royal Postgraduate Medical School in London, announced in *Nature* the discovery of a suppressor similar to enterostatin named *GLP-1* (glucagon-like peptide-1), whose receptors are located in the hypothalamus.

Jeffrey Friedman (*The Brain in the News,* April 2004, p. 5) of the Howard Hughes Medical Institute at Rockefeller University in New York discovered leptin in the 1990s. Leptin, secreted by fat cells, suppresses appetite. Leptin deficiency is associated with overeating in rats, but leptin supplements in humans have not led to the predicted appetite suppression. In a complex balance, the hypothalamus contains two opposing types of cells: *NPY cells,* which, when activated, stimulate appetite, and *POMC cells,* which suppress appetite. Both are constantly active, and the dominance of one or the other determines feeding urges. Leptin deficiency activates the NPY cells, which is why losing weight makes you hungry. This appears to be at least one aspect of the "set point" theory. The trick is for researchers is to learn how to lose fat, and hence leptin, without in turn activating the NPY cells.

On another front, Merck, in partnership with Nastech Pharmaceutical Company, is in trials with a nasal spray that provides a rapid fullness message to the brain by using the natural hormone *Peptide YY$_{3-36}$* (PYY$_{3-36}$). This hormone is made in the intestines in direct proportion to the calorie intake at mealtime. Early results indicate that use of the spray can result in a 30 percent reduction in daily calorie consumption, with an associated 50-pound annual weight loss. Long-term side effects, as well as long-term maintenance requirements, are undetermined at time of publication.

A Stab at Putting All the Appetite Chemicals Together

The spring 1997 issue of the *Harvard Mahoney Neuroscience Institute Letter* announced the identification of leptin receptors in the hypothalamus. Leptin is secreted by *adipose tissue* (fat cells) as a messenger to the hypothalamus with information about whether it wants more fat, less fat, or is just fine, thank you. Obese mice lose their excess fat when injected with leptin. Roger Unger of the University of Texas Southwestern Medical Center at Dallas reported in the *Proceedings of the National Academy of Sciences* that leptin is also active in burning up fat inside the adipose tissue. So leptin performs at least two functions: it metabolizes fat within fat cells, and it sends messages to the hypothalamus. Apparently, although I haven't seen this reported, leptin is the instigator of the hypothalamic secretion of galanin. The overall process, then, is something like this: fat cells send leptin to the hypothalamus, which interprets the information and decides when to send out galanin to fish for fat, which results in the release of enterostatin when the fat hits the pancreas (figure 7.1).

Current Drugs for Appetite Control

Drugs now available for appetite control treat symptoms, not causes. One such symptom is the increase in dopamine and serotonin levels produced by fat consumption—a kind of reward system first discovered by Bartley Hoebel of Princeton University. The triggers and suppressants listed above relate to the causes of good and poor appetite control. Drugs like phentermine (increases dopamine), Prozac (increases serotonin), Orlistat (blocks fat absorption), fenfluramine (increases serotonin), and dexfenfluramine (a component of fenfluramine known commercially as Redux) do not address the root causes of craving and satiety, but rather provide the effect of pleasure from having eaten, thereby covering up the cravings. Recent warnings suggest that only the morbidly obese should use the powerful "Fen-phen" combination of fenfluramine and phentermine; studies show ill effects on the heart, lungs, and brain in both animals and humans. Even the drugs prescribed singly, like Redux (dexfenfluramine by itself), are overprescribed, according to Mark Molliver of Johns Hopkins University School of Medicine. Molliver was quoted in the March 17, 1997, *Dallas Morning News* as saying, "I've gotten calls from patients all over the country. They are 20 pounds overweight and were given Redux. I think

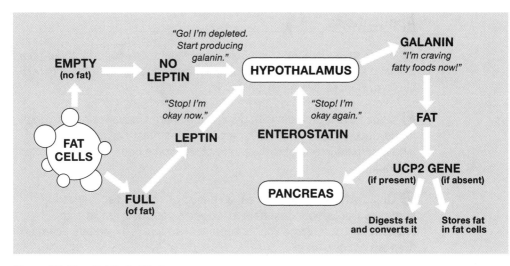

Figure 7.1. How Fat Cells Work

it's being used to a degree that's completely inconsistent with medical ethics." Part of the question has been resolved: in September 1997, the Food and Drug Administration pulled both dexfenfluramine (Redux) and fenfluramine (Pondimin, half of the Fen-phen combination) off the market because of their link to serious heart problems.

Researchers at the Eleanor Roosevelt Institute (University of Denver) have found that overweight mice lose 50 percent of their weight in two weeks when injected with *melanocyte-stimulating hormone* (MSH). Apparently the gene POMC controls MSH production, and mice with the POMC gene turned off fail to make enough MSH, which apparently specializes in burning fatty acids. No ill side effects accompanied the weight loss in the overweight mice. The process is just beginning (in 2004) for human research.

In a recent and related discovery, researchers at the University of California, Davis, announced in *Nature Genetics* the discovery of a gene that governs what one does with excess calories: whether one converts it into normal body heat or stores it as fat to "get through winter or famine." The protein associated with this gene, UCP2, occurs at high levels in animals who do not gain weight from high-fat diets. With the discovery of this process, and of leptin receptors in particular, great strides will surely be made in carrying this new knowledge closer to a harmless drug for appetite control.

Applications

1 If you have a problem with being overweight, ask your doctor or pharmacist if any new drugs either limit galanin production, bind galanin receptors, or increase enterostatin or leptin levels.

2 If you have a problem with being underweight, have your doctor look for products that boost galanin production, stimulate galanin receptors, bind enterostatin or leptin receptors, or use some combination of these techniques.

3 Until better medical intervention based on recent discoveries becomes available, your best help for appetite control is to exercise regularly and to manage your environment so that fatty, sugary alternatives are not available.

4 Save fat consumption for evenings, when desire is strongest for most of us.

5 When eating an early-evening meal, minimize carbohydrate consumption and maximize protein. When eating very late, minimize protein to avoid interference with sleep.

6 When possible, after a stressful episode, dissipate cortisol with exercise before subjecting yourself to the temptations of fatty snacks. For example, during a break, rather than heading for the snacks, try taking a 10-minute brief walk first.

7 Although the research laments that diets have a high failure rate, there seems to be a common cause for such failure—the monotony, or lack of variety, in many diets. I feel that such monotony results from a failure to study the diet plan and search properly for the many ways of fulfilling the spirit of the plan. For example, the controlled carb diets report excellent initial weight loss, but participants tend to lament their boredom with eating steak and eggs every day. This is clearly an overly simplistic interpretation of the plan. The controlled carb approach allows for extensive variety.

TOPIC 7.2   Metabolism

Paul Moe, research leader in the Energy and Protein Nutrition Laboratory of the U.S. Department of Agriculture, reports that in their human experiments in the calorimeter (a nine-by-ten-foot chamber that measures oxygen input and carbon dioxide output with 80,000 sensors to determine total energy expenditure), they found no differences in the efficiency with which different people metabolize food. Their conclusion was that differences in weight can't be blamed on differences in metabolism; they result from excess eating or deficient exercise, or both.

William Bennett (1991) argues, however, that each body has its own "set point," or genetically programmed level of body fat. It would be a lifelong battle to try to maintain a lower set point. For example, if a woman's set point is 150 pounds and she decides to drop 10 pounds, her body will forever be trying to recover the lost fat. Bennett argues that to minimize fat, we should avoid the two things that tend to raise our set point: inadequate exercise and excessive consumption. He's convinced that simple overeating in and of itself is not the culprit. In a study where subjects were overfed 900 calories a day for 14 weeks, identical twins gained weight at about the same rate; gains of 29–92 pounds were reported for unrelated people. Bennett maintains that the metabolisms of any two people at their set point would appear normal. Hence, his findings seem compatible with Moe's.

More recently, a team of scientists from New York's Rockefeller University determined that metabolism maintains a tenacious hold on weight. After losing 10 percent of their body weight, patients expended 15 percent less energy than expected for someone of their newly acquired reduced size. Reporting in the *New England Journal of Medicine,* Kassirer and Angell (1998) explained that the body resists weight change, struggling to return to its former weight. This has been explained as an evolutionary boon to more primitive peoples, subject to famine and spartan winters, but a bane to modern folk plagued with daily abundance. This regulatory system appears to keep everyone at his or her normal weight, whether slim or heavy. In a 1997 Harris poll of overweight adults who dieted, two out of three reached their target, whereas only one in nine kept the weight off (the average loss was 34 pounds, the average rebound gain 31). There is evidence that this set point can be adjusted over a substantial length of time: sustained high-fat diets can raise it and sustained exercise programs can lower it.

Recent research suggests that sleep affects metabolism. Columbia University researchers led by Steven Heymsfield (*Prevention,* May 2005) found from studying the sleep habits of over 18,000 subjects that, in comparison with those getting 7–9 hours of sleep each night:

- Those sleeping for less than 4 hours nightly are 73 percent more likely to be obese.

- Those sleeping around 6 hours nightly are 23 percent more likely to be obese.

- Those sleeping an average of 10 hours nightly are 11 percent less likely to be obese.

Heymsfield explains that sleep deprivation lowers leptin levels and raises ghrelin (a hormone that stimulates appetite) levels with the effect of maintaining fat storage and increasing appetite.

Applications

❶ When there's a choice, walk, don't ride.

❷ When there's a choice, stand, don't sit.

❸ When there's a choice, exercise or escape, don't snack.

❹ Serve smaller portions. A couple in our neighborhood maintain trim profiles without exercising, yet without giving up any favorite foods. We've sworn they had to have a God-given metabolism that allowed this indulgence. A while ago, we had them over for dinner. Because the serving dish was in front of the woman, she served the stew in bowls to the rest of us. To my consternation, I noticed that my portion barely covered the bottom inch of a bowl with a three-inch wall! I looked at my wife, who knowingly smiled back at me. Later that night, we agreed: it isn't just metabolism; it's portion size. We both grew up in homes where large portions were served. If we didn't eat large portions and ask for seconds, our mothers took it as rejection. We have to rescript ourselves to feel all right about eating smaller portions. The task is clear—and uphill!

❺ If you are confident that your exercise and diet levels are appropriate for you, learn to accept your set point and not feel guilty.

❻ Get a good night's sleep.

Miscellaneous Topics, in Alphabetical Order

TOPIC 7.3	Additives

Ben Feingold of the Feingold Association has found that people, especially children, react to food additives that interact with the natural salicylates in good food (A. Winter and R. Winter, 1988). Food additives include artificial sweeteners such as aspartame, artificial colors, artificial flavors, flavor enhancers such as monosodium glutamate, and preservatives such as nitrites. Aluminum-based additives (found in antacids and double-acting baking powder) appear to have especially adverse effects on the nervous system. Reactions include poor concentration, short attention span, fidgeting, aggressiveness, excitability, impulsivity, a low frustration threshold, clumsiness, and insomnia.

Applications

1 Avoid foods with additives for yourself, your loved ones, friends, and co-workers. Just don't make them available. While this subject is still being hotly debated, it would seem wise to minimize or eliminate additives in the diet, especially for expectant mothers and children exhibiting the symptoms described above.

2 Read food labels to check for additives, especially aluminum.

3 Candace Pert (1997) cautions us not to eat any food that is not 4,000 years old! In other words, let the test of time guide food selection.

TOPIC 7.4	Breakfast

Ernesto Pollitt of the University of Texas Health Science Center at Houston compared the school performance of children who skipped breakfast to the performance of those who ate a good breakfast (Pollitt, Leibel, and Greenfield, 1981). Those who ate breakfast made measurably fewer errors as the morning wore on. Other studies of both children and adults have confirmed this finding.

Application

❶ Don't skip breakfast. If you must eat on the fly, grab a banana, a glass of milk, or at least a piece of bread that's not dredged in fat and sugar.

TOPIC 7.5   Chocolate

Much to the delight of the world's chocolate lovers, research (see *Science News,* March 18, 2000) has found that chocolate consumption is healthy. The cocoa bean contains *flavonoids,* a natural antioxidant. One 40-gram serving (about the size of one typical chocolate candy bar) of pure milk chocolate contains about 400 mg of antioxidants, the rough equivalent of that contained in a glass of red wine. One serving of dark chocolate contains more than double the quantity of antioxidants found in one cup of black tea. Furthermore, when matching chocolate molecule for molecule with *ascorbic acid* (vitamin C), chocolate's flavonoids are more powerful at limiting plaque development by preventing the oxidation of cholesterol. Also, chocolate's power pack increases levels of nitric oxide, which work to relax the inner wall of blood vessels, thereby improving circulation and reducing risk of both stroke and heart disease. In fact, say researchers, chocolate's flavonoids appear to have the same anticoagulant effect as that of a mild aspirin. So, as long as we can minimize the butter fats and sugars associated with chocolate, we shouldn't feel guilty about consuming, on average, 12 pounds of chocolate per year in the U.S.!

TOPIC 7.6   Fat

Fats, or more properly, *fatty acids,* are chains of carbon. Some, having a complete set of hydrogen atoms, are said to be "saturated" with hydrogen; hence, they are known as *saturated fatty acids.* Saturated fats are solid under normal conditions; unsaturated fats, which lack one or more hydrogen atoms, are liquids. Those missing only one hydrogen are called *monounsaturated*; those missing more than one, *polyunsaturated.* Saturated fats include animal fat, such as the solid fat surrounding a beef steak. Unsaturated fats include vegetable oils such as olive oil. For the convenience of modern homemakers, a process was invented in the U.S. in 1910 that turned liquid vegetable oils into solids. This process, called *hydrogenation,* had the effect of "saturating" vegetable oils with hydrogen atoms and turning liquids into solids. The resulting product is called a *transformed,* or "trans," fat. Crisco and margarine are prime examples.

Stay away from trans fats—don't put them in your body. Though trans fats are not harmful in small amounts—e.g., the occasional cookie—a steady diet of them has been associated with heart disease, diabetes, cancer, low birth weight, obesity, and immune disfunction. Trans fats also interfere with the proper conversion of the essential fatty acids omega-3 and omega-6 (see topic 7.8), leading to a deficiency of these vital nutrients. The problem is that trans fats are everywhere: baked goods (doughnuts, cookies, pastry), deep-fried foods, imitation cheeses, chips, crackers, and so forth. The word to the wise: consume vegetable oils in their natural, liquid form. Say no to hydrogenated, even so-called "partially" hydrogenated oils. Among the natural fats, prefer unsaturated ones to saturated ones.

Fat is the dietary source of *acetylcholine,* a neurotransmitter that is crucial to maintaining the condition of neural cell membranes. Too much fat is unhealthy, but too little fat is also unhealthy: with too little acetylcholine, the neural cell membranes will become brittle and deteriorate over time. The result of this deterioration is memory loss and a general decrease in brain function. Dietary fat metabolizes into *lecithin,* which further metabolizes into *choline,* which then, with the help of the catalyst *cholinacetyltransferase,* metabolizes into acetylcholine. Some research indicates that doses of choline can improve the problem of severe memory loss.

A series of meta-analyses (DeAngelis, 1992) suggests that low-fat diets, though improving death rates from heart disease, increase death rates that result from suicides, homicides, and accidents. This apparent relationship between low-fat diets and negative affect adds emphasis to the potential dangers to the human system of too little fat.

Dr. Michael Zemel of the University of Tennessee's Nutrition Institute published a study in *Journal of Obesity Research* (April 2004) that found diets with three daily servings of dairy (serving = one cup of milk or yogurt, or 1½ ounces of cheese) resulted in more weight loss than diets either with low dairy or with calcium supplements. Apparently there is a hormone in dairy products that influences the size and quantity of fat cells, resulting in more and larger fat cells in its absence.

Application

❶ Do not eliminate fat from your diet!

TOPIC 7.7   **Mood: The Role of Carbohydrates, Proteins, Fats, and Sugars**

The four food groups act on mood and the brain in the following ways:

Protein (in flesh, legumes, tofu): Contains an abundance of the amino acid *L-tyrosine,* which produces norepinephrine and dopamine (leading to elevated alertness and stable memory).

Complex carbohydrates (in vegetables, grains, fruits): Contain an abundance of the amino acid *L-tryptophan,* which is necessary to produce serotonin (leading to a sense of satiety and relaxation).

Fats (in dairy, meat, oils): Important for the production of acetylcholine, which is crucial for memory formation and general neural integrity (an absence of acetylcholine leads to the breakdown of neural membranes and advanced aging).

Simple carbohydrates (sugars): A quick energy booster, but without the "time-release" quality of complex carbohydrates, which provide glucose for longer periods (sugars alone lead to sluggishness).

Complex carbohydrates—those with a low glycemic index (grains, seeds, beans, fruits, and vegetables)—metabolize more gradually and provide a steadier release of glucose for use by the body. Simple carbohydrates such as sugar, on the other hand, provide a quick rise in blood sugar followed by a letdown.

Haas (1994) points out that the sequencing of proteins and carbohydrates is important. If you're having a "California-style" salad for lunch and want to be alert after lunch, eat the chicken (protein) first, so that the L-tyrosine gets to your brain first. Then eat the rest of the salad, with L-tryptophan lagging. This ensures that you get the energy from the carbohydrates without the sleepiness. If you eat the carbohydrates first or simultaneously with the protein, the tryptophan will dominate and reach the brain first, thus establishing lower arousal and higher relaxation.

A Hebrew University research team led by Nachum Vaisman learned that children 11–13 years old showed improved performance on cognitive tests when they consumed milk and cereal within 30 minutes of the test. Children who had eaten breakfast at home two hours before the test showed no improvement in cognitive performance over children who hadn't eaten breakfast at all. Apparently the boost in brain sugar levels just preceding the test also boosted performance.

Applications

1 Serve primarily carbohydrates and fats before events for which you want people relaxed and easy to please, such as a sales presentation.

2 Serve primarily proteins before events for which you want people alert and analytical, such as a staff meeting. Or put protein out first, carbohydrates later.

3 Save fats for the evening, when you crave them most and when you have the least need for alertness.

4 Time snacks to just precede a time of day when you need a boost in mental performance (a test, a presentation, a meeting, a new learning challenge, an important new sales call).

5 Follow this recommended daily meal and snack content:

> *Breakfast:* complex carbohydrates + protein (skim milk + cereal)
>
> *Mid- to late-morning snack:* complex carbohydrates (fruits or grains)
>
> *Lunch:* protein first (chicken or shrimp cocktail), then complex carbohydrates
>
> *Afternoon snack:* complex carbohydrates (fruits, vegetable juice, or grains)
>
> *Dinner:* complex carbohydrates, fats, minimal protein
>
> *Bedtime snack:* complex carbohydrates, sugar, fats (at last, banana ice cream!)

TOPIC 7.8	Omega-3 Fatty Acids

Omega-3 fatty acids have a well-earned reputation for benefits to the circulatory system and the joints (helps with arthritis), and for treating diabetes, but only recently have they acquired a reputation for addressing issues of the nervous system. Found naturally in fish, flaxseed, canola oil, nuts, and avocados, these essential fatty acids (fats the body can't make, but which are required for optimum health) have shown promise in the prevention and treatment of many nervous system disorders, including depression, bipolar disorder, ADHD, alcoholism, Alzheimer's disease, and postpartum depression. Although the trials are incomplete, the consumption of the foods containing omega-3s is certainly benign, so let's review how they work in the spirit of knowing why we might increase consumption of omega-3-containing foods as a kind of self-treatment.

Omega-3s must stay in balance with omega-6 fatty acids. Omega-3s come in fish, canola oil, and flaxseed. Omega-6s come in oils from soybean, safflower, and corn, as well as meat, poultry, and fish. Over the last 100 years, Americans have undergone a thousandfold increase in the amount of soybean in their diet, with an accompanying overbalance favoring omega-6 that results in higher incidences of depression and heart disease. The solution is to bring omega-3 back into balance by including more omega-3-containing foods in the diet. In support of this notion, countries with the highest fish consumption also have the lowest rates of depression and suicide: Korea, Taiwan, Norway, Portugal, Hong Kong, and Japan; countries with the lowest fish consumption have the highest rates of depression and suicide: the United States, France, West Germany, Canada, New Zealand, Hungary, Bulgaria, and Austria.

Pregnancy entails a double whammy: the embryo's mother is the only source of a particular omega-3 fatty acid, and the child drains the mother of her normal supplies. Postpartum depression can be the result; in countries with lowest fish consumption, postpartum depression is 50 times higher than in countries with higher fish consumption.

Alcoholism depletes supplies of omega-3s, but research to date has not established whether increasing consumption of omega-3 foods can prevent or offset the physical effects of alcoholic excesses.

(Source: Sally Squires, "The Omega Principle," *Washington Post*, August 18, 2003. Available online at www.washingtonpost.com/wp-dyn/articles/A11623-2003Aug18.html.)

Applications

1 Set a goal of averaging one serving of fish daily. Go for variety: canned salmon spreads, canned clam spreads, smoked fish, scrambled with eggs, in tomato sauces, and so forth.

2 Mix 1 tsp of flax seeds with your breakfast, wrap, sandwich, soup, and so forth.

3 Prefer unsalted nuts for snacks and meals.

4 Although olive oil should be your number one source of fat, canola should be number two.

5 At least once a week, slice an avocado onto your salad, sandwich, wrap, as a side, or into your favorite guacamole recipe.

TOPIC 7.9   Peak Physical Performance

At the request of the U.S. Army Research Laboratory's Military Nutrition Division, the National Academy of Sciences' Committee on Military Nutrition Research looked at the contribution of six food groups to various aspects of military performance. The goal: to improve soldiers' physical and mental performance through nutrition by 10–15 percent by fiscal 1998. Their recommendations are listed here as applications.

Applications

1 Use carbohydrates (found in cereals, grains, vegetables, and fruits) to increase your capacity for physical work and reduce anxiety. A special Kool-Aid type of brew boosted with powdered carbohydrates has been found to enhance performance.

2 Use caffeine to increase mental alertness and physical endurance. (For proper dosage, see topic 8.3.)

3 Use tyrosine (this amino acid is found in proteins, especially nuts, and is particularly high in cashews and sesame seeds) to better withstand extreme cold and to better adjust to high altitudes. The Army uses a powdered supplement in a food such as applesauce.

4 Use choline (found in egg yolks, liver, and soybeans) to increase mental clarity. Choline also has been shown to take five minutes off a marathoner's time.

5 Use carnitine (found in red meat, liver, and heart) to increase physical performance over a long period.

6 Use structured lipids (a manufactured product used in hospitals to boost the caloric intake of some patients) to strengthen immune responses and to decrease susceptibility to disease and infection.

7 For more detailed information, as well as a listing of reports published by the NAS committee, visit www.iom.edu/CMS/3788/4615.aspx.

TOPIC 7.10   Sodium

Sodium is not just bad for hypertension and the heart—overconsuming sodium can also lead to electrolyte imbalances and accompanying mental dysfunction. The typical body requires about 1,000 mg of sodium daily and about five times that much potassium. (The balance between sodium and potassium is important for effective neural transmission.) To give you a rough idea of how easy it is to overconsume sodium, one tablespoon of soy sauce contains about 1,000 mg, the recommended daily allowance.

Applications

1 Don't salt your food, or at least limit yourself to one shake or pinch.

2 Use a variety of spices and peppers to compensate tastewise for lessened salt intake.

TOPIC 7.11 Taste

The tongue recognizes different tastes differently. Sweet is identified on the tip of the tongue, sour on the sides, bitter on the back of the tongue (hence the gagging that often accompanies bitter tastes), and salt all over, but especially in the front (Ackerman, 1990).

Applications

1 If you are tasting an unpleasantly sour substance, try to avoid having the substance touch the sides of your tongue.

2 If you are tasting something to determine if it is bitter, understand that you are not getting an accurate reading until the substance hits the back of your tongue. It is then natural to gag it up and out, as that is the only way to bypass the back of your tongue if you don't want further experience with the substance.

3 If you are eating something too sweet or salty and you must continue, avoid placing the substance on the front of your tongue.

TOPIC 7.12 Taste Buds

Researchers have identified three levels of taste bud chemistry: *nontasters, tasters,* and *supertasters.* One's level is determined by two genes: the gene for tasting *PROP* (6-n-propylthiouracil) and the gene for determining the density, or number per unit area, of *fungiform papillae* on the tongue (the housings for taste buds). Nontasters cannot taste PROP (it tastes just like water or paper) and have fewer papillae. Tasters can taste PROP; it tastes bitter to them. Supertasters have denser concentrations of papillae, and PROP tastes extremely bitter to them. Not only does the intensity of taste increase as the number of papillae rises, the number of pain receptors also increases. Roughly 25 percent of people in the United States are nontasters and 25 percent are supertasters, with tasters holding the middle at 50 percent of the population.

Nontasters eat a wider variety of foods than the other two groups. A higher proportion of females, Asians, and blacks are supertasters.

Supertasters tend to have lower cholesterol and to be less obese. To the supertaster, bitter tastes more bitter, sweet tastes more sweet, fat tastes more creamy, and salty tastes more salty. Ginger, alcohol, carbonated beverages, and the capsaicin in chili peppers all create a greater sensation of burning on the supertaster's tongue. Supertasters are more likely to reject bitter foods such as green tea, soy products, grapefruit, coffee, cabbage, broccoli, mustard greens, saccharine, brussels sprouts, and spinach. The University of Michigan's Adam Drewnowski, a professor of environmental and industrial health, is using a National Cancer Institute grant to determine if such taste preferences are causing women with breast cancer to reject foods high in antioxidants. Supertasters appear to experience an advantage in the battle of the bulge. Some research suggests that they find fatty and sugary foods too intense and avoid them (reported in the *APA Monitor,* January 1998, p. 13). Because the aversion to bitter foods in supertasting women increases significantly during the first trimester of pregnancy (when toxins can do the most damage to a fetus), researchers suspect that the supertaster status prevalent among women is an evolutionary advantage.

Understand that preferences and aversions in regard to certain foods are not imaginary; they are genetic. To find out how you stack up, do two things. First, get some phenylthiocarbamide (PTC) paper from your local chemical supply store. Tasting these paper strips will let you know if you can taste PROP. If they just taste like paper, you are 50 percent on your way to being a nontaster. Second, swab your tongue with some blue food coloring. Then find one of the small, circular, lifesaver-like stickers used for reinforcing the holes in notebook paper. Place it in the center of your tongue, toward the tip. Near a mirror, shine a flashlight on the circumscribed area and count the number of papillary bumps (the blue sticks to everything but the bumps). The more bumps, the more of a taster you are. Nontasters tend to have around five bumps, while supertasters can have thirty or more.

Applications

1 If you're a nontaster, you have a natural tendency to shovel it in, hoping that by assaulting your tongue with quantity you will experience pleasant tastes. However, quantity doesn't lead to quality here. Alter your eating habits by highly seasoning your food—if you assault your tongue with spices and peppers and other assorted strong flavors, you are more likely to resist the push for quantity.

② If you're a supertaster, then you are less likely to have a tendency to shovel it in, because your taste buds are more sensitive, easier to please. However, should you have a problem with overeating, you might try seasoning your foods stronger than your comfort level as a way of toning down your cravings.

TOPIC 7.13 **Undernourishment and Performance**

In the February 1996 issue of *Scientific American,* Larry Brown, of the Tufts University Center on Hunger, Poverty and Nutrition Policy, and Ernesto Pollitt, of the University of California, Davis, School of Medicine, reported on a major study involving over 2,000 children in Central America. After providing calories, protein, vitamins, and minerals, researchers observed reverses in poor academic performance that had been attributed to poverty. Other research has demonstrated that a major effect of undernourishment is significantly lessened social interaction, adding lack of exposure to lack of mental energy.

Application

❶ For children in poverty, academic intervention alone is not enough to improve performance. They need protein and calories as well as instruction and caring. Support programs in your region and elsewhere that provide nutritional supplements for children in poverty.

TOPIC 7.14 **Violence and Sugar**

Many studies report drops in violent acts when, for example, residents of detention centers are fed low- or no-sugar diets. Stephen Schoenthaler (1983), of the Social Justice Program at California State College, Stanislaus, reports from a 1980 study at the Tidewater Detention Center in Chesapeake, Virginia, that high-sugar diets promote violence in this way: whenever the limbic system and the cerebral cortex have to vie for scant supplies of glucose, the limbic system always wins. With a high-sugar diet, the body is left depleted of blood sugar when a hit of dietary sugar wears off, because insulin is released to shut down the body's production of glucose; the limbic part of the brain then gobbles up the available glucose, starving the cerebral cortex and thereby making emotional behavior dominant (the limbic system is in control) and pushing rational behavior into the background.

When I taught high school, I once had a violent student in my 11th-grade homeroom. I called his parents in for a conference. The mother (the father was on the road) described a typical day. I noticed that the boy was rising at 5:30 A.M. in order to catch a 6:15 A.M. bus to school. Meanwhile, the mother stayed in bed. The son left the house without human contact or food intake, stopped by a convenience store on the way to the bus stop, grabbed a grape soda and a pack of doughnuts or cookies, and caught the bus. When he arrived at school, therefore, he was on a sugar high and was affable and demonstrative for about one hour; then, after the sugar wore off, he started hitting people. Why didn't his mother fix breakfast? Because he didn't like her breakfasts. I asked what he'd eat if she fixed it. We agreed on a hamburger and a glass of milk, of all things. Within two weeks, his pattern had changed, reverting to that of a reasonably likable 17-year-old. I'm sure that he benefited not only from the substantial breakfast, but from having some contact with his mother before leaving home.

Applications

1 Ensure that sugary foods do not replace healthy foods; at most they should only supplement them.

2 Look for other causes of behavioral problems than sugar and sweeteners.

TOPIC 7.15   Vitamin and Mineral Deficiencies

Vitamin and mineral deficiencies result from either insufficient intake or inadequate absorption. The first can be fixed by a varied and balanced diet composed primarily of fresh or frozen foods. The second can be fixed by appropriate injections administered by a physician. The consequences of a sustained deficiency are fatigue, loss of appetite, poor concentration, failing memory, depression, and insomnia. You can confirm and specify a suspected deficiency through a blood test at a laboratory qualified to test for vitamin and mineral content.

Now that I have said that, consider what Jane E. Brody describes as "Vitamania" (*New York Times,* October 26, 1997). From 1990 to 1997, spending on vitamin and mineral products more than doubled, from roughly $3 billion to $6.5 billion, according to the Council for Responsible Nutrition in Washington, D.C. Yet this buying pattern is not based on any clear results. The notion that vitamin and mineral supplements benefit healthy people who consume a balanced diet is supported by meager evidence. And even for those who need more vitamins and minerals—the elderly, smokers, the undernourished, the sick, pregnant women—the research findings are uncertain. Interestingly, most of the consumers of supplements are active non-smokers who avoid heavy alcohol consumption, eat more fruits and vegetables, are better educated than the norm, and have comfortable incomes. One thing is clear: vitamin takers do not live longer or die less frequently from cancer, based on a 13-year study of over 10,000 Americans by Atlanta's Centers for Disease Control and Prevention, and this 1993 report (available from their website at www.cdc.gov) also found no support for the notion that vitamin and mineral supplements can compensate for slack eating habits.

Brody concludes that consumers are, in essence, voluntary subjects in a national marketing-driven experiment. Enough good, long-term studies on the effects of vitamin and mineral supplements are simply not available, and the jury is still out on their relative helpfulness and harmfulness. A few bits of good news are available: supplements can remedy the deficiencies that cause such diseases as scurvy and rickets. But nothing conclusive is available for cancer, heart disease, osteoporosis, longevity, and overall well-being. In a 20-year study (*The Lancet,* October 2, 2004) of some 170,000 persons at risk for developing gastrointestinal cancers, antioxidant pills (for vitamins A, C, and E) were found to have no effect in reducing cancer risk, further supporting the notion that antioxidants should be taken through normal diet that includes fruits and vegetables. In addition, a considerable list of dangers is emerging, including the following:

- Vitamin E megadoses (a relative term, but suggesting more than the RDA) can interfere with vitamin K (which affects blood clotting).

- Calcium megadoses limit the absorption of iron and perhaps that of other trace elements.

- Although taking 500 mg of vitamin C daily does have an anti-oxidant effect, British doctors at the University of Leicester reported in *Nature* (April 1998) that it also has a pro-oxidant effect, attacking DNA. They join Victor Herbert of Mount Sinai School of Medicine in New York, who has been arguing for decades that extra vitamin C promotes free radicals (unlike the vitamin C in orange juice, which is an antioxidant).

- Zinc megadoses can reduce the body's copper levels, interfere with immune responses, and decrease levels of high-density lipoproteins (the "good" cholesterol).

- Folic acid megadoses can mask vitamin B-12 deficiency and adversely affect anticonvulsant medications.

The one certainty that emerges is the benefit of eating a variety of foods, minimizing fat, and maximizing fruits, vegetables, and complex carbohydrates. And to hedge your bets, take a daily multivitamin. In fact, on April 7, 1998, reversing a trend of discouraging vitamin supplements, the National Academy of Sciences recommended for the first time that the following two groups take specific supplements:

1. Women of childbearing age need 400 micrograms of folic acid daily. That amount is guaranteed in most multivitamins and is difficult to get through a normal diet. Insufficient folic acid in these women increases the chance of birth defects in their offspring.

2. Adults over age 50 need 2.4 micrograms of vitamin B-12 daily in order to minimize the chance of developing anemia. Between 10 and 30 percent of people over the age of 50 lose the ability to absorb B-12 from food.

Applications

 Vitamin supplements are best absorbed when taken with other foods. Caffeine, however, obstructs absorption, so take your multivitamins with a meal that does not include coffee, tea, or caffeinated sodas.

❷ Mineral supplements are best absorbed between meals.

❸ If you think that you have some of the symptoms of a deficiency, take a blood test to determine your vitamin and mineral content.

❹ To get the most nutrition from your foods:

- Replace canned food with fresh or frozen food.

- If you use canned food, retain and use the juices in other dishes, unless you detest high sodium.

- Keep milk and bread in opaque containers.

- Don't leave food in the freezer too long.

- Use fresh juice immediately, preferably the same day it is squeezed.

- Avoid soaking vegetables.

- Choose pressure cooking, steaming, or boiling to cook vegetables, using minimum water, leaving skins on, and cooking the vegetables the shortest amount of time possible.

❺ Factors that obstruct absorption, destroy nutrients, or both include the following:

- Excessively low calorie count

- Alcohol

- Nicotine

- Tannin

- High fiber in the diet

- Aspirin

- Medications

- Overcooking

❻ Hedge your bets and take a multivitamin! I do.

SUGGESTED RESOURCES

Agatston, A. (2003). *The South Beach Diet.* Emmaus, Pa.: Rodale Press.

Bouchard, C., and G. A. Bray (Eds.). (1996). *Regulation of Body Weight: Biological and Behavioral Mechanisms.* New York: Wiley.

Gibbs, W. W. (1996, August). "Gaining on Fat." *Scientific American,* 88–94.

Haas, R. (1994). *Eat Smart, Think Smart.* New York: HarperCollins.

Katahn, M. (1991). *One Meal at a Time.* New York: Norton.

Somer, E. (1995). *Food and Mood.* New York: Henry Holt.

Thomas, P. R. (Ed.). (1995). *Weighing the Options: Criteria for Evaluating Weight-Management Programs.* Washington, D.C.: National Academy of Sciences Press.

Winter, A., and R. Winter. (1988). *Eat Right, Be Bright.* New York: St. Martin's Press.

Winter, R. (1995). *A Consumer's Guide to Medicines in Food.* New York: Crown Trade Paperbacks.

Yepsen, R. B., Jr. (1987). *How to Boost Your Brain Power: Achieving Peak Intelligence, Memory and Creativity.* Emmaus, Pa.: Rodale Press.

8

Powders and Elixirs

Mind-Altering Agents

Leo Tolstoy included in his ethic of love an injunction against consuming anything that detracted from one's normal state of full alertness. Thus, he declined coffee as well as alcohol. This chapter does not make such a demand of its readers; its purpose is to summarize findings related to the impact of various kinds of drug intake on the brain.

The word *drug* comes from the Middle English *drogge* (as well as French and German forms), which means "dry." It refers to the various powders (that is, the dried forms) we know as chemicals, or drugs. I use this word to refer to any consumable substance taken for the purpose of intervening in the normal functioning of the mind-brain. Expectant mothers should read this chapter carefully. According to a 1994 survey by the National Institute on Drug Abuse, among 2,613 mothers giving birth at 52 hospitals, 5.5 percent had used an illegal drug (marijuana or cocaine) during pregnancy, 18.8 percent had used alcohol, and 20.4 percent had used cigarettes.

Drugs act on our bodies in the same way that ligands do. Typically, a drug acts on the same "lock and key" receptor as a corresponding neurotransmitter or peptide. Sylwester and Hasegawa (1989) summarize this in their article, "How to Explain Drugs to Your Students":

- Amphetamines block dopamine and norepinephrine reuptake channels.

- Alcohol mimics and decreases GABA.

- Opiates mimic endorphins.

- Mescaline mimics norepinephrine.

- Phencyclidine (PCP) and gamma hydroxybutyrate (GHB, aka "Georgia Home Boy" and "Goop"), increase dopamine levels.

- Lysergic acid diethylamide (LSD) mimics serotonin.

- Nicotine, muscarine, atropine, and scopolamine mimic acetylcholine.

- Barbiturates mimic GABA.

- Valium enhances GABA's ability to bind to its inhibitory receptors.

- Antipsychotic drugs such as haloperidol block dopamine receptors.

- Cocaine blocks dopamine and norepinephrine reuptake channels.

- Tricyclic antidepressants block reuptake channels for norepinephrine and serotonin.

- Antidepressants inactivate monoamine oxidase (MAO) enzymes.

- Caffeine extends the stimulant action of cyclic AMP.

- Lithium modulates extreme cyclic AMP effects.

- Tetrahydrocannabinol (THC), the active ingredient in marijuana, mimics anandamide, one of the body's naturally recurring pleasure chemicals.

TOPIC 8.1   Alcohol

Alcohol serves as a disinhibitor; that is, it "unlocks" normal inhibitions. It also serves as a depressant, or downer (often followed by coffee, whose caffeine serves as an upper). Alcohol destroys brain cells, primarily in the left hemisphere, the seat of language and logic. The number of cells killed varies according to the amount of alcohol consumed, plus other factors (such as the body's state of hydration). Alcoholics and heavy drinkers kill off about 60,000 more neurons per day than their light-drinking and teetotaling friends. A Reuters news story reported that people who drink heavily for 30–40 years die with brains that weigh 105 grams less than the brains of their light-drinking friends (1,315 grams vs. 1,420 grams). If you drink alcohol, limit the amount to one ounce per day (the equivalent of two regular beers or two small glasses of wine).

Scott Swartzwelder, a psychiatrist at Duke University Medical Center, has found that the equivalent of up to two drinks daily appears to be benign in the adult brain, but the same amount for young people appears to depress NMDA (N-methyl-D-aspartate) receptors, thus interfering with learning and memory. Although the research was performed with rats, parallel results in humans have been confirmed. Alcohol interferes with the link between GABA and NMDA receptors. GABA is an inhibitor, a kind of lock on the gate that fosters quiet and receptivity. NMDA is excitatory, a gate opener that fosters activity and initiation of communication. Alcohol shuts down NMDA and permits GABA to control traffic, thus slowing down communication, beginning with reduced motor coordination and slurred speech and ending in blackout.

Ernest Noble, of the UCLA School of Medicine, has found that two to three drinks a day, four days a week, have an adverse effect on brain function, especially for those over 40. This level of alcohol consumption also causes premature aging. Studies of the brains of alcoholic men show reduced blood flow in the frontal lobe, the seat of memory formation, creativity, and problem solving. Alcohol makes the nerve membrane more fluid and less viscous than normal, which results in structural instability and increased susceptibility to structural changes and damage.

Elizabeth Ginsburg, a gynecologist at Brigham and Women's Hospital in Boston, examined the effect of alcohol consumption on women taking estrogen replacement therapy (ERT). Women who consumed the equivalent of three to five drinks a day showed levels of estradiol (the most potent form of estrogen) that were three times the intended level. Because of the unknown effects of these elevated levels of estradiol (and because of suspected links between long-term ERT and breast cancer), Ginsburg cautions women on ERT to go light on social drinking until more is known.

Some 30 studies point to a strong family effect for alcoholism (Plomin, DeFries, McClearn, and Rutter, 1997, p. 224). Alcoholism in the parent is the best predictor of alcoholism in the child. Among alcoholic families studies, 40 percent of the sons and 20 percent of the daughters of alcoholics were also alcoholic, compared with the general population risk level of 20 percent for males, 5 percent for females. A 1992 University of Minnesota report (cited in Rose, 1998) based on data from 356 twin pairs suggests that the causes of alcoholism are genetic only when it occurs in adolescent males. When alcoholism develops in adult males or in women, the evidence points to environmental causes. Franklin (1987) reports that Japanese researchers have identified two genes that control different alcohol-related enzymes: a slow-acting enzyme that breaks down alcohol slowly, giving its bearer a low tolerance for alcohol and a proneness to get sick before excessive consumption, and a fast-acting enzyme that breaks down alcohol quickly, giving its bearer a high tolerance for alcohol and a proneness to drink large quantities, with an attendant reputation for "being able to hold liquor." The Japanese found that although the two genes were divided 50-50 among the general population, only 2 percent of alcoholics have the slow gene and thus are "sitting ducks for alcoholism" (pp. 166–167). This finding is supported by a U.S. study by Marc Schuckit and Tom Smith, who reported in the March 1996 *Archives of General Psychiatry* that in a father-son study of 358 pairs of men, the best predictor in 20-year-olds of eventual alcoholism, after having an alcoholic father, is having a low physiological and psychological sensitivity to alcohol (the fast-acting gene).

Lead researcher Todd Thiele, professor of psychology at the University of Washington, published in *Nature* (February–March 1999) the results of an experiment with hard-drinking mice. Mice with higher levels of neuropeptide Y (NPY) consumed less alcohol, and those with lower levels consumed more. This was true whether the levels of NPY were genetically bred and controlled, or whether NPY was injected. Lower levels of NPY were associated with hard-drinking mice who preferred ethanol to water, and who held their liquour better, taking longer to show its effects. Higher levels of NPY were clearly associated with getting quickly drunk, hence serving as a protection against heavy alcohol consumption (*BrainWork*, March–April 1999, p. 3).

University of Illinois, Chicago, researchers (reported in *BrainWork*, July–August 2004) have made an association between low levels of the protein CREB during alcohol addiction and low levels of CREB in mice that show anxiety in maze learning. As it turns out, if you give CREB-deficient mice a choice between alcohol and water, they'll choose alcohol. These researchers, led by Subhash Pandey, reason that there must be a common pathway for alcohol, CREB, and anxiety, and they are working to establish a model by which, some day, treatment for alcoholism in humans may be possible using CREB levels in some way.

Like heart disease, alcoholism is not a single disease but a complex of diseases: the fast enzyme, a low pain threshold, chemical malformations, depression, brain wave abnormalities, and low levels of CREB and MAO. When treating alcoholism, more than one of these issues may need to be addressed. For example, low levels of MAO are associated with impulsivity, short attention span, pleasure seeking, and a low pain threshold. Alcoholics who have low MAO tend to exhibit the more violent form of alcoholism. Also, to the degree that an alcoholic has a low pain threshold, treating the source of pain would also partially address the need to drink as a form of self-treatment for disease or pain. I remember consuming alcohol to relieve low back pain. When the pain was finally diagnosed as gout, I discovered that the alcohol was in fact exacerbating the gout. Treating the gout eliminated my need for daily "medication." Depression is another application of the self-medicating quality of alcohol. Barbara Mason reports in the March 13, 1996, *Journal of the American Medical Association* that the tricyclic antidepressant desipramine relieves alcohol-associated depression and also lowers the chances of relapse.

The demographics of alcoholism are changing. The number of women diagnosed with alcoholism has risen to almost 4 million; during the 1970s, the elderly showed an increase of over 50 percent in their incidence of alcoholism. In fact, more than 20 percent of seniors over the age of 65 have problems with alcohol, with an estimated 3 million diagnosed as alcoholics. More seniors are hospitalized for problems with alcohol than for heart problems; of those hospitalized over the age of 60, about 25 percent are diagnosed as alcoholics. That's one-quarter of Medicare costs going to treat alcohol abuse. And that proportion will increase.

Absinthe, a drink now banned in most countries (including France, where it achieved fame, but not in the Czech Republic, where Prague is "the new Paris"), is famed for having driven its consumers to depression and suicide (*Science News,* April 1, 2000, p. 214). The active toxic ingredient is alpha-thujone, which blocks brain receptors for GABA. Denial of GABA's inhibitory effects thus permits neuronal firing with abandon, resulting in extreme highs and extreme lows, including hallucinations.

Applications

❶ In planning a cocktail party or reception, do not allow for more than the equivalent of two beers per person. If individuals want to drink more, you may have it available, but make them pay for it. Don't put yourself in the position of making it easy for a person to consume more than one ounce of alcohol daily.

❷ If you run a bar and are having a "happy hour" (illegal in some states), cut off special prices after the second drink. Have customers pay full price for third and subsequent drinks.

❸ In bars or restaurants, provide information (posters, notices on menus, placards on tables, and so on) cautioning against consumption of more than two alcoholic drinks per day.

❹ Consider medical intervention for male adolescents who show alcoholic tendencies. Counseling alone is not sufficient to counterbalance a genetic predisposition.

❺ If you're pregnant, ideally you should not drink at all, but especially during the first four months (see topic 4.2).

❻ If you're on ERT, limit yourself to a couple of drinks a day until more is known.

❼ The National Council on Alcoholism and Drug Dependence has information on treatment programs around the country. Contact them through their website at www.ncadd.org.

(8) Visit the website of the U.S. Department of Health and Human Services' Center for Substance Abuse Treatment that is maintained by the Substance Abuse and Mental Health Services Administration at csat.samhsa.gov.

(9) Consuming alcohol suppresses REM sleep, so for a better night's sleep, quit drinking early enough to rehydrate your body with several glasses of water—one 8-ounce glass for every ounce of alcohol. For a vivid description of the effect of alcohol on sleep, see Hobson (1994), chapter 15, especially pages 270–276.

(10) Although the few countries that permit the sale of absinthe typically allow only a weakened version, don't drink it.

TOPIC 8.2　Aspirin

Much has been written recently about the ability of aspirin (acetylsalicylic acid) to thin blood and about its potential positive effects on blood pressure and the associated lower risk of heart attack and stroke. However, a recent report based on the Women's Health Study identified a significant sex difference. Specifically, the daily aspirin dose does not reduce the risk of heart problems for women until they reach the age of 65. This does not mean that women should not take the daily aspirin before age 65, for such a dose does in fact reduce risk for stroke from age 45 onward. In addition, the right amount of aspirin can ameliorate dementia (general deterioration of mental ability): one aspirin a day will improve dementia, but two a day worsen it. After one year on one aspirin a day, demented patients showed a 17 percent improvement in tests of cognitive ability; after two years, they showed a 21 percent improvement. (See further discussion of pain medications in topic 15.3.)

Application

(1) If you have a friend or family member who is suffering from dementia and the aspirin treatment has not been suggested, you might arrange to consult with the patient's physician about its appropriateness. Some individuals should not take aspirin. Be aware of possible side effects, such as stomach upset. To minimize tummy troubles, use coated aspirin. Several brands offer a reduced dose for adults taking aspirin daily.

TOPIC 8.3   Caffeine

Caffeine is a stimulant, or "upper," that exists naturally in some 60 plants, the most familiar being kola nuts, tea leaves, cacao beans, coffee beans, maté leaves, and guarana paste. Its effect is heightened physiological arousal, which is similar to arousal caused by stress in that it results in the release of cortisol. Chemically, caffeine belongs to the family of *alkaloids,* plant-derived compounds that typically have both a positive and a negative side. These include cocaine, morphine, strychnine, quinine, nicotine, and atropine. More specifically within that family, it belongs to the subgroup *methylxanthines,* along with *theophylline* and *theobromine,* all of which have the ability to trick the brain into thinking they are the neurotransmitter *adenosine.* Adenosine (see chapter 36) is a relaxant that is required to restore the central nervous system from sympathetic to parasympathetic arousal, or from stress to relaxation. By binding adenosine receptor sites, caffeine prevents the relaxing effects of adenosine and maintains high arousal. Thus, caffeine is an imposter, like a false highway patrolman saying it's okay to keep doing 70 mph in a residential area.

Roger Spealman of Harvard Medical School has identified another specific action caused by caffeine (he also identified its adenosine-blocking action): it inhibits *phosphodiesterase* (PDE). PDE is an enzyme that breaks down adenosine, so inhibiting PDE makes more adenosine available. (If caffeine acts like a false patrolman, it also acts like a seductress who keeps the cop off the highway. Caffeine has multiple personalities!) This results in psychomotor stimulation, increased alertness, faster heart rate, and faster breathing. Caffeine consumption can also trigger panic attacks. Excessive arousal appears to result in errors of commission (for example, typographical errors), whereas deficient arousal appears to result in errors of omission (e.g., skipping a paragraph while typing). Routine tasks are less affected by excess arousal, while more complex, unfamiliar tasks appear to suffer under high-arousal conditions, which can make concentration difficult (see the discussion of the Yerkes-Dodson law in topic 36.2). In addition, in a study of 1,500 college students, higher caffeine consumption was found to be correlated with lower academic performance.

In a National Academy of Sciences study of military nutrition, caffeine's arousing properties were found to be positively associated not only with mental alertness, but also with physical endurance. James Lane, Research Professor of Behavioral Medicine at Duke University, has determined that people who drink caffeine and have stressful jobs experience more health problems than those with stressful jobs who don't consume caffeine. This is because of the double-whammy effect of having cortisol coming from two sources: stress and caffeine (topic 36.1 describes how cortisol works). In a Reuters news release (October 11, 1999), researchers at the Weizmann Institute in Rehovot, Israel, report that caffeine triggers the release of calcium in nerve cells. That is both a good and a bad thing: a moderate release of calcium encourages cell growth and enables memory formation, whereas a greater level of calcium leads to cell collapse. This is one more piece of evidence that one should restrict caffeine intake to one "dose" every six or so hours. The stress-related chemical cortisol also triggers the release of calcium, so continuing to consume caffeine as an antidote to stress actually has a double-whammy effect.

Interestingly, the less impulsive personality generally wakes up in a higher state of cortical arousal. If the less impulsive person consumes caffeinated beverages upon waking, he or she will tend to perform poorly on complex mental tasks. If the more impulsive person tries a complex mental task upon waking before consuming a caffeinated beverage, he or she will tend to perform poorly. Toward the end of the day, this pattern switches: in the evening, less impulsive people perform complex mental tasks better with a hit of caffeine, whereas more impulsive people perform complex tasks better without caffeine.

Takayuki Shibamoto, an environmental toxicologist at the University of California, Davis, reports that coffee beans contain more than 1,000 chemical compounds. Some of these compounds are antioxidants, the chemicals that disarm (or bind) free radicals and inhibit their insatiable appetite for vital cell membranes. This is true of coffee beans in their solid state. After being brewed, regular or decaffeinated coffee produces another 300 chemical compounds that are all antioxidants.

The normal effective dose of caffeine is estimated at 100 mg or, more precisely, at 2 mg per kg of body weight (roughly 1 mg of caffeine per pound of weight). Ten grams is a lethal dose (about 67 cups of regular drip coffee) for adults, but for small children 35 mg per kg of body weight is toxic (that's about 500 mg of caffeine—about 10 soft drinks—for a 30-pound child). Table 8.1 shows some common caffeine levels.

Table 8.1. Common Caffeine Levels

Substance	Amount (mg)
Drip coffee (5 oz.)	150
Percolated coffee (5 oz.)	100
Espresso (2 oz.)	100
Instant coffee (5 oz.)	50
Decaffeinated coffee (5 oz.)	2
Tea (5 oz., brewed 1 min.)	10–30
Tea (5 oz., brewed 5 min.)	20–50
Iced tea (12 oz.)	70
Cocoa (6 oz.)	5–10
Chocolate syrup (2 tbsp.)	5
Milk chocolate (1 oz.)	6
Baking chocolate (1 oz.)	8–35
Chocolate powder mix (3 heaping tbsp.)	8
Soft drinks (12 oz.)	50*
Guarana "Magic Power" (15 ml. alcohol w/5 g. guarana seeds)	250
NoDoz, Vivarin	200
Excedrin	130
Midol, Anacin	65
Dristan, other cold remedies	20–35

Source: Columbia University School of Public Health (1986), *Health and Nutrition Newsletter,* 2(2); National Soft Drink Association (1979), *Journal of American Diet,* 74(28–32); A. D. Bowes (1989), *Bowes and Church's Food Values of Portions Commonly Used,* Philadelphia: Lippincott.

* The actual range is from about 30 mg in Canada Dry Cola to about 59 mg in Sugar-Free Mr. Pibb.

Note that the figures for coffee and tea are averages and represent a wide variation in actual amounts of caffeine.

Some have touted ginseng supplements as a natural way to boost one's energy. Interestingly, researchers at the Rochester Institute of Technology in New York have discovered that caffeine and caffeine-like substances have been added to many ginseng supplements. If you're a ginseng user, check your product out carefully to ensure that you're not getting caffeine instead of active ginseng.

Consumption of 400–500 mg of caffeine per day is associated with dependence (Winter and Winter, 1988). Symptoms of caffeine dependence may include diarrhea, nausea, lightheadedness, irregular heartbeat, irritability, and insomnia. One dramatic warning sign of caffeine dependence is a feeling of dizziness upon standing after having been prone—normal people experience a rise in blood pressure, but caffeine addicts experience a drop. Another symptom is the so-called Yom Kippur headache associated with fasting (and abstaining from coffee) for 12–16 hours.

The arousal effects of one cup of caffeinated coffee last for approximately six hours but vary according to the individual. I'm 6 feet 1½ inches tall, weigh 220 pounds, and am 63 years old. If I drink caffeinated coffee after 5:00 P.M., I have trouble getting to sleep that night. If I drink more than two cups of strongly caffeinated coffee in a short time, I get jittery and have trouble concentrating. My limit is one cup of strong, two cups of moderate, or three cups of weak caffeinated brew.

The length of time that caffeine remains active in one's system is affected by many factors. While on average it stays for about six hours, the following factors will cause it to stay in your system longer: drinking it with alcohol (as Irish coffee), being Asian, being male, being newborn, taking oral contraceptives, having liver damage, being pregnant, and consuming other caffeinated products (including chocolate) along with it. On the other hand, smoking cigarettes, being Caucasian, being female, and being a child all speed up the metabolism of caffeine. Specifically, research shows the average length of time caffeine stays in these human conditions is

- Healthy adults: average of 6 hours, with a range of up to 12
- Pregnant women: 18 hours
- Preterm infants: 65–100 hours
- Term infants: about 80 hours
- 3–4 month olds: about 14 hours

Weinburg and Bealer (2001) describe the effect of childbearing on caffeine metabolism this way (p. 281):

> Caffeine metabolism dramatically slows during gestation. The metabolic rate drops progressively, falling to one-half normal during the second trimester, and to one-third normal during the third trimester, before returning to normal within the week following delivery. This means that caffeine that is ingested by the woman in the last few months of pregnancy will remain in her system three times longer than usual, and, consequently, that the exposure of her unborn child to caffeine will last three times longer.

Though coffee usually produces feelings of energy and motivation (women who drink coffee are less likely to commit suicide than those who don't, according to a report in the *Archives of Internal Medicine*), coffee has a dark side: the American Psychiatric Association's *Diagnostic and Statistical Manual* (DSM-IV) includes four caffeine-related diagnoses: caffeine intoxication, caffeine-related anxiety disorder, caffeine-related sleep disorder, and (in the appendix) caffeine withdrawal. In addition to these problems, caffeine, a stimulant, can wreak havoc with calming prescription drugs such as antidepressants, antianxiety medication, and neuroleptic tranquilizers. Initially suspecting panic disorder and agoraphobia for a woman who came into the Center for Stress and Anxiety Disorders in Albany, New York, doctors were surprised to find that she was on a steady daily diet of 30 cups of coffee!

In addition to the foregoing disorders, studies in which mega-doses of caffeine were given to pregnant rats have produced mixed results regarding birth defects. One reason: studies in the early 1980s force-fed rats through a tube directly into the stomach, while later studies have simply added caffeine to the rats' drinking water. The Food and Drug Administration has concluded that the evidence is not conclusive regarding the danger to human reproduction, but hedging its bets, it recommends that expectant and nursing mothers consume caffeine in moderation. Caffeine also makes its way into breast milk.

> When exposed to caffeine, sperm become more active, and the woman's chance of becoming pregnant doubles!

The myth that a cup of coffee for the road counteracts the effects of alcohol after a night of drinking is just that—a myth. At Hull University, students who had consumed vodka were given two cups of coffee. Those who were given caffeinated coffee made twice as many psychomotor errors as those who drank decaffeinated coffee or no coffee at all.

As with most so-called laws of nature, exceptions abound.

Applications

❶ Know your limit. If you are in doubt, limit yourself to one cup of strong caffeinated brew (or two moderate or three weak cups) every six hours. More physically active people can have somewhat more caffeine and have it more often.

❷ Make noncaffeinated alternatives available to guests, especially for introverts in the morning and extraverts in the evening.

❸ If you are responsible for a meeting, do not provide more than the equivalent of two moderately caffeinated cups of brew per person. If people ask for more, let them purchase it on their own. Don't be responsible for providing them with an excuse for less than effective mental activity. Switch to noncaffeinated alternatives (coffee, tea, bottled water, soft drinks, juice) after the initial allotment runs out. Ideally, people should have a choice between caffeine (green tea is ideal), a complex carbohydrate (for example, V-8 juice), or bottled water.

❹ I've found some hotels and restaurants to be unconcerned about supplying noncaffeinated beverages for breaks. You must be specific in asking for them when you order. (Of course, if you're a "real man," having an assortment to choose from other than "spring mint" can help cushion your sensitive male ego. Perhaps you can find an herbal or decaf selection such as "Buffalo Thunder Morning Wake-Up Wonder" or "Irish Breakfast Tea (Decaf)."

⑤ If you're pregnant, consult your physician about your proper dose of caffeine. Better yet, give it up during your pregnancy. During the months when you're nursing your infant, take care that your caffeine consumption is moderate and occurs shortly after nursing, not before. Caffeine that you consume before nursing will enter your breast milk and provide unnecessary stimulation for your nursing child.

⑥ Check the newsgroup **alt.drugs.caffeine** on the Internet for further information and discussion. A FAQ (frequently asked questions) file is available. It is maintained by Alex Lopez-Ortiz at the University of Waterloo, Ontario, Canada. E-mail him at **alopez-o@daisy.UWaterloo.ca**.

⑦ You've had too much caffeine (the official term is caffeine "intoxication") if you have five or more of these symptoms (*DSM-IV,* p. 213):

- Restlessness
- Nervousness
- Excitement
- Insomnia
- Flushed face
- Diuresis (excessive urination)
- Gastrointestinal disturbance
- Muscle twitching
- Rambling flow of thought and speech
- Tachycardia or cardiac arrhythmia
- Periods of inexhaustibility
- Psychomotor agitation

⑧ Consider the combinative effects of caffeine with sex, age, nationality, and other beverages. For example, realize that having chocolate with regular coffee prolongs the presence of caffeine in your system—better have a good book at bedtime!

⑨ Have a look at **Caffeinedependence.org** for information on the psychological aspects of caffeine addiction.

TOPIC 8.4	Cocaine

When an endorphin neurotransmitter jumps a synapse and lands on a receptor site, a pleasurable sensation ensues. Normally, the endorphins then detach from the receptor sites and return to their presynaptic location. Cocaine attaches itself to the endorphins at the receptor site and prevents their return to the presynaptic site. Thus, (1) the pleasurable effect is maintained and (2) there is a shortage of endorphins when the cocaine is metabolized, resulting in a strong letdown and the urge to use more of the drug. Cocaine constricts blood vessels in the brain. The more cocaine, the more constricted the brain's blood vessels. This constriction leads at a minimum to impaired mental function and at the maximum to brain damage.

As reported in *Science* (Lester, 1998), in an analysis of eight studies of children who were exposed to cocaine when their mothers used it during their pregnancy, Brown University researchers found that

- Cocaine-exposed children averaged 3.26 IQ points lower than nonexposed children.

- The damage is more subtle than was once supposed. There appears to be no severely crippling brain damage.

- The cocaine-exposed children's loss in the ability to understand, or "receive," language was more severe than their IQ loss.

- The annual cost to society of these cocaine-related impairments could be as high as $352 million; it appears in the form of special education requirements for these children.

The Brown researchers observed that a three-point IQ deficit is less noticeable for a high-IQ child than for a borderline child. This loss serves as a double whammy for poor children who suffer decreased mental performance as well as socioeconomic disadvantages. Barry Lester, the lead author, avers that some mental impairments can be partially eradicated by early intervention in the form of specific therapies soon after birth.

European scientists have experimented with BP 897 as a drug to soften rats' craving for cocaine. It helps ease the pain of cocaine withdrawal in two ways: by stimulating the brain, and by regulating dopamine (higher levels of which are associated with the craving for cocaine). Preliminary human trials were occurring in 2004. Other experimenters (such as Kim Janda of the Scripps Research Institute in

La Jolla, California) are creating antibodies that recognize and attach to cocaine molecules, thus preventing them from reaching the brain.

For addiction to heroin and other opiates, a new drug promises improvements over methadone. Buprenorphine, made by Reckitt Benckiser as Suboxone, is available by prescription. It is not as addictive as methadone, it does not provide an increased high above a certain level, and it persists in the system—one pill lasts for three days. All of these factors work together to make it less regulated and more effective.

Applications

❶ Don't!

❷ Maximize the use of natural highs provided by the body. Aerobic exercise and laughter are two good sources of natural highs.

❸ Do whatever is in your power to prevent pregnant women from using cocaine.

❹ In cases where newborns are known to have been exposed to cocaine through their mothers' use, advocate immediate intervention to stimulate language reception skills.

TOPIC 8.5 Ecstasy

Stephen Kish, researcher at Toronto's Centre for Addiction and Mental Health, has reported (in *Neurology,* August 2000) that Ecstasy (MDMA, or methylenedioxymethamphetamine), popular at so-called "rave" parties because of its supposedly benign effects, depletes serotonin levels, with resulting mood, appetite, and sleep disorders. Toronto alone is reporting about one Ecstasy-related death a month, with autopsies revealing 50 to 80 percent decreases from normal in brain serotonin levels. Popularly acclaimed for its 4- to 6-hour euphoria and relatively cheap price tag, Ecstasy now is being reevaluated.

Quartz & Sejnowski (2002) report that Ecstasy, in effect, depletes the brain of serotonin, which then takes weeks to return to its normal levels. If it is taken more than once monthly, the effect of this drug is lessened, due to inadequate opportunity for serotonin levels to recover. Therefore, frequent doses have less to work with. Ecstasy doesn't manufacture serotonin; it just releases your current stores. Over time, use of Ecstasy reduces the number of serotonin receptors. In addition to depleting serotonin, Ecstasy is reported (in *Science,* September 27, 2002) to cause deterioration at the synapse in the *dopaminergic system,* thereby increasing the likelihood of Parkinson's disease, or Parkinson-like symptoms.

Application

❶ No wiggle room here. Just say no!

| TOPIC 8.6 | Marijuana |

Roy Matthew, director of the Duke Alcoholism and Addictions Program, affiliated with Duke University in Durham, North Carolina, reports that steady users of marijuana (10 joints a week for three years) showed a dramatically lower (and permanent) baseline level of cerebral blood flow than nonusers. Cerebral blood flow is a measure of brain activity. Those who smoked once or twice during a three-year period showed no measurable drop in baseline cerebral flow over time. However, the same nonusers and infrequent users showed an immediate measurable drop in cerebral blood flow right after smoking one joint. Continued steady use of marijuana resulted in what Matthew calls the "amotivational syndrome"—lethargic, self-defeating behavior resulting in loss of interest in work or school, abandonment of long-term plans, and loss of pleasure in normal activity.

The active ingredient in marijuana—*tetrahydrocannabinol,* or THC—has a naturally occurring equivalent in the human body. This substance, called *anandamide,* from the Sanskrit for "internal bliss," was discovered in 1992 by William Devane and Raphael Mechoulam of Hebrew University of Jerusalem. Researchers are looking for other THC-like substances that occur in the body naturally, with the hope of making available safe pharmaceutical applications for the control of mood without marijuana's undesirable side effects. At an October 26, 1997, presentation in New Orleans for the Society for Neuroscience, researchers from Brown University, the University of Michigan, and the University of California, San Francisco, reported that animal research demonstrates the effectiveness of *cannabinoids* (a family of drugs that include THC as a primary ingredient) as nonaddictive painkillers.

Application

❶ If effective use of your mind is important to you, don't use marijuana. Legal, controlled uses of its active ingredients are just around the corner.

| TOPIC 8.7 | **Nicotine** |

Nicotine interrupts the flow of oxygen to the brain, particularly in the right hemisphere. The resulting oxygen deprivation is accompanied by decreased metabolism of glucose, which translates into sluggish and faulty memory, ineffective problem solving, and lower mental output in general. Nicotine also elevates levels of cortisol, the stress hormone. On a different front, nicotine appears to release a flood of beta-endorphins and dopamine, which together serve to enhance mood. This finding relates to the work of Caryn Lerman, a psychologist with Georgetown University in Washington, D.C., who has found that upward of 40 percent of smokers entering smoking-cessation programs are depressed. This level of depression is triple that found among nonsmokers. Lerman and others have concluded that these depressed smokers are, in effect, self-medicating for depression with nicotine. Smokers who report depressed moods at the beginning of smoking-cessation programs are the most likely to relapse, and depressed smokers who treat their depression with both talk and pharmaceutical therapy are much more likely to quit smoking and remain nicotine-free. Effective antidepressant and smoking-cessation drugs include buproprion (Zyban) and nortriptyline. Neal Benowitz, a professor at the University of San Francisco's Department of Medicine, says that they both work as well as the nicotine patch or gum (*New England Journal of Medicine,* October 23, 1997). More recent research led by psychiatarist Steven Potkin of the University of California, Irvine, has determined that smoking results in higher activation in the brains of angry, aggressive personalities than in the brains of calmer, more carefree persons. This suggests that the higher risk group for smoking would be teenagers particularly higher in the trait Need for Stability and lower in the trait Accommodation (see topic 33.2).

Motives for smoking are generally not the same for men and women. Ralph Delfino, epidemiologist at the University of California, Irvine, College of Medicine, in a small controlled study (35 men, 25 women), found that men tend to smoke to offset bad mood (anger, anxiety, sadness, exhaustion), with a resulting medicinal effect. Women, more often, tend to smoke in response to social cues, when they feel good, as a part of the interaction process. This parallels other research that shows nicotine increasing men's threshold for pain but leaving women's unaffected.

Andy Parrott, psychologist at the University of East London, writes (in *American Psychologist,* October 1999) that, rather than *soothing* stress, smoking *causes* stress, in two ways. First, when an individual becomes a smoker, his overall stress level and negative mood increase as a result. Second, stress increases measurably between smokes, with the stress continuing to increase the longer the wait until the next hit. The impression that smoking alleviates stress comes from the relief felt at the first smoke after a long period of abstinence, such as first thing upon awaking. Parrott found no empirical evidence that nicotine alleviates stress.

Tests are under way on a vaccine to prevent nicotine from reaching the brain. Reporting in *Pharmacology, Biochemistry, and Behavior* (December 1999), Dr. Paul Pentel of Minneapolis's Hennepin County Medical Center found that, in rats, the amount of nicotine reaching the brain was reduced by more than 60 percent, thereby avoiding the typical increases in blood pressure that normal nicotine intake entails. The size of this reduction precludes the normal "kick" from nicotine, thus robbing it of its addictive power.

Some current twin studies are pointing toward the possibility that depression and nicotine share a common gene. In fact, Margaret Spitz and her colleagues at the M. D. Anderson Cancer Center in Houston have identified a genetic constellation, including a variant of the dopamine-related DRD2 gene, that is common to smokers. They hypothesize that smokers, and possibly other stimulus seekers such as overeaters and alcohol abusers, have a brain pleasure center that is underactive. For them, stimulants are required to generate the endorphins that nonsmokers (or people who do not use stimulants) produce normally. Both the findings and their implications, however, are far from universally agreed upon. Specific preventive and treatment options are still in the future. In the meantime, the use of dopamine-releasing drugs such as bromocriptine and buproprion (and even some drugs used in treating Parkinson's disease) may be helpful in addressing the smoking urge.

We've all heard that women should not smoke during pregnancy. Researchers at Cornell University and the University of Rochester, for example, report that children whose mothers smoked while pregnant have significantly lower IQs; this is attributed to reduced oxygen flow and the effect of some 4,000 chemical components in tobacco smoke that can damage a child's neural development. But recent research suggests that stopping during pregnancy may not be enough. Michael Weitzman of the Rochester (New York) School of Medicine, in a study of the mothers of 2,256 youngsters ages 4–11, found that when mothers smoked after delivery, their children had twice as many behavioral problems and alterations in brain function as children whose mothers did not smoke. In another study, Denise Kandel of Columbia University reported in the *American Journal of Public Health* in 1983 that daughters (but not sons) of mothers who smoked during pregnancy were 3–6 times more likely to smoke (depending on the sample observed) than daughters of mothers who did not smoke during pregnancy. Smokers' infants, on the average, have lower birth weights, smaller brains, and poorer spatial and visual-motor skills. They are also more likely to be left-handed.

As part of a study of osteoporosis, for which white women are at highest risk, Heidi Nelson of the Oregon Health and Science University School of Medicine reported that white women over 65 years old who smoked ($n = 9,704$) performed more poorly on 11 out of 12 tasks, including strength, agility, and balance (Nelson, Nevitt, and Scott, 1994). The overall effect of smoking for these women was to add five years to their apparent physical age.

Jack Henningfield, a psychologist at the National Institute on Drug Abuse Research Center, reports that within four hours after smoking their last cigarette, smokers' accuracy and speed decreases in logical decision making, arithmetic, and short-term memory tasks. This decline in cognitive processing is attributed to changes in the brain's electrical activity. In addition, smokers who've succeeded in quitting permanently show a similar degradation in performance for one to two months after quitting. The latter finding varies widely for individuals, but all apparently recover eventually.

A comment on passive smoke. Mounting evidence, much of it available from the Environmental Protection Agency in a 1993 report (with continuing supplements, available online at www.oehha.org), points to scientific agreement over the following associations with tobacco smoke in one's environment:

- It increases the risk of asthma, bronchitis, and pneumonia.

- It increases the risk of heart disease and heart attack.

- It increases the risk of lung, cervical, nasal sinus, and brain cancer.

- It raises levels of carbon monoxide in the bloodstream, thereby reducing oxygen flow to the heart, brain, and other organs.
- It increases the frequency and duration of ear infections in young children.
- It increases the risk of sudden infant death.

Applications

❶ If you have excess brainpower that you don't want or need, then enjoy smoking. It's a good way to cut your brain down to a more humble performance level. You won't worry so much about heart and lung disease.

❷ If you are a parent or you live or work around children, know that smoking around children has a high likelihood of causing behavioral and mental dysfunction.

❸ If you are involved with a smoking-cessation program, ensure that you screen for depression and treat clients accordingly. If you are a smoker who wants to quit, have yourself evaluated for possible depression and accept appropriate treatment. In either case, nicotine used as a mood elevator must be replaced by other, healthier mood elevators, such as the endorphin rush provided by aerobic exercise.

❹ If you are a smoker who operates machinery, do not do so when you need your next nicotine hit. If you've quit smoking recently, be aware that your performance will be inferior until you've recovered completely. Airplane pilots and other high-performance drivers should be particularly aware of this.

❺ Insist on your rights as a nonsmoker to live, work, and play in a smoke-free environment. Don't live with a smoker who insists on smoking around you, and insist that your employer provide smoke-free work areas.

❻ Recent studies show that the greatest chance of success occurs when smokers use several cessation methods simultaneously (e.g., support group, nicotine gum or patch, and counseling). For a review of treatment guidelines in smoking cessation, see Wetter and others (June 1998).

❼ Obtain the excellent booklet, *Tobacco: Biology & Politics,* by Stanton A. Glantz, published in 1992 by Health Edco (P.O. Box 21207, Waco, Texas 76702-1207, toll-free 800-299-3366). It's also available online; just do a search on the title and you'll find a source. *(Contributed by Glenda Davenport-Cook)*

❽ Target teenagers higher in Need for Stability (angry and reactive) and lower in Accommodation (aggressive and challenging) for smoking prevention efforts.

❾ Consider using differential programming for stop-smoking programs: anger or mood management for men, relationship management for women.

| **TOPIC 8.8** | **Prescription Drugs** |

Nervous system depressants affect brain function. Sleeping pills, tranquilizers, muscle relaxers, and antianxiety drugs all affect the quality of brain function. Cortisone and some arthritis drugs also affect brain function. Valium (diazepam), in particular, affects the ability to drive safely, including staying in one's lane, maintaining a constant speed, braking in a reasonable distance, recognizing signs quickly, and having peripheral awareness (Winter and Winter, 1988). Matthew Muldoon of the University of Pittsburgh reported on a study of the effects of cholesterol-lowering drugs at the November 10, 1997, meeting of the American Heart Association. In a double-blind study of 194 men and women, half got lovastatin (Mevacor), a popularly prescribed cholesterol-lowering drug; the other half got placebos. The scores on attention and mental dexterity were 10 percent lower for the lovastatin group; memory scores were about equal. This difference in attention and dexterity could have a significant effect, for example, on the ability to operate vehicles and equipment in "heavy traffic" situations.

Some, but not all, drugs in several categories tend to impair performance in operating machinery: painkillers, antidepressants, antihistamines, tranquilizers, sedatives, antipsychotics, stimulants, antihypertensives, and anticholinergics. The effects of these drugs are typically worsened when they are taken along with alcohol. Certain combinations of these drugs can produce unpleasant or even lethal side effects.

Recently a new agency was formed to study the differences in body chemistry among ethnic groups. The Center on the Psychobiology of Ethnicity, located in Torrance, California, at the Harbor–University of California, Los Angeles, Medical Center, presented its initial research reports in 1992. For further information, contact Dr. Keh-Ming Lin, Director; The Center on the Psychobiology of Ethnicity; Harbor–UCLA Medical Center; 1124 West Carson Street, B-4 South, Torrance, California 90502 (310-222-4266).

Applications

❶ Try to find a nonpharmaceutical alternative to the prescription drugs listed in this topic. Confer with your physician about how to identify non-pharmaceutical treatments.

❷ Just as unions are sometimes considered a palliative for bad organizational management, so are some pharmaceuticals a palliative for poor self-management. Ensure that you have taken charge of your life with diet, exercise, and stress elimination or reduction before you allow yourself to become drug-dependent. Read Covey (1990) and Sternberg (1988). And read on!

❸ Be a "reluctant chemist," to use J. Allan Hobson's expression (1994, pp. 280–281). He writes:

> Even if . . . individuals have serious problems, their doctors should pre-scribe drugs only as a temporary means to jolt them out of their state and should then turn to scientific humanism for the long-term cure. These individuals may need a drug for a few days or weeks to break their cycles, but then they must use volition to keep themselves healthy. *Only volition can cure them.* [Italics mine.] That's why groups like Alcoholics Anonymous work; there is a collection of people who mutu-ally support each other. There is a collective will. Once the individuals in the group feel the power of their own volition, they can control their states, and the natural healing power of the mind and body will kick in.

TOPIC 8.9	**Brain Nutrient Drugs**

Dean and Morgenthaler (1990) make dramatic claims for a family of drugs called *nootropics* (from the Greek *noos,* or "mind," and *tropos,* or "change"). According to their research, noo-tropic drugs can improve mental function and arrest or even reverse some brain diseases. More recently, this family is being called "smart drugs." Most of the so-called nootropics are chemical efforts to duplicate various neurotransmitters and neuromodulators. Many of these drugs have not been approved for use in the United States. However, at least three kinds of smart drugs are currently in clinical trials:

1. ***Ampakines.*** Cortex Pharmaceuticals, Inc., is developing these drugs with the capability of strengthening electrical signals between neurons, with one particular strain being evaluated by the Department of Defense as a way to offset the effects of sleep deprivation.

2. ***Mem compounds.*** Memory Pharmaceuticals Corp. is developing mem compounds for improving long-term memory and as a possible treatment for Alzheimer's disease. In rats, the drugs improved maze recall to their levels at a much earlier age. Could be on the market by 2008.

3. ***HT-0712.*** Helicon Therapeutics Inc. is developing this drug, which appears to improve one's ability to form long-term memories from short-term, and which should be helpful in recovering from stroke.

Dr. Andrew Scholey, researcher at the University of Northumbria in England, reports on powerful effects of gingko biloba and ginseng, taken separately and together. A dose of 400 mg of ginseng was associated with immediate improvements in memory (including storage, holding, and retrieval), whereas a dose of 360 mg of ginkgo was associated with faster mental reaction times. Taking the two together in a dose of 960 mg (60 percent ginseng and 40 percent gingko) appeared to have a synergistic effect in focusing available mental energy. Subjects in this condition were able to subtract the number seven repeatedly from a variety of figures just as rapidly as they could subtract the number three. Under normal conditions, subtracting sevens is more time-consuming.

Richard Restak (1997) advises generally that nondietary sources of brain nutrients "cannot substitute for a diet rich in fruits and vegetables" (p. 37). (See the discussions in chapter 7.) A much-publicized brain nutrient is the "human growth hormone" (HGH). Restak points to HGH research as an example of the difficulty in interpreting results. Daniel Rudman, an endocrinologist at the Medical College of Wisconsin in Milwaukee, was trying to find a way to reverse the pituitary gland's decreasing production of growth hormone as we age, with 60-year-olds having on average a 90 percent lower level of growth hormone than 40-year-olds. Rudman, working in the 1980s, injected synthesized HGH into elderly subjects and found a virtual "fountain of youth" effect—increased muscle mass, increase sex drive, and so on. But when the research was repeated in the 1990s by physicians at the University of California, San Francisco, the results were not remarkable. What was the difference? Observers, including Rudman's widow, have concluded that the earlier study, in which the subjects knew what they were being given, fell victim to the "self-fulfilling prophecy," whereas the San Francisco study was a blind study in which subjects did not know what the injections contained. Concludes Restak, "I encourage you to cultivate a healthy skepticism" (p. 44).

Applications

❶ As a general rule, for the normal healthy person with no evidence of dementia, I recommend nonpharmaceutical methods for improving brain function (diet, exercise, and training in the many areas described in this book).

❷ For exceptional cases where deterioration of brain function does not respond to available interventions, Dean and Morgenthaler (1990) can help in identifying a doctor who is willing to prescribe nootropic drugs. The book itself will tell you how to become a part of the nootropic network.

❸ If you just have to try an herbal concoction to see if it boosts your memory performance, then try a 960 mg cocktail (60 percent ginseng, 40 percent gingko) shortly before you need peak mental performance. Let me know what you think! You should probably take the concoction before the episode in which you *learn* the material that you will later need to remember.

TOPIC 8.10   Effects of Chemicals on the Elderly

Steffie Woolhandler, of Cambridge Hospital and Harvard Medical School, warned against improper prescriptions for people over the age of 65. Table 8.2 shows some of her findings. For a complete listing of these so-called PIRx's (Potentially Inappropriate Prescriptions), consult the continually updated "Beers List" at the website www.dcri.duke.edu/ccge/curtis/beers.html.

Table 8.2. Potential Problems with Drugs for the Elderly

Drug	Potential Problems
Sleeping Aids and Tranquilizers	
Diazepam (Valium)	Addictive, too long-lasting, drowsiness, falls, confusion
Chlordiazepoxide (Librium, Mitran)	Too long-acting, falls
Flurazepam (Dalmane)	Too long-acting, falls
Meprobamate (Miltown, Equanil)	Addictive, too long-acting, falls
Pentobarbitol (Nembutal)	Addictive, too long-acting
Secobarbitol (Seconal)	Addictive, too long-acting
Antidepressants	
Amitriptyline (Elavil)	Dizziness, drowsiness, inability to urinate
Pain Relievers	
Propoxyphene (Darvon Compound, Darvocet)	Addictive, little better than aspirin, more side effects than morphine, seizures, heart problems
Pentazocine (Talwin)	Addictive, seizures, heart problems
Dementia Treatments	
Cyclandelate (Cyclospasmol)	Not effective
Isoxsuprine (Vasodilan)	Not effective
Antihistamines	
Diphenhydramine (Benadryl, Excedrin PM, Goody's PM)	Strong anticholinergic effects; prefer nonsedating antihistamines
Hydroxyzine (Atarax, Vistaril)	Strong anticholinergic effects; prefer nonsedating antihistamines
Cyproheptadine (Periactin)	Strong anticholinergic effects; prefer nonsedating antihistamines
Bladder Control	
Oxybutynin (Ditropan)	Extended release version has fewer side effects
Iron	
Iron supplements	Accumulation of iron in substantia nigra thought to contribute to Parkinson's disease

Source: Adapted from "Inappropriate Drug Prescribing for the Community-Dwelling Elderly" by S. M. Wilcox, D. U. Himmelstein, and S. Woolhandler (July 27, 1994), *Journal of the American Medical Association*, 272(4), 292–296, and "Potentially Inappropriate Medication Prescriptions among Elderly Nursing Home Residents: Their Scope and Associated Resident and Facility Characteristics" by D. T. Lau, J. D. Kasper, D. E. B. Potter, and A. Lyles (Oct. 2004), *Health Services Research.*

Application

❶ If you or someone close to you is 65 years of age, be sure that any prescription drugs have been prescribed according the most current guidelines and that the prescriptions have minimal or no undesirable side effects. Find the least problematic alternative. For a recent and thorough explanation of the problems associated with prescriptions for the elderly, read D. M. Fick, J. W. Cooper, W. E. Wade, J. L. Waller, J. R. Maclean, M. H. Beers (Dec. 8, 2003), "Updating the Beers Criteria for Potentially Inappropriate Medication Use in Older Adults: Results of a US Consensus Panel of Experts," *Archives of Internal Medicine* 163 (22), 2716–2724. A full-text copy is available on the web at **archinte.ama-assn. org/cgi/content/full/163/22/2716**.

SUGGESTED RESOURCES

Sylwester, R., and C. Hasegawa (1989, January). "How to Explain Drugs to Your Students." *Middle School,* pp. 8–11.

Wilcox, S. M., D. U. Himmelstein, and S. Woolhandler (1994, July 27). "Inappropriate Drug Prescribing for the Community-Dwelling Elderly." *Journal of the American Medical Association,* 272(4), 292–296.

Winter, A., and R. Winter. (1988). *Eat Right, Be Bright.* New York: St. Martin's Press.

Yepsen, R. B., Jr. (1987). *How to Boost Your Brain Power: Achieving Peak Intelligence, Memory and Creativity.* Emmaus, Pa.: Rodale Press.

Website

National Clearinghouse for Alcohol and Drug Information: www.health.org

TOPIC 9.1   The Sleep Cycle

The infant averages 14 hours of sleep, the mature adult 7½ hours, and the senior adult (over 75) averages 6. Before the invention of electric lights, typical adults slept for 9 hours. When all cues to time of day are removed, typical adults will average 10.3 hours of sleep daily, similar to their cousins, the apes and monkeys. However, studies show that the length of sleep is not what causes us to be refreshed upon waking. The key factor is the number of complete sleep cycles we enjoy. Each sleep cycle contains five distinct phases, which exhibit different brain wave patterns (see more in chapter 2):

Pre-sleep: beta waves, or normal alertness.

Phase 1 sleep: alpha waves, the mind at rest, eyes closed, breathing slowed, images beginning to appear; these images can be voluntarily controlled—you are at this point still conscious.

Phase 2 sleep: theta waves, or light sleep.

Phase 3 sleep: delta waves, or deep sleep.

Phase 4 sleep: rapid eye movement (REM) sleep, or dreaming.

Phase 5 sleep: theta waves, or light sleep, signaling the end of a cycle.

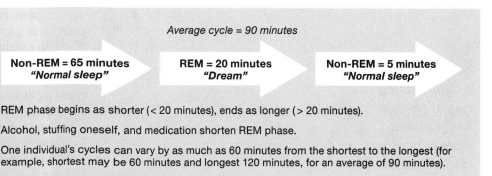

Average cycle = 90 minutes

Non-REM = 65 minutes
"Normal sleep"

REM = 20 minutes
"Dream"

Non-REM = 5 minutes
"Normal sleep"

REM phase begins as shorter (< 20 minutes), ends as longer (> 20 minutes).

Alcohol, stuffing oneself, and medication shorten REM phase.

One individual's cycles can vary by as much as 60 minutes from the shortest to the longest (for example, shortest may be 60 minutes and longest 120 minutes, for an average of 90 minutes).

Between cycles, one is not asleep ("twilight zone").

Figure 9.1. The Sleep Cycle

A Good Night's Sleep

Cycles, Naps, Dreams, and Nightmares

A good night'
should be
a basic hu
Research
nearer to
the purpose of s
example, Rober
(1998), reviewin
sleep and mem
out that among
deprivation pr
formation. Thi
reviews findin
helpful in und
what a good r
and how we c
get one.

9

A Good Night's Sleep

Cycles, Naps, Dreams, and Nightmares

> **66 What a delightful thing rest is! The bed has become a place of luxury to me. I would not exchange it for all the thrones in the world. 99**
>
> —Napoléon Bonaparte

A good night's sleep should be declared a basic human right. Research is growing nearer to establishing the purpose of sleep. For example, Robert Stickgold (1998), reviewing studies on sleep and memory, points out that among rats, sleep deprivation prevents memory formation. This chapter reviews findings that may be helpful in understanding both what a good night's sleep is and how we can manage to get one.

TOPIC 9.1   The Sleep Cycle

The infant averages 14 hours of sleep, the mature adult 7½ hours, and the senior adult (over 75) averages 6. Before the invention of electric lights, typical adults slept for 9 hours. When all cues to time of day are removed, typical adults will average 10.3 hours of sleep daily, similar to their cousins, the apes and monkeys. However, studies show that the length of sleep is not what causes us to be refreshed upon waking. The key factor is the number of complete sleep cycles we enjoy. Each sleep cycle contains five distinct phases, which exhibit different brain wave patterns (see more in chapter 2):

Pre-sleep: beta waves, or normal alertness.

Phase 1 sleep: alpha waves, the mind at rest, eyes closed, breathing slowed, images beginning to appear; these images can be voluntarily controlled—you are at this point still conscious.

Phase 2 sleep: theta waves, or light sleep.

Phase 3 sleep: delta waves, or deep sleep.

Phase 4 sleep: rapid eye movement (REM) sleep, or dreaming.

Phase 5 sleep: theta waves, or light sleep, signaling the end of a cycle.

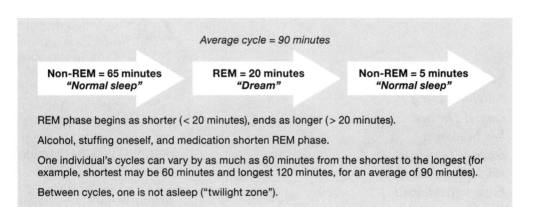

Average cycle = 90 minutes

Non-REM = 65 minutes
"Normal sleep"

REM = 20 minutes
"Dream"

Non-REM = 5 minutes
"Normal sleep"

REM phase begins as shorter (< 20 minutes), ends as longer (> 20 minutes).

Alcohol, stuffing oneself, and medication shorten REM phase.

One individual's cycles can vary by as much as 60 minutes from the shortest to the longest (for example, shortest may be 60 minutes and longest 120 minutes, for an average of 90 minutes).

Between cycles, one is not asleep ("twilight zone").

Figure 9.1. The Sleep Cycle

Phases 1–3 together average 65 minutes, followed by an average of 20 minutes for phase 4 (REM) sleep, with phase 5 lasting only 5 minutes on average. For a complete description, see *The Mind in Sleep* (Arkin, Antrobus, and Ellman, 1978) or *Sleep: The Gentle Tyrant* (Webb, 1992). For our purposes, it suffices to say that one sleep cycle lasts an average of 90 minutes (see figure 9.1).

If we were to sleep completely naturally, with no alarm clocks or other sleep disturbances, we would wake up, on the average, after a multiple of 90 minutes—for example, after 4½ hours, 6 hours, 7½ hours, or 9 hours, but not after 7 or 8 hours, which are not multiples of 90 minutes. In the period between cycles we are not actually sleeping; this is a sort of twilight zone from which, if we are not disturbed (by light, cold, a full bladder, noise), we move into another 90-minute cycle. A person who sleeps only four cycles (6 hours) will feel more rested than someone who has slept for 8–10 hours but who has not been allowed to complete any one cycle because of being awakened before it was completed. Within a single individual, cycles can vary by as much as 60 minutes from the shortest cycle to the longest one. For example, someone whose cycles average 90 minutes might experience cycles that vary in length from 60 to 120 minutes. The standard deviation for adult length of sleep is 1 hour, which means that roughly two-thirds of all adults will sleep between 6½ and 8½ hours, based on an average of 7½ hours.

A friend once told me, "All this stuff about cycles is a bunch of bunk. I wake up every morning when the sun rises." After talking about his sleep patterns, he discovered that he was self-disciplined in such a way that his bedtime was consistently about 7½ hours before sunrise. He was waking between cycles, and the song of a bird, the cry of a baby, or the pressing of a full bladder could have been equally as effective as the sunrise in waking him. All it takes to awaken someone between cycles, especially if he has had sufficient sleep, is a gentle stimulus.

When my alarm goes off during the last half of my cycle, for a few hours I feel as if a truck has hit me. When it goes off during the first half of my cycle, it is like waking after a 15- to 20-minute nap, and I feel refreshed. Our motor output system from the brain is completely shut down during REM sleep; that is why we dream we are moving but don't actually move and why we feel so lifeless when we wake during REM sleep. Our motor output system hasn't kicked back in yet!

Applications

❶ Keep a sleep journal. Record the beginning and waking times for each natural sleep episode that is uninterrupted by an alarm or any other disturbance. Find the common multiple. For example, if your recorded sleep periods were 400, 500, 400, 200, and 700 minutes, the common multiple is 100, so you would conclude that your personal sleep cycle typically lasts for 100 minutes, or about 1.6 hours.

❷ Once you know the length of your typical sleep cycle (if you haven't kept a journal, you might assume 90 minutes), then, where possible, plan your waking accordingly. For example, my cycle is 90 minutes. If I am ready for bed at 11:00 P.M. and I know that I must rise at 6:00 A.M. in order to make a 7:00 breakfast meeting, I read for about 45 minutes to avoid having the alarm go off during the last half of my cycle. Conversely, if I go to bed at midnight, I set my alarm for 6:30 A.M. and rush to get ready, rather than being interrupted toward the end of my fourth cycle.

❸ In support of waking naturally, William Moorcroft of the Luther College sleep laboratory reports that if we get the same amount of sleep each night, we don't really need an alarm clock, except as a backup (*Sleep,* January 1997). Subjects who were asked to visualize their time of waking on an imaginary clock face were generally able to rise at the desired time without an alarm. The key techniques: get the same amount of sleep nightly, choose your own time, visualize before sleep onset, and use a backup (a clock set 15 minutes later than your target rising time).

❹ We all are awake between cycles. However, most of us are not aware of this, because we go straight into the next cycle. When we "wake up" during the night, it is because some sensory stimulus (e.g., cold, heat, noise, or light) has penetrated our consciousness between cycles. It only *appears* that our "sleep" has been disturbed, when in fact we were not asleep at all. Many people worry about these "interruptions" of sleep. Don't. Realize that being awake between cycles is perfectly normal, and just surrender to your next cycle. As we age, it is even more common to be aware of being awake between cycles. Again, don't let it cause worry, as it is perfectly normal.

❺ For an intriguing description of the biology of sleep, see chapter 5 of John Medina's book *The Genetic Inferno* (2000).

Cornell University professor of psychology James B. Maas (in *Power Sleep,* 1998) says sleeping less than a normal night's sleep (e.g., slavishly obeying an alarm clock) negatively affects energy, performance, memory, learning, thinking, alertness, productivity, creativity, safety, health, longevity, and quality of life.

Maas stresses the importance of REM sleep, most of which occurs during the later hours of a night's sleep. Without REM sleep, we lose what we have learned the day preceding sleep. The specific mechanism by which REM sleep transforms experience into long-term memory is the *sleep spindle.* A 1- to 2-second outburst of brain waves at extreme frequencies, a sleep spindle serves (1) to transport memories in the form of neural patterns to the hippocampus, and (2) to resupply one's system with neurotransmitters used up during the previous day. Without REM sleep and this spindling process, memories dissipate. So if you spend good money learning a new tennis stroke and fail to get a natural night's sleep afterwards, Maas says it is like having never had the lesson. You may remember the elements of the new stroke from an academic perspective, but the absence of spindling fails to convert the motor neural patterns into long-term memory.

In related research with rats, Matthew Wilson (MIT) and Allan Hobson (Harvard) found that the brain wave patterns of rats during sleep mimicked the patterns obtained while running a maze the previous day, so much so that the researchers could actually tell what area of the maze the rats were dreaming about by comparing the brain waves to actual maze-running wave patterns. These researchers found that rats deprived of sleep after maze running performed the mazes less well on following days.

Application

❶ Organize your time so that you are able to wake up naturally, in a way that does not disrupt a sleep cycle.

❷ When you have spent effort learning something new, make it a point to get a "natural" night's sleep afterwards, without an alarm clock.

TOPIC 9.3   The Circadian Rhythm

From the Latin *circa* ("about") and *dies* ("days"), the term *circadian* simply means "about a day." Researchers have located the part of the brain that runs our body clock—the *suprachiasmatic nucleus* (SCN). We have assumed for centuries that our bodies' circadian rhythm has a 24-hour cycle. Thus, we should be renewed and refreshed after every 24-hour period. Research by Charles Czeisler of

Table 9.1. An Ideal Sleep-Shift Progression

Day	Shift Starts	Shift Ends	Bedtime	Waking Time
1	12:00 MIDNIGHT	8:00 A.M.	1:30 P.M.	9:00 P.M.
2	(OFF)		2:30 P.M.	10:00 P.M.
3	(OFF)		3:30 P.M.	11:00 P.M.
4	8:00 A.M.	4:00 P.M.	4:30 P.M.	12:00 MIDNIGHT
5	8:00 A.M.	4:00 P.M.	5:30 P.M.	1:00 A.M.
6	8:00 A.M.	4:00 P.M.	6:30 P.M.	2:00 A.M.
7	8:00 A.M.	4:00 P.M.	7:30 P.M.	2:30 A.M.
8	8:00 A.M.	4:00 P.M.	9:30 P.M.	5:00 A.M.
9	(OFF)		10:30 P.M.	6:00 A.M.
10	(OFF)		11:30 P.M.	7:00 A.M.
11	4:00 P.M.	12:00 MIDNIGHT	1:00 A.M.	8:30 A.M.
12	4:00 P.M.	12:00 MIDNIGHT	2:00 A.M.	9:30 A.M.
13	4:00 P.M.	12:00 MIDNIGHT	3:00 A.M.	10:30 A.M.
14	4:00 P.M.	12:00 MIDNIGHT	4:00 A.M.	11:30 A.M.
15	4:00 P.M.	12:00 MIDNIGHT	5:00 A.M.	12:30 P.M.
16	(OFF)		6:30 A.M.	2:00 P.M.
17	(OFF)		7:30 A.M.	3:00 P.M.
18	12:00 MIDNIGHT	8:00 A.M.	9:00 A.M.	4:30 P.M.
19	12:00 MIDNIGHT	8:00 A.M.	10:00 A.M.	5:30 P.M.
20	12:00 MIDNIGHT	8:00 A.M.	11:00 A.M.	6:30 P.M.
21	12:00 MIDNIGHT	8:00 A.M.	12:00 NOON	7:30 P.M.

Harvard University and the Center for Circadian and Sleep Disorders at Brigham and Women's Hospital in Boston, as well as research by others, suggested that in fact many of us have a body clock set for a 25-hour day and most of us have a natural tendency to stay up later and wake later than we do.

Czeisler has discovered that when 24-hour shift work is necessary, there is an optimum schedule based on this 25-hour rhythm. The shifts should progress from day to evening to night, each lasting several weeks, with workers going to sleep progressively later. In this manner, when workers who have worked up to an 11:00 P.M. bedtime end a day shift, they start an evening shift; they keep the 11:00 P.M. bedtime for several days and move to a midnight bedtime, then, after several days, to a 1:00 A.M. bedtime, and so on, until several weeks later they are going to bed at 7:00 A.M. and rising to start an evening shift at 4:00 P.M. This schedule takes advantage of the body's natural tendency to go to bed later and rise later—that is, to live a 25-hour day. (Table 9.1 illustrates how we may take advantage of this 25-hour circadian rhythm while working shifts.)

It was thought that Saturday sleep-ins were symptomatic of this 25-hour cycle. However, Czeisler (*Science,* June 25, 1999) has recently demonstrated that the 25-hour cycle was a premature announcement. In a study with two dozen men and women living in subdued light and no clues as to time of day, the body clock appeared be set at 24 hours, 11 minutes. The tendency to sleep later on the weekend he now attributes not to a 25-hour cycle but rather to exposure to bright lights in the evenings, which apparently sets the body clock forward about 10 minutes for every hour of exposure. He has also found that the urge to sleep becomes strongest at 10:00 P.M., and the urge to wake begins at 4:00 A.M., in conjunction with the times when body temperature begins to fall in the evening and rise in the morning, respectively.

For a person working normal days, the body clock seems to be set as follows:

Time	Effect on Body
6:00 P.M. to midnight	Stomach acid is high; hormone levels drop; blood pressure, pulse rate, and body temperature drop.
Midnight to 6:00 A.M.	Lowest body temperature is between 2:00 and 3:00 A.M. Body is at its lowest level of efficiency between 4:00 and 6:00 A.M. (3:00 to 5:00 A.M. for early birds, 5:00 to 7:00 A.M. for night owls).

	This is a highly accident-prone period, characterized by low body temperature and low kidney, heart, respiratory, and mental functions.
6:00 A.M. to noon	Upon waking, pulse rate and blood pressure rise sharply; body temperature rises; blood clotting activity is high. Rote memory is at its sharpest.
Noon to 6:00 P.M.	The sense of smell is better. Body temperature is at its highest between 2:00 and 3:00 P.M. Grip strength is at its highest. Tolerance for alcohol peaks around 5:00 P.M.

Research is discovering more and more hormones and other body chemicals whose levels rise and fall with circadian regularity, so much so, in fact, that a new term, *chronotherapy,* has arisen to describe the practice of coordinating pharmaceutical and other treatments with time of day. William Hrushesky (1994), of Albany Medical College in New York, summarizes the circadian aspects of several major illnesses:

Rheumatoid arthritis: Worst in morning

Nonrheumatoid arthritis: Worst in evening

Asthma: Worst in early morning (2:00 to 6:00 A.M.)

Cardiovascular disease: Highest risk in morning

Various cancers: Optimal times for treatment are highly rhythmic

See Hrushesky (1994) for a more detailed discussion.

The body's clock can get thrown out of kilter by disease, aging, travel, and other factors. Because the clock seems to be triggered by the daily pattern of sunrise and sunset, it can be reset by the use of bright lights. (Light treatments have also been found effective in relieving winter depression; see topic 19.5.) Czeisler reported in a May 3, 1990, press release that looking into a four-foot-square array of sixteen 40-watt bulbs according to his schedule can successfully reset the body clock up to 10 hours in two days. To set a person's clock back, light treatment should be administered after the body's low-temperature point (4:00 to 6:00 A.M.); to set the body clock forward, light treatment should be administered before the low point. Light inhibits the body's release of melatonin, a neurotransmitter associated with sleep, whereas darkness triggers its release. Czeisler's light treatment apparently resets the body's time for shutting down melatonin release. He also recommends using an eye cover or lightproofing the sleeping quarters of someone who must sleep during the day or in a lighted room. Sleeping in total darkness maximizes the chance of obtaining sufficient melatonin release. According to Scott Campbell (Cornell University Medical College, White Plains, New York), the light does not have to enter the body through the optic nerve. In recent research, Campbell aimed lights behind the knee and achieved the same circadian changes as those achieved through eye-borne light.

On early risers versus those who sleep into the morning, Sydney Harris once commented in his daily syndicated newspaper column, "Some say there are morning people and night people—it isn't so—night people are just teenagers who've never grown up!" Recent research, however, has shown that there really is such a thing as "morningness," or the tendency to awaken as much as two hours before those who don't have morningness. Researchers at Stanford University and the University of Wisconsin report that morningness is genetically controlled (*Sleep,* October 1998). They have identified a specific gene whose variations from individual to individual appear to be associated with whether one is an early bird or a night owl.

Roberts and Kyllonen (1999) explored the relation of morningness to cognitive ability. Using 420 U.S. Air Force recruits in the sixth week of basic training, they found that cognitive ability was positively correlated with eveningness and negatively correlated with morningness. They cite Sternberg's doctrine that flexibility is associated with intelligence, and that adapting to the electrically lighted evening hours would be an example of such flexibility. Interesting, that those of us who, evolutionarily speaking, have adapted to become night owls, and not rigidly adhered to thousands of years of early to rise, early to bed routine, show greater signs of intelligence. I like that!

Applications

❶ Don't get up early (4:00 to 6:00 A.M.) to finish a project; stay up later if you must. Research documents the futility of getting up early. You're fighting your natural tendency to sleep later, as well as working during the period of your body's lowest efficiency.

② As 4:00 A.M. approaches, go to sleep. If you must stay awake and safety is an issue (for example, if you are driving or operating other equipment), then try to have someone to talk to. Social interaction appears to be the best stimulant. Caffeine also helps. Take breaks. Keep cool. Avoid heavy carbohydrate or fatty snacks; stick to proteins and light complex carbohydrates. Bright lights help (especially full-spectrum lights), as does your attitude; think about something that excites you. If you know ahead of time that you will have to be up and alert during these early-morning hours, take a nap the afternoon before. David Dinges, a sleep researcher on the faculty of the University of Pennsylvania, has done research that shows that people who nap before staying up all night perform better than those who don't (Dinges and Broughton, 1989).

③ With around 200 sleep clinics in the United States and many others spread throughout the world, don't accept what you perceive as a problem with sleep. Check yourself in for observation. For information on various sleep programs, contact Associated Professional Sleep Societies, LLC, One Westbrook Corporate Center, Suite 920, Westchester, IL 60154 (www.apss.org).

④ See the applications for topic 9.4.

⑤ If you must sleep during daylight hours, use an eye covering and earplugs to better simulate the darkness and quiet of night.

⑥ Dark places are associated with depression for a reason: they have insufficient light to shut down melatonin production. If you or a friend have a tendency toward depression, avoid dairy products and choose bright, well-lighted, sunny environments.

⑦ Avoid setting your alarm for earlier than 6:00 A.M. Prepare the night before if getting up at 6:00 A.M. will be a rush for you: lay out your clothes; prepare breakfast, such as a bagel or yogurt; put coffee on a timer or premake it and zap it in the microwave at 6:00 A.M. Take a nap the afternoon before if you must rise early.

⑧ If you must regularly get up before 6:00 A.M., reset your body clock by ensuring darkness and quiet for an early-to-bed schedule and waking up to bright lights. Remember, sunrise is the trigger for the typical body clock.

⑨ Adolescents have a sleep cycle different from those of both older and younger individuals. They need to go to sleep later, and wake later. See the specifics at topic 5.4.

⑩ If you or someone close to you suffers from a major illness, ask your physician about the optimal time of day for medication and other forms of treatment. If your doctor is unfamiliar with chronotherapy and the circadian aspects of treatment, you should ask elsewhere. Start with Hrushesky (1994).

⑪ For current sleep information and research results, visit the National Sleep Foundation's website at www.sleepfoundation.org.

TOPIC 9.4   Time Zone Changes

Extraverted people adapt more quickly to time zone and shift changes, whereas the physiology of introverted people resists time changes. The principal problem is resetting the body's clock; introverted people need more help in doing this. The major factors in resetting the body clock are the neurotransmitters serotonin and melatonin. Serotonin can be controlled by diet, melatonin both by diet and by the use of available light. Carbohydrates, fats, and dairy products in general tend to increase serotonin, and total darkness hastens the flow of melatonin. (Incidentally, melatonin is a metabolite of serotonin.)

Applications

❶ If you have a more introverted personality, make an extra effort when you must travel through different time zones or change shifts. Light therapy helps (see topic 19.5); in addition, avoid caffeine, alcohol, artificial sweeteners, and food additives for six hours before you try to sleep after a time-zone change. Consume dairy products, carbohydrates, and fats for maximum facilitation of sleep (milk and cookies, cheese and bread).

❷ If you are responsible for managing shift schedules, remember that more extraverted personalities are less disrupted by time-zone or shift changes. This doesn't mean that introverts can't be called on to work night shifts, but you should (a) be sure that they know the precautions to take for minimum disruption and (b) accept their bodily resistance to time changes as normal and not as an attitude problem.

❸ Try the following pattern, or something like it, if traveling across time zones gets you down. This pattern assumes a 6:00 P.M. departure in the United States from the East Coast and an 8:00 A.M. (local time) arrival in Europe or Africa, with your body operating as though it were actually 2:00 A.M. You are, in essence, being asked to skip one night's sleep. The solution is to sleep once you arrive or to sleep on the plane. Sleeping once you arrive is best, if you can arrange it. Remember, consume no caffeine or other stimulants for six hours before the flight, and use an eye mask and earplugs. In order to sleep on the plane, however, you must trick your body into thinking it's bedtime shortly after you take off. Following this schedule the week before you leave can help (assume a 6:00 P.M. Saturday departure):

Day	Rising Time	Bedtime
Sunday	7:00 A.M.	11:00 P.M.
Monday	6:30 A.M.	10:30 P.M.
Tuesday	6:00 A.M.	10:00 P.M.
Wednesday	5:30 A.M.	9:30 P.M.
Thursday	5:00 A.M.	9:00 P.M.
Friday	4:30 A.M.	8:30 P.M.
Saturday	4:00 A.M.	8:00 P.M. (airborne)

If you can manage this schedule, you should get at least a few 90-minute cycles of sleep; you will feel much better for it. Remember, use an eye mask and earplugs, and consume no caffeine, alcohol, or artificial sweeteners after 1:00 P.M. on the day of departure. Your body will then feel as if it's early morning instead of the middle of the night when you land. And when 10:00 P.M. (local time overseas) rolls around on Sunday, your body clock will feel as if it's about 1:30 A.M. (since, if you were following the above pattern at home, you'd go to sleep about 7:30 P.M., or 1:30 A.M. local time). If you don't follow this pattern, when it's 10:00 P.M. on Sunday night, your body will feel as if it's 4:00 A.M. Clear? It won't work for everyone, but give it a try if eastward overseas flights really bother you. Westward flights don't bother most people because it's just like staying up later but being able to have a normal night's sleep, in accordance with the body's naturally advancing rhythms.

❹ Charles F. Ehret of the Argonne (Illinois) National Laboratory recommends the anti-jet-lag diet (Yepsen, 1987), an alternating pattern of fasting and feasting that proceeds as follows:

- Three days before the flight, have high-protein feasts at breakfast and lunch and consume only complex carbohydrates for supper; take caffeine only between 3:00 and 5:00 P.M.

- Two days before the flight, fast on broth soups, salad, and fruit; follow the same caffeine rule.

- One day before the flight, follow the same pattern and the same caffeine rule as three days before (feast).

- Flight day is fast day: for east-west flights, fast only half a day, with caffeine in the morning; for west-east flights, fast all day, with caffeine between 6:00 and 11:00 P.M.

- Upon arrival, sleep until breakfast; all three meals on the day of arrival are feasts. Begin and continue on the day of arrival with all the lights turned on and remain active.

❺ If you live on the East Coast of the United States and must fly to the West Coast, decide whether you will actually be there long enough to justify going through a change of body clock. Jane Howard says, "Often I will go to a two-day meeting in the West, go to bed on Eastern time, and pretend I'm still in the East with respect to meals and caffeine. I go to bed around 9:00 P.M. West Coast time and wake up around 4:30 A.M. Reentry to the East Coast is a breeze; my body clock remains unchanged. I miss out on night life with this plan, but marrieds should feel okay about that."

❻ Dr. John Hermann, director of the Sleep Disorder Clinic at Children's Medical Center of Dallas, recommends this simple approach to minimizing the disruption of time zone travel (i.e., more efficient resetting of your body clock):

a. Take 6 mg of melatonin (remember, the laboratory kind, not the animal-extracted variety) prior to departure when it is 11:30 P.M. in the destination time zone. In other words, if you're departing at 5:00 P.M. and your destination is five time zones to the east, you would take your melatonin 1½ hours after your departure.

b. As soon as possible after arriving at your destination, immerse yourself in the sun—go for a walk, bicycle ride, sunbathe, you get the idea.

c. In the evening after your arrival, take another 3 mg of melatonin one hour before your desired bedtime.

For your trip back home, follow the same three steps, but with your home town as the destination.

TOPIC 9.5   **Sleep and Exercise**

Exercising tends to elicit cortical alertness—not what you want when going to sleep. Exercise relaxes you after experiencing stress, but good aerobic exercise generally puts your nervous system in a state of moderate arousal. In this condition, you are ideally suited for mental tasks. In order to sleep soon after a workout, you would need to consume carbohydrates and dairy products.

Applications

❶ Exercise no later than several hours before bedtime.

❷ If you must exercise just before retiring for the evening (I know a television sports announcer who exercises after a night game because he's so keyed up), try reading a relatively unemotional book in bed rather than an exciting one (for example, Plato rather than Dan Brown) to help you get to sleep.

TOPIC 9.6   **Sleep and Diet**

Milk products stimulate melatonin production, which improves sleep. Whether skim or fat, milk (like complex carbohydrates) contains *L-tryptophan,* the amino acid that is a precursor of melatonin (and serotonin). The folk remedy of imbibing a cup of warm milk to enable sleep is in fact appropriate—warmer dairy products metabolize more quickly than cooler ones, so they bring on sleep sooner.

Simple sugars and fats decrease the oxygen supply to the brain, which decreases alertness and makes you sleepy.

Alcohol consumption reduces the relative amount of time spent in REM sleep; therefore, sleep following alcohol consumption is not as restful as alcohol-free sleep. The more alcohol we consume, the less REM sleep we get and the less rested we are in the morning.

Food additives in general and artificial sweeteners in particular tend to increase alertness, which interferes with sleep. Eating a large meal in the evening also interferes with sleep.

Applications

1 To maximize the chances of a good night's sleep, avoid snacks with additives or artificial sweeteners before bedtime and eat moderately.

2 To increase your chances of a good night's sleep, have a milk product or light carbohydrate snack shortly before bedtime. *Warning:* If you have the classic warm milk, don't sweeten it with artificial sweetener. Have it plain or with honey, sugar, or some other natural flavoring.

3 If you drink alcohol in the evening, plan to allow at least one hour for the alcohol to metabolize before you go to sleep; allow more time for more consumption. Also, alcohol dehydrates and water rehydrates, so it helps to drink water between the time you stop drinking alcohol and the time you go to bed. For example, if you've been drinking alcohol through-out an evening dinner party at your home, clean up that night, not the next day, as a way of giving the alcohol time to metabolize, and drink water while you're cleaning. Or go for a gentle walk or stroll before retir-ing, then read for a while—and drink water. If you want a restful night's sleep, switch to a nonalcoholic beverage before the evening is over. My rule of thumb is one 8-ounce glass of water for every ounce of alcohol. You may get up a lot to pass the water on to Mother Earth, but you'll feel better the next morning! Besides, your bladder is not waking you up, but rather gently urging you to pay attention to it when you naturally are awake between cycles.

4 When flying across time zones, drink milk rather than caffeine or alcohol.

| TOPIC 9.7 | **Sleep and Weight** |

      The amount of sleep we require is directly related to our body weight—that is, skinnier people require less sleep; heavier people sleep more.

Application

❶ If you would like to require less sleep, get trimmer.

| TOPIC 9.8 | **The Effect of Odors on Sleep** |

      Peter Badia, of Bowling Green State University in Ohio, reports from his sleep lab research that most odors disrupt sleep; the heart rate increases, and brain waves quicken. One odor, *heliotropine,* which has a vanilla-almond fragrance, does not disrupt sleep and may help (Kallan, 1991). (See topic 9.9 on the use of herbal scents and cinnamon in Japanese stress reduction.)

Applications

❶ Try Amaretto liqueur or almond extract in your hot milk before going to sleep. Or try a few drops of vanilla extract in your bedtime milk.

❷ Eliminate strong odors before going to sleep. Sleeping with an open window can help to diffuse odors.

| TOPIC 9.9 | **The Effects of Sleep Deprivation** |

      David Dinges, an award-winning sleep researcher at the University of Pennsylvania School of Medicine, points out (in *Monitor on Psychology,* July–August 2004, p. 61), that three out of five Americans (1) get less than seven hours sleep nightly and (2) have trouble sleeping several nights a week. He notes that three of every four workers in the U.S. consider the quality of their decisions to be negatively affected by sleep deprivation. Sleep-deprived people, according to Dinges, fall into deep sleep just four minutes after shutting their eyes, whereas those with non-sleep-deprived histories take 40 minutes to get to deep sleep, and that continued sleep loss affects performance stability to the same extent as one night without sleep.

People who are significantly deprived of sufficient sleep engage in microsleep, brief periods in which they lose consciousness. Microsleep is not restorative; it is a warning that you have lost control. A person who has begun to microsleep is a safety hazard. It is possible to drift in and out of microsleep and not be aware of it. Torbjorn Akerstedt, who conducts sleep research at the Karolinska Institute in Stockholm, connected 11 railroad operators to wire monitors. He found that six exhibited microsleep (that is, they dozed at the helm according to the electrode measurements), yet only four were aware that they had dozed. Two plowed through warning signals while asleep (Long, 1987).

In the September 11, 1997, issue of the *New England Journal of Medicine,* the same phenomenon was reported for long-haul truck drivers, with half of the drivers studied exhibiting signs of drowsiness for at least 6 minutes during a week on the road. Drivers in the United States get 8 hours off after driving 10. The study shows, however, that they average only 4 hours 47 minutes of sleep, with the other 3 hours devoted to a variety of unwinding activities. Understandably, the drivers don't want to spend all their off time sleeping. Some researchers recommend expanding the off time to 10 hours.

Eve Van Cauter, a sleep researcher at the University of Chicago, has studied the chemical effects of sleep deprivation. She has found that the loss of even an hour or so of sleep for two or three nights in a row results in attendant increases of cortisol and decreases in growth hormone and prolactin. All three of these changes are the opposite of those that occur during a normal good night's sleep (around 7½ to 8 hours for most people). Typically, following a normal night's sleep, prolactin and growth hormone increase while cortisol decreases. Another chemical change involves the reduced production of *adenosine triphosphate* (ATP). During sleep, the body produces ATP to replace what was burned up during the previous waking episode as a source of energy. A by-product of burning ATP is *adenosine,* which, as it accumulates throughout the waking episode, ultimately signals the brain that fatigue is coming on. Failure to get a good night's sleep results in (1) an inadequate supply of ATP for the next waking episode and (2) an excess of fatigue-signaling adenosine. Alexandros Vgontzas, psychiatrist and professor at the Milton S. Hershey Medical Center, Hershey, Pennsylvania, has discovered that one night of sleep deprivation (one night with no sleep preceded by four nights of normal sleep) results in elevated levels of *interleukin-6* (IL-6) during the following day. IL-6 is a *cytokine,* a protein that regulates immune function, and excessive levels of the protein are associated with bone and tissue (especially cardiovascular tissue) damage.

The consequences of all these chemical changes include depletion of the immune system, the growth of fat rather than muscle, possible harm to brain cells, acceleration of the aging process, memory impairment, and an increasing risk of depression. Van Cauter warns that a good night's sleep should be as high a priority for fitness buffs as aerobic exercise and proper nutrition. Many cultures, however, praise those who "need" less sleep and refer to those desirous of a good night's sleep as "wimps" or "wusses."

Amy Wolfson, a psychology professor at the College of Holy Cross, Worcester, Massachusetts, reported at the American Psychological Association's Women's Health Conference in 1996 that women working 40-hour weeks averaged about one hour's less sleep than they needed. The deprivation is greater when children under 18 are at home. Thomas Roth, head of the Sleep Disorders and Research Center at Detroit's Henry Ford Hospital, proposes a simple test for sleep debt: if you fall asleep in less than 6 minutes, the chances are that you are sleep-deprived. People typically take more than 6 minutes and upward of 15 minutes to fall asleep. Of course, exceptions occur.

June Pilcher and Allen Huffcutt, psychologists at Bradley University, Peoria, Illinois, reviewed 19 studies of sleep deprivation, with a total of 1,932 subjects (*Sleep,* June 1996). Their conclusion was that sleep deprivation has the largest effect on mood (it fosters a more negative mood), with a somewhat smaller effect on cognitive tasks and an even smaller effect on physical tasks. Overall, the average performance of sleep-deprived individuals was around the ninth percentile among the 1,932 total subjects.

An Associated Press news article dated July 30, 1999, identifies an increasing recognition of sleep disorders among harried Japanese workers. Attributing it to the stress of crowding, commuting, long work hours, and financial woes, Japanese researchers estimate that one in five workers suffers from insomnia. The male suicide rate is up in Japan, and depression stemming from lack of sleep is viewed as a major cause. An industry is emerging that specializes in stress reduction and sleep induction. Healing Garden, for example, is a salon where the stressed-out get rubdowns, listen to soporific music, and whiff appropriate herbal scents, such as cinnamon, which is known to help achieve sleep onset. In operation since 1994, Healing Garden serves about 1,400 customers monthly. One planetarium holds concerts intended to make people sleep! (See also topic 9.8.)

The safety hazards of severe sleep deprivation—several days without sleep—can be eliminated by one night of natural, uninterrupted sleep (typically 9–10 hours). The effects of long-term sleep deprivation (e.g., less than 7–8 hours a night for 10 years) includes increased risk of heart disease, weight control hormones going out of sync (causing higher fat storage and less efficient burning of fat), depression, anxiety, insulin resistance, and increased risk for accidents (*Prevention,* March 2004, p. 198).

Applications

1 If you must experience severe sleep deprivation, nap whenever possible.

2 If you have experienced severe sleep deprivation and are engaging in a safety-related activity such as driving or operating large machinery, take appropriate safety precautions: alert a backup, take frequent breaks and move around, take deep breaths, sip a caffeine drink, have someone to talk with, talk to yourself, or yawn (a lot!).

3 The maximum sleep deprivation possible without posing a major safety hazard is either (a) two to three days on no sleep, (b) six days with 1½ hours' sleep each day, or (c) nine days with 3 hours' sleep each day (Webb, 1982).

4 Support naps and extended sleep periods for operators of long-haul vehicles.

5 Stand up for your rights. Don't let your peers sneer at you for getting proper sleep. They're the losers. Don't wake up early to have your workout; the stress from sleep loss cancels the benefits of the exercise.

TOPIC 9.10   Sleep and Medication

In the first edition of this book, I pointed out that European research on melatonin as the sleep neurotransmitter was far ahead of research in the United States. I'm happy to report that the United States has now caught up. The production of melatonin, a naturally occurring hormone, is triggered by the pineal gland in the absence of sunlight; the reappearance of sunlight suppresses the production of melatonin (even for the blind). Melatonin is produced by the protein AA-NAT. As the brain perceives darkness, AA-NAT levels rise and so do melatonin levels. When the lights come back on, AA-NAT levels fall, and melatonin falls. (Some researchers call melatonin the "Dracula hormone" because it simulates the effect of nighttime.) Melatonin is available from most health food stores, drugstores, and even supermarkets. The most common dosages range from 0.5 mg to 10 mg. Although no harmful side effects have been reported (people do dream more vividly), most folks are taking too much. Dosage should begin at 0.5 mg and increase by 0.5-mg increments until the optimum level is found. A friend of ours, deprived of melatonin by lactose intolerance (melatonin is also a metabolite of dairy products), started out with a 3-mg capsule and found himself getting a good night's sleep for the first time in years. I encouraged him to cut back and find the lowest possible dosage; he's settled in at 1.5 mg.

Caution: Just to be on the safe side with melatonin, purchase only pills synthesized in the laboratory, and avoid pills extracted from animals. Animal-derived melatonin carries a small chance of bringing along viruses and who knows what else. Check the label and/or consult with your pharmacist. Also, be aware that not everyone has endorsed melatonin as a sleep medication. Clifford Saper (1996), Putnam Professor of Neurology and Neuroscience at Harvard Medical School, writes, "At present, taking melatonin for sleep is both without sound basis and potentially dangerous, as the long term effects of it have never been studied adequately" (p. 3). He is especially concerned about lack of certification that the pills contain no contaminants.

Steve Henriksen, of the Scripps Research Institute in La Jolla, California, reported in *Science,* June 9, 1995, that a compound identified as cis-9,10-octadecenoamide, dubbed *oleamide,* when injected into rats, even well-rested ones, results in a quick, deep sleep. The sleep appears to exhibit the features of natural sleep, including the lowering of body temperature. The compound, a lipid that occurs naturally in the cerebrospinal fluid of cats, rats, and humans, is found at higher levels in sleep-deprived cats, lower levels in rested cats. When injected animals were roused from a deep sleep, they showed no apparent ill ("hangover") effects from the injections. The Scripps laboratory has successfully synthesized oleamide. Eventually, treatment will be available for humans either in the form of oleamide-based pills, which increase levels of oleamide, or *oleamide hydrolase inhibitors,* agents that prevent the breakdown of naturally occurring oleamide, thus optimizing one's natural supply.

The sleeping pills Dalmane and Halcion, while inducing sleep, have a negative effect on brain function, causing memory loss, withdrawal symptoms, and loss of coordination. Some insomniacs are helped by taking a small dose of calcium and magnesium (such as Citracal Plus with Magnesium) at bedtime on an empty stomach. Beware too much magnesium, however, as it can lead to diarrhea. Physician and sleep researcher Andrew Krystal of Duke University found that insomniacs taking the drug Estorra (now called Lunesta) nightly for six months report falling to sleep faster, sleeping longer (by up to 40 minutes), and feeling more alert during the day than other insomniacs taking a placebo. No serious side effects have been reported. Lunesta (made by Sepracor) has proven to be effective when taken for up to a year, with no next-day groggy feelings. Indiplon and Ramelteon are two more recent drugs with good records. Two other drugs, Ambien and Sonata, tend to become addictive after a week or two, can cause dizziness, grogginess, or memory problems the next day, and should not be taken along with alcohol. Both drugs should be taken only when you can sleep for at least four hours afterwards. However, the general recommendation is to take one of these drugs only long enough to break the pattern of insomnia—say, for a week or two.

Applications

❶ People in their 20s should take melatonin infrequently and only for insomnia. Those in their 30s to 50s may take it more frequently for insomnia; those over 60, daily.

❷ Begin with 0.5 mg of melatonin two hours before desired sleep onset, and increase by 0.5 mg until desired sleep quality is attained.

❸ For jet lag associated with travel involving time-zone changes, try 1 mg of melatonin for each time zone crossed. Take your dosage a few hours before bedtime at your destination and again when you return.

❹ Consult your physician if you are taking other medications, or if your dosage of melatonin exceeds 10 mg.

❺ Take melatonin only in the evenings, unless you are taking it for help with sleep problems associated with changing work shifts. In that case, take your dosage two hours before desired sleep onset, regardless of the time of day. A 70-year-old friend lamented that he'd tried melatonin before bedtime, but he still tossed and turned. I asked when he'd taken it. He said, right before I turned out the light. I said, from now on, take it two hours before you turn out the light. He has, and it now works.

6 Prefer natural sleep inducers (see the summary at the end of this chapter) over developing a dependency on prescription medication. If nothing works for you, consult your physician.

7 Blind people should continue to have eye checkups to ensure that they retain the capacity to register light. Otherwise, they lose the regularity of their biorhythms. In particular, they should not replace their natural eyes with artificial eyes that may be more pleasing for others to look at; again, that amounts to cutting off the receptors that tell the pineal gland to stop producing melatonin.

TOPIC 9.11 **Naps**

First, let me be very clear: napping is not sleeping! The goal of napping is to move from beta waves to alpha waves (see final page of chapter 2, and topic 9.1). Alpha waves are associated not with sleep, but rather with a kind of trance or meditative state. I nap every afternoon, usually somewhere around 3 o'clock. I go to our training room (if it is available; otherwise I stay in my office), turn out the lights, and lie on the floor, on my back. I spread-eagle myself and just lie there, thinking about whatever, but allowing my mind to be empty or busy, whatever it chooses. In about 5 or 10 minutes, images start dancing in my mind's eye, images that I can manipulate and play with, making them change and perform to my liking. This is alpha state. No matter how drowsy I am when I lie down, my eyes pop open when I reach alpha state, as if my mind and body were saying, "Thank you, Pierce. I needed that." I then return to my workstation refreshed, usually accompanied by a fresh cup of tea (I put the water in the microwave before lying down!). If you should attempt to nap, and let yourself actually get beyond alpha state and into theta state, you're in trouble! You're then officially asleep, and when you wake (unless you sleep for a full cycle), you'll feel groggy, like a truck had hit you, especially if you stay under long enough to get into delta state, or deep sleep. That's why I sleep on the floor—it is well nigh impossible for me to get to sleep on my back on the floor!

People who nap consistently live longer and show a 30 percent lower incidence of heart disease. My 89-year-old father-in-law (now deceased) took a daily nap after lunch for 70 years and outlived all the men in his family. The ideal time for a nap, according to David Dinges, a University of Pennsylvania sleep researcher, seems to be 12 hours after the midpoint of one's previous night's sleep. So if I sleep from 11:00 P.M. to 6:00 A.M., my nap urge should be around 2:30 P.M. The ideal length seems to be 30 minutes. Evening naps appear to interfere with sleep. The worst time to nap is at the bottom of the circadian rhythm, between 3:00 and 6:00 A.M. (Webb, 1982).

Rossi and Nimmons (1991) talk of "ultradian breaks" and recommend two or three 20-minute naps a day. The urge to nap occurs in a natural rhythm, and denying this urge has a negative effect on health, productivity, and general well-being. This denial occurs most commonly among office workers who stoically resist throughout the day. The result is chronic mild arousal.

Psychologists Mark Rosekind, of the NASA Fatigue Countermeasures Program, and David Dinges, of the University of Pennsylvania Medical School, have teamed up to measure fatigue in pilots crossing multiple time zones (transmeridian flights). They found that pilots who were allowed a planned 40-minute rest period including a nap never lapsed in their performance. Both rested and unrested pilots showed physiological measures of fatigue during the last 90 minutes of flight, but the unrested group had twice as many measurably sleepy episodes as the rested group. Performance was measured by a timed response to a visual cue (*APA Monitor,* May 1996).

Lydia Dotto (1990) points out that the effects of napping are different for the sleep-deprived and the nondeprived. She found that for the sleep-deprived, napping improves performance but not mood; for normal sleepers, napping improves mood but not performance.

Applications

① When possible, take a 15- to 30-minute nap in early to midafternoon to get recharged. Some people practice meditation to achieve the same effect. Minimize your reliance on caffeine for recharging. *Viva la siesta!*

❷ Although naps are generally recommended, they are crucial for people who do not get an uninterrupted night's sleep. The First Napper, Former President Bill Clinton, reportedly sleeps 4–6 hours, then naps at least once daily, anywhere from 5 to 30 minutes, and awakes refreshed. He claims to be able to nap leaning against a wall.

❸ Provide a nap room at work. *(Contributed by Vicki Halsey of Blanchard Training)*

TOPIC 9.12   Dreams

Everybody dreams. Dreaming takes place during REM sleep, which first begins around the 14th to 16th week in the womb. The REM sleep of infants occupies about 45–60 percent of their total sleep time; that of mature and senior adults, about 20–25 percent. During REM, the nervous system's sensory output, external sensory input, and inhibition or control are blocked. Physiologically, this is accompanied by a drastic drop in production of the neurotransmitters serotonin and norepinephrine. Meanwhile, as the inhibiting effect of the serotonin and norepinephrine disappears, the neurotransmitter acetylcholine increases in the brain stem and activates a flood of internal memories and perceptions. The fact that we exert no management of these internal perceptions results in an often bizarre collage of whatever comes to the big screen during this central core dump.

Research by Allan Braun of the National Institutes of Health and Thomas Balkin of Walter Reed Army Institute of Research revealed that brain scans of dreaming subjects contained no activity in the frontal area of the brain, which is involved in planning and higher reasoning, thereby confirming the "unmanaged" nature of dreams. Interestingly, and in additional partial confirmation of the "unmanaged" theory, David Maurice, a professor of ocular biology at New York's Columbia-Presbyterian Medical Center, says that the primary purpose of rapid eye movement is to restore levels of oxygen to the cornea.

Hobson (1988) has defined a theory of dreams he calls the *activation-synthesis model,* which states that dreams are made (synthesized) out of the uncontrolled internal images and perceptions that bounce off each other (are activated) during REM sleep. He argues, accordingly, that "the meaning of dreams . . . is thus transparent rather than opaque. The content of most dreams can be read directly, without decoding. Since the dream state is open-ended, individual dreams are likely to reveal specific cognitive styles, specific aspects of an individual's projective view of the world, and specific historical experiences" (p. 219). Hobson points out that the physiology and content of dreams are similar to those of mental illness. The difference, he says, is that in dreaming we don't expect to have control of our minds, whereas the mentally ill have poor or no control of their memories and images where we would expect control to exist. He also presents a highly readable review of dream research, including its history, a neurobiological description of dreaming, and a discussion of the interpretation of dreams.

Applications

❶ Regard your dreams as a form of brainstorming, in which a flood of unevaluated and unmanaged images and ideas piggyback off each other and merge in often bizarre ways.

❷ Understand that the search for latent, hidden meanings in dreams is a game with a potential for inappropriate results. I had a dream one night about trying to destroy a toy train before a Japanese woman prevented me; my wife was setting the charge as I kicked off on my bicycle. Each of these images represented something I had read about recently: major rail accidents in Manhattan and South Carolina and an article in *Time* magazine about a Japanese executive who was forced to take a vacation. Don't ask *why* these images occur in your dreams; more appropriately, ask *where* they come from. Remember that bizarre combinations can result from zero management control.

TOPIC 9.13   Nightmares

Visualization techniques have proved to be a big help in reducing or eliminating nightmares. They consist of re-creating a visual scene or episode with one's eyes closed and can include actual physical movements; watch Olympic skiers visualize a run with movements before starting. These techniques can be self-taught and self-administered, or they can be learned with the help of a therapist, sleep clinic, or dream specialist.

Applications

❶ If you want to try teaching yourself visualization techniques for nightmare reduction, try the following:

- Recall your most recent nightmare in full detail.

- Alter a significant detail in the nightmare (change a tiger to a cat, a man to a woman, a knife to a feather).

- Play through the complete nightmare, substituting this new detail throughout.

- Continue this sequence until the nightmare stops or becomes acceptable.

❷ Visit a sleep clinic for professional help.

TOPIC 9.14   **Sleep Differences Between the Sexes**

The National Sleep Foundation reports that women are 50 percent more likely to have disturbed sleep than men (www.sleepfoundation.org). An average of 2.5 nights of sleep disturbance are associated with the early stage of menstruation in 71 percent of women, totaling 30 days of poor sleep annually; disturbed sleep is reported by 79 percent of pregnant women; and menopause disrupts an average of five nights monthly in 56 percent of women. For the latter group, estrogen replacement therapy appears to ease insomnia.

Applications

❶ Don't be one of the 7 percent of pregnant women who drink alcohol to help them sleep. It not only doesn't help you sleep (see topic 9.6), it also puts the fetus at risk.

❷ Be aware of the normal tendency for menstruation, menopause, and pregnancy to disrupt normal sleep. Try the specific recommendations listed in this chapter for help in getting to sleep, and see the summary list at the end of this chapter. When sleep disruption persists, reserve the right to take a nap to counter the effects of sleep deprivation.

TOPIC 9.15   Getting Back to Sleep

If you've awakened in the middle of the night and can't get back to sleep, it's a good bet that you've somehow become aroused. What you need to do is shut down your aroused state. Several of the strategies mentioned earlier in this chapter will minimize the chance of your waking. However, if the worst happens and you become wakeful, there are several ways to lower your level of arousal.

Applications

1 Often sleep eludes us because our thoughts race around trying to keep from being forgotten. Keep a pad and pen beside your bed and take a mental dump by writing down all those thoughts that are bumping into each other. You can then sleep peacefully and deal with them tomorrow.

2 Sometimes our sleep is disturbed by an emotionally arousing disturbance, such as a phone call or a surprise intrusion. You need to come down from this state of limbic arousal—in other words, you need to get bored again. Try reading the most sleep-inducing book you can think of.

3 Get out of bed, leave the bedroom, and engage in a constructive but boring activity in subdued light. Getting up to a large dose of bright light will suppress melatonin production, which you don't want to happen. Associate your bed only with sleep.

4 Drink a cup of warm milk with honey; eat cheese, yogurt, ice cream. Recently I awoke in the middle of the night and just couldn't get back to sleep. I got up, went downstairs, got a couple of ounces of cheese and some walnuts, sat in my favorite reading chair, and munched and read for about 45 minutes. I started to get sleepy, returned to bed, and went to sleep immediately. I think I had gone to bed hungry, and when I awoke, my empty tummy interfered with getting back to sleep.

5 Take a melatonin pill.

6 Check to make sure that your room is pitch-black; use wide, long, opaque shades that block out all light, or an eye mask.

7 Meditate.

❽ If you can, simply enjoy resting.

❾ If self-help such as this fails, try finding a therapist who will do cognitive-behavioral therapy (CBT) with you (see chapter 15). Gregg Jacobs, sleep expert with the Sleep Disorders Center at Boston Beth Israel Deaconess Medical Center, in his book *Say Good Night to Insomnia*, suggests a possible joint approach using a pharmaceutical like Ambien or Sonata to help get you started with regular sleeping, but relying on behavior change to complete the job over time, eventually discontinuing drugs. The CBT techniques are similar to many others mentioned elsewhere in this book, from not reading in bed and regular sleep onset times to relaxation techniques.

❿ Get a copy of "Guide to Getting a Good Night's Sleep" for $2 from Graedons' People's Pharmacy, No. I-70, P.O. Box 52027, Durham, North Carolina 27717-2027. Include a stamped (60 cents as of September 2004), self-addressed #10 return envelope.

TOPIC 9.16   Stability in Sleep Patterns

A study that related pilot error in landings to the interval between sleep periods (Webb, 1991) found that the more variable the interval between sleep periods, the more likely a pilot is to make an error in landing. In other words, for a five-day period, if pilot A is up for 17 hours the first day, 12 the second, and then 20, 15, and 21 hours on consecutive days, and pilot B is up for 16, 18, 17, 18, and 16 hours on the same five days, then pilot A will be more likely to make an error in landing (or other similar errors) than pilot B, whose intervals between sleep periods showed less variation from day to day.

Cross-cultural studies by Sara Harkness, an associate professor of human development and anthropology at Pennsylvania State University, found that quality of sleep in infants was related to lifestyle issues. For example, Harkness found that Dutch parents tend to pick up infants less during the day, encourage less stimulating activities during the day (for example, they do not appear to take infants to shopping malls), and put them to bed nightly at the same time. This preference for rest and regularity, according to Harkness, results in Dutch babies sleeping longer than American babies and sleeping through the night at an earlier age than American babies (reported by the Associated Press, February 21, 1995).

Applications

❶ Pilots, and others in jobs with major safety implications that require continuing alertness, should minimize day-to-day variations in the number of hours between getting up and going to sleep.

❷ Be aware that your infant's sleep patterns may reflect your lifestyle. For more regular sleep, prefer a more routine and less stimulating lifestyle.

TOPIC 9.17 **If You *Don't* Want to Sleep!**

Drug manufacturer Cephalon markets Provigil (modafinil), a drug that allows one to stay awake, alert, focused, and able to handle complex issues, for upwards of two days. Modafinil does not entail the bothersome side effects of caffeine and other stimulants. Designed originally for narcoleptics, it was approved by the FDA for other medical conditions. However, experiments have been underway for use with jet lag, military situations, shift work, and other contexts that require relief from the urge to sleep. Perhaps our national leaders should have a supply available for clear thinking in case of a round-the-clock crisis.

Application

❶ If you feel that you have a legitimate need for sleep suppression, consult with your physician about the possibility of prescribing modafinil.

TOPIC 9.18 **Apnea and Restless Legs**

Some people stop breathing repeatedly during sleep. This disorder is called *sleep apnea.* Untreated, apnea can cause high blood pressure, memory problems, weight gain, impotence, headaches, job difficulties, and equipment operation accidents. Apnea can be effectively diagnosed and treated by submitting yourself to a sleep clinic. My wife and several friends all have apnea and use a CPAP (for "continuous positive air pressure") machine for a good night's sleep.

If those who see you sleeping report that you quit breathing from time to time, or if you experience significant drowsiness during the day or the feeling that you can't get a good night's sleep, you should consider going to a sleep clinic for evaluation.

Restless legs has no clearly known cause and no single effective treatment. Those who have the disorder report feeling that their legs (and sometimes arms) are creeping, crawling, tingling, or pulling, or are simply painful, resulting in an irresistible urge to move the affected limb, thus making sleep difficult. The disorder is thought to be associated with anemia, diabetes, kidney problems, Parkinson's disease, and pregnancy, and is often treated by addressing one of these underlying conditions. Other treatments include dietary modifications, exercise, and bathing.

Applications

1 For complete information and support on these two disorders, visit these websites: www.sleepapnea.org and www.restlessleg.net.

2 If you suspect you have sleep apnea, check yourself into a sleep clinic for evaluation.

A Final Word on Sleep

Here are some of the major principles associated with good sleep:

Getting to Sleep
- Consume dairy products (the warmer the better).
- Avoid artificial sweeteners.
- Avoid food additives.
- Avoid caffeine within six hours of bedtime.
- Keep to a regular bedtime.
- Consume carbohydrates and fats.
- Avoid protein.
- Read or view unexciting material.

- Avoid exercise within four hours of bedtime.
- Sleep in absolute darkness (use an eye cover if necessary).
- Maintain quiet (use earplugs if necessary).
- Do not take naps after 3:00 P.M.
- Meditate.
- Avoid beans, raw onions, cruciferous vegetables (broccoli, cauliflower, cabbage), and spicy foods before bedtime.
- Take melatonin pills.

Getting Quality Sleep

- Lose weight.
- Avoid alcohol within three hours of bedtime, and replace each ounce of alcohol with eight ounces of water.
- Plan sleep according to sleep cycles and circadian rhythms.
- Do aerobic exercise regularly, but not close to bedtime.

Getting Back to Sleep

- Write down what's on your mind.
- Read something unexciting.
- Drink warm milk with honey.

SUGGESTED RESOURCES

Arkin, A. M., J. S. Antrobus, and S. J. Ellman (Eds.). (1978). *The Mind in Sleep.* Hillsdale, N.J.: Erlbaum.

Coren, S. (1996). *Sleep Thieves.* New York: Free Press.

Hobson, J. A. (1988). *The Dreaming Brain.* New York: Basic Books.

Sahelian, R. (1997). *Melatonin: Nature's Sleeping Pill* (2nd ed.). Garden City Park, N.Y.: Avery Publishing Group.

Webb, W. B. (1992). *Sleep: The Gentle Tyrant* (2nd ed.). Bolton, Mass.: Anker.

Websites

Associated Professional Sleep Societies:
 www.apss.org

National Sleep Foundation:
 www.sleepfoundation.org

The Body Cognitive

The Effects of Exercise

R esearch is catching up with folk wisdom. From Homer ("Too much rest itself becomes a pain") to Shakespeare ("The labor we delight in physics pain") to Alexander Pope, the contributions of physical activity to mental performance have been touted. But not until recently have research findings supported these claims. This chapter visits some of these findings.

TOPIC 10.1   Physical Activity

Jean Pierre Changeux (1997), of the Pasteur Institute in Paris, and Christopher Henderson, a researcher at the Developmental Biology Institute of Marseilles, found that simple movement of the muscles stimulates the growth of axons, which carry messages between neurons. The number of axons is directly related to intelligence, and people (infants as well as adults) who move about more benefit from greater axonal development. Less movement results in fewer axons. In recent support of Changeux's findings, Carl Cotman and team at the University of California at Irvine show (Quartz and Sejnowski, 2002, p. 250) that regular exercise increases production of neurotrophins in the hippocampus. Moreover, a study of 500 schoolchildren found that those who spent an hour each day in gym class performed better on intelligence tests that those who were inactive, a finding that has been replicated in dozens of studies." Hence, the couch-potato syndrome is associated with lesser intelligence.

Applications

❶ Move it or lose it.

❷ Encourage physical activity from the cradle to the grave. Even people confined to wheelchairs or with limited mobility should move whatever they can. *(Contributed by Jane Howard)*

TOPIC 10.2   Aerobics

Covert Bailey (1991) applies the term *aerobic* to exercise that meets four criteria:

1. It must be nonstop.
2. It must last for a minimum of 12 minutes.
3. It must proceed at a comfortable pace.
4. It must exercise the muscles of the lower body.

He defines "comfortable pace" with a formula: at the conclusion of exercising, your pulse should be 220 minus your age times 0.65 (or 0.8 for athletes). For me, that would mean a pulse of about 102 heartbeats per minute. This formula is intended for the average person (about two-thirds of the population). For a more personal application of the formula, check pages 41–45 in Bailey (1991).

Mentally, aerobic exercise has at least six effects:

1. It clearly improves speed of recall; it is not clear whether aerobic exercise has any effect on the quality of mental functioning or the amount of recall.

2. It releases endorphins, the neurotransmitters that relax us into a state of cortical alertness. This is not the only way to reach cortical alertness (other relaxation methods will work as well), but it is certainly one way. Johns Hopkins's Dr. Solomon Snyder and others are concerned over the lack of substantive research on the so-called runner's high, claiming that the increased endorphins in the blood after running never reach the brain. Calling this connection an urban legend, they contend that the association was an accident caused by the simultaneous popularity of running and the discovery of endorphins. On the other hand, Arne Dietrich (American University of Beirut) has found that a minimum of 20 minutes of aerobic exercise releases significant levels of the cannabinoid *anandamide* in your bloodstream, the same euphoria-producing chemical associated with marijuana. So you must bear with the initial discomfort of aerobic exercise in order to get the ultimate benefit of the runner's high. (No pain, no gain.) We are awaiting clarification. Meanwhile, run on, and enjoy it.

3. As reported in a National Institute of Mental Health study of over 1,900 individuals, people with little or no recreational activity are twice as likely to have depressive symptoms as people who regularly do aerobic exercise.

4. Aerobic exercise increases the number of neurotrophins (agents that stimulate the growth of nerve cells) available to the brain and nervous system, according to the work of Carl Cotman, director of the Institute for Brain Aging and Dementia at the University of California, Irvine. Cotman says that there is an optimum amount of exercise; rats who run five miles, for example, have no more neurotrophins than those who run only two. Kenneth Cooper (Thompson, 1995) underscores this point. Cooper, who started the aerobics craze with the publication of his book *Aerobics* (1968), is concerned that overly vigorous exercising releases excess free radicals. He recommends

the equivalent of walking two miles in under 40 minutes, five times a week. In fact, he remarks, "If you are running more than 15 miles a week, you are running for some other reason than your health" (quoted in Thompson, 1995, p. 136).

5. William Greenough, a professor at the Beckman Institute (University of Illinois) has determined that aerobic exercise results in an increase in capillaries around the neurons in the brain. This translates into more blood and oxygen reaching the brain.

6. Arthur Kramer, a research psychologist who is also with the Beckman Institute, has established that a 45-minute water aerobics class three times a week, lasting for 10 weeks, in people 63–82 years old, results in improved, faster reaction times. He further avows that declines in reaction time appear to be related to declines in fitness more than to aging. The last three studies were summarized in Brink (1995).

Interestingly, Edwin Boyle Jr., director of research at the Miami Heart Institute, found that arteriosclerotic patients with memory loss improved their memory after breathing pure oxygen, with effects lasting up to six months! Aerobic exercise, of course, heightens oxygen intake.

Another series of studies concluded that hunger is inhibited when (1) the brain contains high levels of glucose and serotonin and (2) the blood contains high levels of epinephrine, norepinephrine, and dopamine. Exercise tends to raise levels of all five of these neurotransmitters.

A few words of caution. First, exercise appears to be more effective in preserving mental function that could decline with aging, rather than in improving function among people who have always been sedentary and who, later in life, try to make up for lost time. Second, the benefits of exercise are associated with long-term exercising, rather than brief episodes of several months' duration. And we lose the benefits of having exercised when we stop.

Applications

❶ For maximum benefit, exercise after the most stressful part of the day is over and before a period in which mental alertness is required or desired. For some of us, this may have to be an either-or situation. High stress nullifies the effect of aerobic exercise. You must exercise again after a stressful episode. (Stress releases the toxin cortisol, and aerobic exercise dissipates it. For more discussion of this relationship, see topic 36.1.)

❷ Avoid exercising immediately before bedtime, unless that is the only time you can exercise. It tends to interfere with sleep.

❸ Don't ride when you can walk; don't sit when you can stand.

❹ Learn deep-breathing exercises (breathe in for six counts, hold for four counts, expel for six counts) and isometric exercises for times when you must be sedentary for long periods.

❺ Ensure that you and all your family members get aerobic exercise (brisk walking or its equivalent) for 30–45 minutes a day, at least five days per week.

❻ Exercise your influence to ensure that your local schools are providing daily aerobic exercise for students. According to the President's Council on Physical Fitness and Sports, only 36 percent of kids in grades 1–12 get a daily 30-minute aerobic workout. (Forty percent of five-year-olds already show at least one heart disease risk factor!)

❼ For the maximum benefit of aerobic exercise, engage in the following nonstop activities for an average of 30 minutes, five times weekly: running, bicycling, jogging, brisk walking, distance swimming, skating, jumping rope, rowing, treadmill, dancing, and so forth. Realize that many exercises, while being healthy, are, for a variety of reasons, nonaerobic—for example, basketball (not continuous), sprinting (too brief), golf (low exertion). For a more complete listing, see Bailey (1991).

TOPIC 10.3 **The Importance of Choice**

Norman Cousins (1989) writes of studies that emphasize how choice influences the degree of health benefits of exercise. If an individual is forced to engage in an exercise against his will, the health benefits tend to be reduced. Cousins cites the ineffectiveness of walking on a treadmill, as he had been directed, versus his dramatic improvement after he chose instead to walk on a track.

Apparently the stress of engaging in exercise that is not of our choosing can outweigh its health benefits. As another example of this, my wife's first husband loved playing tennis, especially during hot summer afternoons. She hated it and often sustained headaches when she was pressured into playing with him. Eighteen years later, she still avoids tennis. (See chapter 36 for further discussion of the importance of personal control in managing stress.)

James Gavin, director of the graduate program in applied human sciences at Concordia University in Montreal, has developed a model for prescribing exercise regimens based on personality characteristics. This is related to Cousins's notion of choice in that Gavin maintains that some kind of exercise will appeal to everyone. In his book *The Exercise Habit* (1992), he includes a seven-dimension psychosocial scale to help match exercise with personality.

Related to these findings is the work of Charles Emery, professor of psychology and medicine at Ohio State University, who found (*Prevention,* September 2004) that middle-aged and older cardiac patients (both men and women) experienced cognitive performance boosts when using upbeat music (especially Vivaldi's *Four Seasons*) to accompany their workouts on a treadmill. Those exercising to upbeat music performed twice as well on verbal fluency measures (e.g., how many words can you list in the next two minutes that start with the letter *w?*) as those who exercised unaccompanied. Emery argues that the upbeat musical accompaniment appears to provide an extra boost by organizing mental resources. I suspect that the music may force a quicker tempo that makes more oxygen available to the brain, as well as making the exercise more playful, less punishing, hence less stressful. I am not ready to argue that the music in and of itself caused the boost in performance. However, 'tis a small bother to exercise to upbeat music, so why not? For me, I'll take Bach's *Brandenburg Concerti*—the fast movements, that is.

Applications

1 Avoid engaging in an exercise for its health benefits if you don't really have a positive attitude toward it. Choose an exercise that appeals to you. I've had many friends try to encourage me to take aerobic dance classes. For me, personally, that is a distasteful proposition—I don't like the music most aerobics instructors use to motivate their participants, don't like the follow-the-leader format, don't like the emphasis on dressing out for the event, don't like having to drive there (all this, even though our younger daughter is a jazzercise instructor, and we certainly love her!). Instead, I walk. I love to walk. I could write an essay on why I like walking, but I'd better resist. . . .

 Read Gavin, *The Exercise Habit* (1992).

<hr>

TOPIC 10.4　　**Altering Mood and Cravings**

<hr>

In a study of 16 addicted smokers and 18 regular snackers, Robert Thayer (1989) reported that brisk 10-minute walks reduced their cravings and improved their mood. The walking smokers reported an average increase of 50 percent over the control subjects in the time before they craved a smoke. Those in a poor mood who walked instead of snacking reported significantly higher and longer elevations of mood than nonwalking snackers. In subsequent studies, Thayer and others have found that an intensive workout (a 45-minute jog) has no more effect on mood than a 10-minute brisk walk.

Gregory Mondin, of the Department of Counseling Psychology, University of Wisconsin–Madison, tested 10 volunteers who were accustomed to working out six days a week. After skipping two workouts, all experienced one or more of various mood swings, including anxiety, depression, confusion, and that "blah" feeling. Resuming their exercise routine fixed things right up.

Michael Gallagher, vice-dean of the School of Osteopathic Medicine at the University of Medicine and Dentistry of New Jersey in Newark, has found that participating in regular, nonjarring (that is, not jogging) aerobic exercise (such as swimming, using a stationary bicycle, or walking) improves the chances of avoiding migraine headaches among those prone to suffer from them. Apparently, one precursor of migraines is muscle tension, and the endorphins released by aerobic exercise decrease that tension.

One explanation of exercise's benefits comes from the research of the University of Georgia's Rod Dishman, professor of exercise science, who has identified an increase in epinephrine levels as a result of sustained exercise. Epinephrine permeates the *locus coeruleus,* which is a kind of junction box for the several brain functions associated with mood and emotion. As a result, Dishman theorizes, the increased levels of epinephrine serve to lubricate the individual's mechanism for coping with stress. Interestingly, he points out, several of the antidepressant drugs are associated with elevated levels of epinephrine. Mark Sothman, dean of the School of Allied Health at the Indiana University School of Medicine, says that aerobic exercise, in effect, provides a workout for the body's internal communication system so that when stress occurs, one's physical coping mechanisms are in good order. Both Sothman and Dishman have confirmed these relationships in animal and human experiments (they are summarized in the July 1996 *APA Monitor*).

Dr. Madhukar Trivedi, of the University of Texas Southwestern Medical Center, Dallas, has a four-year, $2.4 million grant from the U.S. National Institute for Mental Health to determine whether supervised exercise will help people being treated with antidepressant medications better combat depression (*Biotech Week,* February 2004). It will be interesting to see whether exercise can augment or even replace SSRI treatment.

Applications

❶ During prolonged sedentary periods or periods of stress, take a brisk 10-minute walk every couple of hours—outdoors, if possible.

❷ During coffee breaks, try taking a 10-minute walk outside instead. The resulting natural arousal will equal or better the arousal you would get from more caffeine and stale office air. Walk by yourself or with a group, whichever pleases you.

❸ If not even a 10-minute walk is possible, at least do a few jumping jacks, sit-ups, push-ups, isometric exercises, or stretches, or just simply meditate, as a way to release the tension build-up accompanying lack of exercise.

TOPIC 10.5   **Extreme Exercise and the Staleness Syndrome**

John Raglin, an Indiana University sports psychologist and kinesiologist, has tagged a condition resulting from continuing high athletic performance and workouts as the "staleness syndrome" (*APA Monitor,* April 1996; see also his "Overtraining and Staleness" in Singer, Murphey, and Tennant, 1993). Around 5–10 percent of athletes who train intensely develop a pattern of irritability, tension, anger, lack of desire to train, sleep disturbance, muscle soreness, decrease in immune function (and accompanying susceptibility to infectious diseases), depression, perceptual changes (for example, routines may suddenly seem harder), and general mental instability. The result is an abrupt halt in the ability to perform. Even short breaks or reduced workout schedules don't relieve the pattern. Only complete rest for several months appears to restore the previous performance level, yet these levels are not always regained. About 60 percent of elite long-distance runners will suffer from staleness at some point. Staleness also affects about 30 percent of sub-Olympic athletes who train seriously, as well as some recreational athletes who train seriously.

Raglin has found that staleness can be avoided by monitoring athletes' moods. In an experiment with swimmers, researchers administered a mood test, the Profile of Mood States (POMS) (McNair, Lorr, and Droppleman, 1971), and varied the swimmers' workout schedules to keep their moods within an optimum range. For the first time in 10 years, no team member developed staleness. Raglin (personal correspondence) reports that scores on the POMS correlate nicely with relevant biological changes, such as muscle glycogen, cortisol, and neuromuscular function, suggesting that the psychological mood changes are symptoms of physical changes. Unfortunately, many athletes misinterpret the staleness symptoms and mistakenly choose to work out harder (with even worse results) rather than to lighten up.

Applications

❶ If you train intensely or are associated with athletes who train intensely, contact Raglin for specific suggestions. Begin by visiting his website at www.indiana.edu/~kines/raglin.htm.

❷ Raglin suggests that because athletes in intense training tend to be honest about physical symptoms and mood states, a simple seven-point scale that measures soreness, general well-being, and perceived exertion can serve as well for self-monitoring as the 72-item, five-minute POMS.

❸ Staleness in exercise bears a remarkable similarity to burnout at work. See the discussion of burnout in topic 36.4 for further understanding and recommendations concerning this phenomenon.

| TOPIC 10.6 | **Exercise and Testosterone** |

Jim Morrison, a psychologist at Iona University in New York, has established that the traditional vigorous workout dramatically increases testosterone levels in men, but not in women. As a result, men who return to the stress of work immediately after a workout are more likely to experience emotional outbursts and acts of aggression. The effect is greater after competitive, nonaerobic workouts like handball than after noncompetitive, aerobic workouts like brisk walking. Men who cool off for 15–20 minutes do not experience such outbursts.

Applications

❶ Men should take a 20-minute "chill" after working out if they anticipate entering a stressful setting. Otherwise, they should be prepared to deal with the consequences of a possible outburst.

❷ When a 20-minute cooldown is not possible, engage in meditation, deep breathing, isometrics, or some other process that assists in refocusing and relaxing.

❸ When exercising before a meeting in which you need to be calm, opt for aerobic exercise. On the other hand, when exercising before a meeting in which you need to be aggressive, choose anaerobic, competitive exercise in which you are likely to win.

| TOPIC 10.7 | **Exercise and Smoking** |

The Cleveland Clinic's Michael Lauer studied 3,000 people and reported in *Circulation* (as cited in the September 27, 1997, *Chicago Tribune*) that the heart rates of a certain category of smokers fail to increase with exercise. Normally, one's body produces epinephrine during exercise, which increases the heartbeat. Nicotine produces a similar effect, and Lauer attributes the lack of rate increase with exercise in some smokers to a kind of tolerance their system builds up toward exercise-induced epinephrine. Because of the constant signals from nicotine, the heart ignores the exercise-induced epinephrine signals. These exercising smokers without rate increases are five times more likely to have a heart attack than are nonsmokers with normal heart-rate reactions to exercise.

Application

❶ This is simply another reason to quit smoking. If you are a smoker and you think your exercise is offsetting the effects of smoking, it isn't. You might check your actual rate before and after exercising to see if you're really getting any circulatory system benefit from the exercise.

TOPIC 10.8   Soccer Headers

Adrienne Witol, an inpatient psychologist at the Medical College of Virginia, and Frank M. Webbe, a professor in the School of Psychology at Florida Institute of Technology, studied 60 male soccer players who were at least 15 years of age and who played five times per week. They determined that players who engaged in "heading" the ball more frequently performed less well on tests of visual searching, attention, mental flexibility, general IQ, and facial recognition than did players who headed the ball infrequently or never. Because the study was not longitudinal, the researchers do not know if the loss of mental function associated with heading the ball is reversible once the players no longer participate in soccer.

Application

❶ If you are a soccer player or associate with soccer players, support the practice of "heading" on an extremely limited basis, if at all. Or wear soccer headgear. Heads are not made for bashing.

TOPIC 10.9   Peak Athletic Performance

Charles Garfield (1984) has described a process that guides athletes into superior performance using mental training.

In fact, he reports that one can reduce one's physical training (for example, running laps) and, by replacing physical training with mental training, increase levels of performance. His process includes visualization, mental rehearsal techniques, goal setting, and volitional self-awareness.

Applications

❶ If you desire to be a peak athletic performer, read Garfield's *Peak Performance.*

❷ Another "mental training" approach to peak athletic performance has been developed by Carol Ann Erickson and Arlene Berkman of the Brain-Body Center for Performance Enhancement, Scarsdale, New York (914-725-2458).

SUGGESTED RESOURCES

Bailey, C. (1991). *The New Fit or Fat.* Boston: Houghton Mifflin.

Brink, S. (1995, May 15). "Smart Moves." *U.S. News & World Report,* 76–85.

Changeux, J.-P. (1997). *Neuronal Man: The Biology of Mind.* (L. Garey, trans.). Princeton, N.J.: Princeton University Press.

Coop, R. H. (1993). *Mind over Golf: Play Your Best by Thinking Smart.* Old Tappan, N.J.: Macmillan.

Garfield, C. A. (1984). *Peak Performance: Mental Training Techniques of the World's Greatest Athletes.* Los Angeles: Tarcher.

Gavin, J. (1992). *The Exercise Habit.* Champaign, Ill.: Human Kinetics.

Morgan, W. P. (Ed.). (1997). *Physical Activity and Mental Health.* Washington, D.C.: Taylor & Francis.

Neeper, S. A., F. Gomez-Pinilla, J. Choi, and C. W. Cotman (1995). "Exercise Raises Brain Neurotrophins." *Nature, 373,* 109.

Singer, R. B., M. Murphey, and L. K. Tennant (Eds.) (1993). *Handbook of Research on Sport Psychology.* Old Tappan, N.J.: Macmillan.

11

Humoring the Mind

Laughter as Free (or Cheap) Medicine

66*Strange, when you come to think of it, that of all the countless folk who have lived before our time on this planet not one is known in history or in legend as having died of laughter.* **99**

— Sir Max Beerbohm

Twenty years ago, humor would not have made its way into a book about brain research. However, we have discovered a dramatic relationship between laughter, a sense of humor, levels of neurochemicals such as endorphins, and the function of the immune system—such a dramatic relationship, in fact, that Norman Cousins used slapstick comedy as a "sleeping pill." Today, increasingly, researchers are trying to get a handle on the nature of humor, and on who benefits from different kinds of humor.

TOPIC 11.1   The Structure of Humor

Willibald Ruch, who teaches in the psychology department of Heinrich Heine University in Düsseldorf, Germany, challenged the psychological research community in 1991 to develop a universal taxonomy of humor. The resulting model of humor appreciation, called the 3WD model ("WD" for "Witz Dimensionen," German for "humor dimensions"), has been validated by researchers in several countries, including the U.S. The three dimensions are *structure, content,* and *response.*

The stimulus, or joke, will fall into one of two *structure* categories plus a content category. The content category describes a joke as either *sexual* or *not sexual,* independent of the structure of the joke: the content overrides the structure. The two structure categories are *incongruity resolution* and *nonsense.* In incongruity resolution, the punch line reveals information that clarifies earlier incongruities. Example: A priest asks the bishop, "Is it permissible to smoke while praying?" The bishop replies, "Certainly not!" Later, a fellow priest, hearing of the first priest's embarrassment at the hands of the bishop, advises: "Next time, ask if it is permissible to pray while smoking." In the nonsense category, the punch line does not clarify earlier incongruities; rather it confounds them by making no resolution at all, by making only a partial resolution, or by introducing even more absurdity or incongruity. Example: Question: "How many psychologists does it take to screw in a lightbulb?" Answer: "Only one, but the light bulb must really want to change."

The response has two conditions: funny or not funny, and aversive or not aversive—which, in effect, adds a fourth dimension. So a joke may be funny yet aversive, funny and not aversive, not funny and aversive, or not funny and not aversive. A funny and aversive joke would be one in which the respondent dislikes, say, a reference to his religion but appreciates the good punch line. Maximum joke appreciation is defined as a judgment of funny and not aversive, minimum appreciation as aversive and not funny. Thus, a joke can be evaluated with the 3WD model and receive scores in four categories (congruous, sexual, funny, aversive), for a total of 16 possible joke "types." These categories and types are illustrated in figure 11.1.

> "With the fearful strain that is on me night and day, if I did not laugh I should die."
>
> —Abraham Lincoln

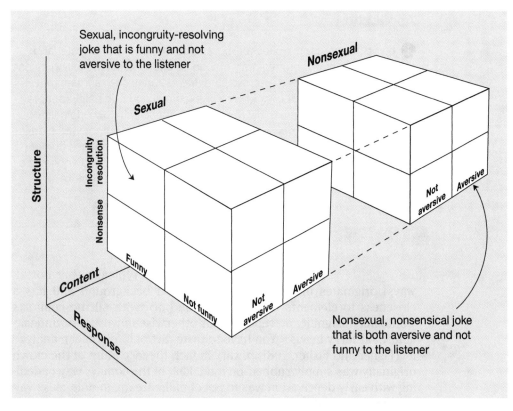

Figure 11.1. The Dimensions of Humor Appreciation

Forabosco and Ruch (1994) report that personality traits (see chapter 33 for complete definitions of personality traits) are associated clearly with appreciation (funny and not aversive) of the three structure and content categories:

- People low in Extraversion and low in Originality prefer incongruity resolution humor.

- People high in Extraversion and high in Originality prefer nonsense humor.

- People high in Need for Stability, Extraversion, and Originality and low in Accommodation enjoy sexual humor.

They also reported that older subjects preferred incongruity resolution humor, while younger subjects preferred nonsense humor.

Application

❶ If you are preparing jokes for a presentation, public or private, and the stakes are high, you might try managing your risk in joke telling by assessing the audience with respect to extraversion (sales representatives are usually higher, engineers lower, for example) and originality (people with high originality are usually more liberal, those with low originality more conservative). Emphasize incongruity resolution humor with older, less outgoing, more conservative groups. Emphasize nonsense humor with younger, more outgoing, more liberal groups. If your audience has a mixture of these characteristics, then mix up the humor structure.

TOPIC 11.2   The Comedic Personality

The comedic personality typically (but not always) originates in some kind of deprived background and has a closeness to elements of life that those born with all the comforts would find insignificant, repulsive, or otherwise unworthy or undesirable. Said Jerry Lewis, "You have to taste dirt before you can analyze it" (Fisher and Fisher, 1981, p. xiii). In fact, the face paint of the clown originally was simply rubbed-on mud. Part of the comic's way of dealing with early deprivation was to reject mainstream, middle-class values and ways of doing things, which made the traditional schoolroom anathema. The adult comedian is likely to have been known in school as a cut-up, a clown, who just couldn't sit still physically, mentally, or emotionally, and who grabbed center stage the best way he knew how, by making people laugh at his noncompliant antics. Consequently, the comic who did well in school tends to be the exception. The school became the comic's first stage, with a captive audience five days a week (Fisher and Fisher, 1981, p. 4). Interestingly, in an effort to determine the relative effects of nature and nurture on comedic tendencies, the Twin Research Unit at St. Thomas's Hospital in London had 254 female twin pairs read the same cartoons (from Gary Larson to more mainstream) and rate them on a 10-point scale. Their conclusion (reported in *Health,* April 1, 2000): similarities in sense of humor among the twins were accounted for by common environmental influences, with genes having no apparent effect.

Joey Bishop identifies curiosity as the *sine qua non* of the comedian (Fisher and Fisher, 1981, p. 9). By constantly picking things up, turning them over, and examining them minutely, the comedian builds on absolutely truthful details. Much like an anthropologist, the comedian scans the everyday for absurd details. But not just objects: the comedian is curious about the motives, thought processes, values, and feelings of people. By staying attuned to what makes others tick, the comic finds the basis for identifying the improbable, the inconsistent, the absurd, the laughable. Hmmm, that reminds me of a joke. . . .

This curious clown is not particularly aggressive or dominating, but rather chooses to be independent in finding his own way, eschewing conformity (p. 138). Psychological testing of comedians finds them impulsive, spontaneous, and energetic. Putting all of this together, we get a Big Five portrait (see chapter 33) of the comedian as N+E+O+A+C-—that is, reactive, outgoing, curious, creative, interested in others, spontaneous, and undisciplined. Although there are exceptions to this profile among decidedly funny people, the presence of all of these traits in one person certainly provides the fuel for comedic behavior. One obvious exception is the hostile, aggressive comic voice (e.g., Rodney Dangerfield, Don Rickles, Roseanne), who is lower in Accommodation.

> Note: When you see cross references to other sections of this book, you may benefit from taking time now to read them; they provide information that will deepen your understanding of the current material.

Applications

1 Practice being curious about things that might not normally interest you, and learn to be amused by what you find, sharing this with others.

2 Develop the habit of chuckling at yourself when you make errors, and resist blaming others or the situation.

TOPIC 11.3 Humor and the Immune System

Norman Cousins (1979, 1989) is known as the founder of *psychoneuroimmunology* (PNI) (see topic 15.2). Originally he called the concept of mentally influencing the immune system "hardiness." One of the four critical ingredients of hardiness is positive emotions, which Cousins defines as maintaining a sense of humor and general joyfulness. He refers to laughter as "internal jogging." Laughter is healthy; it appears to be especially important in recovering from life-threatening illnesses. Cousins (1989) found that even a few moments of laughter can reduce the blood sedimentation rate, which is a measure of inflammation. Lee S. Berk, professor at the Schools of Medicine and Public Health at Loma Linda University in California (*APA Monitor,* September 1997, p. 18), studied two groups of cardiac patients, one of which was asked to watch a half-hour of comedy daily (but otherwise received the same medical treatment as the other group). Results after one year showed, in the comedy-exposed group:

- Enhanced respiration

- An increased number of immune cells

- An increase in immune-cell proliferation

- A decrease in cortisol

- An increase in endorphins

- An increase in salivary immunoglobulin type A concentrations

- Lower blood pressure

- Fewer repeat heart attacks

Tests of problem-solving ability yield better results when they are preceded by laughter. Laughter has a way of turning off posterior hypothalamic activity and allowing the cerebral cortex to carry on stress-free activity. Cousins reports that 10 minutes of laughter can provide a person in pain with two hours of good sleep. David McClelland (1986) has confirmed that salivary *immunoglobulin type A* is significantly higher among people with a stronger sense of humor.

Michelle G. Newman, a psychologist at Pennsylvania State University, reports that people can learn to use humor as a coping device and that this learned humor has marked effects (*APA Monitor,* September 1997, p. 18). She asked people who normally did not use coping humor to make up, impromptu, a comedic monologue to accompany the videotape of a gruesome industrial accident. Those who made up a nonhumorous monologue showed a measurably higher stress response (measured by blood pressure, skin conductance, and skin temperature) than the humorous commentators.

While Newman shows that one can learn to use humor as a coping device, Lee Berk and some associates have developed a computer program that analyzes people's humor preferences, so that a kind of humor prescription can be written for them. He calls the program SMILE (Subjective Multidimensional Interactive Laughter Evaluation). After 10 minutes, using a question-and-answer format, SMILE prints out a humor profile for an individual along with a detailed list of books, videos, comedic personalities, and other resources especially chosen to match his or her profile.

In a fascinating finding during their research on comics, clowns, and actors, Seymour and Rhoda Fisher (1981, p. 148) found that persons who scored higher on their comic survey also scored lower on the Fishers' Symptom Questionnaire. Although those scoring higher on the comic scale tended to have the same number of physical complaints as others, they ended up making significantly fewer visits to doctors or clinics for treatment of those symptoms. This serves as an intriguing confirmation of the recommendations of psychoneuroimmunology (PNI; see topic 15.2), to the effect that humor is healing. As the Fishers quote (p. 148) from Mark Twain's *Tom Sawyer*:

> The old man laughed loudly and joyously, shook up the details of his anatomy from head to foot, and ended by saying that such a laugh was money in a man's pocket, because it cut down the doctor's bills like everything.

The Fishers comment on the essential value of comedy and comedians: "Thus, the comic, for all of his sometimes outlandish positions, may have the effect of encouraging the stability of a system by preventing it from consistently going too far in any one extreme direction" (p. 193).

Rod Martin, psychologist at University of Western Ontario, questions the soundness of research on the effect of humor on immune function. Many of these studies, he says, lack rigor. For example, some studies showing increase in immune function after a 30-minute video comedy weren't controlled to determine whether it was the comedy or the act of watching a video that was associated with the increase. Of course, other studies have included such controls.

Other examples of poor controls include not specifying the kind of humor—for example, light "family" humor versus aggressive, ridiculing, or self-flagellating humor. In a study by psychologist Herbert Lefcourt of the University of Waterloo, Ontario, Canada, laughing women had lower blood pressure than laughing men. Was this because of a more "healthy" humor? Also, the jury is still out on longevity and humor; some say laughers live longer, some say they die earlier (from an Associated Press release, July 12, 1999). Many more studies need to be done with controls for personality traits and type of humor. For example, does matching type of humor with particular personality traits result in different effects on the immune system than merely a shotgun distribution of humor in the oncology ward?

Funded in 2000 by a grant from the Comedy Central television network, researchers at UCLA's Jonsson Cancer Center have launched a five-year study—"Rx Laughter"—to determine the nature and extent of laughter's effect on the immune system, focusing on children with weakened immune systems. Find out more, and keep up with their progress, by visiting their website at www.rxlaughter.org.

Applications

❶ Check out the bibliography on laughter in the back of Cousins (1989). Cousins made the "humor cart" famous. Today many hospital oncology departments have a wide variety of laughter-producing materials available for patients and their families, including comic books, video, audio, and humorous books and magazines.

❷ Give yourself permission to perform the whole range of laughs—from the gut-massaging belly laugh to the social titter.

❸ Consciously develop your sense of humor, both as an originator of humor and as someone who appreciates and reacts to humor. Here are some specific suggestions for developing your sense of humor:

- Keep a humor file—on your computer, in your file cabinet, on your bulletin board or office door, in your brief case or hand bag. Share the funny stuff judiciously; if you don't trust your judgment, check with your spouse or a colleague.

- Whenever you hear something funny that you like, try telling it three times within 24 hours. Then you're likely to remember it. If you have trouble remembering it long enough to tell it the first time, jot down the key words on a piece of paper. My father kept a small, spiral-bound notebook in his coat pocket, and jotted down phrases of every good (to him!) joke he heard during the week so he could tell them later to me and others.

- Explore Internet humor resources; there are plenty of "joke-of-the-day" e-mail lists.

- Read the biographies and autobiographies of your favorite humorists. Pick up techniques from their lives, and share amusing episodes from their lives with your associates.

- Visit, and return frequently, to Steve Wilson's therapeutic laughing website at **www.worldlaughtertour.com**. Wilson offers training for Certified Laughter Leaders who, in turn, start and maintain programs in healthcare facilities.

❹ Order your personal humor profile based on Lee Berk's SMILE software for $9.95 by calling 800-759-1294. There are several websites that contain ordering information for SMILE—simply Google "Lee Berk" and "SMILE" and you'll find them. You can also order the software that generates the reports.

TOPIC 11.4 Humor and Gender

John Martellaro of the *Kansas City Star* reported on an informal survey among stand-up comics. Although the findings reflect a trend and not a clear-cut gender difference, generally these folks who live by their audience savvy agree on certain tendencies toward gender differences with respect to humor. Men have the following preferences:

- The humor doesn't have to be quite so intelligent.

- They appreciate silly or slapstick humor more.

- They typically respond better to dirtier or cruder humor laced with profanities.

- They typically don't laugh at jokes about themselves or about men in general but will laugh about women or about other specific men; that is, they are more likely to laugh at jokes at other people's expense.

- They like anything physical and aggressive.

- They are more reactive and tend to be less patient with longer prologues.

- Specifically, they like the Three Stooges, Tim Allen (*Home Improvement*), cartoons (especially *The Simpsons, Ren and Stimpy,* and the Road Runner), films with Mel Brooks and

Chevy Chase, Jackie Gleason's *Honeymooners, Monty Python,* and John Cleese.

Women have the following preferences:

- They enjoy jokes that involve childbirth and raising children.

- They have a generally "dry" sense of humor.

- They laugh at jokes about themselves and other women as well as jokes about men; that is, they are more likely to laugh at jokes at their own expense.

- They like jokes about relationships and the battle of the sexes.

- They like the person telling a joke to set up a scenario, not just go for the quick punch.

- They like the cute, romantic, sugar-coated stuff.

- They are turned off by the graphically dirty.

- Specifically, they like Jerry Seinfeld, Jay Leno, *Cheers,* John Candy, films with Doris Day and Rock Hudson, *The Andy Griffith Show, Family Ties,* and W. C. Fields.

The comics agreed that "family, food, and sex" are, for the most part, good common ground.

In partial confirmation of the comics' observations, Lefcourt has reported that males and females who use humor to cope with stress tend to experience different results: females' systolic blood pressure falls, that of males rises. Females who joke about their stress have lower blood pressure, males higher blood pressure, than those who don't. Lefcourt attributes this difference to two distinct kinds of humor: females laugh at themselves, males laugh at others. For example, when they make a social blunder, females tend to say something self-deprecating, whereas males tend to say something aggressive. Upon dropping a glass of milk, a female might say, "Oh, my, what a klutz I am!" A male might say, "Did I drown that cockroach yet?" The female's response restores social closeness; the male, in effect, tries to maintain his dominant position in the social hierarchy. The former lowers blood pressure, the latter raises it (*APA Monitor,* September 1997, pp. 18 ff.).

Also contributing to this line of research is Eleanor Maccoby (1998), who finds that males tend to make fun at each other's expense, whereas females tend to make fun of themselves. The result is that male humor often appears hostile, and males often feel as though some females don't have much sense of humor because they don't respond to the teasing and quasi-aggression. Maccoby: "Women can mistake men's humor for genuine hostility, while men can mistake women's for true self-abnegation." (p. 236)

In addition to Lefcourt's work, Robert Provine, director of the neuroscience program at the University of Maryland, Baltimore County; Glenn Weisfeld, psychology professor at Wayne State University in Detroit; and Richard Alexander, Hubbell Professor of Evolutionary Biology at the University of Michigan at Ann Arbor report on their various research efforts on gender differences in humor (*APA Monitor,* September 1997, p. 16). Provine reports that the average speaker laughs 46 percent more than the audience, but women speakers and comics laugh 127 percent more than their male audiences, and male speakers and comics laugh 7 percent less than their female audiences. Provine concludes that the trend is for men to be humor producers, women to be laughers. Alexander elaborates on this trend by theorizing that humor production (jokes and puns, for example) serves to establish the humorist's status, whereas the laugher signals acceptance of, and frequently submission to, the humorist. Laughter creates the social perception of granting status to the humorist. It's dominance and submission all over again.

From an evolutionary psychology point of view, one might suggest that women have adapted to their traditional role as caregivers by naturally emphasizing laughter and self-deprecating humor as a way of nurturing their charges, whereas men have traditionally employed less laughter while on the hunt and, consistent with their role as animal killers, have employed aggressive and blaming humor when the time called for it. Perhaps. . . .

Applications

❶ To develop your sense of humor fully, allow yourself to explore more ranges of humor content. If you fit the stereotypically male or female humor profile, consciously expect humor from heretofore unhumorous sources. Don't just say you don't like Jay Leno; if you find yourself watching Jay Leno involuntarily, allow yourself to be surprised with something really laughter-provoking. Minimize preconceptions about humor.

❷ If some of your humor doesn't work around members of the opposite gender (or members of your own gender, for that matter), realize that the problem may not be your style. They may not like certain humor content, regardless of who's telling it!

❸ If you are a male, understand that using aggressive humor as a way of coping with stressful situations does not help your stress. Practice a more self-deprecating approach: learn stock lines, such as "You know, I never get tired of being wrong," or "That's not the first time, and it won't be the last! Blast!" Observe other males who make aggressive, attacking jokes when they are under stress, and practice rewording or reframing their comments to be self-deprecating. Realize that aggressive, combative humor in stressful situations is not heart-healthy.

❹ If you are a woman who does not use humor to cope in stressful situations, learn some good self-deprecating lines, such as "Well, I sure get the klutz prize today!" or "Infamy, infamy, somebody's got it in for me" (from the Broadway musical *Me and My Girl*), or "I'm just a girl who can't say no!" Realize that using such self-deprecating humor lessens the feeling of stress for you.

❺ If you see yourself as more of a humorist than a laugher, consider the possibility that you hold back laughter as a nonverbal way of refusing to confer status on another person. Be aware of the power of appreciative laughter to make other people feel good about themselves, as well as to lower your own stress level.

SELECTED RESOURCES

Cousins, N. (1979). *Anatomy of an Illness.* New York: Norton.

Cousins, N. (1989). *Head First: The Biology of Hope.* New York: NAL/Dutton.

Fisher, S., and R. L. Fisher (1981). *Pretend the World Is Funny and Forever: A Psychological Analysis of Comedians, Clowns, and Actors.* Hillsdale, N.J.: Lawrence Erlbaum.

Forabosco, G., and W. Ruch (1994). "Sensation Seeking, Social Attitudes and Humor Appreciation in Italy." *Personality and Individual Differences,* 16(4), 515–528.

Ruch, W. (1988). "Sensation Seeking and the Enjoyment of Structure and Content of Humor: Stability of Findings Across Four Samples." *Personality and Individual Differences,* 9, 861–871.

12

Music

...as a Means and as an End

> **Music has charms to soothe a savage breast, To soften rocks, or bend a knotted oak.**
>
> —*William Congreve,*
> The Mourning Bride

*H*istorically, music has been mostly entertainment and, to a lesser degree, a communication tool. From the chamber music of aristocrats to the bugle calls of soldiers, music has cut through the normal channels of words with a stirring directness and immediacy. Increasingly, music has acquired new roles—medicinal, facilitative, and mood-altering. This chapter will explore some of these more recent musical functions.

The probability is that music is not a dedicated, evolutionarily distinct part of the brain, but rather a by-product of other evolved areas, among them auditory discrimination, muscular coordination (the kind needed for tool making), and rhythmic sensitivity (of the sort required to slay a moving animal). However, there is some evidence of a genetically evolved basis for music. Persons unable to detect pitch changes in a melody are nonetheless able to detect pitch differences in language, such as the many inflections of Chinese. It is also true that identical twins demonstrate more similarity in musical performance than do fraternal twins.

> "Music oft hath such a charm
> To make bad good, and good provoke to harm."
>
> —William Shakespeare,
> *Measure for Measure*

Brain scans have not yet succeeded in precisely identifying brain regions dedicated to musical activity. Although the auditory cortex is clearly involved, with extensions to the thalamus, not all musical elements appear to have their own unique processing areas. Some areas appear to be used in both musical and language processing.

The plasticity of the brain applies to music as well as other skill areas. The experience of listening to music differs according to one's specialty: trumpeters' brains are more aroused when listening to trumpets than when listening to other instruments, and similarly for pianists, flutists, and so forth.

TOPIC 12.1 Learning Music

Researchers at the University of Konstanz in Germany have determined through magnetic resonance imaging that the area of the somatosensory cortex allocated to the fingers of the left hand is larger for string players than for nonplayers. Its size is related not to the number of hours of daily practice but to the number of years spent playing the instrument. The window for learning musical instruments appears to be from ages 3 to 10. It is harder to learn after 10 years of age, and concert-quality players generally begin their instrumental study before the age of 10.

Looking for the secret of perfect pitch (the ability to sing a pitch without a preceding musical point of reference, as in "Can you hum an A for me?"), Gottfried Schlaug, a neurological fellow with the Heinrich

Heine University in Düsseldorf, Germany (now with Beth Israel Hospital in Boston), took magnetic resonance images of the brains of 30 musicians, 11 of whom had perfect pitch, and 30 nonmusicians. The 11 musicians with perfect pitch had a *planum temporale* in the left hemisphere that was 40 percent larger than the planum temporale in the right hemisphere. The 19 musicians without perfect pitch had only a slightly enlarged planum temporale, which was not significantly different from that area in the nonmusicians (*Science,* February 3, 1995).

Schlaug reported that the evidence pointed to perfect pitch occurring only among musicians who had been exposed to music before age 7, with the likelihood of acquiring perfect pitch extremely unlikely when initial exposure to music came after 10 years of age. Some people without perfect pitch do have the 40 percent enlarged area; Schlaug concludes that nature and nurture both play a role. The enlargement is necessary but not sufficient for perfect pitch; one must also be exposed to music in a timely manner.

In related research at Montreal's McGill University, brain scans of musicians with perfect pitch showed greater activation in the *left posterior dorsolateral frontal cortex* while listening to musical tones (see appendix A); people who did not have perfect pitch, but who did have relative pitch, showed greater activation in this area only when they were comparing musical notes. Research team leader Robert Zatorre (1998) concluded that this area of the brain is activated when naming notes, and that it is activated spontaneously for people with perfect pitch.

To date, no gene mutation has been associated with tone deafness. If such a gene is discovered, it will begin to clarify the question of whether music is an evolved, dedicated capacity or merely a byproduct. Symptoms of tone deafness (known formally as *congenital amusia*) include

1. Inability to detect a change of one half-step in a test tone.

2. Inability to learn a simple melody.

3. Inability to remember a simple melody.

4. Inability to find emotional displeasure in dissonant or out-of-tune sounds that musicians find unpleasant.

5. Inability to tap in time with music.

(From "Music on the Brain," by Dr. John Medina, *Psychiatric Times*, August 2002; Medina is the director of the Talaris Research Institute in Seattle, which is devoted to research on early learning.)

Applications

1 Encourage young children to sing; sing with them and encourage them to sing with others. Our oldest grandchild was singing "Twinkle, Twinkle, Little Star" with the right tune, right rhythm, right words, and even on the same pitch that his grandparents started with, at the age of 18 months. When we sang a phrase and stopped before the last note of the phrase, the toddler would come in with the right word on the right pitch.

2 If your child shows an interest, get an instrument early—around three years of age. Suzuki violin, piano, and flute instruction begins before school age, and violins are available in appropriate sizes for young children.

3 Expose your child to musical training before the age of seven and continue for the best chance of developing perfect pitch.

4 Remember that children love repetition, unlilke their adult caregivers, who tend to get bored after the third repetition of "Twinkle, Twinkle." Don't think you're expanding the child's repertoire by shifting constantly from tune to tune. Stay with one for a while. The kids are building synapses and networks, and repetition is crucial for establishing these building blocks.

TOPIC 12.2 | **Musical Training and Spatial Ability: The Mozart Effect**

Frances Rauscher and three colleagues at the University of California, Irvine, along with Eric Wright, of the Irvine Conservatory of Music, gave twice-weekly keyboard lessons of 12 minutes each, provided daily 30-minute group singing lessons, and supervised daily practice with 22 three-year-olds for as long as the students desired. The tunes included children's songs and folk melodies. Three other, control, groups were monitored: one with group singing alone, one with computer keyboard training, and a third with no lessons. This program extended over eight months in two Los Angeles preschools. Measuring spatial reasoning by manipulating various objects, Rauscher found that tests administered after four months and again after eight months showed a 35 percent improvement in spatial reasoning among the experimental group. None of the control groups showed pretest to post-test improvement in spatial ability (*APA Monitor*, October 1994, p. 5). At a presentation given as part of the Learning Brain Expo in San Diego, California, October 30, 1998, Gordon Shaw pointed out that the entire experimental group showed improvement, the low-scoring students as well as the high scorers. In other words, if you can visualize the distribution of scores as a normal curve, the entire curve moved to the right about 35 percent.

The preschool study was an extension of earlier research conducted by Rauscher in which 36 college students listened to Mozart's *Sonata for Two Pianos in D Major* (K. 448) for 10 minutes just before taking an intelligence test. The students who listened to Mozart scored, on average, 60 percent higher (equivalent to 8–9 points) than students who had listened to relaxation tapes with Philip Glass's "minimalist" music or who had just meditated silently. However, the benefits disappeared after about 10–15 minutes (*Nature,* October 1993). Researchers see this phenomenon as a kind of warm-up effect, in which the complexity and regularity of classical music activates the neural circuitry of the brain associated with spatial reasoning. Apparently, the effect of music instruction on young children, in whom neural circuitry is more plastic, or changeable, is significantly longer term than the effect of music listening among older learners. In a follow-up study with second-graders, two Los Angeles classrooms received four months of piano keyboard training (three hours of training weekly with no practice). Afterward, they showed a 27 percent increase in scores on fractions and proportional math. After four months of piano or keyboard instruction with more than 20 five- and six-year-olds at the Brighton Heights Horace Mann Elementary School (Pittsburgh Public Schools), youngsters showed marked improvement in abstract and spatial reasoning. Training consisted of two 45-minute music classes each week (plus blocks of time during their kindergarten class for practice) and resulted in learning to play songs, read music, and understand pitch and rhythm. Cognitive criterion measures included concentration, listening skill, and eye-hand coordination.

Fran Rauscher, now an assistant professor of child development at the University of Wisconsin, Oshkosh, played music to groups of rats for 12 hours a day, using a repeating-loop audiotape. One group heard Mozart (the same K. 448!), one listened to Philip Glass, and a third got silence. These lab rats had been performing in mazes on a daily basis. With the addition of music, things changed. The Mozart rats began executing their mazes significantly faster, but the Glass and silent-treatment rats showed no increase in speed. The effect lasted about four hours after the tapes ended.

Researcher Christopher Chabris, Harvard Medical School, urges caution in application of "Mozart effect" research. He reports (in *Nature,* August 26, 1999) on his analysis of 16 Mozart effect studies (714 subjects), concluding that no significant effects emerged in the area of spatial or abstract reasoning. The actual effect was, by his measurement, only 1.4 IQ points. However, it is important to keep in mind that Chabris was measuring total traditional IQ, known as g, whereas Rauscher and others typically measure a specific mental ability, or s, such as spatial reasoning.

One final note. Why Mozart? Why not Brahms, Beethoven, or Stravinsky? In planning the original research, Rauscher and her colleagues reasoned that Mozart is unique in that he exhibits three remarkable characteristics: everybody seems to like his music, he began composing at an early age (4–5 years old), and throughout his prolific output there doesn't seem to be a dud. The conclusion drawn from this is that Mozart's brain was probably ideally suited for writing music, and that he can be regarded as the purest exemplar of satisfying musical composition.

Applications

❶ Consider encouraging all child-care providers in your area to include appropriate periods of music listening (the states of Georgia and Florida have moved in this direction).

❷ Encourage young children to learn piano keyboarding, and in addition, other instruments of their choice.

❸ Encourage people to play Mozart and similarly uncomplicated baroque and classical music as a brain organizer.

❹ Visit the Music Intelligence Neural Development project's website at www.mindinstitute.net for more information on music and neural development. The web manager will respond to requests for reprints.

TOPIC 12.3   When Music Interferes with Learning

Proponents of accelerated learning (see table 21.2) have long argued that learners remember more material when it is taught to the accompaniment of music such as Vivaldi's and Mozart's. The research, however, does not support this claim. In a study by M. J. Wagner and G. Tilney (1983), the accelerated-learning students in two German courses of equal length learned 50 percent less. And in a study by B. J. Bush at the Defense Language Institute in Monterey, California, a 10-week accelerated-learning course in Russian was compared with a 15-week traditional course; the music-accompanied accelerated learners mastered 40 percent less information than those using traditional pedagogy. Part of the explanation must be that the music competes for the attentional focus of the learner. (See the discussion of attention in topic 21.9.)

H. J. Crawford and C. H. Strapp (1994), studying the effects of listening to music on verbal and visual-spatial performance, arrived at the following conclusions:

1. Those who choose to use music to accompany study are much more extraverted (see chapter 33 for explanation of traits).

2. Extraverts in general report that they are less bothered by noise and music.

3. People's perception of the degree to which music and noise bother them is unreliable.

4. Vocal music is more bothersome (i.e., interferes more with attention) than instrumental music.

5. Music interferes more with complex tasks than with simpler tasks, and it interferes more with verbal tasks than with visual-spatial ones.

Applications

❶ When trying to focus on learning, prefer a quiet environment. "White noise" is second best. If you must have some kind of noise, then a regular pattern is less attention-grabbing than an irregular noise (e.g., a constant drip vs. an intermittent drip). Or if you must have music, then play the same piece repeatedly.

❷ In a learning environment, limit music to transitional uses. Don't allow it to compete for attention with the material to be learned.

❸ If you insist on using music to accompany rote learning, use melodies that are universally known by your learners, such as "Twinkle, Twinkle, Little Star." If the melody is a well-established schema for the learner, it is less likely to compete and more likely to support the learning.

❹ When you want to soothe people with music without concern for interrupting their mental focus, use vocal music. When you want to soothe them but still respect those who are attempting to focus mentally, as in the waiting room at the dentist's office, then use only instrumental music. However, when the patient is in the dentist's chair, put a headset on him with vocal music. That will maximally distract him from what the dentist is doing. However, don't play vocal music that the dentist can hear! Let her focus.

TOPIC 12.4   Music and Mathematical Ability

Martin Gardiner, a researcher at the Music School in Providence, Rhode Island, reports in *Nature* (May 23, 1996) on first- and second-graders who took seven months of weekly one-hour Kodály instruction. Twenty-five percent more of these students were at grade level or higher in math aptitude than fellow students who had not taken the Kodály course. The Kodály method involves a structured, sequential learning approach (similar to mathematics instruction) in which one skill is mastered before the next is learned. Apparently it is not just the music and visual arts and group singing that account for the advantage; it's the sequential method itself.

Application

❶ Visit the American Kodály Institute website (they're in Baltimore) at www.american-kodaly-institute.org, or call them at 443-838-5785, and inquire about the Kodály program nearest you.

TOPIC 12.5   Music and the Injured Brain

Michael Rohrbacher, director of music therapy at Shenandoah University, Winchester, Virginia, and consultant to the National Institutes of Health (NIH), reports the preliminary results of an NIH Office of Alternative Medicine study on the effects of music on the emotions of patients with injured brains. By listening to music of their own choosing, especially music they grew up with, brain-injured patients showed an increased ability in emotional empathy, increased lucidity if they were confused, and improved recovery and rehabilitation time. Modern music, especially of the pounding, heavy-metal persuasion, appeared to be less effective.

In related experiments: John Hughes, of the University of Illinois, played Mozart (K. 448 again!) for epileptic patients and found that 29 out of 36 showed a statistically significant decrease in epileptic spiking while listening; popular piano music of the 1940s did not yield the same effect. Physician Gordon Shaw of the University of California, Irvine, reported at the 1998 Jensen Learning Conference in San Diego on an experiment by Johnson and Cotman in which Alzheimer's patients improved on a paper-folding task while listening to Mozart.

Applications

❶ Provide music from a patient's youth (and of her choosing) to enhance recovery. Ah, to convalesce with Little Richard and the Brandenburg Concerti!

❷ Obtain material from these two organizations:

- American Music Therapy Association (AMTA), 8455 Colesville Road, Suite 1000, Silver Spring, Maryland 20910; phone 301-589-3300; website: **www.musictherapy.org**.

- International Society for Music in Medicine (ISMIM), Sportkrankenhaus Hellersen, D-5880 Ludenscheid, Germany, 02351 434219; this organization copublishes the *International Journal of Arts Medicine*.

TOPIC 12.6 **The Effect of Music on Mood**

Here are some general guidelines on the human response to various aspects of music:

- The higher the pitch, the more positive the effect generated.

- Slower, minor keys warm the brain, which fosters both cortical and limbic alertness.

- Faster, major keys cool the brain, which fosters better moods.

- Classical composers (for example, Mozart, Haydn, and Beethoven) and mid- to late Baroque composers except for Bach (for example, Vivaldi, Scarlatti, Handel, and Corelli) are considered universal donors in the musical world—that is, they tend to offend the fewest listeners.

Carl Charnetski, chair of the psychology department at Wilkes University in Wilkes-Barre, Pennsylvania, measured the immunoglobulin A (IgA) production of college students who listened to regular jazz, smooth jazz, alternating clicks and tones, and nothing. Smooth jazz was associated with a 14 percent increase in IgA, regular jazz with a 7 percent increase, clicks and tones with a 19 percent decrease, and nothing with nothing! I'm not sure what to make of this, other than to say that mellow music appears to enhance immune function, and that Wilkes University students find smooth jazz (the Muzak variety) mellow. I suspect that those of us who find Mozart or Vivaldi mellow could expect similar benefits.

James Honeycutt (Louisiana State University) and Michael Eidenmuller (Northwestern State University) report (in *Chronicle of Higher Ed,* February 4, 2000) that couples solve their conflicts more effectively when accompanied by music that reflects their anger. Music that doesn't match one's mood tends to irritate rather than to soothe. In observations of couples fighting with music in the background, "angry" music (such as Stravinsky's *Rite of Spring*) tended to facilitate resolution, and "feel good" music (such as Ravel's *Bolero*) tended to serve as the perfect follow-up to conflict resolution by facilitating renewed positive regard. Music with words had a weaker impact. As a general rule, classical and jazz (wordless in both cases) facilitated conflict resolution more effectively than rock or pop (typically with words), even if both parties liked rock or pop.

Neurologist Barry Bittman of the Mind-Body Wellness Center (Meadville, Maryland) has found that regular attendance at a drumming circle leaves workers feeling more energetic and less depressed and angry. For more info, see www.remo.com/health. Bittman and associates at the center provide training for leading such drumming circles. Other musical or rhythmic outlets (e.g., choir, dance) may provide the same effect.

Glenn Wilson (1994) has found the following:

- Repetitive rhythms, such as Ravel's *Bolero* and the minimalist music of Philip Glass, induce a trancelike state that occasionally borders on ecstasy.

Table 12.1. Musical Elements Associated Cross-Culturally with Specific Moods

Element	Joy	Sadness	Excitement
Frequency	High	Low	Varied
Melodic variation	Strong	Slight	Strong
Tonal course	Moderate, first up, then down	Down	Strongly up, then down
Tonal color	Many overtones	Fewer overtones	Barely any overtones
Tempo	Rapid	Slow	Medium
Volume	Loud	Soft	Highly varied
Rhythm	Irregular	Regular	Very irregular

Source: Adapted from *Psychology for Performing Artists: Butterflies and Bouquets* by G. D. Wilson (1994), London: Jessica Kingsley.

- Musical rhythms liberate the mind from ordinary states, hence the popularity of music in religious and military settings.

- Music that slows gradually has a gradual relaxing effect.

- Lullabies in many cultures imitate the breathing rhythms of sleep.

- The body's rhythms adapt to the rhythms of live, close-up music.

- In all cultures, observers are able to correctly identify the music of other cultures that is intended to convey specific human moods and needs, such as war, mourning, love, hunting, and sleep inducement (that is, lullabies!). Wilson's findings are summarized in table 12.1.

Applications

❶ Following are some appropriate workplace uses of music:

- *Retail stores:* Faster, higher-pitched music in a major key (for example, Vivaldi's *The Four Seasons*), for optimum mood

- *Waiting rooms:* No vocal music or TV, please (so people like me can read)—instrumental music only

- *Workplaces where routine work is done:* Slower, lower-pitched music in a minor key (for example, Barber's *Adagio for Strings*)

❷ Don't play soothing string music (e.g., the Melachrino Strings) in the background hoping that it will facilitate problem solving between angry parties. Prefer more tempestuous yet mature and unintrusive music such as the later Beethoven string quartets.

TOPIC 12.7   Music and Personality

Wilson (1994) reports studies by Glasgow, Little, Zuckerman, Davies, Konecni, and others that begin to build a profile of how people with different personalities respond differently to various aspects of music. Among the findings are these:

- People who score "conservative" on personality tests tend to prefer music that is simpler and more familiar; "liberals" tend to find greater pleasure in more complex and unfamiliar music.

- People who score high on "sensation seeking" tend to prefer more complex and unfamiliar music.

In a survey conducted by G. D. Wilson in 1984, several interesting associations between singers' voices and their personalities emerged (Wilson, 1994, pp. 137 ff.):

- The higher the voice, the greater the singer's emotionality.

- The higher the voice, the more stage fright and variability the singer has from performance to performance.

- Basses have higher testosterone and, along with it, more affairs and greater ambition.

- Tenors miss the most cues, sopranos the fewest.

- Compared with singers, nonsingers are less extraverted, less conceited, more intelligent, more faithful, and more considerate.

Instrumental musicians have been the subject of several studies by Kemp, Piparek, Eysenck, Davies, Wills, Cooper, and Marchant-Haycox. Wilson (1994, pp. 176 ff.) summarizes these studies:

- Instrumentalists are more introverted and more anxious than nonmusicians.

- Brass players are more emotionally stable, more extraverted, less accommodating, and less focused than other instrumentalists (see chapter 33 for definitions of these personality traits).

- String players are more emotionally reactive than other instrumentalists.

- Jazz musicians are more emotionally reactive, higher in originality, less accommodating, and less disciplined than other instrumentalists.

Application

❶ Incorporate personality qualities associated with specific musical interests when entertaining or planning events for musicians. For example, because brass players and singers are more extraverted, plan for lots of party time!

TOPIC 12.8   **Music as Psychotherapy**

Is there evidence that music is truly able to "soothe a savage breast," as William Congreve suggests in *The Mourning Bride*? Glenn Wilson (1994, pp. 218–221) reviews the evidence and reports that music cures in a variety of ways, some more short-lived and others longer-lasting:

- Music provides a nonverbal means of communication for people who have lost the ability to communicate verbally.

- Among the elderly, music, whether in a live concert or via some electronic medium, has the capacity to promote positive reminiscences. The results include positive mood, improved communication, pain relief, improved rate of healing, and generally better health and disposition.

- Among a variety of patients, music can unleash verbal communication that for various reasons was previously suppressed.

- Stories abound of music's ability to moderate pain, such as Pablo Casals's testimony that although he was crippled by arthritis in his later years, playing the cello released him from the pain and stiffness.

- Music appropriate to the patient can calm schizophrenics and depressives.

- Vibroacoustic therapy, which surrounds patients with speakers and vibrators, has shown success in alleviating symptoms in patients with arthritis, cerebral palsy, asthma, back pain, and circulatory disorders. It has also been used as a post-event relaxant for skiers, runners, and business executives.

- In one-on-one music therapy, a musician improvises rhythmic, harmonic, melodic support to accompany the therapist's work with a profoundly disabled or disturbed child.

Applications

1 Begin a service in your community like the Music in Hospitals project in England, in which professional singers and instrumentalists donate their time to communicating with patients in hospitals, hospices, and nursing homes.

2 Provide music in appropriate areas of retirement and nursing homes, respecting, however, the need for residents to get away from it. It should be especially optional in their private rooms. Allow them to have a voice in selecting the kind of music to play and how it should be scheduled. Remember that choice is 80 percent of the game.

3 If you are a medical caregiver, remember that, although music is therapeutic, not all patients may respond to your musical preferences. I remember a recent trip to the dentist in which the team of two (doctor and assistant) took great delight in pointing my attention to a television monitor just three feet from my eyes and cooing with pride at the pop musician playing what sounded to me like a jack-hammer. Their new toy, supposedly patient-friendly, transmogrified me from patient into victim. Right idea, wrong choice! Again, provide a choice wherever possible, as the airlines do with their headsets and multiple channels, from jazz to classical.

4 When in doubt what to play for folks, select Mozart or Vivaldi (or their cohorts)!

SELECTED RESOURCES

Campbell, D. (1997). *The Mozart Effect.* New York: Avon.

Jensen, E. (2000). *Music with the Brain in Mind.* San Diego: The Brain Store.

Jourdain, R. (1997). *Music, the Brain, and Ecstasy: How Music Captures Our Imagination.* New York: Morrow.

Ortiz, J. M. (1997). *The Tao of Music: Sound Psychology.* York Beach, Maine: Samuel Weiser.

Shaw, G. (2000). *Keeping Mozart in Mind.* San Diego: Academic Press.

Tomatis, A. (1991). *The Conscious Ear.* Barrytown, N.Y.: Station Hill Press.

Wilson, G. D. (1994). *Psychology for Performing Artists: Butterflies and Bouquets.* London: Jessica Kingsley.

Websites

American Music Therapy Association home page. Contains a wide variety of resources, including publications and links to other websites: www.musictherapy.org

Mozart Effect Resource Center: www.mozarteffect.com

Music Intelligence Neural Development project: www.mindinst.org

Part Four

The Birds and the Bees

*Sex,
Gender, and
Relationships*

Part Four. The Birds and the Bees
Sex, Gender, and Relationships

13

Sex and Gender

The Wiring Is Different

> **"There is one phase of life that I have never heard discussed in any seminar And that is that all women think men are funny and all men think that weminar."**
>
> —Ogden Nash

We must distinguish from the outset the difference between the *male–female* spectrum and the *masculine–feminine*. The former has to do mostly with anatomy and physiology; the latter describes behavior, attitude, and the mind. Figure 13.1 illustrates this distinction graphically. Graph A is about sex differences, graph B gender differences. Your *sex* is how your body is put together; your *gender* is about the role you engage in daily.

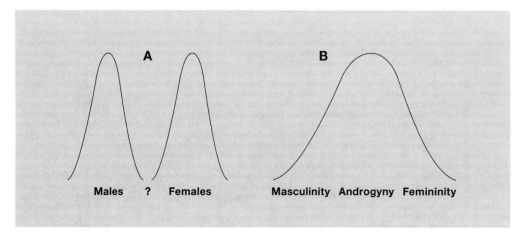

Figure 13.1. How Sex and Gender Are Distributed Differently in the Population
Graph A shows that sexual identity (i.e., body type with regard to procreative function) is bimodally distributed;
graph B illustrates how gender roles are normally distributed.

Having a high amount of estrogen and being able to have babies relate to sex; seeking a career in nursing and being able to do math usually relate to gender.

Males and females are bimodally distributed, with two large clusters at either end of the distribution and fewer in the middle area (graph A above); masculinity and femininity are normally distributed, with many members of the group in the middle area and fewer at the extremes (graph B). Individuals whose body sexuality is somewhat ambiguous are rather uncommon, less than 1 percent of the population, and fall in the middle area of graph A above.

There are not only men and women, but also both men and women with brains that are *male-differentiated, female-differentiated,* or somewhere in between. To the degree that a man exhibits characteristics that are typically "female" (language, emotion, nurture), he is said to have a female-differentiated brain. Conversely, to the degree that a woman exhibits characteristics that are typically "male" (math proficiency, spatial ability, aggression), she is said to have a male-differentiated brain. Men *and* women with male-differentiated brains are said to be more masculine, and are represented by the left side of graph B above; men *and* women with female-differentiated brains are said to be more feminine, and are represented by the right side of graph B.

Sex differences are immutable, except for surgical or pharmaceutical interventions. Gender differences are often based on sex differences, but are also heavily influenced by one's cultural environment. For example, a small difference in brain structure that is associated with a small advantage for one sex (e.g., a larger hippocampus in males helps store more visual-spatial imagery) can be hugely augmented by social demands, expectations, or stereotypes (e.g., the notion that males should be pilots, architects, surgeons, and other occupations that build on visual-spatial ability).

To the degree that a behavior is susceptible to environmental influences that are different for males than for females, it has a gender-related difference, not a sex difference. Sex differences should refer only to those that are attributable exclusively to biological factors. While this sounds simple and clear, it can become despairingly murky. Many differences have both biological and environmental influences. For example, we know that the menstrual cycle affects verbal and math performance in females; this suggests that differential performance on math and verbal scores between males and females is sex-related. But we also know that in countries where legislation has mandated the minimization of opportunity differences between males and females—particularly in the United States and Sweden—differences in math and verbal performance are diminishing significantly. Sandra Bem (1993) expresses these relationships well:

> No matter how many sex differences are someday shown to have a biological component, that knowledge will thus add little or nothing to our understanding of why women and men have universally played such different—and unequal—roles in virtually every society on earth. . . . So yes, women might turn out to be more biologically nurturant than men on the average, but that should make them psychiatrists, not secretaries. And yes, men might also turn out to have a higher aptitude for mathematics than women on the average, but that would not explain why so many more women have a high aptitude for mathematics than have careers requiring one.

This chapter summarizes the findings from cognitive science research on sex and gender differences that have some practical applications. I will endeavor to use the terms *sex* and *gender* properly, reserving *sex differences* to refer only to differences that are biologically established at conception, such as sex differences in height. For differences learned from one's environment, such as who does the cooking, I use *gender* differences. Many gender differences are small sex differences (such as nurturing tendencies) that have been enlarged by cultural expectations or stereotyping (e.g., females "should" be nurses, even non-nurturing females!). I confess in advance, however, that following this distinction is difficult indeed. In appendix B, I have compiled a long list of reported gender differences. Try reviewing the list to get a sense of whether your brain is more male-differentiated (i.e., more masculine), more female-differentiated (more feminine), or more in-between, or undifferentiated (more androgynous or unisex).

A word of warning: Whenever I refer to differences between the sexes, keep in mind that these differences are *averages* unless otherwise specified. This means, for example, that although males have a higher average score on math tests, many males score lower than the average female and many females score higher than the average male. Only time will tell which of these reported differences are free of cultural influences.

TOPIC 13.1 Physical Differences in the Sexes from the Outset

Several biological differences delineate where the brains of men and women begin. Table 13.1 lists these differences. The result is that the two brains are hard-wired differently: the male for "doing"—taking action that is related to goals (called *instrumental functions* by the scholars)—and the female for "talking" or for nurture that is related to relationships (called *agency* or *interpersonal functions* by the scholars). For the record, studies in 39 different countries worldwide exhibit these differences (Halpern, 2000, p. 97).

The male *Doer* tends to become more proficient in what Moir and Jessel (1991) call the five characteristics of the male-differentiated brain: aggression, competition, self-assertion, self-confidence, and self-reliance. All of these characteristics are highly correlated with testosterone levels, whether in males or females, and with math and spatial abilities. Females who excel in math usually also exhibit the five male traits, and females who exhibit the five male traits tend to score higher in math and visual-spatial skills.

The female *Talker* (or *Relater*) tends to gain proficiency in language, sensory awareness, memory, social awareness, and relationships. Much of this is apparently due to the relatively thick *corpus callosum* in the female-differentiated brain, which allows freer communication between the two hemispheres.

Table 13.1 Sex Differences in Brain Structure and Function

Female Brain	Male Brain
Thicker left cerebral cortex	Thicker right cerebral cortex
Corpus callosum is thicker relative to brain weight	Corpus callosum is thinner relative to brain weight
Suprachiasmic nucleus (in the forward hypothalamus) is more ball-like	Suprachiasmic nucleus (in the forward hypothalamus) is more cigar-like
Nuclei up to eight times larger	Smaller nuclei
Hypothalamus works on positive feedback principle (highs get higher, lows get lower)	Hypothalamus works on negative feedback principle (highs and lows return to equilibrium)
Language mechanics (grammar and syntax) engage front of left hemisphere	Language mechanics engage front and back of left hemisphere
Vocabulary work engages front and back of both hemispheres	Vocabulary work engages front and back of left hemisphere
Visual or spatial perception engages both hemispheres	Visual or spatial perception engages right hemisphere
Emotions activate both hemispheres	Emotions activate right hemisphere
Neurons up to 5 percent more densely packed	Brain averages 15 percent larger (about 3 ounces for a 2½-pound brain)
Equal in size to male brain by middle age	Shrinks faster from adolescence onwards
Brain is used more efficiently	Brain more inefficient, more wear and tear
Limbic (i.e., emotional) activation linked to verbal response areas	Limbic activation linked to motor/physical response areas
Estrogen levels variable, especially dropping and rising around estrus	Estrogen levels stable
Testosterone levels relatively stable	Testosterone levels vary widely according to environmental circumstances, in early morning, and in autumn (in northern hemisphere)
Six percent less tissue in the inferior parietal lobule (associated with timing, speed, and 3-D visualization)	Six percent more tissue in the inferior parietal lobule (associated with timing, speed, and 3-D visualization)

One of the differences—the more concentrated activity for language production in females—may account for their verbal superiority as measured by various tests, and the more concentrated activity for visual-spatial perception in males may account for their visual-spatial superiority. Apparently, the advantage of the denser concentration is that fewer possibilities exist for interrupting or interfering with neural activity. Performance is affected not only by density but by separation of function. Male-differentiated brains, in fact, find it easier to handle multitasking, such as talking while building something. Talking, which uses the left hemisphere, doesn't interfere in a major way with building, which is visual-spatial and uses the right hemisphere. Because the female-differentiated brain handles visual-spatial tasks in both hemispheres, building and talking, which both use the left hemisphere, interfere with each other.

One major structure that affects this pattern of specialization is the corpus callosum, which connects the two hemispheres. Theoretically, the larger the corpus callosum, the more efficient the communication between the two hemispheres. Traditional thinking has been that females have the larger corpus callosum, relative to brain size. However, this idea was based on less-than-optimum samples and outdated research methods (e.g., cadaver measurements). More recent studies using better sampling methods and uninvasive measures (such as fMRI) have clouded the issue, with males and females averaging about the same relative corpus callosum size. That said, we can still talk in terms of the "female-differentiated brain," which can occur in males as well as females, and which would include the larger corpus callosum. Possession of a larger corpus callosum would provide the owner with appreciably more connections, or synapses, between the two hemispheres. This degree of connection between the two hemispheres has been shown to be related to articulateness and fluency in language. The male's separation of language specialization in the left hemisphere and emotional specialization in the right helps to explain his traditional ineptness at talking about feelings; the neural basis of his feelings has far fewer connections with his language production. The female, with her emotions seated in both hemispheres and (perhaps) a thicker corpus callosum, has greater access to both her own feelings and the feelings of others as she produces her language. The male, with vocabulary-making powers seated only in the left hemisphere, is more proficient at developing vocabulary (hence the incredible mountains of male-created jargon and technical terminology), yet the female is more proficient at using what vocabulary she has.

Table 13.2. Hormonally Influenced Sexual Developmental Abnormalities

Excess androgen in female embryo	Male-differentiated brain with male appearance and behavior
Excess estrogen (no androgen) in female embryo	Exaggeratedly feminine appearance and behavior
Excess androgen in male embryo	"Super" male (aggressive, hairy, etc.)
Excess estrogen in male embryo	Female-differentiated brain with male appearance and behavior

Apparently the key to differentiation lies in our mothers' hormone levels during pregnancy. The effects are easier to experiment with in animals. If a pregnant rhesus monkey is injected with testosterone, a female offspring will exhibit one or more male traits, such as aggressive play or mounting. The female chaffinch can't sing; she doesn't have the synapses for singing that are present in the male. If male hormones are injected into the female chaffinch, the appropriate synapses develop, along with the ability to sing. When the ovaries of newborn female rats are removed, they develop thicker right hemispheres as adults, with an accompanying increase in spatial ability—a male trait. And when the testes of newborn male rats are removed, a similar check reveals thicker left hemispheres—a female trait.

Studies are revealing that men who behave as if they have female-differentiated brains do, in fact, possess lower levels of testosterone, and women who behave as if they have male-differentiated brains have higher levels of testosterone. In a fascinating line of research, Doreen Kimura, a clinical neuropsychology professor and professor emeritus at the University of Western Ontario in London, Ontario, Canada, has identified a relationship between body asymmetry and gender-related behavior. Namely, men and women with larger right testicles or breasts tend to exhibit more typically masculine behavior (aggression, spatial ability, math proficiency), whereas men and women with larger left testicles or breasts tend to exhibit more typically feminine behavior (nurturance, verbal ability). Table 13.2 shows how variations in androgens (male sex hormones) and estrogens (female sex hormones) in the embryonic stage can affect both body asymmetry and the degree and direction of gender differentiation in the brain.

Events during pregnancy that can affect the hormone level of the unborn child include the following:

- Mutations within the chromosomal matter

- Major or sustained stress (war, rape, bereavement), which suppresses testosterone

- Renal dysfunction, such as *congenital adrenal hyperplasia,* which produces too much testosterone

- Injections, as when mothers take estrogen for diabetes

- Barbiturates (taken by 25 percent of pregnant women from the 1950s through the 1980s)

- An extra chromosome (XXY in a boy yields low testosterone)

- Vigorous exercise (spurt exercise, such as tennis, increases testosterone; sustained exercise, such as a long run, lowers testosterone)

Although the brain is wired in the womb, the differences are most noticeable after puberty, when the brain becomes fully activated as a result of being bathed in hormones.

Applications

1 Do not take any medication during pregnancy until you've carefully discussed the possible consequences with a physician. If you are still in doubt, consult a neuropharmacologist (a specialist in pharmaceuticals for the nervous system). Be especially cautious during the first four months, when neurons are migrating.

2 Be accepting of your level of performance in various areas. Work to improve, always, but accentuate your strengths. If you sense that you are stronger at spatial skills than verbal skills, don't blame fate or your parents or your boss for not having done more to develop your verbal skills. The chances are that the discrepancy in skill level is hard-wired and permanent. Work to improve a skill to its next level, but don't begrudge how far you have to go to be perfect. Have a sense of humor about your natural gifts. There is so much to learn and so little time to learn it; don't moan about what seems impossible to learn. Instead, be attracted to what seems natural. As the Delphic Oracle said, "Know thyself."

❸ On the other hand, do not confuse attitude with ability. If your parents, your friends, your teachers, or society at large seem to expect you to lack a skill, do not let that determine whether or not you in fact possess the skill. Know yourself, and expose yourself to the many kinds of skills (see Gardner's eight talents at topic 34.4).

❹ In all individuals, value feminine characteristics such as cooperation and relationship building, as well as masculine traits such as competitiveness and achievement. Know that all these and many other traits are important for success in today's business environment. Look at them as complementary assets in terms of meeting customers' needs and competing in a continual-improvement business environment.

TOPIC 13.2   **Sexual Identity: How We See Ourselves**

Our sexual makeup is complex and multifaceted. One way of separating this mix of issues, behaviors, feelings, and urges is to group them into three focal areas:

Identity: whether we call ourselves a man (boy) or woman (girl). In other words, do I feel like a man (or woman), regardless of my bodily characteristics?

Orientation: to whom am I attracted romantically—people with a different sexual identify (as in a man desiring a woman), or people with my sexual identity (as in a man desiring another man)?

Behavior: to what degree do I act or behave like others of my sexual identity? For examples, boys who act like most girls (e.g., playing with dolls, displaying effeminate voice, facial expressions, or gestures) are called "sissy," and girls who act like most boys (doing math, playing sports, enjoying hunting or fishing) are called "tomboys."

These three elements of sexuality are independent of each other, in the sense that, for example, a male could see himself as a male and be attracted to females, yet act like a female. Or a male could see himself as a female, be attracted to females, and act like a male. Just because an individual exhibits a particular profile in one of the three areas does not necessarily lead to a particular profile in the other two areas. One of the more common errors in social inference, for example, is concluding that a male with masculine behavior is heterosexual or that a male with feminine behavior is homosexual. These three areas of sexuality are explored, in the order listed above, in this and the following two topics.

Whether we see ourselves as men or as women is determined primarily by our genetic makeup. Brown University developmental geneticist Anne Fausto-Sterling (1993) proposes that sexual identity is really a continuum that ranges from female to male. Bimodal, to be sure, it is nonetheless a distribution, with points in between. Although the medical literature uses the term *intersexual* to describe people who are in between (for example, someone with a penis who menstruates; see her story about Levi Suydam), Fausto-Sterling proposes three intermediate points: *herms* (hermaphrodites, with one testis and one ovary), *merms* (male pseudohermaphrodites with testes, no ovaries, and some form of female genitalia), and *ferms* (female pseudohermaphrodites with ovaries, no testes, and some form of male genitalia). These intersexual categories occur in an estimated 2–4 percent of births. Other writers question Fausto-Sterling's three intersexual categories, preferring to refer to them as a single complex of configurations known as the *transsexual* category.

In spite of the difficulty of nomenclature, there appears to be agreement that the traditional medical practice of performing "clarifying surgery" on intersexuals at an early age serves the community more than the person who is born intersexual. What little evidence is available suggests that the problems accompanying "corrective" surgery (loss of erotic sensitivity and depression over lost body parts, for example) are more detrimental to the intersexual than problems associated with socialization (taking showers in gym class and showing secondary sexual features, for example). Fausto-Sterling and others (see the letters to the editor in *The Sciences,* July–August 1993, pp. 3–4, in response to her March–April article) propose that society should support intersexuals as they learn to accept their sexual identity as something more interesting and complex than being simply male or female.

Case Western Reserve University School of Medicine chair of biochemistry Michael Weiss led a team of researchers in discovering a protein that governs the genes that determine the expression of male vs. female characteristics. Their discovery (reported in *Genes and Development,* July 17, 2000) challenges the traditional assumption that sex characteristics are determined exclusively by testosterone and other sex hormone levels. Although their research was done on *Drosophila* (fruit fly), the mechanism appears to be consistent in other organisms, including humans. In fact, research indicates that the sexual characteristics of some organisms (such as worms) can be reversed by injecting this protein. Ah, brave new world!

A section of the hypothalamus called the BSTc is 50 percent larger among males than among women, regardless of their sexual orientation (that is, whether they are homosexual or heterosexual). However, a Dutch research team led by Dick Swaab at the Netherlands Institute for Brain Research in Amsterdam found that in transsexual men (men who feel that they are really women trapped in the bodies of men), the BSTc is not only smaller on the average than other men's, it is also smaller than women's. Most of these men report feelings of liberation after a sex-change operation.

Applications

❶ If you are a parent or a surgeon faced with deciding whether to surgically "clarify" the sexuality of a newborn or older infant, seek further information from an emerging literature and support service network on transgender and intersexuality issues. Fausto-Sterling concludes that in her ideal world, transgender people should have a say in any medical interventions. Read Fausto-Sterling, *Myths of Gender* (1992), and Fausto-Sterling and Rose, *Love, Power, and Knowledge* (1994). Also see the story of John/Joan, by Milton Diamond and Keith Sigmundson of the University of Hawaii at Manoa's Pacific Center for Sex and Society, in the March 1997 *Archives of Pediatric and Adolescent Medicine.*

❷ Sexual identity consists of more than gonads and other organs. Behavioral patterns and preferences (hairstyle, clothing fashions, mannerisms, nurture vs. aggression) also must be allowed a full range of expression. If an intersexual is comfortable with a variety of gender-related fashions as well as a variety of organs, others should not force such an individual into the Procrustean clarity of a Rhett Butler male or a Scarlett O'Hara female. (Not that old? How about Brad Pitt and Angelina Jolie?)

❸ Contact and/or join the support network of the Intersex Society of North America, 979 Golf Course Drive #282, Rohnert Park, California 94928. Website: www.isna.org.

TOPIC 13.3	**Sexual Orientation: To Whom We Are Attracted**

The emerging evidence points in the direction of a strong genetic basis for sexual orientation—that is, what influences us to find attraction in members of our opposite sex or our same sex. We are all aware of the debate on the choice or inevitability of being homosexual, which is defined as males having sexual relations with males continually, females with females. Such a pattern occurs in about 2–3 percent of the population for males, about 1½ percent for females. As for females, their sexual orientation is typically more flexible than males; females are more likely to be comfortable having sex with either sex (Blum, 1997, p. 128).

Consider the following litany of research findings that point towards a genetic, or biological, basis for sexual orientation:

- Homosexuality runs in families.

- Homosexuality appears randomly in birth order.

- Homosexuals exhibit early childhood gender nonconformity.

- The third interstitial nucleus of the anterior hypothalamus (INAH-3) is of equal size in women and homosexual men but is twice as large in heterosexual men. Homosexual men have fewer neurons in the INAH-3 than heterosexual men, yet more than women.

- Monozygotic (identical) twins have the highest concordance rate; if one is homosexual, there is a 50 percent probability that the other will be too. Michael Bailey reports in the March 1993 *Archives of General Psychiatry* on a study of 71 sets of identical female twins, 37 sets of fraternal female twins, and 35 sets of adoptive sisters, each set including at least one lesbian. For the identical twins, 48 percent of those identifying themselves as lesbian or bisexual also had a sister who was lesbian. For the fraternal twins, this was true of only 16 percent; for the adoptive sisters, only 6 percent.

- Doreen Kimura reports in the December 1994 issue of *Behavioral Neuroscience* that in a study of the fingerprint patterns of 182 heterosexual men and 66 homosexual men, twice as many homosexual men (30 percent) as heterosexual men (16 percent) showed more ridges on the left hand than on the right (most men show more ridges on the right hand). These print patterns are completely formed within four months of conception. Women and gay men have a higher incidence of higher left-hand ridge counts.

- Kimura and Carson (1995) report that both men and women with higher left-hand ridge counts excel at typically feminine tasks such as those involving nurture and verbal skills, and that both men and women with higher right-hand ridge counts excel at typically masculine tasks such as those involving aggression, math, and spatial skills.

- Gays and lesbians have a higher incidence of left-handedness.

- A significant number of gay men hear equally well in both ears (most males hear better through the right ear, most females equally well in both). The latter finding supports earlier findings that homosexual men have larger connections between the two hemispheres.

- Dean Hamer, of the National Cancer Institute, has demonstrated that many gay brothers share a strip of DNA passed down from their mothers. Expanding on this finding, Plomin, DeFries, McClearn, and Rutter (1997) report that such DNA strips—called *linkages* in reference to the unusually close proximity of the genes—in the q28 region of the X chromosome were shared by 67 percent of homosexual brothers but only 22 percent of heterosexual brothers, a significant difference from the 50 percent standard for independence of association. This research builds on the linkage phenomenon whereby two gene locations are close to each other, which is one way of demonstrating genetic influence of behavior.

- Acoustical researchers Dennis McFadden and Edward G. Pasanen and their team at the University of Texas at Austin placed tiny microphones in the ear canals of 60 homosexual or bisexual women and 57 heterosexual women. The former were shown to emit weaker and less frequent spontaneous otoacoustic emissions than the latter. These imperceptible sounds from the homosexual and bisexual women were more like those of men (April 1999 issue of *Journal of the Acoustical Society of America*).

- Laura Allen and Roger Gorski of UCLA reported the results of a study they made of the brain tissue of 34 homosexual men, 75 presumed heterosexual men, and 84 presumed heterosexual women (*Proceedings of the National Academy of Sciences,* August 1992). The *anterior commissures* (a communication link between the two brain hemispheres) of the homosexual men were 34 percent larger than those of heterosexual men and 8 percent larger than those of the women, whereas the anterior commissures of the women were 13 percent larger than those of the heterosexual men. This finding appeared to be confirmed in a later report by Sandra Witelson, a psychiatry professor at McMaster University in Hamilton, Ontario, Canada. Her study was based on a sample of 21 men.

- Four collaborators—laboratories at Stanford University, the University of Texas Southwestern Medical Center at Dallas, Brandeis University, and Oregon State University—have reported (in *Cell,* December 13, 1996) that the male fruit fly (*Drosophila*) possesses a powerful high-level gene that governs his sexual behavior. One mutation of the gene leads to indiscriminate, or bisexual, behavior; another mutation removes the desire to mate; and yet another mutation removes the ability to perform the "courtship buzz." Fruit flies with all three mutations are perfectly healthy otherwise. In the first mutation mentioned, indiscriminate males who are confined together without females all engage in the behaviors of courting and being courted by each other.

- Apparently sex hormones are not the sole determining factor. Although there is a small difference in testosterone levels between heterosexual and homosexual groups, a greater difference exists within groups. In one comparative study, the highest testosterone level belonged to a homosexual male subject.

- Male homosexuals perform more like females on spatial tasks (i.e., lower than male heterosexuals); lesbians do not show the same pattern (i.e., perform more like their own sex).

- Researchers (*Nature,* March 30, 2000) at the University of California at Berkeley found that men's ring fingers tends to be longer than their index fingers, whereas in women these same two fingers tend to be about the same length. Among a sample of 720 adults in San Francisco, lesbians tended to show the typical male proportions, with a longer ring finger. Interestingly, male homosexuals showed a more "masculine" proportion than male heterosexuals, with the homosexuals' index finger even shorter than those of the heterosexuals. Scientists believe that androgen levels account for the difference, with higher levels of androgen during early development of both male and female heterosexuals.

• Among mammals, homosexuality is not an aberration of humans. In a major advance in research, Bruce Bagemihl (1999) has scientifically documented same-sex courting and copulating in more than 450 species of mammals. One of his intriguing, but not universally accepted, interpretations is that of "biological exuberance," or the notion that the world is filled with examples of "excess" resources, such as the sun, that pour out so much of their essence that multiple uses emerge. Thus, the excessive sexual urge of mammals finds expression in behavior oriented in more ways than reproduction. Blum (1997, p. 130) found that homosexual behavior of some sort has been noted in more than 60 species.

Researchers are unsure when sexual orientation is fixed, some believing the fifth month in the womb as the result of a hormonal wash, others holding to a period between two and four years of age. Regardless of where the exact timing lies, Blum comments (p. 142): "Either way, the timing suggests that anyone who argues that sexual orientation is a 'choice' is clueless." Lest we see the evidence as all one way, here is a clear reminder that parts of the animal kingdom present strong evidence for environmental influence. Russell Fernald, a neuroscience professor at Stanford University, has found that male cichlids who reach the top of their dominance hierarchy undergo biological changes: their colors appear, the hypothalamus enlarges, and they become sexually potent. On the other hand, if they fall (or sink) from the top of the hierarchy, they turn brown, their hypothalamus shrinks, and they become impotent. All determined by their environment? Or an environmental trigger for genetically determined programming?

And in a more human vein, Daryl Bem, a Cornell University psychologist, argues for an interactionist interpretation of sexual orientation (D. J. Bem, 1996). Although Bem accepts an inborn biological influence on sexual orientation, he also sees a strong cultural, or environmental, influence. Bem says that we grow up seeing ourselves as more similar to one gender or the other, and the gender we view as different from us is the gender that we view as more exotic. As our hormones urge sexual arousal, this "exotic" attitude is transformed into an "erotic" attitude. More research is required to support this aspect of Bem's theory. His view is certainly more cautious than a purely genetic or purely environmental explanation of sexual orientation. However, sexual orientation, like other life choices (business, religious, dietary, exercise, and academic choices, for example), is built on a biological foundation. Environmental add-ons do not eradicate that foundation, nor does the foundation prevent environmental add-ons.

In support of Bem's argument for cultural influence, at the American Psychological Association's 1998 Annual Conference, Marc Breedlove, a professor of psychology at the University of California at Berkeley, reported new evidence that sexual orientation is subject to environmental manipulation (*APA Monitor,* October 1998, p. 25). In male rodents, the *medial amygdala* is crucial for sexual arousal around female rodents. If the medial amygdala, which detects pheromones, is excised or reduced in size, then arousal doesn't occur. The size of this part of the brain can be controlled by externally manipulating the flow of androgens, with a flood of testosterone restoring the medial amygdala to normal size and, as a consequence, restoring the rodent to full arousal capability. Breedlove concludes that, by extension, it is likely that environmental influences on human androgen levels also affect arousal capability. However, he has not performed the human research, and several questions are unanswered. For example, although the male rodent's medial amygdala is larger than the female's, Breedlove does not report whether the male rodent, in addition to losing interest in females, becomes aroused around other males when his medial amygdala is shrunk to the size of a female's.

Conservatives such as the Family Research Council think tank are advocating "conversion therapy" for changing homosexuals to heterosexuals. The American Psychological Association and the American Psychiatric Association have both issued policy statements opposing conversion therapy. Their opposition is based on their stand that homosexuality is not a mental illness and, hence, not in need of treatment.

Application

❶ Homosexuality appears to have a strong genetic component. To the degree that it is not a choice, it is also not a moral issue. Apparently, homosexuality and heterosexuality are as natural as straight or kinky hair: most folks have straight hair, some have kinky hair, but simply being in the minority does not make it wrong! Medical doctors are a minority, but they are not wrong. Accept homosexuals and heterosexuals as equals, and don't try to change a person's preference or make fun of something that cannot be changed.

TOPIC 13.4   Sexual Role: Our Everyday Behavior

The third aspect of sexuality is the degree to which we engage in everyday behaviors, postures, expressions, fashions, and other habits that are typical of males and females within our culture. This third group (the others being identity and orientation) is apparently determined entirely by our cultural environment and not by our genes or biology. We tend to pick up these behaviors by observing persons we consciously or unconsciously wish to emulate. I remember a college senior who cocked his head and walked with a shuffling gait, only to be emulated by me in more private moments away from his gaze. I will not elaborate on these behaviors, as they are not apparently brain-related, except to the degree that they may reflect identity or orientation. Or not. And, in each culture, the list would be somewhat different. Table 13.3 shows some of the more common differences found in U.S. culture. There are many more, of course, most of which you are familiar with, such as extending the little finger when drinking tea. The point here is that these behaviors are all learned, and they can be unlearned easily enough, however uncomfortable the unlearning may be.

Hormone levels may make certain behaviors more or less natural. For example, *congenital adrenal hyperplasia* (CAH) is a condition in which embryos are exposed to unusually high levels of androgens during gestation. By taking a look at differences in behavior among children affected by CAH and those unaffected, we can get a sense of how stereotypical male or female behavior can in fact be influenced by levels of androgens and estrogens. For example, girls affected by CAH show a much higher incidence of rough-and-tumble play and also of play that covers wider space areas (as opposed to play that is more stationary) than is characteristic of other girls. These CAH-affected girls also engage in substantially less play-parenting (e.g., "I'll be the mommy and you'll be the baby!"), as well as selecting "boy"

Table 13.3. Culturally Influenced Sexual Differences in Behavior

Typical Male Behavior	Typical Female Behavior
Stands with arms akimbo	Stands with one or both arms crossed over abdomen
Stands with feet parallel	Stands with feet asymmetrical, pointed in different directions
Stands relatively straight	Stands in something of an ogival curve, knees slight bent, hips back, chest more forward, head atilt.
When drinking from glass or cup, looks into it, breaking eye contact with others	When drinking from glass or cup, looks out over it, keeping eye contact with others
Likes more distance from other males	Comfortable being closer to other females
Tends to hold an infant with same arm as hand preference	Tends to hold an infant with left arm, regardless of hand preference

toys more frequently than CAH-unaffected girls (Geary, 1998, p. 235). These preferences are related to the larger play theme of elaborated fantasies called *sociodrama,* where boys tend to engage in more competitive, power-oriented episodes such as cowboys and Indians, military re-enactments, and so forth, whereas girls tend to engage in more relational, family-oriented episodes such as tea parties and taking imaginary family trips (p. 239).

The larger consequence of these tendencies is that segregated social groups emerge, owing to the fact that girls just don't typically respond emotionally to the nature of boy play and vice versa (p. 241). We need to remember that exceptions abound, of course. When I was a tender youth in elementary school, I remember fondly playing dolls, dress-up, and "doctor" with two girls in my neighborhood. In fact, pictures exist, which I've hidden from my publicist, that show me in full gypsy dress, complete with turban, in an ogival sway to an imagined balalaika tune, with a broad grin indicating my complete surrender to my feminine side! However, as a general rule, boys' play tends to have as its goal the establishment of dominance within hierarchies, whereas girls' play tends toward establishing stable social relationships with more equal resource distribution (p. 242).

Elenor Maccoby (1998) finds three interesting phenomena that describe how boys and girls develop in gender identity. First, between the ages of 2½ and 6, children form strong preferences for grouping with their own sex. Second, boy groups interact differently from girl groups, with boy groups more competitive, girl groups more cooperative. Third, boy groups tend to exhibit greater solidarity than do girl groups, with boys being much more exclusionary and sexist. "Ooo, he was just talking with a *girl!* Sissy!" However, when boys and girls do interact with the other sex, their characteristic same-sex behaviors do not prevail. Maccoby offers biological, evolutionary, and cultural reasons for these near-universal tendencies. In sum, male and female survival has been traditionally enhanced by the competitive stance of all-male groups and by the cooperative stance of all-female groups.

Across a wide variety of studies (Geary, pp. 165 ff.) that explore the goals of the sexes across cultures, men show a consistently stronger preference for goals that involve hierarchical dominance and competition, whereas women prefer goals that involve building long-term, mutually satisfying relationships with other people. From day one, girls maintain longer eye contact than boys, and at six months boys gaze-avert more often than girls. Beginning young and continuing to develop is the girl's superior memory for faces and the ability to discriminate between similar faces. Also, from one year, girls show more sympathy (by crying, paying attention, offering comfort) for other infants in distress than do boys, who are more likely than girls to show indifference to others' distress. And from one year, though mothers initiate talking equally to boy and girl infants, girls are twice as responsive as boys. Boys are more likely to approach unfamiliar objects than girls, growing to increasing disparity in risk-taking behavior. When novel objects are presented, boys tend to pay more attention to, and remember more, physical details of the objects; girls pay more attention to, and remember more, the reactions of other people to the object.

Taking the Doer and Relater roles (see topic 13.1) to their logical conclusion, Cornell University researchers Jungeen Kim and Phyllis Moen studied 534 retired married men and women. They report (in *APA Monitor,* October 1999) that retirement affects men and women differently. After retiring, men are most happy about themselves and their marriages if they take up part-time employment. For retired women, finding new employment doesn't improve their morale. Rather, they feel best when their marriage relationship is in good order.

Selwyn Becker of the University of Chicago and Alice Eagly of Northwestern University (2004) found a mixed pattern in their study of heroism and gender. They define *heroism* as an act characterized by three qualities:

1. It is voluntary.

2. It is prosocial (for the welfare of one or more others).

3. It involves risk of life or limb.

The research pair explored the question of sex and heroism by analyzing five groups that have exhibited well-documented heroic behavior:

1. Winners of the Carnegie medal (U.S. and Canada)

2. The "Righteous among the Nations"—gentiles in Poland, France, and the Netherlands who aided Jews under Nazism

3. Kidney donors

4. Peace Corps workers

5. Doctors of the World volunteers

In the first group, men outnumbered women (around 1 in 10 were women), whereas women outnumbered men in the latter four (around 6 in 10 were women in these groups). Their explanation:

Men are more likely than women to act heroically when

1. The act requires upper body strength.

2. The action required is immediate.

3. The action is public—viewable by witnesses (associated with opportunity for recognition, and men's tendency to more group-oriented behavior).

4. The action requires emotional control during extreme danger.

5. The men describe themselves as strong, aggressive, principled, and emotional (in the sense of easily aroused to action, yet able to control emotions while acting).

6. The men are larger and more experienced or trained in emergency behavior (as in the military or the Boy Scouts).

Women are more likely to act heroically when

1. The act provides nurture.

2. The act involves maintaining and building relationships (associated with women's tendency to more dyad-oriented behavior).

We think it goes without saying, even though the authors didn't mention it, that women who perceive themselves with the first set of qualities (i.e., lower A) are more likely to act heroically in the first situation, whereas men who perceive themselves as more nurturing and relational (i.e., higher A) are more likely than other men to act in the latter four situations. (See chapter 33 for definitions of high and low A.)

Applications

❶ Understand that so-called masculine or feminine social behaviors are learned, and that they are not necessarily indicative of one's sexual identity or orientation. However, also understand that hormonal levels make certain behaviors easier to learn or unlearn than others.

❷ To the degree that individuals are comfortable in their doing/instrumental role or nurturing/interpersonal role, resist trying to change them. If a man wants to work after retirement, research says it is probably not a bad idea, all other things being equal.

TOPIC 13.5 Gender Medicine

Traditionally, medicine has treated the male and female bodies as equivalent, except for baby-making capabilities. As JoAnn Manson, codirector of Boston's Nurses' Health Study, puts it: "Medical literature and practice have been based on the 70-kilogram man" (*Boston Globe Magazine,* April 27, 1997, p. 13). Recent research, however, has uncovered the need for a more gender-specific approach to medicine. In the forefront of this gender-specific research is the National Institutes of Health, where the $628 million, 15-year Women's Health Initiative is housed. Among its findings is the discovery that women differ from men in a substantial number of medically significant ways. Among them:

- Their immune systems function differently: women have higher immunoglobulin levels for fighting viruses.

- They metabolize drugs differently, including Valium and benzodiazepine, alcohol, acetaminophen, lidocaine, and aspirin.

- Women have a higher prevalence of migraine headaches.

- Women have a higher occurrence of depression.

- Most autoimmune diseases, including multiple sclerosis, lupus, and rheumatoid arthritis, are more common among women.

- Women come around more quickly after anesthesia.

- A woman's heart is two-thirds the size of a man's heart, and it beats faster.

- A woman's risk of heart disease increases fourfold at menopause.

- Same-sex organ transplants are more successful in women.

- Tobacco exposure has more impact on a woman's lungs.

- Men produce estrogen throughout their lives at higher levels than women do after menopause.

- A woman's bone mass decreases at maturity relative to a man's.

- Women live on average seven years longer than men (this gap is widening; it was two to three years at the turn of the century).

- Aspirin reduces a man's risk of stroke, but not a woman's.

- Women are more likely to die after using some heart medications, such as antiarrhythmia drugs.

- Women tend to pursue a different course in response to stress, preferring nurturing, intimate activity over either solitary (i.e., fleeing) or aggressive (i.e., fighting) activity. The typical female self-soothes after stressful episodes by such activities as an intimate talk with a friend or a grooming session with her pet.

Note also the brain differences between men and women cited earlier in this chapter.

Premenopausal women suffer heart disease less often than men, probably due to the palliative effect of abundant estrogen and progesterone, their natural beta-blockers. This, in combination with traditional physicians' tendency to see women's somatic complaints as hysterical, has contributed to women's heart disease symptoms being taken less seriously, As a result, women are more likely to die from their first heart attack than are men, and women are more likely to have a second heart attack within a year of their first.

All of this has led to a revolution in women's medicine, from reproductive medicine to gender medicine. In the forefront of this movement, Columbia University's College of Physicians and Surgeons in New York has instituted the Partnership for Women's Health. The director, Marianne J. Legato, is leading the development of a database that includes sex-based findings about biological differences. Its purpose is primarily educational.

Applications

❶ When you consult your physician about a specific condition or treatment, ask whether there are any sex-specific features that should be considered.

❷ Ensure that your physician is familiar with the Partnership for Women's Health gender medicine database.

❸ Visit and use the Women's Health Initiative website at **www.whi.org**.

TOPIC 13.6 **The Math-Verbal Controversy**

Diane Halpern (2000), professor of psychology at California State University, San Bernardino, identifies three potential physical bases for sex differences in mental ability:

Genetics. To date, there is no evidence for a recessive gene for spatial ability that is sex-linked (p. 147). This is the leading theory for male superiority in spatial ability. If there were a recessive gene for spatial ability on the sex chromosome, then it would take two of them turned "on" for females to have the spatial ability, but only one need be present for males. Hence, it is argued, there would be a genetic basis for the higher male mean. However, no evidence supports this view. Deborah Blum writes (1997, pp. 26–27) that the basis of much of the debate about sex differences in brain and behavior originates in the nature of the so-called "sex chromosomes," *chromosome pair 23* (usually called "chromosome 23" for short), which comprises either two *X chromosomes* (one each from mother and father, resulting in a female embryo) or one X chromosome and one *Y chromosome* (from the mother and father respectively, resulting in a male embryo). Here's where the plot thickens: The female, or X, chromosome has upwards of 5,000 genes passed down to the next generation, whereas the male, or Y, chromosome contributes around 15 genes. The Y chromosome mostly determines the sex of the embryo; the X chromosome is a veritable workhorse, full of disease predispositions, behavioral predilections, and precursors of physical characteristics. Two implications follow from this inequality:

1. If a gene on the X chromosome of a female is defective, the healthy gene on the other X chromosome can take over. Suppose a woman has a bad gene for color vision on one X chromosome, and a good one on the other X chromosome. The result is good color vision. However, if a male has a defective gene for color vision on his single X chromosome, there is no corresponding color vision gene on his Y chromosome part of chromosome 23 to take over. The result is color blindness. It would take two defective genes in a female to produce color blindness.

2. If a gene on chromosome 23 is recessive and takes a "matched pair" in order to be expressed in the next generation, then it cannot be expressed in a male embryo, never, ever.

Hormone levels. One theory is that there is an optimal level of *estradiol* for spatial performance—too much or too little detracts from spatial ability. So, according to the theory, since men are lower and women higher in estradiol, spatial ability could be increased in males by raising estradiol levels and increased in females by lowering them (p. 154). Spatial skills in men also vary with their testosterone levels, both increasing in the early morning and falling off through the day, and, in North America, increasing in the fall and falling off towards spring. (Does this mean you should get your architect to design your building on an early fall morning? I suppose it depends on the architect!)

Structural differences in the brain. One theory is that men, with superior spatial ability and the many mental maps that must be stored in the hippocampus to stay on top of all the "hunting expeditions" entailed by their traditional role, need more space to store these graphic images. After all, we know with computers what memory hogs graphics are! Among animals, those who must do more wandering—regardless of gender—have larger hippocampi in order to accommodate the greater need for storing mental maps. Men's hippocampi decrease in size in proportion to their decreasing spatial ability as they age (see appendix A). Moreover, research supports the ability of changing environmental and hormonal events to modify the structure of the brain. This comes from both animal and human research, with song birds' brains changing size and shape when singing begins, and with humans showing increased density in enriched environments, enlarged corpus callosa from early musical training, as well as shrinking hippocampi from prolonged stress (p. 156).

Neuroscientist Ruben Gur, University of Pennsylvania Medical Center, and his team report (in *Journal of Neuroscience,* May 15, 1999) that superior spatial skills are associated with higher levels of white matter and cerebrospinal fluid in the brain. *White matter* is composed of long axons that link remote parts of the brain, thus facilitating spatial orientation by providing the requisite connectedness between elements of a perceived spatial pattern. Men, on average, have higher concentrations of white matter, affording them a kind of global positioning system; women, on average, have higher concentrations of gray matter, which comprises nerve cell tissue and the many dendrites that form synapses. *Gray matter* is associated with the ability to quickly determine the relationships between a variety of elements in the immediate perceptual field, as in connecting landmarks in a meaningful manner. This relates clearly to the evolutionary psychologists' position that men excelled at long-distance spatial memory for hunting, whereas women excelled at the local spatial memory required for gathering nuts and berries. The amount of white matter is related to cranial size—the larger the skull, the more white matter. In fact, although women's skulls are, on average, smaller than men's, larger-skulled women have commensurately greater spatial ability than smaller-skulled women.

In addition to looking for genetic associations with cognitive sex differences and documenting hard-wired differences in brain structure and their possible impact on math and verbal performance, research continues to explore a close relationship between hormone levels and individual performance. A higher testosterone level results in more sexual activity, more aggression, and higher math and spatial performance (as well as maze performance in rats). In females, performance is related to the menstrual cycle. From day 1 (the first day of menstruation) through ovulation, estrogen starts low and rises. From ovulation through the end of the cycle, progesterone is high and, for the most part, estrogen is high. This relationship is shown in figure 13.2.

Regardless of hormone levels, females, on average, test higher on verbal performance than on fine motor coordination, and they test higher on fine motor coordination than on math and spatial skills (see figure 13.3). When their hormone levels are higher, they have higher average scores on verbal skills and fine motor coordination, but even lower scores on math and spatial skills. In fact, during menstruation (when estrogen and progesterone are at their lowest), women score 50 to 100 percent higher on mental rotation tests.

Also regardless of hormone levels, females perform on average higher on verbal skills and fine motor coordination than males, and lower on math and spatial skills than males (Kimura and Hampson, 1990). This pattern prompts an obvious question: If women as a group are verbally superior, why are there not more famous female writers? Halpern (2000) points out (p. 96) that more than ability makes the writer. Such factors as having sufficient independent income, leisure, and permission to write are important. She cites examples of Emily Dickinson and the Brontë sisters as women with private means as well as ability, opportunity, and encouragement to write. Moreover, the traditional male advantage in mathematics is confounded by the role of verbal skills (as in word problems in math) and the intrusion of spatial tasks in many math problems, especially after the early grades. Girls do better generally than boys in simple computation in the early grades. Then things get murky. The absence of girls from the high-performing ranks is not universal, however—many girls excel in math in China. In fact, David Geary (1998) emphasizes that the vast prevalence of males in math-intensive careers (8:1) cannot be attributed to differences in cognitive

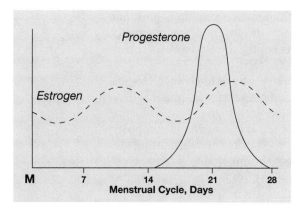

Figure 13.2. Female Hormone Levels Throughout the Monthly Cycle
Source: From *Brain Sex: The Real Difference Between Men and Women* by Anne Moir and David Jessel (1991), New York: Carol Publishing Group/Lyle Stuart. © 1989, 1991 by Anne Moir and David Jessel. Reprinted by permission of Carol Publishing Group. *Note:* M = menstruation.

ability (p. 328). Rather, males and females who enter math-intensive careers have one thing in common (apart from their math proficiency): they have minimal need for social or people contact and prefer theoretical and investigative themes. That is not common for females.

Math-talented women with the typical female bent towards valuing relationship stability are more likely to end up using their math skills in more social and artistic contexts, according to Geary.

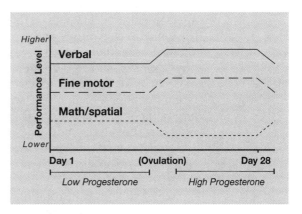

Figure 13.3. Female Hormone Levels and Their Relation to Performance

This same relationship of hormones to performance holds true for males, who should do their best in math and spatial skills in the morning (testosterone levels are highest around 8:00 A.M.) and their best in verbal and fine-motor skills (although not as well as the average female) from midafternoon through early evening (testosterone levels are lowest around 8:00 P.M.). Also, Kimura and Hampson (1990) have found that males score higher on spatial manipulation tests in the spring (when testosterone is lowest) than in the fall (when testosterone is highest). Apparently the relationship is curvilinear: too much testosterone interferes with spatial performance.

Another interesting finding about math performance is that whereas the male-differentiated brain solves math problems nonverbally, the female-differentiated brain tends to solve them by talking through them (hence, the female "Talker"). Females manipulate math concepts with verbal labels; males manipulate the concepts in abstract mental space without conscious use of language. (My wife cannot talk while studying a map in the car; I can.) One consequence of this difference is that the female-differentiated brain typically takes longer to solve a math problem.

Recent studies show that the gap in spatial ability between the sexes remains constant but that the math gap was cut in half between 1982 and 1989. To the degree that the gap is cultural in origin, societies that reduce experiential differences between boys and girls should see these differences diminish. In Charlotte, North Carolina, during the 2004–2005 school year, 318 females enrolled for calculus, compared with 350 males (provided by Dana Wrights, Director of Data Analysis for Charlotte-Mecklenburg Schools). This represents a dramatic increase from the 1950s, when female enrollment was minimal. On the other hand, Larry Hedges and Amy Nowell of the University of Chicago, who examined six major national surveys of U.S. teenagers' mental performance (Hedges and Nowell, 1995), learned that the gaps between boys and girls in math, spatial skills, and reading showed essentially no change from 1960 to 1992. They found that boys' scores showed greater variability, with disproportionately more boys scoring in the extremely high and low ranges, except in reading comprehension and writing, in which a disproportionately large number of boys scored in the low range (but not in the high range, as they did in math).

Evolutionary theorists Irwin Silverman and Marion Eals of York University in Toronto have considered subtests for spatial skills. They theorize that evolutionary necessity accounts for two distinct kinds of spatial skill: mental rotation and spatial memory. Man the hunter was selected for his ability to navigate and find his way home, whereas woman the gatherer was selected for her ability to remember where the good edible plants were to be found. Several lines of recent research tend to confirm this theory. Along with Krista Phillips, also of York, they found that people with higher estrogen (both men and women) perform worse on mental rotation tests: women worse than men, and men with higher estrogen levels worse than men with lower levels. Women score highest on mental rotation tests during menstruation, when estrogen is lowest.

> **Men often use physical strength to dominate hierarchies; women more often use verbal fluency to lubricate relationships.**

In a new protocol in which subjects are asked to peruse a room for a couple of minutes, women remember more objects as well as their locations—unless subjects are told to remember, in which case performance is more similar; women excel at *incidental memory*. In still another confirming vein, women find their way better when using landmarks and concepts (such as "left turn"), whereas men find their way better when using distances and directions (such as "north" and "south"). Further support for this line comes from Heinrich Stumpf and Douglas Jackson (1994), who factor-analyzed cognitive ability for 90,142 female and 96,968 male German medical school applicants. Two of the resulting factors, reasoning and memory, showed clear gender advantages for men and women, respectively.

Diane Halpern concludes from her review of the research: "In general, the majority of the evidence tends to support the idea that females are more verbally precocious than males, but the effects are small and probably of little practical significance" (Halpern, 2000, p. 97). In addition, the math differences are not universal—recall that in China women constitute a large proportion of the professional engineers and scientists. Therefore, a lesson from sex difference studies is that although real trait and ability differences are small, stereotyped perceptions of differences run strong. In a study of 39 countries around the world, researchers found that people identified females as higher on the so-called interpersonal traits (e.g., nurture, warmth), males higher on instrumental traits (goal focus, assertiveness). Based on this, the sex differences in ability and traits should decrease as we (1) improve our educational approaches and (2) break down our stereotypes. Mediocre educational practices and persistent stereotypes are probably the primary causes of sex differences. However, this *may* hold true more for cognitive differences (e.g., spatial ability) than for trait differences (e.g., aggression vs. nurture). Halpern (p. 328) proposes a "biopsychosocial process" model for gender development. In this model, different influences on individual development (family, etc.) have larger or smaller impact at different ages relative to each of the other influences. As you can see in figure 13.4,

> "These data do not support the notion of a smarter sex.... We cannot afford to write off anyone or allow group membership to limit talent development.... Researchers and others need to provide all children with opportunities to develop [skills in all areas]." (Diane Halpern, 2000, pp. 321–322.)

family has greater influence than hormones in early childhood, but this changes during adolescence. Similarly, the influence of peers increases in adolescence relative to the influence of family, then yields back to family in late middle age. Also, notice the gradual increase in genetic influence over time, as we become more true to our nature. As I once heard Nathan Brody say, "Growing up is becoming more like who we are." Halpern concludes, "Development is always in a context" (p. 329). Figure 13.4 is my adaptation of Halpern's version.

Applications

❶ If you are a female and you must take a math test, try to schedule it during the first two weeks of the menstrual cycle, between the first day of

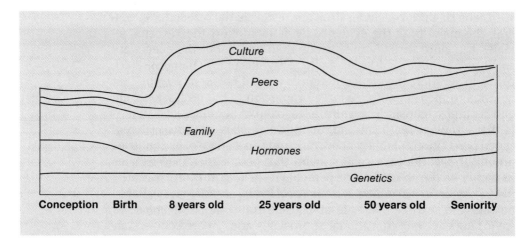

Figure 13.4. The Relative Impact of Different Influences on Human Development over the Lifespan
(Adapted from Halpern, 2000, p. 328.)

your period and ovulation. You will probably achieve higher scores during this time. If you must take a verbal test, such as a graduate oral or written exam, or make a major sales presentation, schedule it during the second two weeks of the menstrual cycle, between ovulation and the beginning of your period. If you must take a test that has both verbal and math components, such as the SAT, GRE, GMAT, or LSAT, schedule it according to which part of the test is your greater priority, math (first half of the cycle) or verbal (second half of the cycle).

❷ If you administer tests—for example, as a human resources selection specialist or a teacher—then be flexible in scheduling the tests, whether with males or females. When possible, permit people to select the time of day and day of the week that best suits them.

❸ The typical school curriculum from kindergarten through adult education is biased toward the female learner, with a predominance of oral and verbal methods and a minimum of visual and hands-on methods. In this environment, the female Talker finds it easier to excel over the male Doer. If you are a teacher or a student, examine your curriculum for its sexual fairness and recommend changes.

❹ Do not administer a timed math test to women (or, actually, to anyone) unless speed at computation is a bona fide occupational qualification.

See Sternberg's definition of intelligence in topic 34.3. He makes a strong case against timed intelligence tests in *The Triarchic Mind* (1988).

❺ If possible, females should put off written reports until the second half of their menstrual cycle, when their verbal ability is higher. *(Contributed by Jane Howard)*

❻ Schedule meetings with men early in the morning when you want alertness and problem-solving ability, late in the afternoon when you want their agreement (males are less aggressive then). *(Contributed by Jane Howard)*

❼ Males should schedule math and spatial tasks early in the day, verbal tasks such as writing and conversation later in the day. *(Contributed by Jane Howard)*

❽ To attract more women into math-intensive careers, find ways to increase the "soft side" of university teaching and laboratory research. For example, make child care and elder care available. Employ collaboration more frequently as a technique (e.g., team teaching, team projects, team research). Emphasize projects and courses that have humanitarian implications. Create support groups across departments. Mathematically and scientifically gifted females tend to be more attracted to medicine and biology where they can work with living creatures; men tend to be more attracted to nonliving things in fields such as physics and engineering (Geary, 1998, p. 329).

❾ It should also be said that having the optimum testosterone level does not insure superior spatial ability. The research suggests one must also have relevant experiences that develop spatial perception and reasoning. Without such experiences (e.g., hunting, fishing, exploring, orienteering), testosterone is necessary, but insufficient, for spatial skill development (Geary, 1998, p. 301). Ensure that your daughters, as well as your sons, experience Lincoln Logs, Erector Sets, Tinkertoys, building blocks, and such manipulative objects, all of which are excellent for learning basic mathematical constructs such as transitivity and associativity. All too often, the traditional girl foregoes the pleasure of such toys, and the only manipulatives (sewing, cooking) come too late to help with mathematical learning in the early grades.

❿ To boost their reading ability, boys need more and earlier practice in learning the correspondence between sounds and letters, which is the essence of the phonics approach to teaching reading. Try games that repeat sounds along with the letters. For example, when we see the letter *p,* I sing or say "Puh-puh-puh pee," or, to the tune of "I like to live in America" (from *West Side Story*), "Puhpuhpuh, puhpuhpuh, puh puh PEE; puhpuhpuh, puhpuhpuh, puh puh PEE."

⑪ To improve their math word problem–solving ability, girls need training in how to visualize the elements of the word problem. For example, give them this word problem: "You have three buckets: a 2-gallon bucket, a 3-gallon bucket, and a 5-gallon bucket. You also have a water source. How can you end up with exactly 1 gallon in the 2-gallon bucket?" Then help them figure out how to draw the problem on paper or board: three buckets of proportionately differing sizes. They can then point to the proper bucket at each step along the way, even drawing additional buckets to help keep track of their progress.

⑫ For a stimulating and provocative discussion of the relationship between sex and proficiency in math or science, study the debate between the two Harvard psychologists Steven Pinker and Elizabeth Spelke at www.edge.org/3rd_culture/debate05/debate05_index.html. You might also read Spelke's argument against innate sex differences in cognitive ability in the December 2005 issue of *American Psychologist.*

TOPIC 13.7 | **Vision**

Research has shown that male-differentiated brains have better visual discrimination in the blue end of the spectrum, female-differentiated brains in the red end. Males have better visual discrimination in bright light (day vision), females in subdued light (night vision).

Applications

❶ Where extremely fine color discrimination is necessary, allow for the fatigue, error, and slowdown that might accompany an attempt to concentrate on an end of the spectrum that is not your "natural" end.

❷ When testing employees for color discrimination, be aware that you will rarely find employees who are equally strong at both ends of the spectrum.

❸ Females may be safer drivers at night, although I have not seen any hard data to support this.

❹ Be aware in workplace design that brightly lit areas are more fatiguing for females and dimly lit areas for males. Allow variations in brightness throughout the facility as much as possible. Vary lighting in break areas to give individuals a choice.

❺ In a romantic setting, don't assume that the male is unromantic because he wants more light or that the female is romantic because she is comfortable with less light. Females can see better with less light than males.

TOPIC 13.8   Space

Studies show that females are more comfortable being in close physical proximity with other females than males with other males. (See also topic 32.12.) As a rule, males require more work space than females. However, this is not a reason for discriminating with regard to space. Understand that accepting a smaller space should not necessarily be taken as a sign of low ambition; some people, especially those with female-differentiated brains, are very comfortable with less space. Conversely, wanting a larger space should not necessarily be taken as a power play; some people, especially those with male-differentiated brains, become uncomfortable, even stressed-out, in a smaller space. It is possible that this difference was genetically favored when women were primarily cave dwellers during the day and men roamed the fields as hunters.

Applications

❶ Allow males to create a comfortable space between themselves and other males.

❷ Trust people to tell you how much space they need in order to be comfortable.

❸ When overnight accommodations are necessary, let people choose single or double rooms if possible. Females will generally feel more comfortable sharing a room than males. *(Contributed by Jane Howard)*

TOPIC 13.9   **The Effects of Odors on Females**

Females are more sensitive to odors than males. It takes a stronger odor to get a typical man's attention than a woman's. This is probably a genetic artifact of natural selection for mothers, who must be alert to olfactory indicators of their infants' distress. This gender difference has been definitely established (remembering, of course, that exceptions are common), but its cause is speculative. Researchers believe that it is related to higher levels of estrogen.

A long-suspected phenomenon among women—*menstrual synchrony*—has been confirmed by researchers at the University of Chicago (*Nature,* March 12, 1998). The senior researcher, Martha McClintock, finds that *pheromones*—odorless and colorless scents found among animals and humans—from one female affect the timing of menstruation of other females. Taking cotton swabs from the underarms of women at different times during menstruation, researchers found that pheromones from specific phases affect other women differently. For example, extracts from the *follicular phase* (early in the cycle) shortened others' cycles, whereas extracts from the *ovarian phase* (midcycle) lengthened others' cycles and those from the *luteal phase* (after ovulation) had no effect. This finding is likely to be the signal for an intense new line of human pheromone research with implications for mate selection, xenophobia, nepotism, dominance struggles, and friendships. (See the related discussion on histocompatibility complexes in topic 14.1.)

Applications

❶ Be sensitive to the fact that some odors may be more offensive to women than to men. They do so because the female-differentiated brain has more alert smell receptors than the male-differentiated brain. Women are not being stereotypically prissy any more than men are being stereotypically macho when they are aggressive—this behavior is a result of their different hormonal makeups.

❷ There are many tasks that require an acute sense of smell: cooking; chemical analysis; safety inspections, such as those for gas leaks; quality inspections, including perfume testing; even lie detection, which measures perspiration. Consider that females as a group have more sensitivity in olfactory detection.

❸ Be aware that it is normal for women who are living in close proximity (roommates, office mates) to experience a convergence in the timing of menstruation. Research is under way to find possible applications for infertility and birth control.

TOPIC 13.10 Gender Differences in Taste

Female-differentiated brains are more sensitive to sweet tastes, male-differentiated brains to salty tastes. Hence, the typical female requires more salt to satisfy her and the typical male needs more sugar. A classic example is my wife's tendency to oversalt food when she cooks and my tendency to oversweeten hot chocolate when I make it from scratch. Notice how, generally, women tend to shake more salt on their meals than men, whereas men tend to add more sugar to their coffee or tea (if they sweeten it at all).

Applications

❶ In food preparation, female chefs should take care not to oversalt their dishes and male chefs not to oversweeten theirs. Diners can always add salt or sugar to suit their taste.

❷ Don't be offended if you're female and a male adds sugar to your prepared dish, or if you're male and a female adds salt!

TOPIC 13.11 Automatization

Males and females who are injected with extra testosterone show an ability to persevere at *automatized behaviors*. These are behaviors that do not demand excessive mental or physical exertion once they have been learned but are subject to fatigue effects over time (Moir and Jessel, 1991). Examples include solving basic arithmetic problems, walking, talking, maintaining balance (for example, standing guard), maintaining observation (being a military sniper or a quality inspector), and writing. Injected groups show a lower decline in skills as the day wears on. Those who are not injected get tired and make more mistakes. The *automatizers,* with extra testosterone, tend to be more focused and single-minded and are more often associated with success and upward mobility. Estrogen is known to suppress automatized behavior, especially just after puberty, when girls' academic performance tends to decline. Boys begin to exhibit automatized behaviors during puberty, when their system ratchets to a new level of testosterone.

Applications

1 Females who are engaging in automatized behaviors will require more frequent breaks to maintain a given skill level.

2 Females can be more consistently productive in nonautomatized areas—for example, sales, research and development, supervision, training and development, planning, analysis, and creative activities.

3 Promotional policies should not be based exclusively on performance at automatized skills. Management tasks do not consist of automatized behavior, so promoting those who are good at it incurs the risk of creating managers who convert their success at these behaviors into inappropriate management behaviors, such as supervising too closely and pushing, pulling, or riding employees without letup. Nonautomatizers are more likely to develop effective coaching, counseling, and listening skills.

A Final Word on Sex and Gender

The final word has not been written on the causes and changeability of sex and gender differences. Keep in mind that all this research deals with averages and that individuals do not obey the law of averages—only groups do. So when we think of sex and gender differences, we should not automatically think that individual X can be described by those differences. It is likely, but not a given, that he or she can be. The fact that men, on average, are not as nurturing as women does not mean that I am either low in nurture or less nurturing than most women. In fact, I love babies and can't resist the opportunity to hold them and go "goo-goo." This does not make me a woman, but it does suggest that I have a "feminine" dimension to my personality.

In a well-written article using rigorous standards, Amy Eagly (1995) of Purdue University wrote in the *American Psychologist* that eight gender differences in behavior pass her test for significance: (1) mental rotation (a type of mental spatial manipulation), (2) facial expressiveness, (3) frequency of filled pauses in speech, (4) incidence of masturbation, (5) attitudes toward casual sexual intercourse, (6) tender-mindedness, (7) nurturant tendencies, and (8) the velocity, distance, and accurateness of throwing a ball. All other gender differences, she finds, are too small to affect our notion of what we view as purely feminine or masculine. Although these differences form the basis of a stereotype, they are not consistently present in only one sex. So even though most women exhibit more expressive faces, there will always be someone like Robin Williams. And although most men have more casual attitudes toward sexual intercourse, there will always be someone like Erica Jong.

SUGGESTED RESOURCES

Bem, S. L. (1993). *The Lenses of Gender: Transforming the Debate on Sexual Inequality.* New Haven: Yale University Press.

Blum, D. (1997). *Sex on the Brain: The Biological Differences Between Men and Women.* New York: Viking.

Caplan, P. J., M. Crawford, J. S. Hyde, and J. T. E. Richardson (1997). *Gender Differences in Human Cognition.* New York: Oxford University Press.

Crawford, M. (1995). *Talking Difference: On Gender and Language.* Thousand Oaks, Calif.: Sage.

Geary, D. C. (1998). *Male, Female: The Evolution of Human Sex Differences.* Washington, D.C.: American Psychological Association.

Halpern, D. F. (2000). *Sex Differences in Cognitive Abilities* (3rd ed.). Mahwah, N.J.: Lawrence Erlbaum.

Maccoby, E. (1998). *The Two Sexes: Growing Up Apart, Coming Together.* Boston: Belknap Press of Harvard.

Moir, A., and D. Jessel (1991). *Brain Sex: The Real Difference Between Men and Women.* New York: Carol Publishing/Lyle Stuart.

14

Love and Relationships

The Wiring Is the Name of the Game

*L*ove and relationships have always been associated with chemistry. Hence, the expression that two people do or do not have "good chemistry together." From Bacchus (alcohol) to Romeo and Juliet (a "potion"), chemicals have enhanced or detracted from the quality of relationships.

> **❝ There are two kinds of sex—for babies, and fore play. ❞**
>
> —P. J. Howard

With the recent "Decade of the Brain" (1990–1999) still fresh in their minds, neuroscientists have enumerated some of the specific roles that chemicals play in the game of love. Here is a partial listing of the "chemicals of desire":

- *Nitric oxide (NO).* Increases blood flow and vessel dilation (associated, e.g., with tumescence).

- *Vasoactive intestinal polypeptide (VIP).* Effects similar to nitric oxide.

- *Pheromones.* Armpit-produced scents that elicit unconscious sexual desire.

- *Epinephrine and norepinephrine.* Cause the heart to beat faster and enhance the effects of NO and VIP.

- *Estrogen.* Creates desire in women (and possibly men) by triggering dopamine release.

- *Dopamine.* This critical ingredient causes the individual to fantasize and consider the possibilities latent in a sexual situation.

- *Serotonin.* Too much before sexual situations tends to suppress sexual arousal, but successful sexual activity results in the pleasureable effects of increased serotonin levels that orgasm entails.

- *Phenylethylamine (PEA).* Associated with feelings of well-being and romance; levels increase during orgasm and ovulation and after exercise; found in chocolate.

- *Alpha melanocyte polypeptide (AMP).* Associated with the beginning of an erection and the heightening of a male's interest in sex.

- *Oxytocin.* Makes possible pelvic contractions during female orgasm; contributes to bonding; often referred to as the "trust" hormone.

- *Testosterone.* Creates desire in both men and women; low testosterone associated in both sexes with minimization or absence of sexual desire.

Now, those are the chemical pieces of the love and relationships puzzle. Let's take a look at how they fit together.

| TOPIC 14.1 | **The Ideal Mate: Factors Influencing Partner Selection** |

Love! What is it? First, it is practically universal. William Jankowiak of the University of Nevada, Las Vegas, and Edward Fischer of Tulane University studied 166 cultures and concluded that at least 147 of them showed evidence of the existence of romantic love. Although it is prevalent around the world, romantic love is not limited to marriage, and marriage is not limited to romantic love; many cultures permit and even encourage arranged marriages.

Several factors appear to influence the initial attraction. Let's start with the nose. Women are more sensitive to pheromones than men, and that includes the odors emitted by one's *major histocompatibility complex* (MHC). The MHC is a reflection of one's immune system, and, evolutionarily, we have learned to be attracted to persons with immune systems unlike our own. Remember, in diversity is survival. Swiss researchers report (*Proceedings of the Royal Society of London,* 1995) that females have clear preferences for certain male body odors. Namely, they prefer the smell emitted by men with an MHC that is most different from their own—in this case, opposites attract. During higher estrogen lev-

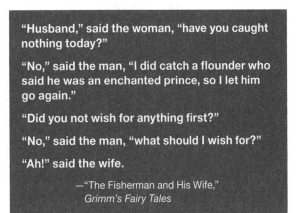

"Husband," said the woman, "have you caught nothing today?"

"No," said the man, "I did catch a flounder who said he was an enchanted prince, so I let him go again."

"Did you not wish for anything first?"

"No," said the man, "what should I wish for?"

"Ah!" said the wife.

—"The Fisherman and His Wife,"
Grimm's Fairy Tales

els, a woman's favorable response to a man with a dissimilar MHC is strongest, thus increasing the chance that she will choose to mate with someone who can increase immune system diversity in her offspring. A complicating factor is that women on the birth control pill prefer men with similar MHCs. So, when a woman who is on the pill unwittingly falls in love with a partner with the same MHC, marries, then goes off the pill when conception no longer needs to be avoided, she will wonder how she got attached to the smelly partner beside her. Interestingly, MHC-dissimilar couples can conceive in two months, compared with an average of five months for MHC-similar couples. Moreover, MHC-dissimilar couples have fewer unaided abortions. Nature appears to have built in a romantic preference for strangers.

Speaking of strangers, Fisher (2004, p. 102) relates that when children live together (as in an Israeli kibbutz), something happens physiologically between the ages of three and six to prevent, or at least minimize, the chance of these individuals forming romantic bonds later in life. Vamoose if you want me to love you!

A third factor was identified by Galdino Pranzarone, a psychologist at Roanoke College in Salem, Virginia, who found that people have established an image of their ideal lover and ideal love behavior patterns by the age of 10 (see the discussion of schemas in topics 21.4 and 28.3).

A fourth factor comes from the anthropologists and sociologists. David Buss (1994), with a group of international collaborators, polled 10,047 men and women from 33 countries across six continents and five islands in an effort to determine what people want in the ideal mate. Buss, who was schooled in the evolutionary biology tradition that sees contemporary behavior as the result of natural selection, found that after intelligence and kindness (which both sexes ranked as the top feature of the ideal mate), men preferred women who were physically beautiful and youthful over women with high earning potential, whereas women preferred good earning capacity and ambition over physical attractiveness. Buss (1992) reports on a study of just U.S. couples, and found that males and females alike prefer mates who "act nice" and who "have a sense of humor." These two behaviors fit nicely into the more global categories of "kind" and "intelligent."

The fifth factor is symmetry. We tend to associate beauty with perfect symmetry. So much so, in fact, that the cosmetics and fashion industries have flourished primarily as a way for women, in particular, to disguise their asymmetrical features. Not only is symmetry associated with beauty—symmetry is associated with several advantages with respect to survival:

- Symmetrical women and men have better immune response.

- Women have more orgasms when with a symmetrical partner.

- Women retain more sperm from symmetrical partners.

- Men looking at images of more symmetrical women show higher increases in testosterone and dopamine.

- Symmetrical men begin having intercourse on average four years earlier, and they have more partners and more extramarital affairs.

- Women's hands, breasts, and ears are more symmetrical during ovulation.

The sixth factor—this one has to do with men's perception of women—is waist-to-hip ratio. A waist to hip ratio of about 70 percent defines the standard. For example, a 28-inch waist paired with a 40-inch hip would yield a precise 70 percent. Here's what we know about women with such ratios. They

- are likely to have babies.

- have higher estrogen relative to testosterone.

- find it easier to get pregnant.

- get pregnant earlier.

- have fewer miscarriages.

- have fewer chronic diseases and personality disorders.

Seventh, what is ideal to a person can depend both on the time of the month and the goals of the individual, as reported in two studies by Dr. David Perrett, psychologist at the University of St. Andrews in Scotland (*Nature,* June 24, 1999). In the first study, 39 Japanese women were shown composite photographs of "blended" faces of men that showed more masculine (jutting chin, bushy eyebrows, square jaw) faces and more feminine faces. Women on birth control pills selected the more feminine faces consistently, daily throughout the month, but women allowed to ovulate showed a marked preference for the "masculinized" faces during the week surrounding ovulation, the time of greatest fertility. In the second study, 65 British women were asked to use a computer "face designer" to compose their ideal man's face, both for the short term and for the long term. The task was repeated with the same women once weekly for a month. When asked to compose the short-term face (for a "fling" experience), like the Japanese women they preferred the more masculinized faces during ovulation, but when they were asked to compose long-term faces, their compositions were more decidedly feminine, regardless of time of month. Dr. Perrett concluded that women prefer more masculine faces on the spur of the moment but more feminine ones for the long haul. This mixed-mating strategy, it is thought, reflects an evolutionary tendency to maximize genetic contributions during sex for procreation (i.e., the more "masculine" faces) and to maximize nurturing contributions for the long-term task of child rearing and relating to one's mate.

In summary, let's take a look at a scientific checklist based on the work of Geoffrey Miller and Peter Todd (1998). Their conclusions are based on the above studies, as well as on other research in cognitive science and evolutionary psychology. According to their studies, four traits dominate mate selection: physical attractiveness, intelligence, social status, and personality. By enumerating the specific indicators under each trait heading, one can create one's very own customized checklist for selecting a mate.

I have taken their recommendations and organized them into a checklist for your consideration (see table 14.1). Miller and Todd, further demonstrating their commitment to a scientific approach,

Table 14.1. Checklist for Mate Selection

Actual Trait Exhibited	Trait Perceived	Indicators	Score (10 = best)
1. Health and fertility	Physical attractiveness	a. Face symmetry b. Waist-to-hip ratio c. Height d. Facial "averageness" ("10" is well above average)	_____ _____ _____ _____
2. Neuro-physiological efficiency	Intelligence	e. Vocabulary f. Wit or humor g. World knowledge h. Creative story-telling ability	_____ _____ _____ _____
3. Provisioning ability and resources	Social status	i. Education j. Job status k. Income l. Possessions and fashion	_____ _____ _____ _____
4. Capacity for cooperative relationship	Personality	m. Kindness n. Adaptability o. Generosity p. Morality	_____ _____ _____ _____
		Total =	_____

Based on Miller and Todd (1998). You may modify the indicators in the third column to suit your personal idiosyncrasies. Maximum point value for these 16 indicators would be 160.

suggest a specific way to set the ideal mate for an individual. Taking their cue from statistical search theory, they suggest that one first estimate the total number of potential mates one will encounter during the period of exploration. Second, make a commitment to resist choosing the first 37 percent of those candidates. From the first 37 percent, fix firmly in mind the best candidate from among them. Then, determine to select as your mate the next candidate who exceeds that ideal! Now, I call that the rational approach. . . .

Helen Fisher (2004) reports that, while viewing photos of their love partners, men's brains activate in areas associated with visual stimuli and sexual arousal, women's brains in regions associated with attention, emotion, and recall. This suggests, in the final analysis, that men are more influenced by appearances, women by memories.

The game gets complicated. What you see in your ideal mate may not all be there. William Tooke of the State University of New York at Plattsburgh found that during courtship, men tend to exaggerate their earning potential and ambition, women their youthfulness and beauty, each relaxing into their more natural levels of ambition and appearance after attachment has been secured. Caveat emptor!

Applications

1 If ambition or appearance is important to you in a mate, be aware of the possibility that your intended is deceiving you in order to win your attachment. Look to the past for his or her natural behavior by interviewing friends and perusing yearbooks.

2 Talk with your intended in order to confirm whether his or her levels of ambition or appearance are authentic or a soon-to-be-abandoned enticement.

3 If you are liberated from these classic needs of your animal and primitive ancestors, then smile at the antics of your anachronistic cousins and get on with your life.

4 If you are a woman taking the birth control pill, before you become irrevocably attracted to someone, spend some time with that person while you're off the pill to ensure histocompatibility. Get a true whiff before you take a hard grip!

TOPIC 14.2   **Lust, Romance, and Attachment: An Overview**

Helen Fisher (2004) identifies three phases, or manifestations, of love: lust, romance, and attachment. Each is an independent system with its own neurotransmitters and associated neural networks. *Lust* is simply a momentary urge for sexual gratification, with no intention of permanence. *Romance* is the "elation and obsession of 'being in love'" (p. xii) that is focused on one individual. *Attachment* entails feelings of "calm, peace, and security one often has for a long-term mate" that evolved to support rearing children. The three are independent— each can exist without the others occurring either previously or concurrently—but the possibility of a 1-2-3 sequence is implied.

For example, sexual intercourse (lust) and needs for fidelity (attachment) are less important to the person "in love" (romance) than the emotional satisfaction that accompanies the conviction that the intensity of one's partner's feelings for one match the intensity of one's feelings for that partner—that is, you love me as much as I love you, you need me as much as I need you, you want to be with me as much as I want to be with you. As Fisher writes (p. 22), "The lover aches to have his or her love returned." In a survey of people who identified themselves as "in love," over three-fourths of both men and women responded that knowing their partner's love matched the intensity of their own was more important than having sex with them.

Let us consider lust, romance, and attachment as the "alphabet" of love, with various combinations of these three systems explaining the many kinds of loving relationships found in everyday life, including film, television, theatre, and literature. John Alan Lee (1973) has examined these many different forms of love and settled upon six. By closely reading his definitions of these six love styles, we can see how each can be explained (see Fisher, 2004, p. 95) as a combination of Fisher's three types of love, similar to selecting letters (three love types) to form words (six love styles):

- *Agape.* Selfless, spiritual, giving

- *Eros.* Passionate, confident, self-disclosing; enjoys intimacy

- *Pragma.* Requires the partner and relationship to satisfy certain preexisting conditions

Table 14.2. The Alphabet of Love: How Lust, Romance, and Attachment Relate to Lee's Six "Love Styles"

Style	Type: Lust	Romance	Attachment	Comments*
Agape: unselfish, giving, and spiritual			•	Big Five: A+C+
Eros: passionate and devoted	•	•		
Pragma: practical relationship that expects balance or perks and responsibility			•	Big Five: N-O-A-
Storge: companions without emotion; sibling/avuncular love			•	Big Five: N-A+
Ludus: playful, as in playing the field	•			
Mania: possessive and obsessive		•		

* In order to discriminate between Storge, Agape, and Pragma, all three of which build primarily on Attachment, we have associated each of them with their most likely Big Five traits. See chapter 33 for more information on personality traits.

- **_Storge._** Companionable, friendship-oriented, reliable

- **_Ludus._** Fun, exciting, non-self-disclosing; prefers multiple partners

- **_Mania._** Dependent, jealous, conflicted; yearns for love but experiences disappointment

People with the first four styles—Agape, Eros, Pragma, and Storge—tend to prefer mates with the same style: for example, Eros mates with Eros. The last two styles, however, are a bit trickier; Ludus and Mania tend to mate with other styles. This makes sense. If both partners avoid intimacy and long-term relationships, as in the case of Ludus, there is less chance of the couple staying together than there would be if at least one member of the pair were less avoidant. Also, if both partners are jealous and dependent, as in the case of Mania, there is less chance that they will stay together than if one partner is more secure.

Phillip Shaver, a psychologist at the University of California, Davis, has conducted extensive research on love, or attachment, styles (see Mallandain and Davies, 1994). By studying twins in the California Twin

Registry, Shaver has concluded that love style is determined primarily by environmental influences.

Applications

❶ Know your attachment style and consider the attachment styles of people with whom you find yourself becoming serious. The likelihood of long-term satisfaction is increased when your styles are compatible, as outlined above. Imagine Storge partnering with Pragma only to find after four years when the "amphetamines" wear off (see topic 14.4) that the companion is no longer available and Storge must look elsewhere for friendship while Pragma pursues his or her own agenda.

❷ Consider conflicts in relationships, when they occur, as more likely to be the result of stylistic incompatibilities in values and expectations than to be intentionally hurtful. Rather than saying, "You don't love me anymore," consider saying, "Your style of loving is different from mine."

❸ Understand that not all persons have the same predominant need for love; some pursue only lust, others romance, yet others attachment. Understand your own needs, and make sure that your partner matches them.

❹ With apologies to Pittsburgh, consider love as something like a Three Rivers Stadium in that the three love "systems"—lust, romance, and attachment—reflect the movement of three sets of chemicals, each set able to interact with the others. In the next three sections, we will explore these three "rivers" in more depth.

TOPIC 14.3   **Lust: The Neurochemistry of the One-Night Stand**

Lust is the desire for sexual release. It is associated with increased levels of testosterone in both sexes. In men, testosterone is highest in the early morning and in the autumn, in women around the time of ovulation. Unlike romance and attachment, when sexual release is found, the desire, in concert with falling testosterone levels, fades, only to rise again when testosterone levels rise. What sparks such rises? In men, it is typically something visual: a provocative décolletage, a pinup, a flash of leg. In women, it is typically something romantic—words and situations that suggest affection and commitment. In addition, both sexes can find lust triggered by danger, novelty, the five senses, music, romantic settings, and direct approaches (Medina, 2000, p. 83).

Applications

❶ If you are the initiator of a lustful encounter, do what you can to communicate to your intended partner the nature of your attraction—a momentary attraction with no strings attached. All the same, be aware that, either for you or for your partner, lust can phase into romance or attachment.

❷ If you are concerned that you initiate lustful encounters too often/too indiscriminately, be aware of the time of day or situation in which you are most likely to feel the urge. Then, plan to avoid the urge by avoiding those situations and/or occupying yourself with otherwise engaging activity—exercise, reading, fishing, and so forth.

❸ If you are on the receiving end of what appears to be a lustful encounter, don't be deceived as to the likelihood that this will be "the one." Enter with the conviction that there's no better than a 50-50 chance that this lustful partner will transform into a romancer or long-hauler. If it doesn't happen, don't take it personally. You're up against genes and chemistry working within a body that does not have completely free will!

❹ For an intriguing description of the physiology of sexual desire, see John Medina's fascinating treatment (2000) in chapter 2 of *The Genetic Inferno*. He incorporates into his discussion four physiological systems, 11 regions of the brain, hundreds of genes, and over 30 neurotransmitters, enzymes, hormones, and other chemicals.

TOPIC 14.4   **Romance: The Neurochemistry of Consuming Adoration**

Dopamine, norepinephrine, testosterone, phenylethylamine (PEA), and serotonin levels are associated with romantic love. Dopamine feeds the fantasy, the imagination, leading to a kind of love-sickness in which the imagination just can't rest. During romance, dopamine increases specifically in the brain's *nucleus accumbens* and *caudate nucleus,* and in the *ventral tegmental area,* the region that forms the reward network (referred to as the *mesolimbic reward system*) that is associated with cravings and addictions. In animal studies, increasing dopamine levels serves as a love potion, causing the subject to fall head over heels for whomever happens to be nearby at the time, just like Titania's hard fall for the donkey-headed Bottom after falling under the spell of Puck's potion in Shakespeare's *Midsummer Night's Dream.* As Fisher (2004) writes, "All of the major addictions are associated with elevated levels of dopamine. Is romantic love an addiction? Yes. . . . " Dopamine is intimately involved with the brain's reward system, and failure to achieve one's romantic love interests serves to ramp up dopamine levels even more, such that the cravings become more intense with the unavailability of one's beloved.

As dopamine levels increase, two other chemicals are affected. Dopamine typically drives up testosterone levels, thereby increasing sexual desire, and dopamine metabolizes into norepinephrine. Norepinephrine supports this imagination-run-wild by providing increased energy and a sense of euphoria, like being on uppers. Who needs sleep and food when all you can think about is your beloved? As norepinephrine levels rise, details of the lover's experience with the beloved are imprinted in long-term memory, because norepinephrine serves as a kind of "fixer" to establish memories, like fixers in old-time photographic darkrooms. So, with romance, it all starts with rising dopamine, which leads to increases in norepinephrine and possibly in testosterone.

An interesting consequence of this chemical confluence is that serotonin levels plummet, causing a discomfiture akin to that of obsessive-compulsive disorder, in which low levels of serotonin permit the obsessive quality of romance to persist, dreams to arise, and business as usual to be forgotten.

Now, this neural romance network is strikingly similar to the network that Dean Hamer identified as the neural underpinnings of spirituality (which he calls *self-transcendence*; see topic 38.5). In both cases—romance and self-transcendence—what Gerald Edelman (1992) calls *basic* or *primary consciousness* (knowing who, where, and when you are) gives way to *higher* or *secondary consciousness* (losing your orientation and being overtaken by the focus of your will or attention). Both of these processes are similar (if not identical) to Csikszentmihalyi's *flow* concept (see topic 37.2), which he describes as the state of total absorption in the activity of the moment to the extent that one loses one's sense of time and space. An attempt to put all of these processes into some perspective is made in topic 37.4.

Applications

❶ Understand that being in love is like an addiction, and that you need to find a way to take objective assessment of the situation.

❷ If you are uncertain whether your beloved returns your feelings, you may use the strategies suggested at topic 14.6 for maintaining relationships, in hopes that maintenance behavior will bring her or him around.

❸ On the other hand, if you get the clear message that your love is not mutual, realize that you need to cure yourself of your addiction. Try the strategies for overcoming rejection suggested in topic 14.14.

TOPIC 14.5 | **Attachment: The Neurochemistry of the Long-Haul Relationship**

It is more common for romance to lead to lust than the other way around. Attachment, however, is another matter. Attachment is for the long haul and may proceed with or without lust or romance. Vasopressin and oxytocin are the chemicals of attachment. Produced in the hypothalamus and the gonads of both sexes, vasopressin and oxytocin are known as the "satisfaction hormones" or the "cuddle chemicals" (LeDoux, 2002, p. 89) and are associated with bonding and exclusivity in relationships. LeDoux points out that oxytocin enhances bonding only in females, whereas the parallel process in males is enhanced by vasopressin. Both are dependent on the presence of their sex-appropriate hormones, estrogen and testosterone, respectively (p. 232). Tom Insel and Larry Young, neuroscientists at Emory University, report (in *Nature,* August 19, 1999) that it is not just the amount of vasopressin present that makes for monogamy, it is the relative number of vasopressin receptors. By taking the gene for vasopressin receptors from prairie voles and activating it in mice, the researchers were able to change the mice from their well-known polygamous patterns to a pattern which, if not strictly monogamous, was characterized by an atypical (for male mice) amount of affiliative activity with the female. Perhaps a touch of vasopressin will make homebodies of us all.

Elevated during sexual intercourse (especially as the nipples and genitals are touched), and especially at orgasm, these chemicals create the sense of closeness that follows intercourse. In addition, they are released during birth and during breastfeeding. And natural evolution has introduced a healthy irony here: as the cuddle chemicals increase, testosterone is typically at minimum. With true attachment comes decreased desire and hence decreased need for straying to satisfy lust. When a man holds an infant, testosterone falls. But in an often cruel alternate scenario, when testosterone rises, the cuddle chemicals tend to recede. So when the mate finds stimulating circumstances away from the life partner, best close one's eyes, about face, and remove oneself lest the testosterone rise and the cuddle chemicals go bye-bye. In passing, recall the animals who exhibit lifelong attachment with no roaming (e.g., the male sparrow): when experimenters inject them with testosterone, they abandon their commitment and look for the first available sex partner. Just as the chemicals of attachment can damp down lust, the chemicals of lust can lessen attachment (p. 91). Thus, a role for choice and intention. Infidelity is not all about hormones, but one must understand what the hormones are doing.

> Animals with similar body size for both sexes tend to be monogamous, evolutionarily related to the ability of the two sexes to swap functions. Bone records from 300,000 years ago show male human skeletons that are twice the size of female skeletons. We appear to be headed toward being a more monogamous species.

Earlier, we said these three systems were independent. Deborah Blum (1997) writes (pp. 94 ff.) about experimenters with prairie voles who, by manipulating the appropriate chemicals, can modify behavior so that voles may or may not play around, and may or may not be monogamous, resulting in four conditions that can be changed with the appropriate injection(s):

1. Married for life with some playing around

2. Married for life with no playing around

3. Unattached for life with playing around

4. Unattached for life with no playing around

Mary Ainsworth (1978) and John Bowlby (1965) found that in their first year infants grow into one of three ways of relating—*secure, anxious,* or *avoidant*—based on how their parents or caregivers treat them. The secure child sees the mother as supportive and feels free to explore the world, the anxious child views the mother as an unpredictable caregiver and commits his or her life to earning the mother's love, and the avoidant child sees the mother as rejecting and consequently discounts his or her own needs. It would appear that the *anxious* attachment style would be characteristic of those of us with varying or inadequate levels of oxytocin or vasopressin, the *avoidant* style associated with consistently low levels of these attachment chemicals.

Donald Kiesler (1996) produced a definitive review of the literature on relationships. He identified two crucial principles for their long-term viability, whether marital or otherwise: the *interpersonal reflex* (p. 6) and the *behavior concordance model* (p. 49). The interpersonal reflex principle states that "any interpersonal act is designed to elicit from a respondent reactions that confirm, reinforce, or validate the actor's self-presentation and that make it more likely that the actor will continue to emit similar interpersonal acts" (p. 6). When Neil Diamond laments, "You don't give me flowers anymore," he is revealing that either (1) he is no longer behaving in a way that encourages the woman to continue giving him flowers, or (2) she has given up on him as a mate and is focusing elsewhere. In either case, things need fixing.

The behavior concordance model has established that "individuals will feel pleasant affect when they behave consistently with their traits" (p. 49) and unpleasant affect when they behave inconsistently with their traits. Have you ever heard of people who were "not happy unless they were unhappy"? Pity the worrier who has nothing to worry about, the gregarious talker who has no ears around, the ambitious worker who has no goal. They are unhappy campers. The relevance to relationships is this: to maximize the chances of your happiness and the happiness of your mate, ensure that you validate the core behaviors (traits, values, interests, attitudes, and skills) of your mate and that your mate validates yours. More important, early in the relationship, learn what these core behaviors are and decide whether you feel good about validating them for a lifetime.

Applications

❶ Be careful that you don't validate someone's behavior unintentionally; you may dig yourself into such a deep hole that you can't get out. A friend faked orgasm with her mate for years. The consequence? He didn't develop as a lover, and she grew resentful.

❷ On the other hand, be careful that you don't invalidate someone's behavior that you wish to maintain. Avoid saying "You shouldn't have done that" when your meaning is "Thank you!" because the other person may, in fact, stop doing that. Or if you wonder why a friend hasn't asked you back for dinner, look for the possibility that you neglected to confirm your enjoyment of the last dinner (by returning the favor, taking a house gift, writing a note, mentioning it favorably at a later date, and so on).

❸ If you are in the beginning phases of a relationship, romantic, work, or otherwise, and you know that you want the relationship to be long-term, learn all you can about the other person's core values and behaviors and share as much of your core values and behaviors as you can. This might not seem important during the honeymoon or "amphetamine" phase, but it makes all the difference in the world when, after the initial euphoria wears off, you are a Willie Nelson groupie left to live life with a Mozart maniac, or a Sierra Club enthusiast tied to an nonrecycler who drives a gas guzzler.

TOPIC 14.6   Maintaining Relationships

We have emphasized that males are wired to do and achieve, females to talk and nurture (Moir and Jessel, 1991). Expecting a male to talk, and only talk, can be highly uncomfortable for the male and rather unproductive as well. Expecting a female to engage in an activity without talking can be equally uncomfortable and unproductive for the female. In order to keep communication between males and females at the maximum, both should attempt to initiate serious conversation when the male is engaged in some form of physical activity, such as walking, trimming his fingernails, or gardening. In a scene from the movie *City of Angels,* the doctor friend of Meg Ryan, advancing his case for a proposal of marriage, recommends that they "get away" for a while. She says, "Why not right now? Let's just spend the next five minutes together, with nothing else on our minds." He says, "Five minutes? Doing what?" As a typical male, he just doesn't get it. She wants to chat intimately with him, but the very thought makes him uncomfortable. He wants to be doing something.

On another front, the University of Washington's John Gottman studied 130 newlyweds for six years to find ways of predicting marital success and failure. A commonsensical finding emerged: men who accepted the influence of their wives, and wives who presented requests, complaints, or suggestions in a warm, even humorous, manner were most likely to be in happy marriages for the long term. The gist of this report (*Journal of Marriage and the Family,* February 1998) is consistent with the behavior common to the midrange of the Accommodation dimension of the Big Five personality model (see chapter 33). In a related finding, Gottman reported that the use of interpersonal listening and communication techniques such as *active listening* were not predictive of marital success. Perhaps this is because therapists teach troubled partners such techniques too late in their downward spiral.

Judith Rich Harris (1998) has found that, by the age of four, children form the ability to attach to someone. If they have no opportunity to form such attachments (with siblings, friends, parents, or other family) and have not therefore exercised their "relationship module" in the brain, then they will have difficulty as adults in forming relationships.

Applications

❶ In most male-female relationships, conflict arises when the female wants to talk and the male wants to act; the classic example is the female preference in lovemaking for greater foreplay and the male preference for immediate release. The solution to this type of conflict is to allow the other person's style to be expressed: the male agrees to talk if he is allowed to continue working in the yard, and the female agrees to work in the yard with him if he will talk with her. Males need to be willing to listen and respond while doing, and females need to be willing to "do" as a stage for talking. For example, a male and female who go to a ball game or museum may discuss family matters during appropriate lulls. Or they may just go for a drive together, with the male driving (doing) while they are talking. An alternative is to set aside exclusive times to talk without doing and vice versa.

❷ Any negotiating team should include females. They provide a willingness to talk and work on relationships that balances the males' desire for a quick fix.

❸ Human resource functions in organizations should include females in decision-making or advisory roles.

❹ One way to get males to talk more is to make something of a game or contest out of it. A traditional male is more likely to engage in talk when he can see communication skills as a set of tools to master. That way he is not just "talking"; he is practicing a skill set.

❺ Neither a doormat nor a deaf ear be. For optimum satisfaction in a long-term relationship, make sure that neither of you gets your way to the exclusion of the other party. Harold Kelley (Kelley and Thibaut, 1978) describes this ideal relationship as "interdependent." Interdependence exists when neither person experiences costs (pain, labor, drudgery) that exceed rewards (life's pleasures).

❻ If you desire a long-term relationship, ensure that you find substantial features about your mate that you respect and admire, so that when the attraction phase wears down after several years, you will still derive your daily dose of endorphins for the long term.

❼ Novelty. Do something new, something exciting or different—the very novelty will increase dopamine levels with their associated tonic effects. Create new memories. Love loves variety.

❽ Sex. Have sexual intercourse in which seminal fluids from a trusted partner are admitted. Seminal fluids contain dopamine, norepinephrine, oxytocin, vasopressin, and testosterone—for all three love chemical groups (lust, romance, and attachment). Plus endorphins!

❾ Space. Don't crowd the other person. Absence of one's beloved heightens dopamine levels and the ensuing sensation of reward expectation.

❿ Danger. Share an experience that has a manageable amount of risk—anything from sailboat racing to hiking the Appalachian Trail.

⓫ For men: talk to your woman, write notes or poems to her, gaze into her eyes, assume a strong posture or pose.

⓬ For women: share activities with your man, stand side by side (don't always insist on eye gazing), appear vulnerable when appropriate (to appeal to many men's need to rescue you).

TOPIC 14.7   **Orgasm**

Not allowed in polite parlor conversation, the topic of quality and quantity of sexual fulfillment is difficult to understand without reading an authoritative resource or searching out a friend or professional who has already studied the subject. Perhaps this humble section of my book will facilitate the quest for knowledge in this much-yearned-for but hard-to-find area of wisdom.

The brain's activation during sexual stimulation is widespread, including the *vagus nerves, the reticular formation, basal ganglia, anterior insular cortex, amygdala, cerebellum,* and *hypothalamus* (see appendix A). In a special section of *Time* magazine (January 19, 2004) devoted to love and romance, writers presented this list (pp. 76–77) of the benefits of frequent sexual orgasm:

- Lowers risk of heart attacks.

- Burns about 200 calories per episode on average.

- Releases endorphins that help with chronic pain problems.

- Reduces vulnerability to depression.

- Calms anxiety.

- Boosts the immune system.

- Releases oxytocin and DHEA that inhibit the development of breast cancers.

- Is associated with increased longevity.

Independent scholar and historian Rachel Maines writes (1999) of the "androcentric" model of sexual relations that has traditionally discounted the need of females for satisfaction in intercourse while affirming the priority of the male's need for satisfaction. This view has been so ingrained that sexually unsatisfied women (most, in the past) had to resort to "hysteria" in order to obtain the respectability of medical intervention. To wit, sexually frustrated wives of the 19th and 20th centuries whose desire for sexual release went unaddressed in the marriage bed gave rise to a set of symptoms then known as hysteria, and now simply known as evidence of sexual frustration—irritability, sleep and appetite disturbance, fainting, fluid retention and associated congestion, muscle spasms, and nervousness (p. 23). Apparently most of these women "hysterics" knew the cause of their problems (husbands who ignored their wives' need for sexual release) and found the only respectable way to obtain sexual release: visit a physician and submit to external massage of the clitoris—that is, assisted masturbation (a task often delegated to a nurse or midwife). Remarkably, after such a "medical" visit, these women returned to their families with grace and equanimity, only to seek further "treatment" at some point in the future. In the middle of the 20th century, with more open acknowledgment of such practices, the "medical treatment" euphemism was dropped and the practice essentially disappeared—along with "hysteria." The Sexual Revolution legitimized masturbation, vibrators, and liberated partners. The illusion that simple male penetration of the vagina could pleasure a woman has given way to the understanding that direct clitoral stimulation is the way of a woman's pleasure.

Applications

1 It is perfectly natural and healthy for a man to bring himself to orgasm through direct self-manipulation, using an appropriate lubricant to avoid penile burn.

2 It is perfectly natural and healthy for a woman to bring herself to orgasm through direct self-manipulation of her clitoris or with the aid of a mechanical device, e.g., a vibrator.

3 To help a woman achieve orgasm, her partner needs to realize that penetration is largely a mythic means, with gentle, steady clitoral stimulation the more efficacious alternative. Be sure to communicate with your partner about what is more pleasing. We can't learn and grow without feedback.

TOPIC 14.8   Jealousy

David Buss (2000b) makes the point that jealousy is different for men and women; men typically become jealous when the woman physically strays, women when the man is emotionally unfaithful. Men interpret women's smiles at them as a come-on; women interpret others' smiles as warmth. Men trigger jealousy in women by making them feel their desirability has diminished, and the jealousy can be assuaged (sometimes) by reaffirming that desirability. Women trigger jealousy in men by making them feel their value as resource provider is inadequate, and can assuage it (sometimes) by affirming their indispensability. Buss maintains that jealousy is a separate emotion, but I sense it is a condition in which all the major negative emotions are activated: fear, anger, depression, disgust, etc. He presents no evidence for its separateness as an emotion.

Application

❶ Women, make him feel indispensable; men, make her feel desirable! Sounds like a great start on a country music song, huh?

TOPIC 14.9   Affairs

There are two aspects of extramarital affairs: the sex act itself and the emotional attachment to another person. Women tend to experience more distress over emotional attachment than to the act itself; the opposite is true for men. Moreover, the woman's reaction to her husband's infidelity is influenced by the menstrual cycle, with higher hormonal levels (during ovulation) engendering more emotional jealousy, and lower hormonal levels (during menstruation) leading to more jealousy of the sexual act itself (Geary, 1998, p. 130).

David Buss (1994) reports that women, 25 percent of whom have extramarital affairs, tend to blame their affairs on dissatisfaction with the marital relationship: they're looking for a replacement. (As a matter of interest, according to Geary [1998, p. 134], when the wife initiates an infidelity, it is more likely to occur at ovulation, when estrogen is at its highest.) Men who have affairs are as likely to feel good about their primary relationship as they are to be unhappy with it. Another sex difference has to do with jealousy. Buss points out that the human female is the only species whose ovulation cannot be observed. Hence, her mate never knows visually when she is fertile. As a result, a man tends to be especially jealous when his woman simply has intercourse with another man, regardless of the seriousness or length of the attachment; if she becomes pregnant, he has no way of knowing whether the child is his, and he risks spending resources on another man's child. (Perhaps in the era of DNA testing, this evolutionary vestige will disappear.) On the other hand, the woman generally cares less if her man has a one-night stand; she is more threatened by a competing serious attachment that could result in her loss of resources. This is all understandable from an evolutionary point of view (D. M. Buss, 1994; H. E. Fisher, 1982, 1995): in the past, the woman needed to keep an extra relationship offstage in case a saber-toothed tiger eliminated her man, yet she fought against her man's keeping up such a relationship for fear that she'd lose her resource provider. The man needed to ensure the survivability of his kind by planting his seed abundantly, but he fought against his woman's exercising her own options, not wanting to rear another man's child. Hence the proverbial double standard.

Applications

❶ If you are a woman, you should understand that, typically, a man's jealousy is triggered not so much by a long-term serious relationship on your part as by the single sex act itself. Consider that your need for an affair may be attributable to dissatisfaction with your marriage. This should be a signal to work on the marriage. Get help.

❷ If you are a man, you should understand that, in most women, jealousy is triggered more strongly by an ongoing relationship on your part than by a one-night stand. If you require any outside relationship, this is a signal that the marriage is in trouble. Get help.

❸ In the case of both men and women, attachment style (see topic 14.2) also plays a part in the need for an intimate relationship with one's partner. For example, if you are a Ludus married to an Eros, you need to give Eros permission to find a deeper relationship elsewhere.

TOPIC 14.10   **The Effects of Marital Discord**

The quality of a marriage affects the parenting of men but not women. When a marriage is deemed unsatisfactory by either a man or a woman, the man is likely to withdraw emotionally or behaviorally from his children, more so toward daughters than toward sons. Women, on the other hand, tend to maintain their level of child involvement regardless of the quality of the marriage (Geary, 1998, p. 107). During adolescence, the consequence of the father's absence affects both sexes in two ways: earlier sexual activity and poorer school performance (p. 114). In addition, the consequence of a father's withdrawal is greater on the son. Adult men who experienced their father's absence show higher levels of the stress hormone cortisol throughout their lifetime, thus affecting general health and exhibiting higher levels of stress throughout the lifespan. As a rule, children reared with both natural parents in a relatively stable home live longer and healthier lives (Geary, 1998, p. 113). On the brighter side for fathers, men who engage in rough-and-tumble play (as well as other, less active play) with their children tend to see their children grow into adulthood with superior emotional control and social skills (p. 115). However, children—girls as well as boys—who experience their mother's absence show elevated levels of cortisol throughout adulthood, more elevated than that of boys who've experienced a father's absence (p. 116).

Application

❶ Mothers *and* fathers, maintain your relationship with your children, in both quantity and quality!

TOPIC 14.11 Sexual Fantasies

Psychologists Harold Leitenberg and Kris Henning of the University of Vermont reported in *Psychological Bulletin* (May 1995) that 95 percent of adults have sexual fantasies and, Freud's views to the contrary notwithstanding, that people with more active sex lives have more fantasies, not the other way around. The median number of daily sexual fantasies for males is seven, five of which are prompted by events (for example, an attractive woman appears on the scene), the other two arising spontaneously from within. For women, the median number is five daily, three from external cues and two from within. Men are more likely to fantasize about having multiple sexual partners, with an average of 1.96 partners per fantasy; women have an average of 1.08 partners per fantasy.

Application

 Accept sexual fantasies as normal and unavoidable.

TOPIC 14.12 | **Personality Traits and Sexual Behavior**

The two most widely researched dimensions of personality are Extraversion (a.k.a. positive emotions) and Need for Stability (a.k.a. neuroticism or emotional stability). (See chapter 33 for further discussion of these dimensions.) G. D. Wilson, in his essay "Personality and Social Behavior" (in Eysenck, 1981), summarized a wide variety of behavioral correlates of personality dimensions. Several of these correlates relate specifically to sexual behaviors. They are listed in table 14.3.

> Note: When you see cross references to other sections of this book, you may benefit from taking time now to read them; they provide information that will deepen your understanding of the current material.

Remember that these associations are not absolutes. Not all highly extraverted persons, for example, demonstrate all the associated behaviors. These are trends, not inevitabilities. It is useful, however, to get a sense of the degree to which one's behavior is typical of that of other people with a similar personality. Many factors can explain exceptions to the trends provided in such tables, including mores, opportunities, incentives, exposure to diverse lifestyles, parenting styles, and limitations resulting from social circumstances.

Application

1 If your partner's sexual behavior is something other than what you prefer, realize that there is a strong likelihood that this difference is attributable to the way your partner's personality is built and is not a reaction to, or judgment of, you. In other words, don't take differences in sexual preferences personally, as a kind of rejection. To the degree that sexual behavior is important to you, realize the importance of partnering with someone whose personality is similar to yours. If you're more introverted, don't date an extravert and then be perturbed because he or she acts consistently with an extravert's nature.

Table 14.3. Sexual Behaviors Correlated with the Personality Dimensions Extraversion and Need for Stability

Low Need for Stablity ("Resilient")	High Need for Stablity ("Reactive")
Males report fewer sexual urges	Males report more sexual urges, more frequent erections, more masturbation
Females report more orgasms during intercourse	Females report fewer orgasms during intercourse
Less sexual pathology and dissatisfaction reported	More sexual pathology and dissatisfaction reported
Less nervous about sex	More nervous about sex
Less easily excited sexually	More easily excited sexually
Less sexual hostility	More sexual hostility
Less guilty concerning sex	More guilty concerning sex
More petting	Less petting
More acts of sexual intercourse	Fewer acts of sexual intercourse
More oral-genital sex	Less oral-genital sex

Low Extraversion ("Introvert")	High Extraversion ("Extravert")
Somewhat less satisfaction with sex	More satisfaction with sex
Less engagement in fellatio and cunnilingus	More engagement in fellatio and cunnilingus
Less sexual foreplay	More sexual foreplay
Averaging fewer than three sexual positions	Averaging more than three sexual positions
Fewer sexual partners over time	More sexual partners over time
Larger proportion are virgins	Smaller proportions are virgins
Less comfortable with physical closeness and touching	Comfortable with more physical closeness and touching
Less pursuit of interpersonal intimacy	Maximum interpersonal intimacy

TOPIC 14.13 Inbreeding

Although mating with a cousin is only slightly riskier than mating with a nonrelative (cousins have a 90 percent chance of producing a healthy offspring; nonrelatives incur a 94 percent chance), inbreeding on a large scale has a significant downside (Jones, 1994). In areas where one founder or a relatively small number of founders established a community that has remained resistant to mingling with the outside world, deadly diseases or undesirable deformities have emerged. Some examples: porphyria among Afrikaners, blindness among the inhabitants of Tristan da Cunha, an enzyme defect among Kurdistan Jews, and a stunted, six-fingered hand among the Pennsylvania Amish. The most dramatic instance of the negative effects of inbreeding is that of the Lake Maracaibo Venezuelans, where 4,000 out of 10,000 people either have Huntington's disease or are at risk of contracting it.

Application

❶ Celebrate mating between people of diverse backgrounds, through which undesirable genes can become extinguished. In diversity is strength.

TOPIC 14.14 **Handling Rejection**

Okay, what to do when it just does not work out? When one's romantic goal is rejected by one's beloved, we tend to pass through two phases before returning, hopefully, to normal. First, we protest and do everything within our power and imagination to get our beloved to reconsider. This phase employs the same neurochemical pathways as romance: elevated dopamine and norepinephrine, lowered serotonin. One often experiences abandonment rage during this phase—anger and love are independent systems and may, as many of us know, occur simultaneously. Second, over time, as the beloved remains inaccessible and the romancer remains rejected, stress increases, cortisol dominates one's system, one's immune response weakens, and protest gives way to depression. At this point, all of the romance chemicals now drop below normal levels. The extremely low levels of serotonin during this second phase of rejection is associated with impulsiveness—sometimes violent, sometimes self-defeating, sometimes directed against others, sometimes against self.

What to do when faced with rejection? How can one recover more quickly? Fisher (1995, pp. 184 ff.) recommends a variety of strategies, all with one common theme: push your memories of the beloved out of consciousness. They are listed below as applications.

Applications

❶ *Clean house.* Get rid of pictures, mementos, gifts.

❷ *Steer clear.* Avoid opportunities to have eye or ear contact with the beloved—avoid known haunts.

❸ *Meditate.* On the negatives of the beloved. On the qualities of an ideal beloved. On another person.

❹ *Keep busy.* Take classes, be with friends and family, establish new goals, start new projects.

❺ *Exercise.* Walk, work out, do yard work, dance, take a pet for a stroll, get a massage.

❻ *Sun therapy.* Get out into the sunlight as much as possible—darkness and artificial light can depress mood.

❼ *Smile.* Put reminders around you to smile, check for your smile in the mirror, have a smiling partner.

❽ *Groups.* Join a 12-step group such as SLAA (Sex and Love Addicts Anonymous).

❾ *Novelty.* Do or learn something new; this raises dopamine levels.

❿ *Sex.* Have sexual intercourse in which seminal fluids from a trusted partner are admitted (see topic 14.6, application 8).

⓫ *Practice optimism.* Count your blessings, practice positive explanatory style (see topic 37.5).

⓬ *Therapy.* Seek talk therapy, either group or individual, and obtain antidepressants if deemed appropriate. However, don't use antidepressants without talk therapy; remember, such drugs enable one to learn new behavior, but are not magic bullets—you've got to change behavior while the pills make you amenable to behavior change. Be aware that your increased serotonin can inhibit production of dopamine and norepinephrine; ask your therapist to provide something to offset this tendency. Otherwise, though you may feel better, you may also feel indifferent toward beginning new relationships (which might not be a bad thing, for a while). Increased serotonin levels can also interfere with sexual response, making orgasm unlikely in both sexes, with the accompanying frustration and miscommunication associated therewith.

SELECTED RESOURCES

Ainsworth, M. D. S., M. Blehar, E. Waters, and S. Wall (1978). *Patterns of Attachment.* Hillsdale, N.J.: Erlbaum.

Bowlby, J. (1965). *Child Care and the Growth of Love* (2nd ed.). London: Penguin Books.

Buss, D. M. (1994). *The Evolution of Desire.* New York: Basic Books.

Diamond, J. (1997b). *Why Is Sex Fun? The Evolution of Human Sexuality.* New York: Basic Books.

Fausto-Sterling, A., and H. Rose (1994). *Love, Power and Knowledge.* Bloomington: Indiana University Press.

Fisher, H. E. (1982). *The Sex Contract.* New York: Morrow.

Fisher, H. E. (1995). *Anatomy of Love: A Natural History of Mating, Marriage, and Why We Stray.* New York: Fawcett.

Fisher, H. E. (2004). *Why We Love: The Nature and Chemistry of Romantic Love.* New York: Henry Holt.

Hatfield, E., and R. L. Rapson (1993). *Love, Sex, and Intimacy: Their Psychology, Biology, and History.* Reading, Mass.: Addison-Wesley.

Kelley, H. H., and J. W. Thibaut (1978). *Interpersonal Relations: A Theory of Interdependence.* New York: Wiley.

Kiesler, D. J. (1996). *Contemporary Interpersonal Theory and Research: Personality, Psychopathology, and Psychotherapy.* New York: Wiley.

Lee, J. A. (1973). *The Colours of Love.* Toronto: New Press.

LeVay, S. (1996). *Queer Science: The Use and Abuse of Research into Homosexuality.* Cambridge, Mass.: MIT Press.

Maines, R. P. (1999). *The Technology of Orgasm.* Baltimore: Johns Hopkins University Press.

Potts, M., and R. Short (1999). *Ever Since Adam and Eve: The Evolution of Human Sexuality.* New York: Cambridge University Press.

Walsh, A. (1996). *The Science of Love: Understanding Love and Its Effects on Mind and Body.* Amherst, N.Y.: Prometheus.

Part Five

Illness
and Injury

*What
We Know
about
Brain
Repair*

Part Five. Illness and Injury

What We Know about Brain Repair

Brain-Related Disorders

Some Big Picture Stuff

*L*ittle Jimmy was five years old and had never spoken a word. His parents had tried every known resource—from speech pathologists to faith healers—to help Jimmy talk. One Saturday morning at breakfast, little Jimmy whined, "My damn eggs are cold!"

His parents exclaimed, "Jimmy, we're certainly glad to hear you finally talk! But why've you waited so long, and only to curse like a little sailor?"

Jimmy replied, "Everything's been all right up 'til now!"

> **"A journey of a thousand miles must begin with a single step."**
>
> —The Way of Lao-tzu

In general, our brains appear to function within acceptable limits. We may be more sleepy than we like, or more nervous than we like, but we're able to hold a job, to advance in our careers, to enjoy long-term relationships, and to entertain ourselves. But sometimes the brain goes awry: that is, it begins to function outside these acceptable limits in a way that makes it hard, and sometimes impossible, to hold a job or manage a relationship.

In December 1999, Dr. David Satcher announced his office's report on the state of mental health in the U.S.: *Mental Health: A Report of the Surgeon General* (complete text available at www.nimh.nih.gov). According to this review of hundreds of studies:

- One-fifth of Americans have a mental disorder in a given year.

- Half of Americans have a disorder at least once in a lifetime.

- Roughly two-thirds with disorders do not seek treatment.

- Effective treatment options are available for almost every type of mental disorder.

- Mental disorders occur in all kinds of families, social classes, and backgrounds.

- Treatment (in 1996) costs $69 billion annually (including $17.7 billion for Alzheimer's disease and $12.6 billion for drug and alcohol abuse treatment).

- One-fifth of all children show signs of a mental disorder, but only about 1 in 20 children show severe adaptive problems.

- Among adults ages 18–54, 14.9 percent have anxiety disorders, 7.1 percent mood disorders, and 1.3 percent schizophrenia.

- Adults over age 65 have the highest suicide rate, with about 1 in 10 showing signs of depression.

- Normal aging is not accompanied by mental disease.

This chapter provides some background on therapeutic approaches to brain disorders; the next four chapters address specific categories of disorders. This chapter also includes a discussion of *psychoneuroimmunology* (PNI), which is not a mental disorder but the study of the nervous system, endocrine system, and immune system considered as if they were a single system. To the degree that we embrace the principles of PNI, we establish the best possible psycho-physical environment for staying physically and psychologically well.

Neurobehavioral Disorders

It should become clear in the next several chapters that neuro-behavioral disorders are not simply "in one's head." For many years, mental disorders from depression to dyslexia were believed attributable solely to childhood mistreatment, lack of discipline or will, or some such nonbiological source. Only something as blatantly palpable as a brain tumor was sufficiently "physical" in nature so that people were willing to 'fess up to it in public. One could say, "My son has a brain tumor" without adversely reflecting on oneself, whereas saying, "My son has a depressive disorder" seemed to admit to a kind of personal failure or inadequacy. We now know better. Sure, environment can play a role, but we have learned that the so-called "mental disorders" are in fact physical.

Ivan Goldberg, a New York City psychiatrist, proposes in an Internet posting that the phrase *neurobehavioral disorder* be substituted for *mental disorder* or *mental disease.* When his patients ask what it means, he says something like this: "It is an illness in which thoughts, feelings, images, and behavior are largely the result of a neurochemical disturbance in the brain." This emphasizes the fact that "there is but one self, not a neurobiological self and a psychological self."

> Warning: Estimates of disease magnitude are usually based on high-end numbers to serve the funding needs of researchers. Actual numbers are typically lower, based on how you define terms and collect data.

In a thoughtful discussion of mental illness in the January 26, 1998, *Newsweek* ("Is Everybody Crazy?"), Sharon Begley describes what psychiatrists and neurologists are calling a continuum of diagnosis. For example, if a dozen or so gene markers are involved in dopamine regulation, then the behavior of people with one or two genetic markers will be less extreme than the behavior of people with all 12 markers. This would be like the difference between someone who is moderately impulsive (with only two or three markers) and someone who continually flirts with disaster.

Treatment Alternatives

Generally speaking, treatment for brain-related illnesses will fall under one or more of five categories: *psychotherapy, pharmacotherapy, mechanotherapy, complementary therapy,* and *autotherapy.* Or, more familiarly: *talk therapy, drug therapy, electronic therapy, nontraditional therapy,* and *self-help.*

Psychotherapy

Traditional wisdom has maintained that psychotherapy is not effective. However, in a major study of the effectiveness of psychotherapy, *Consumer Reports* ("Mental Health," 1995) challenged this stance based on the results of a survey of its readership. Seligman (1996) summarized the report in a special issue of the *American Psychologist,* "Outcome Assessment of Psychotherapy." The key to understanding the *Consumer Reports* findings hinges on an important distinction: academic research vs. field research. In the traditional academic research paradigm, a single treatment is evaluated over a brief period, and the therapist's personality is eliminated through random assignment and control groups. In field research, as typified by the *Consumer Reports* study, the therapist-patient relationship is evaluated over the whole term of their association, whether it lasts two weeks or two years, one day or a lifetime. In academic research, the treatment is the subject of the study; in field research, the therapist-patient relationship is the subject.

Thus, academic research demonstrated that specific therapies—gestalt, transactional analysis, cognitive, behavioral, and other therapies—showed few positive effects. However, when the subject of the study changed to the patient-therapist relationship, dramatic improvements emerged. The difference is this: in the field, therapists don't use just one treatment method, such as gestalt therapy, for a defined period and then quit. Rather, they tend to try a treatment method and, if it doesn't appear to work, switch to another one. Under these more realistic field conditions, patients report highly satisfactory results for psychotherapy. In fact, Seligman (in Horgan, 1996) maintains that only two drugs are superior to talk therapy: lithium for manic depression and tranquilizers for schizophrenia.

Psychotherapy can be divided into two formats: individual talk therapy and group therapy. The former ranges from the so-called brief therapies—one or two sessions—to psychoanalysis, which can go on for years. The latter ranges from informal support groups, in which people with a similar concern (for example, long-term caregivers) get together and talk with the aid of a therapist, to traditional group therapy, in which people with a variety of conditions (for example, control freaks, nonassertives, and the like) confront their problems with the aid of the therapists and each other.

Currently, *cognitive behavior therapy* (CBT) is the talk therapy of choice. Created in the 1960s by Aaron Beck and Albert Ellis, CBT challenged the assumptions of traditional (Freudian) psychoanalysis, replacing depth-diving into past history with shallow wading through current assumptions and negative patterns of behavior. CBT focuses on rumination (repeated self-talk such as "I'm not as worthy as these other people. . . . They're more intelligent than I. . . . They bring more to the table than I. . . . They don't respect me"), dark assumptions ("I'm an undesirable lover" or "I'm slowly dying of cancer"), and negative thought patterns (such as a tendency to regard options as all or nothing—e.g., the "pessimistic" explanatory style described by Seligman (see topic 37.5). CBT replaces these thoughts with more positive, productive, and distracting patterns of self- and other-dialog. CBT has been proved effective in treating depression, hypochondria, chronic fatigue syndrome, and other afflictions. Researchers have documented that such talk therapy produces changes in areas of the brain similar to those induced by drugs such as serotonin reuptake inhibitors (e.g., Prozac). The problem: the lack of trained therapists and the relative expense. The advantage: no side effects, unless positive self-talk disrupts important relationships, which has been known to happen!

Pharmacotherapy

In its ideal form, this type of therapy is practiced by a therapist who is committed to an ongoing relationship with a patient and who prescribes medication as an enhancement of the ongoing individual talk or group therapy. The drugs may be prescription (Prozac) or nonprescription (St. John's Wort, melatonin). Generally, pharmaceuticals are less effective when they are unaccompanied by psychotherapy. All too often, a primary care physician will prescribe a medication such as Ritalin or Prozac, both of which have become fashionable, under one of two conditions: either (1) the patient does not have the disorder and the drug provides only cosmetic relief, or (2) the patient does have the disorder and the drug provides some relief, but the relief is less dramatic and less long-lasting than would be the case if the patient had a continuing relationship with a psychotherapist.

There is a debate concerning the relative effectiveness of drugs alone, versus talk therapy alone, versus drugs and talk therapy combined. Several significant studies have shown no advantage to combining treatment methods, and some researchers, including University of Pittsburgh mood disorders expert Ellen Frank, regard the advocates of combination as myth peddlers. But things are not that simple.

Cornell University psychiatrist and researcher John Markowitz says the "bigger, better" studies (quoted in *BrainWork,* July–August 2004, p. 3) show (1) an advantage for combined treatment and (2) that combined treatment never does worse than either of the two individual treatment modalities used alone. A 2004 NIMH study of adolescent depression found 3 of 4 patients treated by a combination (cognitive-behavioral and fluoxetine [Prozac]) therapy improved, with only 2 of 4 improving when treated with either method alone. The goal of research needs to be to improve our understanding of different kinds of depression, and which modalities are superior for each specific kind. Some evidence indicates, for example, that talk therapy affects brain activity in the cerebral cortex, whereas drug therapy affects activity in lower limbic areas.

A new descriptor is popping up more and more often in the pharmaceutical landscape—that of *rational* drugs. Traditional pharmaceutical research and development could be defined as *pre-genome.* In other words, before the Human Genome Project began in the early 1990s to identify the relationship between specific genes and specific disorders, a hit-or-miss, "shotgun" quality typified much pharmaceutical research. The more recent line of rational drugs has built on the known chemical relationships between one or more genes and a specific disorder. The term "rational" applies to this more deductive form of development— hence, rational drugs. Typically, these drugs are more precise in their aim, so they have fewer adverse side effects. It is as though researchers now have a kind of blueprint for building new drugs.

In contrast to therapy with rational drugs, which treat diseases that are genetic in origin, *gene therapy* uses genes as a distribution system. This remarkable process begins with a benign virus, introduces into its DNA a new gene that will produce the desired chemical, then injects the virus into the desired area of the brain, thus bypassing the blood-brain barrier. The benign virus multiplies, becoming a regional drug factory that deposits increasing and permanent supplies of the desired chemical. As an example, the *adeno-associated virus* (AAV) is modified with the human gene for the enzyme *tyrosine hydroxylase* (TH). Once the AAV has been implanted, TH is released, which in turn converts the amino acid tyrosine into L-dopa, the precursor molecule for dopamine.

David Harder, professor of physiology and director of the Cardiovascular Research Center at the Medical College of Wisconsin, along with his research team, identified in 1999 a gene that manufactures an enzyme that ultimately results in producing a chemical messenger of the *epoxide* family that controls the flow of blood in the brain. Extensive research is underway at both MCW and Johns Hopkins University to confirm Harder's important findings. This research bears significant future implications for Alzheimer's disease, stroke, and other brain conditions.

One of the ongoing obstacles to pharmaceutical treatment of brain disorders is the *blood-brain barrier* (BBB). This filter allows only the smallest particles to enter the brain through the bloodstream, keeping out toxins. Unfortunately, most of the effective drug treatments for brain tumors are larger than the BBB allows to enter. One interesting workaround being tested at the Oregon Health and Science University in Portland is the injection of sugar water, which apparently removes water from the BBB filter, thus allowing about a 30-minute window for drugs to pass into the brain (*Brain in the News,* April 2004, p. 2).

Mechanotherapy

This category includes any electrical (brain-wave machines, biofeedback, vibrators), surgical, mechanical (acupuncture, massage implements), physical (hand massage, Rolfing, various touch techniques), or other devices or procedures other than talk and drugs. One approach currently enjoying wide and diverse exploration is deep brain stimulation (DBS)—an electrode implant with impulse generator, in which an electrode is surgically placed in a specific part of the brain. When it is active, the electrode stimulates neurons that relate to a specific response, such as tremor, mood change, stiffness, appetite, or pain. Medtronic Inc. manufactures these devices. The Food and Drug Administration approved them for general use in August 1997. A typical procedure costs $25,000–$30,000 and is normally covered by insurance.

For disorders like Alzheimer's that involve the destruction of neurons, hope lies in the successful use of stem cells in mice and humans. Researchers name these uncommitted cells *progenitor cells* (or *pluripotent cells*) inasmuch as they give birth to cells that can then be committed to specific purposes. Although human trials are some time in the future, Evan Snyder (lead author), Booma Yandava, and Lori Billinghurst, neurological researchers at Children's Hospital (Boston) and Harvard Medical School, reported (in the *Proceedings of the National Academy of Sciences,* June 1999) successful transplanting of stem cells from mice into other mice with lesions. The stem cells took on the function of the destroyed cells. Different organs make their own stem cells; one can find neural stem cells, blood stem cells, and so forth. Most abundant in the developing fetus, stem cells are manufactured throughout the life span. The exact mechanism by which a stem cell "knows" how to take on a needed function is currently unknown.

Senators Arlen Specter and Tom Harkin have introduced bipartisan legislation that would permit human embryo research employing embryo cells that would otherwise be thrown out by in-vitro fertilization laboratories (since their donors no longer require them). Representatives Mike Castle and Diana DeGette have introduced similar legislation in the U.S. House of Representatives. The House version is likely to come to a vote first. In August 2000, the National Institutes of Health approved the use of federal funds for stem cell research, with the restriction that the extraction of stem cells from embryos must be performed by private laboratories, which will in turn provide the stem cells to government agencies for research purposes. However, President George W. Bush in August 2001 placed a restriction on stem cell research that allows investigations only with the 64 existing genetically diverse stem cell lines. See a history of stem cell use and legislation at www.fedcan.ca/english/fromold/breakfast-bayliss1001.cfm. This debate may be made obsolete by new developments suggesting that cells from a sick person's healthy bone marrow can also serve as stem cells, without the ethical complications associated with embryonic cells.

Transcranial magnetic stimulation (TMS), a more benign variation on *electroconvulsive therapy* (ECT), emits brief magnetic surges into the brain. TMS appears to be able to improve mood and lift depression without damaging memory. Following a 45-minute treatment, the patient may immediately resume normal activity. The procedure involves only mild sensations during treatment and entails no known adverse side effects. Major study is underway in 16 centers across the country in 2004. Early results show a 28 percent reduction in symptoms (*Brain in the News,* April 2004, pp. 1 ff.).

Complementary Therapy

Candace Pert (1997) has documented the beneficial effects of a wide variety of alternative (she prefers the term "complementary") therapies that are not traditionally accepted by mainstream therapist providers or insurance companies. These include, but are not limited to, massage, Rolfing, body psychotherapy, biofeedback, hypnotherapy, acupuncture, Emotional Freedom Techniques (EFT), Ayurveda, naturopathy, macrobiotics, body work, acupressure, bioenergetics, Feldenkrais, Hellerwork, Alexander technique, myotherapy, reflexology, chiropractic, transcendental meditation, therapies using music, art, dance, and humor—the list goes on. Pert sees these "mindbody" therapies as helping promote the free flow of peptides and other "molecules of emotion" that are essential to general health and well-being. She provides an extensive list of resources, by category, in appendix B of her book, *The Molecules of Emotion* (1997).

I would like point out a recently discovered nontraditional approach to working with young folks with special needs. The Allegro Foundation (www.allegrofoundation.net) offers weekly 30-minute dance and movement workouts for children with special needs (e.g., autism, Down syndrome), with a ratio of teachers and adult volunteers to children of about 3:2. Building on the child's natural responsiveness to music and dance or movement, the children slowly move out of their comfort zone to learn cognitive (following instructions, phonics) as well as social (waiting your turn, staying in line) skills, with some remarkable results. One concrete example is shown in figure 15.1.

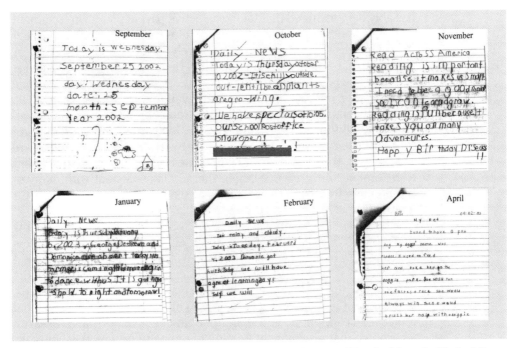

Figure 15.1. Effect of Allegro's Movement Techniques on Quality of Handwriting of a Student Born with Cerebral Palsy, Attention Deficit Disorder, Mental Retardation, and Contractures
Reprinted with permission from Pat Farmer, Founder/Executive Director, Allegro Foundation . . . a Champion for Children with Disabilities (www.allegrofoundation.net).

This eight-year-old student (we've masked the child's name to provide anonymity) was born with cerebral palsy, attention deficit disorder, mental retardation, and contractures. He had severe visual and sensory perception challenges, along with a strong fear of and oversensitivity to demands placed upon him. Over the course of one year's worth of weekly 30-minute sessions of dance therapy, his compliance with directions and overall participation increased and his emotional outbursts decreased, according to his classroom teacher, who is now an advocate for the Allegro approach. Notice in figure 15.1 the dramatic improvement in the quality of his handwriting samples as they progress from September to the following April.

Autotherapy

Power to the people. Never before in history have such informational resources been available to the average individual. From lending libraries to the Internet, we can look up our ailments, try to diagnose them, and, when confident, treat them. Norman Cousins (1979, 1989) has ably demonstrated that taking an active part in your own treatment improves your chances of recovery. A close cousin to self-treatment is attempting to treat, or work positively with, a family member or work associate. Joan Franklin and Kim Freeland have put together, for example, a manual called *Management Strategies: Obtaining Positive Productivity from Problem Personnel,* available from Magnolia Press, Franklin, Tennessee. These clinicians recommend specific interventions for working with 11 different DSM disorders. In roughly two-thirds of the cases, this can't hurt, as two-thirds of all ailments are self-limiting: they will go away with time and respect for the ailment (for example, with rest). Self-help therapy is consistent with many of the findings from the growing field of psychoneuroimmunology (for more information, see topic 15.2).

If you would like information on a topic that is not found in this book, try your local reference librarian or browse the Internet. A keyword search in Google, AskJeeves, GuruNet, or Gigablast can yield a myriad of resources (chat rooms, document repositories, support groups, current information summaries, article and book references, addresses of researchers and scholars) about a multitude of medical topics. Use caution, however, and double-check everything; research has shown that a significant portion of online information is faulty.

The best treatment is probably a combination of elements of all five of these categories of treatment. One clinic that manages to put it all together in a comprehensive therapeutic environment is the Biscayne Institutes in North Miami Beach, Florida, Marie DiCowden, executive director. Their holistic approach to patient care is described in the April 1997 *APA Monitor* (p. 38). Imagine getting a massage before engaging in an hour of psychotherapy!

A Note on Placebos

The word *placebo* comes from the Latin for "I shall please." The placebo effect, therefore, is what happens when the "very act of undergoing treatment—seeing a medical expert, for instance, or taking a pill—helps the patient to recover" (W. A. Brown, 1998, p. 90). Walter Brown, a psychiatrist at the Brown University School of Medicine, recommends the cautious and appropriate use of placebos in treating disorders that research has shown to be affected positively by placebo treatment. These disorders include asthma, angina pectoris, the common cold, high blood pressure, depression, anxiety, and general aches and pains. Placebos are any medically originated interventions that are believed by the physician to be inert—that is, to have no research-documented curative effect. The placebo can be a "sugar pill," an injection of water, something nonprescriptive to ingest (such as herb tea, chicken soup with rice, or a spoonful of honey), an exercise, acupuncture, something externally applied (ice packs, mud packs, brain-wave machines, hot baths), a regimen (a 20-minute nap after lunch, a 30-minute walk before dinner, a cup of warm milk before bed every day), or the experience of the trappings of the medical art itself (using the stethoscope, the reflex hammer, the tongue depressor, or the otoscope). Anne Harrington, a science historian at Harvard, calls them "lies that heal" (*New York Times,* October 13, 1998, p. F1).

Daniel Moerman, medical anthropologist at the University of Michigan–Dearborn, is credited for causing people to take the placebo effect seriously. In a 1975 article, he cited multiple examples of the cultural effects of belief on treatment. For example, Chinese-Americans who believe in the astrological signs and who have ominous signs die younger than persons with life-enhancing signs, and they also die younger than non-astrological-believing Westerners who have the same ominous birth year signs. In Houston, five patients suffering from osteoarthritis got fake knee surgery, and four out of the five reported positive results six months later and recommended it to others. In another study, blood-pressure patients were taken off their regular medication for three weeks in order to try a "new" drug that was a placebo, and their blood pressure decreased to a normal range while taking the inert placebo. Moerman estimates that as many as 50 percent of positive treatment outcomes are due to placebo effects, which could include everything from sugar pills to the therapist's good bedside manner. In 1955, researcher H. K. Beecher of Harvard estimated the effect to be around 30 percent.

Because the research on the effectiveness of placebos is so convincing (in one study, 40 percent of a group of depressed patients improved after taking placebos), Brown believes that physicians should seriously consider prescribing them in place of drugs that may have undesirable costs and side effects. If they don't work, then they can try medications. The success of these interventions is explained by *expectancy theory*. According to this theory, we are trained by classical conditioning to associate certain consequences with specific actions: take a pill; feel better. Hence, if it looks like a pill and we are told it's a pill by an authority figure, we expect it to act like a pill, and our bodies typically anticipate that action. Brown is appropriately cautious concerning the ethics of such interventions. He writes (1998):

> A doctor could explain the situation to a patient in the following manner: "You have several options. One is to take a diuretic. It will probably bring your blood pressure down, but it does have some side effects. There are also other treatments that are less expensive and less likely to cause side effects and that help many people with your condition. Some find that herbal tea twice a day is helpful; others find that taking these pills twice a day is helpful. These pills do not contain any drug. We do not know how the herbal tea or these pills work. They may trigger or stimulate your body's own healing processes. We do know that about 20 percent of the people with your type of high blood pressure get their blood pressure into the normal range using this approach. If you decide to try one of these treatments, I will check your progress every two weeks. If after six weeks your blood pressure is still high, we should consider the diuretic."

Mark Ardis, a retired Veterans Administration psychiatrist, psychiatric administrator, and university professor, has strong reservations concerning the use of placebos. He points out (personal communication) that the health of the relationship between the patient and the therapist is crucial to the successful outcome of treatment. In many cases, if the patient even suspects that the physician is administering placebos, that relationship is likely to deteriorate. On a personal note, in my early 30s I had a debilitating low-back pain that continued to go undiagnosed. My primary care physician prescribed a muscle relaxant. As he was writing the prescription, I commented that I had read that muscle relaxants were placebos. He turned, smiled, shook his head, and tore up the prescription! Lucky for me, my pain was later diagnosed as gout, and I've been pain-free since learning how to treat and manage gout.

It would be an incomplete discussion of the placebo effect not to mention its opposite—the *nocebo effect*. Just as the former involves the coming true of a belief in something's positive agency, so the latter involves the coming true of a belief in something's negative agency. Placebo: this pill will make you better. Nocebo: playing with frogs will make you worse. Both are forms of "self-fulfilling prophecy," so well explored by Robert Rosenthal (see topic 30.3).

TOPIC 15.1   Genetics and Disease

Figure 15.2 illustrates the relationship between environmental nurture and genetic predisposition for genetically based diseases. Generally, the relationship is interactive—the better the nurture and the lower the genetic predisposition, the better the chances are of not contracting a genetically based disease. The poorer the nurture and the higher the predisposition, the better one's chances are of contracting the disease. High nurture combined with a high predisposition and low nurture combined with a low predisposition are each more of a toss-up: high nurture will not guarantee suppression and low nurture will not guarantee expression of a genetically predisposed disease.

Only 3 percent of all human diseases are caused by a single defective gene, and these diseases are not major killers like cancer.

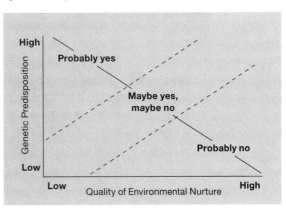

Figure 15.2. The Nature-Nurture Paradigm for Incidence of Genetically Based Diseases

John Rennie points out that more complex diseases "involve a host of genes that merely nudge a person's predisposition to develop an illness" (*Scientific American,* June 1994, p. 90). The notion that single genes cause specific diseases has led to the phrase "myth of genetic determinism," with the accompanying notion that one's genotype equates to one's fate. Because of the complex interaction between multiple genes and multiple environmental effects (diet, drugs, behavior, climate, stress, etc.), Rennie concludes that "genetic tests for [specific] illnesses can never by themselves predict an individual's future with perfect clarity."

Applications

❶ The best nurture can only minimize the chances of getting a disease toward which you are genetically predisposed. When you contract a disease following good nurture, assume a genetic predisposition; don't feel as if the nurture was somehow inadequate. Continued good nurture will facilitate recovery. (See topic 15.2 for a related discussion of psychoneuroimmunology.)

❷ Conversely, don't assume that not getting a disease is the result of excellent nurture; you may simply be genetically resistant.

TOPIC 15.2 The Immune System and Psychoneuroimmunology

Descartes's mind-body dualism has traditionally dominated medical thinking: adjust the body to fix a bodily problem, adjust the mind to fix a mental problem. However, recent research suggests that a single system exists in which mental symptoms (for example, depression) can have either a mental cause (job loss, divorce, death of a close friend) or a physical cause (poor internal regulation of serotonin, for example). This field, called *psychoneuroimmunology* (PNI), is the study of the feedback loop, traced by Karen Bulloch of the University of California, San Diego, between the brain and the immune system— the *lymphocytes* (white blood cells residing in lymph), *thymus, spleen,* and *marrow.* In this system, lymphocytes attack and neutralize invaders, and *natural killer cells* (NKs) fight viruses and tumors.

The loop works like this: the brain can emit chemicals (e.g., *gluco-corticoids*) under stress that depress the immune function, so that stress leads to disease; or the immune system can produce chemicals such as *lymphokines* in the thymus that can cause depression; in this case, disease leads to stress. Edwin Blalock, a physiology professor at the University of Alabama in Birmingham, discovered that the cells of the immune system can produce the same hormones as the brain and that immune-system cells have the same receptors as brain cells. He says that immune cells act like a classic sensory organ, sending messages to the brain the way the eyes and ears do.

> For information on any brain-related disorder not discussed in this book, consult the National Institute of Neurological Disorders and Stroke master index at www.ninds.nih.gov/disorders/disorder_index.htm, which contains hundreds of disorders, with in-depth discussion of symptoms, causes, treatments, and resources.

The original discovery of the mind's control over immune-cell levels was made by psychologist Robert Ader and immunologist Nicholas Cohen at the University of Rochester in the mid-1970s. They gave rats a saccharine solution (which by itself has no effect on the immune system), followed by an injection of cyclophosphamide, which induces nausea and reduces the immune function. After the cyclophosphamide injections were halted, rats who continued drinking the saccharine solution showed a continuing drop in immune function. Ader gave the field its name: psychoneuroimmunology.

Increasing evidence suggests that people's emotional states affect their immune levels. Sandra Levy of the Pittsburgh Cancer Institute found joy level to be the second-best predictor of survival time for patients with recurrent breast cancer. (The best predictor was length of disease-free intervals.) She found that more than half of the fluctuation in the NK level could be attributed to psychological factors, including the patient's perceived social support and how she coped with stress. Other studies by Levy, Lydia Temoshok of UC San Francisco, and Carrie Millon of the University of Miami School of Medicine point to the high correlation between a patient's level of assertiveness and fighting spirit and his or her immune level. Temoshok studied men with AIDS and found that more assertive men had higher immune levels. Millon found that men infected with the AIDS virus had higher immune levels if they were narcissistic and strong-willed.

Robert Schneider, a preventive medicine specialist with the Maharishi University of Management in Fairfield, Iowa, along with UCLA colleagues, followed 60 African Americans with high blood pressure. Taking baseline ultrasounds of their carotid arteries, part of the group proceeded to meditate twice daily, while the other group did not. Seven months later, the meditating group showed a significant decrease in plaque deposits on the artery wall; the nonmeditating patients showed increases. Schneider hails this (in *USA Today,* July 18, 2000, p. 7D) as the first report of a mind-body technique that has actually reversed atherosclerosis.

The *British Medical Journal* in 2002 published a review of 37 studies of optimism-cancer relationships only to conclude that the evidence does not support the long-held assumption that positive mental outlook can prevent or cure cancer. Yes, they found that optimism and a rosy outlook could mitigate pain, but that is different from a cure. Moreover, when cancer treatments fail, a patient who feels guilty and despairing for not having "tried hard enough" to battle the disease with her mental outlook faces an exacerbating condition—for although optimism is not known with certainty to be curative, despair is clearly known to weaken one's immune system. On the other hand, Harvard health psychologist Laura Kubzansky found in her 10-year study of 1,300 men that self-reported optimists showed only 50 percent of the incidence of heart disease as nonoptimists.

The Healing Brain (Ornstein and Sobel, 1987) is a highly readable treatment of this subject. The authors relate amazing stories of the power of the mind's control over the body, including one experiment in which a placebo treatment had the same pain-reducing ability as 8 mg of morphine. They say that the brain is not so much a computer as it is a pharmacy. Another interesting treatment is found in Norman Cousins's *Anatomy of an Illness* (1979, pp. 67–69), where he tells of the witch doctor in Albert Schweitzer's village. The two doctors had an arrangement to provide three levels of service to the villagers: bend, mend, and send. The witch doctor provided two levels: one for those with vague complaints such as stomach pains, which he treated by the traditional methods (for example, "bending" the patient's spirits with incantations), and one for those with simple specific complaints such as cuts and bruises, which he and his assistants treated with modern first aid (for example, "mending" with iodine). For the third level—complex specific complaints such as a broken leg—the villager was referred ("sent") to Albert Schweitzer.

The late Franz Ingelfinger, editor of the *New England Journal of Medicine,* wrote in his last article (Ingelfinger, 1980, p. 45) that he judged 85 percent of all human illnesses to be addressed by the immune system. Ever since Seneca, who wrote, "It is part of the cure to wish to be cured," people have debated the effect of the mind on the healing process. In fact, in many ways, this debate is at the core of cognitive science. Herbert Benson, of the Mind/Body Clinic of New England Deaconess Hospital in Boston, uses the relaxation response—the body's reaction to activities such as meditation and aerobic exercise—on patients with hypertension; he reports that 80 percent are able to reduce either blood pressure or drug dosage. Psychologist Gregg Jacobs of Harvard University's Mind/Body Medical Institute (founded by Benson) reports that it takes only five minutes of the relaxation technique to produce dramatic brain wave changes. Jacobs has used the techniques to cure insomniacs.

David C. McClelland of Boston University (McClelland, 1986; McClelland and Kirshnit, 1988) found *salivary immunoglobulin type A* to be

- low among people with a high need for power when they are stressed and out of control.

- high among people who are experiencing love.

- high among people who are temporarily experiencing positive emotions (as in watching a film about Mother Teresa).

- high among those with a stronger sense of humor.

Cousins (1989) is careful to explain that people should not abandon medical assistance in favor of exclusively concentrating on positive emotions to cure disease. He urges patients to accept medical diagnosis and treatment but to augment it by taking an active role in the healing process. He says that patients who don't deny the diagnosis but defy the verdict seem to do better than others (p. 45). This sense of "defying the verdict" is what Cousins means by "hardiness."

Vanderbilt University's Oakley Ray (2004) reviewed the research on PNI and found three variables that account for the mind's effectiveness in controlling illness, especially upper respiratory illness:

1. The number of viruses in one's environment

2. One's perceived *allostatic load* (i.e., the quantity and severity of stressors)

3. One's actual allostatic load

To the degree that all three are high, Ray concludes that the mind will have minimal effect on maintaining health. Otherwise, Ray points out that what matters in the mind's efforts to maintain health is not whether one actually has good coping skills, but whether one *believes* that one has good coping skills. The four areas of coping that appear to be most effective are

1. *knowledge* (about one's body and one's environment).

2. *inner resources* (one's beliefs, assumptions, and predictions, e.g., optimistic explanatory style).

3. *social support* (the larger one's social support system, the lower the mortality rate).

4. *spirituality* (professing to find strength or comfort from religion).

In fact, in one study of men over 55 with elective heart surgery, men expressing no comfort from religion were three times more likely to die than those who found comfort, and men who did not participate in group activities (i.e., social support) were four times more likely to die than those who participated in group activities.

Applications

1 To ensure maximum functioning of your immune system during both sickness and health, maintain your sense of humor, have positive expectations (hope and trust in medical processes), play an active role in the healing process, and stay relaxed by removing or minimizing your stressors and dissipating stress when it occurs.

2 Several books about PNI are available for both caregivers and seriously ill patients. Start with Cousins (1989), LeShan (1989), Siegel (1987), and Simonton, Simonton, and Creighton (1980). A must-read is *Molecules of Emotion* (1997) by Candace Pert, discoverer of the endorphin receptor.

3 Seek out doctors with a more holistic approach. *(Contributed by Rick Bradley)*

4 Make a commitment for yourself and your close friends, family, and associates to be supportive of one another, spread good humor, and show appropriate optimism.

5 When you are faced with higher-than-expected levels of sickness at home or at work, look to stress as a possible cause. Identify the stressors and eliminate them as much as possible.

6 Encourage yourself to increase the level of humor in your life, both humor that you initiate (tell jokes, be witty, go to comedic plays and movies, be around funny people, read humorous books) and humor that you react to (let yourself belly laugh, don't always hold back). Norman Cousins calls a good belly laugh "internal jogging."

7 Develop a sense that you are in control of your life and a fighting spirit that stays on the lookout for ways to improve your situation. Remember Alcoholics Anonymous's version of the Serenity Prayer: "God, grant me the serenity to accept the things I cannot change *today*, the courage to change the things I can *today*, and the wisdom to know the difference." To accept too much negativity in your life is to be personally responsible for lowering your own immune level. (See more on motivation in chapter 37.)

8 If you have a sick family member or friend, look for funny get-well cards instead of sad, depressing ones. When my mother had cancer, I sent her lots of funny cards. After recovering, she decided they were good "medicine" and now sends this type of card instead of the serious, somber versions. *(Contributed by Jane Howard)*

9 Kiecolt-Glaser and Glaser (1992) identified eight specific behavioral strategies for improving immune function: aerobic exercise, relaxation, social support, learned control such as biofeedback, classical conditioning, cognitive training, therapy, and self-disclosure (talking or writing about one's problems).

10 For pain management, try repeating words or phrases privately while ignoring thoughts that try to intrude on your awareness. Let the words or phrases fully occupy your conscious awareness.

11 If you are a prospective medical student, ensure that your medical school offers course work in nontraditional healing. According to a survey by the Association of American Medical Colleges, a majority of medical schools now offer such programs.

12 Demand that your managed care provider include benefits for nontraditional healing methods. In a 1997 survey of 80 HMOs conducted by Landmark Healthcare, 58 percent indicated that they either currently offered alternative therapies or planned to offer them within one to two years.

13 Subscribe to these resources:

- *Mental Medicine Book/Tape Catalog;* 800-222-4745

- *Mental Medicine Update,* a mind-body health newsletter edited by David Sobel and Robert Ornstein; Center for Health Sciences, Los Altos, California; 800-222-4745.

- *Mind-Body Health News,* a quarterly resource for mind-body study groups; Mind-Body Health Study Group Network, Washington, D.C., 202-393-2210. This and similar resources can be found at www.healthy.net/wellness/mindbody.

⑭ Another excellent summary of PNI and the relationship between stress and disease is in R. M. Sapolsky (1994), *Why Zebras Don't Get Ulcers: A Guide to Stress, Stress-Related Diseases, and Coping.*

TOPIC 15.3   Treatments for Pain

The sources of pain vary from pressure (being hit) to puncture (being stuck), but all pain is communicated through synaptic structures called *nociceptors.* These receptors, which are committed to relaying pain messages, follow two pathways:

1. From the source of potential pain (for example, a fingertip) to the spinal cord and back to the source, resulting in a reflex action (jerking the finger off a hot stove). This is a warning path.

2. From the source of actual pain (for example, the burned area of the finger) to the brain and back, resulting in the sensation of pain. The inflamed area produces *prostaglandins,* which act on the nociceptors to transmit pain messages. How much pain we feel depends on the threshold for activating our nociceptors. This threshold is a function of genetics, physical condition, attitude, and attentional focus (for example, boxers don't really feel the pain of being hit until they stop focusing on the fight itself). The following treatments can be helpful.

Treatments

❶ Narcotic analgesics such as morphine and codeine actually block the pain message at the nociceptor. However, the body develops a tolerance for these drugs, so this is only a short-term solution.

❷ Roughly two-thirds of those who suffer chronic pain experience relief with either cognitive behavioral psychotherapy or nonaddictive drugs. Because of the social toll of untreated chronic pain, doctors are beginning to prescribe narcotics for the other third (*APA Monitor,* December 1996, p. 22).

❸ The PNI literature contains a vast number of suggestions for self-managing pain as well as illness in general (see topic 15.2).

❹ Anesthetics such as novocaine and ether block all sensation, not just pain.

❺ Neurontin (gabapentin), a drug currently on the market for epilepsy, also is effective as a pain reliever.

❻ Hot and cold applications such as heat lamps and ice activate other nerve endings that compete with the nociceptors for attention.

❼ Electrical stimulation such as *transcutaneous electrical nerve stimulation* (TENS) works the same way as heat and cold.

❽ For soothing pain in infants, nursing them, holding them, and feeding them sucrose, alone or in combination, have been shown to be calming (*APA Monitor,* December 1996, p. 21).

❾ Stress-reduction techniques appear to be effective against pain (see topic 36.1).

❿ Patient-controlled analgesia, an intravenous administration, is used for pain.

⓫ Biofeedback uses visual feedback to promote mental self-control of pain.

⓬ Deep relaxation (self-hypnosis) induces a generally numb feeling; for example, fewer pregnant women require epidurals during delivery when they use deep-relaxation techniques (*Journal of Women's Health,* Winter 1993). For a list of hypnotherapists in your area, send a stamped, self-addressed envelope to the American Society of Clinical Hypnosis, 140 North Bloomingdale Road, Bloomingdale, Illinois 60108-1017, or go online to www.asch.net.

⓭ Mild, over-the-counter analgesics such as aspirin work at the site of the pain to reduce inflammation and block production of prostaglandins.

Four classes of over-the-counter analgesics are currently available. Their pros and cons are listed in table 15.1.

⓮ Tips for over-the-counter analgesics:

- Heat and moisture can affect their quality, so store them away from the bathroom in a cool, dry area.

- Avoid "extra-strength" pain relievers; they are more expensive per milligram than normal doses and they make it harder to control precise dosage.

- Avoid products with caffeine mixed with analgesics. Consumers Union questions their effects in the combined form. If you want caffeine with your single-ingredient pain reliever, ingest it as coffee or another product of your choice.

- To ease the effect on your tummy, take analgesics on a full stomach with a full glass of water and avoid lying down for a half hour.

- If you take medicine for high blood pressure, avoid all analgesics but aspirin, as they can elevate blood pressure. Consult your physician if you are unsure.

⓯ To the degree that your pain is stress-related, and to the degree that your stress is attributable to poor fit between your personal qualities and what is being expected of you, make a careful study of chapter 36, and especially appendix L ("My Shapers") to find ways to experience the total mental engagement that Mihalyi Csikszentmihalyi calls *flow*. To the degree that you can enter flow, the chances are that you can find substantial relief from pain.

⓰ Read Wall (1999), *Pain: The Science of Suffering* (part of the series "Maps of the Mind").

⓱ The prescription drug OxyContin (one of 60 or so brand-name drugs containing oxycodone, a synthetic form of morphine) has a double-edged effect. On the positive side: relatively inexpensive, more powerful, and longer-lasting than most other drugs, easy on the stomach, and especially effective with cancer-related pain. On the negative side: you can bypass the 12-hour time-release design of the drug by pestling it into a powder, thus releasing an instant high similar to that of heroine. A standard version of the pill contains 5 mg of oxycodone, but pills are available that are up to 16 times stronger. Doctors have lost their licenses for abusing their prescribing privileges for OxyContin, and abuse has been

Table 15.1. Pros and Cons of Over-the-Counter Analgesics

Class	Trade Names	Advantages	Disadvantages
Aspirin	Bayer, Anacin, Ecotrin, Bufferin	Cheapest; reduces fever, swelling, stiffness; reduces chance of heart attack, stroke, and digestive tract cancer	Hard on stomach; Reye's syndrome when given to young child with flu or chicken pox
Acetaminophen	Tylenol, Aspirin-free Anacin	Reduces fever, easier on stomach, fewest side effects	No effect on swelling and stiffness; liver damage when taken with three alcoholic drinks per day
Ibuprofen	Advil, Nuprin, Motrin IB	Lasts longer than aspirin and acetaminophen; better on stronger pains; reduces fever, swelling, stiffness	Aggravates stomach upset when taken with three alcoholic drinks per day; boosts blood pressure; liver, kidney, stomach disease
Naproxen	Aleve	Lasts longest; best with strongest pain; helps swelling, fever, stiffness	Most expensive; same disadvantages as ibuprofen
COX-2 Inhibitors	Celebrex	Easier on the stomach	Increased risk of heart attack

rampant (Rush Limbaugh being one of the more famous abusers, reputedly having taken as many as 30 pills a day). Yet the truth remains that the pill delivers 12 hours of pain relief for those who need it.

⑱ For more (and free) information, explore the site of the federal National Institute of Neurological Disorders and Stroke at **www.ninds.nih.gov**.

⑲ Follow the work of scientists such as Mich Hein of the Scripps Research Institute, La Jolla, California; Charles Arntzen of Texas A&M University; and Richard Curtis III of Washington University in St. Louis. They are using recombinant DNA technology to develop plants that deliver medication, as in potatoes that prevent gastroenteritis (Arntzen) and alfalfa sprouts that carry a cholera vaccine.

TOPIC 15.4	Caring for Caregivers

Those who fall into the role of providing long-term care (for example, for Alzheimer's patients) develop health problems of their own. The emotional and physical pressures associated with around-the-clock caregiving often lead to the kinds of diseases normally associated with prolonged stress. The Canadian Study of Health and Aging has presented evidence that Alzheimer's caregivers have more health problems than other people of the same age, as well as more health problems than people caring for a loved one at home with a disease other than Alzheimer's. Periodic temporary relief that allows the caregiver to get away for a couple of hours at a time appears to minimize such health complications.

Applications

❶ Two interventions have been found effective in helping caregivers maintain their immune level: teaching them stress-reduction methods, such as relaxation, and providing them with respite when they feel they need it, so they can go to a movie, go shopping, or just walk.

❷ If you are a caregiver, or if you know one, find a support group of people you can call on for short-term relief. Most cities have a clearinghouse that will put you in touch with providers of respite care. Don't be a martyr; it's not healthy.

❸ Two good websites for respite care resources are www.caregiver.org and www.visitingangels.com. Also, browse the Internet for a senior care network in your area.

❹ To keep current on caregiving, get on the mailing list for the Family Caregiver Alliance, 425 Bush Street, Suite 500, San Francisco, California 94108, phone 415-434-3388.

TOPIC 15.5	Cousins: The Four Ingredients of Hardiness

Norman Cousins (1989), who himself recovered from three life-threatening illnesses, became a primary popularizer for the new field of psychoneuroimmunology (see topic 15.2). Cousins summarizes a large body of research and experience with a quote from Seneca: "It is part of the cure to wish to be cured." This attitude—wanting to play an active role in curing oneself—is the essence of the motivated person. Cousins calls it *hardiness* and says that it is composed of four ingredients. I have summarized them as follows:

1. ***Positive expectations (vs. negative expectations):*** expecting successful outcomes for oneself and others

2. ***Relaxation (vs. stress):*** dissipating stress through appropriate methods

3. ***Positive emotions (vs. negative emotions):*** maintaining a sense of humor and joyfulness

4. ***Active role (vs. passive role):*** being a doer, not just being done unto

Applications

❶ Rosenthal and Jacobson (1968) lit the torch on the power of the self-fulfilling prophecy, or the Pygmalion effect. Their lesson is simple: expect bad things, and bad things tend to happen; expect good things, and good things tend to happen. See also topic 30.3.

❷ Topic 36.1 provides abundant information and suggested applications for ways to dissipate stress.

❸ Give yourself permission to be humorous and to enjoy the humor of others. Explore the various ramifications of humor in chapter 11.

❹ Focus on positive emotions. See fewer horror films, more inspirational films; listen to music in a major key. In one study (Rein,   on, and McCraty, 1995), students who were randomly assigned to watch films of Mother Teresa had higher levels of salivary immunoglobulin A, a measure of the level of immune-system functioning, after viewing than did students assigned to watch films of Nazis.

❺ The Society for the Preservation of Barbershop Quartet Singing in America has documented the positive effect of singing on health. Call 800-876-SING for more information, or visit www.barbershop.org. *(Contributed by Jack Wilson)*

❻ Give a damn! Robert Sternberg (see topic 34.3) says that three basic strategies are available to affect the world around us: change me, change thee, and change the situation. Use them. Don't stick with a strategy type that's not working. If you do what you've always done, you'll always get what you've always gotten!

7 The Eastern concept of *chi* is defined as the force we feel when our life is in balance. A study of Eastern philosophy, science, and literature will lead us in the direction of self-control, which is the essence of optimism and hardiness.

SELECTED RESOURCES

Brown, W. A. (1998, January). "The Placebo Effect." *Scientific American,* pp. 90–95.

Cousins, N. (1979). *Anatomy of an Illness.* New York: Norton.

Cousins, N. (1989). *Head First: The Biology of Hope.* New York: NAL/Dutton.

Hafen, B. Q., K. J. Karren, K. J. Frandsen, and N. L. Smith (1996). *Mind/Body Health: The Effects of Attitudes, Emotions, and Relationships.* Needham Heights, Mass.: Allyn & Bacon.

Horgan, J. (1996, December). "Why Freud Isn't Dead." *Scientific American,* pp. 106–111.

"Mental Health: Does Therapy Help?" (1995, November). *Consumer Reports,* pp. 734–739.

Pert, C. B. (1997). *Molecules of Emotion: Why You Feel the Way You Feel.* New York: Scribner.

Seligman, M. E. P. (1994). *What You Can Change and What You Can't.* New York: Knopf.

Seligman, M. E. P. (1996, October). "Science as an Ally of Practice" (Special issue: "Outcome Assessment of Psychotherapy"). *American Psychologist,* 51(10), 1072–1079.

Websites

Charles A. Dana Foundation home page: www.dana.org

U.S. Office of Disease Prevention and Health Promotion: www.healthfinder.gov

Structural Disorders

Bats in Your Belfry

> **“Art thou not,
> fatal vision,
> sensible
> To feeling as to
> sight? or art
> thou but
> A dagger of the
> mind, a false
> creation,
> Proceeding from
> the heat-
> oppressed
> brain?”**
>
> —*William Shakespeare,*
> Macbeth

A combination of genetic and environmental contributions can render the brain structurally— that is, biologically and chemically—out of sorts. The result of structural damage or alteration can slow down or speed up function and can range from the dulling of function in retardation to the massive electrical storms of epilepsy. This chapter explores the state of causal associations and therapeutic possibilities for eight structural disorders:

attention deficit hyperactivity disorder, autism spectrum disorders, dyslexia, epilepsy, retardation, schizophrenia, stuttering, and tumors.

TOPIC 16.1 Attention Deficit Hyperactivity Disorder (ADHD)

Roughly 5 percent of children have attention deficit hyperactivity disorder (ADHD), and most of these are boys (Biederman and Faraone, 1996). It accounts for about half of the referrals to children's psychiatric clinics. No more than one in five of these cases carries over into adulthood. ADHD involves poor regulation of the *catecholamine* family of neurotransmitters, specifically dopamine and norepinephrine, among the synapses in the frontal area of the brain, particularly the right area, and the *basal ganglia* (*Archives of General Psychiatry,* July 1996). These two areas, which are associated with focusing attention, blocking distractions, and inhibiting behavior, are up to 10 percent smaller in ADHD children. In essence, their brains fail to fire inhibitory processes, thus leading to uncontrollable motoric behavior. ADHD occurs in families, pointing to a genetic basis, and is associated with poor environmental conditions. Although 49 percent of ADHD cases involve no other mental disturbance, 51 percent are associated with other disorders: depression (11 percent), anxiety disorders (11 percent), conduct disorders (7 percent), or some combination of the three. A combination of ADHD and conduct disorders predicts later antisocial disorders and alcohol or drug dependence, ADHD and depression predicts later manic depression (bipolar disorder; see topic 19.4), and ADHD and anxiety predicts later anxiety disorders.

The symptoms of ADHD are inattentiveness, impulsivity, and motoric overactivity, starting during the early grades and interfering with social and academic performance. The *Diagnostic and Statistical Manual of Mental Disorders (DSM-IV)* lists 19 specific symptoms, a majority of which must occur in at least two different settings, such as home and school. Doctors typically diagnose ADHD into one of three categories: predominantly inattentive (usually called just "ADD"), predominantly hyperactive, or combined.

In the Charlotte-Mecklenburg (North Carolina) schools, teachers look for the following 14 behaviors as indicators; they must be severe, must have lasted for six months, and must have started before age seven (*Charlotte Observer,* December 5, 1993):

1. Often fidgets or squirms in seat

2. Has difficulty remaining seated

3. Is easily distracted

4. Has difficulty awaiting turn in groups

5. Often blurts out answers to questions

6. Has difficulty following directions

7. Has difficulty sustaining attention to tasks

8. Shifts from one uncompleted activity to another

9. Has difficulty playing quietly

10. Often talks excessively

11. Often interrupts or intrudes on others

12. Often does not seem to listen

13. Often loses things necessary for tasks

14. Often engages in dangerous activity without considering the consequences

Martin Teicher of Harvard Medical School's McLean Hospital reported the results of a protocol to assess for ADHD that is 90 percent accurate (*Journal of the American Academy of Child and Adolescent Psychiatry,* March 1996). In this procedure, a child performs a high-vigilance task with a television screen. The child watches the screen for 15 minutes, only occasionally being asked to respond. This boring procedure intentionally (and unfortunately!) resembles traditional expectations for classroom behavior. Throughout the 15 minutes, an infrared motion-analysis device monitors movements 50 times per second.

Treatments

❶ Ritalin (methylphenidate, an amphetamine) is the treatment drug of choice, with upwards of 2 million prescriptions in the United States, about 90 percent of them for children. Normal doses range from 5 to 20 mg daily. Ritalin works by stimulating the production of neurotransmitters, including dopamine and norepinephrine. In general, ADHD sufferers have low neurotransmitter production, which leads to poor impulse control.

Ritalin attempts to normalize this production. Possible side effects include loss of appetite (which typically vanishes after one month of use), as well as crankiness, headaches, or drowsiness as the drug's effects wear off.

❷ Joe Stegman, a pediatrician in Concord, North Carolina, cautions that taking Ritalin can only calm the brain. It should be accompanied by family counseling so that the family's lifestyle does not foster ADHD any more than necessary. For example, Stegman says ADHD children should avoid violent television programs, candy-coated cereal, long bus rides to school, and other situations that can aggravate the condition. On the other hand, the National Institutes of Health, under the leadership of child psychiatrist Peter Jensen, assembled six teams at sites around the U.S. for the purpose of evaluating Ritalin against behavior modification therapy. The study comprised 579 seven- to nine-year-old children (80 percent of whom were male) over 14 months. Conclusion: adding behavior therapy to Ritalin resulted in no improvement over using Ritalin alone. The study affirms the practice of treating hyperactive children with stimulants. (Reported in December 1999 issue of *Archives of General Psychiatry.*)

❸ Although not all ADHD children take Ritalin, many children who are merely restless take it unnecessarily. Just as Prozac is often prescribed wrongly to help adults take the rough edges off their personality, Ritalin is often prescribed for children's rough edges that do not reflect ADHD. As the ability to maintain reasonably healthy relationships at home and work is one test for genuine depression, so the ability to maintain healthy school and social performance is one test for genuine ADHD.

❹ In adults, we mostly see ADD, wherein symptoms are less overt, more internal, with less apparent hyperactivity. Adult ADD involves difficulty in planning and organizing, procrastination, forgetting appointments, and resistance to repetitive tasks. A six-item self-screening tool for adult ADD is available at www.adultadd.com/2_2_recognizing/screener.jsp. For a comprehensive, current description of what is known about ADHD, see the NIMH website at www.nimh.nih.gov/publicat/adhd.cfm. In addition to finding the right medication, adult ADD can be aided by obtaining vibrating multi-alarm watches and pillboxes, as a way to keep appointments in mind and pills on schedule. A catalog of such devices is available at **www.eadhd.com.**

❺ Researchers at Children's Hospital and Regional Medical Center of Seattle studied 1,345 children (*Pediatrics,* April 2004) and concluded that any television watching during the first two years of life affects the "hardwiring" of the brain. The more a child watches fast-moving images, the more of the brain commits to neural networks that track them. The result: slower-motion patterns, such as social interaction, are crowded out, leaving the child highly susceptible to ADHD. This phenomenon knows no cultural bounds—so-called educational programs have just as strong an effect as junk programming.

6 Low-birth-weight children are at risk for much, including ADHD. In a study (*Journal of Consulting and Clinical Psychology,* Vol. 72, no. 2, 2004) of 2,232 five-year-old-twins, half of whom had low birth weight, those who experienced a warmer, more affectionate relationship with their mothers were at lower risk for developing ADHD and other behavioral problems.

7 Jay Giedd and a team at the National Institute of Mental Health used magnetic resonance imaging to identify brain asymmetries in ADHD boys. Non-ADHD boys have an *anterior frontal area, caudate nucleus,* and *globus pallidus* (see appendix A) that are 4–6 percent larger in the right hemisphere than they are in ADHD boys. Further research must determine whether this asymmetry is a cause of ADHD or a result of treatment. It should be noted that hyperactivity can also occur among people who have a genetic defect associated with a thyroid disorder.

8 An innovative approach being used with some ADHD cases that meet certain requirements is *electroencephalographic neurofeedback.* For specific information on this technology, as well as a position paper on its use with ADHD, check out www.biof.com/neuroarticles.html, Allied Products' website.

9 For the most up-to-date information, check the Attention Deficit Disorder Association website at www.add.org.

10 In one promising line of research for diagnosing ADHD, scientists at Boston's Massachusetts General Hospital report (in *The Lancet,* December 1999) that confirmed ADHD sufferers have levels of dopamine transporters up to 70 percent higher than nonsufferers. Dopamine transporters provide a kind of mopping-up function: they collect extra dopamine, thereby stopping its action. The extra portion of transporters in ADHD patients, however, does not entail a single explanation. On the one hand, extra transporters could suggest a deficiency of dopamine; on the other, an excess. But while the cause-and-effect relationship of transporters to actual dopamine levels is unclear, the presence of the transporters does, in fact, represent a promising method for diagnosing the presence of ADHD.

TOPIC 16.2 Autism Spectrum Disorders

Still a mystery to most researchers, the spectrum of autism disorders is thought to be biological with some degree of genetic origin. On one end of the spectrum we have classic *autism,* symptoms of which include poor language development, the inability to recognize another person's state of mind, unusual preoccupations, and repetitive behaviors (e.g., rocking and hand flapping). At the other end we have *Asperger's syndrome* (AS), with symptoms including moderate to high intelligence in one or more areas but lack of social skills such as reading nonverbal behavior (facial emotional cues, for example). In between are several similar disorders, such as *Rett syndrome* and *Fragile X syndrome.* Disorders across this spectrum afflict some 1.5 million persons in the U.S., according to the Autism Society of America.

For a time, some researchers thought autism was linked to the use of mercury-based thimerosal as a preservative in many vaccines used with young children, but the Institute of Medicine put that to rest, based on the negative findings from research on thousands of children. Some researchers believe autism is caused by the failure to prune sufficient nerve cells, or to prune in the proper manner, in the two months before birth. Humans reach greatest brain density in second trimester, with significant pruning of unnecessary cells in the time remaining before birth. Francesca D'Amato of Italy's National Research Center believes that attachment disorders such as autism may be at least partially attributable to defects in the opioid, or pleasure, center of the brain. Working with rats, D'Amato eliminated key opioid receptors in newborn rats' brains, with the result that the newborn rats failed to emit their accustomed squeals when separated from their mothers. D'Amato hypothesizes that deficient opioid systems deny the newborn any pleasurable association with mother contact, which leads to indifference. Uta Frith of University College London has determined that autism is attributable primarily to connectivity problems rather than specific locational deficiencies—in other words, different parts of the brain simply don't cooperate with one another. This discovery should lead to breakthroughs in treatment.

Asperger's syndrome is genetic. Current thinking is that between 10 and 20 genes, plus some environmental factors, determine the nature of Asperger's. The good news is that one no longer has to blame one's upbringing, but the bad news is that no known treatments or cures are available.

Traditionally thought to be lazy and insensitive, modern "Aspies" (as they often refer to themselves) are pleased to be regarded as disabled rather than merely backward. The most appropriate response to a diagnosis of AS is to learn coping strategies. Support groups and training classes help develop behaviors to offset the effects of their social awkwardness: how far to stand from others, how to tell when someone is angry, timing their monologues, learning to glance away and not stare others down, asking co-workers to send overt signals when they need to stop talking (such as handing them a pencil or a pad).

This hard-to-diagnose syndrome is characterized by a gift in recall of factual information, plus an obsession with one or two domains of knowledge. This combination tends to land Asperger's sufferers in quantitative fields like engineering, mathematics, or computing. They have average or above intelligence (using traditional measures), but they show symptoms such as social awkwardness, difficulty in relationships, difficulty forming emotional bonds with others, and inability to read nonverbal communication (such as facial expressions). Palo Alto psychologist Lori Bond (Children's Health Council) calls it "social dyslexia." Boys account for the vast majority with this disorder, and a typical profile might be described as "spouting off facts and figures, but uninterested in two-way conversation." They have difficulty knowing how to behave when not following an established routine.

These are the AS indicators from *DSM-IV*:

- Preoccupied with one subject or object (airline schedules, dinosaurs, etc.)

- Exceptionally accurate memory for details

- Committed to a routine, resistant to change

- Clumsy in social relations with both children and adults, especially in unstructured situations

- Seldom use imagination when playing

- Avoid eye contact and are not bodily or facially expressive

- Typically unaware of others' feelings

- Unable to reciprocate socially or emotionally

- Unable to be a party in a casual two-way conversation of mutual give-and-take

- Difficulty talking about topics they are not interested in

- Literal in the meaning of spoken and heard conversation

- Though processing conversational language with difficulty, can form complex sentences by age two to three
- Concentrating often accompanied by pacing, fidgeting, or rocking
- Easily taken in by others (naïve, gullible, credulous)
- Extra-sensitive to light, noise, and touch (hence a tendency to avoid hugs and handshakes)
- Clumsy in sports

Treatments

1 Causes and treatment are unknown. Antidepressants provide some relief when combined with years of social skills training and speech therapy.

2 When someone you know is acting antisocial (or just extremely awkward) yet showing flashes of mental brilliance, avoid assuming he is at fault for being boorish, and consider the possibility that he has Asperger's syndrome. Find a way for him to see a neurologist, psychiatrist, or well-informed primary care physician with the request to determine whether he might have AS. Remember that AS runs in families; in fact, many parents are diagnosed after their children first get diagnosed.

3 Encourage AS individuals to join or form an AS support group. Their usually unsatisfied cravings for intimacy can be partially fulfilled by an on-going support group.

4 Among many AS individuals in support groups, there is a tendency to use Cambridge University's "autism quotient" (AQ) test as a point of pride—as in, I got a higher score than you did, or, I'm more autistic than you. To take the test, go to **www.wired.com/wired/archive/9.12/aqtest.html**. The AQ test is also available at other websites.

5 Visit the Autism Society of America website at **www.autism-society.org**.

6 Twelve studies throughout the U.S. are evaluating secretin, a hormone with demonstrated ability to improve some autistic children's cognitive and language skills.

7 See *A Parent's Guide to Asperger's Syndrome and High Functioning Autism* by S. Ozonoff, G. Dawson, and J. McPartland (2002). Sally Ozonoff is an associate professor of psychiatry at the University of California at Davis Health Systems in Sacramento, and on staff at the M.I.N.D. Institute (UCD Health Systems).

⑧ Visit www.aspennj.org, Asperger Syndrome Education Network's website.

⑨ Visit hunter.apana.org.au/~cas/autism/lists.html for a listing of autism electronic mailing lists.

⑩ The discovery of genes on chromosomes 7 and 15 that cause Rett syndrome and Fragile X syndrome give a major clue to regions possibly involved with autism.

TOPIC 16.3   Dyslexia

Once thought to be mostly caused by stress, *dyslexia* (difficulty in reading for biological reasons) has been estimated to afflict up to 15 percent of the population. Research on a large Norwegian family with many dyslexic members has yielded a location for the dyslexia gene, DYX3, on chromosome 2. Dyslexia appears to be related to the poor synchronization of two neural systems in the brain. Dyslexic patients have *magnocellular* layers (large cells in the visual pathway) that are 27 percent smaller and less well organized than comparable areas in the brains of nondyslexic people. On the other hand, dyslexic and nondyslexic individuals have *parvocellular* layers (smaller cells in the visual pathway) of comparable size and organization. Because of their smaller size and disorganization in dyslexics, magnocellular cells transmit more slowly than parvocellular when processing perceptual information (e.g., letters on the printed page). As a result, visual information (printed words) and auditory information (spoken words) don't work together. Auditory content is processed at normal speeds, but visual content is not. Appropriate treatments for dyslexia equalize the speeds of these two perceptual systems. Paula Tallal, codirector of the Center for Molecular and Behavioral Neuroscience at Rutgers University, and Michael Merzenich of the Keck Center for Integrative Neuroscience at the University of California, San Francisco, have developed a computer-based therapy that varies the amplitude and duration of sounds in a video-game format.

Dyslexia acts differently in speakers of Eastern ideogram-based languages than in speakers of Western phoneme-based languages. In Romance language speakers, for example, the misfiring occurs in the left temporal-parietal area, a region that is associated specifically with awareness of the phonemes of one's alphabet. In English, there happen to be 44 phonemes. However, Li-Hai Tan of NIMH and the University of Hong Kong has identified a different region that misfires among Chinese dyslexics: the left middle frontal gyrus, which is associated with symbol interpretation. This discovery suggests that no universal treatment for dyslexia is possible, that treatment must be directed toward either phoneme awareness and production or ideogram awareness and production. The study, which appeared in the September 2004 issue of *Nature,* does not mention whether subjects have been identified who are dyslexic in Chinese but not in English, or vice versa.

For the current status of any clinical trial mentioned in this book, check this website: www.clinicaltrials.gov.

Sally Shaywitz (1996) has identified five myths about dyslexia:

1. Dyslexics engage in mirror writing. (Not necessarily. Mirror writing is a common developmental phenomenon among dyslexics and nondyslexics. Dyslexics have phonological problems, not writing problems.)

2. Dyslexia should be treated with eye training. (There is no evidence to support this.)

3. Boys are more often dyslexic than girls. (No. This is a bias of traditional research methods. Current data show the distribution to be pretty much identical for boys and girls.)

4. One can outgrow dyslexia. (No. For many, it continues into adulthood. They can read, but slowly.)

5. Dyslexics can't be smart. (Wrong. The two are independent. William Butler Yeats, Albert Einstein, and George Patton were dyslexic.)

The classic symptom of dyslexia is a discrepancy between intelligence (or ability) and achievement (or performance). The symptoms differ widely, from spelling problems to hesitant oral reading; different symptoms call for different treatments. The later a child is diagnosed as reading-disabled, the harder it is to teach that child to read and the more likely the disability will leave psychological scars. Louisa Moats, project director of the National Institute of Child Health and Human Development Early Intervention Project in Washington, D.C., identified indicators appearing as early as 30 months of age, including a sloweddown ability to name numbers, colors, or objects, that point to later reading disabilities.

Treatments

1 To treat dyslexia, consult your neurologist for the latest information on how to pharmaceutically or behaviorally equalize the transmission of magno and parvo cells.

2 If you grew up thinking that dyslexia was primarily a reaction to stress, understand that current research indicates most cases of dyslexia have a physical basis. Be sympathetic with dyslexics' need to take their time processing perceptual information. For them, proceeding slowly is not a sign of less intelligence.

3 Because of their phonological deficits, dyslexics respond better to the whole-word method of reading instruction than to the phonics approach. Dyslexics often need surrounding context cues in order to identify a specific word. Therefore, multiple-choice tests, which provide virtually no context, particularly penalize them.

4 Paula Tallal and Michael Merzenich have founded a company, Scientific Learning Principles, based in San Francisco, that has developed a product called "Fast ForWord" that employs their video learning program and is marketed as an interactive CD-ROM. They have a website at www.scilearn.com.

5 Dennis Molfese, psychologist at Southern Illinois University at Carbondale, identified (in *New Scientist,* August 18, 1999) brainwave patterns in 36-hour-old infants who end up dyslexic at age eight. Although 22 of 24 infants so identified were in fact dyslexic, the two who were misidentified cause concern in planning remedial interventions for every newborn so identified.

6 Try getting on the mailing list for the International Dyslexia Society (formerly the Orton Dyslexia Society): www.interdys.org.

7 For information on the broader subject of learning disabilities, visit the website focused on children's learning disabilities at **www.ldonline.org**.

8 Search for "dyslexia" on the Internet. You will find a wide variety of support groups and informational sources for both children and adults. One valuable resource is the National Institute of Neurological Disorders and Stroke at **www.ninds.nih.gov/disorders/dyslexia/dyslexia.htm**. Check the best sites often to keep abreast of newly developing information.

9 Because dyslexia is considered a genetic defect, cures are not realistically expected, but treatments certainly are. One line of research (as yet unproductive) is the development of a drug that equalizes the tempos of the magno and parvo cells.

10 David Pauls of Yale University is part of a research team that has identified two genetic markers for dyslexia, one on human chromosome 15 that is associated with single-word reading and another on chromosome 6 that is associated with phonetic ability. It is hoped that this line of research will lead to increasingly effective treatments for dyslexia.

11 Medical researcher Sally Shaywitz of Yale University established (in *Journal of the American Medical Association*, April 1999) that estrogen replacement in post-menopausal women results in improved verbal performance. Shaywitz and her team at Yale are currently working on determining whether dyslexia is related to low levels of estrogen.

12 NIH has funded five universities to study the biology of learning disabilities: University of Washington at Seattle, Yale, Johns Hopkins, University of Colorado, and Harvard.

13 Experimental psychologist Joel Talcott, University Laboratory of Physiology, Oxford, reports (in *Science News*, March 18, 2000) that two perceptual skills appear to be closely related to reading effectiveness among 10-year-olds. Children able to discriminate shifts in pitch of lower frequency sounds appear to have superior skills in reading and making speech sounds, and those successful at detecting changes in the motion of dots on a computer monitor appear to have the best skills in spelling. Research is underway to determine if early training in these two perceptual skills is effective in minimizing dyslexia.

TOPIC 16.4   Epilepsy

About 1 percent of the U.S. population have *epilepsy,* a brain condition for which no single cause is known. Genes are suspected in half of the cases, but the other half point to an array of causes, including lead poisoning, prenatal problems, disease, tumor, head injury, stroke, infection, and drug or alcohol abuse. Epilepsy describes a pattern of electrical storms called seizures, which are set off by a brief period of electrical firing in the brain up to four times as fast as normal.

Treatments

1 About two-thirds of epileptics improve by taking anticonvulsant drugs such as Tegretol (carbamazepine); others can improve with surgical procedures. However, thousands remain whose epilepsy is impervious to all known treatments.

2 An implant that stimulates the vagus nerve, the "NeuroCybernetic Prosthesis System,"(reported in the *Chicago Tribune,* January 5, 1998, p. 1) is manufactured in Texas by Cyberonics Inc. It consists of a set of coils placed around the vagus nerve and connected to a stopwatch-sized generator surgically implanted under the skin of the chest. The generator sends a 30-second burst of electricity followed by a five-minute lull, continuing in alternation. Apparently, these bursts disrupt seizure patterns, amounting to what some have called a pacemaker for the brain.

3 To increase participation in genetic studies, the Epilepsy Foundation of America has set up a website, **www.epilepsyfoundation.org**, that puts people who think they have inherited epilepsy in touch with researchers. By participating, you may help isolate the genes associated with a dozen or more types of epilepsy. To date, researchers have found only a few genes associated with three or four types of epilepsy. More volunteers are needed. Drugs used to treat epilepsy before 1994 were not based on genetic research; new *rational* drugs such as Gabitril (tiagabine hydrochloride) address specific properties defined by newly identified genes associated with epilepsy (C. A. Walsh, 1997). With the identification of more genes comes the possibility of more and better rational drugs that will close the treatment gap.

❹ Physicians at Boston's Beth Israel Deaconess Medical Center have transplanted 400,000 fetal pig cells into the brain of a middle-aged man with severe epilepsy. Researchers will watch to determine if the animal cells survive and affect the patient's condition. Beth Israel plans additional *xenotransplants* over the next several years.

❺ For an excellent, comprehensive treatment of the subject of epilepsy in both children and adults, get familiar with Shorvon (2005), *Handbook of Epilepsy Treatment* (2nd ed.).

TOPIC 16.5 Retardation

A developmental disorder that afflicts between 1 and 3 percent of the population, *retardation* is defined as a failure of the individual to perform age-appropriate motor, language, intellectual, or self-help behaviors. Its onset, severity, and causation cover a wide range. Onset can be before birth (*prenatal*), during birth (*perinatal*), or up to age 18 (*postnatal*). Roughly 75 percent of cases of retardation have prenatal causes, 10 percent are perinatal, and another 10 percent are postnatal; 5 percent are simply hard to understand and classify. Research attributes mild retardation to genetics, beause siblings of the retarded often exhibit limited IQ. However, moderate to severe and profound retardation are attributed to environmental factors such as birth problems, diet, trauma, and accident (Plomin, DeFries, McClearn, and Rutter, 1997, p. 109). The severity of retardation can range from borderline to severe.

The most common prenatal cause is *Down syndrome,* with congenital rubella and fetal alcohol syndrome also causing many cases. Down syndrome occurs in one out of every 773 live births when chromosome 21 in the egg fails to separate properly, with the result that the embryo receives two chromosome 21's from the mother and the normal one from the father, for a total of three chromosomes, rather than the normal two. This condition is referred to as *trisomy* (or, three chromosomes). For a 20-year-old mother, the risk of trisomy is 1 in 2,000; for a 40-year-old mother, 1 in 100 (Blum, 1997, p. 102).

Perinatal causes of retardation include prematurity and infections, with birth trauma actually accounting for only a small portion. Postnatal causes include trauma and tumors. Causation is extremely complex, with upwards of 40 different causes, some of which are related to trauma, some to disease, some to genetics, and still others to diet, poisons, and environment. Only an estimated 25 percent of cases have a clear-cut causation identified, with the remainder in a huge "unexplained" category.

Treatments

1 Prenatal family genetic screening and counseling can prevent the occurrence of retardation caused by genetic factors. Prenatal counseling can educate parents to avoid dietary, drug, and other causative factors, such as malnutrition and alcohol or lead poisoning. Counseling can also identify diseases that could harm the fetus to which the mother may be prone. She can be taught how to avoid contracting such diseases. Current treatments are aimed at helping the individual learn behaviors at the most advanced possible level. Many retarded individuals are able to live independently, but others must live in a specially structured environment.

2 About one in 20,000 babies is born with *hydrocephalus* (an enlarged head filled with fluid) and virtually no brain function. Untreated, such babies typically remain infantile and die before the age of 10. In March 1999, a team of doctors at Vanderbilt University Medical Center, led by Noel Tulipan and Joseph Bruner, performed a surgical first—brain surgery on a fetus to remove the buildup of water. Physicians had detected the hydrocephalic condition while performing a routine ultrasound examination when the fetus was about 20 weeks old. *In utero* surgery had been used with much success to repair spina bifida lesions on fetuses, but never for brain repair. The infant, born two months later without excess fluid, appeared to be developing normally.

3 Current research is focused on a variety of techniques, including the use of gene therapy, neuronal cell growth factors, and development of rational drugs. Example: Evan Snyder of Children's Hospital Boston and Harvard Medical School has reported his work on *mucopolysaccharidosis* (MPS), caused by an enzyme deficiency in the brain (*Nature,* March 23, 1995). Snyder and his team are experimenting with a process in which good enzyme-producing cells are transplanted into the target area.

4 For current information, visit the many websites dedicated to mental retardation. This one is maintained by NIH's National Library of Medicine: www.nlm.nih.gov/mesh/jablonski/syndrome_db.html.

TOPIC 16.6   Schizophrenia

Schizophrenia typically begins during the teenage or early adult years in upwards of 1 percent of the population. U.S. rates are similar to those in both developed and undeveloped countries. Some of the criteria used to diagnose schizophrenia in the *DSM-IV:*

- Speech and thought disorders
- Hallucinations and delusions
- Psychomotor disturbance (immobile or restless)
- Inappropriate emotional responses
- Bizarre behavior
- Reduced intellectual and self-help ability

Schizophrenia is a chronic condition; symptoms must last for at least six months to earn the diagnosis. Early on, it can be confused with several other disorders, including depression, mania, and substance abuse, and can range from slightly to totally disabling. Based on the different symptom sets, the diagnosis may be for any one of five different subtypes: *catatonic, disorganized, undifferentiated, residual,* or *paranoid.* Some cases last for only one or several episodes with a return to normal or near normal; others slowly improve or get worse. Sex differences in responses to antipsychotic drugs and in age of onset suggest that sex hormones influence the course of the disease—as does socioeconomic status, with three factors playing a significant role:

- Lower income and status
- Urban environment
- Demands for socialization placed on adolescents and young adults

EEG, PET, MRI, and CT evaluations all reveal abnormalities in the brains of schizophrenics, and recent studies indicate that the abnormal brain patterns are present before the onset of symptoms. This suggests that schizophrenia is the result of developmental problems in the brain and nervous system. Although some forms of the disease may be associated with one specific gene, the greater likelihood is that several genes are implicated, suggesting a tangle of causes (genetic and environmental) for each of the subtypes. To date, linkage studies have identified regions on chromosomes 6, 15, and 22 as possible addresses for schizophrenia-related genes (Wyatt and Henter, 1997).

In 1966, Leonard Heston of the University of Washington compared the children of 47 hospitalized female schizophrenics with a matched sample of the offspring of nonschizophrenic women. He found that the risk of developing schizophrenia was the same for schizophrenic mothers' children who had been adopted and reared by nonschizophrenic parents, as for the children of schizophrenic mothers who did their own child rearing. The risk for both groups was around 10 percent. Heston concluded that the environment played no role in causing schizophrenia, and that genetics was the sole causal factor (Plomin, DeFries, McClearn, and Rutter, 1997, p. 70).

Children are at three times higher risk for schizophrenia if their mothers had influenza during the first half of their pregnancy (i.e., first 4½ months).

Treatments

❶ Treatment is aimed at relieving symptoms. Traditional medications have focused on blocking dopamine receptors, as well as targeting specific symptoms such as low affect. More recent medications have been more of a "cocktail" in which multiple ligands, including clozapine, olanzapine, risperidone, and sertindole, are addressed in addition to dopamine. These newer medications have a record of fewer relapses and fewer, and milder, side effects. Pharmacotherapy must be accompanied by psychotherapy, and researchers are improving their knowledge of environmental scenarios that trigger episodes in specific patients.

❷ Gerard Hogarty, the lead researcher of a psychiatric team at the University of Pittsburgh's School of Medicine, reported in the November 1998 issue of the *American Journal of Psychiatry* that a three-year psychotherapy regimen called *personal therapy* resulted in improved adjustment and fewer relapses than pharmacotherapy alone. Unlike psychoanalysis, personal therapy concentrates on the present-day life of the patient. The patients are educated to the idea that their brains are unusually sensitive to stress, and they are trained in ways to recognize stress and cope with it.

❸ Personal therapy sounds similar to what is now being referred to as *recovery therapy*. Psychiatrists Courtenay Harding (University of Colorado) and William Anthony (Boston University), two advocates of the recovery model, are claiming improvement rates upwards of 70 percent, compared with 10–30 percent for traditional methods. The recovery method emphasizes patients' potential, rather than their illness, and trains them in the skills of accessing resources and self-development.

4 If pregnant, or planning to get pregnant, keep your flu shots current.

5 In addition to the well-established dopamine connection to schizophrenia, researchers have discovered that phencyclidine (PCP), when abused as a street drug, can initiate schizophrenia-like behavior. PCP's special action blocks the receptors for glutamate, a critical neurotransmitter involved in intercellular communication. Glutamate's role in the drama is currently under investigation.

6 In addition, researchers are studying why schizophrenics are the heaviest smokers of all those with mental disorders. Apparently, nicotine gives some relief, and that connection is under investigation.

7 As with other disorders of the mind-brain, researchers are using all available imaging devices to localize the active areas of the brain that are unique to specific symptoms. As the areas are mapped, interventions can be designed to address them based on their characteristics.

8 One current area of research is into when to begin aggressively administering antipsychotic medications. Early treatment appears to bring greater improvement in the long term.

9 Increasing evidence seems to associate maternal influences before and during pregnancy with later onset of schizophrenia in the child. These include deficiencies in the mother's nutrition, immunological incompatibilities between mother and fetus, and the effect of influenza contracted by the mother during the second trimester. As evidence accumulates, science and public policy may help reduce or control these factors.

10 For current information on schizophrenia, call the National Alliance for Research on Schizophrenia and Depression at 800-829-8289 or visit its website at www.narsad.org.

11 A number of schizophrenia researchers, including Thomas McGlashan, head of Yale Psychiatric Institute in New Haven, point to a period of "pruning" that occurs in late adolescence as a culprit in the onset of schizophrenia. This pruning is a kind of spring cleaning in which unused synapses atrophy, as adolescents surrender their extra supply of raw material for learning to set the stage for the adult demands of greater efficiency. Brain scans show that normal adolescents prune about 15 percent of their gray matter between pre-puberty and mid-20s; schizophrenics can lose up to 25 percent. This reduction in force could be related to the onset of schizophrenia in one of two ways. First, the superfluity of synapses could mask the effects of an earlier virus, thereafter exposing the virus's effects during spring cleaning. Alternatively, schizophrenia could emerge as the result of excessive, uncontrolled spring cleaning.

⑫ A growing body of evidence points to a viral influence on schizophrenia—not necessarily a "schizophrenia virus" per se, but rather a virus, probably a *retrovirus* (a family of viruses that includes the HIV virus), that interacts with other conditions to result in schizophrenia. Follow the work of Robert H. Yolken, director of the Stanley Division of Developmental Neurovirology, Johns Hopkins University.

⑬ LeDoux (2002) classifies the symptoms of schizophrenia as either positive or negative. Positive symptoms include hallucinations, abnormal thought patterns, paranoia, delusions, agitation, hostility, and bizarre, out-of-context behavior. Negative symptoms include blunted emotions, cognitive deficits in attention and working memory, poor hygiene, poverty of speech, social isolation, and loss of motivation. Different pharmaceuticals appear to be effective in treating the two sets of symptoms: dopamine blockers seem more effective with the positive set, drugs affecting serotonin and norepinephrine with the negatives. In fact, current research suggests that the positive symptoms involve overactivity of one type of dopamine receptor in the basal ganglia (see appendix A), whereas negative symptoms are associated with underactivity of another type of dopamine receptor in the prefrontal cortex (pp. 268–269). The truth of the matter is that schizophrenia is not a single disorder, but rather a family or disorders that present different combinations of symptoms in different people. Future treatment needs to be aimed at finding the specific circuits involved and addressing them with circuit-specific drugs (p. 272).

TOPIC 16.7 **Stuttering**

Stuttering involves threefold interruption of speech: repeated phonemes ("Sh-sh-sh-show me the . . ."), sustained phonemes ("Shhhhhhhhh-ow me the . . ."), and sound stoppages (no sound emerges at all). Roughly 1 percent of the U.S. population is affected, males outnumbering females four to one. Causal factors include one or more of these four: genetics, other language disorders, unusual brain development (some stutterers while talking show activity in different areas of the brain than nonstutterers), and pressure. Emotional trauma is not thought to be a cause. Famous persons who have stuttered include James Earl Jones (the voice of Darth Vader) and Marilyn Monroe.

Research is currently directed toward identifying the genes associated with stuttering. Once these are identified, then rational drugs can be developed. In addition, drugs and other therapies are under investigation for helping stutterers with anatomical abnormalities.

Treatments

❶ As a rule, the best way to communicate with stutterers is by talking at a slow, relaxed tempo. Mr. Rogers (of PBS fame) is often cited as a model. Your tempo should not be too slow, however.

❷ Contact the Stuttering Foundation by calling 800-992-9392 or visiting www.stutteringhelp.org.

❸ If stuttering persists, early treatment is most effective. Consult a speech pathologist who specializes in stuttering. Referrals are available from the Stuttering Foundation.

TOPIC 16.8 | Brain Tumors

Brain tumors (also called *neoplasia*; the field is called *neuro-oncology*) form as the direct result of bad genes (Louis, 1995). Two kinds of genes, *oncogenes,* which promote cell growth, and *suppressor genes,* which retard cell growth, normally act in balanced concert. Tumors form when either the oncogenes are overactive or the suppressor genes are underactive. Tumors can occur in glial cells (*gliomas*), meningeal cells (*meningiomas*), Schwann cells (*schwannomas*), and immune system cells (*lymphomas*), but only rarely in normal neurons, because neurons do not divide after birth. In the U.S., around 17,000 brain tumors are diagnosed annually. Over two-thirds of these are gliomas, the second most frequent type of cancer in children (behind leukemia). More commonly, tumors occur in older people because of the complex mixture of influences—inherited, external environmental (for example, gases), and internal environmental (such as disease)—that interact to start the process.

Treatments

❶ Most gliomas and lymphomas resist therapy and lead to death within several years. Meningiomas and schwannomas are typically benign and capable of surgical removal. The key issue with tumors, however, is "location, location, location." Remote areas of the brain can harbor tumors whose removal would be extremely risky.

One complication of surgical removal is the inevitable destruction of neurons, either from having been crushed by the tumor or from the surgical invasion. Current thinking is that that these lost cells will not regenerate. However, loss of function as a result of neuronal damage can sometimes be recovered using the property of plasticity in neighboring cells. *Plasticity* is the capacity of neurons to take on new functions. Rehabilitation processes are designed according to the nature of the tumor and the outcome of the surgery.

❷ A promising new gene therapy technique is under study at the University of Pennsylvania. Researchers have inserted a gene into a benign virus that later commands the viral cells to manufacture the enzyme *thymidine kinase.* Once the enzyme has been injected into the tumor, it attacks both cancerous and noncancerous cells. The doctor then administers the drug ganciclovir, which the thymidine kinase converts into a powerful toxin that prevents tumor cells from making further DNA, hence arresting further cell division.

❸ An excellent way to keep current is to join a support group, such as the many that are listed with the American Brain Tumor Association (hope.abta.org). Google "brain tumor support group," and you'll find quite a few listed.

❹ For excellent current information, have a look at Al Musella's website, virtualtrials.com/musella.cfm. Al got hooked on the subject when his sister-in-law was diagnosed with a brain tumor. From there, he began posting to his website information on every brain tumor clinical trial going on in the United States.

5 Visit the American Neurological Association website, **www.aneuroa.org**.

SUGGESTED RESOURCES

Biederman, J., and S. Faraone (1996, Winter). "Attention Deficit Hyperactivity Disorder." *On the Brain* (Harvard Mahoney Neuroscience Institute Letter), pp. 4–7.

Livingstone, M. S., G. D. Rosen, F. W. Drislane, and A. M. Galaburda (1991). "Physiological and Anatomical Evidence for a Magnocellular Defect in Developmental Dyslexia." *Proceedings of the National Academy of Science,* 88, 7943–7947.

Pennington, B. F. (1991). *Diagnosing Learning Disorders: A Neuropsychological Framework.* New York: Guilford Press.

Shaywitz, S. E. (1996, November). "Dyslexia." *Scientific American,* pp. 98–104.

Shaywitz, S. E., M. D. Escobar, B. A. Shaywitz, J. M. Fletcher, and R. Makuch (1992). "Evidence That Dyslexia May Represent the Lower Tail of a Normal Distribution of Reading Ability." *New England Journal of Medicine,* 326(3), 145–150.

Walsh, C. A. (1997, Winter). "Epilepsy: Genes May Build the Road to Treatment." *On the Brain* (Harvard Mahoney Neuroscience Institute Letter), pp. 1–3.

Wyatt, R. J., and I. D. Henter (1997, May–June). "Schizophrenia: An Introduction." *BrainWork: The Neuroscience Newsletter* (Charles A. Dana Foundation), 7(3), 1–3, 8.

Insults and Injuries

A Blow-by-Blow Account

Perhaps the Earl of Chesterfield was not thinking of insults and injuries to the brain when he penned his pearl, but a parallel exists. In fact, insults in the form of early childhood abuse appear to have a disturbingly long, often permanent life. This chapter explores brain disorders that can be attributed to injury: abused child syndrome, cerebral palsy, concussion, headaches, spinal cord injury, and stroke.

TOPIC 17.1　Abused Child Syndrome

Intense stress from severe physical or sexual abuse floods the brain with chemicals, including adrenaline, noradrenaline, cortisol, opiates, and others; this results in the eventual shrinkage of the hippocampus. The left hippocampus typically shrinks more than the right, with the former reportedly shrinking up to 26 percent and the latter up to 22 percent of their normal size (Mukerjee, 1995).

Daniel Alkon committed his career to discovering the secret of how to reverse the effects of early abuse, only to become convinced of its impossibility. He reported his findings in *Memory's Voice* (1992). According to Alkon, a kind of neural commitment occurs (pp. 162–164):

> [The result of this lifework] was not what I expected to find when I set out, energized by a sense of mission to wrestle with trauma's grip on the human psyche. . . . I didn't understand then, as I do now, that the actual biology of experience's influence on our brains is not the same in most of adulthood as it is in early childhood. . . . The adult brain's networks are to a significant degree hard-wired. . . . These are not styles that can be trained. They are ingrained, built into a permanent template. When we wish to counsel change in others or consider it for ourselves, it seems essential, therefore, to know the basic terrain of the behavioral landscape. New training and radically different experience may be able to modify familiar behavior, but the networks will not change with learning in adulthood as they can when we are growing up. The chemistry of personality has already been determined. . . . These thoughts do recommend an attitude of humility toward the possibilities of change for people.

The most disturbing part of this hard-wiring process, Alkon points out, is that "the emotional importance of what has been learned in critical periods determines its permanence. If only the brain changes of adult learning were more like those of childhood. Perhaps then we could be more ambitious. As it is, for now, these differences limit our freedom and, to a degree, seal our fate" (p. 164). A person traumatized by abuse, Alkon learned, cannot dissolve the hard-wired networks of increasingly thick *myelination* built up over months and years of emotional trauma. As an adult, such a person must search for a partner who shares these attitudes shaped by abuse, or who does not pose a challenge to the maintenance of these attitudes. Neither surgical, pharmaceutical, nor other therapeutic methods, according to Alkon, have succeeded in overcoming these abuse-built neural networks, glazed with the chemicals of fear, anger, and depression and fired in the kiln of these intense emotions.

Partial confirmation of Alkon's conclusions comes from the Child Emotion Research Laboratory at the University of Wisconsin–Madison. Chief researcher and assistant professor of psychology and psychiatry Seth Pollak, using electrode skullcaps, compared the reactions of 28 abused children with those of nonabused children when shown pictures of angry faces. The abused children involuntarily exhibited wild variations in electrical activity that were not found in the nonabused children.

Up to 20 percent of survivors of abuse suffer from either *dissociation* or *post-traumatic stress disorder* (PTSD). In dissociation, often used by children who are unable to escape the abuse, the victims separate the experience from conscious awareness, in essence feeling detached from the experience in such a way that it doesn't appear to happen at all. On the other hand, in PTSD, the victims relive the abusive or severely stressful memory and try to avoid situations that remind them of it.

Sexually abused girls suffer a dramatically altered developmental pattern. Although there is some variation among them, these girls can be found to mature physically earlier, have different hormonal reactions, and have impaired immune functions (DeAngelis, 1995). They tend to suffer generally higher levels of arousal, as evidenced by sustained higher levels of *catecholamines*. This hyperarousal is associated with sleep disorders, nervousness, depression, and anxiety. Collaborative research into abuse victims is being conducted by Penelope Tricket of the University of Southern California and Frank Putnam of the National Institute of Mental Health's Laboratory of Clinical Psychology.

Treatments

❶ A variety of treatments are being tried, from eye-movement therapy to the "counting method." For an excellent summary of available resources, visit the Wounded Healer Journal, the oldest website devoted to trauma and abuse support and resources: **www.twhj.com**.

❷ If you know a child who appears to be experiencing abuse, know that the longer it goes on the harder its effects will be to reverse. Act now!

❸ For a book that summarizes current prevention and treatment issues, get Wolfe, McMahon, and Peters (1997), *Child Abuse: New Directions in Prevention and Treatment Across the Lifespan*.

❹ For breaking news in the treatment of abuse victims, get on the mailing list for the National Crime Victim's Research and Treatment Center, Medical University of South Carolina, Charleston, South Carolina 29425. Their website is **www.musc.edu/cvc**.

TOPIC 17.2   Cerebral Palsy

About 2–4 out of every 1,000 births result in irreversible damage to brain cells that govern voluntary muscle movements, sensations, and mental faculties. About 1 out of every 20 babies who weigh less than three pounds suffers this damage. These very low birth weight babies account for roughly 28 percent of all cases of *cerebral palsy* (CP). The damage may also be caused by bleeding in the brain or by a dying off of white matter that leaves holes in the midst of various nerve connections. In other cases, the damage occurs in early infancy because of some accident, trauma, or illness.

Symptoms typically appear anywhere from three months of age to as late as age two. The symptoms are nonprogressive and can include one or more of a long list, including spasticity (the most common symptom), paralysis, perceptual abnormalities, speech defects, and seizures. Life expectancy is normal, except for very low birth weight infants with CP, whose average life expectancy is 20 years. Intellectual ability can range from severely retarded to extremely bright.

Treatments

❶ Because there is no cure for CP, the goal is to create the greatest possible independence. This may include use of physical therapy, braces, hearing and seeing aids, drugs, or special schooling. For extreme cases, institutionalization is available. Prescriptions could include muscle relaxants and anticonvulsants. Some cases require surgery to correct joint, muscle, and feeding problems.

❷ Studies are pointing towards the possible preventive effect of introducing magnesium sulfate into mothers with premature delivery.

❸ Keep current with information from the National Institute of Neurological Disorders and Stroke (NINDS) website at www.ninds.nih. gov/disorders/cerebral_palsy.

| TOPIC 17.3 | **Concussion** |

A *concussion* occurs when the head sustains a strong blow that results in loss of consciousness, however brief. After the blow, the brain hits the skull in a "counterblow." In more severe cases, often as the result of twisting the neck during the blow, pressure is put on the brain stem, where basic involuntary life functions are controlled. Bleeding or other damage may occur. Often, people who sustain a concussion cannot remember the events surrounding the blow.

Neuropsychologist Michael Collins, Henry Ford Health System in Detroit, reported (in *Journal of the American Medical Association*, September 8, 1999) that, in a study of 393 college football players, those who had suffered two or more concussions were significantly more likely to evidence problems with headaches, sleep, and concentration. They scored significantly lower on tests that measured word learning, thinking speed, and ability to handle complex tasks. Furthermore, those players who had learning disorders in addition to the two or more concussions performed even lower.

In a related study, amateur soccer players fared worse on tests of memory and planning ability than other amateur athletes. Blows to the head, including "headers," accounted for the difference. In both the football and soccer studies, "concussion" was defined not just as being "knocked out," but also to include blows to the head that resulted in dizziness, headache, confusion, difficulty with balance or memory, or even personality change (see description of grades 1 and 2 below).

Outside the realm of organized sports, similar effects are coming to light: roller coasters, no less! Since 1991, at least 13 documented cases of severe brain injury have been attributed to theme park rides traveling at speeds as high as 90 miles per hour, a speed creating G forces above five, which is greater than that experienced by astronauts on shuttle takeoffs. Injury in these cases comes not from being hit, but rather from the kind of whiplash that happens when severe forces cause the brain to slosh against the inner wall of its carrier. Look for symptoms such as vomiting, pupils that are different sizes, confusion, seizures, coma, muscle weakness, or unusual walking patterns.

Treatments

❶ The American Academy of Neurology has established guidelines for three levels of concussion (note that the examples are drawn from the sports world, which happens to have the highest incidence of concussion):

> *Grade 1:* No perceptible loss of consciousness; mild confusion and loss of coordination; symptoms are gone in 15 minutes. (Check every 5 minutes for symptoms; if they have cleared after 15 minutes, the individual may resume normal activity. If a player in a sport has suffered multiple grade 1 concussions, she may return to play only after a neurological assessment and one symptom-free week.)

> *Grade 2:* No perceptible loss of consciousness; mild confusion and loss of coordination; symptoms last more than 15 minutes. (Remove a player from the game; examine him frequently; conduct a brief neurological assessment. The player may return after one week with no symptoms after rest or exertion. If a player suffers multiple grade 2 concussions, he may return only after being symptom-free for two weeks.)

> *Grade 3:* Loss of consciousness for either seconds or minutes. (Take the patient by ambulance for an emergency neurological examination. With brief unconsciousness, a player may return to a game after one symptom-free week; with longer periods of unconsciousness, the player may return after two symptom-free weeks.) These last two guidelines are for adults. The guidelines differ for young people.

If a young person in an athletic situation has a concussion, typically she should not resume athletics for three months. Immediately after the concussion, the person should be still and quiet. Brain injury rates are higher for those who have sustained prior concussions with unconsciousness. Repeated concussions have a cumulative effect on one or more mental functions. With uncomplicated concussions, full recovery is typical.

For a complete copy of the American Academy of Neurology guidelines, visit their site at **www.aan.com/professionals/practice/guideline/index.cfm**.

❷ Stay current with information on concussions by visiting the National Institute of Neurological Disorders and Stroke website: **www.ninds.nih.gov**. Information is also available from the Brain Injury Association: 202-296-6443 or website **www.biausa.org**.

TOPIC 17.4   Headaches

Migraine headaches afflict roughly 28 million Americans; most are associated with *vasoconstriction* (tightening of the blood vessels). Vasoconstriction can be offset or prevented by limiting consumption of foodstuffs with *tyramine*, an amino acid believed to be associated with vasoconstriction. (See table 17.1 for a list of tyramine-containing, migraine-precipitating foods.) Menstrual migraines can be eliminated by finding the precipitating foods from the list in table 17.1 and avoiding them, starting several days before onset of menses and continuing until it's over. One friend has successfully eliminated her menstrual migraines by cutting out sugar, another by eliminating alcohol consumption, two to three days before the expected onset of menses. For nonmenstrual migraines, an individual would simply eliminate a suspected food until a migraine occurred, then assume that the food hadn't been the cause of the headache, and eliminate another food.

Gallagher (1990) concludes that most headaches can be limited or eliminated by pharmaceutical methods, or by nonpharmaceutical methods such as diet or biofeedback. Once a headache begins, however, dietary methods are ineffective: it's time for drugs.

Treatments

❶ Experiment: Systematically eliminate different foods from the list in table 17.1 before expected headaches. If a headache happens, resume that food, and next time try eliminating another. Or try eliminating combinations of foods.

❷ Consult with your physician for pharmaceutical assistance. If this produces no results, read Gallagher (1990) and discuss some of his recommendations with your physician.

❸ For further information, call the National Headache Foundation at 800-643-5552 or visit their website at **www.headaches.org**.

❹ Significant relief is available for menstrual migraines through a dopamine-related drug called bromocriptine. Also, for migraine, large daily doses (400 mg) of Vitamin B-2 (riboflavin) have been shown to have preventive value: migraine sufferers who took B-2 had 37 percent fewer reported migraines than those who did not take the vitamin (*Neurology,*

February 1998). And when the B-2 takers did have a migraine, the attack was shorter than for a placebo group.

❺ Two relatively new treatments are zolmitriptan (a designer drug acting on serotonin receptors, providing relief within two hours for two-thirds of recipients) and sumatriptan nasal spray (which could begin pain reduction as early as 15 minutes after administration; it helps two-thirds of recipients).

❻ Julian Nash, psychologist and director of the Miriam Hospital's Headache Management Program, Providence, Rhode Island, studied 41 headache victims who averaged a headache at least every other day. After a 10-week behavior therapy program, headaches occurred only every third day and were briefer. The program encouraged lifestyle changes, such as regular meal schedules, regular sleep times, increased exercise, and minimized stress.

❼ Aspartame (Equal, Nutrasweet) can trigger headaches. If you're migraine prone, try a different sweetener, such as sucralose (Splenda).

❽ Though triptans have proven effective in stopping migraines, little has been available to keep these headaches from happening. Prescription drugs, such as antidepressants and blood pressure drugs, can help prevent them but may have undesirable side effects and don't always help. Studies have shown over-the-counter options that appear to be effective in preventing migraines:

- *Coenzyme Q10.* Daily dose of 300 mg, works by activating cell mitochondria.

- *Magnesium.* Doses can range from 360 to 1,000 mg, but should not be taken by persons with kidney problems.

- *Riboflavin (Vitamin B-2).* 400 mg daily; also works on energizing the mitochondria.

- *Feverfew.* This herb (akin to the daisy) appears to prevent blood vessel constriction to some degree but can interact adversely with Coumadin and some other blood thinners.

- *Magnesium-riboflavin-feverfew combination.* The brands MigreLief and MigraHealth recommend two pills daily, totaling 300 mg of magnesium, 400 mg of riboflavin, and 100 mg of feverfew.

- *Butterbur root extract.* In soft gel tablets (brand name Petadolex). This herbal extract appears to be helpful in reducing the intensity

Table 17.1. Migraine-Precipitating Foods

Meat and Fish	Vegetables	Baked Goods
Pickled herring	Fava beans	Fresh-baked breads
Chicken livers	Lima beans	Sourdough
Sausage	Navy beans	
Salami	Pea pods	
Pepperoni	Sauerkraut	**Desserts**
Bologna	Onions	
Hot dogs		Chocolate
Marinated meats	**Beverages**	
Aged, canned, or cured meats		
	Alcoholic	**Other**
Fruits	Caffeine (limit to 2	
	cups/day)	Soy sauce
Canned figs	Chocolate milk	MSG
Raisins	Buttermilk	Meat tenderizer
Papaya		Seasoning salt
Passion fruit	**Dairy**	Canned soups
Avocado		TV dinners
Bananas	Aged, processed cheese	Garlic
Red plums	Yogurt (limit to ½ cup/day)	Nuts
Citrus (limit to ½ cup/day)	Sour cream	

Source: Michael Gallagher (Ed.) (1990), *Drug Therapy for Headache,* New York: Marcel Dekker. © 1991 by Marcel Dekker, Inc. Extracted from the National Headache Foundation Diet, Chicago, Illinois. Reprinted by permission.

and frequency of migraines in both adults and children. Dosage varies, so be careful, starting with lower doses. Butterbur was once taken for plague.

9 Teenagers who have frequent headaches have a tendency to take too many pain killers, such as Advil, Aleve, and Tylenol, without telling parents or doctors. Taking as many as 20 doses weekly can cause rebound headaches, gastrointestinal bleeding, and kidney problems. At the 2004 meeting of the American Headache Society, researchers recommended that children from ages 6 to 18 take only two doses per week.

10 Using the new technique of *voxel-based morphometry,* Peter Goadsby and colleagues (at the Institute of Neurology of the National

Hospital for Neurology and Neurosurgery in London) have found a structural abnormality associated with cluster headaches. Cluster headaches are more intense than migraines and typically appear with regularity, attacking the sufferer at the same time of day or night. Their very predictability has earned them the moniker "alarm-clock" headaches. Using MRI scans, Goadsby has determined that the area of the brain active during cluster headaches is in the region that controls the body clock—the hypothalamus—and that the gray matter in this area is more abundant among cluster sufferers than among normals. Arguing against the traditional vascular explanation, Goadsby concludes (in *Nature Medicine,* July 1, 1999) that the cluster-headache-associated brain activity in the area of the biorhythm controller helps to explain the periodic nature of cluster headaches. Rami Burstein, neurobiologist at Harvard Medical School, and Stewart Tepper, director of the New England Center for Headache, Stamford, Connecticut, concur. Migraines, they say, are caused not by changes in blood flow but by a series of neurological misfires. Once the chain reaction becomes established, say after an hour, treatment appears to have little effect. They recommend the use of triptans (zolmitriptan, rizatriptan) within the first 20 minutes to an hour of the initial attack. Hit 'em hard and early on, they recommend.

⓫ Cleveland plastic surgeon Bahman Guyuron theorizes that migraines are the result of muscles pinching the *trigeminal nerve.* He has had success using a combination of Botox injections and plastic surgery to relieve the pinching. The procedure involves several months of Botox injections before the surgery, then "lifting" the forehead and reshaping the nose.

⓬ The March 1998 issue of *Archives of Neurology* reported that 59 percent of migraine sufferers who took a combination of three nonprescription drugs—acetaminophen, aspirin, and caffeine—within two hours of migraine onset found that their pain subsided or disappeared.

⓭ Martin A. Samuels, chair of the Department of Neurology at Boston's Brigham and Women's Hospital, argues that because migraine sufferers' stomachs do not empty well, oral pills are less effective. He finds that the inexpensive suppository Indocin works almost as well as expensive injections. He recommends that if suppositories don't appeal, a stomach relaxer should be tried along with oral pills to help improve absorption of the active ingredients.

TOPIC 17.5   **Post-Traumatic Stress Disorder (PTSD)**

Post-traumatic stress disorder is what happens to some people after having experienced a life-threatening event, or series of such events, such as combat, natural disaster (e.g., tsunamis), terrorism, serious accidents, or violent personal assaults (e.g., rape). Rescuers and witnesses can get PTSD, too. PTSD sufferers tend to relive the event(s) through flashbacks, intrusive thoughts, and nightmares, with resulting behaviors such as avoidance of activities or places associated with the trauma, emotional numbness, chronic insomnia, sleep disorders, panic attacks, and violent outbursts. A key to treatment of PTSD is early identification of these symptoms. Factors that place one at a higher risk for developing PTSD include a history of childhood abuse, family dysfunction, and preexisting psychological disorders. Around 8 percent of U.S. citizens will suffer from PTSD during their lifetime, with occurrence among women twice that of men. This is a relatively small portion of those who report having experienced a traumatic event in their lives—60 percent of men report experiencing trauma, 51 percent of women.

Rachel Yehuda (Bronx Veterans Affairs Medical Center) finds that PTSD sufferers have lower base levels of cortisol than normals, thus allowing adrenaline to roam free during the trauma. Adrenaline, as we know from the section on memory (chapter 23), serves to help imprint strong emotional events—it acts like a photographic "fixer." Yehuda observes that cortisol levels tend to hold adrenaline levels in check. Therefore, a person with lower base levels of cortisol would be that much more likely to form a strong memory of the trauma. PTSD sufferers also evidence atypical brainwave activity, reduction in the size of the hippocampus, overactivation of the amygdala, excessive arousal of the sympathetic nervous system (i.e., the stress response), and production of higher-than-average levels of bodily opiates (i.e., endorphins). They are very likely to suffer from other disorders, such as depression, alcohol or drug abuse, phobias, or conduct disorders.

Jerome Groopman ("The Grief Industry," *The New Yorker,* January 26, 2004, pp. 30–38) was interested in what it takes to prevent a trauma from leading to PTSD. Specifically, he wanted to know if so-called "group grief counseling" was effective. This approach, developed by Jeffrey Mitchell in the 1970s, builds on the assumption that persons who have experienced a common trauma (such as 9/11) can avoid permanent injury by sharing and reliving the experience. The seven-step approach must occur between 12 and 72 hours after a catastrophe. However, recent research suggests that such reliving or debriefing is at best useless, at worst counterproductive. In one study of persons experiencing severe burns, those receiving group debriefings were more likely to develop PTSD than controls who received no treatment. Some find that the group experience tends to create memories that weren't there—"Did I see that that? I must have. Oh, my goodness, I have not even been aware of that. That's terrible." And so on. It is not helpful to overly psychologize a trauma victim's mental state. Groopman reports that most people recover spontaneously over time after such trauma, without therapeutic intervention. Troublesome behavior immediately after a trauma is regarded as a natural part of the recovery process and not in need of treatment. All that appears to be needed is basic comfort and support; just give the victims time and nurture. In one follow-up study six months after 9/11, only 1.7 percent of New Yorkers were found to have symptoms of PTSD, thus invalidating some grief counselors' claims that all are at high risk. We suspect that there is a certain trait profile that puts one at higher risk, perhaps N+O+A+ (persons who are worriers, imaginative, and caring—see chapter 33 for a discussion of traits).

In support of Groopman's observations, George Bonanno (2004) of Columbia University's Teachers College finds that traditional "grief work" practices—focusing on dredging up negative, painful memories and processing them with the help of a grief counselor or support groups—are actually harmful to the griever. He recommends instead four paths to recovery from trauma (loss of a loved one, near-death experiences) that have been traditionally considered deleterious:

- *Hardiness.* Pursuing a purposive life, believing in one's personal control and power, and believing that one can grow and learn from negative events.

- *Self-enhancement.* Overlooking one's "warts" and seeing oneself, in essence, in a more positive light than others might; Bonanno points out that this characteristic, though helpful for recovery, is not always endearing in relationships—narcissists can be a pain.

- *Repressive coping.* Ignoring or simply not reporting any negative symptoms or experiences, although physiological measures might suggest otherwise; although repression has traditionally been considered harmful, Bonanno finds support for repression as an effective coping strategy for many trauma sufferers, especially sufferers of childhood abuses; such repression appears to aid the trauma victim in adapting to new circumstances, with subsequent better adjustment.

- ***Positive emotion and laughter.*** This is a particularly social strategy; one needs a social support network in order to express optimism and to engage in laughter.

In a large study (*Time,* July 12, 2004, pp. 35–36) of pre- and post-service in Afghanistan and Iraq in 2003, researchers made several key findings:

- About 12 percent of those deployed in Iraq showed symptoms of PTSD (compare this with about 30 percent of those deployed in Vietnam showing symptoms).

- About 6 percent of those deployed in Afghanistan showed PTSD symptoms.

- Risk of PTSD symptoms was correlated with number of firefights experienced, which accounts for the lower incidence of symptoms for Afghanistan deployments.

- Soldiers experiencing one or two firefights showed PTSD symptoms around the 9 percent level; more than five fire fights, around 19 percent.

- Before deployment, about 5 percent of the soldiers showed PTSD symptoms, comparable to the civilian population.

- Soldiers with the most symptoms were least likely to seek treatment.

- Regular army and marines were less likely to show symptoms than national guard personnel, who were typically less intensively prepared.

Treatments

❶ Edna Foa, psychology professor at the University of Pennsylvania, uses cognitive behavioral therapy (CBT; see "Treatment Alternatives," chapter 15). Working particularly with rape victims, she begins the therapy several months after the trauma—and one-on-one, as opposed to the group approach immediately after the trauma, as practiced by Mitchell and his followers. She finds that only 15 percent develop PTSD symptoms, and these are the women with whom she works. She has them narrate the event in its entirety, then again at a subsequent session. Over about 20 hours of therapy, the patient organizes the elements of the event into a cogent narrative, thus gaining the feeling of being in control of the memory of the experience—progressing from a feeling of external "locus of control" to internal (see Seligman on explanatory style, topic 37.5). Along with developing the patient's control over the memory, she also works on desensitizing the patient to the places associated with the event by assigning homework to visit them repeatedly. Foa has also used this technique to prevent PTSD. However, many therapists appear to reject her approach. Groopman opines that this rejection derives from the more mechanical, by-the-book nature of the CBT approach, not so satisfying to the imagination of traditional therapists who are accustomed to dredging up childhood memories and building bridges from them to the present experience. In other words, some therapists find CBT boring. We would suggest, then, that the proper trait profile for CBT practitioners-in-training be low in the Big Five trait of Originality (see chapter 33) or low in Imagination—that is, comfortable pursuing the practical and down-to-earth.

❷ What to do for a trauma victim:

1. Get him to a safe place.

2. Provide water and food.

3. Inform him of the status of family, loved ones, or associates.

As a rule, Groopman says recall what you do to help persons who suffer the death of a loved one—the commonsense approach of advising them to take care of themselves, get sleep, avoid too much alcohol, eat properly, and so forth. A script is unnecessary.

❸ The problem with soldiers is that they fear seeking treatment will adversely affect their careers. To combat this mindset, the combined armed forces have set up a hotline to provide confidential counseling with civilian therapists. The hotline number is 800-464-8107. Treatment includes CBT and pharmacotherapy with Paxil and Zoloft.

❹ Read the definitive work on recovery from rape by Nancy Venable Raine (1998), *After Silence: Rape & My Journey Back*. Raine writes of the need to talk about something that one is not supposed to talk about, and of the therapy of writing about it.

5 The Department of Veterans Affairs maintains the National Center for PTSD, a comprehensive website at **www.ncptsd.va.gov**. Keep an eye on this site for developments in treating PTSD.

TOPIC 17.6   **Spinal Cord Injury**

        Upwards of 10,000 incidents of spinal cord injury (SCI) occur in the United States annually, the majority of them in metropolitan and industrial areas. About 80 percent of the injuries occur to people between the ages of 16 and 30, with males accounting for 82 percent overall. Vehicular accidents cause 40 percent, with sports, assaults, and falls contributing to most of the remainder. Injuries are categorized as either partially or completely severed spinal cords. Completely severed cords cannot be rejoined at present, nor can feeling or movement be regained in body parts below the break. The spinal cord, a long tube of soft matter about the diameter of a bratwurst, occupies the interior of the spinal vertebrae. The fracture results in blood flooding into the nerves and causing swelling, which starves spinal cord cells and brings on inflammation and cell death.

    The much-publicized injury of Christopher Reeve has stimulated heightened interest in spinal cord injury research. Reeve's accident came during a horse-riding competition in 1995 in Culpepper, Virginia. A fracture of the upper cervical vertebrae resulted in paralysis from his shoulders down, allowing breathing only with the aid of a ventilator or respirator. Eight years later, Reeve could breathe without the ventilator for most of the day and had recovered 80 percent of his muscle strength. He exercised in a swimming pool, and he could do "snow angel" moves with his arms and push off with his legs. Reeve died in 2004 as the result of complications from bedsores.

Treatments

1 Although some studies have shown that megadoses of methylprednisolone aid in restoring some degree of neurological function, the precise treatments vary, depending on the point and degree of the separation. A variety of pharmaceutical and orthopedic options are available. For resources, check the website of the National Spinal Cord Injury Association, **www.spinalcord.org**.

② V. R. Edgerton, a neuroscientist at UCLA, bases his experiments on the assumption that the spinal cord (1) has a memory of movements that is independent of the brain and (2) can relearn these movements by simulating them. He works with cats (whose spinal columns are severed) by placing them in a harness on a treadmill and putting them through the paces of walking. After six months of this training, most of the cats are able to walk unaided. Dr. Anton Wernig, a neurophysiologist at the University of Bonn (Germany), has demonstrated the same procedure with humans. In a variation on Wernig's adaptation of Edgerton's approach, Christopher Reeve practiced on a stationary bicycle.

③ Spinal cord researcher John McDonald of Washington University (St. Louis) uses electrical stimulation to assist workouts on treadmills, on bicycles, and in swimming pools. McDonald worked extensively with Reeve.

④ Case Western Reserve University School of Medicine (Cleveland) is involved in a clinical trial with a diaphragm pacemaker that is installed with a laparoscope. Reeve underwent this process, which reduced his need for a respirator to only five hours daily.

⑤ Reeve-Irvine Research Center's Hans Keirstead, experimenting with transplanting human glial cells into rats with damaged spinal cords, is finding that rats with this treatment are subsequently able to stand and in some cases walk.

⑥ Almudena Ramón-Cuerto (of the Spanish Council for Scientific Research in Valencia) has found that transplanting an injured rat's olfactory glial cells (they have the capacity to regenerate themselves) to the damaged spinal cord in fact enables regeneration of the spinal cord. Her research has been confirmed by at least seven other researchers.

⑦ Chinese neurosurgeon Hongyun Huang has taken olfactory glial cells from human fetuses and inserted them into damaged spinal cord areas of around 400 human patients, with some beginning to regain function as soon as three days after the procedure. This $20,000 surgery had, as of November 2003, 6,000 people on the waiting list, including many non-Chinese who travel there from countries (like the U.S.) that disallow research with human fetuses.

⑧ Michal Schwartz of Israel's Weizmann Institute of Science leads a project team that transplants a certain type of human blood cell into the spinal cords of patients within two weeks of their injuries.

⑨ Lars Olson, Henrich Cheng, and Yihai Cao of the Karolinska Institute in Sweden reported a major step in spinal cord reconstruction: the ability to successfully grow nerve cells across gaps in the severed spinal cords of adult rats (*Science,* July 26, 1996). Researchers took nerve cells from the rats' chests, formed them into filaments called "bridges," and fitted these into a ⅕-inch gap in their spinal cords. After several months, their once-motionless, dragging hind legs began to show voluntary movement. Within a year, the rats could partially support their weight and walk to some degree. An unusual feature of this technique that may account for the researchers' dramatic success is that they connected one end of each "bridge" to gray matter (the inner core of the cord) and the other end to white matter (the outer cover). Needless to say, intense efforts are under way to refine the technique and to ultimately experiment with humans.

⑩ For a website with a listing of organizations that provide information and support, try **neurosurgery.mgh.harvard.edu.** For the larger subject of traumatic brain injury, try the NIH's National Institute of Neurological Disorders and Stroke at **www.ninds.nih.gov.**

TOPIC 17.7   Stroke

Strokes (also called *brain attacks* or *ischemia*) hit 700,000 people in the United States annually, making stroke the third most fatal disease, following heart attack and cancer. One in five women over the age of 55 incur a stroke, and one in six men. These rates double with high blood pressure. Other risk factors for stroke include prior stroke, diabetes, heartbeat irregularities, smoking, exposure to second-hand smoke, heart disease, excessive alcohol use, and uncontrolled high cholesterol levels. The attack on the brain is initiated by the circulatory system, which blocks the path of oxygen and other nutrients to the brain because of a disease within the circulatory system itself.

Regarding second-hand smoke: *Time* magazine (May 10, 2004) reported that when Helena, Montana, in 2002 passed an ordinance prohibiting all indoor smoking, the heart attack rate dropped 40 percent within the next six months. After a court order voided the ban and everyone felt free to light up indoors, the rate shot back up to "normal." Even though this study did not look at stroke, certainly the findings should concern those at risk for stroke, as stroke and heart attack are both circulatory phenomena.

Symptoms that an attack has begun may include any or all of the following: headache, numbness or weakness of face, arm, or leg (especially affecting only one side of the body), dizziness, loss of balance or coordination, difficulty swallowing, confusion, visual disturbance, and difficulty in speaking or understanding. If one or more of these signs occurs suddenly, get yourself (or whoever is experiencing them) to the hospital immediately.

The effects of stroke include paralysis, loss of speech, and mood disorders, depending on just where the damage occurs. Research indicates that damage to the left hemisphere results in more depressive moods (activity in the left hemisphere is associated with positive moods), whereas damage to the right hemisphere (associated with more negative moods) results in more manic and hallucinatory moods. Roughly one-third of strokes are fatal, another one-third result in some degree of handicap, and the remainder result in complete (or close to complete) recovery. Quick treatment is essential.

Treatments

❶ The best prevention for stroke is to take maximum care of your circulatory system. After that, many doctors recommend that at a certain point in your life (my doctor recommended that I start at age 55), you take one coated aspirin (use reduced-dose version) each morning as a preventive; aspirin eases blood flow through its thinning, anticoagulant properties. Neither Coumadin nor heparin is any more effective than aspirin in preventing stroke. Megadoses of folic acid, B6, and B12 vitamins do not reduce the risk of stroke recurrence, according to a Wayne State University (Detroit) study of 3,680 adults who had already suffered a mild (nondisabling) stroke. Matthew Gillman of the Harvard Community Health Plan reports that stroke risk declines 22 percent for every three servings of fruits and vegetables eaten daily, where one serving equals 2 cups (*Journal of the American Medical Association,* April 12, 1995).

❷ The treatment for a brain attack depends on the nature of the attacking force. One must first determine the kind of circulatory problem that caused the attack. The initial cell death that occurs within 90 minutes of the attack sets off a program of systematic follow-on destruction that can last for days. If appropriate action can be taken before that 90 minutes are up, the chances of minimizing damage and maximizing recovery are improved. A new drug that dissolves blood clots, a tissue plasminogen activator (tPA), will improve the outcome of stroke if it is administered within two hours of onset. However, Stuart Lipman of Brigham and Women's Hospital reported in the February 1998 issue of *Nature Genetics* that tPA damages nerve cells in addition to breaking up clots.

❸ Broccoli and, especially, broccoli sprouts have been found to lower the risk of stroke and cardiovascular disease in general. University of Saskatchewan researchers fed the antioxidant-rich sprouts to stroke-prone rats, who after 14 weeks showed stronger defense and cardiovascular health.

❹ Researchers at Brigham and Women's Hospital and the Harvard School of Public Health report (in *JAMA*, October 6, 1999) that persons who eat five to six daily servings of fruits and vegetables reduce their chances of stroke by about one-third. One six-ounce serving daily of orange or grapefruit juice alone reduced chances of stroke by 25 percent, and one daily serving of cruciferous vegetables (e.g., broccoli and brussels sprouts) reduced chances of stroke by 32 percent, according to this study that involved over 100,000 men and women. (*Note:* Recall that caffeine interferes with vitamin C absorption.)

❺ In a study of 22,000 men (reported in *New England Journal of Medicine*, November 18, 1999), consuming one to two glasses of wine or beer daily is associated with a 20 percent decrease in risk for ischemic stroke (the most common form). Long known to reduce risk for heart disease, light to moderate alcohol consumption appears to lower stroke incidence the same way, by increasing "good" cholesterol (HDL) and breaking up blood clots.

❻ Concentric Medical of Mountain View, California, offers a "corkscrew" device called the MERCI (mechanical embolus removal in cerebral ischemia) Retrieval System. A catheter is inserted into an artery in the groin, than snaked to the neck, where a smaller extension catheter emerges and reaches into the brain, with a corkscrew-like probe piercing the clot, then backing the clot toward the main catheter in the neck, which then vacuums it up, helped by a kind of balloon that has stopped blood flow.

Studies showed that this device removed the clot in half of the attempts, with 75 percent surviving and 40 percent having little or no disability. Among the remainder, 50 percent survived, with 6 percent having little or no disability.

7 The National Institute of Neurological Disorders and Stroke is conducting clinical trials on the use of amphetamines as an aid to stroke victims in their effort to relearn talking and muscle control after the acute phase of stroke.

8 Using a procedure that has had both positive and negative results, neurosurgeon Douglas Kondziolka of the University of Pittsburgh injected anywhere from 2 million to 6 million laboratory-produced (by Layton BioScience, Atherton, California) brain cells in each of 12 patients (9 men, 3 women). Some who had been nonambulatory were subsequently able to walk; others got worse. Research is underway to determine whether there might be a certain kind of stroke patient who responds best to this treatment (*Neurology*, August 2000).

> **For the current status of any clinical trial mentioned in this book, check this website: www.clinicaltrials.gov.**

9 Neurologist John Milton (University of Chicago) is exploring the effects of visual rehearsal on stroke recovery. By studying the actual location in the brain of visualization among athletes, Milton hopes to learn how to apply visualization techniques to assist stroke patients in, for example, learning to walk.

10 A team at the University of California, San Diego, has been testing on animals a cooling device made by Innercool Therapies for slowing down the death of brain cells in stroke victims.

11 UCSD is also testing a modification of the current drug tPA (tissue plasminogen activator), which has a tendency to cause fatal hemorrhaging. The modification, TNK (Tenecteplase), is designed to reduce the chances of hemorrhage. tPA is used in only about 2 percent of all stroke victims, with higher rates in cities that have stroke teams. It is used only with the milder and more common clot-caused strokes (ischemic attacks), not with the rarer but more crippling hemorrhaging strokes (which comprise about 12 percent of all strokes).

⑫ Stromal bone marrow cells injected into the blood stream have been found to move to the area around dead brain tissue (as the result of stroke) and begin new brain activity. This technique is currently used only in animal research but shows promise, not only for strokes but for other disorders, such as Parkinson's, MS, and spinal cord injury.

⑬ A new clot buster by Eli Lilly, ReoPro, can be used during the three to five hours after ischemic strokes; this treatment is under study.

⑭ Currently being studied is the comparative effectiveness of two different surgical techniques for unblocking clogged carotid arteries in the neck: carotid endarterectomy and carotid artery stenting.

⑮ The problem with tPA is that it must be given within three hours of the beginning of stroke symptoms, and if administered incorrectly can cause terrible bleeding. Only 3–4 percent of U.S. stroke victims arrive at a hospital within that three-hour window of effectiveness. Only 5 percent of stroke victims receive the tPA treatment, and only 1 in 8 of those treated are helped. Researchers have been testing another anticlotting agent, desmoteplase, derived from the saliva of *Desmodus rotundus,* the vampire bat. Desmoteplase can be administered closer to the clot, as well as several hours later, without the disastrous bleeding in other parts of the body associated with tPA. Paion is the German company making the drug and sponsoring its testing.

⑯ The controversy continues over the up and down sides of estrogen boosts for women at menopause. Since a major study was discontinued in 2002 by NIH because estrogen replacement therapy (ERT) was increasing the risk for breast cancer and heart disease, the precise effects of estrogen replacement has been in limbo. One plus in the debate has been the discovery that estrogen lowers the risk for stroke and appears to reduce damage if stroke does occur. Younger women are less at risk for stroke than their male cohorts, but the women lose this advantage at menopause as estrogen levels decline. Researchers such as Patricia Hurn (Oregon Health and Science University in Portland) are exploring just how we might go about ERT so that its positive effects are realized and its negative effects minimized or eliminated.

⑰ A variety of research efforts are under way to determine how such players as glutamates, neurotrophins, free radicals, nitric oxide, and calcium act before, during, and after a brain attack. Another hotly debated topic is the role of fat consumption in stroke. A controversial article in the *Journal of the American Medical Association* (December 24, 1997) reported a positive relationship between *all* kinds of fat that are consumed—saturated, unsaturated, and polyunsaturated—and the absence of stroke: the more fat consumed, the less likely an individual is to have a stroke. This research, based on the Framington Heart Study, was reported by Matthew Gillman, the same person who reported (see above) that every three servings of fruits and veggies reduced stroke chances by 22 percent! We must await clarification. Researchers commonly point to studies conducted in Crete, a region where both heart disease and stroke are low and low levels of saturated fat are coupled with low levels of overweight among the population. Interestingly, the Cretans have a high fat content in their diet, but it is monounsaturated fat, as in olive oil.

⑱ A University of Alabama at Birmingham team has reported excellent results in arm and leg rehabilitation (Pidikiti and others, 1996). The technique involves immobilizing the good arm or leg and forcing use of the damaged one.

⑲ For a listing of links to various stroke resources, visit the Internet Stroke Center site at **www.strokecenter.org**.

SUGGESTED RESOURCES

Alkon, D. L. (1992). *Memory's Voice: Deciphering the Brain-Mind Code.* New York: HarperCollins.

DeAngelis, T. (1995, April). "New Threat Associated with Child Abuse." *APA Monitor,* 26(4), 1, 38.

Mukerjee, M. (1995, October). "Hidden Scars." *Scientific American,* pp. 14, 20.

Wolfe, D. A., R. J. McMahon, and R. D. Peters (1997). *Child Abuse: New Directions in Prevention and Treatment Across the Lifespan.* Thousand Oaks, Calif.: Sage.

18

Degenerative Conditions

Slowly Falling Apart

*I*n a sense, the degenerative conditions discussed in this chapter are like accelerated aging. But even normal aging does not require us to experience the terrifying loss of memory, coordination, and clarity that these conditions can entail. This chapter discusses degenerative diseases: Alzheimer's, Creutzfeldt-Jakob, Huntington's, Lou Gehrig's, Lyme, and Parkinson's diseases, as well as multiple sclerosis.

> **66***Forgive, O Lord, my little jokes on Thee And I'll forgive Thy great big one on me.***99**
>
> —*Robert Frost*

For the most part, cures for these degenerative conditions are dependent on finding ways to replace damaged and deceased neurons. Samuel Weiss and Brent Reynolds of the University of Calgary (Canada) Faculty of Medicine discovered reserves of immature brain cells in adult mice that could be coaxed into dividing into new cells. This phenomenon had been thought possible only in embryos. The implications for humans are now being studied. Fred Gage, along with a team of Swedish scientists, recently announced the successful detection of regenerated brain cells. However, the successful regeneration of human or animal brain cells, although it is a major breakthrough, is just the first step in a long research-and-development process.

TOPIC 18.1   Alzheimer's Disease

At the 1996 meeting of the Society for Neuroscience, attendees could choose from more than 500 presentations on *Alzheimer's disease* (AD). AD afflicts 4 million old people in the U.S. (and almost half of those age 85 and over) and is sure to increase with the aging baby-boom cohort. Women experience AD at the rate of one in four; men, one in six. Apparently, a concatenation of bad genes, poor education, head injury, and normal aging processes work together diabolically to produce *beta amyloid* and *neurofibrillary tangles.* Beta amyloid is a protein composed of 42 amino acids that form toxic deposits, or *plaque,* on the brain's neurons. David Snowdon (2001, p. 129) points out that the problem with amyloid appears related not to the amount of amyloid produced, but rather *how* it is produced. If improperly derived from the *beta amyloid precursor protein* (APP), the amyloid becomes sticky and forms plaques. Several genes, in mutant form, appear to contribute to this malformation of amyloid. Dennis Selkoe, chief investigator and professor of neurology at Harvard Medical School, reports discovery of the protein presenilin that converts normal brain protein into amyloid plaque (*Nature,* April 8, 1999). Research is underway to identify presenilin inhibitors.

The neural tangles result from an abnormal protein, *tau protein,* within the cell that constricts and distorts fibers. Some argue that plaque is the primary culprit, but others say it is the tau protein. Snowdon (2001, p. 130) wryly calls this the debate between the Tauists and the Baptists (from B-eta A-myloid P-rotein)! Nonetheless, these processes appear to be controlled by at least four genes (*Neuron,*

November 15, 1997; *Archives of Neurology,* January 2003): APP, which, when it is flawed, produces amyloid-precursor protein, the raw material for plaque; Presenilin 1, which affects cell repair and cell death; ApoE4 (apolipoprotein E, variant 4), which affects the speed at which plaque is deposited; and CYP46 for late-onset AD—this gene's job is to maintain balanced levels of cholesterol in brain. Apparently, the mutated APP alone is associated with late onset of AD, whereas the other two are associated with earlier onset (Presenilin 1) and rate of onset (ApoE4). Duke researchers find that those with the ApoE4 gene from both parents have eight times the risk for AD as those who don't. Neurogeneticist Rudolph Tanzi of Massachusetts General Hospital (reported in *BrainWork.* March–April 2002) suggests that ApoE4 is a risk factor gene but does not directly cause AD; 50 percent of AD patients do not carry ApoE4, an indication that there are other environmental and genetic factors. Tanzi predicts there might be four to seven more AD genes yet to be discovered. His lab has identified several "hot spots" for potential AD genes, such as chromosomes 9 and 10. Their study used data from the National Institute of Mental Health registry of 437 families.

Huntington Potter, of Harvard Medical School's Department of Neurobiology, reports that these genes apparently do not perform inside neurons but rather work inside the cells of neighboring *microglial cells* and *astrocytes,* which in turn release the free radicals that kill off the nerve cells (*Cell,* October 1997). Others, including Davis Parker, Jr., of the University of Virginia, believe that the process starts in the neuron's mitochondria, where, because of a genetic defect, energy production goes awry and produces free radicals rather than energy. In either case, the brain essentially oxidizes, or slowly burns itself up, leaving plaque and tangled fibers as evidence of what once was. The plaque and tangles begin deep in the brain near the brain stem (Braak stages I and II), progress to the hippocampus and its neighborhood (Braak stages III and IV), finally arriving at the neocortex (Braak stages V and VI). AD stages are named after German researchers Heiko and Eva Braak. Stage 0 is absence of tangles and plaque.

The effect of this toxic process is a progressive, neurodegenerative disease that typically begins in one's 70s or 80s. A variation called early-onset Alzheimer's can begin during middle age. The first symptoms of this buildup of plaque (from beta amyloid protein) and tangled nerve fibers (from tau protein) are memory problems; then, over a period of years, problems develop with personality, cognition, and general physical functioning.

Much discussion has centered on the role of mental exercise—the "Use It or Lose It" factor—in preventing or delaying AD. Yaskov Stern and his colleagues at Columbia University studied 593 New Yorkers at risk for AD. They found that people who either had fewer than eight years of schooling or lower-skilled (i.e., mentally unstimulating) jobs were twice as likely to end up with AD, whereas those with both of these factors were three times as likely to develop dementia as those who were more highly educated and more highly skilled. Amir Soas of Cleveland's Case Western Reserve University Medical School and Mary Haan of the University of Michigan confirm Stern's findings. Specifically, they found that persons who read more, learn more, and who in general are more mentally and physically active throughout life show significantly reduced chances of contracting AD. Particularly effective, according to these researchers, is increasing one's intellectual activity during adulthood.

However, it appears that the foregoing researchers used too broad a measure. David Snowdon (2001, pp. 112–114) writes that an analysis of the autobiographies written by nuns at the beginning of their careers found idea density to be the strongest predictor of cognitive capability in later years, with grammatical complexity a distant second. Around 80 percent of the nuns with low idea density in their 20s scored low enough on cognitive tests in their 80s to be described as impaired, compared with only 10 percent with high idea density in their 20s. Eighty-five of the 93 nuns whose autobiographies were analyzed were college-degreed and engaged as teachers; this weakens the argument that education in and of itself prevents dementia.

The process is complex, with tangles starting early in life and gradually becoming more complex and extensive. It is possible that low idea density in early life is affected by such tangles or possibly by some other aberration in the gray matter. In other words, it is unclear whether idea density prevents AD, or whether the lack of idea density serves as an early symptom. It is possible that plaque and tangles in early development prevent idea density, with the result that such early tangles influence the kind and degree of schooling that individuals pursue. For example, Robert Friedland, neurologist at Case Western Reserve University School of Medicine, reported (in *American Academy of Neurology,* August 2004) the results of studying 357 people over 40 years. The subjects who did not contract AD reported a 33 percent increase in the level of mental demands in their work; those who developed AD reported no such increase. Similarly, subjects working in professional and managerial jobs (supposedly more mentally demanding) developed AD at a significantly lower rate than those working in technical, sales, and administrative jobs (supposedly less demanding). In these two cases, it could be simply that mental demands did not necessarily prevent AD, but rather that the invisible, early tangles of AD prevented one from selecting and engaging in mentally demanding work. Whatever the case, it would not necessarily help to encourage everyone to take on greater mental challenges regardless of age or level of achievement—but it wouldn't hurt.

Snowdon (2001, p. 116) also tried to determine whether emotional content in the autobiographies of nuns made a difference. It didn't; emotional content was unrelated to density or to subsequent cognitive performance. He also tried to determine whether IQ was related. It wasn't; Of course, IQ test scores weren't available for these nuns back in the 1940s and '50s, but they compared grades in academic subjects and found no relation to either density or later performance. However, one flaw in the latter analysis is that grades are typically more reflective of personal discipline and ambition, not necessarily IQ.

Pascale Barberger-Gateau and others (as reported in the *British Journal of Medicine*) suggest that fish and seafood fatty acids lower the risk of dementia. They followed the fish, seafood (both high in polyunsaturated fat), and meat (high in saturated fatty acids) consumption of 1,674 residents of Southwest France (at least 68 years old and without dementia). Controlling for age, sex, and education, results after seven years yielded no evidence that meat affected dementia. Eating fish and seafood at least once a week significantly lowered risk of AD disease and other dementias. Education accounted for part of the reduction—higher education was associated with eating fish at least once a week. Again, not only might the more educated choose to eat fish more frequently, but the eating of more fish early on might, through keeping one's neurons more tangle-free, incline subjects to take on greater educational challenges.

Huntington Potter discovered an early diagnosis for AD, using analogical reasoning. While looking for Down syndrome features that it might be reasonable to expect in AD because they share the same chromosome, Potter found that AD-destined individuals show a hypersensitivity to tropicamide (the synthetic version of atropine), used by eye doctors to dilate pupils in order to have a good look at the retina. AD subjects, both before and after onset of the disease, need only 1/100th of the normal amount of tropicamide for satisfactory pupil dilation. So we now have a rather effective diagnostic procedure (*On the Brain,* Winter 1995).

In the March 23, 1999 issue of *Neurology,* Charles J. Duffy and Sheldon J. Tetewsky, University of Rochester, describe "motion blindness" as an early indicator of AD. AD damages cells that process visual information, causing confusion in perceiving self-movement as well as movement around the self: am I moving, or is the car moving? One then can't interpret visual cues, resulting in trouble navigating: can't remember how to get home, or how one got to where one is. Another early indicator involves early changes in the *entorhinal cortex* (EC). Studying a group of 123 people with "questionable" AD (do not meet clinical criteria, but have memory problems), Marilyn Albert of Harvard Medical School sought to predict who among the group would develop AD. She was able to pinpoint areas that change the most in people who developed AD. MRI scans indicate changes in the EC before full-blown AD appears, which then progress to the hippocampus.

Snowdon (2001, p. 155) writes that strokes increase the likelihood of developing AD, as well as accentuating its effects, whereas the absence of strokes can allow higher mental performance in someone who does develop AD. In a study of 824 Catholic clerics 55 and older (reported in the May 2004 issue of *Archives of Neurology*), persons who have diabetes in middle age increase their risk for AD by some 65 percent. There is an apparent link between insulin problems and beta amyloid accumulation, as well as a link between inefficient glucose metabolism and memory problems.

Richard Mayeux, leader of a study at Columbia University's College of Physicians and Surgeons, and coauthor Ann Saunders of Duke University report in the *New England Journal of Medicine* (February 19, 1998) that a simple blood test for the presence of the ApoE4 gene, coupled with the presence of dementia, can reduce the AD misdiagnosis rate from the 1997 rate of 45 percent to a significantly lower rate of 16 percent.

Scott Small, assistant professor of neurology at Columbia College of Physicians and Surgeons in New York, provides (in the *New York Times,* February 1, 2000, D7) a brief quiz to evaluate the health of one's memory:

1. Does faulty memory adversely affect your work or family responsibilities? *If yes, see a neurologist: could be Alzheimer's or something as serious.*

2. Do you have more trouble remembering recent events than remote events? Or, do you have trouble finding your way around

familiar places? *If yes, could be brain damage; you might want to check things out with a neurologist.*

3. Have you experienced any other decreases in ability to re-member? *If yes, could be either early Alzheimer's or normal memory loss due to such factors as prolonged medication or stress. If no, then you would not appear to have any memory problems.*

For a brief yet insightful story of the progression of AD, read Lawrence Altman's feature story on Ronald Reagan in the *New York Times* (October 5, 1997, pp. 1, 34).

Treatments

❶ Donepezil (Aricept) was approved by the Food and Drug Administration in November 1996. It appears to be effective in slowing down the pace of dementia in AD for at least 18 months. A reversible inhibitor of the enzyme *acetylcholinesterase,* it functions in one of two ways: it either improves memory or slows down the progress of AD by preventing the breakdown of acetylcholine, which is deficient in AD patients. This represents an improvement over Cognex (tacrine), which has a similar purpose but more side effects. Europeans have been treating AD patients with gingko biloba extract (Egb 761), which improves the flow of blood to the brain, although in doing so, it decreases the blood's clotting ability. However, doses are unclear, and it can interact with other treatments such as aspirin, which could cause both excessive blood thinning and anticoagulation.

❷ The best way to influence idea density is to read to your children. Reading increases vocabulary and comprehension, and these two skills influence idea density. Other preventive measures include (as suggested by Snowdon, 2001, pp. 137 ff.):

- Don't smoke.
- Avoid head trauma (use seat belts and helmets, avoid soccer headers).
- Take vitamins.
- Use antioxidants.
- Exercise.
- Maintain healthy heart and circulatory system—low cholesterol and blood pressure.

- Maintain proper weight.

- Maintain low blood sugar.

- Consume lycopenes, i.e., red pigments in tomatoes, guavas, water-melons, pink grapefruit (gourmet note: lycopenes in tomatoes are best when cooked with some oil, as in a marinara sauce).

- Include folic acid in diet (dark green leafy veggies, beans, nuts, citrus, liver; two-thirds of mothers giving birth to nervous system malformations are folate deficient, compared with only one-fifth of mothers with normal babies—and the higher the levels of folate in the blood, the less likely to find significant deterioration in autopsied brains; folate helps breaks down *homocysteine,* which in high levels leads to brain atrophy).

- Eat fresh fruits and veggies.

- Cultivate optimism (positive emotions account for a survival advantage of some seven years!).

- Participate in prayer/meditation/contemplation.

- Be an active participant in a community, family, or other group.

- Accept emotional support.

- Spurn unnecessary physical support.

- Engage in verbal exercise: reading, crosswords, Scrabble.

- Pursue further education, whether just more coursework or additional degrees, licenses, or certificates.

- Learn new, more complex skills, or elaborate on skills you already possess.

❸ The amount of exercise engaged in regularly between the ages of 20 and 59 is inversely related to the risk of AD. In a study of 373 people, including both those with AD and healthy individuals, neurologists Arthur Smith and Robert Friedland, of Case Western Reserve University School of Medicine, compiled an exercise score based on the number of hours of exercise per month multiplied by an intensity factor. The higher the score, the less likely one's chance of developing AD.

❹ Memantine is the first treatment specifically for the later stages. It is not miraculous, but it does help to stabilize patients so that certain functions can be maintained a few months longer. Studies suggest that it gives patients the ability to go to the toilet on their own for six months. Memantine works by blocking excess amounts of glutamate, which causes damage or kills nerve cells.

❺ Vitamins E and C taken together in huge daily doses (at least 400 IU of E and more than 500 mg of C) could reduce the risk of AD by 78 percent (study published in *Archives of Neurology,* 4,740 participants).

❻ In a one-year evaluation of combination therapy, published in the *Journal of the American Medical Association,* more than 400 AD patients were treated with donepezil (Aricept) and memantine (Namenda). These medicines worked better in combination than alone in slowing down the disease. Substantial benefits were evident for patients with moderate to severe AD. Donepezil preserves the neurotransmitter acetylcholine, and memantine blocks overproduction of the harmful brain chemical glutamate.

❼ Pills are being studied that can offset the effect of mutated genes that are relevant to AD.

❽ The Women's Health Initiative reported in June 2004, on a study of some 3,000 women ages 65–79 who had hysterectomies and a five-year daily dose of estrogen pills, that estrogen does not appear to provide any protection against either Alzheimer's disease or lesser forms of dementia. In fact, persons taking placebos show slightly lower rates of dementia than the estrogen takers.

❾ Researchers at Johns Hopkins University and the National Institute on Aging have identified a significant reduction in the risk of getting AD among those who take nonsteroidal antiinflammatory drugs (NSAIDs), such as aspirin, ibuprofen, and naproxyn, for periods of two years. Persons taking aspirin or ibuprofen for several years decrease their risk for AD by about 70 percent (*Neurology*, September 24, 2002). Apparently, such painkillers interfere with the development of beta amyloid. The doses for the different drugs, however, are unknown, and the side effects of inappropriate use could cause people to wind up with a disease or condition, such as kidney failure, other than the one they were perhaps unnecessarily trying to prevent.

❿ In a significant breakthrough, researcher Dale Schenk of Elan Corp. has led a team in synthesizing a beta amyloid peptide look-alike protein composed of the same number of amino acid molecules—42—as amyloid plaque itself. Regular vaccinations of this synthetic plaque apparently tricks Alzheimer's mice into both preventing further plaque accumulation and reversing current levels of the tangly plaque. The outcome of human trials is eagerly awaited.

⑪ One treatment that is close to availability is a new class of drugs—ampakines—being developed by Gary Lynch of the University of California at Irvine. Ampakines intensify the level of *AMPA glutamates,* chemicals necessary for interneuronal communication, and have been shown to improve memory. Clinical trials are under way.

⑫ William Klunk of Western Psychiatric Institute in Pittsburgh is working with a tissue dye called Chrysamine G, which appears to prevent beta amyloid from expressing its toxic effect on brain neurons—a kind of shield, as it were.

⑬ Some suspect that beta amyloid, or possibly the immune system itself, increases free radicals; they are exploring treatment with antioxidants.

⑭ Rachel Neve at McLean Hospital in Belmont, Massachusetts, is pursuing a variation of the beta amyloid molecule joined with molecules associated with APP gene. This combination (called *C-100*) has been shown to be more toxic than beta amyloid in its normal state.

⑮ A team headed by Jeffrey Gray at Maudsley Hospital's Institute of Psychiatry (London) has developed a technique that manufactures brain cells from rat embryos, injects them into diseased rat brains, and then frees them to migrate to the diseased area and repair or replace the damaged cells. Rats so treated have recovered from severe heart attacks and have subsequently learned complex tasks. The researchers have started a company, ReNeuron, dedicated to researching, developing, and eventually selling the product.

⑯ Mark Mattson, a University of Kentucky neurobiologist, leads a team at the university's Sanders-Brown Center on Aging in the investigation of calorie intake's relation to the onset of AD. Mattson's team reported that rats with a restricted calorie intake resisted injected toxins that mimic Alzheimer's, Parkinson's, and Huntington's diseases (*Annals of Neurology,* January 1999). Rats that ate all they pleased showed significantly less resistance to the AD-like agent. In human terms, this would suggest an optimum daily intake of 1,800 to 2,000 calories. The mechanism perhaps involves the fact that stress results from reduced intake, followed by the activation of genes that protect the body during low intake. No mention is made of the long-term effects of such a pattern.

⑰ The July 1998 issue of *Nature Medicine* presented three articles with apparent breakthrough news: the related reports confirm that beta amyloid is the prime nerve cell killer and that a peptide has been developed that arrests and corrects the progress of cell death. This new peptide binds to the good amyloid gone bad, preventing it from twisting further, straightening out the hardened twists to their formerly benign condition. Researchers are confident that both prevention and cure are just around the corner.

⑱ If you have an interest in AD, you should stay informed about all these lines of research. One way is through visiting the Alzheimer's disease website at **www.alzheimers.org**.

⑲ Studies have shown that men with AD had lower testosterone levels than those who did not develop AD. Though all men exhibit decreased testosterone in their seniority, some produce less than others. Studies are underway to determine whether boosting testosterone levels for aging men whose testosterone plummets more than others will in fact reduce their risk for AD.

⑳ Nicolas G. Bazan, Director of the Neuroscience Center of Excellence, Louisiana State University, has developed a drug that is effective with animals in preventing brain cell destruction associated with AD and other neurodegenerative disorders. He isolated the gene—*cyclooxygenase-2* (COX-2)—responsible for manufacturing the protein that causes brain cell death. His drug, in essence, switches the gene off, thereby preventing production of its protein, also known by the name COX-2. The drug entered preclinical trials in 1999.

㉑ Snowdon (2001, p. 123) suggests things to do with AD patients:

- Discuss past events (from childhood, etc.)—the repetition helps their memory, and the activity is intrinsically satisfying.

- Discuss current events.

- Play cards.

- Sing songs.

- Assemble puzzles.

㉒ Conduct an Internet search on "Alzheimer's Café" and learn about this concept, recently introduced in the Netherlands, in which patients, caregivers, and professionals meet over refreshments to share ideas, treatment options, resources, and so forth.

TOPIC 18.2   Creutzfeldt-Jakob Disease

Caused by eating prion-infected beef from cattle with *bovine spongiform encephalopathy* (BSE, a.k.a. "mad cow disease"), this rare killer has taken 137 human lives in the United Kingdom as of January 2004. These U.K. victims consumed domestic beef; no deaths have been traced to U.S. beef. *Prions* are aberrant, deformed proteins that enter cells and cause normal proteins therein to fold improperly. To the immune system they are indistinguishable from normal proteins. Replicating unchecked, prions spread throughout the body, causing massive brain cell loss that results in delirium and death. Symptoms typically appear years after infection has occurred. Normal infection-fighting methods, even heat and acids, are ineffective.

Treatments

❶ For the present, the only sure prevention is abstinence from eating beef (the "just say no" approach).

❷ The next best prevention is excellent beef inspection.

❸ Little is known about prions. At present, research is focused on two areas: developing antibodies that can discriminate between prions and normal proteins, and genetic engineering of cattle.

❹ Monitor the CJD Foundation website at **www.cjdfoundation.org**.

TOPIC 18.3   Huntington's Disease

Huntington's disease (HD) is the result of one single dominant gene; each child of an affected parent has a 50 percent chance of getting the disease. Huntington's typically begins by killing off cells in the *caudate nucleus* (see appendix A) sometime during one's 40s. The result is a gradual loss of control of the intellect, emotions, balance, and speech. Typically, a pattern of involuntary movements, referred to as Huntington's chorea, accompanies the other symptoms. About 50,000 people have the disease in the United States; the normal progression leads to death within 15–20 years of the initial symptoms.

The Huntington's gene, discovered in 1993, produces a protein referred to as *huntingtin.* The normal form of huntingtin typically contains between 10 and 35 glutamine molecules, whereas the mutant version contains a minimum of 38 molecules and up to 100. This repeated sequence has been described as a kind of chemical "stuttering" (*Los Angeles Times,* August 8, 1997, p. A1). The normal version of huntingtin is necessary to sustain life, and apparently 38 molecules is the threshold at which huntingtin transmogrifies and becomes lethal. In 1995, researchers at Johns Hopkins University announced the discovery of a protein that binds to huntingtin and dubbed it *huntingtin-associated protein-1,* or HAP-1 (*Nature,* November 23, 1995). In a related discovery, researchers have determined that the abnormal protein associated with HD acts on a regulatory protein, *p53,* in such as way as to activate many other genes, with the result of damaging mitochondria.

> For the current status of any clinical trial mentioned in this book, check this website: **www.clinicaltrials.gov.**

Treatments

❶ There are no known treatments.

❷ Much current research is aimed at preventing HAP-1 from binding to huntingtin in mice. Researchers are searching for a pharmaceutical that will somehow interact with the HAP-1 protein and the glutamine 38+ chain to prevent the clustering and buildup that eventually kills off brain cells.

❸ Robert Friedlander, a neurosurgeon at the Harvard School of Medicine, has conducted research in mice that delays the onset of a Huntington's-type disease in mice and extends their lives by a factor of as much as 25 percent. His technique involves blocking the enzyme *caspase-1,* which is a member of a family of enzymes that appear to be involved in other neurodegenerative disorders such as Alzheimer's, Parkinson's, ALS (a.k.a. Lou Gehrig's disease), and stroke. All these disorders are characterized by *apoptosis,* a kind of programmed cell death triggered by the deadly enzyme. The search is underway for drugs that block caspase-1 and are suitable for use in humans.

❹ Riken Brain Institute in Japan reports (in *Nature Medicine,* online, January 18, 2004) a type of sugar called *trehalose* that can prevent formation of huntingtin aggregates and improve motor functioning in mice with the disease. A 2 percent solution of trehalose was administered to *transgenic* mice that had both the genes and the symptoms of Huntington's. Their movement improved: they took bigger strides, achieved better walking posture, and completed motor tasks more quickly than untreated mice and those given table sugar (sucrose). They also lived an average of 10 weeks longer. Trehalose is safe and easy to administer (in the mice's drinking water), exists naturally in honey, can be produced from starch in the lab, and is a promising candidate for human clinical trials.

❺ Keep current by visiting the Huntington Disease Association's website at **www.hdsa.org**.

TOPIC 18.4 | **Lou Gehrig's Disease**

In the United States, *Lou Gehrig's disease (amyotrophic lateral sclerosis,* or ALS) is at about 25,000 cases, with about 5,000 new cases each year. It was named after the New York Yankees star who died from it in 1941. ALS attacks the motor neurons of the brain and spinal cord, which control the muscles. This progressive condition affects strength, speech, swallowing, and breathing, but it does not affect intellect, vision, hearing, taste, touch, and smell, and typically it does not affect sexual, bowel, or bladder functions.

Researchers continue to investigate the cause of ALS. Only 10 percent of the cases run in families, and of that 10 percent, only one in five has a known genetic origin. How are the other 98 percent of the cases explained? The best explanation at present is that ALS results from a combination of some kind of genetic predisposition with some kind of environmental assault (such as the inhalation of strong petrochemicals). Some researchers think that ALS is actually a combination of several different diseases.

Treatments

❶ There is no known cure. Two current treatments aimed at slowing the disease's progress involve an implant and an injection. The implant is a genetically engineered capsule of about 100,000 cells of ciliary neurotrophic factor (CNTF) that releases CNTF at a constant rate. It is manufactured by CytoTherapeutics Inc. in Providence, Rhode Island. The injection uses the drug myotrophin, a genetically engineered form of human insulin-like growth factor (IGF-1). It appears to slow the progress of ALS by about 25 percent.

❷ Drugs that have been approved for treating ALS work best early in the history of the disease. Researchers have therefore been searching for markers that identify ALS as early as possible. A promising protein "signature" has been identified by Harvard, Massachusetts General, and University of Pittsburgh researchers. This signature comprises 10 proteins, and the researchers have developed an algorithm that uses these 10 variables to discriminate unmarked ALS samples from non-ALS samples in a small sample with excellent accuracy. After successful use with a larger sample, this may be a giant step toward early identification of ALS in order to allow drugs to realize their full potential.

❸ For information and support, visit the website of Doug Jacobson (he has ALS) at home.earthlink.net/~jakesan.

❹ At a certain point, ALS has done all that it can do, with no further degeneration. At that point, you and your caregivers can figure out how to settle in for the long haul. My friend with ALS, Joe Martin, has written two novels since getting his diagnosis. He explores every device as it is made available. I wrote recently to ask whether he had tried to use a mind-controlled mouse for his computer. Here is his reply:

> I have played with a simple mind-controlled mouse. I could move the cursor left by thinking about Dean Smith, right with Coach K, up with a picnic, down with the Atlanta airport. I didn't have enough time to find out what would happen if the two coaches met in the airport!

❺ In the fall of 1998, an international study began human testing of a hockey-puck-sized pump that delivers brain-derived neurotrophic factor (BDNF) at a steady rate. BDNF, a synthetic protein similar to one that occurs naturally in the brain, has had only minimal effectiveness when administered by injection.

❻ Neuroscientist Christopher Shaw of the University of British Columbia has serendipitously formed a connection between the onset of ALS and the agene bleaching process that was used in making white bread. The agene process, which produces the toxin methionine sulfoximine (MSO), was discontinued in the 1950s and 60s because of bizarre and unpleasant effects in animals and humans. It is possible that toxins remaining in the body after digesting white bread, along with other factors, play a significant role in the onset of ALS.

❼ Researchers at the University of California, Irvine, and the University of Lyon (France) have isolated a virus essentially unique to ALS sufferers. It is found in motor nerves of the spinal cord and resembles the Echo-7 virus that causes meningitis. Look for more.

| TOPIC 18.5 | **Lyme Disease** |

Lyme disease (LD) is one of the most underreported diseases in the U.S. Doctors and insurance companies seem especially reluctant to acknowledge its existence. The bacterium hides in cell walls, and symptoms mimic other disorders: arthritis, fibromyalgia, memory loss, heart palpitations, confusion, fatigue, mood disorders, and, as one of the primary clinical signs, a foggy brain.

Treatments

❶ The standard treatment, long-term (more than a year), high-dose antibiotics, usually improves and sometimes reverses the symptoms.

❷ There are more drastic treatments with more serious potential side effects, but without treatment, chronic Lyme can lead to permanent neurological damage. Helen Hyams, in an e-mail, January 2, 2003, adds: "I probably got [exposed] in my childhood in New England and it remained dormant until about 1988, then became chronic and notched up a plateau this year. However, you can get it almost anywhere in the country, from deer ticks and or dog ticks or fleas, so I might have gotten it as an adult when I lived in Florida or after I moved here [Texas]. Some people never show symptoms, but if someone has some of these symptoms or the other symptoms of Lyme in the literature, it should be considered as a diagnosis."

❸ Keep informed by monitoring the Lyme Disease Foundation website at www.lyme.org.

| TOPIC 18.6 | **Multiple Sclerosis** |

Multiple sclerosis (MS) is the second most common neural disease among young adults, after head injury. MS affects about 300,000 people in the United States, typically beginning between the ages of 20 and 40. An autoimmune dysfunction, MS occurs when the immune system mistakenly identifies brain and spinal cord tissues, and particularly the myelin sheath that covers axons, as foreign invaders and attempts to get rid of them. The result is an eating away of myelin—a *plaque*—in a region that can extend from several millimeters to over a centimeter. In some cases, the attack succeeds in destroying the axon itself. After some time, the process of *inflammatory demyelination* is halted by *suppressor cells* and, depending on the severity of the attack, the processes of *remyelination* and recovery of function may occur, only to be subject to another attack months or years later.

Harvard's Rohit Bakshi is the first to show that the *caudate nucleus* (part of the brain's gray matter) undergoes atrophy in MS. This is unrelated to the conventional marker of destroyed white matter (demyelination). Therefore, another mechanism must be at work in the gray-matter destruction, or neuronal death. MRIs show that the volume of the caudate nucleus in 24 patients was on average 19 percent lower than that of healthy patients (10 subjects). Bakshi posits that iron deposits in the caudate nucleus may be to blame, like the iron deposits seen in Alzheimer's disease and Parkinson's disease.

Major symptoms can include weakness, paralysis, tingling, numbness, disturbed vision, balance and coordination problems, slurred speech, loss of bladder and bowel control, chronic pain, and severe fatigue. Sensations will spontaneously stop, then recur at a different location. Episodes vary in length from days to months. Because diagnosis is based on multiple sites of inflammation at different times, early diagnosis is difficult, but new MRI techniques are making early diagnosis a possibility. Elliot Frohman of the University of Texas Southwestern Medical School, Dallas, reported (in *Neurology*, September 9, 2003) that, in many cases, a single MRI of the brain and spinal cord can predict MS. New guidelines indicate that patients with three or more lesions in specific areas have a better than 80 percent chance of developing MS within 7–10 years.

About one-fourth of the cases of MS are relatively mild, and about one-third are severe. Half of the people with MS are disabled after 10 years, and more than one-third are unable to walk after 30 years (Riskind, 1996). Twice as many women as men contract MS, and Caucasians are more likely to suffer MS than other ethnic groups. Eight or more genes appear to be associated with the disease, with particular focus on a region of chromosome 6 that is associated with the immune system. The concordance rate is rather low between identical twins, however, suggesting that an unknown environmental agent triggers MS.

Treatments

❶ A cure is unavailable at the present. Some relief from the fatigue of MS is available to about half of the MS population through amantadine, a dopamine enhancer.

❷ For severe flare-ups, an adrenal steroid hormone called methyl-prednisolone can shorten the episode but does not appear to slow the overall progress of the disease.

❸ The two drugs mentioned above treat symptoms, whereas beta-interferon (Betaseron, Avonex), a natural immune agent, provides more long-term benefits for some MS patients. Treatment with Avonex within a month after the onset of symptoms delays new symptoms by more than two years. The study included 203 patients, half receiving Avonex immediately after showing initial symptoms, half receiving it after their second attack. Prompt treatment led to a 43 percent reduction in the number of relapses. Patients who began treatment immediately were more likely to be symptom-free 4–5 years after the first symptoms. Immediate and early intervention may prevent development of the disability for over five years.

❹ Given in the early stages, a new drug—copolymer 1 (Copaxone)—can reduce both the rate of flare-ups and the overall progress of the disease for patients with milder MS.

❺ Seventy-five to 90 percent of people with MS experience fatigue every day. Kottil W. Rammohan, Ohio State University Medical Center, finds that modafinil may provide relief (currently used to treat narcolepsy—daytime sleepiness). Modafinil was tested against a placebo in 72 people with MS (age 18–65). During weeks 1 and 2 only a placebo was administered; weeks 3 and 4, 200 mg/day of modafinil; weeks 5 and 6, 400 mg/day of modafinil; and weeks 7-9, again only a placebo. Participants rated their own fatigue. Results indicated that a 200 mg dose of modafinil showed significant improvement, with common but tolerable side effects including headache and nausea.

❻ Current research is exploring a variety of possible environmental triggers in several different areas, including immune cells from mutant genes, viruses, and pregnancy (particularly prolactin production). The British biotechnology group Plc is currently at work on a new drug based on a major discovery. Steven Jacobson, principal investigator for the Viral Immunology Section of the National Institute of Neurological Disorders and Stroke (NINDS), strongly suspects that a version of the human herpes virus may be the trigger that initiates MS in many cases (*BrainWork: The Neuroscience Newsletter,* January–February 1998).

❼ To keep current, visit the website of the International Federation for Multiple Sclerosis at **www.msif.org**.

TOPIC 18.7 **Parkinson's Disease**

Around 1.5 million people in the United States suffer from Parkinson's disease (PD), most of them over 40. Men have twice the risk for PD as women. While the initiating cause of PD is unknown, Caroline M. Tanner and associates at the Parkinson's Institute in Sunnyvale report, in the January 27, 1999 issue of *JAMA* on a study of 19,842 male twins, that PD has little or no genetic origin, but that it is due to the effect of as yet unknown chemicals in the environment. This is consistent with the higher risk for men, who as a group tend to be more frequently exposed to environmental toxins. People exposed to paints, glues and petroleum products in the workplace developed symptoms of Parkinson's an average of three years earlier than those without exposure. The greater the exposure, the more severe the symptoms. The research team is trying to find a pattern among Parkinson's sufferers that identifies the chemical culprit(s). Onset is associated with the death of cells in the *substantia nigra* and the *striatum*. We start off life with about 1 million so-called dopamine cells;

through normal aging we lose about half of them. In PD, one's portion of dopamine cells drops dangerously low, to somewhere between 50,000 and 100,000. As a consequence, the level of dopamine, which is crucial for coordinated muscle movements, may be 80 percent less than normal. Because of this dopamine dropoff, the balance between acetylcholine and dopamine becomes out of kilter. Apparently, this balance is also crucial for coordination of movement. Interaction with other neurotransmitters such as serotonin, norepinephrine, and GABA, as well as deficiencies in these neurotransmitters, may also be involved.

The symptoms that signal PD include stiffness, tremor, slowness, reduced movement, and problems with balance and walking. More symptoms occur as the disease progresses, and survival after onset is typically 10–15 years. Famous persons experiencing PD include Janet Reno, Michael J. Fox, and Muhammed Ali.

Parkinson-like symptoms have resulted from the illegal use by several young people of a drug called MPTP, which was found to damage cells directly in the pyramidal tract of motor neurons. Some think that PD may in fact produce a chemical similar to MPTP, and that hunch forms one line of current research toward better understanding the disease.

Treatments

❶ Because there is no definite cure, treatment is aimed at reducing the symptoms. The most common treatment for PD is levodopa, or L-dopa, which the body transforms into dopamine. Others are amantadine (believed to release dopamine), carbidopa (which prevents the breakdown of dopamine by the enzyme MAO-B), bromocriptine (which stimulates the three different dopamine receptors), and pramipexole or Mirapex (which controls tremor). The newer class of drugs for treating PD symptoms are dopamine agonists (such as Requip from SmithKline Beecham and Mirapex from Pharmacia & Upjohn). Although levodopa alleviates symptoms, its effect wanes over time, and it causes symptoms of its own called dyskinesias (involuntary movements). In a five-year study, 36 percent of levodopa-treated PD patients developed dyskinesias, but only 5 percent of Requip-treated patients.

❷ The occurrence of PD-like symptoms among young people who took MPTP has spawned an exciting new line of inquiry. Researchers have injected MPTP into monkeys and induced PD symptoms, then looked for an agent that would reverse the symptoms. They have apparently found it in "glial-cell-line-derived neurotrophic factor" (GDNF; see *Nature,* April 1996). GDNF appears not only to prevent MPTP from destroying substantia nigra cells, but also to resuscitate the useless dopamine-producing cells to some degree; however, the effects last only a month in monkeys, so repeated injections are necessary. Clinical trials with humans are now underway. GDNF will not pass the blood-brain barrier, but gene therapy appears to be an effective way to introduce GDNF into the target neurons. Researchers led by Stephen S. Gill of Frenchay Hospital in Bristol, England, surgically treated five Parkinson's patients by infusing them with GDNF through the putamen, a small nucleus of cells within a region that controls complex movements, through an implanted catheter. No significant side effects were reported, and all patients improved in movement and daily activities. A 64 percent reduction in involuntary movements (dyskinesia) was found among the four patients who experienced these problems (as a result of previous treatment with levodopa). This was considered an "open-label" study because no control group was used, and it might not yield significant results in double-blind studies.

❸ In 1988, the first implants of six- to eight-week-old human fetal tissue were placed in the brains of PD patients. Over time, these young cells started producing dopamine to various degrees. Curt Freed, director of the University of Colorado's National Parkinson Foundation Center of Excellence, has completed a few dozen of these procedures. A third were unsuccessful, a third were moderately successful (patients still needed about 70 percent of their original drug dosages), and the final third were totally successful: patients regained normal movement with minimal or, in one case, no use of drugs. Legal and ethical concerns currently hamper development of this process.

❹ Another (and legal) course of trial implants involves the use of pig dopamine cells. Beginning in 1995 and continuing through 1997, 12 PD patients at Harvard University Medical School were implanted with fetal pig brain cells from the area where dopamine synthesis is highest, receiving some 12 million cells each (six patients with Huntington's disease were also implanted). *Science News,* March 25, 2000, reports the outcome of the 10 patients (two must have dropped out of the study) who received transplants: three improved dramatically, three improved moderately, and the remaining four either remained the same or declined somewhat. The improvements were observable about one year after the surgery, and three-year follow-up data show continuing benefits from the transplants.

Although preliminary results are exciting, researchers estimate that release for mainstream use is probably a decade away.

⑤ Another procedure being developed is the pallidotomy, which involves partial destruction of the cells in the globus pallidus. Low dopamine levels cause that area to become overactive, and the pallidotomy brings the levels under control, according to the lead researcher, Mahlon DeLong of Emory University. Other sites currently doing pallidotomies include the Loma Linda University Medical Center, Massachusetts General Hospital, Boston University, Deaconess Hospital in Boston, New York University, the University of Arkansas Center for Medical Sciences, and Mt. Sinai School of Medicine in New York City. Pallidotomies were popular before the availability of L-dopa in the 1960s, when the procedure was all but abandoned. Swedish neurosurgeon Lauri Laitinen caused a revival of the pallidotomy with a published research report in 1992 (*Boston Globe,* June 19, 1995, p. 29). The revival of pallidotomies is based on the availability of improved imaging methods that better pinpoint the lesions. However, pallidotomies bring at best, and at present, only temporary relief from symptoms and not a cure. Refinements of the procedure may improve results and reduce side effects.

⑥ Among other experimental approaches is the implantation of electrodes in various areas. The Movement Disorders Program at Allegheny General Hospital in Pittsburgh, for example, is treating Parkinson tremors by implanting an electrode in the thalamus through a dime-sized hole drilled in the skull. A lead wire runs under the skin's surface to an impulse generator implanted near the collarbone (*Pittsburgh Post-Gazette,* September 2, 1997, p. C1). Called a thalamic stimulator, this device is similar in look and concept to the heart pacemaker. It is made by Medtronic Inc. and is intended not just for Parkinson's tremors but for non-Parkinson's tremors as well. The technique was pioneered by Richard Trosch, a neurologist at the Detroit Medical Center (*Detroit News,* August 25, 1997, p. D1).

⑦ At least one version of PD—referred to as "familial Parkinson's"—is thought to be inherited, and research is underway to identify the gene and its nature. A team headed by Roger Duvoisin of Robert Wood Johnson Medical School, New Brunswick, New Jersey, and Mihael Polymeropoulos of the National Institutes of Health has reported that the gene is located in a small region of chromosome 4 (*Science,* November 15, 1996). Once the gene's specific address is isolated, research can begin on possible ways to prevent or treat familial PD.

Demetrius Maraganore of the Mayo Clinic (Rochester, Minnesota) is re-searching the possibility that just the right variant of two specific genes (alpha-synuclein and UCHLI) cause the disease in women.

8 Also under evaluation is transcranial magnetic stimulation (TMS), a noninvasive method for diagnosis and treatment. It is based on the princi-ple that changing the magnetic field in a local area of the brain can iden-tify as well as influence function in that area.

9 To keep current, browse the Internet for "Parkinson's" websites. The best for general information is "The Parkinson's Web," Harvard's site, **pdweb.mgh.harvard.edu**. You can also call the American Parkinson's Disease Association at 800-223-2732 or visit the Association's website: **www.apdaparkinson.org/user/index.asp**. See also **www.apdaparkinson.com**.

SUGGESTED RESOURCES

Snowdon, David (2001). *Aging with Grace: What the Nun Study Teaches Us about Leading Longer, Healthier, and More Meaningful Lives.* New York: Bantam Books.

Website

National Institute of Neurological Disorders and Stroke (NIH) website and database (for all disorders): www.ninds.nih.gov

19

Mood Disorders and Addictions

Chemicals Gone Haywire

*D*epression, anxiety, addiction, and bulimia all have at least one thing in common: they result from chemical peculiarities and can be treated chemically. Whether the peculiarity stems from environmental pollution, weather conditions, genetic pranks, an unbalanced diet, or insufficient or inappropriate exercise, these disorders, which were once thought to be "in one's head" and evidence of a failure of will, all stem from

427

excesses or deficiencies of some naturally occurring chemical. We will look at six disorders: addictions, anxiety, depression, manic-depressive illness (bipolar disorder), seasonal affective disorder, and eating disorders.

TOPIC 19.1   Addictions

Around 30 million Americans are addicted to some substance, whether it's alcohol, cocaine, or some other substance. Addiction is defined as a compulsive craving for a substance in spite of destructive consequences for oneself and others. George Koob, director of psychopharmacology at Scripps Research Center, adds to this definition by stipulating that true withdrawal from addiction involves a negative affect during the absence of the preferred stimulus. Recent research has revealed that no matter which substance is involved, nicotine or alcohol, heroin or amphetamines (or chocolates and sex!), all abused substances activate the same circuit for pleasure. Originally identified through PET scans of cocaine-addicted patients, this circuit runs from the *amygdala* and *anterior cingulum* to the outer reaches of the two temporal lobes (see appendix A). The circuit is called the *median forebrain bundle* or, more popularly, the "hedonic highway." The one kind of cell that is common among sites along this circuit is the D2 dopamine receptor. Three to four weeks after the addict's last cocaine dose, for example, this pleasure circuit shows unusually low activity on a PET scan. Cocaine, amphetamines, Ritalin, nicotine, and marijuana all inhibit reuptake of dopamine, thus achieving their pleasure effect or "high" by maximizing levels of dopamine. (Addiction to caffeine does not follow this pathway; caffeine gets its effect by blocking the sedative adenosine.)

Apparently, the repeated episodes of unnaturally intense baths of dopamine provided by the cocaine or other addictive substance damage the effectiveness of the dopamine delivery system. This could be the result of reduced dopamine supply, deadened receptors, or shrunken cells with D2 dopamine receptor sites. In fact, Eric Nestler, of Yale University School of Medicine's Laboratory of Molecular Psychiatry, has found that the dopamine cells along this pathway in doping rats shrink by 25 percent (Goleman, 1996). Often addicts take their drugs not to feel high, but just to feel normal, to stop the craving caused by decreased dopamine function. The craving typically subsides after 1–12 years, but many researchers believe that the pleasure circuit, once damaged, never completely returns to normal.

George Koob refers to this increased threshold as *allostasis* (*Science,* October 1997). The new set point established by addiction requires increased volumes of the preferred stimulus. During withdrawal, or absence of the stimulus, levels of dopamine, opioids, serotonin, and GABA all decrease, while cortisol—the stress hormone—increases. All of this activity leads to pain, anxiety, dysphoria, and panic attacks.

Treatments

1 The craving apparently cannot be eliminated; it can only be displaced through some combination of autotherapy (as in 12-step self-help groups), psychotherapy, and pharmacotherapy. Because each addictive drug follows a slightly different path along the median forebrain bundle (also called the *mesolimbic dopamine system*), no single drug can work to restore dopamine balance. The real challenge is getting the addict to stay off the substance for at least a year, preferably 18 months. Any program must provide the support necessary to get through that withdrawal period. Two school-based programs get positive reviews in the literature (*APA Monitor,* September 1997, p. 30): Life Skills Training (LST) and the Midwestern Prevention Project (Project STAR). LST was developed by Gilbert Botvin of the Cornell University Medical College Project. STAR was developed by psychologists at the University of Southern California and has been fully implemented in the Indianapolis schools. Both use secondary school teachers to train students in specific coping skills and have yielded good results in stopping smoking, alcohol, and drug abuse. Both programs also build on the practice of encouraging extracurricular organizations to sponsor activities such as drug-free sports events, smoke-outs, and parental involvement. Another highly touted program, Drug Abuse Resistance Education (DARE), apparently fails to do more than reduce cigarette smoking (*Health Education and Behavior,* April 1997, pp. 165–176).

2 Naltrexone blocks the effects of alcohol on the opioid system by binding opioid receptors. Alcohol enhances GABA (an inhibitor)—thereby slowing one's responses, and making one more accident prone. Alcohol also activates endorphins and dopamine. Naltrexone stands guard, preventing these three chemical reactions.

3 Acamprosate (Campral, by Merck), used in Europe since the early 1990s and now available in the U.S., is thought to reduce the craving for alcohol during recovery. It should be given shortly after stopping drinking, and continued for about one year. Apparently it removes chemical imbalances that result from alcoholism. It should be accompanied by counseling.

④ Alan Leshner, director of the National Institute on Drug Abuse, believes that there will never be a "silver bullet"—one drug that addresses all addictions (Goleman, 1996). Rather, he feels that eventually a kind of "neurochemical cocktail" will be available for restoring balance to the dopamine system for each of the different addicting substances.

⑤ Researchers at the Brookhaven National Laboratory in Upton, New York, report encouraging results with a new drug—GVG (gamma-vinyl-GABA)—that in rodents and primates appears able to block both the high of cocaine and the craving for it. Human trials began in 1998, but were interrupted because of reported visual complications. Clinical trials resumed in January 2005, but GVG is already approved for use in Mexico and Europe. Watch for the results on **www.clinicaltrials.gov**. GVG is an epilepsy drug that controls dopamine levels. Higher dopamine levels are associated with the cocaine high, and GVG appears to prevent these elevated levels.

TOPIC 19.2   Anxiety: A Family of Disorders

Fear: of being in death's hands (*panic disorder*), of being covered with germs and obligated to continually wash oneself clean of them (*obsessive-compulsive disorder*), of being in airplanes (*pteromerhanophobia*). These fears, plus many others, belong to a family of anxiety disorders that appears to be traceable to a common gene. Klaus-Peter Lesch and Armin Heils, of the University of Würzburg, reported in *Science* (January 1997) that one variant of this "worry gene" leads to more serotonin production, another variant to less. Discovery of this anxiety gene should expedite and clarify decisions regarding the nature of specific anxiety disorders and treatments for them.

Simple fear occurs when one reacts to a concrete and immediate threat (e.g., someone in a mask pointing a gun at you). Anxiety occurs when one reacts to a more remote possibility of threats that might occur (Ledoux, 2002, p. 289): for example, reluctance to leave one's house because of such a possibility, even though there is no information to suggest its imminence. About 25 percent of all Americans experience an anxiety disorder at least once in their lifetime, with women experiencing anxiety disorders at three times the rate of men. Annually, 25 million people in the United States suffer from anxiety disorders. Because of the stigma attached to overt acknowledgment and treatment of mental disorders, many people who suffer from anxiety disorders attempt to "self-medicate" with alcohol, tobacco, and nonprescription drugs. This contributes to an estimated $250 billion in lost wages and productivity for American employers.

Anxiety disorders have the following symptoms:

- ***Obsessive-compulsive disorder:*** Repeated thoughts that intrude throughout the day and cause worry. They are typically accompanied by a repetitive series of behaviors. There are over 5 million cases of OCD in the United States. Some are apparently caused by bacterial infections. For information, visit www.ocfoundation.org.

- ***Phobias:*** The experience of crippling worry and tension in specific settings (such as snakes, airplanes, heights, or tests), often accompanied by trembling, stomach problems, headache, and muscle tension. Around 8 million people in the United States have phobias. For information, review the site at: www.nlm.nih.gov/medlineplus/phobias.html. Many other websites cover the subject, including several aimed at self-treatment and support.

- ***Panic disorder:*** A paralyzing sense of terror that strikes without warning, often accompanied by dizziness, racing heart, hyperventilation, and chest pain. Researchers suspect that panic disorder is closely related to disturbances, probably genetic, in the *vestibular system* of the brain, which controls our sense of balance. Panic attacks may be set off by a hypersensitive "suffocation alarm" in the body. Around 6 million people in the United States suffer from panic disorder, and it occurs twice as frequently in women as in men. Researchers at the Royal Ottawa Hospital (Canada) have discovered a gene that apparently controls the predisposition to panic attacks. ROH's chief of psychiatry Jacques Bradwejn finds that this "panic gene" controls the number of receptors for the peptide *cholecystokinin* (CCK). When CCK is injected into panic-prone people, an attack results within 20 seconds. A similar mechanism is at work with bulimia sufferers (see discussion at topic 19.6), who appear to have lower levels than nonbulimic persons after having a snack. It is the sense of panic produced by out of kilter CCK levels that apparently influences the binge-and-purge bulimia pattern. However, Bradwejn's research found high levels of CCK associated with panic, but bulimia researchers found low levels of CCK associated with binging. Clearly CCK is involved, but the exact mechanism is not yet clear. For information, review the American Psychological Association's online brochure at www.apa.org/pubinfo/panic.html.

• *Generalized anxiety disorder (GAD):* A tendency to expect the worst without clear evidence, with particular worries about health, finances, job, and family. Individuals often can't relax, sleep, or concentrate on the task at hand. This disorder affects the quality of work and home life. The approximately 7 million Americans with GAD know that their worry is excessive but feel they can't do anything about it. Information is available at www.mentalhealthchannel.net/gad.

Treatments

❶ Most anxiety disorders can be treated effectively with a combination of psychotherapy (especially cognitive and behavioral therapy) and pharmacotherapy (especially benzodiazepines and antianxiety agents such as Xanax and Valium and antidepressants such as Zoloft, Prozac, Paxil, and Luvox). Some anxiety disorders can be treated successfully with psychotherapy alone. Check with a therapist for specific treatment recommendations. Or take a look at Edward Hallowell's *Worry: Controlling It and Using It Wisely* (1997). LeDoux (2002, p. 284) points out that antianxiety drugs typically work by enhancing the function of GABA in order to inhibit the excitatory work of glutamate that leads to overarousal. Propranolol works to reduce the physical symptoms of fear, such as heart rate.

❷ For a description of the physiology of anxiety and how it relates to other behaviors, such as greed, see John Medina's fascinating treatment (2000) in chapter 4 of his *The Genetic Inferno*.

❸ Clearly more than one gene is involved in setting the stage for the various anxiety disorders. Each gene makes its own protein, and ultimately pharmaceuticals will be available to address specific gene activity.

❹ To keep current on anxiety-related disorders, monitor the website of the Anxiety Disorders Association of America at **www.adaa.org**.

TOPIC 19.3 **Depression**

A survey of over 200,000 Americans (reported in *Time,* August 9, 2004) found that adults felt sad, blue, or depressed an average of three days during any given month. Women and young adults averaged a bit higher, men and seniors somewhat lower. Such blue days were associated with either bad habits (drinking, laziness) or unfortunate circumstances (separation, job change). Interestingly, *underweight* adults reported twice as many blue days as overweight adults.

Depression is thought to be a malfunction of the *monoamine* neurotransmitters, including norepinephrine, serotonin, and dopamine. About 17 million people experience one or more episodes of depression annually. One person in six will experience at least one depressive episode in a lifetime; the incidence within a depressive's family is even higher. Depression attacks all ages. Out of every six people whose depression is serious enough for hospitalization, one dies from suicide. Risk factors for depression include heart disease, Parkinson's disease, stroke, immune dysfunction, previous depressive episodes, and substance abuse. Factors that adversely affect an individual's chances for recovery include continual stress, coexisting medical and psychological problems, alcohol and substance abuse, and adverse socioeconomic circumstances.

Evolutionary psychologists suggest that the origins of depression for men and women differ according to the unique paths the two sexes have trod over thousands of years. Men have secured (or lost) their sense of identity through successful competition in dominance struggles, while women have established (or weakened) their identity through successful long-term maintenance of relationships. When something or someone disrupts a man's dominance, depression or anxiety is more likely to ensue, whereas a woman is more likely to experience depression or anxiety when something disrupts or threatens her primary relationships (e.g., with spouse or children).

University of Michigan nursing professors Reg Williams and Bonnie Hagerty report (in *Nursing Research,* July–August 1999) that a sense of being connected to others and belonging to them in a significant way is a major factor in avoiding depression. Following 410 subjects, the researchers found that, of the four most common predictors of depression—loneliness, conflict, lack of social support, and lack of a sense of belonging—the last is clearly the most powerful. Subjects most likely to show depressive symptoms feel that no one will attend their funeral when they die, that they don't fit in with any individuals or groups in their lives, and that others don't accept them as likeable.

Randolph M. Nesse, director of the Evolution and Human Adaptation program at the University of Michigan's Institute for Social Research, wrote (in *Archives of General Psychiatry,* January 2000) that depression, like many other diseases, does have some positive, adaptive value. He has found many cases in which depression appears to serve as an alarm to an individual caught up in a losing pursuit. Rather than using antidepressives exclusively in order to mask symptoms, Nesse encourages therapists and patients alike to consider the symptoms as a warning. Search the individual's environment to identify a possible hopeless endeavor (relationship, career, job) from which she should disentangle herself. As a rule, Nesse argues, moods serve to encourage us to spend more time on things that are working for us and less time on those that aren't. In cases such as these, drugs can have a role in easing the disengagement and transition but should not be taken without the accompanying change in goal pursuit.

The longer that symptoms go without diagnosis and treatment, the more resistant they become to treatment. About two-thirds of depressives seek help, yet about 90 percent of those seeking help are undertreated (for example, with a single visit and prescription from a primary care physician). One difficulty in treating depression is that the results of therapy are not immediate. Typically, improvement is not noticed for three to four weeks, and, with the expense of treatment, many depressives abandon therapy. Researchers at the Dean Foundation in Madison, Wisconsin, estimated almost a decade ago that the average daily cost of treating depression was about $12.25 per patient per day but was offset by a cost of $13.28 in unnecessary medical services sought out by depressives who were not being treated for depression (reported in Veggeberg, 1997). Moreover, employers lose over $23 billion annually because of lost production and absenteeism associated with depression.

In a related series of findings, researchers have found that men with low cholesterol are three times as likely to experience depression and high stress and to die a violent death, including suicide (*British Medical Journal,* September 14, 1996, pp. 637 ff.). Both men with naturally low cholesterol (below 160) and men who have reduced their cholesterol by diet or medication show this tendency. Traditionally, we have thought that the lower the cholesterol, the better. But recent research suggests that the optimal level is between 160 and 199. Less is apparently not better. This phenomenon is attributed to its association with low serotonin, which is a metabolite of animal fat, along with cholesterol. Can't win for losing! (I am not aware of a similar study done with women. However, the same principle should work. Low cholesterol is associated with lower serotonin levels, and increasing serotonin is a treatment for depression.)

While we're on the subject of men and depression, men suffer depression at half the rate that women do, but they more often fail to get treatment. Depression is seen by many as "unmanly." Recent open discussions of male depression by such public figures as Buzz Aldrin, Dick Cavett, William Styron, and Mike Wallace have paved the way for a higher proportion of afflicted men to seek help. A good book on the subject of male depression is Terrence Real's *I Don't Want to Talk About It: Overcoming the Secret Legacy of Male Depression* (1997). Dick Cavett (1992) has written about his recovery from depression through psychopharmacology combined with talking therapy.

One mitigating factor that accounts for the lower incidence of depression among men was discovered in 1998 by researchers at McGill University in Montreal. Using positron emission tomography, they found that men produce serotonin at a rate 52 percent higher than women. They speculated that in the past, warring and hunting men were subject to more stressors, so an abundance of serotonin became an adaptive trait with high survival value.

The symptoms of depression, based on Jerrold F. Rosenbaum, in *On the Brain* (Harvard Mahoney Neuroscience Institute Letter), (Spring 1996); Medina (2000); and Scott Veggeberg, in *BrainWork: The Neuroscience Newsletter* (September–October 1997), include two or more weeks of

- depressed mood
- loss of interest or pleasure
- excessive guilt
- impaired concentration
- fatigue and loss of energy
- appetite and sleep changes
- agitated or retarded motor behavior
- suicidal or morbid thoughts

- unexplained—and disabling—aches and pains
- unexplained crying spells
- indifference toward former interests
- social withdrawal
- memory disruption
- feelings of hopelessness
- indecisiveness
- feelings of worthlessness or emptiness
- overall negative affect, including anger, worry, agitation, anxiety, irritability, and pessimism

Four or five of these symptoms experienced daily over a two-week period should alert an individual to the possibility of being in a depressed state. *Dysthymia,* a milder form of depression, is characterized by the same symptoms but in less severe form; these less severe symptoms can last for more than two years.

Apparently, although some genetic causes have been acknowledged, depression is largely environmental in origin, as evidenced by the large variation in incidence rates across cultures. Myrna Weissman, a professor in the School of Public Health at Columbia University, headed up a 10-nation survey of depression (*Scientific American,* November 1996, pp. 24–25), using the same methods for all of the countries. (Note that the list doesn't distinguish between rural and urban areas. It would be interesting to know whether rural areas have a lower incidence than urban areas.) The research revealed that the percentage of the population in each locale that would experience at least one depressive episode lasting one year or more was as follows:

Country	Percentage
Taiwan	1.5
Korea	2.9
Puerto Rico	4.3
United States	5.2
Germany	9.2
Canada (Edmonton, Alberta)	9.6
New Zealand (Christchurch)	11.6
Italy (Florence)	12.4
France (Paris)	16.4
Lebanon (Beirut)	19.0

This wide range of occurrence for depression certainly argues for strong cultural influences. On the other hand, Weissman (e-mail: mmw3@columbia.edu) found several patterns that held true for all 10 countries:

1. Each country's rate was highly correlated with its divorce and separation rates, except for Lebanon, which suffered war for the previous 15 years. (Note to reader: Look for a decrease in Lebanese depression in the wake of Syria's recent pullout.)

2. Women were twice as likely as men to suffer depression.

3. Separated or divorced men were more likely to suffer depression than separated or divorced women.

4. The average age of first depression fell into a fairly narrow range, from 34 in Italy down to 24 in Canada.

5. Manic depression (*bipolar disorder*) showed much less magnitude and variability across the 10 countries, ranging from 0.3 percent in Taiwan to 1.5 percent in New Zealand. This confirms other studies that have posited a stronger genetic component for bipolar depression than for *unipolar* depression.

Jackie Gollan, clinical psychologist at Brown University Medical School, assessed the personality profiles of 78 depressed patients and concluded (as reported in *APA Monitor,* February 2000) that the following four traits were the most significant risk factors for depression:

1. Hostility

2. Aggression

3. Low dependence on others

4. Low enjoyment of recreational activities

A Note on Depression in Children

Though the safety of antidepressant medications for preschoolers is still in debate, the prescriptions for this age group are on the rise. According to the April 2004 issue of *Psychiatric Services,* the number of preschool girls on antidepressants doubled from 1998 to 2002, while the number of boys in the same age bracket increased 64 percent. Overall, 0.5 percent of preschoolers are on antidepressants—1 in 200.

Regardless of the uncertainty of using these drugs with the five-and-under depressives, environmental and behavioral modification should accompany the drugs, if not completely replace them. Both Paxil and Zoloft appear to be associated with a high risk of suicidal thoughts in children. However, Prozac, in combination with talk therapy, appears to be a winning combination. Any child taking antidepressant medication should be monitored by parents and professionals. Again, the drug should not replace talk therapy, but rather facilitate it.

A Note on Postpartum Depression

The Brooke Shields–Tom Cruise media spat has recently brought attention to postpartum depression, a condition that one of ten mothers will experience anywhere from shortly after birth up to one year later. It is caused by fluctuations in hormonal levels both during pregnancy and afterwards. Read Shields's book, *Down Came the Rain* (2005). Symptoms include fatigue, hopeless feelings, sleep and appetite disturbance, confusion, uncontrollable crying, apathy towards the infant, fear of harming self or baby, and mood swings (American Psychiatric Association). Most at risk are women with severe premenstrual syndrome or a family history of mood disorder. Postpartum depression is easily treated by drug and talk therapy. It should not be confused with the normal "baby blues" that typically occur for several days to several weeks after delivery for seven out of ten mothers.

Treatments

❶ In a review in *Professional Psychology: Research and Practice* (December 1996), David Antonuccio and William Danton, both of the University of Nevada School of Medicine, and Garland DeNelsky of the Cleveland Clinic Foundation reported that psychotherapy, particularly cognitive-behavioral therapy or interpersonal psychotherapy, should be the treatment of choice for unipolar depression because of its superior long-term outcome and lower medical risk than either drugs alone or drugs combined with psychotherapy. Psychotherapy, then, is at least as effective as pharmacotherapy, even for severe depression. Furthermore, they assert, there is no evidence that drug treatment can improve the results of psychotherapy for depression, although psychotherapy can improve the results of drug treatment. Considering that the relapse rate for treating depression with drugs alone is upward of 60 percent, psychotherapy should always accompany pharmacotherapy. Antonuccio, Danton, and DeNelsky argue that medication should not be used to treat depressive children or adolescents and should be prescribed with caution for adults.

2 Three classes of drugs are associated with the treatment of depression: tricyclic antidepressants (TCAs), monoamine oxydase (MAO) inhibitors, and selective serotonin reuptake inhibitors (SSRIs). The older tricyclics (Elavil, Pamelor) and lithium had unpleasant side effects and have been replaced by the SSRI drugs—Prozac, Zoloft, and Paxil (fluoxetine, sertraline, and paroxetine)—and MAO inhibitors (including the increasingly popular herb St. John's Wort). Monoamine oxydase gobbles up extra neurotransmitters (including serotonin) in the synapse, and MAO inhibitors prevent such a feast, thus making more serotonin (among other neurotransmitters) available in the synapse. SSRI drugs supposedly work by preventing serotonin in the synapse that has not been absorbed by postsynaptic receptors from being reabsorbed by presynaptic receptors, thus keeping it available in the synapse for immediate and future absorption. Thus, if one has a low supply of serotonin, the proportion available for use is maximized. It is a bit like taking a bottle of water out of the refrigerator, taking a swig, and keeping it with you in case you want more, rather than putting it back in the fridge.

However, the monoamine system is complex, and its workings are not apparent. There are at least 14 different subtypes of monoamine receptors, and it is terribly easy, and tempting, to oversimplify what happens: "Raise serotonin levels and you'll be happy." Yeah, right! It's not that simple. In fact, Ivan Goldberg of Columbia University, in an Internet posting (e-mail: **ikgl@columbia.edu**), writes, "It is very clear that SSRIs do not work as antidepressants by inhibiting the reuptake of serotonin. It is clearly established that 1 mg/day of fluoxetine is all that is needed to fully block the reuptake of serotonin. If blocking the reuptake of serotonin were both necessary and sufficient, patients would not need higher doses to get over their depressions. I know no patient who has had an optimal response to such a low dose."

Normally, patients take one 20 mg capsule of SSRI (the actual range of doses is from 5 to 300 mg daily) for no more than one year, although some take it for longer periods. The possible side effects include

- weight loss (in fact, SSRIs have been found successful in treating some cases of bulimia)

- delay in achieving orgasm (SSRIs have been prescribed to help some men with premature ejaculation problems) or failure to reach orgasm, although many accept this side effect because they are glad to feel good enough to have sex in the first place!

- akathisia, or outbursts of temper or violence

- gastrointestinal problems, fatigue, and nervousness

Many experts feel that SSRIs are overprescribed. Over 60 percent of SSRI prescriptions are written by primary care physicians or obstetrician-gynecologists who do not follow up with talk therapy and evaluation. Of the more than 15 million SSRI prescriptions written annually, many are not written for depression but are given by sympathetic physicians to patients who are unsatisfied with the rough edges on their personality. Thus, SSRI drugs have become something of a cult phenomenon, a kind of plastic surgery for the persona, for people who want a quick fix to achieve social and career success.

Julian Whitaker, in his newsletter *Health and Healing* (January 1998), points out that over time SSRIs can reduce the overall supply of serotonin. He prescribes instead tryptophan (an amino acid), which is the precursor of 5-HTP (5-hydroxytryptophan), or 5-HTP, which is the precursor of serotonin. Whitaker comments that supplying these raw materials to increase the production of serotonin has only a few mild side effects, the worst being occasional diarrhea. He says that daily doses of 50–100 mg of 5-HTP on an empty stomach are helpful for most people; some take 100 mg three times a day; others may take up to 900 mg daily. He recommends starting the prescription in the evenings, because 5-HTP can cause drowsiness.

In a study of 536 adult depressives, a research team led by Gregory Simon of the Center for Health Studies in Seattle compared three treatment groups, two using tricyclics (desipramine or imipramine) and one using an SSRI, fluoxetine (reported in the *Journal of the American Medical Association,* June 26, 1996). Their findings after six months of treatment were as follows:

- There was no difference among the three groups in the overall effectiveness of the drugs.

- There was no difference in the length of time it took the drugs to become effective.

- There was no difference in total cost.

- There was no difference in remission rates.

- Tricyclic users reported more side effects.

- Twenty-seven percent of tricyclic users discontinued medication early, compared with 9 percent of fluoxetine users.

- Forty percent of tricyclic users switched to another medication, compared with 20 percent of fluoxetine users.

Their conclusion: the patient and physician may choose whichever drug they prefer. Note that Paxil (paroxetine) appears to be the antidepressant of choice for patients suffering depression as a direct result of a heart attack (*Journal of the American Medical Association,* January 28, 1998).

❸ Robert Hirschfeld, a psychiatrist with the University of Texas Medical Branch in Galveston, insists that the family of a depressive must become involved with the treatment. He believes that treatment for depressives whose families have not bought into the process is prone to failure (reported in Veggeberg, 1997).

❹ Apparently women respond better to drugs that address serotonin only, whereas men respond better to drugs that address both noradrenaline and serotonin. This is part of a growing body of research, such as that of Susan Kornstein of the Medical College of Virginia, on how the sexes and their respective hormonal profiles respond differently to drugs.

❺ Many depressives self-medicate themselves by resorting to nicotine (see topic 8.7). Others self-medicate by abusing alcohol or drugs. Summarizing recent findings on the co-occurrence of substance abuse and mood disorders, Brenda Patoine (*BrainWork: The Neuroscience Newsletter,* May–June 1998) recommends the following for people suffering from both disorders:

- Stop drinking alcohol, even moderately; it interferes with depression medication.

- Get treatment from someone with expertise in both areas.

- Don't assume that treating one disorder will also treat the other one.

❻ Leslie Taylor of the Dean Foundation in Madison, Wisconsin, is confident that 80 percent of depressives can be satisfactorily treated but says that 35 percent of those who are treated abandon treatment within the first month. Taylor recommends intense follow-up and monitoring, such as scheduling visits in advance and having the therapist phone the patient from his office. In one study (reported in Veggeberg, 1997), Taylor found that 20 patients all completed a six-month treatment program that included such intense follow-up and monitoring of compliance.

❼ McLean Hospital in Belmont, Massachusetts, is testing the use of a patch to deliver antidepressants. The patch delivers MAO inhibitors directly to the bloodstream, bypassing the stomach and avoiding the typical intestinal distress. This method appears to reduce time to relief from three weeks to one week.

❽ Another trend in the treatment of depression is to administer drugs that prevent the release and accumulation of cortisol. Clearly, stress is associated with depression, and the cortisol released by stressful conditions affects circuits related to depression. Research shows that reducing cortisol levels can improve depression. See a more complete discussion of this relationship in chapter 10 of Joseph LeDoux's *Synaptic Self* (2002, p. 279).

❾ Depressed patients need to learn the skills of working on relationships and of identifying the relationships most likely to benefit from the work.

❿ Find a group for a depressive that lacks something she has—a skill, an attitude, a trait.

⓫ In treating the needs of depressive patients, psychotherapists need to emphasize relationship development and satisfying group membership.

⓬ See the discussion on relationships in chapter 14, especially topic 14.14.

⓭ Read Stephen Covey's *The Seven Habits of Highly Effective People* to gain an understanding of relationship development.

⓮ Fifteen hospitals around the U.S. were given permission in 1999 to study an electrical implant for relief of depression. This was based on the successful procedure performed by Mark George of the Medical University of South Carolina. George describes the implant as a kind of "brain pacemaker." The silver-dollar-sized stimulator is implanted in the chest with a wire stretching up to the vagus nerve, which gets zapped every few minutes. About half of the 30 depressed patients studied reported significant improvement in mood. The device is now officially approved.

⑮ Researchers at the University of California, Irvine, report (in *American Journal of Psychiatry,* August 1999) that some patients can be jolted out of depressive moods by staying up all night. Apparently, jolting and resetting the body clock helps to reset mood, at least for some.

⑯ Some success has been reported in providing temporary relief using repetitive transcranial magnetic stimulation (rTMS). A strong magnet held on the scalp stimulates neural activity, which depressed patients lack. There are no apparent ill effects, except for occasional mild seizures, but the treatment wears off over time. It appears to be a more benign form of electroshock therapy (ECT). Follow the research. The New York State Psychiatric Institute at Columbia University is one site that is using this therapy.

⑰ A variety of researchers report that persons who strongly identify with sports teams have less depression and higher self-esteem than persons who are not sports fans. In addition, fans show increases in testosterone and optimism after wins, and decreases after losses, just as do the athletes themselves. See particularly the work of James Dabbs (Georgia State University), Robert Cialdini (Arizona State University), Charles Hillman (University of Illinois), Edward Hirt (University of Indiana), and Daniel Wann (Murray State University).

⑱ For a description of the chemicals, neural systems, and bodily structures involved in depression and how they interact, read chapter 7 in John Medina's *The Genetic Inferno* (2000, Cambridge University Press). Medina goes into some detail in describing how the hypothalamus, pituitary gland, and adrenal gland interact to affect cortisol levels.

⑲ In addition to close monitoring and follow-up, another promising approach is what Martin Seligman of the University of Pennsylvania has dubbed a depression "vaccine" (*APA Monitor,* October 1994; see chapter 37 for more information on his work). He proposes that we train young people in optimism or, more precisely, in a positive explanatory style (see topic 37.5). Seligman's research has shown that a negative explanatory style is associated with depression and that his model for a positive explanatory style is (1) learnable and (2) effective in reversing and preventing depression. In experiments with 10- and 11-year-olds and also with college freshmen, two years after learning the optimism model the younger subjects showed a 50–100 percent reduction in their depression rate compared with controls; the 18-year-olds showed just a slight to moderate reduction. He is convinced that teaching a positive explanatory style at an early age, in effect, "immunizes" children against depression and possibly against other mental problems. With childhood depression rates roughly 10 times greater now than two generations back, we should regard this finding as something of a mandate. In fact, the California legislature has mandated training in self-esteem as a weapon to crack the welfare cycle. Seligman says that self-esteem training misses the mark but his explanatory style model doesn't.

20 For many centuries, Europeans have been using the herb *Hypericum perforatum* (St. John's Wort) to treat depression. It has few, mild side effects and enhances serotonin, norepinephrine, and dopamine. However, Duke University psychiatrists conducted a randomized, multisite, double-blind study to evaluate St. John's Wort and found it no more effective than a placebo.

21 One new line of research comes from Wayne Drevets of the University of Pittsburgh, who led a team that has discovered that the brains of depressive patients, compared with nondepressives' brains, are missing 40–90 percent of their glial cells in the anterior cingulum of the prefrontal cortex (a part of the "hedonic highway"—see topic 19.1). On the other hand, these same depressive patients' regular neurons were all intact; just the glial cells were depleted. Glial cells provide structural support for neurons, as well as growth nutrients that provide the "fuel" that drives neurotransmitter production (*Newsday,* October 21, 1997, p. A8).

22 New York Medical College researchers report that approximately 25 percent of people who are hospitalized for depression or suicidal behavior appear to carry the gene for *Wolfram syndrome* (a form of diabetes that entails deterioration of eyesight) (*Molecular Psychiatry,* January 1998, pp. 86–91). Research is underway to determine how this knowledge can help in the treatment of depression.

23 Merck & Co. researchers reported in the September 11, 1998, issue of *Science* that a new drug code-named MK-869 appears to be a robust treatment for depression. It targets a heretofore mysterious chemical called *substance P,* which is involved with pain transmission and abundant in the area of the brain associated with the negative emotions. The new drug appears to block substance P with far fewer side effects than Paxil or Prozac. Preclinical results as of summer 2005 have been excellent. Watch for release news.

24 On the dietary front, researchers at the National Institutes of Health report a strong relationship between low levels of omega-3 fatty acids and depression, as well as other mental disorders. Omega-3 polyunsaturated fatty acids are found primarily in fish. A few fish high in omega-3 fatty acids are listed here:

Fish	Grams of Omega-3 Fatty Acids per 200-gram Serving of Fish
Raw mackerel	10
Raw salmon	8
Marinated salmon	8
Smoked salmon	6
Fillet of herring	6
Tuna in oil	4

In Asia, where fish consumption is high, depression levels are low. In several recent studies, fatty acid supplements led to a decrease in depressive symptoms and a decrease in schizophrenic hallucinations.

25 Recent reports that antidepressants are no more effective than placebos are tricky to interpret. For one thing, the fact that placebos have *increased* their effectiveness in treating depression can be related to the ongoing track record of antidepressants, which has had the effect of increasing the suffering public's confidence in treatment in general. So, culturally, depressives tend to be more confident in their treatment these days. Second, clinical studies are often briefer and more focused on single-treatment protocols than are real-life treatments. In real life, therapists work with patients for longer periods and try more protocols, often with good results. Look for future clarification. I suspect that, as our genetic sophistication increases, we will find pharmaceutical researchers designing rational drugs that are more effective with fewer side effects and that are clearly superior to placebos.

26 LeDoux (2002, p. 277) points out that depression, like schizophrenia and many other diagnoses, is not a single disorder but rather has many combinations of symptoms reflecting different combinations of neural circuits. Likewise, there is not just one type of serotonin receptor. Consequently, research and treatment need to focus on finding pharmaceuticals that work on specific circuits and their specific receptor types. The more specific the treatment is to the disorder, the fewer the side effects. Broad treatments work well on one circuit but make other circuits go haywire.

27 For the most current information on depression, monitor the website of the International Foundation for Research and Education on Depression at www.ifred.org.

TOPIC 19.4 Manic-Depressive Illness

Affecting about 1 percent of the population, *manic-depressive illness* (MDI, or *bipolar disorder*) is a less common form of depression (see topic 19.3) in which an exhilarating period of heightened physical and mental energy, which can last from days to weeks and can spin out of control into a delusional state, which then typically crashes into a major depressive episode. The process is cyclical, with manic and depressive phases interspersed with normal periods. The composer Robert Schumann suffered from it, and achieved with it, until his suicide by starvation in 1856. At present, the only known cause of the manic phase of MDI is the excessive presence of *inositol,* an enzyme that participates in communication between neurons.

The depressive phase of manic depression involves the same symptoms reported for depression (see topic 19.3). Symptoms of the manic phase may include "exaggerated optimism . . . decreased need for sleep without feeling fatigue, grandiose delusions . . . excessive irritability, aggressive behavior, increased physical and mental activity, racing speech, flight of ideas, impulsiveness, poor judgment, easily distracted [and] reckless behavior, i.e., spending sprees, rash business decisions, erratic driving, flagrant affairs" (Veggeberg, 1997, p. 2).

Treatments

1 Lithium is used to bind inositol in order to make it unusable, thus calming neuron communication. Anticonvulsives are also prescribed for the manic phase. Antidepressants are sometimes used for the depressive phase, but drugs such as Prozac and Zoloft can trigger a manic episode. Different treatment is required for the two phases of the disease. For the manic phase, in addition to lithium carbonate, doctors are using Depakote (divalproex, an anticonvulsive), Zyprexa (olanzapine, an antipsychotic; these first two are the most effective), Geodon (ziprasidone),

Risperdal (risperidone), Tegretol (carbamazepine), and Trileptal (oxcarbazepine). Zyprexa and a newer drug, Lamictal (lamotrigine) work to prevent both manic and depressive episodes.

❷ Even though lithium salts have proven effective in leveling out MD's mood swings, social factors appear to have a significant triggering effect. Psychologist Noreen A. Reilly-Harrington of Boston's Harvard Medical School identifies (in *Science News*, April 8, 2000, pp. 232–233) four primary social triggers—negative thinking, personal misfortune, disturbance of one's daily routine, and disturbance of one's sleep patterns—each of which can apparently trigger the manic phase of MD. Disturbances of routine include travel across multiple time zones and extended periods of unemployment. Regular sleep and wake times appear to decrease the chance of mania. Reducing external stimulation upon the onset of mania can soften the symptoms. The therapist should assist the MD in both planning stable routines and adhering to them. Psychologist Ellen Frank of the University of Pittsburgh School of Medicine has had particular success with this approach.

❸ Increasing diagnoses are being made for preschoolers. Read this book for a definitive treatment of childhood bipolar disorder: Demitri and Janice Papolos, *The Bipolar Child* (2002).

❹ Researchers around the world are attempting to isolate the genes associated with manic depression. Studies of twins and of close communities such as the Amish lend support to the hunt; most of the evidence is pointing toward genes 6, 13, and 15.

❺ For current information, monitor the Depression and Bipolar Support Alliance website at **www.dbsalliance.org**.

TOPIC 19.5   Seasonal Affective Disorder

Also called "winter depression," *seasonal affective disorder* (SAD) apparently results from the inefficiency of the body's system that produces melatonin (see topic 9.10). Normally, the *pineal gland,* even for blind persons, produces melatonin in the absence of sunlight. This flooding of melatonin is apparently critical for sleep. In the morning, with sunrise, the presence of natural light (you can do the same thing with a good lamp) signals the pineal gland to shut down production of melatonin. This leads to alert wakefulness. In SAD, apparently, the pineal gland, fooled in some people by winter's darkness, continues to produce melatonin into the day, with a resulting inability to shake off the night's slumber.

Symptoms of SAD include inactivity, negative affect, weight gain, craving for carbohydrates, increased sleep time, decreased libido, and daytime sleepiness (Thayer, 1996). This disorder affects about 5 percent of the population, females more than males. It tends to let up in spring and summer, although a summer variant has been noted.

Treatments

❶ Upon waking, the person with SAD is exposed to bright light of about 2,500 lux (roughly equal to a window open to normal sunlight) for two hours or so, looking directly at the light source from time to time. The individual, apparently "starved" for light, should experience a resetting of the body clock and an attendant return of a normal mood.

❷ To avoid SAD, wake up and begin your morning tasks around light bulbs or lamps that have a CRI of 90 or greater. (See discussion at topic 32.2.)

TOPIC 19.6   Eating Disorders

Statistics on eating disorders are difficult to assess, with some estimating that upwards of one-third of all people in the U.S. suffer from one of the eating disorders to some degree. *Anorexia nervosa* (starving oneself), *bulimia nervosa* (dieting, binging, and purging), *binge eating disorder* (compulsive eating), *anorexia athletica* (compulsive exercising), *night-eating syndrome* (consuming over one-half of one's daily food after 7:00 P.M.), and *nocturnal sleep-related eating disorder* each have a complex set of causes, including biological, social, family, and psychological sources. Although anorexia and bulimia primarily afflict females between 10 and 35 years old (somewhere between 5 and 10 percent of anorexia and bulimia patients are males), cases have been reported from as young as 6 years of age to as old as 76. The lower incidence among males is attributed to societal approval of the strong, muscular, more bulky image for males. In fact, many believe that the primary cause of eating disorders is the ideal image that daily forces itself upon readers, listeners, and viewers of the popular media. In South Korea, as recently as the 1970s, the ideal image for a female was full-figured. These women were thought to be more sexy, more beautiful, and more able to bear healthy children. But decontrol of broadcasting has unleashed a flood of Western body image material throughout the culture, so that today the diet industry in Korea is flourishing, with entrepreneurs hawking everything from diet pills to liposuction. The statistics for South Korea now roughly parallel those of the United States (*Los Angeles Times* article, October 26, 1997).

Symptoms for each of the disorders are complex and are best not summarized. They include such diverse behaviors as skipping meals, experiencing relationship problems, and talking excessively about food. Excellent profiles of the symptoms for each disorder are available at the website for Anorexia Nervosa and Related Eating Disorders Inc.: www.anred.com.

Treatments

❶ Without treatment, one out of five people with eating disorders will die prematurely. Treatment reduces that rate to one out of 30 to 50. About 60 percent of those who are treated recover, but not all make a full recovery. Current treatment could include one or more of the following: hospitalization, medication, dental work, individual counseling, group counseling, family counseling, nutritional counseling, and support groups. Consult a physician or mental health professional for specific recommendations.

❷ Although little research evaluation is available, a promising new approach has been taken by Peggy Claude-Pierre. She has labeled eating disorders the *confirmed negativity condition* and has established a therapeutic environment that consists of 24-hour unconditional love and support. The Montreux Counseling Centre in Victoria, British Columbia, is her residential treatment site. Treatment is expensive, has a high staff-to-patient ratio, and is based on a five-step process. Read about it in her book *The Secret Language of Eating Disorders* (1998) (www.randomhouse.com).

❸ Stanford University's James Lock proposes a new treatment for anorexia nervosa developed by British therapists Christopher Dare and

Ivan Eisler of Maudsley Hospital, London. The treatment sees family not as cause, but rather as ally, in getting the patient to eat more, return to a more normal weight, and establish control of her eating patterns. The treatment proceeds by observing family interactions and coming up with ways for the parents to help the child eat more. In essence, the therapists train the parents to become nurses for their child. Daniel LeGrange, director of the Eating Disorders Program at the University of Chicago, also is using and studying the treatment.

For the current status of any clinical trial mentioned in this book, check this website: www.clinicaltrials.gov.

❹ Expect major discoveries in the next 10 years in this new field. Follow new developments with these websites: **www.eating-disorder.com** and **www.anred.com**.

❺ Watch specifically for research on the enzyme *cholecystokinin,* which is lower in bulimic patients. The level of this enzyme typically increases when eating, with the result of stimulating the production of digestive enzymes that send us the message that we're no longer hungry. Apparently bulimics fail to get this chemical message, and keep on eating.

SUGGESTED RESOURCES

Castle, L. R. (2003). *Bipolar Disorder Demystified.* New York: Marlowe & Company.

Claude-Pierre, P. (1999). *The Secret Language of Eating Disorders: The Revolutionary New Approach to Understanding and Curing Anorexia and Bulimia.* New York: Vintage Books.

Foreman, J. (1996, December 17). "Anxiety: It's Not Just a State of Mind." *Boston Globe,* p. C1.

Goleman, D. (1996, August 13). "Brain Images of Addiction in Action Show Its Neural Basis." *New York Times,* p. C1.

Hallowell, E. M. (1997). *Worry: Controlling It and Using It Wisely.* New York: Pantheon Books.

Nemeroff, C. B. (1998, June). "The Neurobiology of Depression." *Scientific American,* pp. 42–49.

Real, T. (1997). *I Don't Want to Talk About It: Overcoming the Secret Legacy of Male Depression.* New York: Scribner.

Seligman, M. E. P. (1991). *Learned Optimism.* New York: Knopf.

Veggeberg, S. K. (1997, September–October). "The Big Story in Depression: What Isn't Happening." *BrainWork: The Neuroscience Newsletter* (Charles A. Dana Foundation), 7(4), 1–3.

Whybrow, P. C. (1997). *A Mood Apart: Depression, Mania, and Other Afflictions of Self.* New York: Basic Books.

Websites

National Institute of Mental health site on anxiety disorders and obsessive-compulsive disorders: www.nimh.nih.gov

Obsessive-compulsive disorders: www.ocdresource.com

20

Violence and Aggression

Running Hot and Cold in a Global Society

*I*n his *On Human Nature* (1995), Edmund O. Wilson describes six different ways in which humans use anger:

- To dominate a group
- To fight off a predator
- To enforce the moral rules of culture
- To defend or acquire territory
- To obtain material goods forcefully
- To force another into sexual submission

“*H*atred is a failure of the imagination. ”

—*Graham Greene,*
The Power and the Glory

Wilson is writing as an observer of angry, violent behavior. Behind each of these overt acts of anger, however, lurks a motive or a core belief that justifies the violent act to the actor. Roy (University of Pennsylvania) and Judy Eidelson (2003) have identified five such core beliefs associated with conflict and aggression. Each core belief operates on both an individual and a group level. Four of them work to increase the likelihood of open conflict, the fifth to minimize conflict:

1. *Superiority.* The belief that one's culture is superior to all other cultures in every possible way.

2. *Injustice.* The belief that one, either as an individual or a group, has a legitimate grievance against another individual or group.

3. *Vulnerability.* The belief that one is subject to annihilation at the hands of aggressive others.

4. *Distrust.* The belief that another individual or group will not honor their commitments.

5. *Hopelessness.* The belief that one cannot expect to improve one's condition, either as an individual or as a group.

Clearly the first four of these core beliefs can lead to aggression, the last to self-destruction.

According to Quartz and Sejnowski (2002), aggression starts early and depends on cultural influence for taming. Citing the work of the University of Montreal's Richard Tremblay, they point out that "the typical two-year-old engages in eight to nine aggressive acts an hour" (p. 194). Typically, we are more aggressive between the ages of two and two and a half years than at any other period in our lives. "During the course of normal development, the typical child learns how to inhibit this aggressive behavior and replace it with cooperative and peacemaking strategies, which lie at the core of social competence. From the perspective of cultural biology, this suggests that one path to violence may lie in veering from this normal journey" (p. 195).

Medina points out that the Iowa adoption studies (*not* twin studies) of children taken at birth by genetically unrelated parents reveal the following two patterns:

- Children whose biological parents were stable mostly remained stable as adults, regardless of the stability of their adoptive homes.

- Children whose biological parents were unstable also grew up to be unstable if adopted into an unstable home; however, if kids whose biological parents were unstable were adopted into stable homes, they tended to grow up to be stable themselves (Medina, 2000, p. 196; also see Cadoret, 1978).

In research into twins studies, Medina (2000, p. 201) looked at studies exploring the timing of aggressive behavior. In other words, does the time of life—a person's age—make a difference in genetic effects on violent behavior? The answer is a resounding yes. Twins—fraternal as well as identical—subjected to violent neighborhoods in their youth are highly concordant for delinquent behavior, but when those twins become adults, the incidence of violent behavior drops by half, with identical twins showing twice the concordance for aggressive behavior as adults, compared with fraternal twins. In other words, regardless of your genes, it is difficult to avoid delinquency as a teen when living in a delinquency-filled neighborhood. However, when you age up, move out, and reach your stride as an adult, your genes fight in your behalf to establish you as a good citizen. Or, as Medina puts it: "A kid might end up in 'juvy' because of his parents [or peer group], but, in his adult configuration, the kid will end up in the 'state pen' because of his genes."

Males are arrested for around 90 percent of all violent crimes, except for rape, where males account for 99 percent of those arrested. Eleanor Maccoby (1998) points out that most males are not violent, and that those who are tend to take their aggression out on other males. Moreover, they tend to respond more violently to aggression from males than to aggression initiated by females.

No culture in the world has been identified in which the degree of deadly female violence comes even close to that of male-perpetrated violence. In research covering records over a seven-century period, on average males kill other males 30–40 times more frequently than females kill females (Daly and Wilson, 1988). Most of these murders occur during the period when men are seeking a mate—from the late teen years through the mid-20s. The inciting cause for most of them comes from male-male competition for dominance, resources, and mate selection (Geary, 1998, p. 318). Researchers suggest that increased educational and employment opportunities would address many of the causes of violence (p. 325; see also Gilligan, 1997).

With respect to age of the perpetrator, violent-crime arrests are at the maximum for 18-year-olds and decline steadily from that point on. This is, of course, an average. Different kinds of violent crimes have different peak age levels associated with them, with robbery, for example, peaking earlier (about age 17) than assault (around 24). In their monumental study of violence, the National Research Council reported (1993–1994) that alcohol consumption is probably not a major cause of violence, but rather a facilitating factor.

Neil Alan Weiner and Marvin E. Wolfgang (in Weiner, Zahn, Sagi, and Merton, 1990, pp. 281–294, "Explaining Violent Behavior"), in surveying the full spectrum of violent behavior, find these physical (biological) causes (p. 284) accounting for most episodes:

- Tumors and other assorted disruptions affecting the limbic system

- Epileptic seizures (the violence can occur just before or after)

- Endocrine abnormalities

- Birth complications

- Nervous system abnormalities such as MBD (*minimal brain dysfunction*) and extreme EKGs (either very fast or very slow brain waves)

- Hyperactivity

- Genetic abnormalities (violence is strongly heritable)

- Body type (e.g., the juvenile offender body type is more muscular, athletic, and bony)

- Learning disorders

- Personality disorders

- Absence of anxiety about possible harm to self or others among psychopaths and hardcore juvenile offenders (i.e., low autonomic activity)

- Disconnect between limbic area and inhibiting areas in the frontal cortex

- Low blood sugar (research here lacks convincing consistency)

- Disinhibiting effects of alcohol and psychoactive drug consumption

In addition to these physical roots of violence, Weiner and Wolfgang found psychological causes (pp. 287 ff.):

- Prolonged frustration (disruption of goal seeking)

- In a larger sense, stress, or the discrepancy between demands placed on a person and his ability to deliver (cf. *flow*)

- Socially learned behavior

- Combined effect of all environmental forces that seem to invite a violent response

- Combined effect of various rewards for violent behavior, including subculture support

- Combined effect of all inhibitory forces, internal and external

- Strength of the immediate situation with respect to triggering the offender

- Lack of alternative nonviolent responses available to the offender (i.e., doesn't know how else to behave in the situation)

- Cultural inversion, or reaction formation: "If I can't be middle class, I'll be a terror to the middle classes (hedonistic, destructive, other values opposite traditional middle-class values)"

For a thorough description of the physiology of angry aggression, see John Medina's treatment (2000) in chapter 7 of his book *The Genetic Inferno.*

TOPIC 20.1   The Origins of Violence

Wrangham and Peterson (1996) write that among the primates, the capacity for violent aggression (including battering, rape, and infanticide) has been common to all, but its actual expression is a function of vulnerability. Vulnerability itself is a function of one's degree of social protection. Apes who live in smaller groups, such as orangutans and chimpanzees (the latter live in groups of two to nine), experience more violence, because the individual apes have fewer resources for forming protective alliances. Those who live in larger groups, such as bonobos (pygmy chimpanzees, with an average group size of 17) and gorillas, benefit from the social protection available from the implicit alliances in the larger group. Safety is found in numbers (p. 143).

The forces that cause a species to evolve into larger groups have to do with the "costs" associated with grouping. These costs include the availability of snack food from the jungle floor. Groups are easier to form when abundant snack food is available. Bonobos developed into peaceable, nonaggressive colonies because of the topography of their homeland south of the Zaire River, where tree fruits and floor plants abound: lots of snacks, lots of cohorts, lots of alliances and friendships, and lots of peace. Chimps, on the other hand, evolved north of the Zaire River, where the dearth of floor plants forced them to split up in order to forage: lack of snacks, competition for scarcer foods, few alliances to prevent aggression. Humans evolved 3 million years ago in a savanna near the chimps. Our need to forage makes us more like the chimps and less like the peaceable bonobos.

This pattern is an excellent example of the interaction of nature and nurture. Although aggression is common to all apes (nature), some had social protection and some didn't (nurture), resulting in the more peaceable bonobo and the more aggressive chimps and humans. Wrangham and Peterson (1996) point out that specific acts of aggression are caused by pride in one's status. If this status (for example, the status of the alpha male or an All-American running back) is never challenged, then there is no need for violence. One's nature doesn't express itself. But dominant primates, especially males, do not like to grovel. So when their dominance, or position in the hierarchy, is challenged, a quick mental calculation ensues, something like this:

1. The status quo is disturbed by a perceived threat.

2. The dominant member evaluates the threat: "Can I win or not?"

3. If the dominant member feels confident of winning, then aggression takes place.

4. If the dominant member feels unsure of winning, then he or she avoids immediate engagement, delaying until an effective coalition can be formed.

Treatment

❶ Understand that a very effective way to deal with aggression is often to form alliances. When you are vulnerable to the aggressive advances of someone else, form friendships and alliances that are publicly visible to your aggressor. There is safety in numbers. Consider the aggressor-boss in the movie *9 to 5* and the effective coalition formed by the three secretaries! Remember that once an alliance has been formed, whether to aid or thwart aggression, the members need ongoing "grooming" for long-term stability and dependability. Grooming among primates typically involves picking nits; among humans, this would translate into subservient behaviors, such as offering to help with some unpleasant chore—covering the phones, washing dishes, and the like.

TOPIC 20.2   Violence as Bad Chemistry

Researchers are finding aggression to be a complex process. Serotonin levels have been shown to be highly subject to nature-nurture interaction (*APA Monitor,* April 1997). Stress combined with severe living conditions or a harsh upbringing can lower levels of serotonin. Low levels of serotonin are associated with poor impulse control and have been shown to accompany alcoholism, aggression, depression, and suicide. In addition to low serotonin levels, researchers (e.g., Stephen Gammie, *Journal of Neuroscience,* September 15, 1999) have identified another neurotransmitter that affects aggression and sexual violence—nitric oxide (NO). Rats low in NO are missing the gene that encodes for the enzyme *nitric oxide synthase,* from which NO emerges. Lower levels of NO in male rats—but not female—are associated with violent behavior. In addition, the enzyme *monoamine oxidase A* (MAO-A) is known to break down chemicals that lead to overreactivity to stress, such as adrenaline. MAO-A is lower in more violent men. The gene encoded for MAO-A, which is sex-linked, has been identified by researchers at Massachusetts General Hospital (*Science,* October 22, 1993). So, lower serotonin, lower NO, and lower MAO-A have the cumulative effect of poor impulse control.

Quartz and Sejnowski (2002, p. 196) relate that high levels of childhood stress lead to higher levels of noradrenaline, and low levels of maternal nurture lead to lower levels of serotonin, a one-two punch that leads to violent antisocial tendencies. With high levels of noradrenaline and low levels of serotonin, one tends to see threats in situations that others see only as normal. Hence, they live life with a constant quick trigger. This makes it difficult to learn cultural norms that promote social competency. Furthermore, prolonged stress pumps corticosteroids that accumulate and damage the hippocampus, thus affecting memory and the sense of self, further exacerbating the tendency to lash out inappropriately.

Psychopathologist Adrian Raine and colleagues at the University of Southern California report (in *Archives of General Psychiatry,* February 1, 2000) that a study of 21 men diagnosed with antisocial personality disorder revealed that they possess 11–14 percent less gray matter in their prefrontal cortex than normals—about two teaspoons' worth. The consequence of this deficit is generally lower levels of arousal, with an attending need for stronger stimulation. Gilligan (1997) points out that most prison injuries are self-inflicted. He associates this with the reduced capacity of the sociopath to feel emotions, thus resorting to self-mutilation in preference to feeling nothing.

Keith McBurnett, a psychiatry professor at the University of Chicago, led a team in a four-year study of boys with behavioral problems. He discovered that the boys with lowest salivary cortisol levels were the most violent and antisocial. Frequently named the meanest in their class, these low-cortisol boys match what we know about adults with antisocial personality disorder: they are fearless and guilt-free. This study suggests that one reason persons with antisocial disorder feel no remorse is that they feel no stress. Their systems do not pump cortisol like the rest of us. Cortisol is a glucocorticoid that is a part of the stress response. These low-cortisol boys in essence have ice in their veins, thus failing to go into the fight-or-flight response under stress. In fact, one would logically conclude that they don't experience stress. What stresses the rest of us doesn't ruffle their feathers; if they don't like it, they aggress it—kill it, beat it, or take it out of commission.

For the current status of any clinical trial or study mentioned in this book, check this website: www.clinicaltrials.gov.

Sex hormones and their relation to behavior have come under intense study in recent years. A raging debate among physicians, psychotherapists, drug manufacturers, and feminists continues over the nature and treatment of *premenstrual syndrome* (PMS) and *premenstrual dysphoric disorder* (PMDD). Although symptoms of these two disorders are similar to major depression, the difference is that PMS and PMDD are cyclical, occurring prior to the onset of menses. And the difference between PMS and PMDD is that the latter is crippling, causing roughly 3–9 percent of women such severe symptoms that they cannot carry on with normal routines until menses begins and the symptoms disappear. Approximately 50 percent of females' psychiatric and medical emergency hospital admissions and 50 percent of females' criminal acts occur at this time; most assignments of females to solitary confinement in prison take place during the premenstrual period. The debate rages over whether PMDD is a mental disorder, raging hormones, or symptoms of personal stress in need of resolution. Regardless of its nature, however, women experiencing crippling cyclical premenstrual symptoms need relief, whether through drugs or through behavioral or life style changes. Pills are available, but may serve only to mask causes. Causes could be sleep deprivation, spousal abuse or dysfunction, dietary abnormalities (e.g., blood sugar out of control), and so forth. A therapist should first attempt to explore possible causes, then prescribe medication only as a facilitator to help deal with them. As with ADHD and other disorders, the drug helps dispose oneself to learning new behaviors and enacting lifestyle changes.

Blum (1997, chapter 7) writes of the similar, yet different effects of stability and variation of testosterone and estradiol in men and women. These effects are summarized below:

	Males	**Females**
Testosterone	Variable*	Stable
Estradiol	Stable	Variable**

* *Varies because of environment, competition, etc., as well as time of day and year*

** *Varies because of monthly cycle*

To spell it out, levels of testosterone do not vary much at all in females, just as estradiol is stable in males. However, testosterone levels can vary greatly in men, and the variation is attributable to changes in the environment, such as losing a competition or serving in a demeaning position. On the other hand, estradiol levels vary in women, but only in response to bodily changes associated with the menstrual cycle. During the several days preceding the onset of the monthly menstrual period, the woman's body experiences a dramatic drop in progesterone and estrogen production. This is an example of *positive feedback,* in which changes tend to increase in their initial direction of change, as opposed to *negative feedback,* in which changes tend to return to the original state. The result of this positive-feedback phenomenon is emotional volatility. However, the relative changes in level of testosterone in men are only around 100–150 percent, whereas changes in estradiol in women (see figure 13.2) range from a lowest recorded fluctuation of 650 percent to a highest recorded change of 4,900 percent! (Blum, p. 207.)

For males, the equivalent (in terms of its relation to violence) of a woman's hormone depletion in a man is an excess of testosterone. The normal peaks in male testosterone levels are (1) early in the morning (they are 25 percent lower in evening hours), (2) during rapid-eye-movement (REM, or dream) sleep, and (3) in early autumn (they are lowest in spring). Males experience six or seven peaks in their testosterone level each day, with accompanying variations in the five male characteristics of behavior (competition, aggression, self-reliance, self-assertion, and self-confidence; see topic 13.1). Excessive testosterone takes these characteristics to a grotesque extreme: the cocksure (extreme self-confidence) loner (extreme self-reliance), driven (extreme self-assertion) to dominate (extreme aggression), whatever the cost (extreme competitiveness). Testosterone production soars in the teenage years; as a result, the highest crime rates are among 13- to 17-year-olds. Moir and Jessel (1991) talk of the two equivalent mood disorders as PMT (*premenstrual tension*) and VMT (*violent male testosterone*). Heino Meyer-Bahlburg of the New York State Psychiatric Institute, however, finds that castration has little effect on male violence in general, only on sexual violence. This points to the contribution of other factors, such as low serotonin and GABA levels, in combination with testosterone.

Men's limbic or emotional activation is linked to physical response areas of the brain, women's to verbal response areas. Love me, caress me; love me, talk to me. Hate me, fight me; hate me, argue with me. Preeminent male Bear Bryant: "Make something happen." Preeminent female Sappho: "Equal to the gods seems to me that man who sits facing you and hears you nearby sweetly speaking and softly laughing. This sets my heart to fluttering in my breast. . . ." Accordingly, says Blum (p. 62), "men are more likely to strike out physically and women to strike out verbally."

Stanford University neuroscience professor Robert Sapolsky (1997, pp. 147–159), points out that testosterone and other members of the male hormone family do not cause aggression, they intensify it. Testosterone doesn't cause aggression—it aggravates (in intensity) what is already there (in terms of frequency). In other words, variation in levels of testosterone will not affect the frequency of aggression, just its intensity. For example, castrated rats do not cease being violent, they simply decrease their level of violence. Certainly, the more testosterone, the more violent and aggressive a violent and aggressive person will be. But tons of testosterone will not make a nonviolent person violent. Watch out for secondary sex characteristics, however!

Deborah Blum (1997, pp. 180–182) suggests that the hormonal basis of anger is twofold: levels of testosterone appear to influence primarily how angry one feels, whereas levels of noradrenalin influence primarily the degree to which one expresses, or acts on, that anger. Much of this view is based on a Dutch study following female athletes given testosterone: they ended up more testy and grouchy with people around them, but they didn't get physically reactive, as in pushing people about.

Treatments

❶ Pioneering work by British researcher Katharina Dalton (1987) has yielded two significant findings relative to PMT: (1) administration of progesterone calms the rage center of the brain, and (2) a drop in blood sugar results in a rise in adrenaline and a drop in progesterone. Holly Anderson has opened a clinic based on this research: the PMS Treatment Center in Arcadia, California. A simple, self-administered remedy for women with troublesome mood swings is to try snacking every two to three hours to maintain blood sugar levels throughout the day. Women might also try a low-carbohydrate lifestyle to maintain blood sugar at a lower overall level smoothly, without peaks and valleys. Other women with PMS have benefited from four daily servings of calcium- and vitamin D–rich nutrients, such as dairy and orange juice. Women with a tendency toward violent moods that won't go away should consult an endocrinologist for both pharmaceutical and nonpharmaceutical treatment.

❷ Women who have a tendency toward violent mood swings need to understand this reality. They also should mention to others their tendency to have mood swings and deal with them with appropriate humor after the fact. Men (and other women) need to avoid taking a woman's premenstrual mood swings personally; it helps if they can find appropriate ways to respond (such as "Wow! You're furious!" or "You have a right to be mad" or "You're right; good point") and then get on with things.

❸ Men who have a tendency to "take no prisoners" need to understand this reality. They should follow up such episodes with humorous or self-deprecating comments (such as "Boy! I just couldn't let go of my position, could I? I was a real bastard"). To minimize the possibility of exhibiting killer behavior when an important high-risk situation is coming up, they should try preceding the situation with long, strenuous exercise—for example, a 45-minute run or lap swim or a 60-minute brisk walk.

4 It is important for both males and females to pick up the pieces after their hormone-driven outbursts. At a minimum, they should say, "I'm sorry," or its equivalent (such as giving flowers or some other token). At another level, decisions made during outbursts should be reconsidered.

5 In September 1991, the U.S. Department of Agriculture reported that elevated (1,300 mg) daily doses of calcium relieve some of these symptoms; American women average about 600 mg of calcium per day. It is not clear how the calcium works. Women experiencing mood swings might try consuming more calcium products, such as milk or yogurt, before their periods.

6 For current information on PMS/PMT, contact Women's Health America, a national organization for women's health information in Madison, Wisconsin, on their website at www.womenshealth.com.

7 The bad moods associated with PMS can be elevated by getting out of bed (and staying up) around 3:00 A.M. five days or so before the start of one's period. Apparently these effects are related to ineffective body-clock regulators, with sleep deprivation providing a kind of reset.

8 Find a way to boost the serotonin levels of significant people in your life who are prone to aggression: dietary fats, aerobic exercise, serotonin reuptake inhibitors, and success experiences are several options.

9 Provide opportunities for young people (who would otherwise gain status through gang behavior) to gain acceptable status vis-à-vis their peers through various community or neighborhood programs.

10 Individuals with poor impulse control can improve their behavior with prescription medications.

11 Individuals with poor impulse control, if they are unconcerned about the consequences of their behavior, need to be placed in a safe, structured environment with few provocations from others.

⑫ Raine and colleagues suggest that one way to prevent future anti-social behavior is through identifying those with deficient prefrontal cortexes early and then channeling these high-risk children into highly stimulating—but socially acceptable—activities and careers, such as bomb-disposal expert, firefighter, and test pilot, each of whom perform better when unhampered by fear.

⑬ Weiner, Zahn, Sagi, and Merton (pp. 415 ff.) describe the use of Depo-Provera (medroxyprogesterone acetate, an antiandrogenic agent) in the treatment of *paraphilia,* the persistent craving for deviant sex. Injected into the muscle, it lowers blood testosterone levels, as well as apparently acting directly on the brain itself. While on the medication, patients exhibited reduced cravings and an 85 percent rate of abstinence from abnormal sexual behavior. Side effects may include weight gain, cold sweats, nightmares, hyperglycemia, labored breathing, hypogonadism, and leg cramps.

⑭ To defuse a potentially violent situation

- with a woman, engage her in her comfort zone, which is dialog. Talk, and listen.

- with a man, engage him in his comfort zone, which is action. Go for a walk or a bicycle ride.

TOPIC 20.3 **The Role of Peers in Shaping Violence**

Judith Rich Harris (1998) points out that the peer group is the primary environmental (or nurture) influence on what a child becomes (see more in my chapter 33). To the extent that a child is "born violent," the peer group can soften or accentuate that violence. The peer group works its magic through the *group contrast effect,* in which members of the group work hard to differentiate themselves from other groups and the rest of the world. Harris's proposals for schools and parents in managing the controlling effects of groups are listed below as "treatments."

In support of Judith Rich Harris's work, Thomas Dishion (of the Oregon Social Learning Center and University of Oregon) and his associates report (in *American Psychologist,* September 1999) that interventions designed to place delinquent youths together result in increased, not decreased, acts of violence and substance abuse, both long-term and short-term. In related research (e.g., Shermer, 2004; Kurzban and Leary, 2001), evidence is mounting that we are hard-wired to hate. The good news is that, from a genetic and evolutionary point of view, we are not hard-wired to hate a specific group, but the bad news is that we do appear to be hard-wired to hate. This, in the sense that humans have a strong tendency to see others as belonging to the in-group or the out-group. However, who belongs to one person's out-group is not only learnable but changeable. When we think of "us" vs. "them," we are reflecting learned behavior with respect to who belongs to the "them" group, while reflecting genetic wiring by stigmatizing "them," or the out-group, in the first place. Who belongs in a person's out-group can change many times in a lifetime: racial groups, neighborhood members, church affiliations, music preferences, political leanings, and so forth.

Quartz and Sejnowski (2002, pp. 206–207) clarify that individual, sociopathic violence is associated with low levels of activity in the *orbitofrontal cortex*—i.e., absence of feeling. The opposite, however, appears to be true for group violence. Itzhak Fried of UCLA has labeled a set of symptoms associated with group violence as *Syndrome E*: "obsessive ideation, compulsive repetition, rapid desensitization to violence, blunting of emotional response, and hyperarousal, together acting like a contagion that spreads through the whole group." Here the orbitofrontal cortex is hyperaroused, thus appearing to numb the group members to their normal feelings for fellow creatures. What is disconcerting here is that group violence appears to be normal socialization gone awry. The same forces that lead to group social achievement can lead to group social violence (pp. 214–215):

> As Patricia Hersch documented so poignantly in her book *A Tribe Apart,* the life of adolescents in America is far more lonely than violent. The violence that some adolescents turn to is in part a symptom of the larger problem of how modern society structures adolescent life so that it lacks adult involvement at a time when their struggle to form a coherent self-image requires guidance. Some of them, overwhelmed by the challenge of navigating that adolescent world by themselves, create worlds of violent fantasy that spill over to shatter everyone's reality.

Treatments:

❶ School program designers can turn the *group contrast effect* on its tail by using it for good:

- Eliminate all competing groups within a school (as in an all-female school, or everyone being on a sports team, or everyone being a writer, musician, etc.). The practice of requiring a standard school uniform incorporates this principle.

- Within a class, have many groups that are constantly changing, so that pupils feel a part of "Mrs. McGillicuddy's Fourth Grade Class" as a kind of meta-group that contrasts itself in a healthy way with the rest of the school and world.

- Teachers can use benign groups that acquire no superior or inferior status vis-à-vis each other: Porpoises vs. Dolphins, Writers vs. Speakers.

- Forming a benign common enemy, as in one group competing against another group in an interscholastic competition.

❷ Parents can work the group contrast effect to their child's welfare in several ways:

- Minimize a child's differences with respect to a positive peer group (kids don't want to be different from other kids in their peer group with regard to such things as dress, hair, spending money, nickname, braces, skin doctor, plastic surgery, etc.).

- Move to a new neighborhood or city if you have no other way to get away from a bad peer group.

- With large families, create strong leadership within the family with a strong identity, norms, and boundaries: "We're the Butlers, and we're lookin' good!"

- Move one child to the home of a relative.

- Consider home schooling.

- Change schools.

- Develop a new peer group and plan how the child can win respect within its hierarchy (like the time my mother and her friends created a Friday night ballroom dancing class with a dance teacher and a group of kids—including me—they wanted to be a peer group).

- Teach skills to your children—cooking, sewing, crafts, wood-work, gardening, landscaping, plumbing, electrical wiring, fishing, sports, makeup, and so on.

- Support your child's achievement.

- Provide a lifelong relationship that is satisfying and a good model.

- Respect your child's membership in a good peer group—do what you can to stabilize it by supporting it financially, by volunteering (one of my friends' mothers ALWAYS made yummy popcorn and Kool-Aid for us when we went to his house to play basketball, and we all wanted to go back!), or by resisting a move to a "better" neighborhood or city when it would mean breaking up the peer group.

- As Ms. Harris warns, make it fun, not work!

❸ To the degree that "us vs. them" behavior is natural, it behooves us to encourage folks to use their stigmatizing energy in the most benign way possible. For example, rally folks behind an athletic team, rather than rallying them behind ethnic group membership!

TOPIC 20.4   **Violence in Schools**

Much of school violence doesn't hit the front pages or the TV evening news. Arnold Goldstein believes, however, that these lesser forms of violence—name-calling, bullying, physical attacks, threats, sexual harassment, theft, rumor spreading, racial slurs, and shunning—must not be minimized, for their impact is cumulative. Goldstein, director of Syracuse University's Center for Research on Aggression, cautions (in *APA Monitor,* October 1994, p. 45) that most school violence programs are characterized by three attributes that don't work:

- Punishment, because it is only temporary

- Catharsis, because venting doesn't eradicate a learned behavior

- Cohabitation, or living with it, which is just not acceptable

Goldstein recommends that effective school violence programs have three characteristics that are known to be effective:

- Complex enough to address age levels, family members, peer groups, and the nature of the violence, because one policy doesn't fit all situations

- Prescriptive, or designed for the specific individual

- Situational, take into account such factors as timing, environment, and location

During the 1995–1996 school year, Mark Singer (*Pediatrics*, October 1999), researcher at Case Western Reserve University in Cleveland, Ohio, looked for precursors of violence in 2,245 public school children ages 7–15. The three strongest predictors: exposure to violence, lack of parental oversight, and television viewing habits (more than 20 percent reported viewing in excess of six hours a day).

Treatments

1 Goldstein has developed a school violence intervention program called "Aggression Replacement Training" for elementary and secondary schools. It emphasizes three approaches: handling conflict without aggression, controlling anger, and reasoning through moral issues.

2 Parent training, social work, and other programs aimed at curbing violence among schoolchildren need to emphasize ways to reduce exposure to violence, to increase parental oversight, and to reduce television viewing.

TOPIC 20.5   Television Watching and Video Gaming

In the U.S., preschoolers average one hour of television a day, school-age children three hours. By the time a child finishes high school, she will have witnessed more than 13,000 violent deaths on television. Research (Weiner, Zahn, Sagi, and Merton, 1990) shows that the more television a kid watches, the more likely she is to aver that it is okay to hit people "if you are mad at them for a good reason" (p. 329). People with heavy television viewing habits simply see the world differently than light viewers: they think there is much more violence out there than there actually is, they are more afraid of violence than others, and they see violence as more inevitable (p. 331).

In *Archives of Pediatrics & Adolescent Medicine* (July 2005), studies revealed that third-graders with television sets in their rooms had verbal and math scores eight points lower than those without TVs. Further, children with home computers and no TV scored higher than the TV-possessed, and children with a TV but no computer scored lower than children with both TV and computer. The studies also revealed that 26-year-olds who watched much TV in their childhood had lower educational levels, and that children watching television more than three hours a day before their third birthday scored worse on first-grade school tests that kids who watched less than three hours a day. It is important to note, however, that children who watch educational television programming do show gains in school achievement.

Psychologist Jeanne Funk and her University of Toledo colleagues studied the impact of violent vs. nonviolent video games on the self-reported temperament of 35 eight- to twelve-year-olds. They reported (at the August 2000 meeting of the American Psychological Association) that playing a violent video game did not increase a child's self-reported aggressiveness, but that a child's self-reported aggressiveness did determine whether a child preferred the more violent games over the nonviolent games.

Lieutenant Colonel Dave Grossman, a professor of military science, relates in his *On Killing: The Psychological Costs of Learning to Kill in War and Society* (1995) that in World War I most soldiers never fired their weapons in combat. In World War II, only 15–20 percent fired; in Korea, 50 percent; Vietnam, 95 percent. The difference: training changed, from stationary bullseyes to popup and falldown human targets. Grossman discouragingly points out the parallel of these training techniques to current video shooting games.

Treatments

❶ Schools need to educate both students and parents on how to view television critically, through asking questions, making personal comparisons, and generally having dialog and discussion, not just accepting the action as presented.

2 Violence is cheap content for television programs. We need new policies that make more civilized resources available. To the degree that television remains dependent on advertising, violence is almost assured.

3 Follow articles by George Gerbner, Larry Gross, and others in the *Journal of Communication* (more at **joc.oupjournals.org**).

4 Hilary Clinton and others are trying to limit the publication of and access to such violent video games as *Grand Theft Auto.* Support these legislators.

Part Six

Learning

The Brain
as Student

Part Six. Learning
The Brain as Student

21

Designing Instruction

Building Blocks for Learners

*T*he findings from cognitive research presented in this chapter all relate to how we learn. These findings will be applicable to you to the degree that you have an interest in influencing the learning of others (as well as your own!). Clearly, not every finding and every suggested application will find its way into your learning experiences. One of the major foundations of sound learning design that should permeate your approach to learning is closely related to Addison's quote here.

Michelangelo reputedly referred to a block of stone as "containing" the statue that he would "reveal" by chipping away the unnecessary stone. His emphasis was on intimately understanding the composition of the block, so that all he had to do as a sculptor was remove the excess, thus revealing the figure within. Each of us has a learner within that is defined by, for example, the eight Gardner talents (topic 34.4) or the Big Five personality dimensions (chapter 33). The experiences of an introverted intrapersonal learner will be different from those of someone who is extraverted and kinesthetic. In chapter 37, I present a comprehensive model for describing how each of us is put together, along with a worksheet (called "My Shapers" as appendix L) for each of us to use in defining how we are similar to and different from others.

One warning to those who design learning: Much has been said and written about the generally higher test results of Japanese schoolchildren. Apparently a major reason for this superiority is that the Japanese curriculum planners attempt a much narrower list of learning objectives than do, say, those in the United States. Where the Japanese might attempt 20 distinct mathematics skills in one year, U.S. educators might try 30. The resulting increase in practice time per skill for the Japanese students explains much of their superiority in test performance. The lesson is clear: attempt less in breadth, demand more in depth, if what you want is higher performance in specific skills.

One note of concern. First, the bad news: much of the research in this section comes out of the academic psychology departments, and there is no direct conduit to educators in our schools. Now the good news: beefed-up resources for the Department of Education's Office of Educational Research and Improvement are making many new grants contingent on cooperative research projects involving both psychologists and educators; both must be represented for the money to be awarded. Another bright light on the horizon is the efforts of John Bransford and others to establish a "cumulative knowledge base on learning and teaching." Bransford is a professor in the College of Education in the University of Washington at Seattle. This effort is described in chapter 11 of his book *How People Learn,* which was a collaborative effort sponsored by the National Research Council. Periodically, we should all do a web search on both the name of John Bransford and the phrase "cumulative knowledge base on learning and teaching" to see if progress has occurred. It is a massive undertaking in which many universities are collaborating, including Vanderbilt, Bank Street, and MIT.

Note also that I do not take time here to describe the actual neuro-chemistry of the learning process. This is available in all "Introduction to Psychology" texts. I will mention that an excellent, detailed description of the process involved in learning, also called *plasticity,* is available in chapter 6 of Joseph LeDoux's *Synaptic Self* (2002). LeDoux describes all the chemicals, structures, and processes involved in creating the new synaptic connections that form the basis of learning, including traditional processes such as classical and operant conditioning, and the details of the process referred to as *long-term potentiation.*

This chapter focuses on findings that relate to the design of learning experiences in general. Subsequent chapters in this section treat other aspects of learning: the role of the teacher, memory, learning styles, giftedness, and language development. Treat these chapters as a sort of cafeteria line or smorgasbord from which you take what you need today and to which you return later to take something different as your learning needs change. As a way of helping you evaluate your learning experiences overall, I have provided appendix C, "Evaluating Your Learning Practices." Enjoy.

TOPIC 21.1   Chunking

Make an effort to limit the introduction of new information to groupings of about seven of anything. G. A. Miller (1956) has demonstrated that seven new and previously unassociated bits of information (like those found in a telephone number) are about as much as most people can work with. Once the seven or so bits of information have been mastered, they become a chunk and behave as one bit. See more about Miller and the "magical number seven" at topic 23.1.

Applications

1 If you want people to remember a list of 10 or more items, either (a) somehow reduce the list to 9 or fewer items (preferably 7) or (b) break up the list into two or more units of 7 chunks each, master the first list of 7 before moving on to the second, and so on.

2 Where possible, take a longer list of, say, 15 or 20 items and reduce it to about 7 by identifying the biggest categories. Then learn the original list as subcategories of the shorter one. Work on the 7 main categories until they have been mastered; then work on the sets of subcategories one by one until you have learned the entire list.

❸ For verbal passages, start by mastering the first 5–9 words or chunks. (A familiar phrase such as "Old MacDonald Had a Farm" counts as one chunk.) Then learn the next 5–9 words or chunks. Put them all together and continue in the same way. For example, treat the sentence "'Old MacDonald Had a Farm' is one of my favorite childhood songs" as 8 bits—the song title itself counts only as 1 bit, as the original 5 bits of the title have become routinized, and are now a "chunk," or a single memory element—the 5 have become 1.

❹ For lists of numbers, look for combinations that can serve as chunks for you. For example, with the list of 611959, I could remember it as two chunks: my height (6'1") and my high school graduation year (1959).

TOPIC 21.2   **Testing as a Learning Process**

Classroom testing generally comes in two types: formative and summative. *Formative testing* provides feedback on the degree to which the learner is forming correct notions of the content; *summative testing* is typically done at the end of the unit or course to measure the sum, or final state, of the learner's knowledge of the subject. This section is about formative testing, which we will refer to simply as "testing."

Testing learners helps them to remember, according to Ronald P. Fisher of Florida International University. Some of his findings:

- Learners who take pretests do better on their finals.

- Learners who take pretests with fill-in-the-blank questions do better on their finals than those who take pretests with multiple-choice questions.

- Learners who take pretests with inferential multiple-choice questions do better on their finals than those who take pretests with factual multiple-choice questions.

Apparently, testing gives the learner an opportunity to practice several effective learning procedures simultaneously. Tests do not have to be punitive, or even graded, to be effective. It is the act of taking the test that is helpful. As Bransford et al. (2000) put it, "Feedback is most valuable when students have the opportunity to use it to revise their thinking as they are working on a unit or project" (p. 141).

Bruce Tuckman, psychologist at Ohio State University, compared three treatment groups: spot quizzes, homework, and classwork only. Spot-quiz students outperformed the homework students by 16 percent and the classwork-only group by 24 percent. He further found (reported in *APA Monitor,* October 1999) that students with low grade averages showed the most improvement. Students prone to procrastinate also showed more improvement than students not prone to procrastinate.

L. A. Hart (1983) argues that *nondirective tests* (in which the learner must figure out the relevant patterns and programs, as in essay, short answer, and fill-in-the-blank questions) are superior to *directive tests* (in which the key patterns and programs are presented to the learner). In a multiple choice test, for example, the pattern is explicitly presented, as in "J. S. Bach composed music in which style or period?" and the program options are clearly delineated, as in "a. Classical, b. Romantic, c. Baroque, d. Renaissance." A purely nondirective form of the question would be: "Based on your knowledge of the history of music, list a minimum of five composers in each of the major historical periods of musical composition." These nondirective questions are superior, according to Hart, because learners have to identify patterns and select programs, thus strengthening the neural pathways necessary for retrieval.

Applications

❶ Use the beginning of a class session to review content from previous sessions. For example, in reviewing a decision-making process, you might ask a series of questions such as "What is the first step?" "Why does it come first?" "What step is most frequently skipped?" "Why is it hard to remember?" This is a good way to use time while waiting for everyone to get back from a break.

❷ Use group competition in tests. For example, divide the learners into small groups and have them make a list of the steps of a process you taught in a previous session. Let the group that finishes first recite the steps to the other groups. If they make an error, let another small group recite from that point, and so on.

❸ Place learners in small groups and have each group construct a test to give to the other groups. This builds on the principle of "Handle It!" (see topic 21.6).

❹ Use card sorts to see if the steps of a process have been learned. For example, in an organization with an elaborate 17-step performance appraisal process, the trainer made decks of 17 cards each, with each card containing an unnumbered step of the process. The learners had to arrange the cards in the proper sequence, as individuals and as groups, and were allowed to review one another's work until they all thought they were right. The preferred solution was then revealed. You should be open to the possibility that in such a case the class may come up with an improvement to the process!

❺ If possible, choose tests that require the learner to identify a pattern (for example, somebody doing a poor job of listening to someone else) and then to identify an appropriate *program* to apply (for example, a clarifying question).

❻ Start a training session with a pretest that includes some of the more unusual points you will cover in your session. *(Contributed by Jane Howard)*

TOPIC 21.3   What Makes Good Textbooks?

Apart from the content of the written material used in learning, two factors seem particularly important: *style* and *organization.* In regard to style, Suzanne Wade, a professor of education at the University of Utah, reported in a presentation to the American Education Research Association in April 1993 that concrete details and visual descriptive passages are more effective in making material interesting than are amusing anecdotes and sidebars. The former make the material not only more enjoyable, but more understandable; the latter may even interfere with learning by detracting from the in-depth pursuit of information. Wade found that technical language interfered with interest and understanding at more basic levels, whereas concrete and visual language aided interest and understanding (*APA Monitor,* July 1993).

In regard to organization, Walter Kintsch (1994) has found that *advance organizers,* when they are arranged the same way as the target text, lead to higher scores on recall of information (see topic 22.1). However, when advance organizers are arranged differently from the target text, learners show higher scores on comprehension. Apparently, the latter condition forces more participation from the reader, hence deeper understanding. Kinsch also found that low-knowledge readers learn better from well-organized texts, whereas high-knowledge readers learn better from more loosely organized texts that do not spell everything out. Apparently, when more knowledgeable readers and learners see a well-organized text, they assume that they know most of it and opt not to "get involved" with the material. More loosely organized texts, such as casebooks, edited collections, and sourcebooks, are more inviting to the knowledgeable reader.

Applications

1 For beginners, prefer texts and written materials that are well organized and that employ a concrete, visual style. Avoid highly technical language. Use advance organizers that parallel the organization of the text.

2 For more advanced readers, prefer texts that are more loosely organized and that use a more technical style. Advance organizers should not be arranged in the same way as the text. Make advanced readers grapple and get involved with the material.

TOPIC 21.4   Schemas

British psychologist Frederick Bartlett (1932) was the first person to propose a theory of abstract cognitive structures called schemas. A *schema* is an outline, a skeleton, a map that defines the essential structure, the logic, for a particular type of experience. For example, I have a schema for preparing scrambled eggs. My schema may or may not be similar to your schema for scrambling eggs. When schemas are similar to an actual experience, they render our memories of that experience accurate; if they are different, they color our memories accordingly. In other words, if I depart from the way I normally cook eggs, perhaps because of a telephone interruption, then later in the day when I attempt to recall my egg scrambling, I am likely to remember the cooking not as it actually occurred, but rather to conform with my schema. The biological basis of a schema is a neural pathway that represents the schematic diagram of a specific cognitive process. We have schemas for telling stories or jokes, giving directions, and solving problems. We may even have several different schemas for each task. David Rumelhart (H. Gardner, 1985, p. 125) describes the standard schema for storytelling; I have summarized his description as follows:

1. State the goal.

2. Enumerate the steps to the goal (e.g., "Once upon a time, Little Red Riding Hood set out to visit her grandmother").

3. Relate the reactions along the way.

4. Describe and comment on the success or failure in reaching the goal.

Our schemas differ from each other's just as our experiences do. Someone who has learned the Chinese language will have different schemas from someone who hasn't. In one sense, the story of our mental life is the story of either (1) forming new schemas or (2) accommodating new experiences to old schemas. Most learning appears to be a process of fitting new information into old schemas. Unless we work hard to establish new schemas, our existing schemas tend to determine how we evaluate and shape new information.

John Bransford, co-director of Vanderbilt University's Learning Technology Center, has determined that schemas play such a strong role in coloring new learning that learners can't help but modify what they hear and see according to their prior experience. Learners who hear "The doctor's son greeted his father" will typically tend to accommodate this statement to their schema about doctoring and see the son shaking hands with a father who is a doctor, rather than allowing for the possibility that the doctor is actually the mother, standing by and watching her son greet his father, who is not a doctor. In this sense, stereotypes are schemas. Bransford says that this tendency is so strong and so pervasive that the instructor must take responsibility for listening to students discuss their newfound knowledge and clarify instances of inappropriate accommodation to previous schemas. As Hodgson's law says, we tend to remember a thing the way we want to remember it.

An example of this is a story educator John Holt tells of visiting an elementary school and observing a geography lesson. The fifth-grade teacher was pointing to a wall map of the United States and was questioning students about points of the compass. Holt, on a hunch, approached the wall map, removed it, and laid it flat on the floor. He then asked, "Which way is north?" All the students pointed toward the ceiling!

L. A. Hart (1983) defines learning as the acquisition of useful schemas, which he calls *programs*. He defines a program or schema as a sequence used for attaining a preselected goal. Programs are triggered when the learner recognizes a pattern or situation that somehow fits with the program or schema. For example, when I see a whining child (pattern), I use my "distract the child" routine (program), in which I move through my repertoire of quacking like a duck, making clicking noises with my tongue, crowing like a rooster, and so forth. If the program works (that is, the learner achieves the goal), fine; otherwise, the learner tries another program or looks for another pattern.

Mary Crawford (1995) has clarified the influence of gender differences in learning schemas. According to her research, many females acquire certain schemas that males are less likely to acquire, such as "how to mend a shirt," while many males acquire certain schemas that females are less likely to acquire, such as "how to build a workbench." She has found gender differences in the amount of detail recalled when two groups are told the same story but given different titles, with each title representing a gender-specific schema. For example, most females will remember more detail from a story entitled "How to Mend a Shirt" than one entitled "How to Build a Workbench," even when the two stories are identical except for the title (that is, the story is about building a workbench that is used to mend a shirt).

Janet Kolodnor (1997) builds on the idea of schemas by demonstrating the effectiveness of analogous situations as a teaching tool. By relating new concepts structurally to familiar situations or schemas, learners demonstrate greater understanding and retention. For example, teaching the concept of how the multiple points of view in the Continental Congress in the early United States were satisfied might be simplified by convening a class meeting about a similarly divisive subject, such as how the school should or could treat the needs and desires of students and their families with respect to different religious traditions and holidays.

Applications

❶ Before teaching someone a new skill or body of knowledge, first find out what the learner already knows that is similar. Then proceed with your instruction, pointing out the ways in which this new learning is similar to or different from the learner's existing schemas. For example, if the learner is to learn arc welding, find out whether she has had experience with other kinds of welding machines, soldering irons, and so on. This is a normal part of the technical training model called *job instruction training* (see Eckles, Carmichael, and Sarchet, 1981, p. 340).

❷ As we get older, we have more complex and more numerous schemas to build on. This is particularly helpful in the *peg-word technique* for memorizing lists. Say that you want to memorize the 10 largest cities in the world. You start by making a list of rhyming words for the numbers 1 to 10. You then think of an association between the rhyming word (the peg word) and the name of the city; the more whimsical or outrageous the association is, the easier it will be to remember. For example:

Number	Rhyme	City	Association
One	Bun	Tokyo	*Looks like the bow on the traditional Japanese kimono*
Two	Shoe	Mexico City	*Mexico as the shoe of the body of the North American continent*
Three	Tree	São Paulo	*The land of rain forests*
Four	Door	New York	*The traditional door to the United States for immigrants*
Five	Hive	Seoul	*A beehive of political activity*
Six	Sticks	Osaka	*"O sock-a me with the sticks"*
Seven	Heaven	Buenos Aires	*Heaven is good air ("buenos aires" = "good air")*
Eight	Gate	Calcutta	*"Cut a" gate into the fence*
Nine	Line	Bombay	*The coastline around the bay*
Ten	Pin	Rio de Janeiro	*Pin (blame) it on Rio (movie title)*

Once you've memorized the peg words (bun, shoe, and so on), all you have to do is form good visual associations between the peg word and the related item on the list you're trying to memorize. The mind can easily relate the schema of bun, for example, to both sweet rolls and the bow on the back of the kimono. See examples in Lorayne and Lucas (1974) and Buzan (1991).

❸ When you think a common schema exists for everyone in a group, you might refer to it in front of the whole class. For example, if you are talking about performance appraisal, you might discuss how it is similar to and different from traditional school report cards.

❹ Ask questions and provide examples that relate to the experiences of the learners. Help them to see the connection between their experiences and what you are teaching.

❺ Allow your learners time for exploration. Help them verbalize both the patterns they recognize and the programs and schemas they choose to apply (L. A. Hart, 1983). Here's a model of the process:

1. Recognize the pattern.

2. Implement the program.

3. Evaluate the program. If it fails, reinterpret the pattern, look for a new pattern, try a new program, or try a variation on the failed program.

❻ When using familiar schemas (basketball, cars, cooking, sewing) to explain a concept (for example, how to find a percentage), remember that some students will be unfamiliar with some of the schemas. Be sure to use a representative set of schemas in order to give all the learners an equal chance to learn the concept. Try to find more gender-neutral schemas (such as eating, swimming, or reading) to use as a basis for new learning. Test the intended schema with the group by asking whether everyone is familiar with it.

TOPIC 21.5 **Two Modes of Processing Information**

Seymour Epstein (1994), in reviewing more than 30 different studies on human information processing, has identified two independent yet interactive methods that individuals use: *experiential* and *rational.* These two modes have been given various names over the last century; seeing all these different names together (table 21.1) is a powerful argument for their prominent role in human learning.

People who are strong in one mode may be weaker in the other. Even when learners are strong in both modes, redundancy in instructional design will result in greater learning by the greater number of learners. Consider your favorite speaker (lecturer, rabbi, mullah, and so forth); one reason you like him is probably that he balances abstract points with concrete examples, and not too much of either. An excellent example of this balance, at least in the domain of writing, is the work of the *New York Times* international affairs writer Thomas Friedman. In his works, such as *From Beirut to Lebanon* and *The Lexus and the Olive Tree* (on globalization), he begins each chapter with an abstract point, then proceeds to illustrate it abundantly with concrete stories and other examples.

The experiential mode could be described as more right-brained, the rational mode more left-brained. Arthur Glenberg, psychologist at the University of Wisconsin–Madison, has developed the *embodiment theory* of memory—that human memory is designed to remember action, not the abstract. Elaborating on this idea in "What Memory Is For," his paper in the journal *Behavioral and Brain Sciences* (1997), Glenberg says this explains why people are more likely to remember how a machine operates after seeing it demonstrated than after only reading about it. Glenberg's theory seems to relate to the two modes of Epstein—and the two hemispheres, especially concentrating on the experiential mode.

Applications

❶ Ensure that your learning design contains a balance of experiential and rational learning strategies. For example, for every expository definition given to the learner, provide a story that illustrates it.

❷ For every point you explain, tell a story to illustrate it.

❸ For every essay you write, find a narrative or story to illustrate the concept. For every story you write or tell, identify the concept or point that it illustrates. This is the technique for Aesop's fables, in which each story ends with an aphorism.

❹ For every drama, review criticism.

❺ For every activity, talk about it (called "processing" in human relations parlance).

Table 21.1. Two Modes of Human Information Processing

Mode	Experiential/Narrative (Learning Feelings and Behaviors Through Schemas)	Rational/Expository (Learning Attitudes and Beliefs Through Language)
Defining Characteristics	Unconscious, emotionally engaging, personally convincing, interpersonal, automatic, independent of intelligence and age, storylike, concrete, specific, promitive, simpler, perceptual, positive, imagistic, rapid, more effective in changing feelings and behavior	Analytical, conscious, formal, theoretical, more complex, general, removed from direct experience, capable of negation, abstract, public, logical, structural, organized, comceptual, more related to verbal, numerical, and spatial intelligence
Traditional Synonyms for Mode Title	Unconscious	Conscious
	Nonverbal	Verbal
	Procedural	Declarative
	Contextual	Propositional
	Prototypical	Logical
	Episodic/procedural	Semantic
	Tacit/implicit	Explicit
	Mythos	Logos
	Natural	Extensional
	Automatic	Reflective
	Heuristic	Effortful
	Direct, behavioral experience	Indirect, nonbehavioral experience
	Narrative	Propositional
	Biological	Conceptual
	Implicit	Self-attributed
	Biological	Linguistic
	Prewired	Intentional
Typical Learning Strategies Associated with Mode	Stories, settings, intentions, emotions, actions, scripts, narratives, plots, moods, five senses, images, pictures, acting, movement, feedback mechanisms, metaphors	Charts, tables, exposition, diagrams (non-narrative), formulas, systems analysis, symbol systems, organizational methods, process designs

Source: Adapted from "Integration of the Cognitive and the Psychodynamic Unconscious" by Seymour Epstein (August 1994), *American Psychologist, 49*(8), 709–724.

❻ For every lecture, conduct an experiment. For example, if you are lecturing on African history, get the class to make some predictions about their peers' knowledge, then confirm by asking, for example, "How many of you know where Nigeria is located?"

❼ For additional ideas on how to balance the two modes, read Don Norman's *Things That Make Us Smart* (1993).

TOPIC 21.6   Handle It!

One of the best ways to learn a body of information is to manipulate it in such a way as to make it yours. I have a friend who understood this principle in undergraduate school. After each lecture, he would return to his room with his notes, then sit at his typewriter and rewrite the notes in an outline form that was meaningful to him. Four years later, he had earned his Phi Beta Kappa key! To get a handle on it, handle it.

Another dimension of this learning principle was expressed by UCLA's Robert Bjork (1994, p. 192): "Manipulations that speed the rate of acquisition during training can fail to support long-term post-training performance, while other manipulations that appear to introduce difficulties for the learner during training can enhance post-training performance." I'm reminded of the passage from Aeschylus's *Agamemnon* that is variously translated as "Man must suffer to be wise" and "He who learns must suffer." Nothing new, that passage by Bjork. Easy come, easy go. The easier, more pain-free the practice is in the classroom, the more difficult it will be to transfer the information to the street, home, or workplace. After students show initial understanding, the instructional design should include variations, interference, distractions, and other difficulties that require the learner to struggle with the deep, essential structure of a new learning and not be content with just its surface structure.

In a study reported in the *Journal of Experimental Psychology: Learning, Memory, and Cognition* (July 2001), Dominic Simon (McMaster University, Hamilton, Ontario) and Bjork (UCLA) compared different sets of skills learned in separate blocks versus randomly interleaved. Persons who learned in blocks felt they had better mastery, and they performed better the next day on a post-test than the interleaved learners. In fact, although the block learners *did* do better on the day of instruction, they performed measurably worse overall than the interleaved learners. Interleaving, such as by interrupting the learning or introducing difficulties, is worse for the short term, better for the long term. This is of significance for persons such as surgeons, who must learn separate skills over time but must ultimately use them together.

Bjork (1994, p. 188) recommends that learned material be *multiply encoded,* using multiple models, paraphrases, and examples rather than a single version: "The research is unambiguous: A variety of manipulations that impede performance during training facilitate performance on the long term" (p. 192). This principle of learning is often violated for several reasons:

1. Trainers and teachers are evaluated on a short-term basis.

2. Trainers and teachers typically don't see the long-term effects of the learning.

3. Follow-up is not usually done by the original trainer or teacher.

4. Trainers and teachers often confuse current success with future success.

Applications

❶ If you are a teacher and want to hand out an outline of your material, wait until after you've covered it. This forces the learners to write their own notes and struggle with the wording and outline. The act of having to "handle" the material helps the learners to build on their existing schemas. Alternatively, show the outline as an advance organizer (see topic 22.1), especially for learners unfamiliar with the content, but don't keep the outline available to them. Release it to them later.

❷ If the material forms some kind of list or chart, put the elements on cards. Then have either individuals or groups arrange the cards in a correct or meaningful order.

❸ Have small groups generate their own examples of the point you are making.

❹ Use role playing.

5 Have the learners write their own case studies.

6 If the learners are to apply a skill (such as constructive criticism) to a job, have them write out a script to use.

7 Examine books on the subject of TRICA (teaching reading in the content areas). These texts contain hands-on activities and are meant for high school teachers with students who do not read well. The activities work well as an adult learning technique, regardless of reading level.

8 Have the learners prepare a presentation for each other. (Remember, the best way to learn something is to teach it.)

9 Suggest that the learners make a presentation back on the job to others who are unable to attend. Allow time in class to begin work on such a presentation.

10 Give the learners, alone or in groups, an unorganized list of all the elements of your presentation and let them decide how they'd like to organize it.

11 Have individuals or groups rank a list of items according to some criterion. This helps them to grapple with the concepts.

12 Vary the conditions of practice: schedule practice in a random fashion, minimize order and predictability, and vary the length, scope, distance, order, resources, context, or subject.

13 Interrupt practice with both related and unrelated events and information.

14 Introduce the model (for example, with advance organizers) by using an outline that is inconsistent with the practice model.

15 Used spaced and distributed practice rather than massed practice (see topic 22.2).

16 Reduce feedback: use summary feedback after several trials, rather than feedback after each trial.

TOPIC 21.7	Transfer: Applying Classroom Ideas to the Real World

Whenever you teach a theory or concept, give the learners time to apply it to specific situations. Many learners are unable intellectually or unwilling motivationally to apply an idea to an everyday situation. Detterman and Sternberg (1993) paint a discouraging picture of training in the workplace. They distinguish between *learning* and *transfer of learning*. Learning has occurred when one is able to repeat a new behavior in nearly identical situations close in time to the original learning event. Transfer of learning has occurred when one is able to repeat a new behavior in different kinds of situations that are remote in time—that is, when the learner sees a new *pattern* that fits with the *program* in some way (see topic 21.4). Detterman and Sternberg distinguish *near* and *far* transfer. Near transfer occurs when one repeats a behavior in a similar situation that is remote in time; far transfer occurs when one repeats a behavior in a different situation that is remote in time. Following a thorough review of the literature, they maintain that far transfer is unlikely to occur. Or, as Bransford et al. (2000) put it: "Simply learning to perform procedures, and learning in only a single context, does not promote flexible transfer" (p. 77).

Roughly $100 billion is spent annually on training in the workplace. Detterman and Sternberg estimate that only about 10 percent of that training actually transfers to the workers' jobs. Baldwin and Ford (1988) confirm these numbers; in addition, they state that this 10 percent is only of the "near" variety. An example of near transfer would be learning a counseling skill in a classroom role play involving an employee who repeatedly arrives late to work, then actually using that counseling skill back on the job with an employee who is repeatedly tardy. Applying that skill to a different situation, like that of an employee who never puts his or her tools back in the right place, would be far transfer, and Detterman and Sternberg (1993) say that this just doesn't happen:

> When I [Sternberg] began teaching, I thought it was important to make things as hard as possible for students so they would discover the principles themselves. I thought the discovery of principles was a fundamental skill that students needed to learn and transfer to new situations. Now I view education, even graduate education, as the learning of information. I try to make it as easy

for students as possible. Where before I was ambiguous about what a good paper was, I now provide examples of the best papers from past classes. Before, I expected students to infer the general conclusion from specific examples. Now, I provide the general conclusion and support it with specific examples. In general, I subscribe to the principle that you should teach people exactly what you want them to learn in a situation as close as possible to the one in which the learning will be applied. I don't count on transfer and I don't try to promote it except by explicitly pointing out where taught skills may apply. . . . There is no good evidence that people produce significant amounts of transfer or that they can be taught to do so. There is, on the other hand, substantial evidence . . . that favors the idea that what people learn are specific examples. Experts are experts because they have learned many more examples than novices. . . . Current evidence suggests all that is necessary to be an expert is time, basic ability, and the opportunity to learn a large body of exemplars by experience [p. 17].

[An expert's] knowledge is so ample and elaborately structured that it is hard to present an expert with a problem that is not already represented therein [p. 174].

People who know a lot about something are not experts because of their ability to transfer but because they know a lot about something [p. 18].

The lesson learned from studies of transfer is that if you want people to learn something, teach it to them. Don't teach them something else and expect them to figure out what you really want them to do [p. 21].

Robert Bjork (1994) extends this thought by commenting that "perceived similarity, or the lack thereof, of new tasks to old tasks is a critical factor in the transfer of training. . . . To the extent feasible, a training program should provide a learned representation that permits the learner to recognize when the knowledge and skills acquired during training are and are not applicable to new problems" (p. 186). Bjork emphasizes that retrieval practice during the training session is critical in assuring future transfer and retrieval: "Retrieval information becomes more recallable in the future than it would have been without having been accessed. In that sense, the act of retrieval is a 'memory modifier.' . . . As a learning event, in fact, it appears that a successful retrieval can be considerably more potent than an additional study opportunity, particularly in terms of facilitating long-term recall" (p. 188). To relate this to L. A. Hart's (1983) model, retrieval, or transfer, is the act of identifying a pattern that calls for a specific program.

Applications

❶ Use printed, video, or audio examples. For example, "Interpersonal Management Skills" (IMS), an excellent course developed at Xerox, provides printed worksheets with good and bad examples of the skills applied in different settings (plant, office, home, etc.), an audiotape with examples and practice exercises, and a videotape with both positive and negative examples. The IMS program is available from Learning International Inc., 225 High Ridge Road, Stamford, Connecticut 06905.

❷ Using your schemas, give examples from your personal experience to illustrate a concept, then ask the learners to generate other examples in small groups, building on their schemas.

❸ If you want the learners to apply a concept or skill you are teaching to some situation far away from the classroom, then think up some likely scenarios and have the learners apply the concept or skill in those settings through role play, small-group work, or individual work.

❹ Whenever possible, use real situations in the classroom for the learners to copy later in other situations. Don't just use generic case studies. In my problem-solving classes, for example, I have students write up a list of problems they'd like help in solving; then we pick the ones my techniques apply to and work on them.

❺ Broad and Newstrom (1992) have found that the manager, the trainer, and the learner each play an important role in transferring learning back to the job. Further, they find that the timing of the involvement of these three roles is different. Although all three should be involved with the learner before, during, and after the learning episode, it is especially critical for the learner to be involved *before* the learning (with preparatory work and advance organizers), for the manager to be involved *during* the learning (with observation, input, feedback, and support), and for the trainer to be involved *after* the learning (with follow-through practice, support, and feedback).

❻ Bransford and others (2000) describe a variety of new curriculum resources that use technology to bring the outside world into the classroom. This is certainly one way to make sure that classroom learning relates to the outside world! Listed below are several of these projects. Find out more by reading chapter 9 in Bransford's book, which was sponsored by the National Research Council, or by searching on the web for these titles:

- The Voyage of the Mimi (Bank Street College)
- Jasper Woodbury Problem Solving Series (Vanderbilt)
- Global Lab
- Project GLOBE (Global Learning and Observations to Benefit the Environment)
- Learning Through Collaborative Visualization (CoVis) Project
- Middle School Mathematics Through Applications Projects (MMAP)
- Little Planet Literacy Series
- The Belvedere System
- STELLA
- GenScope Project
- SMART (Special Multimedia Arenas for Refining Thinking)
- DIAGNOSER
- Classtalk
- CSILE (Computer-Supported Intentional Learning Environments, a.k.a. Knowledge Forum)
- Challenge 2000 Multimedia Project
- Sherlock Project
- Geometry Tutor
- PUMP (Pittsburgh Urban Mathematics Program)
- PAT (PUMP Algebra Tutor)
- Kids as Global Scientists (KGS) Research Project

- American Schools Directory (www.asd.com; has a page for every K–12 school in the U.S., both public and private, with opportunities for cross learning and cross fertilization with such services as a wish list for requesting help, along with a free e-mail address option for any student or teacher)

- Teacher groups:

  LabNet Project (physics)

  Bank Street College's Mathematics Learning project

  QUILL (Alaskan writing teachers)

  HumBio Project (biology)

  WEBCSILE

  TAPPED IN (Teacher Professional Development Institute)

- Resource databases such as that provided by the Indiana University and the North Central Regional Educational Laboratory at www.ncrel.org.

TOPIC 21.8 | **Practice**

Allow ample time for practice. Supervised practice provides the feedback necessary to refine the learning, and practice in and of itself is crucial in converting the learning from short- to long-term memory (see chapter 23). Practice clarifies and strengthens the neural connections that are formed while learning. But practice should not be mindless, as topic 21.6 points out. Appropriate complications in the practice program help build a deeper understanding of the schema underlying the new learning.

Robert Bjork (1994) comments that "people learn by making and correcting mistakes. We have known at least since [1955, in a paper by Estes] that it may be necessary to induce forgetting during training to enhance learning. Training conditions that prevent certain mistakes from happening (and give trainers a false optimism about their level of comprehension and competence) can defer those mistakes to a post-training setting where they really matter" (p. 201). Bjork warns that the principle of introducing mistakes into training is especially important in such roles as public safety officers, nuclear power plant operators, military personnel, and transportation workers. For these and other jobs, it is crucial that we look for *mistakes* during training, not the absence of mistakes. In a similar vein, Quartz and Sejnowski (2002, p. 244) write: "Experiments with animals demonstrate that the largest brain changes occur when novelty is maintained by regularly rearranging and changing the objects in the animal's environment, keeping the animals in a constant state of learning."

Applications

1 Role playing is an effective way to practice, especially for interpersonal skills. Try to make it less intimidating by having several pairs or groups of three do the role play at the same time and then discuss the results together, rather than putting two individuals on the spot in front of the class.

2 Provide case studies, both off-the-shelf and real. They give learners the opportunity to practice applying their learning under your supervision.

3 Introduce appropriate distractions, irrelevant information, and other real-world properties that make practice more mindful. For example, in role-playing a seven-step counseling interview, have the interviewee purposely lead the interviewer forward or backward in the process, so the interviewer develops a sense of understanding and control concerning the importance of managing the process firmly.

4 When using a simulator (such as a flight simulator) for practice, the most important element is randomness, not physical appearance. The simulator should be psychologically faithful to the real world, not just faithful in an engineering sense.

5 In batting practice, randomly varied pitches give better performance results than blocks of pitches (for example, 15 curves followed by 15 sliders).

6 Practice skills that require identical performance conditions in a way that varies the conditions; for example, practice jump shots in basketball at varying distances and heights, practice point-after-touchdown conversions in football at different distances, timings, angles, widths, and heights.

TOPIC 21.9   Focus and Attention

Notwithstanding teenagers' claims that they can do homework in front of the television set, the brain cannot focus on more than one stimulus at a time. What may appear to be multitasking, or simultaneous focusing, is in fact a rapid alternation of focus. The more routine a stimulus is, the less it interferes with rival stimuli. So if you're listening to the news while driving on the interstate with moderate traffic, you will miss far less of the news than when you are driving around the Place de l'Étoile in Paris trying to maneuver across eight lanes of circular traffic. To underscore this point, University of Toronto physicians Donald Redelmeier and Robert Tibshirani reported that automobile drivers were 4.3 times more likely to have an accident while using a cell phone than when the unit was not in use. They reported that hands-free phone operation provided no safety advantage over hand-held sets (*New England Journal of Medicine,* February 13, 1997). Also, Geoffrey Woodman and Steven Luck, psychologists at the University of Iowa (Iowa City), have offered convincing evidence (in *Nature,* August 26, 1999) that supports the notion that we pay attention to items serially, not in parallel (two or more at a time). Electrophysiological measurements revealed rapid changes in event-related potential as the brains of subjects searched for particular elements in an array.

Much has been made of "information overload" in the 1990s. I don't buy it. Oprah Winfrey was concerned about forgetting the security codes to Harpo Studios in Chicago and about forgetting on Thursday the subject of Tuesday's show. Her producers called and asked if I'd care to come to the show and explain what they were referring to as "Yuppie Alzheimer's." Certainly. I explained that information overload, or Yuppie Alzheimer's, did not exist. There has always been abundant information vying for our attention. The hunter-gatherers who survived and made our existence possible were those who paid attention to the source of berries, seeds, and other nutrients. Can you imagine a gatherer in 10,000 B.C. wandering around a new terrain, finding berries, and *not* making it a point to remember the location? The next day, he'd make a beeline to yesterday's berry source. The gatherers who mindlessly skipped from bush to tree, from berry to nut, without paying effortful attention to remembering their locations, were doomed, at worst, to languish tomorrow in hunger or, at best, to waste precious time in having to relocate the stash.

So what did I tell Oprah and her viewers? "Stop and smell the roses. If you really want to remember something, make a point of remembering it. Focus, intend, practice." To make my point, I looked at her intensely and said, "I'm going to make a point of remembering exactly what you look like today. I know people will ask me. Well, you are wearing gold knot earrings with three strands woven in a pattern about three-quarters of an inch in diameter. You are wearing a two-piece tan knit suit, with the dress floor length (almost) and the jacket open and three-quarter length." By intending to remember, and by really *focusing* on her attire, I still remember it some 10 years later. And because so many people ask me about the show, I keep recalling it, which further reinforces the memory. Oprah can improve her recall with similar efforts at focused attention with the intention of remembering. It's funny: when we were in school, we made a point of trying to remember. As adults, we casually read or observe without similar efforts at remembering, such as taking notes or reviewing, and then we lament that we are "losing our memory" when we can't remember! For example, an executive reads *The Wall Street Journal* over breakfast, then later in the day tries unsuccessfully to recall the name of a person featured in a news story. She laments: "Oh my! I am getting old. My memory is going." Balderdash. We're expecting results like those of our schooldays without exerting a similar effort. There's something wrong with that picture.

Attention is maximized by learning design elements such as "Handle It!" (topic 21.6) and "Practice" (topic 21.8).

Applications

❶ Avoid playing music if you want the learner to concentrate. My wife and I once attended a workshop together. The leader asked us to complete a worksheet individually and silently. As we began our seat work, the leader started to play some background music—I believe it was a '50s tune. Well, my wife knew every word to that and each succeeding tune, silently sang along with them, and found it impossible to concentrate on the worksheet. The background music became foreground for her.

❷ Don't introduce a new skill on top of a prior one until the prior skill has become routinized. Practice the skills separately until one is mastered; then you may build on it. My daughter understood this well when, at the age of eight, she took Suzuki violin lessons. One day, as I was supervising her practice, she lost patience with my approach and glared at me, saying, "I'll keep my wrist right, or I'll keep my feet right. Take your pick. But don't make me do them both at the same time."

❸ Avoid using your cell phone when the car is in motion. When you must use your phone while driving, inform the other party that you're driving and that you may have to refrain from talking or listening if the traffic gets difficult. Avoid using your phone when you're approaching an intersection or when you're passing or being passed. Use it instead when you're cruising down a highway or major road with moderate traffic. If you're talking on the phone and approach an intersection, simply tell the other party, "Please hold for a second until I clear this intersection."

❹ Remember, doing two things at once is an illusion; you're actually doing the two things in alternating streams.

❺ If you really want to remember something, stop and pay attention to it. Don't create competing distractions.

TOPIC 21.10　Visualization

When you're preparing for an event, remember the importance and effectiveness of visual and mental rehearsal in combination with physical rehearsal and practice. Visualization, also referred to as mental practice, has been shown to be effective in improving motor skills, although there is no evidence that it improves cognitive and behavioral skills (see Druckman and Bjork, 1991, and Gawain, 1978). University of Chicago neurologist John Milton has used EEG measures to study the effectiveness of visualization techniques on athletic performance. While helping Olympic golfers improve their swing technique, he observed that subjects showed the more active beta waves on the left (more analytical) side of their brain while mentally rehearsing a shot, and calmer alpha waves on the right side of the brain while actually executing the shot just visualized. He refers to this shift from beta to alpha as going from active concentration into a kind of "zone" associated with peak performance (see Csikszentmihalyi on "flow" in chapter 37). Milton found that the golfer's accuracy increased after these visual rehearsals.

Application

❶ If you are an athlete, executive, actor—anyone wanting to achieve a smooth, masterful performance—close your eyes and internally simulate the performance in your mind. Allow yourself to accompany this visualization with approximate physical movements or pantomime.

TOPIC 21.11 Modalities

Much has been written over the last 30 years advocating the use of multiple sensory channels, or modes, for conveying instruction. Most individuals have a stronger, or preferred, mode—visual, auditory, or kinesthetic. Accordingly, if a teacher or trainer uses both visual and auditory modes to present information, the chances are enhanced that people who prefer one of these modes will learn. This is related to Howard Gardner's work on multiple intelligences (see topic 34.4). In a recent study, researchers at the University of New South Wales reported that two simultaneous modes of presentation can often enhance learning (*Journal of Experimental Psychology: Applied,* December 1997, pp. 257–287). For example, a learner could follow visual instructions and diagrams on a television monitor with auditory reinforcement of key points. The New South Wales researchers found that when two simultaneous modes each present complete details, one interferes with the other. It is better for one mode to present the complete set of instructions, with the second mode simultaneously presenting only bare, skeletal (schema-like) information that reinforces the key points of the primary mode. Two simultaneous presentation modes, each with abundant detail, violate the principle of attention (see topic 21.9).

Applications

❶ When you are lecturing or orally presenting information, ensure that your visual aids contain only key points. Otherwise, the details in the visuals will interfere with the details in the spoken presentation. When you need to switch modes in order to present complicated visual information, as in a large, row-by-column table, then you should slow your speech to make only key points while the learners focus on the details of the table.

❷ When you are presenting information kinesthetically, as in demonstrating a movement with the learners moving along with you, don't be tempted to fill in the silence by talking the entire time; speak only to make key points.

❸ When you are presenting information visually, as in a videotape or DVD, the most effective sound track will make sparing commentary, and only to emphasize key points to focus the learners' attention. Don't distract learners with chatter. If you need to talk, let the visual mode subside by using a freeze-frame or some repetitive action.

TOPIC 21.12   Strategies for Learning

Claire Ellen Weinstein has made lemonade of lemons. When she was a Brooklyn teacher, she found that her father and siblings were inefficient learners. In her efforts to teach them strategies they could use to improve their learning efficiency, she ultimately won a doctorate from the University of Texas at Austin that was based on her assessment of learning strategies and her accompanying developmental recommendations. Students who benefit from her model show remarkable improvements in high school and college course outcomes. The graduation rate of the at-risk students at the University of Texas at Austin who experience her model is 71 percent, compared with 55 percent for the student body at large (*APA Monitor,* April 1998, p. 36). Her instrument, LASSI (Learning and Study Strategies Inventory), is used by more than half the colleges in the United States and has been translated into more than 30 languages.

The LASSI model is tripartite: skills, will, and self-regulation. The 177-item assessment measures the student learner in 10 areas:

1. Information processing
2. Selection of main ideas
3. Test strategies
4. Attitude
5. Motivation
6. Anxiety
7. Time management
8. Concentration
9. Study aids
10. Self-testing

Application

❶ Obtain a copy of LASSI and assess your learning effectiveness or that of someone close to you. Request a sample from H & H Publishing Company Inc., Clearwater, Florida; phone 800-366-4079 or e-mail your request to hhservice@hhpublishing.com; or visit www.hhpublishing.com and order LASSI in the quantity desired. Their website includes an online sample survey and report.

Some Myths about Learning

In 1984, the U.S. Army Research Institute asked the National Academy of Sciences to form a committee to evaluate "nonordinary" techniques for improving human performance. This request followed the urging of some who felt that "New Age" educational technologies that had been developed outside the mainstream might have some basis for their claims of achieving high results. The defense establishment was willing to consider any technique that might provide a competitive edge in the armed services. John Swets, a consultant from Cambridge, Massachusetts, was appointed chair of the committee, and Daniel Druckman, formerly of the consulting firm of Booz Allen Hamilton, was appointed study director. Their results were published as *Enhancing Human Performance: Issues, Theories, and Techniques* (Druckman and Swets, 1988).

During the next two years, reaction to this publication was intense and widespread. As a result, the committee re-formed in 1990 to evaluate areas that had not been included in the earlier study and to address concerns raised by that study. Robert Bjork was brought in as committee chair and Druckman was retained as study director. Their findings were published as *In the Mind's Eye: Enhancing Human Performance* (Druckman and Bjork, 1991). Several of the findings in these two books have been presented in this and other chapters. Table 21.2 focuses on some "myths" about learning—learning methodologies that claimed positive results but didn't stand up to the scrutiny of these two committees.

Table 21.2. Some Myths about Learning

Method	Conclusion and Comments
Learning during sleep	There is no evidence of this with verified sleep. There is some evidence with light sleep. It is difficult to verify sleep stages. This technique is worth a second look. Disturbing sleep raises ethical issues.
Accelerated learning (SALTT, Suggestopedia, SuperLearning)	Of 11 elements identified, only two were nontraditional and both were found to be ineffective: relaxation (too much of it causes lack of focus) and re-view with music (it interferes with attention). No basis was found for the high claims. Good accelerated learning is basically no different from good teaching generally. Claims of 5- to 50-fold improvements were based on poor research designs. The two best studies (Bush, 1986; Wagner and Tilney, 1983) found that SALTT produced 40–50 percent lower results than traditional methods. The other nine elements of accelerated learning were all deemed to be traditional characteristics of effective teaching already in mainstream use: advance organizers, dramatic presentation, spacing, practice, mnemonic aids, student-generated elaborations, tests, imagery, and cooperation in groups.
Altered consciousness	This is an optimal arousal concept worth further research. Devices such as Hemi-Sync that stimulate a specific hemisphere appparently do not enhance learning. A satisfactory methodology is unavailable for researching these claims.
Neurolinguistic programming (NLP)	There is no evidence that one person can inflluence another as a result of matching representational systems. It is difficult to isolate individual variables in NLP research. There are poor dependent variables in much of the research (for example, "client-therapist empathy" is a vague dependent variable).
Parapsychology	It doesn't work. Existing programs at Stanford University, Princeton University, and Brooklyn's Maimonides Medical Center, and in San Antonio, should be monitored. Researchers need to agree on a research methodology.
Subliminal self-help	There is no evidence, either theoretical or experimental, for the effectiveness of this technique.
Meditation	Meditation is no more effective in reducing arousal than just resting quietly. There is no evidence that soldiers can be taught "soldier-saint" superhuman skills by yogis.

SUGGESTED RESOURCES

Bransford, J. D., et al. (2000). *How People Learn: Brain, Mind, Experience, and School.* Washington, D.C.: National Academy Press.

Broad, M. L. (Ed.) (1997). *In Action: Transferring Learning to the Workplace.* Alexandria, Va.: American Society for Training and Development.

Broad, M. L., and J. W. Newstrom (1992). *Transfer of Training: Action-Packed Strategies to Ensure High Payoff from Training Investments.* Reading, Mass.: Addison-Wesley.

Buzan, T. (1991). *Use Your Perfect Memory* (3rd ed.). New York: Penguin Books.

Caine, R. N., and G. Caine (1991). *Making Connections: Teaching and the Human Brain.* Alexandria, Va.: Association for Supervision and Curriculum Development.

Druckman, D., and R. A. Bjork (Eds.) (1991). *In the Mind's Eye: Enhancing Human Performance.* Washington, D.C.: National Academy Press.

Druckman, D., and J. A. Swets (Eds.) (1988). *Enhancing Human Performance: Issues, Theories, and Techniques.* Washington, D.C.: National Academy Press.

Hart, L. A. (1983). *Human Brain and Human Learning.* White Plains, N.Y.: Longman.

Lorayne, H., and J. Lucas (1974). *The Memory Book.* New York: Stein & Day.

Metcalfe, J., and A. P. Shimamura (Eds.) (1994). *Metacognition: Knowing about Knowing.* Cambridge, Mass.: MIT Press.

Norman, D. A. (1993). *Things That Make Us Smart.* Reading, Mass.: Perseus Books.

Sternberg, R. J., and J. E. Davidson (Eds.) (1995). *The Nature of Insight.* Cambridge, Mass.: MIT Press.

22

The Role of the Teacher

How to Facilitate Learning

> **The teacher's task is not to talk, but to prepare and arrange a series of motives for cultural activity in a special environment made for the child**
>
> —Maria Montessori,
> The Absorbent Mind

Not only have we all experienced classroom learning, but many of us will have the opportunity in the near or distant future to teach something to a group. Sales representatives teach their prospects as a part of their sales presentations. Other people may conduct a training class for employees, teach an elementary or secondary school class, teach at the university, conduct an evening class at the community college, give religious instruction, orient new employees, train employees on the job in new skills and technologies, or teach (that is, persuade) power brokers to pursue a certain path. This chapter is intended for the teacher in all of us.

The best lesson plan in the world is less effective than it could be if the teacher using it fails to bring to the plan what only good teachers can bring. That is the role of the teacher: to present content for learning in a way that makes students most likely to learn. I distinguish here between the design of learning experiences (which I treated in chapter 21) and the role of the teacher. Clearly there is some overlap; however, one can design learning but never teach it, and one can teach without having designed. This chapter looks at what brain research says about the teacher's role as a facilitator of learning, regardless of whether or not the teacher designs the learning.

> "Those who educate children well are more to be honored than even their parents, for these only give them life, those the art of living well."
>
> —Aristotle

L. A. Hart (1983) suggests that any educational environment should be characterized by the following four general features:

1. High expectations

2. A nonthreatening ambience

3. A goal of 100 percent mastery

4. An air of reality (that is, it consists of more than just books)

Of course, we should all keep in mind that the learner is often the best teacher. Just because we focus in this chapter on the role of the teacher, don't ignore these principles if you're not a teacher. We are all learners, so many of these ideas apply to us as we teach ourselves.

TOPIC 22.1   Advance Organizers

Students tend to learn more when they are given some warning about what they are to learn. Perhaps this brings relevant schemas into the foreground or at least prepares them to put forth an appropriate effort to form new ones. Techniques used to alert learners about the nature of an upcoming learning episode are called *advance organizers* because they help them to call up relevant schemas in preparation for learning.

Applications

❶ Send out preliminary reading materials.

❷ Provide an outline or agenda of the learning experience both in advance of the session and at the beginning of the session.

❸ Review the objectives at the beginning of the session.

❹ Tell people what you are getting ready to do. Abruptly moving into an activity is disturbing to many people.

❺ Before class, have the attendees meet with their supervisor or team members to agree on expectations.

❻ At the beginning of the session, give the participants some kind of big-picture overview of the material to be covered; this provides a map for the terrain.

❼ Ask the participants what their expectations are. *(Contributed by Jane Howard)*

❽ Choose appropriate textbooks (see the applications for topic 21.3).

❾ In chapter 12 we learned about the Mozart effect, or how playing Mozart-type music prepares the mind for spatial reasoning tasks. That is a kind of advance organizer.

TOPIC 22.2 Spacing

In a classic 1978 experiment in educational psychology, British postal workers learned to use a new machine. Those who studied 1 hour a day learned twice as fast as those who studied 4 hours a day in two 2-hour sessions. The 2-hour group learned to use the machine in half as many days but spent twice as many hours learning. In other words, the more hours per day they spent in instruction, the more total time they required. Clearly this would be desirable only under a deadline. Prefer spaced to massed learning where possible. Learning is *spaced* if it is composed of multiple modules with a significant time lapse between the modules. Spaced learning for a given quantity of learning consists of shorter modules with time for practice and assimilation between the modules.

Harry Bahrick, a psychologist at Ohio Wesleyan University, believes that teachers should institutionalize spacing concepts. His research establishes the superior effect of cumulative learning. The more that people study and review, the more they remember. He found that high school Spanish students who took five courses remembered about 60 percent of the vocabulary 25 years after finishing high school, whereas students taking only one course remembered almost none, in spite of the fact that neither group had used Spanish to a significant degree after high school. Again controlling for usage, he compared 1,726 adults who had finished high school 50 years earlier and found that those who had gone on from high school algebra and geometry to take college-level math at or above the level of calculus scored 80 percent correct on an algebra test. Those who took only high school algebra and geometry and did as well as the college math group in their high school math courses managed to score only slightly better than a control group who had taken no algebra or geometry at all in high school or anywhere else! Bahrick laments that we spend millions helping people learn, then let them forget what they learned.

Applications

❶ Try to schedule learning modules of no more than two to four hours per day; allow time and space for practice between sessions. If this isn't possible, build in frequent breaks.

❷ If you must have an all-day seminar, take extra care to allow participants time to read in advance and to practice and review afterward. Also, during the period of instruction, don't just keep presenting new information and skills. Allow ample time for assimilation (as in relating new information to previous information) and practice (as in role play, case study, and exercises).

❸ Schools should change from the quarter system to the semester system, and from longer class periods to more but shorter class periods.

❹ Schools and other learning organizations should require review of prior material both during the course and in subsequent courses.

❺ Schools should include cumulative courses that review and integrate prior courses and should give cumulative final examinations.

❻ Schools should offer courses that meet, for example, once a week for two or three years, rather than three times a week for four months. The general rule should be to spread out learning as much as possible—with frequent review—to maximize retention.

❼ Carefully plan training for new employees over time to avoid overwhelming them during their first days on the job. *(Contributed by Rick Bradley)*

❽ Schedule more frequent, shorter staff meetings.

❾ As an alternative or supplement to all-day seminars and workshops, use the Internet as a way to space out learning. Use such online learning platforms as eCollege, EdTek, Breeze, WebCT, Scribe Studio, and Blackboard to present both information and practice, saving in-class time for critical discussions, demonstrations, and other activities.

TOPIC 22.3 | **Breaks**

Research reveals at least two good reasons to take breaks after each learning module. First, new neural connections formed by learning need time to fix and strengthen themselves without competition from additional novel stimuli. A simple walk around the block can provide such jelling time. This is like the need in darkroom photography for a "fixing" chemical to stabilize the photographic image. Second, because of fatigue factors, errors increase as break time decreases.

Applications

❶ Some form of exercise is an excellent follow-up to a learning episode because of the impact of the extra epinephrine on the formation of neuronal connections. Perhaps you could lead your students in stretching, bending, and breathing exercises after a learning episode.

➋ The best time of day to take in new material is just before going to sleep. Research indicates that material studied just prior to sleep onset tends to be remembered better. Sleep, in one sense, is another way to take a break. Encourage learners to do memory work before going to sleep.

➌ In classes of adults, announce that students can leave the room whenever they wish, but also have periodic, scheduled breaks. *(Contributed by Jack Wilson)*

TOPIC 22.4 | Incubation

To come up with creative responses to problems, allow time for the information to incubate. As Louis Pasteur remarked, "Chance favors only the mind that is prepared." Do your homework; then let intuition work on it. When I was a first-year student at Davidson College, I had a tennis class under Coach Lefty Driesell. One day, after Lefty hit a ball past me, I shouted out, playfully, "LUCK!" Driesell stopped dead in his tracks, glared at me, and said, "There's no such thing as luck, Howard. It's preparation meeting the opportunity." For a more extensive treatment of incubation in terms of how it fits in with the four-phase model of the creative process, see topic 27.4.

Applications

➊ Allow for a substantial break, when possible, after problem-defining activity and before idea-generating activity.

➋ Many of us participate in team-building retreats. The best use of these overnight problem-solving sessions is to present the information (attitude survey results and so on) before bedtime, then, in the morning, after it has incubated, come up with creative responses in a planning session.

➌ Teams and departments often push through meeting agendas, grasping at the first suggestion that develops in order to get to the next item. Make it a group norm to allow for more incubation time when a matter is not urgent. Better planning is often the result.

TOPIC 22.5 Follow-Up

The best way to ensure that classroom learning will be forgotten is by failing to provide opportunities for follow-up and follow-through. Studies show that a larger portion of the material learned in a classroom setting is retained when the learner or the teacher makes provisions for follow-up.

Applications

1 Have learners write "goal letters" (e.g., "Here's how I plan to use my new learning from this experience, and what I hope to accomplish") to themselves and turn them in to you; then mail them out several months later. These "letters from the conscience" remind them of what they intended to work on after the training session.

2 Make sure that, after returning to the job, the learners schedule a conference with their supervisor or team to review their accomplishments and the possibilities for applying their learning on the job.

3 Develop refresher modules of short duration for students to take periodically.

4 Hold class reunions.

5 When using a series of spaced modules, provide homework assignments (practice or reading) between sessions. Review the homework, sharing successes and failures at the beginning of each session.

6 Plan during class how each participant will apply new learning to the job—for example, by writing scripts, developing implementation schedules, identifying obstacles to success, or writing personal development plans.

7 Send out audio- or videotapes or CDs that recap the major points of the training session.

8 For schoolchildren, suggest to parents how they might follow up classroom learning by at-home applications and exercises. An excellent example of this is the series of CDs developed by Frances Van Voorhis and Joyce Epstein of Johns Hopkins University and presented in their book *School, Family, and Community Partnerships* (2nd ed.).

TOPIC 22.6   Control

The teacher is the one person most able to influence the learner's sense of control over the learning process. If the learner feels in control, a wider range of learning, both rote and meaningful, can occur. If the learner feels highly controlled, only rote learning can occur. Caine and Caine (1991) call this *taxon* (list) and *locale* (map) learning. Locale learning encourages creativity, analysis, synthesis, planning, problem solving, and complex decision making. When the learner feels relaxed and in control, the cortex is fully functional and this higher-level, more meaningful learning is possible. When the learner feels out of control of the learning process, he or she "downshifts" (Caine and Caine, 1991) from cortical locale learning to the limbic system's taxon, or rote, learning. In this condition, the cortex essentially shuts down. The only learning possible involves rote memorization or learning of simple skills, and the only creativity or problem-solving possible is that which is based on habits, instincts, or other already learned routinized behaviors.

I do not advocate giving *complete* control to the learner—that can result in frustration. In a review of the research on discovery learning, Richard Mayer (2004) of the University of California, Santa Barbara, concludes that pure discovery learning—allowing students to explore material entirely on their own in hopes of spontaneous insight—yields lower student performance than guided discovery, in which teachers guide the exploration and nudge students toward discovery and insight.

> Note: When you see cross references to other sections of this book, you may benefit from taking time now to read them; they provide information that will deepen your understanding of the current material.

Sometimes stress, rather than lack of ability, is the reason people appear able to learn only simple, routine skills. Away from the sources of stress, they can be more creative and complex in their learning behavior. A stressful learning environment or classroom can itself prevent cortical learning, whether the stress is real or only perceived. Make sure that your classroom does not force downshifting. (For more on stress and control issues, see chapter 36.)

Applications

1 At the beginning of a class, clearly establish learner control by reviewing class norms. For example, you might say, "Feel free to take a break when you need to," "Please let me know if you're physically uncomfortable, and I'll see what can be done about it," or "Please feel free to ask any questions whenever the need arises; the only dumb question is the unasked question."

2 Help learners set their own goals for learning.

3 Use effective listening techniques, such as active and reflective listening, paraphrasing, and clarifying, that have the effect of focusing on the learners and underscoring their control.

4 Ask open-ended questions, which invite the learner to be more involved in the process. Avoid questions with yes-or-no responses, because they discourage involvement. And avoid questions starting with "Why . . . ?" This type of question tends to create stress in learners and make them defensive (see Flanders, 1970).

5 Respect differences in learning styles by accommodating students' stylistic differences as much as possible: their need for cool or warm temperatures, preference for dim or full light, desire for snacks, or need for physical activity.

6 Build in opportunities for participant involvement, such as role playing, case studies, simulations, investigations, interviews, construction, and small-group work. *(Contributed by Rick Bradley)*

7 Don't assign seats; let participants select their own seats. If you want to mix the learners up after a break, ask them to select new seats with new people on either side. They will still maintain the same sense of control.

TOPIC 22.7   Relaxation

As discussed in topic 22.6, encouraging the learner to feel in control is a major strategy in preventing downshifting—that is, moving from cortical alertness to limbic arousal (stress).

Another strategy would be to help learners who are already under stress (for example, those coming into your class after a bad encounter) to "upshift"— move from limbic fight-or-flight arousal into cortical arousal and alertness. When a person comes to your learning experience full of stress, that stress must be relieved before meaningful learning can occur. The primary strategy to use in the classroom is relaxation. Remember, however, that too much relaxation is not conducive to learning. For further consideration of this point, see topic 36.2, which discusses stress and arousal and the Yerkes-Dodson law; see also the comments on accelerated learning in table 21.2.

Applications

❶ Play tapes with sounds of nature—rainstorms, desert winds, the beach, birds—before class, during breaks, or during silent individual work like reading or filling out worksheets. Nature sounds have a way of refocusing a person away from absent stress into the here and now.

❷ Play tapes with simple classical music (Mozart is a good common denominator) before class or during breaks, as a way of helping people refocus. Don't play music during individual work, however.

❸ If you are the teacher, lighten up from time to time in a way that is appropriate for you (e.g., wear funny glasses, a silly hat, and so forth). This keeps students alert and prevents them from downshifting.

❹ If you are a student, practice some of the relaxation techniques described in the applications for topic 36.1.

TOPIC 22.8 Rapport

Researchers, particularly in the field of *neurolinguistic programming* (NLP), have tried to identify why some therapists seem to work magic on clients. They have found that effective therapists tend to establish rapport with clients by matching and pacing—in other words, by mirroring the clients' posture and following their tempo. The research suggests that matching and pacing another person has the effect of establishing rapport and increasing trust and openness.

Applications

1 When you have a student who seems to be resisting your help, identify the biggest differences between the two of you and see if you can eliminate some of these differences or at least minimize their effects. For example, get on your knees to talk eye-to-eye with a young child, or slow down your speaking tempo to match a more reserved student.

2 Move toward a participant who is asking a question or making a comment; establish rapport by getting closer and using eye contact. *(Contributed by Jane Howard)*

TOPIC 22.9 Positive Expectations

Rosenthal and Jacobson (1968) established that positive expectations tend to yield positive results and negative expectations yield negative results. They call this the *Pygmalion effect*, or the self-fulfilling prophecy. As told by the poet Ovid, Pygmalion was a sculptor who fell in love with his creation, named Galatea, and pleaded to Venus to make her human. Venus acceded. (See topic 30.3 for more on this subject.)

Applications

1 Communicate clearly to all students that you have confidence in their ability to excel.

2 Communicate to all students your confidence in your own ability to teach effectively.

3 Communicate to all students your confidence in previous students' successful application of classroom learning to the real world.

4 Resist the temptation to give up on some students; maintain high expectations for all of them. Remember, you may have some students who've been told all their lives that they're failures, so don't be discouraged if you don't make much of a dent in their self-concept. If enough of us treat them with positive expectations, we increase the chances of their success.

❺ If it is appropriate, mention other groups, classes, or organizations that have successfully completed the program.

❻ For specific suggestions on employing positive expectations in a work context, read Thomas Connellan's *Bringing Out the Best in Others!* (2003).

TOPIC 22.10 **Habituation**

Habituation is the psychological term for "enough is enough." Our sensory receptors become aroused when a new stimulus begins, but if the new stimulus continues without variation in quality or quantity, our sensory receptors shut down from their aroused state, having become habituated, or accustomed, to the monotonous stimulus. A change in the quality or quantity of the stimulus will arouse the receptors again. This is why, for example, it is hard to pay attention to someone who speaks in a monotone. It is also why people dining often add salt, pepper, or other seasoning after several bites. Druckman and Bjork (1991) emphasize the importance of varying training conditions to prevent habituation and its attendant inefficiency in learning.

City University of New York professor Tracey Revenson attests to the value of varying presentation style by emphasizing the importance of acting ability to good teaching (*APA Monitor,* January 1994, p. 40). She constantly varies energy level, perspective and role, pace, accent, mood, and more. In the same article in the *APA Monitor,* University of Southern Indiana professor Joseph Palladino stresses the effectiveness of using appropriate humor—that is, humor that fits the context. He teaches the concept of *successive approximation* (estimating the value of an unknown quantity by repeated comparison to a sequence of known quantities) by getting down on all fours and bleating like a sheep until the class successfully trains him to their desired objective.

Another approach to this topic is called *mindfulness,* which uses frequent changes in auditory and visual attention to maintain alertness. Borysenko (1987), Langer (1989), and Cooper (1991) each suggest specific techniques for avoiding the fatigue that results from sustained attention. A facilitator of learning should teach these techniques to the learners. Avoiding habituation, or attentional fatigue, is a two-way responsibility. The teacher can certainly provide a variety of stimuli, but the learner can also take preventive action. Mindfulness appears to be the flip side of the concept of "monkey mind," described in topic 36.1, application 7.

Applications

❶ Have yourself videotaped while teaching. Review the tape; critique yourself for signs of repetitive behaviors that might tend to lessen the alertness of your students: talking at the same pitch, the same volume, or the same speed (never even slowing down to make a dramatic point); using the same vocabulary (complex Greek- or Latin-derived words rather than simple Anglo-Saxon ones); standing or sitting in the same place; walking in the same pattern (desk to window, window to desk, desk to window, and so on); limiting eye contact (always looking at the same three or four students or from window to ceiling and back); or waving your arm the same way for emphasis.

❷ Seek out authentic ways to vary your behavior to maximize students' alertness. Remember when the teacher played by Robin Williams in *Dead Poets Society* jumped up on his desk or walked the class into the hall to view a picture? He knew how to avoid habituation. Fight it like the pLaGuE!

❸ Minimize learning tasks that exceed five to ten minutes, and search for ways to vary tasks to maximize the students' arousal: contrast lecture with discussion, whole-group or small-group learning with individual seat work, reading with writing, standing with sitting, computer work with face-to-face interaction, remembering and mastering with creating, practicing with critiquing.

❹ After each break, encourage the learners to take a seat in a different part of the room.

❺ Jump, clap, shout, throw, wave, stomp, roll, whisper.

❻ Offer graphs to trainers for feedback on how well they do with this habituation paradigm. I once was asked to observe a superintendent of schools as he conducted a staff meeting. He had a reputation for horrible meetings. The first thing I noticed was his monotone. I charted his variation in pitch, volume, tempo, vocabulary, posture, and gesture over time. The resulting graph showed nothing but a group of flat lines. It made the point; he understood why and how to improve.

7 As a learner, keep shifting focus to avoid visual fatigue: don't focus on the same point for more than a few seconds; study an object for one minute, close your eyes and try to reproduce it in your mind's eye, then open your eyes and compare; remember to blink frequently; practice scanning by looking for all the examples of one specific letter or number on a page; refresh your scanning skills by doing crosswords and jigsaw puzzles.

8 When learning, practice selective focus as a way of avoiding auditory fatigue. Pick out one of several auditory signals in your environment and focus on it exclusively, then pick another; when listening to music, select one instrument and focus on it for a while to the exclusion of other instruments, then shift to another instrument. When you are faced with the cacophony of two speakers blaring different voices or music, try alternating your focus between the two different signals.

TOPIC 22.11   Developing Prestige

In their research, Caine and Caine (1991) found that students perform better when they perceive the teacher to be prestigious. They further found that this prestige comes primarily from two perceptions: that the teacher has expertise and that she or he is caring. Expertise is assumed from the appearance that the teacher has mastered the subject, is not dependent on notes (except to help in sticking to the subject), and has practiced what is being preached. Caring is assumed from the appearance that the teacher accepts and values each student as a human being.

Applications

1 Practice the applications in topics 22.8 and 22.9.

② Try visualizing the class process in much the same way that a skier visualizes a downhill sequence before jumping off. Keep notes on potential problems you spot while visualizing, then solve them after you finish.

③ Try a dry run in which you move through the class process rapidly, again keeping notes on potential problems.

④ Try putting notes on the borders of your transparencies to avoid the distraction of looking down at notes in your hand.

⑤ Try out the lesson plan first on a test group (office mates, your family, a group of employees, or even paid guinea pigs). Have them critique you or simply serve as a live test audience.

⑥ Arrive early and greet people by name; don't rush away as soon as the lesson is over.

⑦ During breaks, mix and mingle.

⑧ Lightly pencil your notes onto blank flip-chart pages before class. The notes will go unnoticed by participants, and you'll be seen as well versed in your subject. *(Contributed by Rick Bradley)*

⑨ When seeking input from a group, capture their responses on a flip chart or transparency. *(Contributed by Rick Bradley)*

⑩ Acknowledge input from the group. *(Contributed by Rick Bradley)*

⑪ Work hard to understand your audience and their issues and concerns. Use this understanding to build class outlines. Use real-life examples they can relate to.

⑫ If you have been brought into an organization as an outside expert or guest, have someone from the organization introduce you to the group. *(Contributed by Jane Howard)*

⑬ Display or mention licenses, certificates, apprenticeships, degrees, and awards.

⑭ Whenever possible, bring current information from a recent newspaper, television show, journal, or other information source. This contributes to your learners' perception of you as keeping abreast of your field.

⑮ Award-winning professor Charles Brewer of Furman University says that teachers must show a "passion for their discipline, and a passion for sharing what they know about it with their classes. . . . That's what separates gifted teachers from those who merely teach" (*APA Monitor,* January 1994, p. 39).

⑯ Give the class a brief handout that includes a curriculum vitae and other relevant information about you and your qualifications, along with a contact phone number or e-mail address, for later reference. *(Contributed by Helen Hyams)*

TOPIC 22.12   Atmosphere

Research has identified a long list of learning atmosphere variables, each of which suggests its own applications. See more on workplace design in chapters 31 and 32.

Applications

❶ Faber Birren, in *Color and Human Response* (1978a), has suggested the many effects of color on people. See topic 32.3 for a listing of these effects.

❷ Ensure abundant light, especially at the beginning of a session, for those who may not be fully awake.

❸ Remember that a moderate amount of background noise (so-called white noise) is helpful for concentration. If the room is too quiet when participants are working silently at their seats, you can run the fan of an overhead projector. *(Contributed by Jane Howard)* Paradoxically, white noise can also be helpful in eliminating distractions when you are trying to fall asleep or stay asleep. An air filter with an audible fan works well. *(Added by Helen Hyams)*

❹ You can take advantage of the knowledge that arousal (both limbic and cortical) is associated with a warmer brain, pleasant moods with a cooler brain. Robert Zajonc, of the University of Michigan, has found that slow, minor-key music warms the brain and breathing through the nose cools the brain (Izard, Kagan, and Zajonc, 1984).

❺ Provide places and opportunities for adult learners to contact their offices. Also have phone lines or phone jacks available for those who need to check e-mail, as well as outlets for recharging cell phones and laptops.

❻ Avoid serving high-glycemic carbohydrate foods (sugary cookies and pastries) for snacks; they produce a pleasant mood and subsequent sleepiness. Choose proteins and low-glycemic carbohydrate foods like fruits, vegetables, whole-grain crackers or breads, and nonfat dips, all of which are better for mental activity. Supply juices, bottled water, and diet sodas in addition to regular sugared colas. See more about nutrition and mood at topic 7.7.

❼ Make sure that ample caffeine-free beverages are available to prevent overarousal, which makes concentration difficult. Many hotels that host seminars fail to provide enough decaffeinated beverage options.

❽ Encourage participants to sit in a different place after each break; research indicates that this improves participation and freshens the participants' perspective.

❾ Allow 50 square feet per person in the classroom; less is stressful.

❿ Plan the lighting in the room carefully when you are using slides or an overhead projector. Develop alternative presentation methods if the room must be darkened too much.

⓫ An article on class size in *Scientific American* (November 2001) concluded that class size has no consistent impact on student learning, with the exception of smaller class size being associated with benefits for minority students in the early grades.

TOPIC 22.13   Richness

Mark Rosenzweig of the University of California, Berkeley, conducted a classic experiment in which two groups of rats were compared for the impact of environmental richness on brain development. One group was placed in a dull cage, the other in an enriched, "Disneyland" cage. The brains of the highly stimulated rats grew larger and developed denser concentrations of synapses. Other research, including research on humans, has confirmed these findings. See particularly the work of Marian Diamond (1988), also of Berkeley, who concludes that synaptic structures show growth from enriched environments throughout the life span, including old age.

Parallel to Diamond's work, Fred H. Gage and a team of researchers at the Salk Institute for Biological Studies report that enriched environments actually result in increases not only in synaptic complexity but also in the total number of neurons, or brain cells. Gage found a 15 percent increase in brain cells in the mice from enriched cages compared with brain cells in mice from dull cages (*Nature,* April 1997). This research, along with that of William T. Greenough of the University of Illinois, who has shown that aerobic exercise in rats increases the number of neurons (see the information on exercise in chapter 10), demonstrates that with proper management we can *replace* some of the cells lost as a result of natural aging, disease, alcohol, and other brain toxins. Gage has reported that he and a Swedish team have actually observed the generation of new brain cells in humans (*Nature Medicine,* November 1998). This sets the stage for generalizing Greenough's and others' research to humans.

Applications

❶ Put up a variety of posters, corporate and otherwise, such as "The dogs bark, but the caravan moves on," on the walls of the classroom.

❷ As you complete flip-chart diagrams, lists, and so on, tear them off and tape them to the wall for visual reinforcement.

❸ Place games and puzzles around the border of the room and on the students' tables for manipulation during idle moments.

❹ Have a computer around for experimentation with relevant software, or for playing games during breaks.

❺ Hang photographs and artwork in the classroom and nearby hallways.

❻ Have books and newspapers for browsing in the classroom.

❼ Place mirrors in appropriate locations for self-stimulation. Mirrors enhance self-concept among infants and relieve boredom among adults. In one amusing incident, tenants of an office tower complained of long elevator waits. The owners installed mirrors in the elevator waiting area and the complaints disappeared. Preening makes the wait grow shorter!

❽ Post information about local resources such as restaurants and shopping centers. Include maps.

❾ If appropriate, have participants bring in and display some of their own work. As an example, in Bank of America Quality Team meetings, which bring facilitators from across the company together for two- or three-day seminars, participants are asked to show how quality is being visibly promoted in their area. The walls and tables are filled with posters, buttons, banners, T-shirts, memos, job aids, and team pictures. It creates real excitement. *(Contributed by Rick Bradley)*

❿ Use graphics and color on overhead projections, slides, participant guides, and so on. With PowerPoint presentations, take the time to find the right clip art by searching web resources, not just the gallery provided on your hard drive. *(Contributed by Rick Bradley)*

⓫ Ditch the black flip-chart marker. Use a variety of colors. *(Contributed by Rick Bradley)*

⓬ When you are headed for a particularly boring meeting, make sure to carry along at least three colors of ink pens and colored paper for taking notes. *(Contributed by Rick Bradley)*

⓭ Include extra, relevant reading materials such as articles for participants to read if they finish individual tasks before other people are done. *(Contributed by Jane Howard)*

TOPIC 22.14   **Peer Feedback**

Peer feedback is more influential than teacher feedback in obtaining lasting performance results; too much of the latter can be harmful (Druckman and Swets, 1988). Apparently the approval or disapproval of one's peers is the best reinforcer. Excess feedback from the teacher can be perceived as being insincere if it is too effusive or demotivating if it is too discouraging.

Applications

❶ Emphasize peer feedback for student performance in small groups or one-on-one interaction.

❷ One effective technique is to have graduates of a seminar meet in pairs over breakfast or lunch six months later for a follow-up session in which they discuss their successes and failures in implementing the class concepts and skills.

❸ In role plays, have all the participants do the exercise at the same time in groups of three—two to actually play the roles and one to help by making suggestions to a participant who is stuck and by providing feedback. *(Contributed by Jane Howard)*

TOPIC 22.15   **Self-Explanation**

Michelene Chi (Chi, de Leeuw, Chiu, and LaVancher, 1994) reported on the effectiveness of allowing learners to explain what they have learned. Learners who give explanations of what they have learned achieve at higher levels; those who receive explanations from the teacher achieve at lower levels. This relationship holds true regardless of ability: both high- and low-ability learners who self-explain show 30 percent increases in achievement after learning, compared with only 20 percent for those who do not self-explain; the more explanation given (people who do this are called *high explainers*), the higher the gain. So high self-explainers achieve more than low self-explainers, and low self-explainers gain more than those who do not self-explain at all. This topic actually serves as an elaboration of topic 21.6 ("Handle It!"): verbal self-explanation is a way to personally become involved with content by handling information.

Applications

1 Ask learners to explain what they have learned, both during and at the conclusion of a learning episode. Encourage them to put it in their own words.

2 A variation on application 1 is to ask learners who've arrived at a wrong or unacceptable conclusion or solution to explain the process that led them to the wrong answer. By talking through the process, either the learner or you as the listener-facilitator can identify errors in the process that account for the unacceptable answer. Educator John Holt advocated this practice in his book *How Children Fail* (1983). I once had the opportunity to tutor a neighbor's middle school daughter in mathematics. My strategy was simply to have her talk through the steps she had used for each of the problems the teacher had marked as wrong. In each of the wrong answers, we were able to spot an error in her process of problem solving. About halfway through the session, she remarked to me, "This is fun! I've never done this before." I asked what it was that she hadn't done before. She replied, "The teacher always goes over our wrong answers. I've never had a chance to talk about how I solve them with the teacher listening to me!"

3 Occasionally, even though a learner has arrived at an acceptable answer, you are not certain that the process that got her there was sound; in other words, the learner may have been lucky. In such a case, asking her to give a self-explanation by narrating how the conclusion was reached would help to clarify whether the result was luck or skill.

4 Employ learning activities (either spoken or written) that engage the learner in summarizing or paraphrasing an experience.

TOPIC 22.16   **Stereotypes and Performance**

Claude Steele (1997), a professor in the psychology department at Stanford University, has studied the way stereotypes affect the performance of African Americans in college and the performance of females in the mathematical sciences. He has studied other stereotyped groups as well, but these two are his primary focus. Steele is interested in a particularly puzzling phenomenon: why do capable women and African Americans underperform? Or, expressed another way, why do women who are excellent at mathematics (and who positively identify with the field of mathematics) perform worse in the first two years of college than their SAT and ACT math scores would predict? In a parallel vein, why do African Americans who are high achievers in high school, and who have high SAT and ACT verbal scores, achieve a significantly lower grade point average in the first two years of college than would be predicted by their scores?

Steele hypothesized that these two groups were underperforming because of the effect of *stereotype threat.* Subtly, or not so subtly, he suspected, these two groups were receiving the message that they did not belong. To test his hypothesis, he administered difficult SAT math questions to capable college women and difficult SAT verbal questions to capable college African Americans. The experimental groups were told that the answers to the questions would in no way reflect on them as a gender or racial group. For example, in order to remove the performance threat associated with stereotyping, students in the experimental groups might be told that the questions were being evaluated for readability. The control groups were allowed to complete the questions with no special instructions; in other words, they answered the questions with any assumptions they made about stereotype threats fully in effect.

The result was that the experimental groups outperformed the control groups and performed at the levels that had been predicted. Steele concluded that teachers and program administrators can remove the barriers to performance in groups affected by stereotype threat by intervening in a way that makes the students feel included, capable, valued, and successful. In a program designed to test his treatment assumptions, Steele and others carried out an intervention at the University of Michigan called "Twenty-First Century," with dramatically successful results. The applications below list specific strategies.

Applications

❶ Teachers and administrators must exhibit optimistic behaviors and attitudes toward students who are subject to stereotype threat (see the discussion of optimism in topic 37.5).

2 Eliminate the stigma of "remedial" work, preferring instead programs that accept students at their current level of achievement and supportively challenge them to tackle progressively more demanding work.

3 Through a variety of means, such as posters and conversation, communicate to students that ability is not a fixed quality. Emphasize that people can incrementally increase their ability.

4 Affirm that stereotype-threatened groups (women in math courses, African Americans in college honors programs, men participating in interpersonal sensitivity training) belong in their chosen domains by providing role models and other signs of inclusion. Steele emphasizes that in this case, intellectual belonging is substantially more important than social belonging.

5 Value and employ a variety of approaches to the subject matter.

6 For students who do not positively relate to the stereotyped subject (for example, women who do not see themselves as mathematicians), emphasize nonjudgmental acceptance of their efforts, preferring a Socratic dialogue to an emphasis on right or wrong answers. Until a pattern of success emerges, prefer acceptance to praise. Above all, build the students' sense of competence, level by level.

A Final Word on the Role of the Teacher

Harvard psychologist Ellen Langer (1997) has launched a major initiative to change classroom education from a world based on right answers to one based on flexible thinking. Accordingly, she proposes that seven myths permeating classroom education seriously curtail the learning process (*APA Monitor,* August 1997, p. 97). Following is my adaptation of the list of myths that she challenges:

- *Myth 1.* The basics should be learned so well that they become second nature. (*Fact:* Overlearning stifles creativity and individual expression.)

- *Myth 2.* Paying attention means staying focused on one thing. (*Fact:* Novelty, as in examining unfamiliar aspects of familiar objects, persons, and things, holds attention.)

- *Myth 3.* Delaying gratification is important. (*Fact:* Keeping the fun in learning leads to more meaningful learning.)

- *Myth 4.* Rote memorization is necessary in education. (*Fact:* Students who relate material to personal experience do better than memorizers on tests of comprehension.)

- *Myth 5.* Forgetting is a problem. (*Fact:* Memory can be a straitjacket, preventing the formation of novel uses and applications.)

- *Myth 6.* Intelligence is knowing "what's out there." (*Fact:* Lifelong learners, not know-it-alls, are the true experts.)

- *Myth 7.* There are right and wrong answers. (*Fact:* Correctness is dependent on context.)

In a masterful summary of the effectiveness of training, Robert Bjork (1994) points out that current research challenges two traditional—and incorrect—assumptions about training: that it should be relatively risk-free (that is, it should protect the learner from the pain of making errors) and that it should be orderly (with no skipping around). Bjork argues that simple and orderly learning provides good short-term results, such as A's on tests at the end of the course and high marks for the teacher. However, "simple and orderly" does not establish memories that last for the long term. Learners need multiple ways of experiencing a new concept or skill, and unpredictable opportunities to practice it, in order to understand it and have access to it for the long term.

Bjork supports his argument with two storylike experiments. A control group of batters on a California State University baseball team practiced hitting first 15 curve balls, then 15 sliders, then 15 fastballs. The experimental group practiced hitting 45 pitches, but in random order. The latter group outbatted the group with the simple and orderly batting practice. In the second experiment, two groups of eight-year-olds practiced throwing beanbags into a bucket. They were to be tested at a distance of three feet. The control group practiced all throws from a distance of three feet; the experimental group practiced some throws from two feet, others from four feet, and *none* from three feet. Guess what? The latter group outperformed the former, even though the experimental group had never had an opportunity to throw from the distance used in the final test.

SUGGESTED RESOURCES

Bjork, R. (1994). "Memory and Metamemory Considerations in the Training of Human Beings." In J. Metcalfe and A. P. Shimamura (Eds.), *Metacognition: Knowing about Knowing* (pp. 185–206). Cambridge, Mass.: MIT Press.

Borysenko, J. (1987). *Minding the Body, Mending the Body.* Reading, Mass.: Addison-Wesley.

Bransford, J. D., et al. (2000). *How People Learn: Brain, Mind, Experience, and School.* Washington, D.C.: National Academy Press.

Caine, R. N., and G. Caine (1991). *Making Connections: Teaching and the Human Brain.* Alexandria, Va.: Association for Supervision and Curriculum Development.

Cooper, R. (1991). *The Performance Edge.* Boston: Houghton Mifflin.

Diamond, M. (1988). *Enriching Heredity: The Impact of the Environment on the Anatomy of the Brain.* New York: Free Press.

Druckman, D., and R. A. Bjork (Eds.) (1991). *In the Mind's Eye: Understanding Human Performance.* Washington, D.C.: National Academy Press.

Druckman, D., and J. A. Swets (Eds.) (1988). *Enhancing Human Performance: Issues, Theories, and Techniques.* Washington, D.C.: National Academy Press.

Hart, L. A. (1983). *Human Brain and Human Learning.* White Plains, N.Y.: Longman.

Langer, E. (1989). *Mindfulness.* Reading, Mass.: Addison-Wesley.

Langer, E. (1997). *The Power of Mindful Learning.* Reading, Mass.: Addison-Wesley.

Rosenthal, R., and L. Jacobson (1968). *Pygmalion in the Classroom.* Austin, Tex.: Holt, Rinehart and Winston.

Sylwester, R. (1995). *A Celebration of Neurons: An Educator's Guide to the Human Brain.* Alexandria, Va.: Association for Supervision and Curriculum Development.

23

Learning That Sticks

Insights for Enhancing Memory

66My memory is the thing I forget with. 99

—a schoolchild

Research on memory has taken a significant turn in recent years. Memory used to be regarded as a structure; now it is seen as a process. A memory was thought of as a single unit with an identifiable place of residence somewhere in the brain that could be recalled when necessary. Now a memory is viewed as a reconstruction from many different chunks stored redundantly throughout the brain (see topic 23.1). Bartlett (1932, p. 213) foresaw this development when he wrote:

> Remembering is not the re-excitation of innumerable fixed, life-less, and fragmentary traces. It is an imaginative reconstruction, or construction, built out of the relation of our attitude towards a whole active mass of organized past reactions or experience, and to a little outstanding detail which commonly appears in image or in language form. It is thus hardly ever really exact, even in the most rudimentary cases of rote recapitulation, and it is not at all important that it should be so.

This new view of memory was brought dramatically to the public's awareness after John Dean's testimony at the Watergate hearings. Viewers were initially impressed with Dean's avowed excellent memory for detail. But when his testimony was later compared with accurate records of conversations, viewers (and Dean himself) were flabbergasted to learn that most of his testimony was at best flawed and at worst made up.

Defining Memory

Memory is learning that sticks. Before memory, potential new learnings linger briefly in a kind of "scratchpad" about the size of a postage stamp that is located in the right prefrontal cortex, above the right eye and about one inch behind the forehead. This working-memory area can hold the proverbial seven plus or minus two bits of information (see topic 21.1) until such time as we decide to make a permanent record of it. When we decide to remember it, new synapses form, old synapses are strengthened, or both. These new or strengthened connections are the new learning. The synaptic connections are the molecular equivalent of a chunk of newly learned material, such as a telephone number. Initially, as we learn, a protein called *kinase C* (PKC) is deposited among certain hippocampal neurons, according to Daniel Alkon of the Marine Biological Laboratory, Woods Hole, Massachusetts. (*Note:* Neuroscientist Aryeh Routtenberg of Northwestern University has put forth a rival explanation, in which new proteins are not what form the new synapse, but rather a reshaping of existing ones. Watch for more on this.) Apparently, kinase C causes the branches of the brain cells to narrow. When they have narrowed and formed new synapses, learning has occurred. Unless the learning is converted into long-term memory, however, it will disappear, just as new muscle fiber will break down if it is not used. Again, we must use it or lose it.

Researchers on a team drawn from both the University of Texas Medical School at Houston and the University of Houston have reported the discovery of *transforming growth factor B* (TGF-B), a protein that works as a kind of congealing agent to solidify new synapses (*Science,* March 1997). In research with snails, the Texas team discovered that the presence of TGF-B was associated with substantially higher electrical charges, hence stronger responses to stimuli. The discovery of this protein shows that, in addition to "use it or lose it," we also need the proper chemical makeup. Watch this line of research; it could well lead to breakthroughs in the treatment of Alzheimer's disease and other memory disorders.

With continued use, the hippocampal cells extend the storage of the new learning to the cerebral cortex, which then becomes the primary location of long-term storage and retrieval (see appendix A). When a new learning chunk reaches the cerebral cortex, it apparently is stored for the long term. Larry Squire, of the University of California, San Diego, describes the hippocampus as a kind of broker that binds memory until the cortex takes over and becomes its handler. And Gazzaniga (1988) reports that memory occurs not just in the brain but throughout the nervous system. In animal research, animals lacking a hippocampus can remember remote items but not recent items, whereas animals with intact hippocampi remember recent items better than remote items, which is the normal condition. Anders Bjorklund of the University of Lund in Sweden has demonstrated that aging rats with deteriorated hippocampi are unable to learn new skills, yet they are able to learn and remember after receiving transplants of good hippocampal cells from young rats.

What we know about memory formation is shown in figure 23.1. The perception of an event triggers activity at the synapse. The quality of this activity depends on the person's readiness (fatigue, stress, medication) and volition (intention to remember, emotional arousal). Assuming that the person is ready and waiting to capture the event as a memory, protein kinase C is released and settles around the synapse, thus forming the basis of memory (or, as Routtenberg suggests, existing proteins are reshaped). With subsequent recall and practice, the new connection strengthens.

Memory appears to be fully developed by eight years of age. At that point, we remember an average of one bit of information out of

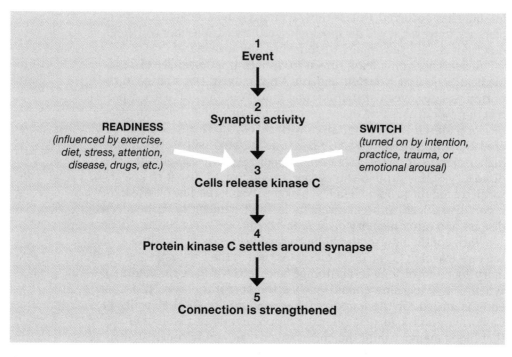

Figure 23.1. The Process of Memory Formation

every 100 we receive. There is some debate about the relationship of memory to IQ, but I agree with those who hold that they are apparently unrelated. As I read the research, I am convinced that if memory and IQ appear to be directly related, it is because those with higher IQs usually try to acquire more learning than those with lower IQs. In a competition between adult humans and five-year-old rhesus monkeys, the University of Texas Health Science Center in Houston reported that after viewing a series of slides, humans and monkeys both got 86 percent right on a 10-item test in which they were shown the slides with new slides mixed in and asked to press a lever when they recognized a familiar slide. One of the reasons that people who score high on conventional IQ tests also have excellent memories is that conventional IQ tests include so many questions whose correct answers rely on a good memory. A purer IQ test would separate memory as just one variable. Of course, this all depends on how one defines intelligence. My attempt to define a comprehensive, integrated view of intelligence is presented in chapter 34.

Remember that it is not sufficient to learn a new concept, skill, or body of information; you must convert it into long-term memory. In other words, if you take the time to read a book or article, say, on how to be a better listener, you probably will not remember the skills or concepts unless you practice one or more of the three strategies described in topic 23.4.

TOPIC 23.1   **The Three Stages of Memory Formation**

Forming a chunk of memory is like making a photograph. Regard photography as a three-stage process: (1) capturing the image on light-sensitive film, (2) developing the film with chemicals, (3) fixing the image permanently with chemicals. A similar process happens in memory-chunk formation: capturing the chunk (immediate memory), developing it (short-term memory), and fixing it (long-term memory).

Immediate memory is a kind of buffer area that can hold thousands of pieces of data for two seconds or less. For example, when you look up a telephone number that you've never seen before, you'll forget it a few seconds later unless you keep repeating it. New information will push out old unless the old is paid attention to.

Short-term memory—often referred to now as *working memory*—appears to function in the hippocampus as a kind of broker that selects chunks of data to remember. A chunk is defined as an unfamiliar array of seven (plus or minus two) pieces, or bits, of information—for example, a seven-digit telephone number, a new word such as *phlyxma* (I made this up!), or a new definition composed of familiar words. George Miller (1956), in a classic article in *Psychological Review,* first identified the fact that people learn most efficiently in units of seven plus or minus two. He calls it the "magical number seven." Groups of seven occur throughout literature and history (the Seven Wonders of the World, the Seven Mortal Sins, the Seven Virtues). The Australian aborigines have only seven words for numbers, equivalent to one, two, three, four, five, six, and seven. Another word means simply "many," or more than seven. It is perhaps because the aborigines have little or no need for long-term memory that they recall only what is reinforced daily. The word for "three" surely would occur every day, or at least every other day, whereas a word for "sixty-three" wouldn't get a chance to be reinforced every two days. Therefore, "three" would remain in short-term memory, but "sixty-three" would disappear and have to be reinvented.

More recently, Nelson Cowan has modified Miller's "seven plus or minus two" to the round number of four (*Trends in Cognitive Science,* March 1998, p. 77). Cowan points out that some chunks are more easily assimilated than others. For example, easily pronounced nonsense words like "wyk" are more easily assimilated than hard-to-pronounce cousins like "wcxik." Cowan urges that four chunks (plus or minus two) are a more realistic target than Miller's seven.

Decision theorist Herbert Simon says that it takes about eight seconds of attention to add one new chunk to short-term memory. Once a chunk has been completely mastered, it becomes a bit and can then be combined with other bits to become a new chunk. In other words, a new chunk loses its identity as a chunk after it becomes second nature to us. Chunks become bits, just as images on film become printable negatives after developing.

Long-term memory appears to be located in the cerebral cortex. Apparently, hippocampal short-term memory communicates with the cortex through what we call simple human will or effort; over time, it establishes chunks in long-term storage. Using a device that measures blood flow, Henry Holcomb, a memory researcher in Johns Hopkins University's Department of Radiology, has determined that the memory for a new motor skill takes five to six hours to move from temporary storage in the front of the brain to permanent storage in the rear of the brain. Attempting to learn another new skill before this five- to six-hour period is up will cause problems for the prior learning. Holcomb recommends that new learnings be followed by more familiar, routine activity. Much more research is required before we know if this principle also applies to nonmotor memory.

A key to the formation of long-term memory is the level of the neurotransmitters epinephrine and norepinephrine. James McGaugh, a psychobiologist at the University of California, Irvine, showed that rats with low epinephrine levels had poor recall ability, but that booster shots of epinephrine after they had learned something improved their retention. He further found that injecting older rats after they had learned a maze improved their memory. Larry Stein, also at Irvine, shocked rats when they stepped off a platform that was surrounded by water. Weeks later, when the rats were put back on the platform, they remembered and didn't step off. However, when he blocked their norepinephrine, he found that although they could *learn* not to step off, they couldn't *remember,* and they stepped off into repeated shocks.

When we have a strong experience, norepinephrine tells the brain to print it, and we hang onto the memory. Apparently, trivial experiences, about which we don't get juiced up, are lost. Blocking norepinephrine prevents us from remembering new information. This is why some people with amnesia can remember distant events but not recent ones.

Epinephrine and norepinephrine are released by the adrenal medulla when the body is subjected to physical or emotional stress. In addition to increasing blood flow, this release causes extra glucose production. The rate of glucose breakdown is a measure of cortical activity. So although you can relax when you are reading, you need to put in a little sweat equity (known as grunting and groaning) in order to convert what you learn into long-term memory.

We acquire one or two bits of information per second during concentrated study; by midlife we have acquired roughly 10^9 bits. Our average brain capacity is 2.8×10^{20}, or approximately 10 million volumes (books) of 1,000 pages each. This outrageous capacity mandates humility. I've heard people lament that they couldn't learn anymore, that their "brain is full." Yeah, right! There is no way that their brain is full. They have simply reached a point of fatigue and need a break for things to settle. Then, just as the body yearns for more once the last meal has been digested, we are always ready to learn more. I've never met the person who has reached the limits of his or her capacity to learn. I *have,* however, met plenty of folks who have quit learning.

Daniel Alkon (1992, p. 208) writes: "Once a memory link is formed, there is a short period of perhaps hours to days during which the responsible cellular changes can reverse. Then the cellular changes become permanent." In other words, if we fail to review the learning, it will probably disappear. Once the memory or learning has become firmly established, however, "the old memory cannot be erased. Instead, to modify the meaning of the older memory, new memories must be added." As a bleak testimony to the persistence of memory, Alkon laments that memories of early painful and intense abuse are doomed to be permanent. He does not foresee any surgical, pharmacological, or psychotherapeutic cure. Instead, he finds that victims must comfort themselves with three common strategies for avoiding such memories: compulsive behavior, fantasizing, or dulling the senses (p. 213). More recently, James McGaugh, director of the Center for Neurobiology of Learning and Memory at the University of California, Irvine, has found that propranolol appears to be helpful in softening the effects of traumatic memories that keep one awake nights. It doesn't erase the memory, but rather tones it down.

Forget about forgetting: life is a constant struggle of new learning that strives to coexist with the old. Sometimes it appears to us that old memories have been lost, but Alkon points out that "when they are forgotten, the records are not erased but inhibited" (p. 209). Further, he suggests that "the brain is not like a computer that can be reprogrammed after the deletion of old programs. The new programs have to be reconciled with the old. . . . Whatever pharmacological tools we can devise to facilitate remembering, forgetting, and learning anew, they will not replace the memory banks themselves, or the steps by which they are acquired" (pp. 224–225). Because of this persistence of memory (remember Salvador Dali's "wilting watch"?), some of us will succumb to its familiar voice and give up on new learning.

Stanford University Psychiatry Professor Emeritus Karl Pribram writes of the holographic structure of long-term memory. Each memory seems to be stored throughout the brain, rather than in a single confined location. Apparently, memories hook onto related networks of other memories, so that, for example, redheads are all somehow loosely tied together in your storage, and you can dump out a long list of redheads upon request. These networks become diffuse and interdependent. Neal Cohen, an associate professor at the University of Illinois at Urbana's Beckman Institute, trained rats to learn a maze, then operated on them. If less than one-fifth of the cortex was removed, regardless of where it came from, the rats exhibited no memory loss. If more than one-fifth of the cortex was removed, a proportional loss of memory occurred. So there appears to be no one location within the cortex for memory storage; instead, each memory seems to have an extensive set of backups.

Not all memory slip-ups are to be considered problematic. Memory researcher Daniel L. Schacter of Harvard has identified (1999) seven so-called "sins" of memory—shortcomings of an otherwise powerful record of the past:

- *Transience.* Some memories grow less accessible over time.

- *Absent-mindedness.* Some memories were processed casually and never took root.

- *Blocking.* Temporary unavailability of otherwise stored memory.

- *Misattribution.* Naming the wrong source for an idea or memory.

- *Suggestibility.* Allowing a leading question or comment to establish a memory-like content as real.

- *Bias.* Allowing present views to distort older content.

- *Persistence.* What we would forget, we can't.

The first three involve kinds of forgetting, the second three involve inaccuracies, and the final one involves memory being too strong in the mind. Schacter makes the case that not all memory "faults" are weaknesses of the memory system that evolution overlooked; rather, they are strengths that have adaptive value, even though at times they can be pesky. Consider:

- *Transience.* What if we remembered absolutely everything, even after it was no longer useful or enjoyable?

- *Absent-mindedness.* What if we didn't have to focus and work at remembering, and our minds were like flypaper, and we remembered everything we encountered?

- *Blocking.* What if we had constant access to everything conceivably related to the issue at hand and were flooded with data?

- *Misattribution.* What if we remembered all the peripheral information related to a core memory? Typically all we need is the core, not the context. Socially, I need to remember the joke, not the person I learned it from.

- *Suggestibility.* Often we need to know only the gist, not the grist. We allow ourselves sometimes to be led to recalling more detail than we should because it enhances our "credibility."

- *Bias.* Currently held schemas serve to help us organize information, and the more compatible past information is with current schemas, the better we feel about ourselves—so it is natural to aid the past in fitting the present.

- *Persistence.* What if we too easily forgot traumatic events and were daily doomed to approach trauma-producing situations with no sense of forewarning?

Applications

1 After a learning episode of an hour or so, take a break and do something to pump up your epinephrine levels: walk about, do isometrics, climb some stairs, do laundry, move some boxes—anything that will generate epinephrine and norepinephrine to help fix the memory. Then go back and review the old material before going on to something new.

② Making the effort to reorganize new material you've read or heard about is, in itself, a form of stress that will help you to convert the material to long-term memory.

③ Take notes on material you wish to remember. *(Contributed by Rick Bradley)*

④ In order to retrieve inhibited memories—ones you know are there but can't find—try some method that "uninhibits" the mind, such as hypnosis, relaxation exercises, free-association techniques, or visualization. Try to think of a possible cue that would be associated with the inaccessible memory. For example, if you can't remember someone's name from last night's party, focus on what she was wearing, drinking, talking about, her hair style, where you were standing or sitting with her, who else joined your conversation, and so forth. The act of pulling in all these cues is likely to bring with them the person's name. In her novel *Déjà Dead*, author Kathy Reichs suggests leaving a recall effort when stuck, and clearing the slate with something unrelated:

> I punched in the code for the security system, but in my building excitement I got the numbers wrong and had to start over. After messing up a second time, I stopped, closed my eyes, and recited every word of "I Wonder What the King Is Doing Tonight." Clear the mind with an exercise in trivia. It was a trick I'd learned in grad school, and, as usual, it worked. The time-out in Camelot helped me reestablish control. I entered the code without a slip, and left the apartment [p. 140].

⑤ Try to organize your day so that new learnings occur at one of three times: shortly after first waking, shortly before sleeping, and approximately halfway in between. Caution: Remember that exactly halfway between waking and sleep onset is the low point in your circadian rhythm, so you'll be better off timing the new learning a couple of hours before or after that point. For example, if I rise at 7:00 A.M. and retire at 11:00 P.M., my low point—and a good time for a nap—would be around 3:00 P.M. New learnings could be timed for around 8:00 A.M., 1:30 P.M. (or 4:30 P.M.), and 9:00 or 10:00 P.M., depending on when the afternoon session occurred.

6 Accept faulty memory not as a limitation but as providing a service. Understand that, just like food, memories are often present when we neither need nor want them. React with a sense of humor when otherwise useful memory "failings" play in your field.

TOPIC 23.2   **Maintenance Requirements**

Once a long-term memory has been formed, three major factors interfere with retrieving it: clogging at the synapse, deterioration of the neuronal pathways involved, and stress. Clogging at the synapse occurs over time as protein particles accumulate on both sides of the synaptic gap; it consists of pregap or *dendritic* clogging and postgap or *axonic* clogging. This clogging is similar to the protein accumulation on contact lenses. Just as this protein accumulation can be removed by soaking and baking, synaptic clogging is removed by the neurotransmitter *calpain,* found in calcium. Another finding, by Richard Wurtman, director of the Clinical Research Center at MIT, is that Alzheimer's patients have buildups of rock-hard amyloid protein and a deficiency of acetylcholine, which is necessary to break down amyloid protein. In another line of research, Ming-Yi Chiang and a team at the Salk Institute have found that vitamin A enhances the transmission efficiency, hence the learning and memory function, of specific receptors in the hippocampus (*BrainWork,* March–April 1999, p. 6).

Some deterioration of the neuronal pathways occurs naturally through aging (see topic 6.1 for a list of factors that contribute to the deterioration of neurons), but there is one source of deterioration over which we have control: the lack of production of the neurotransmitter acetylcholine, whose presence is crucial to the maintenance of neuronal membranes. With insufficient acetylcholine, these cell membranes become brittle and fall away. The dietary source of acetylcholine is fat. Diets with levels of fat below the recommended daily allowance represent a threat to acetylcholine levels. Normal or even high fat content in your diet, however, does not ensure sufficient acetylcholine. Other factors, such as genetics, disease, medication, and stress, can influence acetylcholine levels negatively.

Stress causes the limbic system to work in the foreground, thus drastically reducing the availability of the cortical system. As a result, memory retrieval is highly ineffective and unreliable during stressful episodes. For example, when I make a presentation, I experience stress. If I am prepared and speak from well-organized notes, the presentation goes well. On the other hand, if I haven't organized my presentation, have no notes or outline, and am winging it, I do less well. The difference is not how thoroughly I know the material—I know it equally well in both cases. The difference is that I cannot access or retrieve the material as effectively when I am under stress. The notes help to guide the retrieval, and this has the added effect of reducing the stress. I once lunched with our younger daughter's friend, a college sophomore who wanted to transfer to a more prestigious university. He needed to make an A in his history course but couldn't crack a B. However, he said he know the material cold. After hearing that his professor asked all essay questions—three or four to be answered in one hour—I suggested that he do a mind map (see topic 29.3, application 1) on each question for a couple of minutes before trying to write. I showed him how to do one quickly on a napkin. I assured him that, if he were to take two minutes to do a quick mind map of the key points to use in answering a question and rapidly sequence them, he could write three to four times as much as usual. He ended up making an A in the course and attributed it to the mind map. It was the stress of trying to get it all out that obscured his memory. By doing a "dump" and organizing it, he no longer felt stress; everything he needed to say was available to him without digging. He now had a map, so the journey was a breeze.

Electroshock can improve memory by approximately 300 percent, with effects that last for about three weeks. Apparently electroshock shakes some of the protein off the synapse. Some improvement of memory is possible with the drug physostigmine, which inhibits the formation of *cholinesterase,* an enzyme that breaks down neurotransmitters such as acetylcholine. Improvements have also been seen in studies at Northwestern University Medical School with a drug called nimodipine, which appears to inhibit calcium buildup in people who consume too much calcium. In experiments with rabbits, older rabbits learned more quickly after taking nimodipine. More recently, researchers at Northwestern University Medical School have found that cycloserine and monoclonal antibodies appear to have profoundly positive effects, improving and speeding up memory as well as mitigating memory disorders such as Alzheimer's disease. These two chemicals act on the nimodipine receptors in the hippocampus, allowing calcium to enter and help form new synapses.

Older citizens often lament what they perceive as deteriorating memory. Grandparents can sit around reminiscing about World War II, yet they can't remember to fulfill a recent request. They say they just can't make new memories. But the real difference between short-term and long-term memory is the difference between learning a telephone number long enough to dial it immediately and learning it long enough to dial it a week later. That distinction is often confused in people who seem to remember remote events but can't remember something they were told yesterday. Bolles (1988, p. 234) writes: "Memories for recent and for long-ago events depend on the same constructive abilities and the same emotional, factual, and interpretive levels of memory. If a person can still remember past events well and still tell interesting stories about the long ago, he has the equipment to do the same for more recent events. Failure to remember the present in such cases suggests a failure to pay attention to the present, not an inability to learn new details." This suggests that for many, what may appear to be poor short-term memory may in fact be a symptom of depression. Depressed people may not pay much attention to events or care enough about them to remember them.

Short-term memory problems can also be a symptom of stress. John Newcomer, with other researchers at Washington University in Saint Louis, administered glucocorticoids (stress hormones) to a test group for four days. Subjects were not aware of their ensuing memory dysfunction, but the researchers observed a sharp drop in memory. After they stopped administering the hormones, the memory dysfunction disappeared within one week. My father-in-law was a case in point. In his 80s, he moved from his home state of Alabama to North Carolina. Uprooted from his church and friends, he fell into a mild depression. His wife would ask him to go to the grocery store and pick up milk and bread, and he'd return with coke and cookies! He couldn't seem to form any short-term memory, yet he could remember all the details of his childhood and the geography of his home state. However, if my wife (his youngest daughter) called and suggested they go get an ice cream, and that she'd pick him up in front of the retirement home at 4:00 P.M., he'd be out front by 3:45 eagerly awaiting her arrival— no problems with short-term memory there! He paid attention, got aroused, the adrenaline formed the memory, and he acted on it.

Applications

1 If you want others to think they have your attention, focus on what they are telling you, including their name. Saying "I have to hear a name three times before I remember it" just doesn't wash; it simply leaves you sounding like someone who doesn't pay attention. If you don't want to forget a name, keep saying it to yourself, associate it with other images, and ask questions about it, such as "Is it a popular name in your family?" "What part of the world does it come from?" "Is it a nickname?"

2 If someone, particularly an older person, appears forgetful, remember that it could be something as simple as his or her mind having wandered momentarily or something as major as depression, dementia, or other disease.

3 When problems with short-term memory appear, look for stressors that could be chemically interfering with memory formation. Engage in activities that either remove the source of stress or combat the symptoms.

4 Maintain the recommended daily allowances for fat and calcium.

5 Minimize the stress in your life (see topic 36.1).

6 Consult your neurologist for possible experimental drug treatment of memory problems.

7 If someone you know, especially an older adult, seems confused or is having memory problems, have a physician check for an excess or deficiency of dietary calcium.

TOPIC 23.3   The Two Kinds of Memory Chunks

Joseph LeDoux (2002) summarizes research on the kinds of memory by identifying two large families: declarative and nondeclarative. *Declarative* memories are memories that you can express in a declarative sentence: "I spent last weekend in the mountains," "Montpelier is the capital of Vermont." Declarative memory chunks, also known as *explicit* memory, come in two kinds: episodic and semantic. The weekend-in-the-mountains example above is episodic, the Montpelier sentence semantic. *Episodic* deals with experiences and events; *semantic* deals with facts (names, dates, places). Both kinds of declarative memories are associated primarily with the hippocampus and are not specific to any domain of knowledge (visual, kinesthetic, mathematical, etc.). *Nondeclarative* memory chunks, also known as *implicit* or *procedural* memory, involve routines or skills that cannot be captured by a declarative sentence. Examples are how to ride a bicycle, how to sing properly, how to form a grammatically correct sentence, and so forth. These nondeclarative memories are not restricted to the hippocampus, and they are heavily associated with neural processes in the sections of the brain that house their knowledge domain. LeDoux points out that nondeclarative memory doesn't require conscious recall (for example, a melody or a tennis serve) and works within the confines of a specific domain (e.g., musical, linguistic, kinesthetic), whereas

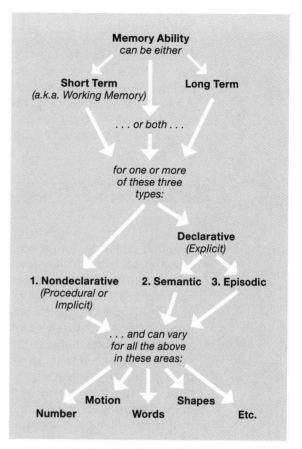

Figure 23.2. A Map of the Kinds of Memory Ability

declarative memories are formed independent of specific domains (e.g., where you vacationed last summer, the name of your neighbors, telephone numbers). To help keep these different kinds of memory straight, refer to figure 23.2.

Skill learning is associated primarily with the limbic (animal) brain, whereas fact learning is primarily associated with the cerebral cortex, which develops after the limbic area does. Perhaps this is why we can't remember much from the first several years of life—why it is easier to remember how to walk, but not how to say a word. Interestingly, damage to the hippocampus (see appendix A) prevents learning of new facts but allows learning of new skills.

Application

❶ It is possible that you have more strength in one kind of memory unit than in another. If so, emphasize your strengths rather than regretting your weakness. I am sure that my skill (visual-spatial) memory is superior to my fact (language) memory. So I should abandon the frustrating pastime of trying to keep my foreign language ability up and enjoy my ability to learn to play new musical instruments.

TOPIC 23.4   Three Strategies for Remembering

Minninger (1984) has categorized the many memorization gimmicks into three categories: *intend, file,* and *rehearse.* This approach has been around for some time. Erasmus wrote in 1512, "Though I do not deny that memory can be helped by places and images [referring to Simonides's *loci* technique, discussed below in application 2, bullet 6], yet the best memory is based on three important things: namely study [rehearse], order [file], and care [intend]." Intend to remember something; that is, don't assume that it'll just stick after exposure; you need to make a point of wanting to remember it. File it by organizing it and playing with it in your own special way. Rehearse it, or practice it, as a way of showing that you intend to remember it. Do it and say it repeatedly. These three generic strategies are the means by which we convert short-term memory to long-term memory. For related information and suggestions, see topic 21.9 on attention and focus.

Applications

❶ Here are some ways to apply the *intend* strategy:

- Before reading an article or book, "pre-read" it by examining the section headings, pictures, charts, graphs, figures, appendixes, and bibliography to get a feeling for how it is laid out and what it covers. This will serve as a kind of advance organizer that will make the reading more meaningful.

- Before taking a course or workshop, do all you can to be ready to receive the material: read the course syllabus, outline, agenda, handouts, and bibliography; read relevant material suggested by a librarian, the instructor, the bibliography, graduates of the course, or common sense. Contact past participants to hear what they learned.

- Consciously decide to remember something; then select a way to file it (see application 2 below). D. J. Herrmann (1991) provides many good suggestions in his book *Super Memory: A Quick-Action Program for Memory Improvement.* His approach is not as technical as those of Buzan (1991) and Lorayne and Lucas (1974).

- Once you've decided to memorize information, one way to show your intention is to chunk it (see topic 21.1) and learn the chunks. Divide and conquer.

- Understand and practice the concept of state dependence described in topic 23.5.

2 Here are some ways to apply the *file* strategy:

- Make a flowchart, Pareto chart (see topic 29.3), or any other kind of graphic that structures what you've learned in a way that's meaningful to you.

- Using self-sticking notes or a material like flannel board, write out single chunks of what you've learned on their own sheets. Then arrange the chunks on a wall in a way that makes sense to you. Restudy the arrangement from time to time and rearrange the notes as needed. When you've fixed the organization the way you like it, make a flowchart or some other kind of chart or outline and put it away for easy review or retrieval. Keep it in your portable notebook for frequent rehearsal.

- Describe the person or object you want to remember in a way that evokes the name of the object. For example, you might associate the name Ann Woodward with this description: "She who keeps the extra timber for repairs to Green Gables."

- Substitute words (perhaps with rhymes) as an aid to remembering a name. Try to make the words graphically visual. For example, if Harvey Darrow has bad acne, associate the name with the substitutes "larvae barrow" while visualizing a wheelbarrow containing dirt filled with larvae (acne). At a party, if you want to remember the name Ted Miller, and Ted is extremely lacking in personality, remember him as the Dead Miller. I invite folks who reverse my first and last names to remember my name as rhyming with the "fierce coward" (Pierce Howard). See *The Memory Book* (Lorayne and Lucas, 1974) and *Use Your Perfect Memory* (Buzan, 1991) for many ideas on visualization techniques for memory. These authors remind us that our memory for images is better than our memory for words, and our memory for concrete words is better than our memory for abstract words.

- Lorayne and Lucas (1974) recommend another technique called *linking,* which is a way to remember a list of things. If you need to stop by the grocery store to pick up milk, bread, hose, and shrimp, link each word to the next one on the list by some exaggerated visual connection. For example, a huge carton of milk has a loaf of bread for a stopper, with a pair of hose connected to the bread to pull it out in order to pour the milk into a saucepan to boil the shrimp. Once you've made these admittedly outlandish linking associations, all you have to remember is the first image—the big bottle of milk—and the rest follows.

- Use the peg-word technique, described in topic 21.4, application 2. The peg-word technique is actually a variation on the *loci* technique of Simonides, the ancient Greek orator. Simonides associated parts of a speech with parts of familiar places (*loci*); for example, each spot in a familiar walkway or building would be associated with a paragraph or subtopic of the speech.

- To remember a number, such as a telephone number, substitute the phonetic consonant equivalents for the numbers and fill in with vowels to make up words. To substitute consonants, try these possibilities:

1 = *d* or *t* or *th* (one vertical stroke)

2 = *n* (two vertical strokes)

3 = *m* (three vertical strokes)

4 = *r* (last letter of the sound of four)

5 = *L* (Roman numeral for 500)

6 = *j,* soft *g, sh,* or *ch* (*J* and *6* are mirror images; the others sound like the *s* or *x*)

7 = *k,* hard *g,* or hard *c* (angular, like a *7; g* and *c* sound like *k*)

8 = *f, v,* or *ph* (cursive *f* looks like an *8; v* and *ph* sound like *f*)

9 = *b* or *p* (*b* looks like an upside-down *9 and p* like a backward *9; b* and *p* sound alike: they are labial consonants)

0 = *z, s,* or soft *c* (first letter in *zero*)

To remember the telephone number for our favorite Indian restaurant, I came up with Lub Duk Tiki-Ba, or 591-7179 (LBD-KTKB). Leave out the vowels and substitute numbers for consonants according to the above list (or think up your own). See Lorayne and Lucas (1974), Buzan (1991), and Minninger (1984) for more examples. Try to create outrageous, gruesome, or bawdy images—they're easier to recall and can be your private joke on the world.

❸ Here are some ways to apply the *rehearse* strategy:

- Obtain or create the material on CD or audiotape and review it while driving, jogging, walking, or riding the bus.

- Create a tickle file. Assign a file folder for each month, week, or day and insert notes you want to review in the appropriate folder.

- While reading, use a highlighter or pen to note sections for review; then periodically review the highlighted sections.

- When you are idle (stopped at a red light, walking, and so on), recall recently memorized material and rehearse it. Review this material with a walking or jogging partner.

- Make a set of flash cards of the steps in a process or some other sequential list of items you want to remember, with the correct sequence of each card indicated on the back side. Shuffle the cards and sort them.

- For many additional suggestions, information, and training opportunities, get on the mailing list of The Buzan Centre of Palm Beach Inc., 415 Federal Highway, Lake Park, Florida 33403 (800-964-6362 or 800-Y-MINDMAP, www.mind-map.com).

TOPIC 23.5　State Dependence

People recall information more readily when they can remember the state in which they learned that information. This is the basis of the old advice to play back in your mind everywhere you've been in the last 30 minutes when you want to find an object you've lost in that time period. In one research study, subjects memorized a list in the basement of a building and were tested. When they were moved to one of the upper floors of the building and were given the same test, they scored poorly. They then were asked to visualize the basement in which the memory task occurred, and their scores improved; when they were returned to the actual basement room where they had memorized the list and were tested again, their scores improved even more. This phenomenon is called *state dependence,* the theory that recall of learning can depend on the state or other situation that existed when the learning took place.

State dependence is reported to hold true for place (as in the basement example), mood (if you were angry when you learned, remember the anger), odors (remember that the olfactory sense is located in the limbic system), and physical condition (if you were drinking coffee while you were learning, you will remember better whenever you drink coffee). Why? Apparently, the synapses formed to create a specific memory are connected to neural networks that form the basis of the conditions associated with the time and place of learning. Recalling the place (for example, a specific room in a house) where you learned a person's name will help you to access the name, because the two are connected by neural networks. This is similar to taking a photo of a person against a distinctive background.

Applications

❶ When you are with someone who is having a hard time remembering something you both want to remember, get the other person to focus on the place, the mood, and his or her physical condition when the information was learned. The same goes for you if you're trying to remember something.

❷ Make an effort to learn things under conditions that are easy to replicate when you need to remember what you've learned.

❸ When you are trying to teach job-related skills, create a learning environment that approximates the conditions on the job. *(Contributed by Rick Bradley)*

TOPIC 23.6 Memory and Emotion

The role that emotion plays in the formation and recall of memory is not clear. We know that some minimal level of arousal, hence emotional activity, is necessary to pump sufficient adrenaline and noradrenaline into one's system to cause the memory to "take." On the other hand, we know that intense emotional experiences appear to interfere with memory formation. Marcia Johnson, a professor of psychology at Princeton University, has found in her research that experiences with intense emotional components appear to be remembered with fewer perceptual details (*APA Monitor,* October 1995). She also has found that focusing on the emotional aspect of a memory results in recall of less detail. More important, she has found that focusing on the emotional aspect of both real and imagined memories blurs the source of the memory.

Applications

❶ When you are attempting to reconstruct a memory that has a strong emotional component, be aware that you may have a tendency to supply details that are not, in fact, details of the experience (the emotions block acquisition of the actual details). Where possible, seek corroboration from another person.

❷ In an emotionally intense situation in which memory is important, try to find a moment of composure to focus on elements you need to remember.

TOPIC 23.7 | **Real vs. Imagined Memories**

Elizabeth Loftus and Katherine Ketcham, in their 1994 work *The Myth of Repressed Memory,* have offered a damning indictment of psychotherapists and others who engage in what the authors refer to as *iatrogenic implantation,* in which a healer or therapist plants the seed of a memory in a patient and, by this process of suggestion, aids the patient in creating a full-blown "recovered memory." The result is not a memory, nor is it recovered.

Memory is malleable. The authors lay a solid background composed of vignettes that illustrate the malleability of memory processes:

- Ulrich Neisser of Cornell University's psychology department interviewed and recorded the circumstances of 44 students at the time of the January 1986 *Challenger* explosion. Two and one-half years later, the memories of where they were had changed: not one was 100 percent accurate, and over one-third were severely inaccurate. The students with inaccurate memories couldn't recognize or accept the authenticity of the written records from only 2½ years earlier.

- Pitcher Jack Hamilton of the Los Angeles Angels threw a ball that crushed the left side of Boston's Tony Conigliaro's face. Neither Conigliaro nor Hamilton were the same after this life-changing event. Though we usually believe that our memories of such events are accurate, Hamilton's memory of the event 22 years later was severely flawed. In an interview with the *New York Times* upon Conigliaro's death in 1990, Hamilton relayed the wrong inning for the bad pitch, the wrong score, the wrong position in the batting order, the wrong time of year, and recalled it as a day game when in fact it was a night game!

Searching for ways to establish the malleability of memory in order to lay a groundwork for discrediting the "recovery" movement, Loftus recounted the now well-known "lost at the mall" story. She asked a friend if he could convince his eight-year-old daughter that she had been lost in a mall at the age of five, when in fact she had never been lost. The friend said that his daughter would never go along with such a planted memory. But to the friend's amazement, after some encouragement, his eight-year-old bought the implanted memory hook, line, and sinker, so much so that she pointed out to her father that he had been "not as scared as I was."

Loftus and Ketcham conclude that there is no such thing as repression, that people don't conveniently select traumatic episodes to be removed from conscious memory and file them away in "special, inaccessible memory drawers." There are four kinds of amnesia, but they differ significantly from so-called repression:

1. ***Anterograde amnesia,*** in which patients exhibit a reduced ability to recall events occurring after a brain injury, as in the famous Central Park jogger rape case.

2. ***Retrograde amnesia,*** in which patients exhibit a reduced ability to recall events preceding brain injury.

3. ***Psychogenic amnesia,*** in which a traumatic event interferes with memory storage and results in fragmentary recall.

4. ***Source amnesia,*** in which one cannot remember the source of a memory, as in who related specific information to you or where you bought a particular product.

None of these four forms of amnesia show anything like the selective elimination of complete episodes claimed by "recovery" therapists. Loftus and Ketchum conclude that repression is nothing more than the invention of the therapist in forced cooperation with the patient. The result of a highly trusting patient in the hands of a suggestive therapist is *pseudomemories.* These "recovered" memories of early abuse have a way of blossoming from nowhere. They spring from the same therapists and their "support" groups, like children who are always sent to the principal's office by the same teachers. These therapists and their ongoing groups have a vested interest in uncovering new supplies of "repressed" memories.

The scientifically accepted phenomenon closest to what is called repression is psychogenic amnesia. But, as the authors point out, in psychogenic amnesia memories are fragmented, not completely eliminated, and over time they tend to become clear. Loftus tells the story of a daring attempt to document iatrogenic implantation, or therapist-induced "memories," by a journalist (I think it was a journalist!) who had himself wired (I think it was a male!) and then went to a therapist who had a reputation for recovering memories of childhood abuse among patients. The resulting transcriptions clearly documented the therapist's leading questions and suggestions. With a patient suffering from depression or anxiety, these implantations could easily form the core of a constructed "memory." Just as lawyers may not lead witnesses, so therapists may not lead patients.

Marcia Johnson (see topic 23.6) has found that real memories tend to have significantly more detail than imagined ones. Memories founded in actual perception usually have more sensory detail; memories originating in the imagination have more information about thoughts and feelings. An individual can develop a knack for identifying memories that possess more perceptual detail, lending more credence to their having a basis in real experience. Johnson calls this process *source monitoring* (*APA Monitor,* October 1995, p. 31). Stephen Kosslyn (1994), a professor of psychology at Harvard University, has determined that these two processes, which he calls *perception* and *imagery,* occur in the same area of the brain. This helps to explain why some subjects may think they actually witnessed an image when in fact they only imagined it, which is of interest to those who study the reliability of eyewitness testimony.

Eric and Minouche Kandel (*Discover,* May 1994) report that the release of the body's natural painkillers—the opioids—interferes with memory formation. They further speculate that under certain circumstances, as in early abuse, when the pain from an experience becomes so intense that it triggers the release of opioids, the memory formation associated with that event is impeded by the painkillers. Under such circumstances, they maintain, memories of early abuse may never become strongly established. The result is not repression or forgetting, but rather weak or nonexistent neural pathways.

One line of research by Daniel Schacter of Harvard University has established that positron emission tomography (PET) reveals a distinct pattern: true memories are associated with a higher level of brain activity than false memories. This higher level results from the greater detail associated with real memories and is clearly visible in PET scans in the hippocampal and temporoparietal regions. This finding, reported in the August 1996 issue of *Neuron,* is regarded as a major breakthrough in understanding false memory, but the process is complex and costly and will probably not be available for everyday verification in the near future. However, it is conceivable that we may eventually ascertain the veracity of memories through such brain scans. In fact, Lawrence Farwell has developed such a technique—Farwell Brain Fingerprinting—but it is not yet admissible in the courts.

Applications

❶ When you are in doubt about the veracity of a memory, compare the perceptual details in your mind's eye with the details of a memory for which you have corroboration. If the doubtful memory has fewer perceptual details (such as colors, smells, and shapes) than confident memories, be distrustful of it.

❷ In attempting to manage the testimony of an eyewitness, establish baseline levels of perceptual detail (by having the eyewitness relate details from memories known to originate in perception) before exploring the eyewitness testimony. Comparing the two levels of detail should help establish the degree of reliability of the testimony.

❸ The best way to establish the veracity (or falseness) of a memory that is uncertain is to corroborate it through the testimony of other reliable observers—memory partners, as it were. I have seen several references in the literature to the healthful habit of ceasing to rely solely on one's own memory or reconstruction of events, and instead soliciting the complementary support of a memory partner in the form of a family member, friend, or co-worker.

④ If you become involved in a serious charge that concerns an unverifiable memory, consult a neurologist to see if PET technology is an option for clarifying the nature of the memory.

⑤ For an excellent review of the literature on false memory syndrome, read Kenneth S. Pope's article "Memory, Abuse, and Science" (*American Psychologist,* September 1996).

TOPIC 23.8 Helping Others Remember

Research into witness management has led to some interesting techniques for eliciting latent memories from others. For example, build on a witness's schemas (see topic 23.4) by identifying something in the witness's background that she can relate to the scene of the memories in question. A witness who likes working with wood should focus on the qualities of the wooden furniture in the scene about which she is trying to recall details. The witness is likely to have paid close attention to the wood and is then more apt to recall other details. Another witness management technique is to minimize questions, asking only a few open-ended questions from which the witness can reveal his schemas. The interviewer then builds on whatever information the witness has volunteered.

Weingardt, Leonesio, and Loftus (1994) write about *eyewitness metacognition* and form several conclusions about the actual and perceived accuracy and trustworthiness of eyewitness testimony:

1. Peripheral details are more likely to be contaminated by misleading postevent information than is central detail.

2. Misleading information is more damaging or influential when it is related in complex sentences than when it is stated simply and obviously.

3. People who receive misleading information make more errors in memory and are more confident about the misinformation than the original information.

4. The more spatial, temporal, sensory, and semantic details that are provided, the more likely a memory is to be based on

perception and not on imagination, and the more likely it is to be perceived to be based on perception.

5. People who see their memory as poor tend to put more faith in written accounts.

6. People tend to think that they're good at remembering what they said in the past (even if they aren't), so if they don't remember it, they tend to think that someone else said it.

7. Juries report a greater belief in witnesses who seem confident.

8. Weingardt, Leonesio, and Loftus's meta-analysis based on 35 studies shows that the correlation between witness confidence and accuracy is low (+.25).

9. The major factors associated with accurate self-confidence in identifying a criminal are the personality of the witness, previous feedback to the witness on his accuracy, and the perpetrator's use of disguise.

In a recent survey of 64 experts on the reliability of eyewitness testimony, Saul Kassin and his team reported (Kassin, Tubb, Hosch, and Memon, May 2001) on the evidence for reliability of 30 conventional propositions about the accuracy of eyewitness testimony. In table 23.1, we present the propositions, with a comment as to the degree of support each proposition found among the experts.

Another clue to the reliability of event memory is knowing whether the individual has experienced the event as one of a kind in his lifetime, versus repeated experiences of it over time. Memories refer to three such degrees of scope: *specific event* (my first writing weekend in the mountains), a *general event* (all of my writing weekends in the mountains), and a *general period or category* (all writing weekends since I first began writing, whether in the mountains, beach, city, at a resort, or at home). Those specific events that are associated with general events and also with general periods tend to lose accuracy in retrieval. It is easier for one who has experienced only one Thanksgiving dinner to remember details from it than for one who has experienced 30 of them to remember details from any one of them. Figure 23.3 provides examples of these three levels of scope and how they relate to the three kinds of memory: declarative-episodic, declarative-semantic, and nondeclarative. Note that for each of the three kinds of memory I provide two examples for each level of scope.

Table 23.1. Thirty Eyewitness Propositions and Their Degree of Support

Conventional Propositions About Eyewitness Reliability	Evidence in Support
1. High stress impairs accuracy.	Moderate
2. Presence of a weapon impairs face identification.	Strong
3. One person "showup" (vs. full lineup) increases risk of misidentification.	Moderate
4. The more lineup faces resembling the suspect, the more reliable the identification.	Moderate
5. Police instructions affect willingness to make a lineup identification.	Very Strong
6. The less time an event is observed, the less well it is remembered.	Strong
7. Rate of memory loss greatest just after the event, then levels off.	Strong
8. Confidence does not predict accuracy.	Strong
9. Memory of an event often reflects information gained after the event.	Very Strong
10. Color judgments under monochromatic light (e.g., orange light) are unreliable.	Moderate
11. Memory can be affected by the way a question is worded.	Very Strong
12. On occasion, eyewitnesses identify as the culprit someone they have seen in another situation.	Strong
13. Police and other trained observers are no more reliable as eyewitnesses than the average person.	Weak
14. Hypnosis increases accuracy.	Weak
15. Hypnosis increases suggestibility.	Very Strong
16. Perception of an event can be affected by one's attitudes or expectations.	Very Strong
17. Violent events are harder to remember than nonviolent ones.	Weak
18. One is more accurate when identifying members of one's own race.	Very Strong
19. One's confidence can be affected by issues unrelated to accuracy.	Very Strong
20. Intoxication impairs future recall.	Very Strong
21. Exposure to a mug shot increases chances of a subsequent lineup identification.	Very Strong
22. Traumatic experiences can be repressed for years, then later recovered.	Weak
23. Memories recovered from childhood are often false or distorted in some way.	Moderate
24. True and false memories can be reliably discriminated.	Weak
25. Young children are less reliable than adults.	Moderate
26. Young children are more susceptible than adults to suggestion and peer influence.	Very Strong
27. The more a description resembles members of a lineup, the more accurate an identification will be.	Moderate
28. Simultaneous lineups yield more misidentifications than sequential lineups.	Strong
29. Elderly eyewitnesses are less reliable than younger adults.	Weak
30. The quicker a lineup identification, the more reliable it is.	Weak

(Very Strong: ≥ 90% Regard as Reliable; Strong: ≥ 75%; Moderate: ≥ 50%; Weak Support: < 50%; based on the judgment of 64 experts; adapted from Kassin, Tubb, Hosch, & Memon, May 2001)

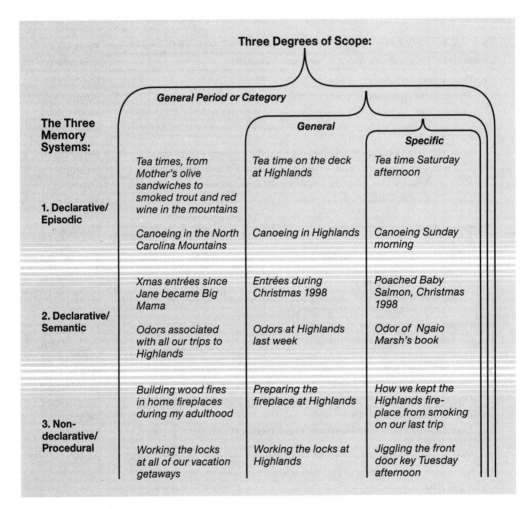

Figure 23.3. The Structure of Memory

The figure shows "Three Degrees of Scope:" branching into "General Period or Category," "General," and "Specific" across "The Three Memory Systems:"

The Three Memory Systems:	General Period or Category	General	Specific
1. Declarative/ Episodic	Tea times, from Mother's olive sandwiches to smoked trout and red wine in the mountains	Tea time on the deck at Highlands	Tea time Saturday afternoon
	Canoeing in the North Carolina Mountains	Canoeing in Highlands	Canoeing Sunday morning
2. Declarative/ Semantic	Xmas entrées since Jane became Big Mama	Entrées during Christmas 1998	Poached Baby Salmon, Christmas 1998
	Odors associated with all our trips to Highlands	Odors at Highlands last week	Odor of Ngaio Marsh's book
3. Non- declarative/ Procedural	Building wood fires in home fireplaces during my adulthood	Preparing the fireplace at Highlands	How we kept the Highlands fireplace from smoking on our last trip
	Working the locks at all of our vacation getaways	Working the locks at Highlands	Jiggling the front door key Tuesday afternoon

Applications

1 Use a person's interests to elicit memories. For example, if the person is a soap opera addict, ask first, "Was there a television set in the room? Describe it. What was on top of it? Beside it? On the wall above it?" Use the TV set to retrieve images of the rest of the room. If you start with an impersonal question that the person cannot immediately relate to his or her experience, you are less likely to get the desired level of detail. Ask someone who's bookish about printed matter, an artist about artwork, a musician about a piano, and so on.

❷ Ask open-ended questions beginning with words like *when, where, how many, how long,* and *what.* Starting questions like these are more likely to get people talking and to exploit their memory than closed-ended questions that typically elicit yes-or-no responses, such as "Did you arrive before 8:00 P.M.?"

❸ In preparing witnesses, develop written accounts when possible.

❹ To maximize perceived credibility, develop as much spatial, temporal, sensory, and semantic detail as possible.

❺ Key witnesses whose credibility may be strained should be coached in nonverbal presentation of self-confidence (eye contact, speaking out, a comfortable posture).

❻ Remember that of the three levels of memory (specific event, repeated event, and larger category of event), one's memory is less trustworthy as you move from a specific one-time event (e.g., a Japanese tea ceremony you attended in Tokyo) to a multiply repeated event (going home for family holidays over a 30-year period).

TOPIC 23.9 **Roundup of Memory Boosters**

To help organize some of the major findings on memory, here is a roundup of accepted memory boosters. Just as the "Roundup" chemical treatment can eliminate weeds from legitimate vegetation patches, these boosters will help you make the most of your memory capacity, with respect to both developing your memory and maintaining it.

Applications

❶ Get sufficient sleep.

❷ Consume the minimum daily fat allowance; don't eliminate fat from your diet.

❸ Minimize consumption of alcohol and caffeine.

❹ Minimize reliance on prescription medications, using exercise, sleep, diet, and fresh air as medicines.

❺ The herb sage (*Salvia officinalis*) prevents acetylcholinesterase from accomplishing its normal mission of breaking down acetylcholine. Shortly before an activity requiring recall (an exam, a press conference, a sales presentation), prepare a sage cocktail by adding one teaspoon of dried sage (from your spice rack) to one cup of boiling water. Mash for five minutes, strain, and enjoy. If the taste is aversive, try combining with bouillon or something satisfying.

❻ Get 30–60 minutes of aerobic exercise five days a week.

❼ Consume at least the recommended daily allowance of calcium, but not to excess.

❽ Get your daily allowances of vitamin A and folic acid.

❾ Intend to remember, organize the material, and practice it.

❿ After learning important new material, work with familiar material for several hours so new won't drive out old.

⓫ Rely on state dependence and other methods for using cues to access memories. My favorite is saying the alphabet silently and slowly (see topic 26.7) until the first letter of the name (or other item) that I'm trying to remember connects with the rest of the word.

⓬ Do your homework before an experience in which you must use your memory—prepare mind maps, note cards, outlines, and so forth.

⓭ Use multiple encoding, such as getting several points of reference as to where you parked your car at the coliseum.

⓮ Minimize the amount of stress in your life.

⓯ Don't put absolute trust in your memory (i.e., be humble), and rely on memory partners.

A Final Word on Memory

Bolles (1988, p. 23) describes the process of memory this way: "We remember what we understand; we understand only what we pay attention to; we pay attention to what we want." In other words, experience arouses emotion, which fixes attention and leads to understanding and insight, which results in memory. Bolles continues: "Attention is like digestion. We do not store the food we eat; we break it down so that it becomes part of our body. Attention selects parts of experience and uses [them] to nourish our memories. We do not store this experience, we use it. Of course, we eat many things that we do not digest and we also experience many things without paying them any attention" (p. 183).

SUGGESTED RESOURCES

Alkon, D. L. (1992). *Memory's Voice: Deciphering the Brain-Mind Code.* New York: HarperCollins.

Bolles, E. B. (1988). *Remembering and Forgetting: An Inquiry into the Nature of Memory.* New York: Walker.

Buzan, T. (1991). *Use Your Perfect Memory* (3rd ed.). New York: Penguin Books.

Edelman, G. M. (1987). *Neural Darwinism: The Theory of Neuronal Group Selection.* New York: Basic Books.

Gordon, B. (1995). *Memory: Remembering and Forgetting in Everyday Life.* New York: MasterMedia.

Loftus, E., and K. Ketcham (1994). *The Myth of Repressed Memory.* New York: St. Martin's Press.

Lorayne, H., and J. Lucas (1974). *The Memory Book.* New York: Stein & Day.

Schacter, D. (1996). *Searching for Memory.* New York: Basic Books.

Weingardt, K. R., R. J. Leonesio, and E. F. Loftus (1994). "On Eyewitness Metacognition." In J. Metcalfe and A. P. Shimamura (Eds.), *Metacognition: Knowing about Knowing* (pp. 155–184). Cambridge, Mass.: MIT Press.

24

A Matter of Style

Our Different Ways of Learning

The second half of the 20th century has seen a virtual alphabet soup of personal learning style models, variously called learning styles, thinking styles, teaching styles, and cognitive styles, with the last typically viewed as the most inclusive category. Thinking styles typically include both learning styles

Table 24.1. Models for Differences in Learning Style

Name of the Model	How the Model Names the Style	Source
Conceptual Tempo	Reflectivity Impulsivity	Kagan (1966)
Psychological Differentiation	Field dependence Field independence	Witkin & Goodenough (1981)
Theory of Types	Extraversion/Introversion Sensing/Intuition Feeling/Thinking Judging/Perceiving	Myers & McCaulley (1985)
Gregorc's Energic Model	Use of space (concrete/abstract) Use of time (sequential/random)	Gregorc (1982)
Teaching Methods	Projects Drill and recitation Peer teaching Discussion Teaching games Independent study Programmed instruction Lecture Simulation	Renzulli & Smith (1978)
Scope	Deep/depth Elaborative/breadth	Schmeck (1983)
Dunn and Dunn	Environmental (sound/light) Emotional (motivation/responsibility) Sociological (peers/self) Physical (perceptual/mobility)	Dunn & Dunn (1978)
Holland Hexagon	Realistic Investigative Artistic Social Enterprising Conventional	Holland (1985)
Kolb	Converging/Diverging Assimilating/Accommodating	Kolb (1978)
Teaching Range	Wide/Narrow	Joyce & Hodges (1966)
Teaching Styles	Task-oriented Cooperative planner Child-centered Subject-centered Learning-centered Emotionally exciting	Henson & Borthwick (1984)
Kirton	Adaptation/Innovation	Kirton (1977)

Table 24.1. Models for Differences in Learning Style (continued)

Name of the Model	How the Model Names the Style	Source
Achievement Pattern	High honors Subject cup Extracurricular Getting by	Howard & Howard (1993)
Social Style	Independet study Contract learning Tutorial Traditional classroom	Howard & Howard (1993)
Honey and Mumford	Activists Reflectors Theorists Pragmatists	Honey & Mumford (1982)
Whetten and Cameron	Receptive/Preceptive Systematic/Intuitive Active/Reflective	Whetten & Cameron (1984)
Modalities	Visual Auditory Kinesthetic Olfactory Gustatory Tactile Group/Alone	Griffin (unpublished)
Neurodevelopmental Systems	Attention Temporal-sequential ordering Spatial ordering Memory Language Neuromotor functions Social cognition Higher-order cognition	Levine (2002, 2003)
Beliefs about Intelligence	Fixed entity—performance oriented Malleable—risk oriented	Dweck (1989)
Organization of Knowledge	Artisans—skilled in traditional way Virtuosos—creatively adaptive	Bransford et al. (2000)

and teaching styles as subsets. For the purpose of this chapter, I will use the term *learning style,* and I will include thinking, teaching, and learning as changing aspects of the characteristic way that individuals go about processing new information. Table 24.1 lists some of the more frequently cited models that have been proposed to explain individual differences in learning style.

Plainly, the domain of learning styles has been shaped and re-shaped in many ways. What was missing for a long time was a grand theory to integrate this domain—until Robert Sternberg came to the rescue. In an article entitled "Are Cognitive Styles Still in Style?" (*American Psychologist,* July 1997), Sternberg and Elena Grigorenko mapped out their "theory of mental self-government" approach to learning style. They presented a model that built on Sternberg's triarchic theory of intelligence (see topic 34.3), employing a metaphor derived from government, with executive, legislative, and judicial branches.

TOPIC 24.1   The Mental Self-Government Model of Learning Style

Sternberg and Grigorenko (p. 707) portray the domain of learning style with a five-part model, shown in table 24.2. They clearly assume that the way people manage their learning is similar to the way the government runs the country. They find that every individual "possesses every style to some degree." Some people are more flexible than others. Although the styles are not fixed but fluid, some individuals persist in a style when one would expect them to alter their style according to the circumstances. This resistance to changes in circumstance suggests that "there may be preprogrammed dispositions that are difficult to change" (p. 708). In other words, learning styles have both a genetic and an environmental component, and the environmental part is most subject to change.

We can see that Sternberg and Grigorenko have incorporated many of the models shown in table 24.1 into their integrative approach. The test that is used to measure the presence of these styles is the Thinking Styles Inventory (Sternberg and Wagner, 1991; Sternberg, 1997c), a self-report instrument that employs a nine-point scale. In addition, Sternberg and Grigorenko have devised a series of instruments for use by educators (the Thinking Styles Questionnaire for Teachers, Set of Thinking Styles Tasks for Students, and Students' Thinking Styles Evaluated by Teachers). These tools, though unpublished, are available from the authors: Robert Sternberg and Elena Grigorenko, Department of Psychology, Yale University, P.O. Box 208205, New Haven, Connecticut 06520 (203-432-4633, robert.sternberg@yale.edu). All these tests have good reliability and validity. They correlate with neither traditional IQ

Table 24.2. Sternberg and Grigorenko's Learning Style Model

Aspects of the Model	Specific Styles for the Aspect	Characteristics of Each Style
Functions	Legislative	Creates one's own rules, formulates one's own structures and approaches; avoids the prestructured
	Executive	Is an implementer; follows rules; relies on existing structures and predefined rules
	Judicial	Prefers to evaluate, judge, and analyze existing rules and ideas
Forms	Monarchic	Focuses on a single goal or task until it is completed
	Hierarchic	Has multiple goals with varying priorities; is comfortable with systematically getting things done
	Oligarchic	Has multiple goals with equal priorities; has difficulty setting priorities for getting things done
	Anarchic	Does not like to be tied down to the current way of doing things; tends to be opposed to existing systems or ways without always having an alternative; has a random approach that often leads to unusual connections
Levels	Local	Prefers specific, concrete details that require precision in execution
	Global	Prefers general problems that require abstract thinking and conceptualization in the world of ideas
Scope	Internal	Prefers working alone, independently of others and on one's own
	External	Prefers to work with and interact with other people.
Leanings	Liberal	Goes beyond the current way and permits change from traditional methods (as opposed to the Legislative style, the new ideas do not have to be one's own)
	Conservative	Prefers to follow the traditional and the familiar (may think up one's own ideas, but they are consistent with custom)

measures nor grade point average, so they appear to be measuring something different from intelligence or aptitude.

Sternberg and Grigorenko conducted a series of studies in which they correlated scores on the Thinking Styles Inventory with other measures using a number of analyses. They compared students and faculty from four different kinds of schools: urban public, prestigious traditional private, Catholic parochial, and progressive avant-garde private. The following applications are based on findings from these studies.

Applications

❶ Teachers in the lower grades are more legislative and less executive; hence, they must find ways that may not be natural for them to work with students who have an executive (structured) style. Teachers in the upper grades are more executive than legislative and hence must find ways that may not be natural for them to work with students who have the legislative (creative) style.

❷ Older teachers are more executive, local, and conservative; hence, they typically must work harder to find ways to appeal to students who are legislative, judicial, global, and liberal. Younger teachers, who are more legislative, judicial, global, and liberal, must work harder to find ways to appeal to students who are more executive, local, and conservative.

❸ Science teachers tend to score as more local, humanities teachers more liberal. Thus, science teachers must typically work harder to appeal to students who are more global (abstract), and humanities teachers must typically work harder to appeal to students who are more conservative.

❹ Teachers' styles have a tendency to match the style of their school. Therefore, school leaders need to be aware of the stylistic profile of their overall program and pay special attention to students who clearly do not fit that profile. The faculty will not naturally design learning experiences that these atypical students will find comfortable.

❺ There is a strong inclination for students' styles to match their teachers' styles, which suggests that students recognize their teachers' styles and adapt to them. Teachers need to make a special effort to include or accommodate students whose styles clearly depart from theirs. Being aware of stylistic differences and communicating a knowledge of those differences to the students can lead to successful adaptations.

❻ The lower the educational and occupational levels of the students' fathers, the more likely the students are to be judicial, local, conservative, and oligarchic. In schools where parents are predominantly less educated and less successful, a curriculum should be designed that appeals to those four styles. In schools where parents are better educated and more successful, the curriculum should primarily appeal to the legislative, global, and liberal styles.

7 Teachers and parents need to understand that siblings naturally differ in their styles. Therefore, teachers should not always expect a child to match the style of a sibling they taught earlier.

8 Teachers are inclined to evaluate and grade more favorably students who match their styles. Schools as a whole grade students higher whose styles match that of the school. Teachers and schools, then, should be mindful of their tendency to downgrade and devalue students whose styles differ from their own. Philosophically—yes, even ethically—teachers and school administrators need to be aware of this tendency to devalue nonmatching students. To compound this effect, Sternberg and Grigorenko also found that teachers often overestimate how close their students are to them in style. As a result, they may encourage students in teacher-compatible stylistic patterns that are based on projections rather than on reality. Teachers must be diligent in adjusting for this blind spot. In support of this pattern, consider that across schools, neither IQ scores nor grade point averages correlate with any of the styles. However, within each school, strong correlations exist between grade point averages and styles. These correlations range from –.42 to +.58.

TOPIC 24.2 **The Relationship of Learning Style to Personality**

I have a special interest in the way personality traits relate to other constructs. Upon close inspection of the definitions for Sternberg and Grigorenko's styles, I have tried my hand at estimating the Big Five infrastructure that underlies learning style and am conducting research that will confirm or clarify these associations. The associations in the following list are based on the personality traits of the WorkPlace Big Five ProFile (Howard and Howard, 2001), as described in topic 33.2. The intent of this list is to suggest the

Note: When you see cross references to other sections of this book, you may benefit from taking time now to read them; they provide information that will deepen your understanding of the current material.

probable personality trait infrastructure that is associated with each of the learning styles. A plus sign in the list indicates that the style is associated with high scores for a factor or facet, a minus sign with low scores, and an equal sign with medium-range scores.

Learning Style	Five-Factor Infrastructure
Functions:	
Legislative	O+C–
Executive	O–C+
Judicial	O–A–C+
Forms:	
Monarchic	O–C+
Hierarchic	O+C+
Oligarchic	O+C–
Anarchic	N+O+A–C–
Levels:	
Local	O1–O2–
Global	O1+O2+
Scope:	
Internal	N–E–E1–E2–A–
External	N+E+E1+E2+A+
Leanings:	
Liberal	O1+O2+O3+
Conservative	O1–O2–O3–

The degree of flexibility for each set of attributes can be associated with the actual scores on the specified WorkPlace Big Five ProFile supertraits and subtraits: midrange scores (45–55, on a scale of 1 to 100) would be more flexible and fluid, extreme scores (below 45 and above 55) more fixed, less situational, and less adaptive to pressure. I remember a professor in graduate school who, on the first night of class, revealed that he was executive and conservative to the extreme and that students veering from his requirements would find it tough going. I, being legislative, judicial, and liberal, refused to stay in the course, although it was required for graduation. Luckily, and due to my persistence and that of several of my cohorts, we were able to form an ad hoc independent study group under the tutelage of a less rigid professor.

Applications

❶ If you have Big Five scores available on teachers and students, try using them to estimate learning styles. The Center for Applied Cognitive

Studies (800-BIG-5555, or visit our website at www.centacs.com) has a software program (*The Learner*) that estimates scores on the Sternberg-Wagner model as well as on other learning style models. These estimates are based on scores from either the NEO PI-R (Costa and McCrae, 1992) or the WorkPlace Big Five ProFile (Howard and Howard, 2001) scores.

❷ Be aware that personality traits as measured by the Big Five are associated with differences in learning style. If you know your Big Five profile, use that knowledge to assess your blind spots as a facilitator of learning. Be aware that you are most likely to undervalue the performance of learners who are different from you. The learning and teaching strategies associated with each of the Big Five traits are spelled out in chapter 17 ("Learning Styles") of Pierce and Jane Howard's *Owner's Manual for Personality at Work* (2000).

TOPIC 24.3 ## The Development of Thinking During College

Harvard's William Perry Jr. set out to describe (1970) the nature of intellectual growth that typically takes place during the college years. In so doing, Perry in effect identified three significantly different phases (with subphases) that amount to developmental stages or even styles:

1. *Dualism,* in which the entering college student tends to see the world in terms of right and wrong, or good and bad, and searches throughout most freshman and sophomore courses to find the right answers.

2. *Relativism,* in which the maturing college student tends to eschew the notion of a single right approach or answer, instead embracing a pluralism in which multiple points of view and value systems may be simultaneously good or right.

3. *Commitment,* in which the mature college student, while continuing intellectually, or epistemologically, to embrace relativism and pluralism, nonetheless affirms a personal set of values. This commitment, however, is integrative and accepting of other systems, unlike earlier commitments, which were unexamined and based on unquestioned authority.

In a parallel work, Mary Belenky and others (1997) found that the traditional female in the U.S. entered college with no voice of her own, accepting instead her authorities' word for what was right and good. Belenky traces the process of such women (and, for that matter, men) discovering their voice. The stages are similar to Perry's.

How does one move a young person from dualism to relativism? In the mid-1990s I attended a workshop called "Critical Thinking for College Students" that was led by biology professor Craig Nelson of Indiana University (who, in recognition of his efforts in improving college teaching, was named "U.S. Professor of the Year" in 2000 by the Carnegie Foundation for the Advancement of Teaching). After reviewing the models of Perry and Belenky, Nelson pointed out that the mechanism for moving a young person in the direction of discovering her own voice was through the use of the "tools" of a discipline. By learning to use these, the student begins to think like a biologist, or a linguist, or a historian, and thus discovers her own voice.

I decided to make a list of the tools used in my primary discipline—industrial and organizational psychology. Here is a partial list:

- Key word/statement format
- "Two by" grids
- Row-by-column matrix
- Weighted row-by-column matrix (decision matrix)
- Flow chart
- Ishikawa chart
- Circular flow
- Mind map
- Open-ended questions
- Graph
- Likert scale
- Anchor
- Executive summary
- Continuum
- Time line (Gantt chart, etc.)

- Action plan
- Stepwise listing
- Consensus
- Itemized response/force field
- Diagram

From time to time, I teach undergraduate and graduate versions of an introductory course in industrial and organizational psychology, and teaching toward mastery of these tools is the basis of the course structure.

Tools vary somewhat from discipline to discipline. As Bransford and others (2000) put it: "The teaching of metacognitive activities must be incorporated into the subject matter that students are learning. . . . These strategies are not generic across subjects, and attempts to teach them as generic can lead to failure to transfer. Teaching metacognitive strategies [i.e., what I'm calling 'tools'] has been shown to improve understanding [in a wide variety of subject areas]." The student of biology learns taxonomic hierarchies and drawing techniques; of philosophy, the syllogism and the Venn diagram; of history, research tools for ascertaining facts. Across disciplines, one learns such tools as the flow chart, the decision matrix, and concept mapping. By using these tools, the student learns to approach the content of a field the way a scholar would, eschewing textbook answers and instead finding solutions independently. Nelson has found in his own controlled studies that students actually master more content when the instructor emphasizes mastery of tools rather than the content itself.

Applications

❶ If you are a teacher or a manager, identify the tools of your discipline, then show your students or subordinates how to use these tools. Their success is directly related to tool mastery. Mastery of the tools should be a major component by which both students and workers are evaluated.

❷ For a way to start identifying both tools that are unique to your discipline and tools that are common to other disciplines, review my *Visual Tools for Knowledge Workers* (Howard, 2000).

A Note on Genetics and Learning

Researchers are discovering specific genes that affect various aspects of the learning process (*APA Monitor,* May 1997, p. 29). For example, the gene named *Linott* is associated with the ability to form a new learning; fruit flies (*Drosophila*) whose Linott gene is missing are unable to form new learnings, but flies whose Linott was removed in infancy are able to learn new tasks when the gene is restored in adulthood. The gene called *Creb* is associated with the ability to retain a new learning over the long haul—that is, to store it in long-term memory. Fruit flies with Linott but without Creb can form new learnings but cannot remember them. Intensive research is underway for possible applications to human learners. It is not clear at this time whether these genes affect the learning styles presented in this chapter. Certainly, how one goes about learning, and the relative effectiveness of one's learning styles, must be considered to be a combination of genetic (nature) effects on the one hand and environmental (nurture) effects on the other.

SUGGESTED RESOURCES

Howard, P. J., and J. M. Howard (2005). *The Learner: An Excel Workbook.* Charlotte, N.C.: Center for Applied Cognitive Studies (*Cent*ACS).

Howard, P. J., and J. M. Howard (2000). *The Owner's Manual for Personality at Work.* Austin: Bard Press.

Sternberg, R. J. (1997c). *Thinking Styles.* New York: Cambridge University Press.

Sternberg, R. J., and E. L. Grigorenko (1997, July). "Are Cognitive Styles Still in Style?" *American Psychologist,* 52(7), 700–712.

Sternberg, R. J., and R. K. Wagner (1991). "MSG Thinking Styles Inventory Manual." Unpublished test manual. New Haven, Conn.: Yale University Department of Psychology.

Website

The Center for the Study of Learning and Teaching Styles at St. John's University hosts the "Learning Styles Network" at this address: www.learningstyles.net

25

Giftedness

Letting the Genius Out of the Bottle

66 *Stupid is as stupid does.* **99**

—*Forrest Gump*

R esponding to the gifted individual is a dilemma for a democracy. The desire to treat each individual the same and to provide equal resources for all has been the hallmark of societies that wish to abandon the elitist aristocracies of yesteryear. In a pure democracy, in the tradition of the U.S. experiment called the American Dream, each individual is to have an equal opportunity to achieve. None are to be given special advantages by the government (though that is not to say that parents can't provide special advantages for their children). The turf must be even, at least with respect to government's role.

In spite of this philosophical commitment in our democracy, voices have been raised in advocacy for special groups, and the gifted are a particularly problematic special group. Parents who lobby to have different or extra attention paid to their exceptionally intelligent children are frequently viewed as elitist or pushy, as self-indulgently bragging, or as seeking attention.

A gifted child is a problem. Easily bored and immensely talented in one or more fields, he often languishes in the typical classroom. Because he represents only a small tail in the normal distribution of ability, he is usually one of a kind in his classes. All too often, unmoved by his ennui, other students and teachers will respond, "If he's so smart, let him find a way to make the humdrum interesting." On the other hand, gifted children don't appear to drop out of school at a rate any different than other children. *Time* reported (September 27, 2004, "Saving the Smart Kids") that, in a study following over 3,000 gifted students, 5 percent dropped out after eighth grade, compared with a 5.2 percent dropout rate for the remainder of the student population.

Ellen Winner of Boston College's Department of Education and the Harvard Graduate School of Education's Project Zero accepts the societal commitment to gifted children, as long as the resources do not exceed those available to others. Winner (1997) points out that giftedness is troublesome to define. As Robert Sternberg and Howard Gardner portray intelligence (see chapter 34), giftedness can be understood as *modular*. With modular gifts, an individual might be gifted in one or more of several areas, such as verbal, musical (auditory), or kinesthetic skills, or in one or more of several aspects of intelligence, such as creativity, street smarts, or informational encoding. But as tradition would have it, intelligence, hence giftedness, is a unitary concept called *g,* for "general." This traditional definition of intelligence is used by Winner and most other writers on the subject of giftedness; we will use it here for the convenience of understanding the research findings.

> "If a man has a talent and cannot use it, he has failed. If he has a talent and uses only half of it, he has partly failed. If he has a talent and learns somehow to use the whole of it, he has gloriously succeeded, and won a satisfaction and a triumph few men ever know."
>
> Thomas Wolfe, *The Web and the Rock*

Traditional intelligence and giftedness are made up of verbal, numerical, and spatial reasoning. One's ability to solve problems in these three areas is referred to as *IQ*. The average IQ is by definition 100. A score of 100 suggests that an individual's verbal, numerical, and spatial abilities are comparable to those of most people in his or her cohort, or age group. Winner identifies two levels of giftedness: *moderately gifted* and *profoundly gifted*. Moderately gifted schoolchildren have measured IQs somewhere around 130–150 and typically perform about one to two years ahead of their cohort. The primary difference between average children and moderately gifted children appears to be one of degree: moderately gifted children remember more, calculate faster, and solve problems more quickly.

Profoundly gifted children have IQs in the region of 180. They are not only different from average children; they are different from moderately gifted children. Winner suspects that profoundly gifted children are different in kind of intelligence, not just in degree, from both average and moderately gifted children. Examples of feats performed by the profoundly gifted include situations in which four-year-olds, unaided, have figured out the rules of algebra, memorized an entire musical score in a moment, or discovered how to identify all the prime numbers. The profoundly gifted, according to Winner, would appear to have two markers: an intrinsic drive to master a particular domain and a prodigious problem-solving and memory apparatus that, unaided, has the capacity for breakthrough thinking.

Thomas Oakland, educational psychology professor at the University of Florida, tested 1,554 gifted and nongifted students ranging in age from 8 to 17, with the Student Styles Questionnaire, a measure of extraversion, creativity, decision style, and preference for order (reported in *Gifted Child Quarterly,* July 2000). His findings:

- Gifted students are 29 percent more likely to have active imaginations than nongifted students.

- Gifted girls are 55 percent more likely to have active imaginations than nongifted girls.

- Girls of both groups preferred making decisions on the basis of values rather than logic.

- Gifted boys are 28 percent more likely to prefer making decisions on the basis of values (rather than on logic), as compared with nongifted boys.

- Although more girls than boys prefer organized styles to a more flexible style, gifted students in general do not show a preference for organization over flexibility.

- Gifted and nongifted students show no differences on measures of extraversion.

One general finding: kids, gifted or not, do better in school when their parents and teachers understand their individual personality trait profile (see chapter 33). Kids do better when their unique temperament is not only accepted but actively engaged in their home and school life.

TOPIC 25.1   Recognizing Giftedness

Children with both moderate and profound giftedness show early signs, such as these (Winner, 1997, p. 1,072):

- A long attention span

- A preference for novelty

- Overreactivity to physical sensations

- A good memory for recognition of previous experience

- Early onset of language

- Intense curiosity, drive, and persistence

- Obsessive interests

- Metacognitive ability (that is, the gifted think about how they think and can talk about their learning and problem-solving strategies)

- Typically, the ability to read one or two years before beginning kindergarten

- The ability to excel at abstract logical thinking

- A fascination with numbers and numerical patterns

- Typically, a more solitary or introverted nature

- A preference for older children

- Difficulty finding compatible peers of any age

- Twice as many social or emotional problems as average children

- A fiercely independent and nonconformist nature

- The ability to derive pleasure from work

- Positive self-esteem about their intellectual ability

Winner points out that not all gifted children follow the same developmental story line. Many hide their talents until they are older (she cites Charles Darwin as an example). Often parents or the school fail to stimulate a child with challenges, and some gifted children who are more needful of external guidance languish until such a challenge appears.

Although many children are gifted globally, not all are. In one study of 1,000 gifted teenagers, over 95 percent showed a marked discrepancy between their math and verbal performance. Moreover, gifted children who have creative strength in a particular domain need to be treated differently from those who have analytic strength in the same domain (give the former the challenge of inventing a new formula, the latter a tough problem to solve). Finally, a child gifted in one domain can have a learning disability in another.

Applications

1 Review the kinds of intelligence in chapter 34. Find a way to provide challenging experiences—in school, outside of school, or both—for children who demonstrate a strong interest and quick learning ability in one or more of the modules in the Gardner-Sternberg Job Matrix (see table 34.4). At a minimum, find a mentor.

2 Consult with a local education professional who specializes in the academically gifted about resources to use with a gifted child.

3 Explore these web resources:

www.kidsource.com/kidsource/pages/ed.gifted.html

amby.com/educate/gifted.html

www.sofweb.vic.edu.au/gifted

www.hoagiesgifted.org

④ Read Sternberg's *The Triarchic Mind* (1988; see topic 34.3) and Thomas Armstrong's *Multiple Intelligences in the Classroom* (1994).

TOPIC 25.2 **Supplementing the Curriculum for Gifted Children**

Two different kinds of supplementary programs are available for gifted children: (1) pullout programs and (2) summer and weekend programs. Three-fourths of all school districts in the United States use pullout programs, in which children experience regular classrooms for most of the day and are "pulled out" into special enrichment classes with other gifted children. Pullout programs typically emphasize one of three areas: *process, content,* or *project.* Process courses train students in problem solving and critical thinking and typically do not emphasize a specific subject area such as math or history. (Recall, however, as we discussed in topic 24.3, that each domain has a different set of critical thinking tools.) Content courses offer advanced study in a specific subject, such as literature or biology. Project courses focus on completion of a project that might culminate in a presentation or other tangible product. Winner observes that pullout enrichment programs are often criticized for being superficial and unsystematic, yet the research does show modest gains in achievement scores for gifted children who participate.

The other supplementary intervention, consisting of summer and weekend programs, is often called *talent search.* This process selects high scorers on normally administered achievement tests, then administers the Scholastic Aptitude Test to these youngsters. Those who do well are invited to attend special weekend and summer programs. Julian Stanley developed the first program, in mathematics, at Johns Hopkins University. Today, programs are available at Duke University, Northwestern University, and the University of Denver, serving over 150,000 students annually. These talent search programs yield impressive results. In one study, 85 percent of talent search graduates finished college with an excellent record and attitude.

Applications

❶ Encourage regular classroom teachers to incorporate the best features of pullout programs into the standard classroom. There is no reason, for example, that a regular classroom teacher cannot design a long-term project on which a gifted child can work along with her non-gifted peers. However, some gifted children will prefer a more solitary and independent mode of learning, and others will resent the tendency of other students to let them do most of the work.

② Check with the education department at your local college or university and inquire about special weekend and summer programs for gifted youth.

❸ Some good information on talent search is available online at www.cmu.edu/cmites/talentsearch.html.

TOPIC 25.3 | **Changing the System of Education for Gifted Children**

The system in which a gifted child receives an education can be changed in four ways: *ability grouping, special schools, acceleration,* and *home schooling.* Ability grouping needs to be contrasted with tracking. In *tracking,* students are permanently placed in classes with peers of similar ability. In ability grouping, the grouping is ad hoc and not rigid. A special one-semester course in advanced science might be offered, then disbanded. Ability grouping can include in-class arrangements in which students at similar levels in the same classroom work together. These groupings are flexible and can change from subject to subject. Winner reports that 90 percent of U.S. elementary schools use such groupings.

A variant of ability grouping, *cooperative learning,* places a gifted child with several nongifted children. Research reports are not kind about the effects of cooperative learning on the gifted child. Although cooperative learning appears to work well with many students, gifted children tend to prefer more solitary, independent, and competitive styles; they frequently lament that they end up doing most of the work while less gifted class members remain passive. They also report being bored or resentful at having to constantly explain subtleties to less able students. Another form of ability grouping clusters gifted students from different grades and classes in a special class that is only for the gifted. The research shows that ability grouping per se achieves only modest gains. However, when it is accompanied by an appropriately challenging curriculum for the gifted students, more dramatic gains emerge.

The second method of systemic change is the special school for gifted children. Private schools have long sought out more intelligent students, but public schools for the gifted are rare except at the senior high school level. The North Carolina School for Math and Science, founded in 1980, is a model for such schools, with imitators in Texas, Illinois, and Louisiana. Although no research is available to assess the effect of these programs (research would require random assignment to these schools and to control groups, which, as Winner points out, would be politically horrendous), the dramatic success of their graduates speaks well for their effectiveness.

The third method of systemic change is acceleration. The theory behind acceleration is that moderately gifted students work more quickly than others, so they should be given a course that advances them at an accelerated pace—a year of math in a quarter, for example. Other forms of acceleration include letting students enter school early or skip grades. These techniques all seem to work well for moderately gifted students, but placing profoundly gifted children with average children several years older results in matched speed but unmatched ability in critical thinking, insight, and memory. Some gains in the speed of mental processing come with age, and putting faster young kids with older kids makes sense in that case. But the profoundly gifted are not just faster, like a computer with more processing speed. They have a different "operating system," like a computer that can perform operations, independent of speed, that lesser computers can't fathom. One possible piece of research that might explain this difference was reported in *Neuropsychology* (Vol. 18, No.2), in which mathematically gifted 13- and 14-year-olds were more able to coordinate information between the two hemispheres, or between the left and right visual fields, than ordinary students. The researchers were uncertain whether this was causal or not. More research needs to be done; now, it is just a correlation.

Jan and Bob Davidson's *Genius Denied: How to Stop Wasting Our Brightest Young Minds* (2004) and *A Nation Deceived: How Schools Hold Back America's Brightest Students,* by Nicholas Colangelo and others (full report at www.nationdeceived.org) argue that accelerating the gifted student is worth the risk of the child's losing time with age peers. Milton Gold, in his *Education of the Intellectually Gifted* (1965), wrote that "we are not aware of any other educational practice that is so well researched yet so rarely implemented." In one longitudinal study of

Australian students who had jumped at least three grade levels, the "accelerants" were more likely to attain graduate degrees than comparably gifted students who moved with their original cohorts. High-IQ cohort-bound students score on a par with younger gifted students who have been accelerated to their level, suggesting that the cohort-bound have not advanced. Accelerants score well on personal adjustment inventories and participate in extracurricular activities. Gifted children entering college tend to be isolated at the beginning of the first year but in general are reasonably well integrated by the end of that year. The key in minimizing social isolation for accelerated students is in (1) screening of accelerated candidates to see if they are sufficiently motivated and have the emotional and physical maturity to undergo the experience, and (2) careful placement and orientation by parents and professionals. In one study of adults who had experienced significant acceleration, 70 percent felt good about it; about half of the other 30 percent wished they had jumped more levels, not fewer.

Grade skipping is risky. Although some studies do show modest gains in gifted children who've skipped grades, studies also reveal an alarming number of cases in which these students develop depression and extreme stress through being placed among older students who are physically and emotionally more mature. Also, the more creative form of giftedness is based not on speed of processing but on *uniqueness* of processing. So grade skipping for many gifted children does not accomplish anything.

Many families who wish for acceleration get frustrated and opt for home schooling. With increased Internet resources and supportive agencies such as the Davidson Institute for Talent Development (Reno, Nevada; www.ditd.org), home schooling is successful for a growing number of students who would otherwise be held with their cohort because of local policy. For arguments pro and con and to identify resources, do a web search on "home schooling for gifted children."

Applications

❶ The single-shot strategy most likely to benefit all students—the gifted included—is the promotion of higher standards. Both average, moderately gifted, and profoundly gifted students at all levels would benefit from the challenge of overall higher standards of performance. Far fewer programs for the gifted are found in many Western European and East Asian school systems. These countries have generally higher standards, hence less need for gifted programs.

2 Another strategy that benefits all students, including the gifted, is flexible ability grouping. Winner (1997) calls for flexible ability grouping across grade levels, with changing placements based on need, interest, and performance.

3 Abandon the elitist term "gifted class" in favor of "advanced class" for such students.

4 Abandon IQ testing as a criterion for placement in advanced groupings, preferring evidence of interest and ability observed in the student's initial curricular experiences.

5 Encourage the formation of special schools and programs that bring the profoundly gifted together in similar age groupings.

6 On an individual level, find mentors and after-school programs that challenge young people in their area of talent.

TOPIC 25.4 Genius in Adults

As mentioned earlier, not all gifted children acquit themselves in adulthood as major contributors to society. Whether or not adult geniuses were in fact gifted as children, these preeminent minds would seem to merit discussion in a chapter about giftedness. One issue we've not addressed is whether giftedness and genius are inherited or acquired; is genius born or made—or both? Professor Michael Howe of Exeter University in England believes that the role of inheritance is overplayed. His research suggests that hard work is a big factor. He finds that geniuses share a strong sense of purpose, a strong motivation to achieve, the ability to concentrate for long periods, and the ability to resist distractions and concentrate their efforts toward specific goals. This, he argues, is evidence that one is not born with genius but rather makes oneself a genius. What Professor Howe himself underplays, however, is the role of genetics in accounting for these very traits that produce genius (see topic 33.1, topic 34.1, and "The Nature-Nurture Debate" in chapter 1). The evidence would support Howe's assertion that we are not born as accomplished geniuses, but some of us *are* born with the wherewithal to get there, whether we use it or not.

Malcolm Gladwell (in the *New Yorker,* August 2, 1999, pp. 56–65, "The Physical Genius") sought to find the common explanation of the genius of a brilliant neurosurgeon (Charlie Wilson), hockey player (Wayne Gretzky), and cellist (Yo-Yo Ma). He found that technical ability or skill was insufficient to accomplish greatness at the performance of complex physical tasks: "These abilities . . . are of little use if you don't have the right sort of personality . . . a practical-minded obsession with the possibility and the consequences of failure" (p. 60). He cites Charles Bosk, sociologist at the University of Pennsylvania, who concluded:

> When I interviewed the surgeons who were fired, I used to leave the interview shaking. . . . I would hear these horrible stories about what they did wrong, but the thing was that they didn't *know* that what they did was wrong. In my interviewing, I began to develop what I thought was an indicator of whether someone was going to be a good surgeon or not. It was a couple of simple questions: Have you ever made a mistake? And, if so, what was your worst mistake? The people who said, "Gee, I haven't really had one," or, "I've had a couple of bad outcomes but they were due to things beyond my control"—invariably those were the worst candidates. And the residents who said, "I make mistakes all the time. There was this horrible thing that happened just yesterday and here's what it was." They were the best. They had the ability to rethink everything that they'd done and imagine how they might have done it differently.

Gladwell found that his three geniuses all put in extra hours practicing basic skills in "single-minded pursuit of some fractional improvement in [their] performance. This kind of obsessive preparation does two things. It creates consistency. . . . More important, practice changes the *way* a task is perceived. A chess master, for example, can look at a game in progress for a few seconds and then perfectly reconstruct that same position on a blank chessboard. That's not because chess masters have great memories (they don't have the same knack when faced with a random arrangement of pieces) but because hours and hours of chess playing have enabled them to do what psychologists call 'chunking.'" (See topic 21.1.) He goes on to point out that the truly great physical performers, the Michael Jordans, are so practiced that they have formed hundreds and thousands of chunks, and that these chunks become so second nature, so familiar, that they are viewed as a single gestalt rather than as a collection of elements. Or, as phrased by John Bransford et al. (2000, pp. 16–17) in the National Research Council's *How People Learn*:

> A pronounced difference between experts and novices is that experts' command of concepts shapes their understanding of new information: it allows them to see patterns, relationships, or discrepancies that are not apparent to novices. They do not necessarily have better overall memories than other people. But their conceptual understanding allows them to extract a level of meaning from information that is not apparent to novices, and this helps them select and remember relevant information.

When driving through Manhattan recently, I gasped as a cab darted from lane to lane in reckless pursuit of his fare's deadline. I thought of this article, and of how the cabbie had "chunked" a vast litany of traffic configurations. Each traffic chunk he encountered was so familiar that he could instantly recognize and employ the right maneuver to get beyond it—much like the well-practiced neurosurgeon, who can be fast, daring, even creative, in performing maneuvers in the brain that less practiced surgeons would have to take step by step. As de Groot (1965, pp. 33–34) says:

> We know that increasing experience and knowledge in a specific field . . . has the effect that things . . . which, at earlier stages, had to be abstracted, or even inferred, are apt to be immediately perceived at later stages. To a rather large extent, abstraction is replaced by perception. . . . As an effect of this replacement, a so-called "given" problem situation is not really given since it is seen differently by an expert than it is perceived by an inexperienced person.

Gladwell writes that Wayne Gretzky, "hockey's greatest chunker," plays differently from most offensive players. The merely above-average hockey player gets in front of the action and makes offense a matter of a duel between himself and the goalie. Gretzky, on the other hand, holds back, letting most of the action go on between him and the goalie. Like a chess master, Gretzky is able to recognize a familiar pattern, or chunk, and instantly slam the puck either directly or indirectly to the net. "He wasn't seeing all eleven other players individually; he was seeing only chunks" (p. 63). Gladwell cites Peter Gzowski's *The Game of Our Lives*: "[Gretzky] sees not so much a set of moving players as a number of situations." In other words, Gretzky perceives immediately a pattern that others would have to study and abstract from raw data.

This intimate familiarity with one's physical environment allows the physical genius to visualize—before, during, or after—the complete process. Harvard University psychologist Stephen Kosslyn has identified four abilities that comprise this capacity to visualize:

1. To reconstruct the visual image of something on demand, or whenever one wishes to

2. To inspect the mental image closely in detail

3. To maintain the image, "in focus," for some time

4. To rotate the image, turning it around in one's mind to see what's on the other side

All four of these elements must be present for the physical genius to be creative. The capacity to visualize appears to be specific for individuals for a particular environment. For example, Gladwell relates that although brain surgeon Charlie Wilson can visualize the intricacies of what's inside the human skull, he cannot visualize the simple ballistic path of a tennis ball. Though he can be breathtakingly efficient and creative in his maneuvering around the visual image of his patient's brain, he has been unable to perform the same level of mastery in tennis; a genius at neurosurgery, he is merely competent at tennis. Chunking allows mastery but does not guarantee it. There appears to be an element of native ability, talent, or insight that permits some to attain the highest levels of mastery—but does not guarantee it. Gladwell (p. 65) quotes Yo-Yo Ma: "[I] decided I would always opt for expression over perfection." Gladwell adds, "The most successful performers improvise. They create, in Ma's words, 'something living.' Ma says he spends 90 percent of his time 'looking at the score, figuring it out—who's saying this, who wrote this and why,' letting his mind wander, and only 10 percent on the instrument itself. Like [Michael] Jordan, his genius originates principally in his imagination. If he spent less time dreaming and more time playing, he would be Karl Malone."

In summary, Gladwell argues that the physical genius—Ma, Jordan, Dr. Wilson, Gretzky—must have one thing "before any of the other layers of expertise fall into place: he had stumbled onto the one thing that, on some profound aesthetic level, made him happy" (p. 65). Figure 25.1 portrays the relationship of these ingredients of physical genius.

In his recent work, *Blink,* Gladwell (2005) writes about what enables some people—art experts, basketball stars, and so forth—to make accurate judgments based on "thin slices" of evidence. In other

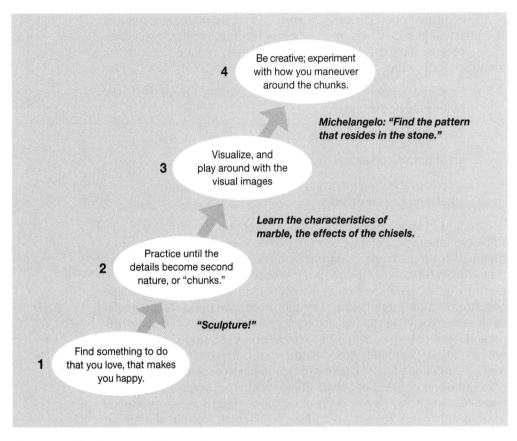

Figure 25.1. The Elements of Physical Genius

words, why is the snap judgment of some of us superior to the snap judgment of others? He concludes (p. 114) that three factors distinguish them from those who are less effective at "thin-slicing":

1. They are well-trained (similar to his description of physical geniuses in the 1999 article).

2. They practice extensively, even overpractice (also similar to the physical genius description).

3. They operate with certain rules that have become internalized (e.g., forgers of classic paintings make clean edges, whereas original artists leave rough edges).

Persons fitting such conditions are able to do such things as

- detect art forgeries with just a glance

- rate teachers' effectiveness with a two-second videotape sample

- identify personality traits by perusing someone's apartment

- correctly identify which doctors will be sued for malpractice by viewing brief videotapes of their interactions with patients

- correctly select which married couples will end up in divorce by viewing a three-minute videotape of them talking about a problem topic

- identify a tennis player about to double-fault by viewing her serve up to the point where her racket contacts the ball

Gladwell concludes that one can develop the ability to make such quick decisions, but that one must be aware of contexts in which they need to approach a decision more cautiously and thoroughly. In short, he urges a balance of thin-slicing and multi-slicing, with the guiding principle that less information is often better than more. The crucial choice for the decision maker is when to trust the more intuitive approach and when to rely on a more analytical one. When do we trust our immediate perception of patterns to be reliable? When should we pause, study, and look for the pattern that is not immediately apparent to us, that is, to abstract it from the information at hand? The guidelines of training, rules, and practice determine when and what to thin-slice.

In support of Gladwell's observations, psychology professors Justin Kruger (University of Illinois at Urbana–Champaign) and David Dunning (Cornell University) report (in the *Journal of Personality and Social Psychology,* December 1999) that competent people tend to *underestimate* their actual level of performance, and that less-than-competent people are clueless. Apparently, Kruger and Dunning conclude, the skills required for competence (critical thinking, self-assessment, receptivity to feedback, and so forth) are deficient in the less-than-competent, and provoke a double-whammy effect: deficiency in these skills limits not only the ability to improve, but the ability to recognize the need for improvement! To test this hypothesis, he assessed the less-than-competent who overestimated their ability. He administered tests on logic, grammar, and humor, and these "clueless" subjects scored in the bottom quartile on each. On the positive side, Dunning has found that training the less-than-competent in critical thinking appears to help them abandon, at least partially and temporarily, their inflated, unrealistic notions of themselves. Psychologists refer to the assumption of competence in the absence of clear evidence to the contrary as the *false consensus effect.* One of the more effective training techniques was to have the clueless persons compare their own work (grammar, humor, logic) directly with the work of more competent persons. Had quite a sobering effect!

This line of thinking is further supported by Winner (2000), who concludes that giftedness is the result of native ability coupled with hard work. She also emphasizes that giftedness is typically limited to a domain and is not a blank ticket. In support of Gladwell, Oliver Sacks (2004) describes the high-performance athlete: "In a bicycle race, cyclists may be moving at nearly 40 miles per hour, separated only by inches. The situation, to an onlooker, looks precarious in the extreme, and, indeed, the cyclists may be mere milliseconds away from each other. The slightest error may lead to a multiple crash. But to the cyclists themselves, concentrating intensely, everything seems to be moving in relatively slow motion, and there is ample room and time, enough to allow improvisation and intricate maneuverings. . . . The expertise of athletes (whatever their innate gifts) is only to be acquired by years of dedicated practice and training. At first, an intense conscious effort and attention are necessary to learn every nuance of technique and timing. But at some point the basic skills and their neural representation become so ingrained in the nervous system as to be almost second nature, no longer in need of conscious effort or decision. One level of brain activity may be working automatically, while another, the conscious level, is fashioning a perception of time, a perception which is elastic, and can be compressed or expanded" (p. 63). Sacks continues: "The dazzling performances of chess masters, lightning-speed calculators, musical improvisers, and other virtuosos may have less to do with basic neural speed than with the vast range of knowledge, memorized patterns and strategies, and hugely sophisticated skills they can call upon. . . . And this is equally so of a comic genius like Robin Williams, whose explosive, incandescent flights of association and wit seem to take off and hurtle along at rocket-like speeds. Yet here, presumably, one is dealing not with the speeds of individual nerve cells and simple circuits but with neural networks of a much higher order, exceeding the complexity of the largest supercomputer" (p. 69).

Applications

❶ Be aware of the areas of your professional or personal life in which you possess the three requirements for snap judgments. In what areas have you (a) been trained extensively, (b) formulated reliable rules for informing judgment, and (c) practiced applying your training and rules with a record of good judgments?

❷ If you aspire to genius, you must be prepared to overpractice, to put in the hours that the merely above-average do not, and especially to be keenly aware of your imperfections, of opportunities for improvement.

Giftedness, Adulthood, and Eminence

Unfortunately, giftedness does not necessarily lead to eminence in adulthood. A high IQ in youth does not automatically translate into major contributions to one's field as an adult. Barron and Harrington (1981) have found that when IQ scores exceed 120, they fail to predict adult eminence. To quote Winner (1997, p. 1073): "[People] with IQs of 170 or above were no more likely to become eminent than were those with lower IQs. . . . Most gifted children do not grow into eminent adults and do not ever make major contributions to the way people think about a particular domain."

Why is this true? Two explanations push to the fore. First, eminence is based on more than verbal, numerical, and spatial reasoning, which is the bulk of what traditional IQ tests measure. What Sternberg calls "successful" intelligence does not require high scores on verbal and numerical reasoning. Rather, it requires a profound ability to sense the unique needs of a situation and to arrive at the interventions that will advance toward the goals implicit in that situation. So the first explanation has to do with the narrow definition currently used for giftedness: we do not identify as gifted, for example, young people who have profound gifts on the leadership scale.

Second, again quoting Winner, eminence requires "creativity, dissatisfaction with the status quo, and a desire to shake things up, and these personality traits are not necessarily reflected in high academic achievement or high IQ" (p. 1073). Often, the problems gifted children have in social development lead them wide of the path of social contribution.

SUGGESTED RESOURCES

Barron, F., and D. M. Harrington (1981). "Creativity, Intelligence, and Personality." *Annual Review of Psychology,* 32, 439–476.

Rogers, K. B. (1986). "Do the Gifted Think and Learn Differently? A Review of Recent Research and Its Implications for Instruction." *Journal for the Education of the Gifted,* 10, 17–39.

Winner, E. (1996). *Gifted Children: Myths and Realities.* New York: Basic Books.

Winner, E. (1997, October). "Exceptionally High Intelligence and Schooling." *American Psychologist,* 52(10), 1070–1081.

26

Building Babel

Acquiring and Developing Language

> **❝Sticks and stones may break my bones, but words will never hurt me. ❞**
>
> —Children's rhyme

> **❝Words are heavy things. If birds talked, they couldn't fly. ❞**
>
> —Marilyn, in Northern Exposure

The first of the two opening quotations for this chapter reflects the old thinking about language; the second is closer to what we know today about the mind-body relationship. Language clearly has the force to alter the physical composition of the body. Malevolent, adulatory, and romantic words alike have the power to alter the balance of chemical neurotransmitters.

Stroking words provide the glue that holds groups together. In fact, Robin Dunbar, in his book *Grooming, Gossip, and the Evolution of Language* (1997), proposes that by measuring the size of the neocortex in various mammals, we can estimate the maximum size of a group in which a mammal can sustain enough grooming behavior to keep the group cooing. According to his formula, the human's neocortex can handle a group of about 150. Beyond that size, he maintains, an individual would have to spend an inordinate amount of time making lubricative chitchat. Chitchat, of course, is a form of grooming—the human equivalent of chimps checking each other for nits. Threatening and hateful words can so disorient the hearer that poisonous toxins affect the sense of balance and timing, leading to accidents that break bones. Indeed, words can be heavy things.

If the eyes are windows to the soul, then words are windows to the self. In fact, the paradigm for personality traits that is sweeping the field of personality research—the Five-Factor Model (see chapter 33)—is based on the assumption that there is sufficient information in language to describe individual differences in personality. That is, the synonym clusters found by factor-analyzing language can adequately describe similarities and differences in personality. Other theories are nothing more than interacting patterns of synonym clusters, and any theory of personality must take these clusters into account.

This chapter serves to highlight current knowledge about how we acquire and develop language. Before presenting specific findings, let's take a brief look at the physical structures that are responsible for language. Most of the action occurs in the *perisylvian area* of the left hemisphere (see appendix A). The front of this area (*Broca's area*) is primarily responsible for grammar and speech, the rear part (*Wernicke's area*) for word sounds and meanings. This holds for sign language as well as spoken language. Because the right hemisphere is the site of visual-spatial activity, one might logically (but incorrectly!) assume that sign language is associated with right-hemisphere activity. However, as Steven Pinker (1994, p. 302) puts it, "Language, whether by ear and mouth or by eye and hand, is controlled by the left hemisphere."

Hormones also play a significant role in language development and mastery. As mentioned in topic 13.6, the quality of language execution in both sexes can vary with estrogen levels, higher levels being associated with better "languaging," just as higher levels of androgens are associated with better "mathing." Medical researcher Sally Shaywitz of Yale University has established (in *JAMA,* April 1999) that estrogen replacement in postmenopausal women results in improved verbal performance. Shaywitz and her team are studying whether dyslexia, which is more common among males, is related to lower levels of estrogen.

Traditionally, philosophers and artists have proclaimed that language was what made us uniquely human. In recent years, animal trainers have asserted that chimps and other primates can be taught both sign language and spoken language. Pinker evaluates these claims with a resounding *Nyet!* and declares that chimp talk is now a "thing of the past" (1994, p. 341). At some point in our ancestry, around 200,000 years ago, a series of minute changes over time resulted in our gift of language: "the ability to dispatch an infinite number of precisely structured thoughts from head to head by modulating exhaled breath" (p. 362).

TOPIC 26.1   How Language Grows Up

Pinker (1994) writes that live spoken language is critical to the child's learning. In studies where deaf parents had their hearing children listen to television, the children did not learn the language. "Motherese" is best; it is slower, more grammatical, more varied in pitch, and pointed more directly to the here and now of the child than is "televisionese." The language does not have to be mother's speech, however: in some cultures, older children are expected to train the wee ones, with the mother putting off her chat with the new child until it can hold its own.

Betty Hart, an assistant professor of human development, and Todd Risley, an adjunct professor of human development, both at the University of Kansas at Lawrence, studied 42 children of welfare, professional, and working-class parents (reported by Sandra Blakeslee in the *New York Times,* April 17, 1997, p. 21D). They describe the following patterns during the first 2½ years of life:

- Children of professional parents hear an average of 2,100 words per hour.

- Children of working-class parents hear 1,200 words per hour.

- Children of welfare parents hear 600 words per hour.

- Professional parents talk directly to their children three times as much as parents in the other two categories.

- Children of professional parents get positive feedback ("Atta-kid!") 30 times per hour, twice as frequently as working-class children and five times more than welfare children.

Hart and Risley (1995) conclude that these language patterns account for much of the large gap that favors professional parents' children in measurements of mental ability at age three.

Although human talk is mandatory for language learning in infants, apparently the correction of grammatical mistakes is not a requirement. As Pinker reports, the research leaves no doubt that children tune out others' evaluation of their grammar. The primary corrective role of the parent appears to be to clarify the truthfulness and propriety of what the child says. In response to a child's "She not here—she gone," for example, a parent might respond either "Yes" or "No, I think *she's* in the bedroom." Apparently, explicit corrections do not affect the learning of standard forms; it is the effect of hearing the standard form enough times for it to stick.

Well, let's start at the beginning of language acquisition. The following list traces the significant steps involved in the development of individual language ability:

In the womb. Pinker (1994, p. 264) cites evidence that the embryo learns the *prosody* (melody and rhythm) of its mother's tongue while in the womb.

Birth. Children are born with the ability to discriminate phonemes (p. 264); they must babble in order to ultimately be able to match the sounds made by their parents. Peter Jusczyk, a Johns Hopkins University professor of psychology, has established that infants in the first year learn to recognize and then store names (or words) before actually associating them with particular objects (Beth Azar, in *APA Monitor*, January 1996, p. 20).

Twelve months. Children begin to learn and use single words (half are for objects, the remainder for actions and social routines). The one-word stage lasts from two months to a year. Some infants show a preference for object words, others for social-routine words. (This is probably related to personality traits.) Phonetic discrimination begins to decrease (see topic 26.8 for a discussion of neuronal commitment).

Eighteen months. Children begin to learn and use two-word phrases; they are now learning words at a minimum of one every two hours.

Thirty-three to forty-two months. Sentence length increases, and sentence types increase exponentially, with children attaining several thousand sentence types by age three. Pinker says, "For any [grammatical] rule you choose, three-year-olds obey it most of the time" (1994, p. 271).

Four years. Every language—German, Chinese, Thompson, English, Arabic—is acquired by a native language learner with ease by the age of four.

Six years. Children have an average vocabulary of 13,000 words, with a word being equal to one root (*sail, sailboat,* and *boat* would count as two words) or one derivative (a word that cannot be understood from the root alone, as in *forestaysail,* a type of triangular sail); this is a rather conservative estimate.

Seven years. Immigrants joining a new language culture up to the age of seven can learn the new language's grammar like a native. From age eight onward, one's ability to learn to speak a new language like a native steadily decreases. For fine phonetic discriminations, learning ability decreases around 10 months to one year. According to University of Chicago researchers Peter Huttenlocher and Arun Dabholkar, however, the auditory cortex continues with a high level of activity until around the age of 12. They have found that young people can learn to speak a language accent-free until then, with, of course, a range of individual differences. Using functional magnetic resonance imaging (fMRI) techniques, Joy Hirsch, a neuroscientist and head of the fMRI Lab at Memorial Sloan-Kettering Hospital, found that bilingual adults who learned two languages as infants had one single brain area—Broca's area—for both languages, whereas those who learned two languages at age 11 had two separate areas, one Broca's area for each language, although they were similar in size and near each other (*Nature,* July 1997).

Eighteen years. The average high school graduate knows 60,000 words (with probably twice as many for brighter students who read more); this pace would entail learning about 10 words each day, roughly one each hour and a half (excluding sleep).

The University of Kansas conducted a study in which parents tape-recorded all their interactions with their children from infancy (*Science,* August 17, 1996, pp. 100 ff.). Researchers measured the children's intelligence at ages three and nine. They found that "total talk

time" was a better predictor of children's IQ than parents' socioeconomic status, employment status, or degree of education.

Applications

❶ In order to learn a language (spoken or signed) like a native, the
learner must start by the age of six.

❷ Do not rely on television, radio, or other electronic media to teach language to your children. Talk with them and allow them to be around others who will talk with them.

❸ Realize that children learn a new word every 1½–2 hours. Don't rest
on your laurels when your child learns a new word. You've got about nine
more to go for the day!

❹ When a child makes a grammatical error, do not make a point of correcting the error. Simply continue to speak correctly, and the child will
pick it up. If you cannot resist the urge to correct a child's grammar, try
restating the error in a low-key, correct manner. For example, when a
child says, "The cat goed away," say matter-of-factly, "Yes, the cat went
to find a rat." Make explicit corrections only for errors of fact ("No, the cat
is in the corner") or propriety (if the child says, "I pulls the tail on the cat,"
say, "No, don't pull the cat's tail. It might hurt him"). Priorities become obvious when the child makes an error in grammar and fact or propriety at
the same time, as in "I wants to play in the oven." Clearly you shouldn't
confuse the child by replying, "No, you *want* to play in the oven."

❺ Support any legislation or other social initiative that increases the
quality and quantity of adult language that children of working-class and
welfare parents hear and interact with. I remember the day I dropped off
our two girls at a new day care program. I walked the two—ages three
and five—into the center, only to see the welcoming staffer whisk them
into a dark room where all were watching noneducational television.
I immediately took the girls back to the car and to work with me, back
to the drawing board for finding a proper option. We ended up with Mrs.
Freeman's Little Folks, a no-TV program that featured gardening, make-
your-own-snacks, Wendy house, and so forth.

TOPIC 26.2   The Case for a Universal Grammar

Steven Pinker (1994) makes a compelling case that a single "universal grammar" explains how all languages work with just two rules. The first rule states: "A phrase consists of an optional subject, followed by an X-bar, followed by any number of modifiers" (p. 110). The second rule states: "An X-bar consists of a head X [noun, verb, preposition, or adjective] and any number of role-players, in either order" (p. 111).

These rules are true for every language (p. 111), according to Pinker. And, although this suggests a universal genetic predisposition toward these two rules for the human species, there is no relationship between genetic structure and the ability to learn a specific language. Up through the time of neuronal commitment (see topic 26.8), any child can learn any language, given a normal brain. As Pinker enjoys commenting, much to the chagrin of Francophiles, French genes are not required for learning French! The learning of a specific grammar is purely environmental. Or, as Pinker puts it: "People store genes in their gonads and pass them to their children through their genitals; they store grammars in their brains and pass them to their children through their mouths" (p. 258).

Application

❶ Be assured that any child can learn any language, independent of the child's genetic makeup. All children have a language instinct based on a universal grammar, and all languages reflect this universal grammar.

TOPIC 26.3   Teaching Reading

Two rival approaches to the teaching of reading—*phonics* and *whole language*—have struggled for ascendancy in the form of publishers who wish to dominate the textbook market. Research slightly favors the whole-language approach, yet an enlightened approach would appear to use a combination of word-attack skills (phonics, in which students are taught, for example, that *p* is said as "puh") and word-recognition (whole-language) skills. A research project conducted by Jenifer Katahira of Pasadena, California (who teaches kindergarten as well as teachers of reading), and psychologist Virginia Berninger of the

University of Washington established the superiority of the whole-language approach in raising student achievement. Berninger is teaming up with Wendy Raskind, a geneticist at the University of Washington School of Medicine, to investigate the possibility of identifying potentially poor readers through brain scan techniques and treating them with gene replacement therapy. Look for the results!

Application

❶ When teaching reading, emphasize word-recognition (whole-language) techniques, but teach word-attack skills (phonics) to the students who respond well to it. Don't browbeat kids who find phonics aversive; just focus on whole-language techniques.

TOPIC 26.4   "Speed" Reading

Back in the 1950s, the U.S. Department of the Navy studied the effectiveness of so-called speed reading programs and found that they were neither more nor less than skimming techniques. Students were trained to read topic sentences (the first and last in the paragraph), and the comprehension tests used to evaluate the training only questioned the content in these sentences. When students were tested on material that was scattered randomly throughout the reading passages, comprehension plummeted.

More recently, University of Missouri at Kansas City educational psychologist Ronald Carver (1990) published a review of research on reading speed. Several findings emerged:

- The normal reading speed is 200 to 300 words per minute.

- Faster speeds involve skipping words.

- Skipping words results in decreased comprehension.

Applications

❶ When you are reading only to find new information on a subject you are already familiar with, then skimming (reading faster than 300 words per minute) makes sense.

2 When you are reading for detailed understanding of a more unfamiliar subject, you should slow down your reading, probably below 200 words per minute.

3 For most other reading, accept the typical rate of 200 to 300 words per minute.

4 Don't claim to read at a thousand or more words per minute. That's not reading, according to research; it's skimming. Calling it "speed reading" is like referring to microwaving a dinner-in-a-box as "cooking." It's not; it's nuking or warming.

TOPIC 26.5 | Writer's Block

The principle of focused attention (see topic 21.9) applies to the common problem of *writer's block*—the experience of wanting to write yet failing to come up with the requisite words. Albert Joseph, in his popular business writing workshop entitled "Put It in Writing," advises the would-be writer that this inability to get words to flow can be attributed to the attempt to do two things at once—namely, to determine both the *how* and the *what.* The *what* refers to the content (facts, concepts, and stories); the *how* refers to the style (word choice, sentence structure, and point of view). Joseph argues that the brain is trying to do two things at once, like listening to the radio and reading a book. Joseph suggests that first establishing the *what* will remedy the problem.

Application

1 When you face a writing task and can't quite get started, try making a list of all the subjects you want to cover. Then sequence the items in the list. The "mind map" (see topic 29.3) is an effective technique for this kind of outlining. It employs a much more forgiving format than the traditional outline (I.a., I.b., II.a., II.b. . . .).

TOPIC 26.6   Language and Mood

Activity in the left hemisphere of the brain (measured as glucose consumption) accompanies positive emotions such as cheerfulness and approach behaviors (see the closing comments in chapter 2). Negative emotions and avoidance behaviors are associated with right-brain activity (Fox, 1991; Gazzaniga, 1985). The language region of the brain is located in the vicinity of the left *perisylvian fissure,* and the evidence points to the positive effect of language (reading, talking, writing) on mood.

Application

❶ Try writing (letters, a journal, your autobiography, a biography, or some other genre) or talking (to a friend, family member, child, stranger in a pub, or other person) as a way to improve your mood. Talking or writing typically gets you out of the doldrums.

TOPIC 26.7   Language and Memory

William Levelt, director of the Max Planck Institute for Psycholinguistics in Nijmegen, the Netherlands, has identified three interactive networks that account for the process of thinking up words to use in everyday speech (reported by Sandra Blakeslee in the *New York Times,* September 26, 1995, p. Cl). He calls these systems the lexical network, the lemma network, and the lexeme network. The *lexical network* is the first to activate as we think up what we want to say. This node stores meanings, or definitions, but not the words themselves. That is why, when we are trying to think up a word, we can see, smell, or hear what the word we want is associated with. Speakers who use gender words (*le* and *la*; *der, die,* and *das*) can even know the gender without knowing the word! This lexical node includes links with synonyms.

The *lemma network* applies the speaker's language syntax rules (such as verb form, case, and gender) to the meaning. Often, when we have many associations with the sought-after word, we experience the "tip of the tongue" (or, for the deaf, the "tip of the finger") sensation. Competition occurs, and the word we want does not always make it to consciousness. Then we have to "reboot" in hopes that a fresh start will permit the desired word to surface.

The third network, the *lexeme network,* applies sounds, or *phonemes,* to the word-meaning that wins the competition, and—voilà!—we say the word. This helps to explain how, when we are unable to form a word, we can often uncover it by running mentally through the alphabet. This alphabet run-through helps us tag the right phoneme to the one word-meaning out of several that are vying for attention. Levelt argues that the speed of neuronal transmission does not slow down as we age, but the larger number of associations we have, combined with some loss of connections and remoteness of the use of a given word, typically require more processing time. Levelt finds that a speaker can generally form two to three words per second—10 to 15 syllables. The average time required for naming is 0.07 seconds.

Application

❶ Don't worry when you can't form a word; just be amused at the silent competition being waged in your left hemisphere. Leave it and come back to it later; often, just giving it time will work. If all else fails, silently say the letters of the alphabet slowly from *a* to *z* (or whatever the letters are in your current language) once, then a second time if necessary. These silent phonemes act like magnets to draw out the word-meanings vying for recognition. Be patient: remember that more commonly used words take less time and effort to form. As we age, the number of our associations, hence the scope of the competition, becomes immense, so the processing time is longer.

TOPIC 26.8 **Neuronal Commitment and Later Language Learning**

A kind of commitment of neurons—those involved in hearing subtle differences in sounds—appears to be made in humans sometime between 8 and 12 months of age. Once they are committed, the neurons ignore unfamiliar stimuli. Janet Werker of the University of British Columbia in Vancouver finds that babies who are exposed only to English from birth can recognize consonants that do not occur in English from the language of the Thompson tribe (located in the Thompson and Fraser valleys of southwest British Columbia) up until 8 months of age, but at 12 months they can no longer distinguish them. Steven Pinker (1994) reports that with less drastic subtleties in phonetic differences, one can learn to speak a non-native language like a native speaker up through age seven. Apparently, then, different levels of neuronal commitment are operating.

Jay McClelland, professor of cognitive neuroscience at Carnegie-Mellon and co-director of Pittsburgh's Center for the Neural Basis of Cognition, is leading a research team studying brain plasticity. Intrigued by the difficulty adult non-native language learners have in learning such sounds as the English *th,* the Spanish *d,* and the Finnish *o,* they designed a protocol aimed at breaking through the non-native's neural commitment to make room for new sounds. In a protocol for Japanese natives to learn the English *l* and *r,* three 20-minute sessions using headphones and audiotapes progressed from computer-generated exaggerated, slowed-down sounds that highlighted the components of the two sounds, through to normal speech, and on to the more difficult sounds of slang, regional, and substandard speech. This experimental group showed significant gains, while controls stayed the same or got worse. The control group also heard tapes, but using only standard speech. McClelland believes this intense, multi-sided approach has promise for other problems of apparent neuronal commitment and lack of plasticity, such as stereotypes and low self-esteem. I'm reminded of its similarity to two other techniques: brain-washing and successive approximation (the "shaping" response used in phobia and anxiety reduction). The goal of these trainings has one purpose in common: to provide the individual with a new set of neural connections that can stand on their own against previous learning.

In related research, Quartz and Sejnowski (2002, pp. 42–43), report that Paula Tallal and Mike Merzenich have found that stretching out sounds, then successively speeding them up, helps students with reading problems learn to recognize basic phonic elements. They have developed a computer program that uses this procedure to apparently restructure the brains of reading-impaired students (reported in *Science,* Vol. 271, 1996, pp. 81–84). Their company, Scientific Learning Corporation, sells this and other programs as their Fast ForWord series. For the more than 100,000 students who have benefited from it, reading has improved from one to four grade levels, with accompanying visible changes in brain processes.

Applications

❶ Expose your infants repeatedly to the universe of sounds that he will need to use later in life—not just language, but musical instruments, bird-song, and other sounds.

❷ Identify the languages that your children will most benefit from speaking later in life, and get them started speaking them before the age of seven.

❸ For adults having trouble learning the sounds of a second language, either figure out on your own how to implement McClelland's approach, or find out more by visiting his site at **www.cnbc.cmu.edu/~jlm**, where he lists articles, books, and software. He calls his approach "Parallel Distributed Processing."

❹ Find out more about Fast ForWord at **www.scilearn.com**. Or just slow things down!

SUGGESTED RESOURCES

Carver, R. (1990). *Reading Rate: A Review of Research and Theory.* Orlando: Academic Press.

Dunbar, R. (1997). *Grooming, Gossip, and the Evolution of Language.* Cambridge, Mass.: Harvard University Press.

Hart, B., and T. Risley (1995). *Meaningful Differences in the Everyday Experiences of Young American Children.* Baltimore: P. H. Brooks.

Pinker, S. (1994). *The Language Instinct.* New York: Morrow.

Part Seven

Creativity and Problem Solving

*Making
Mountains
Out of Hills*

Part Seven. Creativity and Problem Solving
Making Mountains Out of Hills

27

Getting to New You

The Psychobiology of Creativity

> 66 *'Tis wise*
> *to learn;*
> *'tis godlike*
> *to create!* 99
>
> —*John Godfrey Saxe*

*T*he call for creativity strikes fear in some while arousing enthusiasm in others. Why? This chapter addresses that question, based on the current state of research on creativity.

TOPIC 27.1   The Creative Act

Teresa Amabile, a leading researcher in creativity, has defined creativity conceptually as follows (1983, p. 33): "A product or response will be judged as creative to the extent that (a) it is both a novel and appropriate, useful, correct or valuable response to the task at hand, and (b) the task is heuristic rather than algorithmic" (see topic 29.4). She then identifies three criteria for distinguishing more creative contributions from less creative ones: (1) novelty (we haven't seen or heard this before), (2) relevance (it relates to satisfying the need that originally prompted the contribution), and (3) spontaneity (the contributor didn't use a formula to "mechanically" come up with the contribution).

Margaret Boden (1990), thinking in parallel with Amabile, distinguishes between *psychological creativity* and *historical creativity*. The first is merely something new for the individual doing the creating; the second is something new for humanity. To quote Boden: "A merely novel idea is one which can be described and/or produced by the same set of generative rules as are other, familiar ideas. A genuinely original, or creative, idea is one which cannot" (p. 40). Robert Sternberg (in *Review of General Psychology,* Vol. 3, No. 2, 1999, pp. 83–100) expands on the nature of relevance by specifying seven different ways that a creative act can relate to the tradition of an ongoing domain:

1. *Conceptual replication,* in which one attempts to repeat an earlier study to determine whether its results were a fluke or are here to stay.

2. *Redefinition,* in which one finds a new meaning or application for an established entity.

3. *Forward incrementation,* in which one takes an established paradigm to a higher level.

4. *Advance forward incrementation,* in which one takes an established paradigm to a level higher than its advocates are willing to take it.

5. *Redirection,* in which one builds on previous work, but in a different direction.

6. *Reconstruction and redirection,* in which one takes a defunct entity, resurrects it, modernizes it, and claims that it still has value.

7. *Re-initiation,* in which one approaches something in a radically different way and direction from current practice.

Sternberg points out that the first three tend to be nonthreatening and are relatively easy to accept, whereas the last four tend to be resisted because they threaten those currently at work in the field.

How do we know whether or not a contribution possesses novelty, relevance, and spontaneity? Amabile (1983, p. 31) proposes a consensual definition: "A product or response is creative to the extent that appropriate observers independently agree it is creative. Appropriate observers are those familiar with the domain in which the product was created or the response articulated." Her definition reflects Aristotle's comment in the *Rhetoric* that he can't tell how to make good art; he can only describe the art that observers over the ages have agreed upon as good.

Application

❶ The merely novel is often represented to us as being creative. Novelty by itself, however, is an insufficient basis on which to judge something as being creative. Novelty without relevance falls somewhere between whimsy and the psychotic. Novelty without spontaneity is tiresomely formulaic; it leads viewers to respond, "I could have done that myself"—for example, after seeing a painting with a repeating pattern of colors and squares or hearing a 12-tone-row composition. The classic example of nonspontaneous art is "painting by the numbers." Stress the necessity for all three elements—novelty, relevance, and spontaniety—either in your own creative processes or in those of your students, co-workers, and children.

TOPIC 27.2 **The Psychology of the Creative Personality**

Amabile (1983) identifies three components of creativity in individuals: *domain-relevant skills, creativity-relevant skills,* and *task motivation.* These three components must all be present for an individual to be fully creative.

To have domain-relevant skills, the individual must possess the knowledge, technical skills, and special talents peculiar to the domain in which he wishes to be creative. Without this, it may be easy to create novel and spontaneous contributions, but relevance will be, at best, random. The presence of these skills depends on innate logical ability and information-processing skills, as well as on formal and informal education. Amabile defines a *talent* as a skill in which an individual has an apparently natural ability. Thus, someone can play the piano technically well but have no talent for it, leaving listeners less than impressed. Or a person can master the technical side of a welding process but, without a talent for it, can be frustratingly error-prone. This definition of talent fits well with Gardner's definition of the eight domains of intelligence (summarized in topic 34.4).

Amabile identifies three groups of creativity-relevant skills:

1. ***Cognitive style.*** This area includes the ability and willingness to break perceptual sets (as opposed to functional fixedness), be comfortable with complexity, hold options open and not push for closure, suspend judgment rather than reacting to things as good or bad, be comfortable with wider categories, develop an accurate memory, abandon or suspend performance scripts, and see things differently from others.

2. ***Knowledge of heuristics.*** *Heuristics* are insightful tips for coming up with new ideas (for a more detailed treatment of heuristics, see topic 29.4). Probably the most famous heuristic comes out of the neurolinguistic programming literature: "If what you're doing is not working, try something different." This is based on the axiom "If you always do what you've always done, you'll always get what you've always gotten." A dated but highly effective introduction to heuristics is Zuce Kogan's *Essentials in Problem Solving* (1956). Also full of insightful tips are Adams (1980), Bandler and Grinder (1982), de Bono (1967), M. Fisher (1981), P. Goldberg (1983), and von Oech (1983).

3. ***Work style.*** A positive work style consists of the ability to sustain long periods of concentration, the ability to abandon nonproductive approaches, persistence during difficulty, a high energy level, and a willingness to work hard.

Amabile finds that two prerequisites determine our level of performance in these three areas of creativity-relevant skills: *experience* and *personality traits*. Experience in generating ideas in and out of the classroom contributes heavily to a person's creativity. You can't do it unless you've done it! Among the personality traits critical to creativity-relevant skills are

- Self-discipline

- Delay of gratification

- Perseverance

- Independent judgment

- Tolerance for ambiguity

- Autonomy

- Absence of sex-role stereotyping

- Internal locus of control (seeing self as responsible for one's own fate)

- Willingness to take risks

- Ability to be a self-starter

- Absence of conformity to social pressure

Amabile has found that the creative personality must also have task motivation, or a positive attitude toward the task—that is, she must want to do it. An unwillingness to do a task results in measurably lower creativity, using the standards of novelty, relevance, and spontaneity. Research has also conclusively demonstrated that internal motivation (see topic 30.2) is a prerequisite for creative behavior. Internal motivation (doing something because we want to) produces greater novelty, domain relevance, and spontaneity than external motivation (doing something because a boss, spouse, or teacher wants us to). If we perceive that we are doing something because we want to, even if another person wants it also, then creativity is enhanced. The highest creativity occurs when we discover the need for a creative response ourselves and choose to contribute independent of any possible external constraints. When external constraints, such as deadlines, rewards, or punishers, are imposed on a personally desirable task, creativity can still flourish if we are able to cognitively minimize the constraints. When we are unable to forget about them, creativity suffers.

Eisenberger and Cameron (1996) offer a different view on the subject of rewards. Their analysis suggests that the only detrimental effects of rewards on creative behavior occur when the rewards are handed out regardless of the quality of the creative output. I must qualify their finding, however, by observing that their article reads more like a diatribe against cognitive science and an apologia for behaviorism.

The one exception to the negative effect of external motivation is a situation in which the guidelines for success are carefully spelled out. For example, a school art contest or a sales force contest with specific rules and guidelines can generate creative behavior. The guidelines can free us to be spontaneous and novel within a clearly defined playing field. Apparently, the rules have the effect of increasing both the perceived fairness of the contest and our perceived chances of winning.

More recent research has added nuance to Amabile's findings. Eisenberger and Cameron (1996) report that it is not rewards for excellent performance but the less discriminating rewards for daily effort that deter creative achievement. However, Carol Dweck, a psychologist at Columbia University, has found that rewards for effort are more encouraging in the long run than rewards for success. Research suggests that no one general rule defines the best way to encourage creative excellence. People are different. Do what works. To encourage creativity in a person, choose rewards that appeal to her personality. Reward extraverts with a party, introverts with a good book! However, if I had to state a general rule, it would go something like this: avoid overly controlling people, emphasize verbal encouragement, and limit rewards to exceptional occasions (of either special effort or special achievement).

Applications

❶ If you expect others to be creative, take the time to develop their buy-in. Negotiate with them until you perceive that they want to do the task and feel in control of the process. Avoid setting goals and methods *for* others if you expect creative behavior; set them *with* others in joint discussions and mutual agreements. Setting goals unilaterally typically breeds fears and resentments that stifle creativity.

❷ In looking for creative talent, value technical expertise (domain-relevant skills) as much as the more creative behaviors.

❸ In looking for creative talent, look for indications that the individual is a self-starter who can work without close supervision.

❹ Reward creativity after the fact rather than before. Working for a reward generally stifles creativity, whereas unexpected rewards encourage further creativity. On the other hand, always rewarding creativity will stifle it in the long run, because the reward becomes expected. Usually, it is best to just be comfortable accepting creative people's own satisfaction with their contribution. Many creative people report discomfort, even resentment, when a to-do is made over their contributions. It is the creative process itself that is rewarding, and they are eager to return to it.

⑤ If you are commissioning a problem-solving team, ensure that they understand their goal and have management support to implement their solution. If their solution has limits (for example, the project can't cost over $10,000), state them up front. *(Contributed by Rick Bradley)*

⑥ Review the discussion of genius at topic 25.4. The difference between creativity and genius is primarily one of degree, with the requirements for creativity outlined in this chapter taken to the extreme.

TOPIC 27.3 **The Biology of the Creative Personality**

Whatever finally comes to be established as the biological basis of creativity, it will certainly be a composite of three of the Big Five personality factors (see chapter 33): the Explorer, the Challenger, and the Flexible. Although the precise biological foundation has not been finally defined, many elements of that foundation have been tentatively identified. The Explorer trait (high in the Originality trait) is probably related to higher acetylcholine, calpain, and kinase C levels, with the key biological difference between Exploring and Preserving lying in the degree of complexity of the synaptic connections. Inasmuch as the corpus callosum (see appendix A) is thicker in right-brain-dominant people, we will probably find it thicker in creative minds. In addition, research has revealed that more imaginative people have higher levels of dopamine, a neurotransmitter associated with inducing the state of mind that (1) visualizes easily (daydreams, hallucinates, and so forth), and (2) continually invites one to ask the question, "What if I. . . ?" Dopamine has often been referred to as the "curiosity" chemical. The Challenger trait will probably be found to have as its basis low serotonin and endorphin levels. In fact, many creative personalities (see Amabile, 1983) report the need to calm down for work by doing something special, such as meditation or music. This suggests less active opioid receptors than the norm. Challenger behaviors in both men and women are associated with levels of testosterone that are higher than normal, relative to estrogen levels. Finally, the Flexible trait is related to lower testosterone and higher dopamine levels (Geen, Beatty, and Arkin, 1984). Candace Pert, who led the Johns Hopkins University team that isolated endorphin receptors in the brain, reportedly is working on a "creativity pill" that could enhance one's ability, for example, to *bisociate*—that is, to combine features of two distinct objects to form a third, new one, as when Gutenberg conceived the printing press from features of the grape press and the coin stamp. Pert was celebrated in the movie *What the Bleep Do We Know?*

On a molecular plane, creativity can be described as a function of alpha waves, which occur somewhere between alertness and sleep (Goleman, Kaufman, and Ray, 1992). Thomas Edison built this fact into his Menlo Park invention center in the following manner: he would sit in a comfortable chair, arms draped over the sides, holding heavy metal balls in his hands poised directly above two metal pans. He would attempt to doze, until he was startled into waking by the sound of the balls landing in the pans. At this moment, he reports, he had his best creative insights. Robert Epstein (1996) relates that Salvador Dali would lie on a sofa, hold a spoon so that it balanced lightly over the edge of a glass on the floor, then try to reach the "hypnagogic" state. When the spoon clanked into the glass, he roused himself and captured any ideas that had been generated. I wonder if one learned from the other? At any rate, we relinquish control of our mental processes in this brain state. On the continuum from tight mental self-control to the loss of control we experience in sleep, creativity occurs toward the sleep end of the continuum. I personally find that napping serves the same purpose. I like to time my daily 10-minute naps (really just lying down on the floor and settling into alpha state) to follow a time of intense preparation and to precede a need for creative insight and analysis.

Applications

1 The diet to increase creativity is no different from the diet recommended for overall good health (see table 7.1). A word of warning, however: consumption of high-glycemic carbohydrates and fats tends to interfere with creative activity by reducing arousal, whereas consumption of proteins and low-glycemic carbohydrates, unless it is excessive, has no apparent negative impact on arousal.

2 Creative episodes are most productive when they are preceded by some form of meditation or aerobic exertion. Richard Restak (1991) calls this an *attentional*—as opposed to *intentional*—mental space.

❸ Schedule a physical group activity (team building, an icebreaker, an Outward Bound type of initiative) before a brainstorming session; see Fluegelman (1976) for ideas. *(Contributed by Rick Bradley)*

❹ More introverted people will probably be at their creative best in the morning, more extraverted people in the evening (see the discussion of extraversion, arousal, and caffeine in topic 8.3).

❺ When you are trying hard to come up with a new idea and are feeling frustrated by it, try letting go of your control by walking or dozing, or by relaxing in other ways.

TOPIC 27.4   **The Four Stages of the Creative Process**

Graham Wallas (1926) identified four phases of the creative process, which are still accepted today. Using the common language of more recent writers, I would summarize them as follows:

1. *Preparation.* Doing research, gathering facts, assembling people or materials—whatever is needed to have all domain-specific information at our disposal before the creative act. Chick Thompson (1992) reports that Yoshiro NakaMats, professional Japanese inventor and the holder of more than 3,000 patents (number one in the history of the world; Thomas Edison is second, at 1,083), sees memory work as the basis of the freedom necessary for creativity.

2. *Incubation.* Allowing the collected materials to gestate, to be assimilated into our preexisting schemas, and to interplay unconsciously or consciously in our minds without the stress of having to produce. Incubation can be as short as a 15-minute break or as long as a lifetime. It asks us to let go of the data long enough to gain some perspective. A commonly reported form of incubation is dreaming. Elias Howe dreamed of primitives with spears that had eyes at the end, which led to the invention of the sewing machine; Friedrich August Kekulé's dream of snakes biting their own tails led to the discovery of the benzene molecule.

3. *Inspiration.* The actual "Aha!" or "Eureka!" moment when preparation and incubation produce inspiration. This stage

has also been called *illumination* and *discovery*. It can take the form of focusing our attention on coming up with a solution through the sheer force of our will, or it can consist of merely participating in a structured idea-generating session such as brainstorming.

4. ***Evaluation.*** The attempt to verify that the proposed solution is domain-relevant and logically fits the requirement of the original need or stimulus. This stage is also called confirmation. The question asked is "Will it work?"

Mihalyi Csikszentmihalyi illustrates these phases by portraying several contemporary creative geniuses at work (1996). One particularly illuminating example is that of physicist Freeman Dyson (p. 82):

It was the summer of 1948, so I was then 24. . . . And at that time the big problem was called quantum electrodynamics, which was a theory of radiation and atoms, and the theory was in a mess and nobody knew how to calculate with it. It was a sort of a logjam for all kinds of further developments. . . . At that moment there appeared two great ideas which were associated with two people, Schwinger and Feynman. . . . Each of them produced a new theory of radiation, which looked as though it was going to work, although there were difficulties with both of them. I was in the happy position of being familiar with both of them and I got to know both of them and I got to work. [Beginning of Phase I, Preparation] I spent six months working very hard to understand both of them clearly, and that meant simply [the] hard, hard work of calculating. I would sit down for days and days with large stacks of papers doing calculations so that I could understand. . . . [Beginning of Phase II, Incubation] And at the end of six months, I went off on a vacation. I took a Greyhound bus to California and spent a couple of weeks just bumming around. . . . [Emergence of Phase III, Inspiration] I got on the bus to come back to Princeton, and suddenly in the middle of the night when we were going through Kansas, the whole sort of suddenly became crystal clear, and so that was sort of the big revelation for me, it was the Eureka experience or whatever you call it. Suddenly the whole picture became clear, and Schwinger fit into it beautifully and Feynman fit into it beautifully and the result was a theory that actually was useful. That was the big creative moment of my life. [Beginning of Phase IV, Evaluation] Then I had to spend another six months working out the details and writing it up and so forth. It finally ended up with two long papers in the *Physical Review,* and that was my passport to the world of science.

Amabile integrates these four stages of the creative process into a flowchart (figure 27.1) that includes the three components of creativity: *task motivation* (incubation), *domain relevance* (preparation and evaluation), and *creativity skills* (inspiration). The solid-line arrows (between the numbered boxes) indicate the sequence of events of the creative process; the dotted lines show where each of the three components of creativity has its greatest impact on the process.

Csikszentmihalyi (1996) adds a fifth stage to Wallas's four: *elaboration.* Based on Thomas Edison's quip that "genius is one percent inspiration and ninety-nine percent perspiration," elaboration involves the painstaking process of taking the evaluated idea and converting it in all of its detail into a fully realized entity.

Chick Thompson (1992, pp. xi–xviii) tells the story of inventor Yoshiro NakaMats and his three-phase philosophy of creativity:

1. ***Suji (knowledge),*** similar to Wallas's preparation step

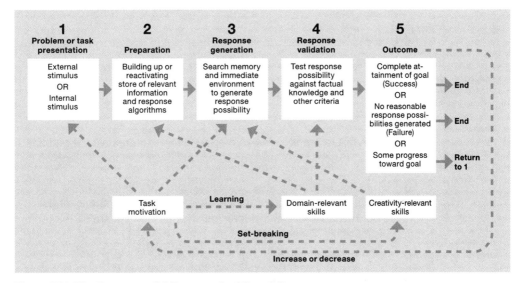

Figure 27.1. The Componential Framework of Creativity
Source: From *The Social Psychology of Creativity* by T. M. Amabile (1983), New York: Springer-Verlag. Reprinted by permission of Springer-Verlag.

2. ***Pika (inspiration),*** similar to the incubation and illumination steps combined

3. ***Iki (practicality),*** similar to the evaluation step

Thompson describes this process as "Ready, Fire, Aim." NakaMats has a static room consisting only of natural materials (plants, natural fibers, and wood, but no plastic) and a dynamic room with music, video, and other media for stimulation. After spending *pika* time in these two rooms, he goes for a swim, during which he expects to have his inspiration, much like Thomas Edison's ball-in-the-pan method (see topic 27.3).

Twyla Tharp (2003, p. 120) summarizes it this way:

> Habitually creative people are, in E. B. White's phrase, "prepared to be lucky." The key words here are "prepared" and "lucky." They're inseparable. You don't get lucky without preparation, and there's no sense in being prepared if you're not open to the possibility of a glorious accident. . . . Some people resent the idea of luck. Accepting the role of chance in our lives suggests that our creations and triumphs are not entirely our own, and that in some way we're undeserving of our success. I say, Get over it. This is how the world works. In creative endeavors luck is a skill.

Applications

❶ When you expect yourself or someone else to come up with a creative contribution, be sure to allow adequate time for preparation and incubation. Ask "What information or material is needed before action can be taken?"

❷ Always take a break between preparing for your creative act and actually trying to execute it. There's good scientific support for sleeping on it!

❸ Many structured exercises are available to assist in the process of idea generation. One element they have in common is that they find a way to hold judgment in abeyance until all contributions are on the table for consideration. These exercises are based on research showing that evaluative activity is stressful and thus activates the limbic system (see chapter 2). When the limbic system is activated, the cerebral cortex is significantly suppressed, inhibiting creative production. Two of the more common exercises are *brainstorming* (excellent for extraverts) and *brainwriting* (excellent for introverts); they are included as appendixes D and E.

❹ Identify your places of greatest inspirational moments and keep paper and pencil there for quick recording. For me, these locations are the bathroom, car, bedroom, and shirt pocket.

TOPIC 27.5 Creative Giants

Mihalyi Csikszentmihalyi, in his book *Creativity* (1996), reported on the findings from interviews with 91 individuals—from physicists to sculptors—who had made exceptional contributions to their fields. He defined exceptional creative contributions as the interaction of a system with three elements:

1. A *culture* (such as genetics or symphonic composition) with an identifiable set of symbolic rules that govern participation in that culture

2. A person with the capability of interacting with the culture in a novel way

3. Experts who recognize and place their stamp of approval on the innovation of this exceptional person

This interaction changes the culture in a significant way, so that subsequent participation in the culture is no longer what it used to be. Csikszentmihalyi distinguishes this paradigm-shifting, culture-changing contribution from the merely brilliant or insightful behavior of scintillating conversationalists who are able to see the world in new ways.

The personality of these creative giants—Stephen Jay Gould, Jack Anderson, Nadine Gordimer, and John Hope Franklin, to name but four—requires a singular commitment to mastering the domain, as Amabile described it in topic 27.2. Other than hard work and dedication to one's domain, Csikszentmihalyi (1996) found two significant features that distinguished these giants from the merely brilliant and insightful: *curiosity* and *complexity*. Listen as he describes the first (p. 11):

> Each of us is born with two contradictory sets of instructions: a conservative tendency, made up of instincts for self-preservation, self-aggrandizement, and saving energy, and an expansive tendency made up of instincts for exploring, for enjoying novelty and risk—the curiosity that leads to creativity belongs to this set. We need both of these programs. But whereas the first tendency requires little encouragement or support from outside to motivate behavior, the second can wilt if it is not cultivated.

He describes the second feature, *complexity,* at greater length (p. 57):

> By this I mean that they show tendencies of thought and action that in most people are segregated. They contain contradictory extremes—instead of being an "individual," each of them is a "multitude." Like the color white that includes all the hues in the spectrum, they tend to bring together the entire range of human possibilities within themselves.

> These qualities are present in all of us, but usually we are trained to develop only one pole of the dialectic. We might grow up cultivating the aggressive, competitive side of our nature, and disdain or repress the nurturant, cooperative side. A creative individual is more likely to be both aggressive and cooperative, either at the same time or at different times, depending on the situation. Having a complex personality means being able to express the full range of traits that are potentially present in the human repertoire but usually atrophy because we think that one or the other pole is "good," whereas the other extreme is "bad."

Csikszentmihalyi identifies 10 polar opposite personality traits that creative giants hold in a "dialectical tension" (p. 58). Adherence to these traits is not merely "wishy-washy," as in being moderately nurturing and moderately competitive, but both fiercely competitive and intensely nurturing; not just a midpoint on a continuum but an alternating embrace of the extremes. Whereas much of the population exhibits a preference for one end of the continuum over the other, this embracing of polarity makes creative giants more complex. Csikszentmihalyi's 10 pairs of antithetical traits (pp. 58–76) are

1. Energy vs. rest
2. Smart vs. naïve
3. Disciplined vs. playful
4. Fantasy vs. realism
5. Extraversion vs. introversion
6. Humble vs. proud
7. Masculine vs. feminine
8. Traditional vs. rebellious
9. Passionate vs. objective
10. Enjoyment vs. suffering

To translate this model into a simpler format, it would appear that Csikszentmihalyi could describe his curiosity component as a high score on Originality in the Big Five Model of personality (see chapter 33), with the 10 polarities representing equal tendencies at the two extremes of each of the other four Big Five personality dimensions (Need for Stability, Extraversion, Accommodation, and Consolidation). With the exception of the second pair of antithetical traits—smart vs. naïve—which relates to intelligence rather than being a personality trait, each of the other nine relate clearly to Big Five traits:

Need for Stability 9, 10

Extraversion 1, 5, 10

Originality (facet 1: Imagination). 4

Originality (facet 3: Change) 8

Accommodation 6, 7

Consolidation 3

The Curiosity component relates to all four subtraits of the Originality dimension: *imagination, complexity, change,* and *scope*. See topic 4.4 and chapter 33 for more discussion of the Big Five. By understanding the basic structure of personality and how it relates to the dynamics of the creative giant, we may gain greater understanding, acceptance, and control of the drive toward creative greatness in ourselves and others.

Csikszentmihalyi summarizes his extended discussion of the 10 polarities in this manner: "Therefore, the novelty that survives to change a domain is usually the work of someone who can operate at both ends of these polarities—and that is the kind of person we call 'creative'" (p. 76).

Application

❶ If you aspire to make great contributions or to live around someone who does, make your peace now with these many conflicting demands. If you have a strong preference for the big picture, for example, realize that you must cultivate a strong enthusiasm, or at least acceptance, for the role of detail. Consider the soaring imagination of Michelangelo coupled with patient attention to detail.

TOPIC 27.6	**Creativity and Madness**

Throughout history, writers have linked creativity and mental derangement. Consider:

[People] outstanding in philosophy, poetry, and the arts are melancholic.
—Aristotle

Great wits are sure to madness near allied,
And thin partitions do their bounds divide."
—John Dryden

The lunatic, the lover, and the poet,
Are of imagination all compact."
—William Shakespeare

Ruth Richards, in the April 1992 *Harvard Health Letter,* reviews studies that show a high incidence of mood disorders among more creative personalities. There is growing evidence that creative outlets in and of themselves have a therapeutic benefit for those with mood disorders. Mood disorders represent a loss of self-control, just as creativity is associated with a loosening of self-control.

Applications

❶ Encourage creative responsibilities for those with bothersome mood swings.

❷ Do not insist that creative personalities have perfect mood control.

TOPIC 27.7	**Assessing for Creativity**

Amabile (1983) reviews the various personality, biographical, and behavioral inventories that have purported to measure aspects of creativity. Most measure aspects of only one component, creativity-relevant skills. For the most part, they do not measure either domain-relevant skills or task motivation (see topic 27.2 for definitions).

Applications

❶ The WorkPlace Big Five ProFile and the NEO PI-R, both described in chapter 33, can give as good a profile of the personality traits relevant to creativity as any other inventory. Most multifactor personality tests today have creativity scores that are derived from scores on the individual scales related to creativity.

❷ Global Creativity Corporation (a.k.a. Global Dharma Center; P.O. Box 294, Mill Valley, California 94942; 415-331-4823; www.globaldharma.org) has developed the Innovation Styles profile, a brief, 28-question questionnaire that yields a descriptive profile of how the respondent might typically approach the creative act. The same information could be derived from a multifactor inventory, but if all you want to do is measure creativity styles, this is an effective instrument. Other brief instruments are included in many of the books written about creativity, such as Milton Fisher's "Test Your Intuitive Quotient" in his book *Intuition* (1981).

❸ If you want to measure creative behaviors (the tests in applications 1 and 2 measure only creativity-related traits), then you must turn to the Torrance Tests of Creative Thinking (also called the Minnesota Tests of Creative Thinking; Scholastic Testing Service), developed by E. Paul Torrance (1974).

❹ Martin Seligman (see the discussion of his learned-optimism theory of motivation in topic 37.5) has developed the Seligman Attributional Style Questionnaire, available by calling Martin Seligman or Peter Schulman at 215-898-2748 (see also www.positivepsychology.org). In my judgment, this is the best instrument available for measuring extrinsic and intrinsic motivation. Another version of the test is available in his book *Learned Optimism* (1991).

❺ I know of no one test that purports to measure completely all three components of creativity as Amabile has described them. I suggest that you review the specific facets of the three components listed in topic 27.2 (and in Amabile, 1983) in order to identify which of them are most relevant to your measurement problem. Then piece together a testing protocol to measure those facets.

❻ Daniel Cappon measures intuition in his Intuition Quotient Test in his book *Intuition Management* (1994a).

❼ Weston H. Agor includes an assessment instrument for intuition in his book *Intuition in Organizations: Leading and Managing Productively* (1989). He includes national norms by management level, gender, ethnic background, and occupational specialty.

❽ In their review of creativity research, Sternberg and Lubart (1996) recommend several different approaches to the measurement of creativity.

SUGGESTED RESOURCES

Amabile, T. M. (1983). *The Social Psychology of Creativity.* New York: Springer-Verlag.

Boden, M. A. (1990). *The Creative Mind: Myths and Mechanisms.* New York: Basic Books.

Csikszentmihalyi, M. (1990). *Flow: The Psychology of Optimal Experience.* New York: HarperCollins.

Csikszentmihalyi, M. (1996). *Creativity: Flow and the Psychology of Discovery and Invention.* New York: HarperCollins.

Eisenberger, R., and J. Cameron (1996). "Detrimental Effects of Reward: Reality or Myth?" *American Psychologist,* 51(11), 1153–1166.

Goleman, D., P. Kaufman, and M. Ray (1992). *The Creative Spirit.* New York: NAL/Dutton.

Koestler, A. (1964). *The Act of Creation.* Old Tappan, N.J.: Macmillan.

Sternberg, R. J., and J. E. Davidson (Eds.) (1995). *The Nature of Insight.* Cambridge, Mass.: MIT Press.

Sternberg, R. J., and T. I. Lubart (July 1996). "Investing in Creativity." *American Psychologist,* 51(7), 677–688.

Tharp, T. (2003). *The Creative Habit.* New York: Simon and Schuster.

Thompson, C. (1992). *What a Great Idea! The Key Steps Creative People Take.* New York: HarperCollins.

28

Chipping Off the Old Block

Removing Barriers to Creativity

"One must be something to be able to do something."

—Johann Wolfgang von Goethe

Chapter 27 was concerned with the definition and measurement of creativity. For many people, the greatest obstacle to creativity is simply not knowing how to access their creative potential. Creative people know that their ideas don't just always pop into consciousness. An element of intention helps to lubricate the idea pathway. This chapter will address the "how to" of accessing one's creativity.

TOPIC 28.1   General Principles for Developing Creativity

The presence of creativity in individuals will, of course, be founded on the development of their domain-relevant skills, creativity-relevant skills, and task motivation. The methods for developing domain-relevant skills are well known: schoolwork, reading, professional associations, mentoring, training classes, coaching, and counseling. Chapters 21–26 describe the most effective ways to use these methods. The methods for developing intrinsic motivation are also covered in some detail in topic 30.2.

Amabile (1983, pp. 161–164) reports several principles concerning the development of creativity in young children, which I summarize here:

- Ability grouping benefits only higher-ability students.

- Parents' and teachers' expectations significantly determine creativity (see topic 30.3 for Rosenthal's work on the self-fulfilling prophecy).

- Teachers tend to wrongly perceive boys as having the greatest variability in creativity—that is, they see them as having both the most and the least creativity, with girls seen as having average creativity. If you are a teacher, beware of this tendency!

- More informal classrooms generate more creativity.

At the university level, Amabile identifies the differences between professors who are successful in facilitating creativity and those who inhibit it. I summarize her discussion (p. 164) as follows. Facilitating professors do the following:

- See students as individuals

- Encourage independence

- Model creative behavior

- Spend time with students outside class

- Expect excellence of students

- Maintain enthusiasm for the subject and for learning

- Accept students as equals

- Recognize student competence

- Are interesting lecturers

- Are good one-on-one

Inhibiting professors, on the other hand:

- Discourage students' ideas

- Are insecure

- Have low energy

- Emphasize rote learning

- Are dogmatic

- Are not up-to-date

- Have narrow interests

- Are unavailable outside the classroom

Amabile also identifies several guidelines for establishing an environment in the workplace that will result in increased creativity (pp. 166–167). I summarize them as follows:

- Give employees the responsibility for initiating new activities.

- Empower employees to hire assistants (allow a budget for doing the less creative work, such as number crunching or assembly).

- Provide freedom from administrative interference.

- Provide job security.

- Remove time pressures; as time allotted for a task decreases, workers tend to choose the simpler path and let go of the more creative or elegant.

Combine the following applications with the suggestions in chapters 21–26 for developing creative behaviors.

Applications

❶ When working with groups, use techniques for suspending judgment, such as brainstorming (instructions are given in appendix D) and brainwriting (see appendix E).

② To get unstuck and find inspiration for the moment, use heuristic techniques, such as those in J. L. Adams (1980), Bandler and Grinder (1982), de Bono (1967), M. Fisher (1981), P. Goldberg (1983), Kogan (1956), Senge (1990), and von Oech (1983).

③ Explore the works of writers who deal in paradox and perceptual flexibility, such as Escher (1983), Falletta (1983), M. Gardner (1979), Hofstadter (1979), Korzybski (1948), Michalko (1991), Polya (1971), Poundstone (1988), Tharp (2003), and Zdenek (1985). These are only a few of many such works, but they represent an excellent start. Digesting these volumes will result in an impatience with conventional assumptions and a greater tolerance for ambiguity.

④ Allow yourself and others long periods of uninterrupted concentration. Constant disruption is the enemy of creativity. Quality circles are an attempt to provide workers with periods of concentration so that they can creatively solve nagging problems in the workplace.

⑤ Develop the habit of bringing your assumptions to the surface and questioning them. Three excellent readings in this area are Kuhn (1970), Senge (1990), and Watzlawick, Weakland, and Fisch (1974).

⑥ Explore ways in which two or more ideas or objects can be combined to produce new ideas or objects. Koestler (1964) calls this *bisociation*; Robert Epstein (1996) calls it *generativity*. Some examples of bisociation from the history of invention are listed in table 28.1.

⑦ Build the habit of playing creative games such as charades, Cranium, Facts 'n' Five, and Pictionary; ask at your library, bookstore, or game store for help in identifying more such games and learning how to play them. Many books for children are filled with creative games and exercises.

⑧ Many books provide specific methods for lessening dependence on so-called left-brain activity. Chick Thompson (1992) describes techniques that are helpful for developing creativity in a wide range of business and personal settings. Betty Edwards (1989) provides hints on more right-brained approaches to learning to draw.

⑨ Get on the Intuition Network mailing list. Write to Jeffrey Mishlove at friend@intuition.org or visit the Network's website at www.intuition.org.

Table 28.1. Examples of Bisociation

Person	Idea A	Idea B	Result of Bisociation
Archimedes	Measuring gold content of Tyro's crown	Overflowing bathtub	Displacement theory
Pythagoras	Musical pitch	Blacksmith forging iron rod	Discovery of relation of length to pitch in music
Alexander Fleming	Mucus from nose falls into culture	Spore flies in window and lands in culture dish	Penicillin
Blaise Pascal	Mathematics	Gambling	Probability theory
Friedrich August Kekulé	Chemistry	Dream of snakes swallowing each other's tails	Benzene ring
Johannes Gutenberg	Grape press	Coin stamp	Printing press

❿ Csikszentmihalyi concludes his book *Creativity* (1996) with a chapter entitled "Enhancing Personal Creativity." The steps he prescribes are an excellent summary of much of what is known about developing creativity in oneself and others. For the full meaning of these steps, I recommend that you read the chapter. Otherwise, this simple listing will give you a hint as to the demands he makes on someone who would aspire to creative greatness:

- Try to be surprised by something every day.
- Try to surprise at least one person every day.
- Write down each day what surprised you and how you surprised others.
- When something strikes a spark of interest, follow it.
- Wake up in the morning with a specific goal to look forward to.
- Commit to doing things well.
- Continually increase the level of challenge.
- Take charge of your schedule.

- Make time for reflection and relaxation.
- Shape your space.
- Start doing more of what you love, less of what you hate.
- Develop what you lack and want.
- Shift often from openness to closure, closure to openness.
- Find a way to express what moves you.
- Look at problems from as many viewpoints as possible.

TOPIC 28.2 Obstacles to Creativity

Over the years, I have maintained a list of what I call obstacles to creative behavior, which I have used with various workshop populations. Each obstacle can be evaluated in many ways. For example, fear is a known obstacle to creativity. But fear can emanate from any one of many sources: ourselves, our co-workers, our spouse, our boss, the corporate culture, the neighborhood, and more. To deal with fear as an obstacle, we must first be clear as to its source. Following are specific obstacles to creativity:

- *A critical nature.* An overly critical nature serves as an inhibitor of creativity. Goleman, Kaufman, and Ray (1992) call this *psychosclerosis,* or hardening of the attitudes! It is especially active during the preparation phase and is often referred to as the voice of judgment or functional fixedness.

- *Personality traits.* Creativity is minimized among the Preserver ("Stick with what works"), Adapter ("Don't rock the boat"), and Focused ("We need it yesterday") personality types. See chapter 33 for information on these traits.

- *Poor diet.* A normal, healthy diet is imperative (see chapter 7), with a special caution against excessive high-glycemic carbohydrates and fats and insufficient protein and low-glycemic carbohydrates.

- *Poor physical condition.* Although you don't have to be a marathoner to be creative, you must be sufficiently active and healthy to maintain the alertness necessary for creativity.

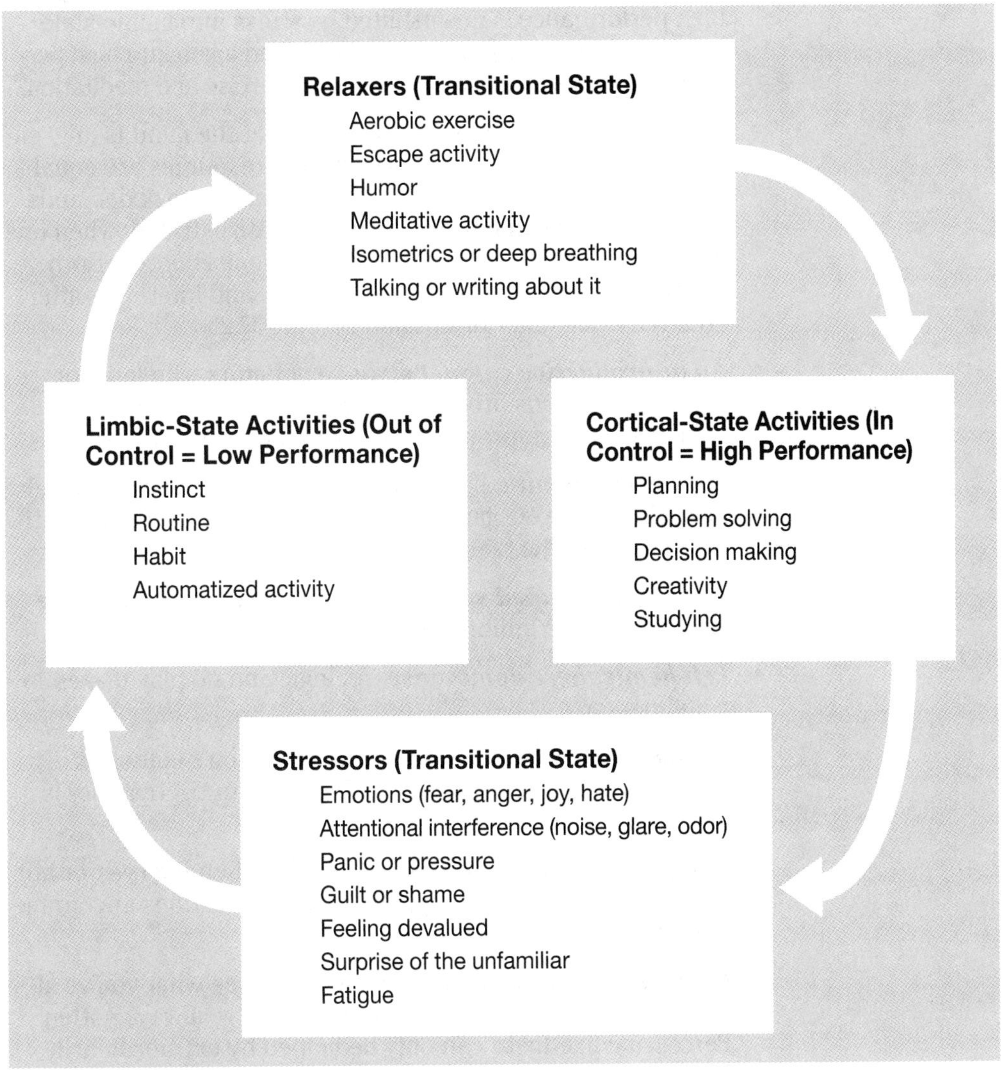

Relaxers (Transitional State)
Aerobic exercise
Escape activity
Humor
Meditative activity
Isometrics or deep breathing
Talking or writing about it

Limbic-State Activities (Out of Control = Low Performance)
Instinct
Routine
Habit
Automatized activity

Cortical-State Activities (In Control = High Performance)
Planning
Problem solving
Decision making
Creativity
Studying

Stressors (Transitional State)
Emotions (fear, anger, joy, hate)
Attentional interference (noise, glare, odor)
Panic or pressure
Guilt or shame
Feeling devalued
Surprise of the unfamiliar
Fatigue

Figure 28.1. The Performance Cycle

- *Fear.* Fear activates the limbic system and proportionally shuts down the cerebral cortex, the center of creative activity. Fear is often accompanied by lack of faith in one's ability. The relationship between fear (and other stressors) and creativity is portrayed in the performance cycle in figure 28.1. Cortical-state high performance is downshifted by stress into limbic-state lower performance, but it can be upshifted again into high performance by relaxers such as aerobic exercise and meditation.

- *Out of flow.* Csikszentmihalyi writes that the mind is fully engaged and in *flow* when one's skills and resources are equal to the demands of the task at hand. When the task demands more than one can muster, one becomes frustrated; when one brings more to the task that it requires, one is bored. Both frustration and boredom are out of flow, and interfere with creativity. See fuller discussion at topic 37.2.

- *An unproductive conflict style.* Negotiators who look for win-win situations breed more creativity than Avoiders, Submissives, Compromisers, or Dictators (see chapter 33).

- *Poor group health.* If the team with which you are involved (a work group, your family) is functioning poorly, your creativity and that of the team will be inhibited.

- *A highly developed superego.* An overly active conscience (full of "don'ts") inhibits creativity.

- *Left-hemisphere dominance.* All logic and no play makes Jo a dull person.

- *A conservative culture.* If your organization's culture is characterized by celebration of the status quo, creativity is inhibited.

- *Inappropriate questioning skills.* Closed-ended (yes-or-no) questions inhibit creativity; open-ended questions encourage creativity.

- *Perceptual fixedness.* If you continue to see what you've always seen, you'll continue to get what you've always gotten. Perceptual fixedness can only be helped by extraordinarily close and precise observation—by seeing what is there, not what you expect to be there.

- *An unchanging perspective.* If you continue to look at the mountain from the same side, you'll always see the same mountain.

- *A need for power and control.* Control freaks, those who must always be right ("My way or the highway!"), are the

ultimate obstacle to creativity, both for others and for
themselves.

- *Pessimism.* Seligman (see topic 37.5) has demonstrated conclusively that personal, pervasive, and permanent pessimism results in less productivity, including creative productivity.

- *Time pressures.* Amabile warns that one of the biggest killers of creativity is unnecessary time constraints. This is a special problem if you're trying to encourage creativity during a brief period of time during a school day.

- *External rewards.* Enticing someone with external rewards to produce creative results tends to be less effective than encouraging creativity for its own sake. See the discussion on the psychology of creativity in topic 27.2.

Application

❶ Identify the obstacles to creativity in your life. Develop a plan to eliminate or minimize these obstacles in areas where you wish to be more creative.

TOPIC 28.3 **The Persistence of the Past in Present Creative Acts**

In a series of experiments, Thomas Ward of
Texas A&M University, Cristina Cacciari of the University of Bologna,
Italy, and Raymond Gibbs of the University of California, Santa Cruz,
have established that people invariably create "new" concepts that
are based on their old concepts (*APA Monitor,* August 1995, pp. 1, 20).
Gibbs calls the elements of old concepts that persist in the formation
of new ones *image schemas.* As an example of this phenomenon, consider the invention of the streetcar. The first streetcar designers had
the stagecoach firmly in their minds—it was the basis of their image
schema for mass land transit in the city. Failing to consider the uniqueness of the streetcar in contrast to the stagecoach, the designers carried forward the schema so that the conductor was seated forward
and on top of the streetcar. As a result, several conductors died when
they were thrown from their perch after braking. In another example,
when schoolchildren are told to create a completely new, imaginary,

different kind of house or animal, they always include the central elements of their image schemas for a house and animal: windows, door, and chimney for the one and four legs, head, and tail for the other.

Applications

❶ When you ask people to create a completely new concept, help them to become aware of possible schemas that might keep them from arriving at concepts that are truly novel, then focus on the key principles involved in the creative act.

❷ In any important undertaking, identify your assumptions. Next, throw out the assumptions that are not useful for the present task or that will potentially interfere with your creativity for the task. Then consciously create new assumptions that might further liberate your thinking and creativity for the task at hand. Others have called this "removing the constraints." You can always put such constraints as budget and permission back in place *after* you've finished being creative, and let your creativity then negotiate with the constraining forces (managers, parents, spouse, and others).

TOPIC 28.4   The Influence of Social Networks on Creativity

Dean Keith Simonton, a psychologist at the University of California, Davis, has studied the lives of scientists, artists, philosophers, and composers to determine the influence of social factors on their creativity. His research has led to the discovery that mentors play a critical role in the development of creative talent (*APA Monitor,* August 1995, p. 21). The artists he studied were exposed to role models at an early age. In adulthood, these creative talents thrived most when they were around colleagues and competitors who could "feed off each other." Simonton points to the absence of mentors as the primary reason for low creative output during the Dark Ages. Kevin Dunbar, a psychologist at McGill University in Montreal, extends this finding by pointing out that researchers in the more creative scientific laboratories thrive in the presence of colleagues with dissimilar backgrounds and specialties. Dunbar argues that this diversity of researchers allows reasoning from analogous situations.

Analogous situations suggest novel approaches, whereas laboratories that are staffed with researchers who have similar backgrounds and specialties lack this fecund source of insights.

Applications

1 Expose your children to role models with talents that you suspect the children possess.

2 Where creative output is necessary, ensure that diverse resources are allowed to mingle. Don't put a team composed only of electrical engineers together to create a new electrical design; include diverse perspectives so team members will feed off each other's ideas.

3 Visit the Edward de Bono site and participate in the thinking club, discussion group, and other features: **www.edwarddebono.com**.

| **TOPIC 28.5** | **Hypnosis and Creativity** |

Weston Agor, founder of the Intuition Network (see more at www.intuition.org), has used hypnosis to access creative ideas among business leaders. In controlled experiments, he divides a group into *intuitives* and *analyticals,* with the intuitives excelling in brainstorming. He then uses an audiotape to induce a hypnotic state. Both groups have claimed to be exhausted of ideas; however, the members of both groups supply substantially more ideas after the

> Note: When you see cross references to other sections of this book, you may benefit from taking time now to read them; they provide information that will deepen your understanding of the current material.

tape, with the intuitives again excelling. The use of the terms *intuitive* and *analytical* may be explained by reference to the Big Five personality dimensions (see chapter 33). Intuitives are high in Originality and low in Consolidation, analyticals vice versa.

Application

1 In situations that demand greater creativity, if the stakes are high and the people involved have given it their all, try importing a clinician who is properly trained in hypnosis. You may obtain guidelines for using hypnosis from the American Society of Clinical Hypnosis, 140 North Bloomingdale Road, Bloomingdale, Illinois 60108-1017; 630-980-4740, fax 630-351-8490; info@asch.net, www.asch.net.

TOPIC 28.6   **Epstein on Barriers to Creativity**

Robert Epstein (1996) argues that no ideas are new, in the sense that all ideas build on previous knowledge. He insists that everyone can be creative and that four obstacles account for most of the blocked creativity:

1. The lack of a method or habit for capturing creative ideas when they occur

2. Reticence about taking on challenging, creative tasks that seem impossible or overwhelming

3. Failure to learn any significantly new subject matter (the more you know, the more likely that bisociation will occur)

4. Living and working in environments that do not inspire

Applications

1 Keep tape recorders, pads and pencils, or other recording devices with you in places where you tend to get or lose the most ideas. I keep dozens of notepads at my desk, more at my bedside, in the bathroom, in my shirt pocket, and in the car (but *not* while you're driving!). As I write this, I'm at the end of a roughly two-hour drive from Charlotte to Durham, North Carolina. I had six notepads on the front seat with me, and the first two or three pages of three of them are full. By the time I return home tomorrow, all six will probably have served faithful duty.

2 From time to time, take on an "impossible" problem in need of new ideas, not necessarily with the hope of finding the right idea, but with the enjoyment of practicing idea generation. Occasionally, my wife and I like to come up with bizarre ideas on how to change someone's bad habit.

3 Learn a new subject from time to time. Or learn a new aspect of a familiar subject. I learned to play classical trumpet several years ago.

Recently, I've taken lessons in jazz trumpet. Learning jazz improvisation and technique is a significantly different experience from playing and reading classical music.

④ Change your environment occasionally by adding, changing, or removing something in a way that modifies your daily perspective.

TOPIC 28.7 **Using Synesthesia to Move from the Humdrum to the Creative**

Diane Ackerman (1990) points out that creative people throughout history have used a variety of gimmicks to force their minds from the ordinary concerns of daily living into more creative realms. The common thread among these tricks is the use of *synesthesia,* the phenomenon whereby immersing oneself in one of the senses tends to stimulate associations with the other senses. As an example, low sounds tend to elicit visual images of dark colors, and high sounds tend to lead one to images of light, bright colors. I had read about the use of these synesthetic transport techniques: for example, William Faulkner took a jug of whiskey into the hayloft for inspiration. To help me get into a writer's mood, I used to wear a garish pink baseball cap that my wife, Jane, gave me on my 50th birthday with the phrase "50-Year-Old Kid" printed on the front. I had to quit wearing it when, upon picking me up for a business lunch after a morning I had spent writing, she observed my "hat hair." So I switched to burning a big fat red candle—it was the holiday season, and the candle was ready at hand. I've been using the burning candle ever since as a gimmick to transport me into the writing world.

The following applications are examples of synesthetic transport gimmicks used by writers throughout history, as listed by Diane Ackerman.

Applications

❶ Dame Edith Sitwell lay in a casket.

❷ William Wordsworth, A. E. Housman, and Bertrand Russell were walkers.

3 Friedrich von Schiller placed rotten apples in his desk drawer.

4 Amy Lowell and George Sand smoked cigars (Lowell once ordered ten thousand from Manila). George Sand also wrote right after making love.

5 Samuel Johnson and W. H. Auden drank tea.

6 Colette picked fleas from her cat.

7 Victor Hugo and Benjamin Franklin worked in the nude (Franklin sat in a tub).

8 Hart Crane listened to Latin music.

9 Willa Cather read the Bible.

10 Stendhal read relevant books for the novels he wrote (as in the French Civil Code for the *Charterhouse of Parma*).

11 Alexandre Dumas père wrote nonfiction on rose paper, fiction on blue, poetry on yellow; he ate an apple daily at 7:00 A.M. under the Arc de Triomphe.

12 Rudyard Kipling had a fetish for the blackest of India inks.

13 Voltaire used his lover's naked back as a writing desk.

14 Robert Louis Stevenson, Mark Twain, and Truman Capote all wrote lying down.

15 Karl Marx, Ernest Hemingway, Thomas Wolfe, Virginia Woolf, and Lewis Carroll all wrote while standing.

16 Hemingway sharpened a bunch of pencils first. (My friend Sandy Welton does this too.)

17 Edgar Allan Poe perched his cat on his shoulder.

18 Aldous Huxley wrote with his nose.

SUGGESTED RESOURCES

Amabile, T. M. (1983). *The Social Psychology of Creativity.* New York: Springer-Verlag.

Csikszentmihalyi, M. (1990). *Flow: The Psychology of Optimal Experience.* New York: HarperCollins.

de Bono, E. (1967). *New Think.* New York: Basic Books.

de Bono, E. (1970). *Lateral Thinking: Creativity Step by Step.* New York: HarperCollins.

de Bono, E. (1994). *De Bono's Thinking Course.* New York: Facts on File.

Goleman, D., P. Kaufman, and M. Ray (1992). *The Creative Spirit.* New York: NAL/Dutton.

Koestler, A. (1964). *The Act of Creation.* Old Tappan, N.J.: Macmillan.

Michalko, M. (1991). *Thinkertoys: A Handbook of Business Creativity for the '90s.* Berkeley, Calif.: Ten Speed Press.

Seligman, M. E. P. (1991). *Learned Optimism.* New York: Knopf.

Sternberg, R. J., and J. E. Davidson (Eds.) (1995). *The Nature of Insight.* Cambridge, Mass.: MIT Press.

Tharp, T. (2003). *The Creative Habit.* New York: Simon and Schuster.

Thompson, C. (1992). *What a Great Idea! The Key Steps Creative People Take.* New York: HarperCollins.

Torrance, E. P. (1974). *Torrance Tests of Creative Thinking.* Bensenville, Ill.: Scholastic Testing Service.

Websites

Brain Store site (Eric and Dianne Jensen's catalog):
www.thebrainstore.com

Edward de Bono's site:
www.edwarddebono.com

The Intuition Network:
www.intuition.com

2. Problems where the cause is known, or is unknown and irrelevant

An example of the first category would be a blown fuse or a tripped circuit breaker. If you do not discover the cause of the electrical overload, you risk fire (at most) or the unavailability of that electrical circuit (at least). An example of the second category would be having a flat tire in the desert with no jack available. The cause of the flat is most likely irrelevant; you just need some good ideas.

Problems for which the best solution is not obvious can be subdivided into three categories. Although these situations are frequently referred to (erroneously, I think) as *problems,* they are more aptly called *decisions.* The verb *decide* comes from the Latin *de-* ("off") and *caedere* ("to cut"), or "to cut off." In other words, decision time is the time to cut off debate and affirm the solution to the problem at hand. In its purest form, then, a problem is a mess without a solution, and a decision situation is a mess with two or more possible solutions. The three classes of solution are

1. Solutions with certain outcomes

2. Solutions with uncertain outcomes

3. Solutions in need of being prioritized

An example of the first type is deciding which home to buy; the outcome is certain, in the sense that its features are plain to the eye. An example of the second type is deciding whether or not to risk major surgery; the outcome is unknown, although to some degree it is predictable. The third type could be having a list of 20 projects that need to be undertaken, yet having a budget for only a few of them.

Applications

❶ When you commit to trying to solve a problem, first determine what kind of problem it is. Once you know that, you will know your objective. This information is summarized in table 29.2.

❷ Often, it is not enough to figure out what kind of problem you are facing. You must also determine an appropriate technique to use in solving that problem. Refer to table 29.1 for the names of possible techniques to use in solving each kind of problem and resources for learning these techniques.

| TOPIC 29.3 | **Describing the Problem** |

The first step in any problem-solving process is taking time to describe the problem as presented. All too often, in the American "pioneer" spirit, we concentrate on the quick fix and take pride in coming up with solutions immediately upon discovering a problem. But research continues to support the thesis that the time taken to plan at the front end is inversely proportional to the time required for execution. In other words, the effectiveness of problem solving is enhanced by the time you spend understanding and gaining consensus about the problem at the front end.

Lemieux and Bordage (1992) make the case that time taken in medical diagnosis, especially, helps to eliminate irrelevant problem information. They distinguish between *linear* (horizontal) problem solving and *semantic* (vertical) problem solving. Linear problem solving is a logical, "if-then" type, where one piece of information is supposed to lead inferentially to the next. They propose that semantic problem solving, although it is perhaps a bit more unwieldy, is more thorough in leading the diagnostician toward the most relevant problem information and away from irrelevant information. This semantic process is

Table 29.2. Kinds of Problems and the Nature of Their Solutions

Kind of Problem	Nature of Appropriate Problem-Solving Activity
Problem with unknown cause	Finding the cause
Problem with known cause or cause irrelevant	Generating ideas that could fix the problem
Decision between solutions with certain outcomes	Deciding on one best solution
Decision between solutions with undertain outcomes	Deciding which solution has the highest probability of success
A jumbled list	Determining the priority order

based on the use of *continua* (also called *axes* or *opposites*). They find that better medical diagnosticians use a series of continua to describe a specific medical problem and then base their diagnosis on whether or not the diagnosis fits the description.

The first five of the following applications present the more popular and effective techniques for describing problems.

Applications

❶ *Mind mapping* (see figure 29.1) is a technique attributed to Tony Buzan (1991). In the middle of a page, write down the main problem you're trying to describe. Circle that problem; then think of everything that might be related to the problem, jotting down words and phrases around the page and linking smaller concepts to bigger concepts. This is a free-form method of outlining that is modeled on the image we have of neural networks in the brain.

❷ The *Ishikawa (fishbone) diagram,* also known as the *cause-and-effect*

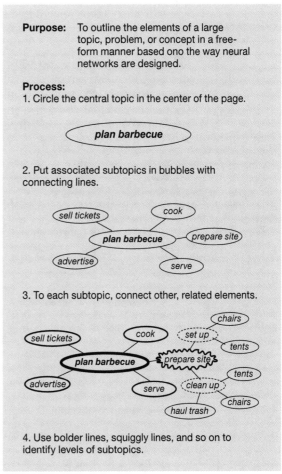

Purpose: To outline the elements of a large topic, problem, or concept in a free-form manner based ono the way neural networks are designed.

Process:
1. Circle the central topic in the center of the page.

2. Put associated subtopics in bubbles with connecting lines.

3. To each subtopic, connect other, related elements.

4. Use bolder lines, squiggly lines, and so on to identify levels of subtopics.

Figure 29.1. Mind Mapping

diagram, has become popular in world business through the total quality revolution. A simple treatment of it is available in Walton (1986); see also Gitlow, Gitlow, Oppenheim, and Oppenheim (1989). The fishbone chart is a cross between traditional outlining and mind mapping; it is not as logically restrictive as outlining and not as free-form as mind mapping. The chart assumes that any given problem will have about four major areas (commonly, but not always, identified as *people, methods, machinery,* and *materials*). These four areas become the "bones" attached to the spine of a fish. Ideas related to the big ideas become smaller bones branching off the larger ones (see figure 29.2).

❸ The *Pareto chart* is also known as the Eighty-Twenty Rule, or the Law of the Mighty Few. Simply put, it is a frequency distribution of problems that enables you to identify the mighty few (usually about 20 percent of your problems) that could give you the maximum payoff (reduce your problems by about 80 percent) if they were fixed. Other common phrasings of the Pareto principle are "Which 20 percent of your sales prospects could get you 80 percent of your sales goals?" and "Which 20 percent of your quality problems account for 80 percent of your cost variances?" For examples of the Pareto principle, see Walton (1986).

❹ The comparison of *actual vs. ideal,* also referred to as "current state vs. desired state," "is vs. should," and "performance vs. standard," has become the most common way of beginning a problem-solving process. Simply put, you first list all the details associated with the current problem (the actual problem situation). Second, you describe what the situation would look like (or sound like or smell like) if the problem were fixed (the ideal). This contrast between actual and ideal provides the focus for generating ideas that might solve the problem, allowing you to move from the actual to the ideal state.

❺ The *Cause and Effect Diagram with the Addition of Cards* (CEDAC) was developed by Productivity Design Inc. in Boston. It is a variation on the Ishikawa diagram (see application 2) in which cards

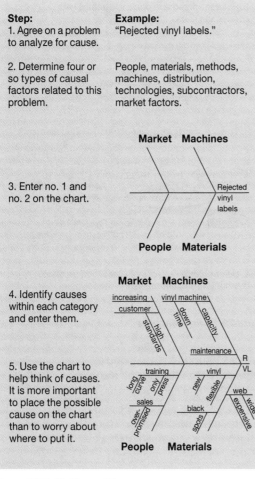

Step:

1. Agree on a problem to analyze for cause.

2. Determine four or so types of causal factors related to this problem.

3. Enter no. 1 and no. 2 on the chart.

4. Identify causes within each category and enter them.

5. Use the chart to help think of causes. It is more important to place the possible cause on the chart than to worry about where to put it.

Example:

"Rejected vinyl labels."

People, materials, methods, machines, distribution, technologies, subcontractors, market factors.

Figure 29.2. Fishbone Diagram

or self-sticking notes are used for greater ease of movement. For information, contact Nate Apkon, President; Productivity Design Inc.; 648 Beacon Street, Sixth Floor; Boston, Massachusetts 02215; 617-262-1717.

6 Describe a problem, particularly a medical problem, using continua like those that follow:

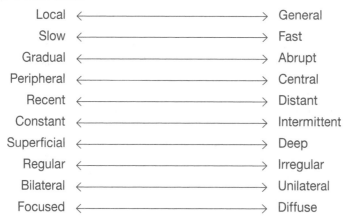

Local	General
Slow	Fast
Gradual	Abrupt
Peripheral	Central
Recent	Distant
Constant	Intermittent
Superficial	Deep
Regular	Irregular
Bilateral	Unilateral
Focused	Diffuse

7 Many software programs are available to assist in "process mapping." Some program names to look for are Decision Explorer, Inspiration, Visio (my personal favorite), IDEF-O, and COPE. For information on Inspiration plus links to other tools and sites, visit the Computer Assisted Qualitative Data Analysis Software website at caqdas.soc.surrey.ac.uk. For information on Decision Explorer, visit **www.banxia.com**.

TOPIC 29.4   **Reaching Solutions: Algorithms and Heuristics**

Research on human attention has demonstrated strongly that we cannot concentrate on more than one focal point at a time. This truth can be built into our approach to problem solving if we focus on one aspect of the problem at a time. *Algorithmic* methods do this naturally by dividing problem solving into steps.

Many will argue that the practice of proceeding one step at a time kills creativity. These people use heuristic problem-solving methods to approach a problem more globally. For example, "If pushing doesn't work, try pulling" is a classic heuristic approach to problem solving. It encourages a big-picture approach in which we think about all aspects of the problem at once. This works best for experts who are intimately familiar with the technical details of the problem and can draw on extensive mental networks.

The word *heuristic* comes from the Greek *heuriskein,* meaning "to find or discover"; Archimedes supposedly said "Eureka!" or "I found it!" when he discovered the specific-gravity method for determining the purity of gold. When heuristic methods fail to yield a solution, an algorithmic (stepwise) approach should be tried. Ellen Langer, a professor of psychology at Harvard University, proposes a compromise between the algorithmic and heuristic approaches that she calls *mindfulness* (*APA Monitor,* September 1994, p. 28). Mindfulness allows the individual problem solver or decision maker to remain in control of the process, rather than being passively led through the stepwise sequence of an algorithm. We accomplish this by collecting a reasonable amount of information (or thinking up some on our own), stopping short of certainty, and then actively making a decision. She cautions, however, against *cognitive commitment,* which can cause a person to hold beliefs rigidly without modifying them when new, relevant data emerge.

Applications

❶ Use the most common algorithms. Of the many problem-solving methods identified in table 29.1, four are particularly noteworthy for their attention to breaking the problem-solving process down into discrete parts: root-cause analysis, matrix-decision analysis, the decision tree, and the precedence chart.

❷ Otherwise, use heuristics. The more familiar you are with the details of the problem, the more likely you are to have success with heuristic approaches. Heuristic techniques are really just rules of thumb for approaching problems. Here is an assortment of these rules of thumb:

- To detach something, attach it to something else.
- If you can't remove it, counteract it.
- Find a similar problem. Is its solution applicable?
- Reframe the problem. A different definition can yield new possible solutions.
- Simulate the problem to understand it better.
- Work backward from the actual state to the former ideal state.

- Remove the unnecessary.
- Dream: fantasize a solution assuming that all restrictions have been removed.
- Simplify by removing some variables.
- Establish subgoals; break the problem into smaller ones.
- List your assumptions and challenge them.
- Study, then incubate.
- Expand, reduce, reverse, substitute, rearrange, regroup, and alternate.
- Make overt the covert.
- Try less of the same.
- Try advertising instead of concealing.
- When one way fails, try the opposite.

❸ For more heuristic techniques, see J. L. Adams (1980, 1986), Bandler and Grinder (1982), de Bono (1967), M. Fisher (1981), P. Goldberg (1983), Kogan (1956), and Nierenberg (1985). Also get yourself on the mailing lists of these excellent resources for problem solving:

Mindware ("Brainy Toys for Kids of All Ages") (catalog); 1803 Mission Street, Suite 414; Santa Cruz, California 95060; phone: 800-447-0477. Online: **www.mindwareonline.com**.

Shamrock Press (catalog); 1277 Garnet Avenue; San Diego, California 92109; 619-272-3880.

❹ When heuristic techniques don't work, try a more algorithmic approach.

❺ Make a poster with your favorite heuristics or algorithms as a way of keeping them in front of you when you may need them.

TOPIC 29.5 **Games and Problem-Solving Ability**

A wide variety of games, puzzles, and toys come under the heading of brainteasers, including such items as Rubik's Cube, the tangram, the Tower of Hanoi, Sudoku, Jim Fixx's word-game books, and Martin Gardner's math and logic puzzle books. These games are helpful in maintaining flexibility in approaching problems. People who report that they enjoy and play these games also score higher on problem-solving tests.

Robert Sternberg discusses at length the role of puzzles, games, brainteasers, and insight-oriented exercises in *Intelligence Applied: Understanding and Increasing Your Intellectual Skills* (1986).

Applications

1 Make a habit of giving games and puzzles to your children starting at an early age, with the games becoming gradually more sophisticated.

2 Do not tease adults for being attracted to brainteasers; they are avoiding perceptual fixedness and developing their mental flexibility.

3 If you work in a facility with a waiting area, consider putting out games and puzzles as well as magazines.

4 Encourage the appropriate use of games and puzzles in the workplace.

TOPIC 29.6   Sleep, Relaxation, and Problem Solving

Often, a problem on your mind interferes with sleep and relaxation. One way to eliminate this bother is to do a mental dump: write down everything in your mind related to the problem or concern. By writing it down, you will be able to rest, knowing that the elements will not be forgotten.

Sleep also serves as a good break between the data collection and solution aspects of problem solving. By collecting all relevant data and then sleeping, you allow unconscious forces to develop a pattern, insight, or inspiration relative to the data.

If sleep time is not available, simply engage in a relaxing activity after finishing the preliminary problem solving and before trying to come up with a solution. Patterns will emerge in this gestation period. Napping or sleeping, in fact, is an excellent way to employ step 3 of the creativity process—"Incubation"—that is described in topic 27.4.

Applications

❶ Keep writing materials at your bedside in case you need to do a mental dump.

❷ When you are trying to solve a problem, take a break (sleep, nap, walk, have lunch) before trying to come up with a final solution.

| TOPIC 29.7 | **Trust the Experts** |

As I pointed out at the beginning of this chapter, research on the effectiveness of various problem-solving techniques suggests that experts are generally better than techniques. In other words, before you take the time to learn a problem-solving technique to solve an electrical engineering problem, first go to an electrical engineer who is familiar with the situation or the workers who are actually doing the work and see if they can spot the cause and offer a solution.

Applications

❶ If you are teaching problem-solving techniques, caution students that the techniques are a last resort and should be used only when experts are unavailable or have been stumped by the problem.

❷ Include a task expert on a problem-solving team or consult someone who is actually doing the job. *(Contributed by Rick Bradley)*

| TOPIC 29.8 | **How to Select the Right Technique** |

From both my experience and my reading, it has become apparent to me that we have gained nothing if we have learned techniques but not how to recognize the situations that would benefit from applying them, and which ones to apply. In the situation I described at the beginning of this chapter in which I helped to solve

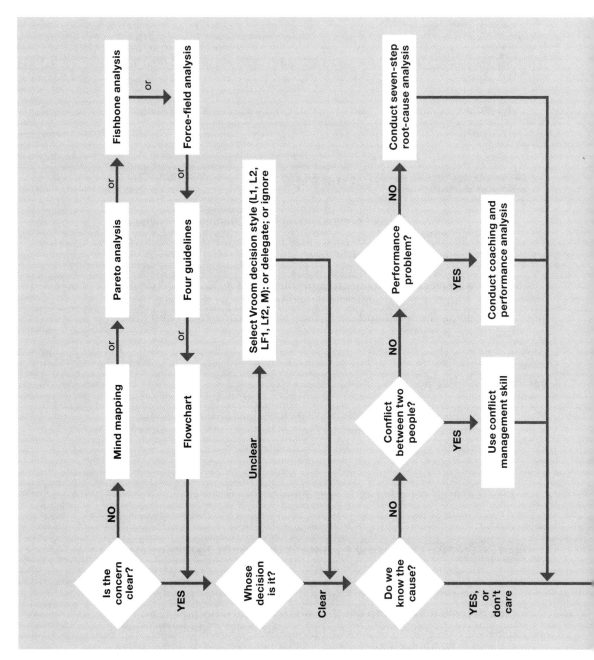

Figure 29.3. Concern Analysis

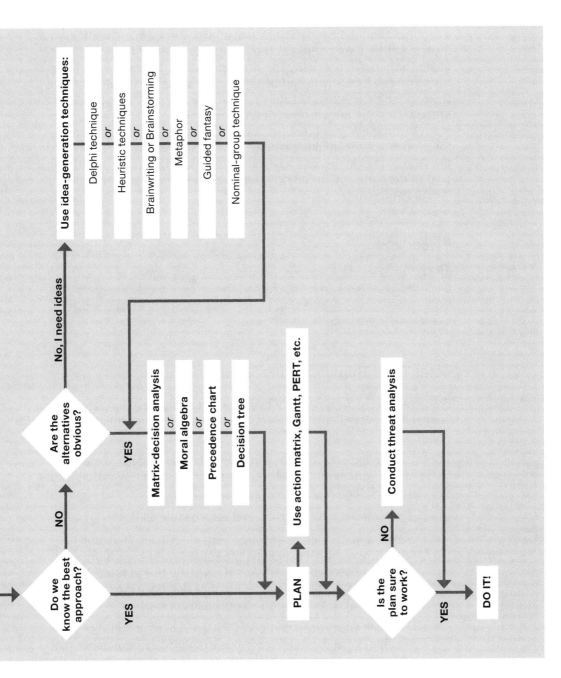

a problem that had been nagging a manufacturer for nine months, we discovered that six people in the group had studied the same technique that I used in solving the problem. All of them were manufacturing professionals who had been trying to solve the problem during the entire nine months, but they had not recognized the applicability of the technique in question: root-cause analysis. It is not enough to learn techniques; you must practice spotting opportunities to apply them. In a critical thinking course I teach from time to time, we use the flowchart in figure 29.3 as an aid in diagnosing concerns, with the goal of deciding which interventions would be most appropriate for specific problems.

Application

❶ Don't just learn techniques. Practice. Find case studies and read them. Try techniques on situations and see if they work. After considerable practice, you will develop the ability to recognize situations that would benefit from specific techniques.

Some Final Thoughts on Problem Solving

Problem solving is made up of many elements. If I were forced to recommend an overall approach—one that would fit most situations—it would be the following:

1. Ask an expert. Consider carefully who the possible experts are (a worker on the job, a consultant). If no one is available or helpful, then . . .

2. Decide what kind of problem it is (see table 29.1).

3. Select a method to use for that kind of problem (see table 29.1). If you are an expert on the subject, first try a more holistic approach (see the list of heuristic tips in topic 29.4, application 2). If heuristic techniques don't work, or if you're not an expert, then try an algorithmic approach.

4. Evaluate your recommended solution in light of Sternberg's flexible domain of intelligence (see topic 34.3). Remember that you can change yourself, the other person, or the situation. If one approach doesn't work, shift to another venue!

SUGGESTED RESOURCES

Adams, J. L. (1980). *Conceptual Blockbusting: A Guide to Better Ideas* (2nd ed.). New York: Norton.

Adams, J. L. (1986). *The Care and Feeding of Ideas: A Guide to Encouraging Creativity.* Reading, Mass.: Addison-Wesley.

Bandler, R., and J. Grinder (1982). *ReFraming: Neuro-Linguistic Programming and the Transformation of Meaning.* Moab, Utah: Real People Press.

Basadur, M., G. Graen, and M. Wakabayashi (1990). "Identifying Differences in Creative Problem Solving Style." *Journal of Creative Behavior,* 24(2), 111–131.

Buzan, T. (1996). *The Mind Map Book.* New York: Plume.

Gitlow, H., S. Gitlow, A. Oppenheim, and R. Oppenheim (1989). *Tools and Methods for the Improvement of Quality.* Burr Ridge, Ill.: Irwin.

Hayes, J. R. (1989). *The Complete Problem Solver* (2nd ed.). Hillsdale, N.J.: Erlbaum.

Metcalfe, J., and A. P. Shimamura (Eds.) (1994). *Metacognition: Knowing about Knowing.* Cambridge, Mass.: MIT Press.

Moody, P. E. (1983). *Decision Making: Proven Methods for Better Decisions.* New York: McGraw-Hill.

Plunkett, L. C., and G. A. Hale (1982). *The Proactive Manager: The Complete Book of Problem Solving and Decision Making.* New York: Wiley.

Sternberg, R. J. (1986). *Intelligence Applied: Understanding and Increasing Your Intellectual Skills.* Orlando: Harcourt Brace.

Part Eight

Working Smarter

*The Brain
in the
Workplace*

Part Eight. Working Smarter
The Brain in the Workplace

30

From Waltz to Tango

Brain-Friendly Approaches to Change

66International government does not mean the end of nations, any more than an orchestra means the end of violins. 99

—Golda Meir

Change. Without it there is only death. Life is change. Cell division, new synapses, digestion. Whether we talk of individuals or organizations, growth is not possible without change. The organization is an extension of the individual. The health of the organization, whether it is a marriage, a business, a team, or a bridge club, is directly related to the health of the individuals within it. Peter Senge (1990, p. 139) writes, "Organizations learn only through individuals who learn. Individual learning does not guarantee organizational learning. But without it no organizational learning occurs."

Without learning, there is no growth. Japanese entrepreneur Kazuo Inamori, founder and chairman emeritus of Kyocera Corporation, asserts: "If employees themselves are not sufficiently motivated to challenge, there will simply be no growth" (Senge, 1990, pp. 139–140). To decide that we have arrived at the right answers for all time is to decide that growth is no longer important. In fact, our pronouncements are at best approximations of the truth. Every day we do what we can to get one micron closer. The quest is eternal. We should, and will, never arrive at final answers. Bernard Phillips, a Quaker preacher, once gave a sermon entitled "The Search Will Make You Free." Personal mastery is one of Senge's five disciplines necessary to the learning organization. He writes, "People with a high level of personal mastery live in a continual learning mode. They never 'arrive'" (p. 142). John Kotter, a Harvard Business School professor and researcher on leadership, identified 12 crucial ingredients of successful leaders. Some years later, he acknowledged an oversight and added one more: *lifelong learning.* In some ways, it is silly to write a chapter on change, because change is incessant.

> **"If you don't know where you're going, it doesn't matter how you get there."**
> —Common management adage

One of the motives that drives conscious individual and organizational change is the pursuit of the ideal, of utopia, of perfection. Of course, there is a sense in which we will never know the secret truths of the universe. Cautions against any scientist's arrogant presumption of omniscience are spelled out by Capra (1984), Gleick (1987), and Heisenberg (1962). We can never know with certainty; at best we can estimate probabilities. We can continually improve our estimates, but when we tamper with a system to improve it, our intervention can cause unforeseen, unpredictable turbulence in the system. We must learn to be comfortable with chaos. Control is an illusion. In Michael Crichton's apocalyptic novel *Jurassic Park* (1990, p. 313), the scientist Malcolm says:

> And now chaos theory proves that unpredictability is built into our daily lives. It is as mundane as the rainstorm we cannot predict. And so the grand vision of science, hundreds of years old—the dream of total control—has died, in our century. And with it

much of the justification, the rationale for science to do what it does. And for us to listen to it. Science has always said that it may not know everything now but it will know, eventually. But now we see that isn't true. It is an idle boast. As foolish, and as misguided, as the child who jumps off a building because he believes he can fly.

I do not mean to sound the death knell of science—only an end to the illusion of omniscience. Laurence Gonzales, in his riveting work about what it takes to survive under extreme circumstances (*Deep Survival,* 2003), points out that as you make improvements on complex systems, progressively eliminating more slack and chance for error, in fact you increase the probability for and magnitude of error by making the system too taut, with too little "margin for error." Between the extremes of Aristotle and Plato there is the voice of W. Edwards Deming. Aristotle would confine us to the realities of the way things are; Plato would propel us toward the clouds of the unknowable. In between, Deming urges us to ask daily, "What can I do to improve today?"

The first part of this chapter will describe findings from brain research that are relevant to facilitating change and that would appear to hold true for both individuals and organizations. Later topics will cover other factors that affect primarily organizational change.

TOPIC 30.1   Kuhn: The Shifting Paradigm

It has become the vogue to talk about paradigm shifts. Thomas Kuhn started it all in *The Structure of Scientific Revolutions* (1970). In this insightful study of the history of science, he gave the world a new verbal toy to play with. The word *paradigm* comes from the Greek *para* ("beside") and *deigma* ("shown"). A paradigm is something shown beside the real thing; it is a pattern or model, like a set of drawings that explains the structure underlying specific phenomena. Kuhn gets more specific when he defines paradigms as "universally recognized scientific achievements that for a time provide model problems and solutions to a community of practitioners" (p. viii). New paradigms emerge because of their capacity to solve more problems, especially problems the old paradigms couldn't solve. As Kuhn writes: "The failure of existing rules . . . is the prelude to the search for new ones" (p. 68). A paradigm shift is generally preceded by a proliferation of theories that try to explain what the old paradigm can't. Kuhn traces in some detail the shift from Priestley's phlogiston theory to Lavoisier's oxygen theory, from Newton's ether to Einstein's relativity, from corpuscular theory to wave theory.

Because paradigm shifts generally require major "retooling," the people affected by the potential shift tend to resist strongly. They wish to forestall the expense and learning curve associated with accepting a new paradigm. Retooling is an extravagance, so when it takes place, it suggests that a new paradigm has emerged. This perfectly explains the transition from the assembly-line production paradigm, which held strongly around the world through the 1950s, to what now appears to be the continual-improvement paradigm of the 1990s. Over the last 40 years, gurus have proposed a variety of theories to explain what the old production paradigm couldn't. Theories such as Theory XY, Theory Z, statistical process control, and DIRTFOOT (Do It Right The First Time) have all vied to replace the time-and-motion studies of the production paradigm in the business world.

Kuhn points out that new paradigms tend to be defined by younger people or people new to the field. In both cases, the pushers of the new paradigm are not wedded to the conventional ways of doing things. Hence, the Japanese, with a past record of poor quality in manufacturing, have pushed the quality paradigm.

Lance Morrow wrote a feature essay in *Time* magazine entitled "Old Paradigm, New Paradigm" (January 14, 1991, pp. 65–66), in which he listed examples of old and new paradigms. Here are several of his plus several of mine:

Old Paradigms	**New Paradigms**
Fidel Castro	Vaclav Havel
Apartheid	F. W. de Klerk and Nelson Mandela
The American Century	The Pacific Rim
Cigarette smoking	Smoke-free spaces
Labor unions	Self-directed work teams
CBS News	Cable News Network
Knowledge	Information
Northern Ireland	The new Germany
Letter writing	E-mail and faxing
Nationalism	Pluralism
Communism	Democracy

Applications

❶ Paradigms are useful frameworks for solving problems. Be open to the possibility that a new paradigm may emerge in your lifetime that will increase your effectiveness. It doesn't matter whether you invent or discover the new paradigm yourself or follow another person's lead; just don't get caught holding onto an old paradigm for loyalty's sake. If a new set of guidelines appears able to answer more questions than the current set, go for it.

❷ Paradigms will shift more frequently now and in the future than in the history that Kuhn described. W. Edwards Deming's dictum of continuing improvement is a paradigm in and of itself and calls for constant attention to opportunities for modifying paradigms.

❸ In problem-solving situations, allow your paradigms to surface and be examined. *(Contributed by Rick Bradley)*

❹ View the five-video series narrated by Joel Barker, *Paradigm Mastery,* available from the publisher, StarThrower, at www.starthrower.com. Show this series to a group that needs to change and discuss it with them. It stresses the importance of questioning our assumptions by taking a fresh look at things.

TOPIC 30.2   Empowerment

The apparent consensus of current thinking on motivation revolves around the question of who sets a course of action: *external (extrinsic) motivation* refers to courses of action set by others, *internal (intrinsic) motivation* to courses of action set by oneself. Listed in table 30.1 are some examples of motivational situations (those in which an individual is expected to act in some way), with both external and internal versions of the motivational stimulus.

Consistently, internal motivators yield higher performance than external motivators. Amabile (1983) notes one exception: when clear guidelines are presented that call for essentially rote performance, then external motivators yield superior results. She also identifies a variation on this principle—rewards that convey competency information, as in "A panel of art experts mistakenly judged the copy of the Van Gogh you painted to be the original." External motivators are more effective with algorithmic, or step-by-step, tasks; internal motivators are more effective with heuristic, or experimental, ones. I am reminded of a now-discontinued (I hope) incentive program by an NFL team in which $1,000 bonuses were allegedly handed out after each game for every player on the opposing team who was put out of commission (for example, if a tackler broke the leg of a pass receiver).

Caine and Caine (1991) point out that, under conditions of continuous stress, internal motivation becomes more and more difficult to generate as people begin to see themselves fulfilling only goals formed by others. Amabile (1983) extensively documents the harmful effects of extrinsic motivation on creativity and problem solving. Gazzaniga (1985) has found that people who are learning to perform a skill under external conditions begin to perform that skill only when the reward possibilities continue to be presented. If you give a person a day off for a job well done, his or her future good performance will tend to become tied to continuing rewards. Give what you've always given, and you'll get what you've always gotten. Stop giving, and you stop getting. Research supports the benefits of mutually discussing possible rewards, rather than paternalistically doling out what you think people want.

Internal motivators are developed when people participate in goal setting and problem solving, as opposed to allowing others to set their goals, make their decisions, and solve their problems. In the summer of 1990, while walking down the coast of Sunset Beach, North Carolina, my wife and I asked each other what bothers could be removed to

Table 30.1. External vs. Internal Motivation

Call for Action	External Version	Internal Version
Sales goals	Manager or company sets goals for representatives	Manager and representative set goals together and mutually agree on them
Incentives	Company announces incentives	Employees negotiate incentives
Child discipline	Parent determines consequences of misbehavior	Child and parent together negotiate appropriate consequences
Class award	Teacher announces award before competition, presents award afterward	Award is announced only after work is completed
Work design	Management designs and monitors	Workers design, management supports

make life more enjoyable. Jane's top bother was feeling guilty about not providing her share of the caregiving for her parents, who were living six hours away by car in Opelika, Alabama. I suggested that she make a conference call to her two sisters—one in Alabama, the other in Minnesota—and discuss the problem. I remember that we emphasized the wisdom of trying to figure out a solution before her parents experienced another crisis (her mother had recently broken a hip) and our options became severely limited and, in fact, thrust upon us.

The call and subsequent research resulted in several options that were mutually agreeable to the three sisters. Jane, as spokesperson, called her parents to discuss the options, one of which was to maintain the status quo. They were also invited to identify other possible options. As it turned out, her parents became very excited about one particular option: to move to a retirement community located about five minutes from our home in Charlotte, with the two sisters retiring to our region (one to the mountains, the other to the beach) within about five years. My wife's mother brightly queried, "When do we leave?"

Although the move did not happen without some sadness, regret, and fear, my wife's parents did settle in and make new friends and new church homes. My wife's mother, a former church organist, played more piano than ever and entertained almost daily in the parlor after dinner. At the age of 77, she gave a one-hour organ recital for over 40 residents of the retirement community. Both parents grew healthier and more vigorous, and Jane's guilt vanished. If our hand had been forced by a crisis, such as a massive stroke, it is highly possible that guilt would have been transmogrified into resentment and anger. I see this episode as a testament to participation in internal motivation.

Gazzaniga (1985), Caine and Caine (1991), Amabile (1983), and Seligman (1991) all call for an end to external motivators. We have been operating since the 1940s under the paradigm of the behavioral contingency model of externally imposed rewards and punishments. Now the time has come to eliminate them, to encourage the new paradigm of empowerment through self- or mutually developed action planning. Gazzaniga goes so far as to decry bureaucracy and institutionalization as the enemy of internal motivation. He sees institutional relief of the symptoms of social ills as the opposite of caring: "I am claiming that a culture becomes more caring and humane the more its citizens feel themselves to be part of the problems that beset their lives. The only sure way to bring them close to such problems is to structure a culture where they deal with the problems at a personal level" (1985, p. 198).

From a societal perspective, what these researchers are saying is consistent with the current preoccupation of many social philosophers with treating root causes, not symptoms. In a recent task force on our aging population, the group coalesced around the need to address causes but agreed that we can't ignore symptoms. For example, to ensure that each senior citizen gets at least one hot meal a day, we need to back up and treat the causes of malnutrition among that population. Our inability to provide such meals is actually both a symptom and a cause—a symptom of poor public transportation and a cause of malnutrition. The resources are there, but access is limited. So we must fix the infrastructure.

Applications

❶ If you are a parent or a teacher, don't assume that you always know the right rewards and punishments. When appropriate, consult with your children or students. Read Glasser (1990) and Dreikurs and Cassel (1972) for ideas.

❷ If you are a manager who is responsible for the performance of others, talk with them to learn what's important to them and what their career goals are. Don't assume that you know the best way to reward them or the best direction for them in their careers. A former manager of mine assumed that I was motivated by the desire to earn more and more money, even after I explained that I was more motivated by challenging projects than by big bucks. My eventual departure from that company was largely based on his failure to abandon his externally imposed rewards for me (higher salaries) and accept my need for challenging and interesting projects. Bucks don't always have bang!

❸ Build an empowered workforce. If you are part of a management team, explore ways to give people more responsibility and opportunities to solve their own problems, make their own decisions, formulate their own plans, establish their own goals, negotiate their own rewards, and even describe their own jobs. Mutually agree on goals, then get out of their way. Don't be an intervener with your people, coming down like an avenging god. Instead, be a supporter, and be there when they need you for resources and consultation. For further ideas on empowerment, read *The Empowered Manager* by Peter Block (1987) and *Developing Superior Work Teams* by D. C. Kinlaw (1990).

4 Be more consultant, less boss. As a spouse or friend, help people understand dilemmas rather than "fixing things" for them. Allow them, or lead them, to solve problems on their own. Over the long term, internally generated solutions keep their power longer and are more likely to work. "Teach a person how to fish, and . . ."

5 Do not protect alcoholics or other addictive personalities from the consequences of their binges. Such protectors used to be called "patsies"; now, they're "enablers." A considerable literature has emerged on this subject as a part of the Adult Children of Alcoholics movement. Write for information, a bibliography, catalogs, and reading material to the following groups:

- National Association for Children of Alcoholics, 11426 Rockville Pike, Suite 301, Rockville, Maryland 20852, 888-554-2627 or 301-468-0985, fax 301-468-0987, www.nacoa.org

- Adult Children of Alcoholics, P.O. Box 3216, Torrance, California 90510 (send a stamped, self-addressed envelope for a schedule of meetings), 310-534-1815, www.adultchildren.org

6 Amabile (1983) identifies several indicators for judging whether or not a person is intrinsically motivated. I summarize four of them as follows:

- The individual is curious or stimulated by the task.

- The individual gains a sense of competence from the task itself.

- The individual perceives the task as being free of strong external controls.

- The individual feels as if he is at play, not at work.

7 In one corporation where I am currently consulting, management doles out recognition cards as rewards. Employees then exchange the cards for gifts of their choosing. Many employees have confided that they would much rather receive a verbal recognition statement specifying what they did well and the impact it had on the company. Stay close enough to the people around you to know what rewards they really value.

8 In training classes, don't use "off-the-shelf" cases exclusively. Build in opportunities for trainees to identify real-time, back-home cases where they can apply their newly acquired skills, concepts, knowledge, or attitude.

TOPIC 30.3   The Pygmalion Effect

Many regard Robert Rosenthal as the prophet of the Pygmalion effect (also known as the self-fulfilling prophecy). According to the myth, Pygmalion created a female statue, named her Galatea, and treated her with such affection that, through Aphrodite's intervention, the statue came to life and responded to him. Such is the essence of the self-fulfilling prophecy: what we expect tends to come true. In a famous report (Rosenthal and Jacobson, 1968), Rosenthal describes a case in which a researcher told teachers that a testing program had identified some students as having high potential and others as having low potential. In fact, the students had been picked randomly and assigned to one of the two groups. The results after a year in school: the "high-potential" group showed significant gains in achievement and ability as measured by standardized tests; the "normal" group showed no significant gains.

Rosenthal's initial report has been followed by 20 years of research exploring the limits of the self-fulfilling prophecy. According to today's thinking, although we can't think a statue into coming to life, we can certainly influence our level of performance and that of others by our expectations. Cousins (1989) includes positive expectations as one of the four key ingredients of hardiness as it relates to psychoneuroimmunology (see more at topic 15.2). The concept of the self-fulfilling prophecy is also very close to Seligman's concept of the optimistic explanatory style; in some ways, Seligman's research has subsumed Rosenthal's. Rosenthal identifies six ways to communicate expectations. I have summarized them and provided examples in table 30.2.

Applications

1 Be aware that negative expectations of yourself or others are likely to produce negative results. Although positive expectations ("I think I can" or "You can do it") cannot guarantee success, they certainly increase its chances.

2 Think of a particular person in your life who performs at a lower level than you'd like to see. Examine the six communication methods in table 30.2 and see if you may be communicating negative expectations without meaning to. Work on being as positive with this person as you can in each of the six ways. Write out a script for yourself with sample comments in each of the six areas.

Table 30.2. Rosenthal's Six Methods for Communicating Expectations

Communication Method	Positive Versions	Negative Versions
1. *Expressing confidence in my ability to help you*	"I know I can train you." "Stick with me—I make winners." "I've got the Midas touch."	"I'm not sure I know how to train you." "I'm not very good at training."
2. *Expressing confidence in your ability*	"I know you can do it."	"I'm not sure you can do it."
3. *Nonverbals: tone of voice, eye contact, energy level*	Smile, nod, pat, eye contact, upbeat energy	Looking away, tentative tone of voice, distant
4. *Feedback: specific and ample; mentioning the good with the bad*	"Good coverage, yet a couple of technical flaws."	"Try harder." "All wrong." "Reread it; you'll see what I mean."
5. *Input: amount of information given to person*	"Let's go over it in detail."	"I don't have time to go over it."
6. *Output: amount of production encouraged*	"Here's a new challenge."	"Better try the same thing again."

❸ View the video *Pygmalion Effect: The Power of Expectations Program,* available from CRM Learning (2215 Faraday Avenue, Carlsbad, California 92008, 800-421-0833). Check with your regional media distributor for ordering information. Discuss its implications for your situation.

❹ Keep the idea of a self-fulfilling prophecy in mind when you are working with teams. Be positive in your approach to problem-solving and work toward win-win situations or compromises. Keep the team asking, "How can we make this work?" In many situations, one positive person can turn the entire team around. *(Contributed by Jane Howard)*

TOPIC 30.4   Using Gap Analysis to Define Goals

Festinger (1953) and others have built a solid tradition of research on the subject of *cognitive dissonance.* In a nutshell (the pathway of this book is littered with many nutshells—hope you're not allergic!), this tradition has established that human organisms naturally work to reduce any discrepancy between the way they perceive themselves (for example, smart, attractive, and capable) and the way their significant others perceive them. In the world of work, an industry has emerged out of this tradition, commonly referred to by two labels: *gap analysis* and *the 360°*. The term *gap analysis* is used to refer to the measurement of two gaps: the discrepancy between how people see themselves and how others perceive them, and the discrepancy between the importance of a specific performance competency to a person's job and how well the person actually performs that competency. So two kinds of gaps may emerge: *perception gaps* and *performance gaps*. The inclusion of other raters in addition to the person being rated makes it a 360°, because the subject is in essence encircled, surrounded by people who are knowledgeable about his or her performance—a boss, peers, subordinates, customers, and the like. Without the other raters, the perception gap cannot be measured. I should point out that the performance gap *can* be measured by questioning only the subject of the analysis; however, the concept of performance gap and perception gap are normally combined, and this requires a small group of raters as well as the subject.

People receiving feedback from such gap analysis and 360° tools typically form action plans aimed at reducing both the perceptual and actual performance gaps.

Applications

❶ An excellent introduction to the "how to" of gap analysis is found in Tornow and London (1998).

❷ An excellent source of gap analysis information on the Internet is www.themanager.org/Knowledgebase/HR/Feedback.htm.

❸ Other resources include Brutus, Fleenor, and London (1998), Fleenor and Prince (1997), and Leslie and Fleenor (1998).

TOPIC 30.5 | **How to Formulate Effective Goals**

In chapter 37, I cover a grand theory of motivation that is based on goals. Everything we do originates with a goal; some are very small or trivial ("Clean my room"), others large or significant ("Build my own cabin in the mountains"). Some goals are more attainable than others because they are formulated better. Since effective goal formation is so important to the world of work, I am placing here (rather than in chapter 37) this summary of what we know about effective goal-making (this information comes primarily from three sources: Latham and Yukl, 1975; Gollwitzer, 1999; and Locke and Latham, 2002):

1. Any goal is better than no goal at all.

2. Difficult goals produce the highest levels of effort and performance (i.e., difficult goals are better than easier goals).

3. Specific goals lead to higher performance than the general exhortation to "do your best."

4. People with higher self-efficacy (i.e., feeling capable in a specific domain)

   • set higher goals than those with lower self-efficacy.

   • are more committed to assigned goals.

   • find and use better strategies.

   • respond more positively to negative feedback.

5. Goals influence performance in four ways:

   • fostering focus and minimizing distractions.

   • providing energy for the task (higher goals generate more energy and effort).

   • yielding greater persistence and more time on task.

   • entailing pursuit of greater task-relevant knowledge and strategy.

6. For very large or complex goals, it helps to set learning goals (i.e., create or identify strategies, ways to approach the performance goal).

7. Goals must be mutually accepted by manager and associate.

8. Assigned goals are just as effective as participative goals *if* the rationale has been explained, but less effective if peremptorily assigned: "Here, just do it."

9. The benefit of participating in goal setting is cognitive, inasmuch as participation creates more information sharing, e.g., around strategies.

10. The more money offered, the more commitment to goal attainment with difficult goals, but if it is all or nothing, people will quit when attainment seems hopeless; money is more effective when the goal is only moderately difficult or when paying a piece rate for performance.

11. Leaders can increase the self-efficacy of followers by

    • providing necessary training.

    • providing models.

    • communicating belief in the worker.

12. Goals with feedback are more effective than goals alone.

13. After attaining a goal, people typically set a higher goal.

14. For complex goals or tasks, proximal goals are effective (i.e., setting incremental goals for quicker, small victories en route to the larger, more distant goal).

15. People who attain lower goals are more satisfied than those who attain higher goals, because the latter are more self-critical (see related discussion at topic 25.4.)

16. In selection interviews where the candidate is asked to set goals based on a scenario, the tendency to set more ambitious goals is a good predictor of higher goal setting and attainment after employment.

17. Satisfaction is the effect, not the cause, of goal attainment, assuming that appropriate compensation is forthcoming.

18. When individual goals are consistent with group goals, group goals benefit; if they are inconsistent, the group goals suffer.

19. Feedback to associates on their progress helps them attain goals.

20. Goals framed as positive achievements are more achievable than ones formulated as negatives or things to avoid or prevent (e.g., "Respond with humor" rather than "Respond without getting angry").

21. Goals are more achievable when persons can remove seductive distractions and competing goals.

22. A goal is more achievable when conjoined creatively with another, synergistic goal—for example, "Build a deck *and* get to know my neighbor (by asking for help)."

If the preceding conditions describe prerequisites for effective goal setting, what do we know about circumstances when goal setting does not work? The research suggests that goal setting does not work when

- goals are formed that are not consistent with how performance is measured.

- initial commitment to the goal is not obtained.

- the relationship of the goal to personal goals is not considered.

- knowledge of how to accomplish the task is not shared.

- performance goals (i.e., number of widgets per hour) are used when learning goals (i.e., how to make widgets) are needed.

- proximal (i.e., short-term) goals are missing (in an uncertain environment).

- goals are too difficult for the individual involved.

Gollwitzer goes into some depth on the subject of what he calls *implementation planning*. It is not enough, he says, to set a goal: one must also plan how to reach it. In a series of experiments, he shows that goals are more likely to be attained when the goal-setter identifies the steps required—that is, formulates a plan. He demonstrates that attainment is more likely when the goal-setter deals with potential distractors by formulating a plan to ignore them, rather than simply redoubling her effort in the presence of a distractor. The more strongly she believes in the goal ("I really, strongly want to write a book on X"), and the more strongly she believes in the implementation plan ("I really, strongly want to spend three hours on Monday and Thursday nights, and three hours on Saturday afternoons, at the library with my laptop"), the more likely she is to reach her goal. Now, let us look at these two lines of research.

First, implementation planning. It is not enough just to say, "I want to write a book." Although this statement has several of the qualities of a good goal (specificity, difficulty, desirability), it is more likely to be attained if the goal-setter specifies the "what, when, and where"—

specific behaviors necessary to get the job done. Gollwitzer asked some of his college students to write him a letter within 48 hours after December 24 describing their Christmas Eve experiences. Half of them were asked to specify precisely when and where they would do the chore. Of the latter group, three-quarters of them successfully completed the assignment, whereas only one-third of the controls wrote him. Gollwitzer cites experiment after experiment, each one showing the dramatic effects of simply specifying when and where one would perform a task. Some groups presented a special challenge. Working with a group of drug addicts in withdrawal, he asked them to write a résumé by a certain time; half were asked, in addition, to specify when and where they would write the résumé. Those who did so were disproportionately successful.

Gollwitzer identifies two ways to address potential distractors: task facilitating and distraction inhibiting. For the goal "Lose 10 pounds in two months," the implementation plan might include "Keep high-fiber cereal with me at all times for snacking." A potential source of distraction would be pastries offered at the many meetings one attends. A distraction-inhibiting implementation plan would be something like "Ignore pastries—they are imaginary and not really there." A typical task-facilitating implementation might be "Focus really hard on visualizing your body 10 pounds lighter, and redouble your commitment." Gollwitzer finds that the latter is much less effective than the former. Focus your energy on avoiding the distractor rather than on redoubling your goal effort.

The effectiveness of implementation planning is founded on the belief that the plan triggers one or more psychological processes, particularly schemas (see topic 21.4), that make goal-directed behavior more natural or automatic. To think it is to do it, or at least to increase the likelihood that one will do it. It is important, in order for the implementation plan to actually trigger the schema, that the plan contain specific environmental cues. For example, for the goal, "I will stop misplacing my keys," one might formulate a plan for, upon entering the door of one's home, placing the keys in a bowl on the front hall table, then checking the bowl whenever passing it to ensure that the keys are there. Like the traditional string tied around one's finger, the bowl becomes a memory trigger: upon entering the house, seeing the bowl reminds one to place one's keys in it. There is, of course, one important difference: the string is nonspecific (it could be used for any of a number of goals), but the bowl is goal-specific.

Applications

① For each goal, whether major (write a book, get elected to office) or minor (visit the nursing home on Saturday, review current journals in the library), in order to maximize the chance of achieving it, decide that you feel *strongly* about it, then use the following checklist (which I call "A Checklist for Formulating Goals That Are Likely to Get Achieved") to evaluate how to formulate it.

1. Is the goal stated as specifically as possible?

2. Is the goal too easy, as more difficult or challenging goals tend to be taken more seriously?

3. Has the goal been accepted or agreed to by the relevant stakeholders (family, co-workers, boss, and so on)?

4. Have you provided for opportunities to get feedback on your progress towards the goal?

5. Have you established monetary or other tangible rewards for you upon partial or complete attainment of the goal?

6. If the goal is long-term, have you broken it down into a series of short-term goals?

7. Can you frame the goal as a learning task, not just as a performance task?

8. Can you frame the goal as a positive achievement ("to celebrate my spouse's achievements") rather than as a negative one ("to stop being threatened by my spouse's achievements")?

9. Can you combine this goal synergistically with another one?

10. Have you identified potential or actual distractors and made plans to avoid them?

11. Have you identified any goals that actually conflict with this goal, and can you eliminate, modify, or minimize the conflict?

12. Have you formed specific implementation plans (what, when, and where) for the goal?

13. Have you made up your mind that you have *really strong feelings* about attaining this goal?

② For each goal, create one or more specific implementation plans that identify *what, when,* and *where* you will perform specific actions aimed at reaching your goal. Make up your mind that you feel *strongly* about the implementation plan(s).

❸ For each goal, identify specific potential distractors and determine to avoid or ignore them. Treat them as though they didn't exist. I have employed this strategy as a way to keep off the 60 pounds I lost as the result of my low-carbohydrate diet. I have internalized the concept of "faux foods": I simply regard white flour, white sugar, and white rice not as food but as dirt, or paper, or wood, or some other nonedible part of my environment.

TOPIC 30.6   **Increments vs. Leaps**

In his Pulitzer prize–winning work *Guns, Germs, and Steel* (1997a), Jared Diamond describes the course of most major changes, discoveries, and inventions. Let us listen to Diamond: "My two main conclusions are that technology develops cumulatively, rather than in isolated heroic acts, and that it finds most of its uses after it has been invented, rather than being invented to meet a foreseen need" (pp. 245–246). In support of this, he recounts a series of incremental technology developments in chapter 13 of his book, "Necessity's Mother." For example, James Watt gets the credit for patenting the steam engine in 1769, but he only improved on a version by Thomas Newcomen some six decades earlier, which in turn was an improvement on Thomas Savery's steam engine of 1698, which was preceded (this is beginning to sound like the "begats") by steam engines built by the Frenchman Denis Papin, the Dutchman Christiaan Huygens, and others. Or the case of Thomas Edison, who was displeased when entrepreneurs debased his phonograph by using it to play recorded music! Diamond goes on: "But the question for our purposes is whether the broad pattern of world history would have been altered significantly if some genius inventor had not been born at a particular place and time. The answer is clear: there has never been any such person. All recognized famous inventors had capable predecessors and successors and made their improvements at a time when society was capable of using their product" (p. 245).

Application

❶ In planning individual and organizational change, think of increments and not of leaps. Increments of change are based on current technology or ideas that have an immediate new use: the chances of success are maximal, the chances of backsliding are minimal. Leaps, on the other hand, are based on untested technologies or ideas that might satisfy a long-standing need, but the chances of success are minimal, the chances of backsliding maximal.

T O P I C   30.7   **Group Size and Cohesion**

Robin Dunbar has reported on research that relates brain size to group size. He identifies four interrelated findings from animal and human research (1997, p. 192):

1. Among primates, social group size appears to be limited by the size of the species' neocortex.

2. The size of human social networks appears to be limited for similar reasons to a value of around 150.

3. The time devoted to social grooming by primates is directly related to group size because it plays a crucial role in bonding groups.

4. It is suggested that language evolved among humans to replace social grooming because the grooming time required by our large groups made impossible demands on our time. Language evolved to fill the gap because it allows us to use more efficiently the time we have available for social interaction.

Dunbar's theory accounts for previous research that estimated between 100 and 150 as the maximum size of a cohesive human group. It also explains why most employee opinion surveys tend to fault communication practices in their organizations; you can never communicate too much, especially when the work-group size is too large.

Applications

❶ Every organization should be partitioned into communities of no more than about 150 people. Schools, churches, banks, and plants should evolve in a manner that permits each member to feel a part of a group with no more than 150 members. Each of these communities should be allowed to develop its own identity through workplace design, social and recreational practices, carpools, and internal communication organs.

❷ Every organization should have a process that continually monitors the effectiveness of communication practices (newsletters, bulletin boards, meetings, etc.) throughout all the communities within the organization.

<hr>

TOPIC 30.8   **The Ideal Manager of Change**

<hr>

Robert McDaniel (1992) studied 62 managers of change projects in a West Coast electronics firm of some 8,000 employees. A clear pattern emerged that differentiated effective managers of change from ineffective ones. The effective managers were socially confident (they were not easily embarrassed), assertive (one didn't have to try to read their minds), open to new ideas (they were not tied to the tried-and-true), and conscientious (they were reliable, prepared, ambitious, disciplined, cautious, and well organized). These qualities are measured, respectively, in the Big Five dimensions called A5, A4, O3, and C (see chapter 33).

Elliott Jaques (see topic 34.6) has found that an effective manager must have sufficient mental complexity, as measured by the time span of work, to be a resource to those who report to her. If a manager cannot handle a longer, more complex time span than her reports, she may flounder, unable to be a resource because of an inability to see how all the issues interrelate.

Application

❶ When you must find an individual or a team to lead a change project, ensure that the appropriate personality traits and mental capabilities are present. If one or more qualities are absent, plan how you will compensate for their absence.

TOPIC 30.9 Appreciative Inquiry vs. Problem Solving

David Cooperrider and others argue that when people need to change, they work better with an ideal model than without one (Cooperrider and Dutton, 1998; Hammond, 1996). Traditional methods of problem solving do not customarily use ideal models; instead, they focus on what is wrong and how to fix it. Cooperrider has encouraged a kind of *best practices* approach, in which people who are responsible for a process that is not going well are exposed to a model of a group that is performing the process satisfactorily. Thus the name of this approach, *appreciative inquiry*—appreciating someone else's excellent performance and inquiring about his keys to success.

I once read a case study in which a hospital-related hotel (for families of patients) failed to make a profit. The change agent identified a successful, noncompeting hospital hotel in another part of the country and secured permission for representatives of each department of the nonperforming hotel to visit the model hotel for several days. After a day or so of observation, the visitors sat down with the model hotel's employees and each other and created an agenda for taking home the best of what they saw.

Applications

1 Read Cooperrider and Dutton (1998) and Hammond (1996) to learn more about appreciative inquiry.

2 Visit Sue Hammond's Thin Book Publishing Company website at www.thinbook.com.

The Elements of Successful Change

To help organizations go through major change, it is necessary to find outside change agents who know how to put all the research together and facilitate effective change programs. One such consulting firm is Rapid Change Technologies (www.rapidchange.com). Magaly d. Rodriguez, the company's CEO, follows brain research discoveries and integrates them into her intervention model. She has described this model in her promotional material as "experiences designed to stimulate imagination, reduce stress, bond teams and clear toxic relationships." Specifically, she works with her clients through a five-phase process:

1. Relieve distress by creating emotional safety.

2. Enrich "people environments."

3. Grow leaders bigger.

4. Commit to sound management of business *and* people.

5. Take ideas to action quickly.

Programs like that of Rapid Change Technologies incorporate not only the explicit change elements discussed in this chapter; they also incorporate ancillary elements such as approaches to stress reduction (see chapter 36), emotional intelligence (see chapter 35), and communication skills. What effective change programs have in common is the ability to help people set aside business as usual and think afresh about tapping their inner resources to identify what it takes to move to the next level.

Evolution involves three elements: variation, replication, and differential "fitness" (Dennett, 1995, p. 343). Genes mutate, the mutations are reproduced, and those that are more compatible with the current environment survive and continue to replicate. In organizations, the equivalent of genes is ideas. If an organization is to evolve, ideas must change and replicate throughout the organization. Those that are most compatible with the current organization's needs will survive and continue to replicate. In order for new and potentially beneficial ideas to emerge, language must flow freely in the organization. Language is the medium of ideas. When language is constrained, ideas are stillborn. Language breeds change and life, just as silence is the agent of stasis.

At topic 36.1, we see that stress is the symptom of an individual's loss of personal control, and prolonged stress leads to burnout. Organizational stress is the result of large-scale constraints intentionally or unintentionally placed on the flow of ideas; long-term organizational stress leads to organizational failure. Organizational constraints on the flow of information could be the result of something as benign and simple as the inertia of people who are just doing their individual jobs 40 hours a week without ever stopping to talk about how they are doing, or something as complex and sinister as managers who are control freaks and deeply afraid of change.

I cannot imagine a relationship that is more full of growth and change—yet stable and grounded—than the one I have with my wife, Jane. She is totally courageous, unafraid of new ideas, totally loving yet absolutely free of the urge to put constraints on me. I work hard to be as freeing with her as she is with me. Recently, I discovered William's Blake's four-line gem "Eternity," a perfect summary of how I feel about Jane, the ideal relationship, the ideal organization, and the prerequisite for change:

Eternity

He who binds to himself a joy

Does the winged life destroy;

But he who kisses the joy as it flies

Lives in eternity's sun rise.

SUGGESTED RESOURCES

Amabile, T. M. (1983). *The Social Psychology of Creativity.* New York: Springer-Verlag.

Cooperrider, D. L., and J. E. Dutton (1998). *Organizational Dimensions of Global Change.* Thousand Oaks, Calif.: Sage.

Cummings, T. G., and C. G. Worley (1997). *Organization Development and Change* (6th ed.). Cincinnati: South-Western.

Dennett, D. C. (1995). *Darwin's Dangerous Idea: Evolution and the Meanings of Life.* New York: Simon & Schuster.

Diamond, J. (1997a). *Guns, Germs, and Steel: The Fates of Human Societies.* New York: Norton.

Dunbar, R. (1996). *Grooming, Gossip, and the Evolution of Language.* Cambridge, Mass.: Harvard University Press.

Kuhn, T. S. (1970). *The Structure of Scientific Revolutions* (2nd ed.). Chicago: University of Chicago Press.

Rosenthal, R., and Jacobson, L. (1968). *Pygmalion in the Classroom.* Austin, Tex.: Holt, Rinehart and Winston.

Senge, P. (1990). *The Fifth Discipline.* New York: Doubleday/Currency.

31

Brain Ergonomics

Workplace Design for Quality and Productivity

*E*rgonomics is the study of how to adapt the workplace to the worker. It comes from the Greek root *ergon,* or "work," and is also referred to as human-factors engineering. Its efforts are aimed at making the workplace more user-friendly for human workers by minimizing or eliminating harmful stress on their bodies and minds. An ergonomics specialist, for example, would figure out how to make my keyboard bend outward from the middle in a way that would eliminate the stress on my wrist that causes tennis elbow.

This chapter deals with one specific domain of ergonomics: how the brain responds to the workplace. Here we are looking at the elements of workplace design that specifically affect the brain and nervous system. We will not talk about the proper shape of a chair for optimal back support, but about such things as the effect of light on mood and wakefulness. Remember that many of the findings in this chapter are equally applicable to the home, which is a workplace for all of us. I have organized these topics so that the first four deal with issues related to time and the remainder with other factors, such as space and temperature.

Temporal Considerations (Topics 31.1–31.4)

The mind is like a moving picture: you can't stop it. If you stop a moving picture, you have a photograph; if you stop your mind, you have a corpse. Time is inextricably woven into the fabric of mental activity. Some even define intelligence as speed of response. Several aspects of time affect the functioning of the brain at work.

TOPIC 31.1 | Time Out!

We have long known the importance of breaks for minimizing error and fatigue and maximizing productivity, quality, and morale. Okogbaa and Shell (1986) summarized this research, offering specific guidelines for minimizing fatigue in computer operators.

As a rule, workers need 5- to 10-minute breaks every one to two hours. The frequency and duration of these breaks depend on the nature of the work and the worker. To determine the need for breaks, try (1) asking the worker and (2) keeping error logs.

Breaks also support the need in thought processes for *chunking* (see topic 21.1) and *spacing* (see topic 22.2). Work involving higher mental functions, such as analysis and synthesis, needs to be spaced out to allow new neural connections to solidify. New learning drives out old learning when insufficient time intervenes.

Applications

1 Allow yourself and your workers to establish optimal periods for breaks. As a simple guideline, when you become aware of more errors or fatigue, take a break.

2 Keep records on error rates over time. Talk with your workers, sharing these records with them. Establish a mutually agreeable policy that is based on the need for taking a break just before the time that one could expect a spike in error rate.

3 Where possible, avoid rigidly mandating the length of time between breaks. Fatigue may set in earlier or later than your fixed work period, and workers need to recognize it and respond to it promptly. Workers differ: some require longer work periods with longer breaks, others need shorter periods with shorter breaks. Workers need the authority and responsibility to take a break when they feel the onset of fatigue, particularly where safety issues are involved (for example, driving, operating heavy equipment, or lifting loads).

4 The ideal break involves some level of exercise, such as throwing horseshoes, walking, or playing basketball. This can dissipate the results of overarousal or stimulate people out of boredom or underarousal.

5 During breaks, mind workers should avoid high-glycemic carbohydrates and fats (this includes most candy bars and other sweets), which cause sleepiness; proteins and low-glycemic carbohydrates such as nuts and fruits are fine.

6 Too much caffeine (more than one "dose"—one mg/lb of body weight—every six hours) causes errors of commission; mind workers are more subject to this phenomenon than muscle workers, who burn off excess caffeine more quickly. On the other hand, too little caffeine can cause drowsiness and errors of omission. This could be a serious safety issue for operators of heavy equipment.

7 Display signs like the following ones in break areas to remind workers of the guidelines in applications 3–6:

Been sitting all day? Take a stroll outside!

Been standing all day? Take a load off your feet!

Feeling tense and shaky? Get some exercise.
(Show pictures of people throwing horseshoes or
jumping rope.)

Feeling drowsy? Try exercise, fresh air, light, caffeine.

❽ Offer a lunchtime training program to give information on breaks to people.

TOPIC 31.2   Shift Work

For workers who must work a night shift, such as midnight to 8:00 A.M., two issues are important: (1) ensuring good sleep and (2) ensuring alertness at work. Because the body appears to work on a cycle of just over 24 hours (see topic 9.3), rotating shifts should advance, not regress; in other words, day shifts should be followed by afternoon shifts, then by night shifts. Following a day shift with a night shift conflicts with the natural body clock.

Timothy Monk, a psychiatry professor at the University of Pittsburgh School of Medicine, has identified eight common risks associated with rotating shift work (Slon, 1997):

1. Chronic fatigue

2. Depression and loneliness

3. Susceptibility to colds and flu

4. Stomach problems

5. Erratic menstrual cycles

6. Obesity

7. Heart disease

8. Accidents

Physician Acacia Aguirre reports that the 24 million Americans who work night shifts are at five times greater risk for stomach ulcers, twice as likely to smoke or use stimulants, at higher risk for high blood pressure, heart attack, and breast cancer, and, if they have kids, are three to six times more likely to divorce. He recommends sleep, exercise, and limiting oneself to one dose of caffeine (1 mg/lb of body weight) during any seven-hour period of being awake, or, two doses daily.

Long term, the best remedy is to relieve your body of the stress of night work. Ichiro Kawachi, an associate professor of health and social behavior at the Harvard School of Public Health, has found that working the night shift for more than six years nonstop results in a 50 percent increase in the risk of heart disease (Slon, 1997). Timothy Monk reports that many career night-shift workers "hit the wall" and lose their adaptability to night work. When this happens, they should find day work.

For the many other factors that affect the quality of sleep, browse through chapter 9.

Applications

1 Monk has a variety of recommendations for helping rotating shift workers maximize the chances of a good night's sleep, including these:

- Take sleep seriously: avoid TV, don't fall asleep on the couch.

- Prepare a quiet room. Ensure total darkness: use blindfolds; avoid clocks that glow in the dark, or put tape over the glow; use black window shades, even black garbage bags and duct tape if necessary. Use earplugs (some foam rubber plugs are form-fitting and unnoticeable); disable telephone and doorbell ringers; buy a "white noise" machine to mask a variety of sounds; listen to a tape recording of waterfalls or something equally soothing.

- Use a "do not disturb" sign (or a sign that says, "Quiet! Shift worker sleeping inside").

- Set the thermostat so the bedroom is 65–68° F when you try to sleep; cooler temperatures make sleeping easier.

- If you don't sleep a full episode, try napping during the afternoon lull between 2:00 and 4:00 P.M. (15–30 minutes if you've slept 4 cycles or about 6 hours; 1½ hours if you've only slept 2–3 cycles or about 3–4½ hours).

- Avoid exercising just before going to sleep; instead, exercise upon waking. The exercise makes you alert, not sleepy.

- Expose yourself to bright lights while at work at night; full-spectrum light is best (see a discussion of full-spectrum light and the color rendering index in topic 32.2, especially application 1).

- Don't drink caffeinated drinks within six hours of desired sleep onset; it takes that long for the caffeine to metabolize.

- Eat your largest meal at "lunch" during the night shift, then eat a light "dinner" with carbohydrates and your daily fat allowance (see the discussion of nutrition and alertness in topic 7.7). If healthy snacks are unavailable, take small portions of fresh fruit and veg-etables, low-fat yogurt, air-popped popcorn, or some other snack that does not contribute to the tendency to gain weight during night work.

- Try taking a 10-minute brisk walk during breaks. You will burn calories and increase alertness, rather than consuming them and getting sleepy, even around 4:00 A.M., when circadian rhythms fos-ter sleepiness.

- Avoid sunlight as much as possible on the drive home in the morn-ing (drive on shady streets) so daylight doesn't get a foothold on your biorhythms. Monk recommends welder's goggles, but they are unsafe for driving, so try close-fitting wraparound sunglasses.

- Resist eating a big meal in the morning before going to bed. It in-terferes with sleep, causes indigestion, and leads to weight gain (you have no exertion afterward to burn off the calories).

- Go straight to bed. Don't do chores or watch TV; instead, read something with the aid of a weak light.

- Avoid alcohol as a sleep inducer: it deprives you of rapid-eye-movement (REM), or dream-stage, sleep, and although you might get to sleep more quickly, it prevents the most relaxing form of sleep.

❷ Wake up to bright lights to help reset your body clock. (See topic 9.3 for the recommended light strength and pattern.) Work areas, break areas, and toilets should be especially well lit for shift workers.

❸ For an ideal 21-day shift progression built on the 24-plus-hour cycle, refer to table 9.1 in topic 9.3, "The Circadian Rhythm."

❹ Monk recommends going to bed the same time every night (or day). If you are working nights during the week and you want to catch a daytime activity with your family on Saturday, then go to bed on Saturday morning at the regular time, get up for the event, and take a long nap afterward. That way, your body doesn't have to keep resetting its clock.

❺ Monk says that the ideal shift work is "rapid change forward" shifts: two "on" days, two "on" evenings, two "on" nights, then several days off; just make sure to go to bed the same time every night and catch up on the sleep you miss on the two night shifts.

❻ The French have a reputation for treating night workers well. One key, apparently, is their tendency to ask night workers what would help to reduce their stress. The workers ask, for example, to have more flexibility in taking time off for vacations and holidays. This gives them a greater sense of control (and we know that this is a major stress reducer).

❼ Provide protein snacks for night workers to minimize the drowsiness that results from consuming fats and high-glycemic carbohydrates.

TOPIC 31.3   **Naps at Work**

Rossi and Nimmons (1991) cite support for two or three 20-minute naps per day. That is the ideal number for maximum quality, productivity, sense of well-being, and overall health and longevity. Studies show that nappers outproduce non-nappers; however, a goal of three naps a day is out of reach for most people. Perhaps a minimum of one 15- to 30-minute nap per day should be voted a basic human right.

Neurologist Roger Broughton of the University of Ottawa concludes from his 20 years of sleep research that "humans are born to nap" (*BrainWork: The Neuroscience Newsletter,* March–April 1998). He suggests about a 20-minute timed nap that occurs about 12 hours after the midpoint of the previous night's sleep. The improvement in alertness from such a brief nap is being acknowledged by the corporate world, as witnessed by the *Wall Street Journal*'s report that several companies are providing employee nap rooms. See more in chapter 9.

Applications

❶ Many companies have official policies that prohibit employees from napping during the workday. These policies serve public relations purposes and are not consistent with research on productivity. Don't associate reasonable napping with laziness; associate it with productivity.

❷ Some people should not be permitted to nap for safety reasons, but even they would be safer workers if they were allowed to go off-duty for a short nap.

❸ If you are a citizen and spot a public worker napping, resist calling in to report it as laziness and a waste of the taxpayers' dollars. Appreciate the productivity, quality, safety, and health benefits associated with a nap. Of course, if you see a public worker snoozing the day away, that's another matter!

TOPIC 31.4   Multitasking

Ergonomics researcher Christopher Wickens, director of the University of Illinois Aviation Research Laboratory, says (see *APA Monitor,* January 1994, pp. 16 ff.) that when a worker must pay attention to multiple inputs or tasks, it helps if the inputs involve brain resources that are different ("noncompeting"). For example, if one must pay attention to two visual inputs, that is more difficult than paying attention to one visual and one auditory input. He has identified three "dimensions"—i.e., sets of resource trade-offs common throughout a variety of workplace settings: visual vs. auditory, verbal-linguistic vs. spatial-manipulative, and response vs. perception-cognition.

Applications

❶ If you must follow two television monitors, turn down the audio on one, then attend to the visual of one and the audio of the other.

❷ In designing multiple information sources, whether for pilots, surgical teams, or security guards, try to select from opposites on Wickens's three dimensions. Design, for example, one of two critical inputs for a surgical team to be visual, spatial, and response-demanding (as in a map of the surgical area), and the other to be auditory, verbal, and cognition-demanding (as in vital systems monitors).

Nontemporal Considerations (Topics 31.5–31.11)

The mind not only works over time: it works in the context of the quality of the moment. The immediate quality of the environment can significantly affect mental function. This section explores some of the environmental qualities that have an immediate impact on the brain.

TOPIC 31.5 **Negative Ions**

The atmosphere we breathe is normally full of positive and negative ions. Air conditioning, lack of ventilation, and long dry spells remove negative ions, which usually serve to latch onto airborne dirt particles and wrestle them to the floor, rendering the air purer. Roughly one-third of the population seems to be particularly sensitive to negative-ion depletion. The proportion of negative ions is highest around moving water (storms, ocean, rivers, waterfalls)—it's no wonder that we feel so energized at the beach. The best ratios of negative to positive ions are associated with waterfalls and the time before, during, and after storms. The worst are found in windowless rooms and closed, moving vehicles. Some air purifiers work by emitting negative ions, which purify room air by attaching to impurities and escorting them to the floor.

High concentrations of negative ions are associated with high energy and positive mood (Thayer, 1996). In fact, Marian Diamond, a professor of neuroanatomy at the University of California, Berkeley, has found that levels of negative ions are inversely related to levels of serotonin in the brain. Negative ions suppress serotonin levels in much the same way that natural sunlight suppresses melatonin. Hence the invigorating effect of fresh air and sunshine and the correspondingly depressed feelings associated with being closed in and dark. If you deplete the air of negative ions, you experience an increase in serotonin and its attendant drowsiness and relaxation—not what you want when mental agility is demanded. Diamond's research (1988), along with other information on ions, is summarized in Yepsen (1987).

In an interesting twist, Josh Backon, a member of the Department of Cardiology, The Hebrew University of Jerusalem, writes in an Internet posting (his e-mail address is backon@vms.huji.ac.il) that in order to increase left-hemisphere activity (linear, language, logical), one can block the left nostril and engage in "forced unilateral nostril breathing." Likewise, to increase right-hemisphere activity (creative, holistic, emotional), the right nostril should be blocked. This practice increases the supply of negative ions to a specific hemisphere.

A note of caution: Underwriters Laboratory and *Consumer Reports* magazine have conducted tests on ionizing air purifiers, only to discover that many machines emit dangerous levels of ozone. At indoor ozone levels greater than 50 ppb (parts per billion), according to the Environmental Protection Agency, one can suffer wheezing, coughing, chest pain, and shortness of breath in the short term, and permanent lung damage and even premature death in the long term. According to the tests, some machines emit over 300 ppb within inches of the machine, but this level drops at greater distances.

Applications

1 Don't live or work in a space with no fresh air unless the air conditioning system contains an ion generator. Periodically check ozone levels.

2 Take frequent breaks in fresh air, and when you can't, open the window!

3 Purchase an ion generator for the room where you spend the most time, and run it when you are not getting any outside air. Place the machine as far away from you as possible, as in a corner opposite where you will be working. Specifically *not* recommended by the testers were

- Brookstone Pure-Ion V2
- Sharper Image Professional Series Ionic Breeze Quadra S1737 SNX
- Ionic Pro CL-369
- IonizAir P4620
- Surround Air XJ-2000

Favorable recommendations were accorded to

- Friedrich C-90A
- Whirlpool 45030

Look for future studies by *Consumer Reports.* For any ionizing machines not mentioned here, ask for ozone-emitting information before buying.

TOPIC 31.6   Stress in the Workplace

J. Donald Millar, director of the National Institute of Occupational Safety and Health, in a presentation at the 1991 American Psychological Association convention in San Francisco, reported that workers' compensation claims for stress-related problems rose 700 percent in California from 1979 to 1988. Nationally, stress-related claims have recently accounted for 12 percent of all workers' compensation claims. During the 1980s, roughly one-fourth of all Social Security disability claims were for mental disorders—that's 600,000 people each year.

Millar cites several sources of this increase of stress in the workplace, including an unpredictable economy, conversion from manufacturing jobs to service jobs, and the increasing role of computers (Bales, 1991, p. 32). He also refers to a greater use of contract workers as a way to beat rising medical costs. His recommendations are listed below as applications. Additional information on the causes and remedies of stress is given elsewhere in this chapter as well as in chapter 36.

Bond, Galinsky, and Swanberg (1998) reported in the *1997 National Study of the Changing Workforce* that extensive research using 3,000 interviews identified workplace stress as the primary cause of home stress, and not the other way around. In fact, they found that stress tends to originate at work, spread to the home, then boomerang to the workplace in an intensified form. Interviewees reported that poor working conditions were more stressful than poor pay and benefits. Job stress has had a greater negative effect on productivity than stress caused by child care or eldercare. The four most significant requirements for job satisfaction emerged as

1. Job autonomy

2. Learning opportunities

3. Supportive supervisors

4. Flexible work arrangements

Women, as a group, have special work-related stress concerns. For example, Amy Wolfson of the College of the Holy Cross, Worcester, Massachusetts, found that in a survey of 184 professional women, 92 percent failed to get a good night's sleep during the week, reporting at least one hour less per night than optimum (*APA Monitor,* November 1996, p. 41). Women who worked 35 hours or more each week slept less and rose earlier than women who worked less. The women reporting sleep loss also reported associated physical complaints and decreased alertness. Wolfson's interviews revealed that the women felt they had to sacrifice sleep in order to work the longer hours.

Paralleling Wolfson's study, researchers at the Center for Health Promotion and Disease Prevention at the University of North Carolina at Chapel Hill studied women's health habits at eight factories across the state. Here are some of their findings:

- One-third of the women smoked.

- Around 70 percent ate no low-fat foods.

- Ninety percent failed to eat the daily minimum of five servings of fruits and vegetables.

- Fifty-three percent said that they had too little time to exercise.

- Forty-three percent lacked the will to go to a gym after work.

The women cited lack of time, support, and education as the primary reason for their poor health habits. Time and support both played a role in a common complaint: as working mothers, they simply didn't have the time or energy to exercise and cook healthy meals.

The Chapel Hill group designed an intervention for these women: they published a personalized magazine based on the information from the survey, with specific recommendations on how to find time, will, support, education, and energy. The program, entitled "Health Works for Women," was presented at the American Psychological Association's Women's Health Conference in 1996; it was summarized in the *APA Monitor* (November 1996, p. 41; more information available at www.hpdp.unc.edu/Research/HWW. pdf?CFID=12310&CFTOKEN=66396148).

Researchers (*Cox News Service,* March 23, 1993) at the University of Manchester in England rated stress levels for a variety of jobs on a 10-point scale. Criteria included pay, control of activities, physical environment, and absenteeism, among others. Here are their findings:

Miner	8.3
Police officer	7.7
Prison officer	7.5
Construction worker	7.5
Airline pilot	7.5
Journalist	7.5
Advertising executive	7.3
Dentist	7.3
Actor	6.8
Nurse	6.5
Firefighter	6.3
Teacher	6.2
Social worker	6.0
Bus driver	5.4
Postal worker	4.0

Applications

❶ Design healthy jobs. This includes everything from applying principles of ergonomics to asking workers how their jobs could be improved.

❷ Monitor jobs to ensure that workers stay healthy. This includes conducting attitude surveys and employing a variety of participative management techniques.

❸ Educate managers and the public on the causes and consequences of stress in the workplace.

❹ Improve the availability of mental health services.

❺ Notify management about stressors on the job. *(Contributed by Rick Bradley)*

❻ Be as concerned about the job-related stress of your employees as you are about their stressors off the job, such as those addressed by employee assistance programs. Some kind of grievance procedure, whistle-blower policy, or other recourse for employees who are experiencing various forms of job stress should be available.

7 Encourage the use of gym facilities by employees during the workday. Better yet, provide workout facilities and showers at work.

8 Follow the work of George Mason University psychology professor Raja Parasuraman, who proposed a field called "neuroergonomics," based on brain scan technology. He wants people with high-stress, high-fatigue, high-risk jobs, such as air traffic controllers and baggage screeners, to undergo brain scans to help identify brain patterns that suggest heightened risk of errors due to fatigue and underattention.

9 If you're highly susceptible to stress (i.e., someone who scores higher on the N scale of the Big Five—see chapter 33), prefer a career with one of the lower ratings. Otherwise, go for mining, police work, construction, or go fly an airplane.

10 Read Martin Moore-Ede (1993), *The Twenty-Four Hour Society: Understanding Human Limits in a World That Never Stops.*

TOPIC 31.7   **Testosterone and the Achievement Syndrome**

Moir and Jessel (1991) summarize the research on the relationship between testosterone level and what might be called the achievement syndrome. They find that automatized behaviors—repetitive behaviors that require little mental or physical effort—typically drop off over time because of fatigue or boredom. However, the performance level for these behaviors does not drop over time in people with higher testosterone levels—they make fewer mistakes and don't tire as quickly. Examples of such behaviors are math computation, walking, talking, keeping balance, maintaining observation, and copying. In several controlled studies, subjects injected with testosterone showed significantly less decline in skill performance as time passed. Those who were not injected showed an increase in mistakes and fatigue. No level of testosterone is directly related to degree of persistence, which is defined as a combination of focus and energy. This phenomenon equates to the Five-Factor Model personality trait of high Consolidation (see chapter 33).

Applications

1 Testosterone level can be increased by participating in competitive sports and winning—so if you feel you need a boost in testosterone and resist the idea of injections, try finding a tennis (or basketball, handball, etc.) opponent you can beat before automatized behavior is required.

2 Redford Williams's research (R. Williams, 1989) showed that two kinds of arousal can be generated by the mind's reaction to the environment: energy to focus and concentrate, which results from increased testosterone production, and energy to fight, flee, or freeze, which results from increased cortisol (from the epinephrine-norepinephrine chain). The latter suppresses the former; as cortisol production increases, testosterone decreases. So if automatized behavior is important to you, you need to dissipate the cortisol (i.e., stress) in your body.

TOPIC 31.8   Temperature and Mood

Craig Anderson writes that hot temperatures affect mood (*APA Monitor,* February 1998, p. 8). Whether it is a hot day in the plant (defined as a day when the temperature reaches at least 90° Fahrenheit) or a hot day on the streets, hot temperatures are associated with hot tempers. More precisely, Anderson reports, as global warming occurs, for every 1° increase in average daily temperature in the United States, we can expect an increase in murder and assaults of 3.68 incidents per 100,000 of population.

Applications

1 Make special provisions for workers who must experience temperatures in excess of 90° F (or lower, if humidity is high). I know a plant in Kentucky where, when temperatures reach the boiling point, the human resources manager instructs the neighborhood grocer to send over enough ice cream to give all the workers as much as they want, as long as the temperature exceeds 90° F, at no cost to the workers.

2 Discipline yourself to practice and encourage lower fossil fuel consumption and be willing to pay extra for cleaner energy and fuel-efficient transportation.

TOPIC 31.9   Handedness

About 10 percent of the population is left-handed, a proportion that appears to persist across generations, socioeconomic conditions, and race. Of these left-handers, 60 percent are male and 40 percent female. Handedness appears to be related both to our specific genetic inheritance and to the stress and trauma associated with pregnancy and birth. On one "hand," if both parents are left-handed, one out of two offspring will be left-handed; if one parent is left-handed, the ratio will be one out of six; and if neither parent is left-handed, only one out of sixteen offspring will be left-handed. On the other hand, because the left brain is more sensitive to oxygen deprivation in the womb, functions such as handedness may be shifted to the right hemisphere, causing left-handedness.

Left-handedness is associated with right-brain qualities: lefties tend to be more creative and imaginative, better at visual-spatial tasks, and better at mathematics. Left-handedness is also associated with a higher accident and injury rate (surely, some of these statistics can be attributed to lefties having to deal with a world built by and for righties); left-handers have 20 percent more sports-related injuries, 25 percent more work-related accidents, a 49 percent higher risk of home accidents, a 54 percent higher risk while using tools, and an 85 percent higher risk while driving a car. Gerald Larson of San Diego's Navy Personnel Research and Development Center studied 2,379 Navy enlisted men and found that the lefties among them reported a significantly higher incidence of "mental lapses" (Associated Press article, August 23, 1993). These lapses include moments when one loses focus or attentiveness, as in not seeing something in plain view; forgetting a well-known name; or forgetting why one moved from one room to another. Larson attributes lefties' higher accident rate to the same biological infrastructure that resulted in these lapses.

This accident-proneness may explain why righties outlive lefties by five years (females) to ten years (males). Challenging these statistics, Stanley Coren (1992), a member of the University of British Columbia's psychology department, says that they're based on the old days when lefties were forced to be right-handed; therefore, there are simply not as many left-handers proportionately among seniors today as there will be in several decades. In fact, Lauren Julius Harris, a professor of neuropsychology at Michigan State University, reported the results of a survey that showed an increase in left-handedness in North America from 4 percent in 1928 to 13 percent in 1983 (*APA Monitor,* April 1997, p. 13). And in a 1993 *Neuropsychologica* study of the elderly, many respondents indicated that because of urging by teachers and parents, they switched early on from left- to right-handedness. The true relationship between handedness and longevity will not be known until such time in the 21st century as the effects of the stigma against left-handedness have disappeared.

It's not easy being left-handed in a right-handed world; however, some parts of our environment favor left-handers. The standard "qwerty" keyboard, for example (the odd moniker stands for the sequence of letters on the left side of the top row), places the most frequently used letter, *e,* on the left side, as well as other highly popular typing letters: *a, r, t, s, d, c,* and *b.* Maybe that's why I (a rightie) developed tendonitis in my left arm

> Most left-handers have dominant motor control in their right hemisphere. This has led some left-handers to conclude that they are the only ones in their right mind.

from keyboarding and had to wear a brace on my left wrist when I was going to be typing for more than 30 minutes. Since I began using an "ergonomic keyboard" that entails almost no bending at the wrist, I no longer have to use the brace.

Applications

❶ If you are left-handed, find tools and equipment that are user-friendly for lefties. If you are responsible for buying things for lefties or training them, put yourself in their position before making purchasing decisions. Better yet, ask them! Too many of us make decisions affecting left-handers without assessing their strengths and weaknesses.

2 For further ideas and information, call or write Lefthanders International, P.O. Box 8249, Topeka, Kansas 66608 (913-234-2177). This organization boasts of over 30,000 members and publishes *Lefthander Magazine,* which is organized from back to front.

3 If you're a right-handed keyboarder, use a left-wrist brace to minimize stress on the left arm while keyboarding for long periods. You might also try using a Dvorak keyboard, in which the most frequently used keys are assigned to the strongest fingers, rather than a qwerty keyboard. If you're a leftie, stick with qwerty.

4 Check out the Usenet bulletin board at alt.lefthanders.

5 Explore the website at www.lefthandzone.com.

6 Begin using an ergonomic keyboard at your computer. I've been using one now for three years—awkward at first, but soon comfy.

TOPIC 31.10 Simultaneous Tasks That Are Close in Space

Christopher Wickens (see topic 31.4) has developed the theory of proximity-compatibility. According to this theory, when multiple inputs are critical for decision making, those inputs should be close in proximity and similar in color and design, so that the brain can instantly recognize their relationship.

Applications

1 Determine the most commonly paired data inputs and find ways to group them close together. The use of font size, font design, and font color can also direct the eye to related inputs.

2 Review the work of Chong Chiu, president of FPI (Failure Prevention and Investigation) International, San Clemente, California. *(Provided by Mary Joy, Duke Energy Corp.)*

TOPIC 31.11   The Cost of Being Out of Flow

      In a startling affirmation of the findings of Csikszentmihalyi's *flow* research (see primary discussion at topic 37.2), Greg Oldham and Benjamin Gordon, researchers at the University of Illinois at Urbana-Champaign, find that workers who are over- or under-challenged by their work tend to partake in cigarettes, alcohol, and marijuana at a greater rate than their co-workers whose cognitive ability matched the complexity level of their jobs. Their study (in *Journal of Health and Social Behavior,* September 1999) used data collected on 7,000 workers interviewed during the National Longitudinal Survey of Youth. Researchers compared job complexity, self-reported drug use, and ability test results. Workers whose ability exceeded or fell short of the demands of their jobs tended to use drugs more. The conclusion: ability-demand mismatches are a breeding ground for substance abuse.

Application

❶ Through employee surveys, performance appraisal, career counseling, or other mechanisms, check out workers' levels of *boredom* (ability exceeds job demand) and *frustration* (ability falls short of job demand) and adjust their jobs to bring job complexity more in line with their ability.

SUGGESTED RESOURCES

Bond, J. T., E. Galinsky, and J. E. Swanberg (1998). *The 1997 National Study of the Changing Workforce.* New York: Families and Work Institute. (See also www.familiesandwork.org.)

Coren, S. (1992). *The Left-Hander Syndrome: The Causes and Consequences of Left-Handedness.* New York: Free Press.

Druckman, D., and J. A. Swets (Eds.). (1988). *Enhancing Human Performance: Issues, Theories, and Techniques.* Washington, D.C.: National Academy Press.

Rossi, E. L., and D. Nimmons (1991). *The 20-Minute Break: Using the New Science of Ultradian Rhythms.* Los Angeles: Tarcher.

Slon, S. (1997, June) "Night Moves." *Prevention,* pp. 106–113.

Thayer, R. E. (1996). *The Origin of Everyday Moods: Managing Energy, Tension, and Stress.* New York: Oxford University Press.

Yepsen, R. B. Jr. (1987). *How to Boost Your Brain Power: Achieving Peak Intelligence, Memory and Creativity.* Emmaus, Pa.: Rodale.

32

Stop, Look, and Listen

The Five Senses in the Workplace

"It is shameful for a man to rest in ignorance of the structure of his own body, especially when the knowledge of it mainly conduces to his welfare, and directs his application of his own powers."

—Philipp Melanchthon

The five senses directly affect our presence of mind. This chapter explores how the input of our five sensory channels affects our minds at work and play. In turn, we will examine the impact on the mind of the visual, auditory, olfactory (smell; see topics 7.11 and 7.12 for gustatory, or taste), and kinesthetic senses. Kinesthetics is the study of touch, space, and motion. You've often heard that you can learn by hearing, by seeing, and by doing. Kinesthetic learning is learning by doing. We will look at four specific aspects of kinesthetics in the workplace: proxemics, room arrangement, touch, and temperature. For those interested in extracurricular reading, Diane Ackerman has provided an entertaining summary of research on the five senses in *A Natural History of the Senses* (1990).

T O P I C 3 2 . 1   **Sensory Input in the Workplace**

Each of us is constantly taking in sensory data as the *afferent nerves* send visual, auditory, olfactory, tactile, and gustatory messages to the brain. These messages vie for attention with other mental activities such as creativity, analysis, and inspection, all of which can be interrupted by sensory data. Make sure that sensory input in your workplace is not driving productive mental activity out of your workers.

As a rule, extraverted people have a higher threshold for sensory stimulation, and introverted people prefer less stimulation. See chapter 33 for further discussion of personality dimensions.

Applications

❶ Talk with your workers to find out whether they have noticed any sensory distractions (e.g., noises, glares, smells, tastes, other physical discomforts) that take their mind off the task at hand, however momentarily. Distractions, even pleasant ones, beget errors.

❷ Include questions about sensory distractions in your annual employee attitude survey.

❸ When you conduct walkthroughs, imagine yourself in the workers' shoes and try to identify sensory distractions that might cause them to make errors.

❹ Identify and remove any sensory distractions that hinder your own performance. *(Contributed by Rick Bradley)*

❺ More introverted people are highly sensitive to input through the five senses; hence, they require relatively little sensation before they've had enough. Moreover, they are easily distracted by the senses. Bright lights and loud noises can wear out highly introverted people, whereas more extraverted people typically can take much more of the "madding crowd" before they feel a need to be "far from" it. The peripheral nervous systems of these two extremes in personality have different thresholds for sensation. Keep the workplace quiet and still for more introverted people, such as (typically) engineers, computer professionals, bookkeepers, and librarians. More extraverted people tend to be comfortable with a moderate hubbub around them.

TOPIC 32.2   The Effect of Light

Light affects mood and alertness by shutting down the production of melatonin, the sleep inducer. Darkness triggers the pineal gland, in the base of the brain, to secrete melatonin (see the discussion in topic 9.10). Because alertness is important for safety and productivity, the work environment should be well lit. If a low degree of alertness, or even drowsiness, is acceptable, then brightness is not as important. Full-spectrum lights are best. Weatherall (1987) points out that most lights are concentrated in the wrong part of the spectrum (orange-violet-red), although blue-green is the most vital part. Absence of this part of the spectrum leads to measurable fatigue and eyestrain.

Light deprivation not only affects performance; it can also lead to a form of depression. So-called winter depression, or *seasonal affective disorder* (SAD), which is associated with the shorter days and longer periods of darkness of winter, has been successfully treated with light therapy (see topic 19.5).

For travelers passing through several time zones, exposure to bright lights several "mornings" in a row in the new time zone can reset the body clock. In September 1991, our family hosted the matron of the King's College Chapel Choir from Cambridge, England. Charlotte was the choir's first stop in the United States. The group was whisked from the airport to our church, and then straight to our several homes. We arrived at our home around 9:00 P.M. (which was about 2:00 A.M. for Dorothy, the matron). We had a full schedule the following day, so we called Dorothy to tea at 7:30 A.M., turning on every light in the house to help her reset her body clock. We didn't tell her why we were so light-happy, but she reported later that this was one of her best trips ever, and that she had felt unexpectedly refreshed.

In an unusual experiment, Timothy Monk and Julie Carrier of the Western Psychiatric Institute and Clinic in Pittsburgh had young adults stay awake for 36 hours beginning at 9:00 A.M. (*Sleep,* September 1997). Although the researchers found that the subjects' measured accuracy was stable from day to night (with night performance somewhat slower), they were surprised to discover that the subjects performed more speedily on cognitive tasks during the second day, after having been up all night, than they did during the prior night. They concluded that the mind is generally sharper during daylight hours than during the night.

Architects now refer to the incorporation of natural sunlight into work and learning environments as "daylighting." Architectural schools such as the one at the University of North Carolina at Charlotte are building "daylighting rooms" for research and teaching. Three elementary schools in Johnston County, North Carolina, have all-natural lighting and report 5–14 percent higher scores on standardized tests than traditionally designed and lighted schools.

You can find more on light and sleep in chapter 9 and topic 31.2.

Applications

❶ Ensure adequate lighting in the workplace. Skimping on lighting can affect morale, quality of work, and productivity. Weatherall (1987) suggests using the color rendering index (CRI) as a measure of the adequacy of artificial light. In this index, natural light equals 100; the higher the numerical light rating, the lower the need to take a physical sample to a window to determine its correct color. Ask at your local lighting supply company for fluorescent or incandescent bulbs with a CRI of 90 or higher. Any lamps with a CRI of less than 90 will be missing part or all of the blue area of the light spectrum, and receiving the blue part of the spectrum is essential for maximum alertness.

❷ Provide extra lighting for workers on night shifts. This lighting can be turned off during the day, but on dark, overcast days, use it to help shake off the doldrums.

❸ In training sessions, plan carefully when you use transparencies or slides requiring subdued lighting. If it is not possible to lower the lights, plan a break or activity immediately following the presentation to rest the audience's eyes.

4 If your employer doesn't see fit to provide you with full-spectrum light when natural sunlight is unavailable, you can buy your own high-intensity light box for maximum alertness. For information, contact the Society for Light Treatment and Biological Rhythms. Their website: www.sltbr.org.

5 Visit the website for Vita-Lite at www.naturallighting.com.

6 In designing new buildings or renovating old ones, maximize the use of natural sunlight. In some European countries, building codes specify that all work areas must have outside views, i.e., must be exposed to the sun's rays.

7 Full-spectrum lighting is especially important in such contexts as nurses' assessments of newborns' skin color (using Apgar scoring) and in any work that requires excellent visual acuity.

TOPIC 32.3　　**The Effect of Color**

Faber Birren, in *Color and Human Response* (1978a), reports specific tendencies in people's responses to various colors. I summarize them as follows:

Color	Response
Red	Good for creative thinking, short-term high energy
Green	Good for productivity, long-term energy
Yellow, orange, or coral	Conducive to physical work, exercising; elicits positive moods
Blue	Slows pulse and lowers blood pressure; conducive to studying, deep thinking, concentration; accent with red for keener insights
Purple	Tranquilizing; good for appetite control
Pink	Restful; calming
Lighter colors	All-purpose; provide minimum disruption across all moods and mental activities
White	Disrupting, like snow-blindness; avoid

Birren recommends lighter colors for most situations and warns against all-white schemes, which can be disruptive.

Here are some other points of general interest from Birren's studies:

- Most people like primary colors.

- Discriminating people like purple, blue-green, and pink.

- Brown, white, gray, and black are the least preferred colors; they tend to attract the mentally disturbed.

- Extraverts, brunets, and Latins prefer warmer colors such as red or orange. (Red is "warm" because the lens adjusts to red shapes at a closer distance than with other colors, so they appear to leap out at us.)

- Introverts, blonds, and Nordics prefer cool colors such as blue or green. (Blue is "cool" because the lens adjusts to blue objects farther away than it does with other objects, so blue objects appear to recede.)

I recommend that you approach these findings with caution. Birren does not offer detailed research citations in support of his conclusions, and some of the color research is contradictory. For example, according to some reports, yellow walls elicit positive moods; another report finds that yellow walls in hospital rooms are associated with patients who require more pain-killing medication.

Application

❶ Evaluate the colors used throughout your workplace in terms of the nature of the work performed in each area. Here are some apparently winning combinations:

Cafeteria	Purple
Sales room	Yellow, orange, or coral
Conference rooms	Red
Offices	Blue with a tinge of red
Production areas	Green (it's energizing)
Waiting areas	Green (it's restful)
Rooms with overly active children	Pink (it tends to calm them)
Alleviation of tremors	Blue lighting
Need to increase strength	Red lighting

TOPIC 32.4   **The Effect of Shapes and Designs**

Beginning in the crib, all humans benefit from a visually enriched environment, with mirrors, artwork, games, posters, colors, and diverse shapes (see more at topic 22.13). To the degree that your workforce will benefit from cortical alertness, provide them with food for the eyes. Consult with them to determine the practicality of your ideas, however. I remember the choral rehearsal room in the Cunningham Fine Arts Building on the Davidson College campus in Davidson, North Carolina. It was beautifully designed, with black wire mesh on the wall behind the conductor, punctuated with thin, vertical teak strips, but we singers developed headaches from the dizzying effect created when the conductor moved back and forth in front of the strips. Your best intentions for visual design may have unintended consequences on the people who have to live and work with them. Follow up with interviews, and adjust the designs as needed.

Applications

❶ Dot the walls of your meeting rooms with appropriate posters containing philosophical or other thoughtful or amusing statements. IBM has done a good job of this, with posters reminding workers that "the individual comes first" or "today is the first day of the rest of your life." These posters are available free from the IBM Gallery of Science and Art, 590 Madison Avenue, New York, New York 10022. *(Contributed by Jack Wilson)*

❷ Provide a budget for artwork and allow employee participation in making selections.

❸ Put yourself in the position of your workers and identify overly distracting or boring visual areas in their workplace. Better yet, ask them how to improve the view that meets their eyes at work.

TOPIC 32.5   **Differences in Visual and Auditory Perception**

Research has shown that males, with their larger right hemisphere, tend to demonstrate better visual perception and discrimination, which is centered in the right hemisphere. Females tend to demonstrate greater auditory perception, which is centered in the left hemisphere.

Applications

❶ In setting up work assignments, remember that females tend to make fewer errors in auditory tasks, such as talking on the telephone, taking dictation, interviewing others, or listening for malfunction indicators in machinery. Males tend to make fewer errors in visual tasks, such as proofreading, visual scanning, or looking for malfunction indicators in machinery.

❷ Also remember that because they are more sensitive to auditory stimuli, females become fatigued more readily in a noisy environment. Males don't, but they do become fatigued more readily in a visually chaotic environment.

TOPIC 32.6 Sound and Concentration

The brain responds to organized and unorganized sounds. The first we call music; the second, noise. One person's music can be another's noise. As a general rule, neither music nor noise should be present where careful mental work is required. As Robert Pirsig comments in *Zen and the Art of Motorcycle Maintenance* (1974), don't trust a mechanic who listens to music while working on your car. If you're listening to music, then you're not listening to the engine. So-called background music does not stay in the background. I write more quickly and effectively when the stereo is off; I find it impossible to create a sentence and listen to a passage of Bach at the same time. If I'm trying to do both, then I'm actually alternating between the two, inevitably adding time and errors to my writing and thinking.

Applications

❶ Background music should accompany only routinized tasks and other situations in which the mind is not actively engaged and in which safety and errors are unimportant and inconsequential. I've seen it used effectively in transitional areas (hallways, restrooms, elevators, cafeterias); in work areas I don't recommend public music—headsets only. Don't provide background music for mental work, because it will inevitably occupy the foreground. For example, when I'm placed on telephone hold, I prefer that no music be piped into my ear. Why? Because I try to do miscellaneous paperwork while I'm waiting, and the music is distracting.

❷ Remember that people have different tastes in music. What pleases one person may be intrusive for another. I've known retail workers who came to hate holiday music when their stores played the same tapes repeatedly for a month. My dentist tries with the best of intentions to entertain patients with music in the waiting area and on DVDs during procedures. However, the former interferes with my reading, and the latter is more offensive than distracting. Ah, taste!

❸ See chapter 12 for a discussion of music and the mind.

TOPIC 32.7 **Noise in the Workplace**

Noise can be the bane of a mind worker's existence—from conversation to clacking equipment, from dripping water to occasional footsteps. Research indicates that so-called white noise, a low-pitched, sustained noise of low volume, serves to mask all other noises. Such an effect can be created by fluorescent light fixtures! One day in the Davis Library on the campus of the University of North Carolina at Chapel Hill, I was totally absorbed in reading a series of journal articles back in the bowels of the stacks. Just as I finished an article on the positive effect of white noise in masking out distractions, I became aware of a low, sustained buzz emanating from somewhere above. I wondered—did the designer of this library know about white noise, or was this just a lucky accident?

Predictable noise patterns are less bothersome than unpredictable ones. If the kitchen faucet is dripping with a regular rhythm, I can adjust to it. However, if the drips are irregular, I have a hard time ignoring them.

Continued exposure to loud noise, especially a chronic noise, damages the cochlear hairs in the ear (Ackerman, 1990). Consuming sufficient fat in the diet, reducing caffeine, and avoiding smoking will improve such hearing loss—and, of course, avoiding continued exposure to the loud noise! In addition to damaging the hearing mechanism, continual noise increases aggressive behavior and reduces healthy behavior. In one elementary school experiment, children 11 months behind in their reading scores who were sent to a remedial reading teacher found that the gap disappeared after being away from constant noise.

The National Institutes of Health estimates that more than 10 million Americans show some degree of permanent hearing loss that is related to excessive noise. The National Institute of Occupational Safety and Health estimates that around 30 million Americans are exposed daily to noises that will someday lead to permanent hearing loss. Among children between the ages of 6 and 19, one in eight shows some degree of permanent hearing loss, and adults who are going deaf are doing so at earlier ages than in the past. At least 20 percent of U.S. workers are exposed to excessive noise, 90 percent of coal miners show hearing loss by the age of 50, and 75 percent of farmers suffer permanent hearing loss (*Time,* April 5, 2004). Sustained noise at 85 db will damage hearing, at 75 db can lead to hypertension, and at 65 db can lead to stress, heart damage, and depression. And how's this: one motorcycle can wake up a couple of hundred thousand sleepers while tooling through a big city at night.

As we age, our hearing ability bifurcates: we can maintain normal hearing levels, as in catching all of a one-person-speaking-at-a-time conversation in an office or living room with no other noise or simultaneous conversation. However, introduce competing noise, and our ability to separate the primary auditory signal from the background noise decreases. That is why seniors often have trouble carrying on a conversation in large gatherings, restaurants, and so forth. This is a case in which the ear is as good as it ever was, but the gradual deterioration of brain cells affects the ability to distinguish signal from noise.

The Occupational Safety and Health Administration (OSHA) recommends wearing safety earplugs when one is exposed to noise levels above 89 decibels. Listed below are some common sounds and their decibel levels (Yepsen, 1987; H.E.A.R.; Sight and Hearing Association):

Sound	Decibel Level
Dripping faucet	40
Moderate rainfall	40
Chirping birds	60
Piano practice	60–70
Vacuum cleaner	70–75
Cocktail party (100 people)	70–85
Busy traffic	75–85
Diesel truck	80
Telephone dial tone	80
Ringing telephone	80
Window air conditioner	80
Electric shaver	85
OSHA Threshold	*89*
Hair dryer	90
Toy xylophone	92
Typical headset or radio at medium setting	94
Screaming child	90–115
Amplified rock music	90–130
Subway or outside at 200 feet	95
Little People Mixie the Cement Truck	98
Chainsaw	100
Jackhammer	100
Motorcycle	100
Inside a subway train	100
Power mower	100–105
Leap Frog Alphabet Pal	102
Barney Bend-a-Tune Trumpet	104
Wiggles Musical Guitar	107
Home Depot Workman's Screwdriver	112
Barney "Songs" book	115
Hockey game crowd	120
Loud thunder	120
Ambulance siren	120
Symphonic music at high point	120–130
Jet engine at takeoff	120–140
Air-raid siren	130

In contrast to noise, listening to our favorite music triggers endorphin release. In studies where endorphins were blocked with nalaxone, listening to one's favorite music failed to produce pleasurable results.

Application

❶ Consult an acoustical engineer about the proper way to mask noises that represent potential distractions for your mind workers. Machines are available that generate such white noise, as well as audio tapes and CDs. You might try perusing the options on **www.sleepwellbaby.com**.

❷ Ask your favorite theatres, restaurants, clubs, etc. to post their maximum allowed decibel levels, or to provide ear plugs.

❸ Make highways more porous—for instance, by mixing in some rubber with the asphalt.

❹ Protect residential and work areas from highway traffic noise with high walls. Cost: about $1 million per mile. Effect: reduces noise by about 7 db—not a huge amount, but makes a difference.

❺ Get airports to use runways that entail nonresidential flight paths as their default takeoff and landing preferences.

❻ Get pilots to use a gradual angle rather than the "stairstep" method for landing, which involves throttling and its associated noise.

❼ Get pilots to try to perform noisy banking maneuvers over bodies of water where possible.

❽ Get your local government to hand out fines for noise violators, such as in New York City's "Operation Silent Night" program.

❾ Support and learn from the European Union's "noise map" initiative, whereby each member nation must produce noise maps for each major city to guide future planning and construction.

❿ Support Tulane University professor Ted Rueter's Noise Free America initiative. See more at **www.noisefree.org**.

TOPIC 32.8   Smell and the Limbic System

The conventional view until 1995 was that the sense of smell was the only one of the five senses with a direct link to the limbic system. However, in the October 1995 issue of *Scientific American,* Richard Axel pointed out that we have two noses: the smell nose and the sex nose. The *vomeronasal organ* ("sex nose"), which detects pheromones—the scent essential for mating—is attached directly to the limbic system. The other, nonsexual smell organs are connected to the higher cognitive centers, hitting the limbic system only after they've passed through the higher centers. Thus, they are under greater control. After reviewing recent literature on pheromones (*Monitor on Psychology,* October 2002, pp. 46. ff.), Etienne Benson concluded that, although pheromones are known to exist in animals, the case for human pheromones is still out to jury. Pheromones are chemicals secreted through the sweat glands and detected by the vomeronasal organ (two tiny ducts in the nasal septum) of animals. The chemical messenger sends sexual communications. However, exactly how the process works remains a mystery. Many perfume manufacturers advertise the presence of "human pheromones" in their products that will make you more attractive to the opposite sex. However, the research neither acknowledges that humans have such secretions and detection organs, nor that the perfumes have any effect other than that of a placebo, making one feel more confident.

Axel, in his excellent summary of research on how we perceive scents, points out that in humans, 1,000 genes encode 1,000 distinct odor receptor systems (each system containing thousands of neurons) that enable us to recognize some 10,000 different odors. In contrast, we have only three color receptors on the retina that work together to discriminate between several hundred hues.

Ackerman (1990) identifies seven categories of smell: minty, floral, ethereal (for example, a pear), musky, resinous (camphor), foul or putrid (rotten eggs), and acrid or pungent (vinegar). There are traditionally only four taste categories: sweet, sour, salty, and bitter; all other, more complex taste sensations are actually attributable to smell. Ackerman suggests that in order to determine the basic taste of something, one should try exhaling while chewing. Researchers claim (in *Nature Neuroscience,* February 2000) to have identified a fifth taste— *umami*—in addition to the traditional four. The umami taste involves a receptor for glutamate in the tongue. The nature of this taste is similar to that of *monosodium glutamate* (MSG), which imparts flavor to many

Asian dishes. It is highly concentrated in the many varieties of Asian fish sauce and was used by the Romans in their own fish sauce, *garum,* a condiment that was widely distributed across their empire but forgotten by Europeans in the Dark Ages.

Humidity and low barometric pressure heighten the sense of smell. So in stormy, inclement, or pressure-inverted weather, wear and use less perfume and other odors; they can become offensive, especially to people with particularly sensitive schnozzes (like me).

Applications

❶ Be particularly sympathetic to others' complaints about bothersome smells, such as perfume, food, or smoke. Not all people are sensitive to the same odors, and sensitivities can be extremely disruptive.

❷ In topic 23.5, I wrote about state dependence, the phenomenon whereby people tend to remember more effectively if they recall the state they were in when the memory was acquired. This principle holds true for smell. In order to remember the details of a passage you were reading, for example, recall the odor of the leather chair in which you reclined while reading. The neural networks associated with the aroma, feel, and sight of the leather chair tend to trigger other networks (such as what you were reading or studying at the time) associated with them.

❸ Alan Hirsch, director of the Smell and Taste Treatment and Research Foundation in Chicago, has found that the odor of barbecue smoke makes a room seem smaller than it is. On the other hand, the odor of green apples tends to make the same room feel larger. More at www.scienceofsmell.com.

❹ Don't fall for perfumes advertising sex appeal based on pheromone content, unless you're trying to appeal to animals! Spend your money elsewhere. Use exercise, diet, sleep, and education to make you feel better about yourself and more attractive to others.

TOPIC 32.9   The Effect of Odors on Productivity

Fragrances improve performance at about the same rate as a cup of coffee, according to William Dember, a professor of psychology at the University of Cincinnati, and Raja Parasuraman, director of the Cognitive Science Laboratory at the Catholic University of America. At a meeting of the American Association for the Advancement of Science, they reported that on a 40-minute test of vigilance (like the test needed for air traffic control or distance driving), 30-second bursts of peppermint or muguet (lily of the valley) scent every five minutes resulted in a 15–25 percent improvement in performance. One interesting aspect of the study is that workers who received scented bursts showed less decline in performance as the task continued. In other studies, lavender scents have been associated with increases in metabolism and alertness.

In the same meeting at which Dember and Parasuraman presented their findings, Robert Baron, a professor of psychology at Rensselaer Polytechnic Institute in Troy, New York, reported that pleasant fragrances cause people to be more efficient, increase their risk level, form more challenging goals, negotiate more agreeably, and behave less combatively.

Along the same lines, Shimizu Technology Center reported that keypunch operators improved 21 percent with lavender bursts, 33 percent with jasmine, and 54 percent with lemon. Similarly, Robert Baron reported that pleasant cooking odors (baking cookies, perking coffee) elicit higher helping behavior in a mall (for example, people are more likely to respond when someone asks, "Hey, buddy, do you have change for a dollar?") (*Personal and Social Psychology Bulletin,* May 1997, pp. 498–503).

Aroma-Sys of Minneapolis and Holmes Products Corporation of Milford, Massachusetts, have each developed scent technologies. Aroma-Sys sells the EPA-1000 aroma diffusion system, which is used by retail stores, corporate offices, beauty salons, spas, healthcare facilities, and numerous fine hotels. Their device takes a scent cartridge of your choice and emits bursts in your large air distribution system. Holmes sells the Indoor Quality System, or "I.Q. System." It is a freestanding appliance based on a device patented by Robert Baron. The Aroma-Sys device is designed for larger industrial systems, the Holmes appliance for personal use.

Research continues on the effectiveness of these scent distribution systems. In an article in the March 1995 *APA Monitor,* Susan Knasko of the Monell Chemical Senses Center in Philadelphia spoke of 11 studies that reported on attempts to establish a connection between scents and productivity: 5 showed no influence, 3 had positive results, and 3 had negative results. Apparently, many variables affect the influence of scents, including the nature of the work performed, competing aromas, a tendency to become accustomed to scents, and individual differences among customers and workers. So ask your workers and customers whether they experience any odors that are distracting, offensive, or otherwise undesirable.

Larry Cahill and fellow researchers at the University of California, Irvine, report (in *New Scientist,* January 2000) that the right nostril provides a more emotional response to odor, whereas the left nostril is more accurate at discriminating between and identifying odors.

Applications

❶ For larger system uses, as in office buildings, hospitals, or plants, call Mark Peltier at Aroma-Sys (612-924-0336) for more information on the EPA-1000 (www.aromasys.com).

❷ For personal, single-room use, call Holmes Products at 508-634-8050 for more information on the I.Q. System, or call the inventor, Robert Baron, at Rensselaer Polytechnic Institute (518-276-2864). Baron is selling his own version by mail order; it's called the PPS, for Personal Productivity/ Privacy System. Holmes's website: www.holmesproducts.com.

❸ In Japan, Shimizu Corporation sells a process that emits bursts of fragrance through existing ventilation ducts. The system, which has been sold to Japanese hotels, banks, nursing homes, and offices, sells for $10,000. Site: www.shimz.co.jp/english.

❹ In designing fragrances for entertaining particular nationalities, employ these known associations:

Germans	Pine
French	Floral
Japanese	Delicate
North Americans	Strong
South Americans	Stronger (for example, Venezuelan floor cleaners contain a pine odor that is measurably 10 times stronger than that of floor cleaners used in the United States)

❺ When wishing to minimize reaction to odor (around unpleasant smells, for instance, or like Ulysses trying to resist the Sirens), try blocking off the right nostril.

❻ When wishing to identify an odor accurately, try blocking off the right nostril so that the emotional reaction does not interfere with discrimination.

❼ Bryan Raudenbush of Wheeling (West Virginia) Jesuit University studies the effect of scents on sleep and athletic performance. He has found that

- jasmine is associated with sleeping more restfully than lavender or no scent, and upon waking, feeling less anxious and performing cognitive tasks more effectively.
- peppermint is associated with enhanced athletic performance.
- lavender eases depression.
- peppermint lifts the spirits.

TOPIC 32.10   The Effect of Odors on Relaxation

Lavender-chamomile scents reportedly reduce stress; lemon, jasmine, and cypress scents induce a positive mood; basil, peppermint, pine, eucalyptus, and clove are "refreshing . . . invigorating," according to Junichi Yagi of Shimizu Technology Center America. Gary Schwartz, of the University of Arizona in Tucson, finds that within one minute, spiced apple scent yields more relaxed brain waves and an average drop in blood pressure of 5 mm. Spiced apple scent has also been associated with the prevention of panic attacks (Ackerman, 1990).

William H. Redd of the Memorial Sloan-Kettering Cancer Center in New York has experimented with bursts of heliotropine to relax patients undergoing magnetic resonance imaging. These patients frequently suffer anxiety, panic, and claustrophobic attacks, causing delays that cost U.S. health care providers millions of dollars annually. At the March 1991 meeting of the Society of Behavioral Medicine in Washington, D.C., Redd reported that among 85 patients, the heliotropine-receiving group exhibited 63 percent less anxiety than the controls.

Applications

❶ Chamomile, spiced apple, lemon, jasmine, eucalyptus, and peppermint are available in tea-bag form. Consider offering them for breaks as a hot-drink alternative to decaffeinated coffee.

❷ In waiting rooms, entry halls, and other areas where you would like to put people at ease, consider naturally fragrant wood furniture (such as cedar or cypress), home-style fragrances (clove balls or potpourri), natural objects (pine needles or cones, a potted miniature pine tree, a bowl of apples), and oils (e.g., lavender) for a continuous source of relaxing fragrance. Hospitals in particular should work to rid waiting areas of that unique hospital smell; though I have no research data to back me up, I'm sure it is anxiety-producing.

❸ Use, where possible, tools having a natural texture and odor; there's too much plastic in the world. Picking up a ruler made of wood can add a bit of pleasurable fragrance to an otherwise cold and lackluster act. I've played on an aluminum harpsichord, and it just doesn't offer the same pleasure as performing on a fragrant wooden instrument. I keep a plastic recorder for use on camping trips, but I never play it at home because it doesn't have the pleasing taste or smell of my rosewood version redolent of linseed oil.

❹ The odor of barbecue smoke makes a room feel smaller; the scent of green apples makes the same room feel larger. Since we know that most women are more comfortable in smaller spaces and most men in larger spaces, try adjusting the perception of room size by freshening women's space with barbecue smoke, men's with green apple!

TOPIC 32.11   **Toxic Effects of Smell**

The use of petrochemicals in perfumes is causing a rash (yes, that's right) of adverse reactions, in addition to the intended positive, or seductive, reaction. According to Samuel Epstein of the University of Illinois in Chicago, 95 percent of perfumes are made from petrochemicals that give off volatile organic compounds similar to the vapors of dry cleaning materials and paint strippers. The results:

- Eye irritation
- Throat irritation
- Skin rashes
- Nose irritation
- Asthma attacks
- Headaches
- Loss of coordination
- Nausea
- Liver damage
- Kidney damage
- Central nervous system damage
- Cancer

In addition to the poisonous effects of petrochemical perfumes, another toxic effect known as *multiple chemical sensitivity* (MCS) has emerged. MCS involves extreme sensitivity to odors that don't bother most people. Symptoms include

- Rash
- Headache
- Joint or muscle pain
- Memory impairment
- Fatigue

MCS affects about 4 percent of the population and is uncertain in origin, possibly related to traumatic prolonged exposure to chemicals, combined with other sources of stress (*Prevention,* September 2004).

Applications

❶ Epstein recommends using perfumed products (such as cologne, soap, skin lotion) with natural ingredients from sources such as flowers and animals. See his (along with David Steinman) "The Safe Shopper's Bible: A Consumer's Guide to Nontoxic Household Products, Cosmetics and Food."

❷ To report a perfumed product's adverse reaction, contact the FDA at 800-332-1088 or check their website at www.fda.gov/medwatch.

❸ Help is available for MCS. Get a copy of Pamela Reed Gibson's *Multiple Chemical Sensitivity: A Survival Guide.*

TOPIC 32.12   Proxemics

Proxemics is the study of how people physically distance themselves from others. Here are several general rules:

- Generally, women are more comfortable at close distances from other women; men are more comfortable at greater distances from other men. This is probably a relic dating from a time when men were genetically selected for their ability to function as isolated hunters outdoors, whereas women were genetically selected for their comfort in more crowded conditions back in the cave and when nursing and caring for their young.

- The smaller the enclosed space, the farther people will want to sit or stand from each other.

- When two people stand face to face, they communicate that they like each other. As the imaginary angle between them increases from 0° to 180° (back to back), less liking is communicated.

- The closer two people stand to one another, the more they communicate mutual liking.

- Moderate eye contact communicates liking; excessive eye contact communicates hostility (as in staring your opponent down); sparse eye contact means apathy or aversion.

- Cultural differences exist concerning comfortable distances and gazing patterns. If people from a different culture from yours appear to be standing farther or closer than is comfortable for you, the chances are that it's more comfortable for them. If you adjust the space between you, they will immediately return to the previous distance. I once taught with a man from Jamaica who would talk to me standing closer than was comfortable for me. At first I interpreted this as a sexual advance. After learning that Jamaicans generally stand closer to others, I felt more comfortable.

- Anthropologist Ray Birdwhistell (1970) has established that in American culture, masculinity is communicated nonverbally by standing with arms akimbo, feet parallel in the same plane, and the bottom of the pelvis rotated forward (tummy in); femininity by arms folded together, feet planted asymmetrically, and pelvis rotated backward (tummy out).

Applications

1 Generally, men require a larger work space than women (see topic 13.8). If you allow people to self-select how much space they need to perform their work, women will select less space, men more.

2 In small offices, meeting rooms, or waiting areas, place chairs and sofas as far apart as possible to give people more space. Using wider chairs accomplishes a similar purpose.

3 When you wish to communicate to people that you like them (for instance, in a performance appraisal or sales call), stand or sit face-to-face at a minimal comfortable distance with moderate eye contact. Avoid either staring them down or excessively gazing away (for example, looking out the window).

4 If a person of the opposite sex is coming on to you in an unwanted manner, try using the three nonverbal sexuality communicators of your opposite sex: a woman, for example, to "turn off" a man, would stand with feet planted parallel, arms akimbo, and pelvis rotated forward.

TOPIC 32.13 Room Arrangement

C. L. Williams and others (1985), in *The Negotiable Environment,* demonstrate that different personality temperaments respond better to different room or office arrangements. Shown in figure 32.1 are office arrangements for the Preserver, the Explorer, the Challenger, and the Adapter (these personality temperaments are described in chapter 33). See if you can identify which is which.

Application

❶ When you are designing office environments, take into account the preferences of people with different temperaments. In general:

- Explorers prefer more books and artwork.
- Preservers prefer more action-oriented pictures and objects (cars, airplanes, horses).
- Challengers prefer computers and other sources of data.
- Adapters prefer to have an area set aside for group meetings (a round table, a corner sofa).
- Flexibles like to have lots of surface space for all their piles.
- Focused people prefer elaborate storage equipment; staying organized is a must.
- Extraverts like lots of eye contact; they prefer windows, open offices, and low walls.
- Introverts like to be able to close the door and isolate themselves for extended periods.
- Reactives will let you know their wants, which will probably change from time to time.
- Resilients will probably not care that much about their office arrangement.

TOPIC 32.14   The Sense of Touch

For some people, the sense of touch is an important element of motivation for work. Be aware that artificial touch sensations can demotivate some workers. For some, glass is preferable to plastic, wood or metal to plastic, wood to metal, natural fibers to synthetic fibers, natural plants to artificial plants, china to plastic or paper plates, leather to plastic, and so on.

Dudley Flood, a human relations consultant in the North Carolina public schools during school integration in the 1960s and 1970s, lamented the prohibition against touch at school and work. Trying to find a safe middle ground with the "P.C. police," Flood opined that it is okay to touch the "hard areas," such as the top of the shoulder,

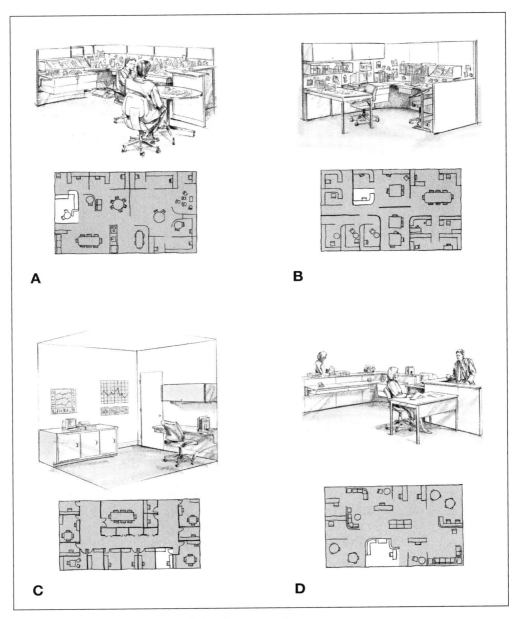

Figure 32.1. Personality Traits and Office Arrangement
Source: C. L. Williams and others (1985), *The Negotiable Environment: People, White-Collar Work, and the Office,* Ann Arbor, Mich.: Miller, Herman. © 1985 by Miller, Herman, Inc. Reprinted by permission.
Note: (*A*) Preserver; (*B*) Explorer; (*C*) Challenger; (*D*) Adapter.

the elbow, the kneecap, the top of the head, and the hands. Touching the other, softer areas is unwelcome except in more intimate relationships. Ackerman (1990) writes about "unnoticed touching," as in the touch of a waiter when making change or a librarian when handing over a book. In these circumstances, unnoticed touching results in a better outlook, including higher sympathy, on the part of the touched person toward the toucher. Wait staff who touch get higher tips; librarians who touch get more smiles.

In what amounts to a review of research, the University of Miami School of Medicine's Tiffany Field establishes the basis for the healthful effects of touch in her article, "Massage Therapy Effects" (1998).

Applications

1 Consult with workers about what's important to them in their work environment. Ask about what materials they prefer and the importance of tactile sensations. If how their materials, equipment, and furniture feel to their touch is not important to them, then there is no need to change them.

2 Find appropriate ways to touch that are "unnoticed," or natural and momentary. Limit yourself to the "hard areas."

TOPIC 32.15 Temperature

The cooler your brain is, the more relaxed you are. The warmer your brain, the more aroused you are (this arousal can be either limbic or cortical). Hence the stereotypes of the cool, unflappable Londoner and the passionate, hot resident of the equatorial zones. Robert Zajonc, professor emeritus of psychology at the University of Michigan, reports that higher brain temperatures can affect the level of neurotransmitters in the neurocirculatory system, especially the level of norepinephrine (*APA Monitor,* October 1990). In an interesting and related study, Zajonc reports that breathing through the nose cools the brain.

Applications

1 One simple way to relax at work is to breathe slowly through your nose.

2 In areas where cortical alertness is necessary, keep room temperatures in the upper range of the comfort zone. Too cool a meeting room shuts down cortical functions and induces drowsiness.

3 In areas where you want people to be relaxed (waiting areas, sales presentation rooms, cafeterias, break areas), keep temperatures in the lower range of the comfort zone.

SUGGESTED RESOURCES

Ackerman, D. (1990). *A Natural History of the Senses.* New York: Random House.

Axel, R. (1995, October). "The Molecular Logic of Smell." *Scientific American,* pp. 154–159.

Vroon, P. (1997). *Smell: The Secret Seducer.* New York: Farrar, Straus & Giroux.

Yepsen, R. B. Jr. (1987). *How to Boost Your Brain Power: Achieving Peak Intelligence, Memory and Creativity.* Emmaus, Pa.: Rodale.

Part Nine

Putting It All Together

*How We
Differ, and
What Makes
Us Tick*

Part Nine. Putting It All Together

How We Differ, and What Makes Us Tick

33

The Big Five

At Last, a Universal Language for Personality Traits

> **"Should one tell you that a mountain had changed its place, you are at liberty to doubt it; but if anyone tells you that a man has changed his character, do not believe it."**
>
> —Muhammad

This section comprises five chapters, beginning with an in-depth look at personality traits, continuing by way of intelligence, basic emotions, and stress, and culminating with a grand theory of motivation. This is an effort to make sense out of the many separate treatments throughout this book—an attempt to explain what makes us tick. You will see how motivation has to do with goals—little goals, huge goals, conflicting goals, coordinated goals, selfish goals, altruistic goals. Goals represent the purpose of our efforts. If we exert no effort, then logically we can be said to have no goal in mind, unless the goal happens to be to take a rest, and our stillness is the result of having achieved our goal of resting. To be motivated is to be in pursuit of a goal, no matter how major or minor. In fact, the word *motivate* comes from the Latin *motivus,* which in turn comes from *movere,* which means "to move." To be motivated is to be moving, to be in pursuit of a goal—the opposite of being a couch potato. You will see that your goals are based on, and are reflective of, your basic personality infrastructure, and that your emotions play two important roles in the process of motivation: (1) pushing you toward some goals and away from others, and (2) giving you feedback on progress towards your goals.

The word *personality* stems from the Latin *persona,* which referred to the masks worn by actors in early drama. These masks provided clues to the enduring behaviors by which a specific actor could be recognized throughout the play; recall the paired face masks—one frowning, one smiling—adorning theatrical facilities and publications.

> "If there be light, then there is darkness; if cold, then heat; if height, depth also; if solid, then fluid; hardness and softness; roughness and smoothness; calm and tempest; prosperity and adversity; life and death."
>
> —Pythagoras

Today, the term *personality* refers to the sets of predictable behaviors by which others recognize us as ourselves. These sets of behaviors go by the name of *traits.* As we will see, personality includes more than traits. In fact, four primary sets of personal qualities form the core of our person: *traits, abilities, memories,* and *physical characteristics* ("TAMP"). The next chapter presents material about abilities, and in chapter 37 we show how these four sets of qualities form the *shapers*—the infrastructure that influences all of our choices.

In 1925, John Watson asserted: "Give me a dozen healthy infants, well-formed, and my own specified world to bring them up in, and I'll guarantee to take any one at random and train him to become any type of specialist I might select—doctor, lawyer, artist, merchant-chief, and yes, even beggar-man and thief, regardless of his talents, penchants, tendencies, and abilities, vocations, and race of his ancestors." This dictum formed the essence of behaviorism for the next half-century—the notion that all behavior is learned, that there is no such thing as an inherited trait or ability. This view was especially strong right after World War II, in sharp contrast to Hitler's policies of eugenics and the breeding of the master race. To view behavior as anything other than learned was to be a racist, and to view behavior as learned was the humanist's credo. Walter Mischel's *Personality and Assessment* (1968) presented the classic rationale against the existence of heritable traits. Mischel's argument runs something like this: Say that procrastination is offered as a trait. Well, there are literally thousands of situations in which we may or may not procrastinate: mailing holiday gifts, depositing paychecks, cooking dinner, reading a professional book, scheduling a physical examination, writing a letter. . . . The list could go on indefinitely. In addition, each item on the list could be subdivided: procrastinating at cooking dinner for unwanted guests, for our boss, for our lover, and so on. And even these could be subdivided: procrastinating at cooking dinner for our lover when we desire to break off the relationship, when we want to impress our lover with culinary flamboyance, when we want the chance to work closely together in the kitchen, when we hope that cooking will be abandoned in favor of dining out, or when we hope that if there is no food it will lead to quicker sex—with food following!

What Mischel means to say is that people act differently in different situations and never (well, hardly ever) exhibit a single behavior in every possible situation that could elicit it. Therefore, says Mischel, to label someone a procrastinator is not only irresponsible, it is impossible to prove. We would have to enumerate thousands of situations, with subdivisions, in order to say with confidence that a person is a procrastinator. Personality tests that attempt to measure the degree of a person's tendency toward a particular trait only ask a sample of 10–15 questions out of the universe of tens of thousands in order to make a statement like "Fran Doe is a procrastinator about 82 percent of the time." Says Mischel: "Poppycock!"

Those of us who argue for the existence of personality traits, which are also called *temperaments* (see Buss, 1989, for an excellent summary), will grant that it is risky to use a dozen or so questionnaire items to form a conclusion about the degree of a particular temperament in a person (see a brief discussion of temperament in children in topic 4.4). However, we can minimize that risk by careful selection, choosing only questions that all people can identify with in some way, such as "People tell me that they can depend on me to finish things when I say I will." In addition, by presenting two statements and asking which is more like the person most of the time (for example, "I prefer parties" and "I enjoy parties with lots of people"), we can ask the respondent to subjectively rewind the tape of his recent life and form a judgment as to which statement is a better fit. By using carefully selected items and question formats, we can obtain valid and reliable estimates concerning how a person will tend to respond across situations that invite behaviors related to a particular temperament. "If personality was primarily inconsistent," says Seymour Epstein (1997, p. 14), "then human behavior would be essentially unpredictable. One might as well select a spouse at random from a telephone book. The concept of responsibility would be meaningless, so one might as well imprison or release people at random. One could not write meaningful letters of recommendation, as it would be pointless to describe a person as conscientious, cooperative, aggressive, lacking in a sense of humor, and so forth, as none of these would have any predictive value."

The concept of the personality trait is widely accepted today. A *trait* is a dimension of personality that has the quality of a continuum. *Gregariousness* is a trait that describes a continuum of behavior on which people find themselves stretched out, ranging from a troglodyte like Ted Kaczynski to a rabble-rouser like Howard Stern, with people like you and me in between.

A popular, but receding, school of thought, as expressed in the literature surrounding the Myers-Briggs Type Indicator (MBTI) (Myers and McCaulley, 1985), has seen labels like *extravert* as bipolar; in other words, one either is or is not gregarious. I, and many of the researchers cited in this chapter, reject that dichotomization as simplistic and inadequate to describe the abundant diversity of our species. John Loehlin (1992, p.119) explains:

> An old issue in personality theory is whether human personality comes in distinct subvarieties—personality *types*—or is best conceptualized as varying continuously along dimensions—personality *traits*. Evolutionary biology has something to say on this point. For example, Tooby and Cosmides . . . argue that the nature of human reproduction makes the emergence of genetically based personality types unlikely. That is because parental genes get reshuffled into new combinations in every generation, so that it becomes extremely unlikely that a system depending on a coherent set of genes could be transmitted as a unit from parent to child. What we should find, argue Tooby and Cosmides, is a general human nature, with variations on it provided by variation in individual genes that affect such things as thresholds of behavioral

expression. About the only possibility of true emergent types would be on the basis of single genes that could act as switches between alternate courses of development.

A Warning about Using Labels

I think it is appropriate, when we talk about personality characteristics, to recall Paul Valéry's comment: "Seeing is forgetting the name of the thing one sees." Valéry is talking about the tendency to substitute labels for the thing itself. He urges us to beware of labels. Labels originate at the point where a careful observer has arrived at a single word or phrase to express a complex set of attributes that are under observation. Those who come upon the label at a later time must choose whether to reexamine the attributes before accepting the label or to simply accept the label on faith. If the stakes are high, it pays to reexamine the real thing, rather than automatically accepting the label. Here are two simple examples:

1. I label my feelings for my wife as love, but rather than simply repeating "I love you" to convey my feelings, I should reexamine my behavior from time to time to see if it is still saying what I mean by love. The Neil Diamond and Barbra Streisand song "You Don't Send Me Flowers Anymore" is evidence of a label that has lost touch with its origins.

2. A death occurred in a major regional medical center because of excessive trust in labels. An inaccurately labeled drug container was sent from the pharmacy to the operating room, and because of assumptions by a pharmacist's technician and a surgeon that the label was correct, a patient died. Simply looking closely at the drug or smelling it would have prevented this unnecessary loss of life.

After presenting this warning, I must push on to insist that labels are a necessary shortcut. We simply do not have the time or energy to look freshly at everything; we must be selective. And the fact that our world is full of differences requires us to develop a language to talk about them. We could take pains to describe everyone we meet with the objective, descriptive detail of an anthropologist, but then we'd all have to be anthropologists. Indira Gandhi reportedly commented on the subject of diversity with the observation that an orchestra of one hundred violins does not hold our interest with anywhere near the power of the multi-instrument orchestra. Having acknowledged that we are different, let us proceed with learning a language to describe those differences.

But wait. Some, such as Mischel (1968), complain that we should avoid the use of labels, maintaining that there are simply not enough labels to go around to describe the billions of people on the Earth. Others, such as Hans Eysenck (1967, 1970, 1981; Eysenck and Eysenck, 1985), have defended the use of personality labels. In the study of color, we find 340,000 discriminable points, each of which can be defined as a unique intersection of the three variables of hue, tint, and saturation. Likewise, if we were to propose 10 personality variables, each with 10 degrees of variation, that would be sufficient to describe 10 billion unique individuals. This is more than enough to label everyone currently on this planet with no need for repetition. Our labels will be words like *extravert* and *accommodating.* Each label can vary in strength: just as we can have a 30 percent or 90 percent solution of hydrochloric acid, we also can have differing degrees of extraversion and accommodation.

Labels are a kind of shorthand. The label *industrious* is like a computer macro that refers to a complex set of elements. We should never reify a label and give it a status equivalent to that of the behavior it refers to. But without the label, we would have no time to do many things. I simply cannot take the time to write a letter of reference for someone if I must specify the 40 or 50 incidents that led me to describe that individual as industrious. I must use the shorthand of the label.

The Equalizer Model of Personality

I hereby propose the "equalizer" model of personality description. You know what an equalizer is—a series of knobs that go up and down to create different qualities and quantities of sound production. Imagine a huge equalizer designed to create multisensory experiences. The machine would have five channels—Sight, Sound, Touch and Motion, Smell, and Taste—and each channel would have several component controls. Sight would have three components (hue, tint, and saturation); Sound four (pitch, rhythm, volume, and timbre); Touch and Motion six (shape, size, texture, temperature, direction, and speed); Smell seven (minty, floral, ethereal, musky, resinous, foul, and acrid); and Taste five (salty, sweet, sour, bitter, and *umami*—see topic 32.8). Ackerman (1990) has given a readable and complete description of the senses.

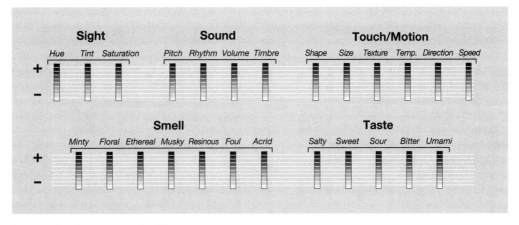

Figure 33.1. An Equalizer for Multisensory Experience

Some of the components might be subdivided further; for example, shape could be divided into curve, length, and other subcomponents. By varying the control knobs, we could create a specific multisensory experience, such as "having wine and cheese in the late afternoon at an outdoor café on the Champs Élysées." If we were to add another channel—Language—we could even have conversation in the background and foreground. Every multisensory experience can be described by determining the point on each scale that fits the experience. The illustration in figure 33.1 tries to capture such an equalizer.

Now take the same idea and apply it to personality (see figure 33.2). The channels would be Traits, Abilities, Memories, and Physical Characteristics. Each channel would have components: Traits would have five (need for stability, extraversion, originality, accommodation, and consolidation), Abilities would have (at least) eight (linguistic, musical, logical and mathematical, spatial, interpersonal, intrapersonal, kinesthetic, and natural observation), Memories could be divided into chronological categories (early childhood through the present), and Physical Characteristics would include features such as height, weight, speed, strength, dexterity, and so forth. Each person could be described by reference to points on each of the scales of the equalizer.

The difference between the two equalizers is crucial: whereas the multisensory-experience machine is hooked up to wires, microchips, lights, and amplifiers, the personality equalizer is hooked up to the central nervous system, the circulatory system, the endocrine system,

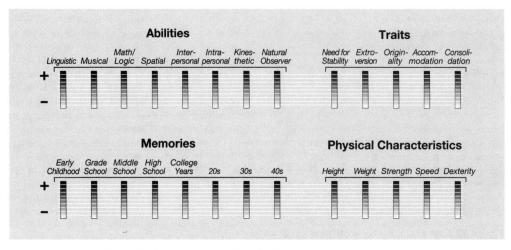

Figure 33.2. An Equalizer Model of Personality

and the musculoskeletal system, all of which, in turn, are hooked up to the external environment. This invites a logical question: to what degree are we free as individuals to modify the positions of our knobs? Moreover, as teachers, therapists, managers, friends, and members of families, to what degree can we modify the positions of the knobs of our children, spouse, students, patients, friends, subordinates—and bosses? Traditionally, personality has comprised four biologically based temperaments. We will discuss them next, then place them in the light of current genetic theory.

A History of Temperament Theory

Western civilization has operated under the paradigm of four personality temperaments since the early Greeks enumerated the four elements of air, fire, earth, and water, along with their associated personality traits (for a discussion of paradigms, see Kuhn, 1970). The fixedness of this paradigm in the minds of Western thinkers is evident in table 33.1, which lists the various manifestations of the four temperaments over the last several thousand years. Because the definitions of each set of four traits are not consistent from model to model, it is not possible to place, for example, all "sanguine"-related traits in the same column. Don't attempt to find the commonality within each column; you'll get Excedrin headache number 4!

This four-factor model of temperament still persists. The most compelling argument to support it is made in Hans Eysenck, *The Structure of Human Personality* (1970). Eysenck presents the psychological dimensions of Extraversion and Neuroticism as the basis of his four-factor model (figure 33.3). Each of the two dimensions forms an axis of a two-by-two grid, with the vectors that emerge from each of the four quadrants defining the four temperaments. But even Eysenck's work shows this four-factor model breaking

Table 33.1. The Four Temperaments from Early Greece to the Present

Source	Air	Fire	Earth	Water
Mythology	Apollo	Hermes	Zeus	Dionysus
Hippocrates	Phlegmatic	Melancholic	Sanguine	Choleric
The Elizabethans (also Galen & Wundt)	Phlegmatic	Melancholic	Sanguine	Choleric
Native American	East/Eagle	West/Bear	South/Squirrel	North/Buffalo
Herrmann (1989)	Cerebral left	Cerebral right	Limbic left	Limbic right
Lefton, Buzzotta, & Sherberg (1985)	Q2, Submissive-Hostile	Q1, Dominant-Hostile	Q3, Submissive-Warm	Q4, Dominant-Warm
Hersey & Blanchard (1976)	S-1, Telling	S-4, Delegating	S-2, Selling	S-3, Participating
LIFO[a] (Atkins, 1978)	Conserving/Holding	Adapting/Dealing	Controlling/Taking	Supporting/Giving
AVA[b] (Clarke, 1956)	V3, Stability	V4, Structure	V1, Dominance	V2, Sociability
DISC[c] (Marston, 1987)	Dominance	Influence	Steadiness	Compliance
Keirsey & Bates (1978)	Troubleshooter	Visionary	Traditionalist	Catalyst
Social Styles (Merrill & Reid, 1981)	Analytic	Expressive	Driver	Amiable
Jung (1971)	Thinker	Intuitor	Sensor	Feeler
MBTI[d] (Myers & McCaulley, 1985)	Extravert/Introvert	Sensor/Intuitor	Thinker/Feeler	Judger/Perceiver
Kolbe (1990)	Follow through	Quick start	Implementor	Fact finder

[a]LIFO = life orientation; [b]AVA = activity vector analysis; [c]DISC = dominance, influence, steadiness, compliance; [d]MBTI = Myers-Briggs Type Indicator

down. In subsequent writings (Eysenck and Kamin, 1981; Eysenck and Eysenck, 1985), he portrays three dimensions (the third being Psychoticism) and their various combinations.

In the 1930s, Gordon Allport (Allport and Odbert, 1936) threw out a challenge to the psychological community: find the common synonym clusters in the roughly 4,500 words in Webster's unabridged dictionary that describe variations in normal human personality. Over the next 40 years, many tried. The solution did not become apparent, however, until the availability of personal computers and of factor analysis programs designed to work on them. In the early 1980s, something approaching consensus emerged in the community of personality scholars: five, not four, factors best account for the broad categories of variability in human personality. As early as 1963, W. T. Norman defined these five factors, based on his careful factor analysis, as Emotional Stability, Extraversion, Culture, Accommodation, and Consolidation (see topic 33.2). An excellent summary of the research leading up to the definition of what we now know as the Big Five, or the Five-Factor Model, can be found in John, Angleitner, and Ostendorf (1988). Digman and Inouye (1986, p. 116) summarize this trend in personality research as follows: "A series of research studies of personality traits has led to a finding consistent enough to approach the status of law. The finding is this: If a large number of rating scales is used and if the scope of the scales is very broad, the domain of personality descriptors is almost completely accounted for by five robust factors."

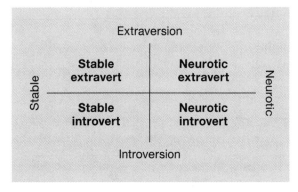

Figure 33.3. Eysenck's Four-Factor Model

The most important difference between the four-factor model as measured by the MBTI (Myers and McCaulley, 1985) and the Five-Factor Model is that the MBTI provides no direct measure of the first factor, Need for Stability (Norman's Emotional Stability, Costa and McCrae's Neuroticism). Yet, after Extraversion, it is the most extensively documented factor. McCrae and Costa (1989) have written an excellent article explaining the differences in the two models.

Six attributes of Big Five research help to explain the wide acceptance of the Five-Factor Model among personality researchers:

1. The same five factors emerge regardless of what factor analysis program is used.

2. The same five factors emerge regardless of the type of item used in testing: sentences, phrases, or words.

3. The same five factors emerge regardless of the people doing the ratings: professional psychologists, self-reports, spouse ratings, or peer ratings.

4. The same five factors emerge regardless of the language used.

5. The same five factors emerge regardless of the subjects tested (old or young, male or female, more or less educated).

6. An extremely high coefficient alpha (a measure of internal consistency) of .90 is associated with the five factors.

TOPIC 33.1 The Inherited Basis of Personality Traits

Neubauer and Neubauer (1990, pp. 38 ff.) write of the research on the genetic origins of personality traits (see the discussion in chapter 1). Among the traits for which strong evidence of an inherited basis exists are the following (see topics 13.1–13.3 for information on the heritability of sexuality):

Aggressiveness	Excitability	Quickness to anger
Alcoholism (see topic 8.1)	Imagination	Shyness
	Language facility	Susceptibility to addiction
Autism	Leadership	
Depression	Maturation rate	Traditionalism
Empathy	Obsessions	Vulnerability to stress
Engageability (aggressive pursuit of one's needs)	Person-vs.-object orientation	Weakness of will

I must take pains to point out that one does not inherit the gene for a trait, or even the trait itself. The term *trait* is a shorthand way to refer to a correlated set of attributes—behaviors, attitudes, and values that tend to occur together in the same individual. These attributes are composed of habits, specific behavioral responses that are persistent over time, such as blushing. The specific behavioral responses are associated with the complex interaction of specific genes and environmental experiences. Even such a behavior as blushing might be influenced by as many as several dozen genes. Most genetic diseases are controlled by a single gene (called the *OGOD principle:* "One gene, one disease"), but behaviors are influenced by multiple genes (*MyGOB:* "Many genes, one behavior"). For an extended description of the relationship between genes, habits, and traits, see Zuckerman (1991) or Loehlin (1992).

One gene's (or trait's) prominence can often mask another's. Albino mice, for example, are less active in the open field than other mice, but if you put them in the dark with a red light, they are just as active as other mice. Albinism entails sensitivity to light, leading one to the conclusion that albino mice are less active, when in fact they are just avoiding being in the light. Similarly, timid infants are often assumed to be less curious. However, once a timid infant becomes comfortable in her surroundings, curiosity emerges—if the trait is there, of course. The timidity masks the curiosity until the time is right (Plomin, DeFries, McClearn, and Rutter, 1997, p. 88).

It is important to note that heritability studies using self-report personality trait inventories have never found a trait that shows only minimal or no heritability. In other words, traits are inherited—period—with some add-ons from our upbringing.

Continuing research is aimed at determining both the makeup and the degree of heritability of personality factors: which factors seem to be especially influenced genetically and to what degree. Tesser and Crelia (1994), for example, have reported on the greater rigidity of attitudes that have high heritability components. Wright (1994, p. 81), on the other hand, argues that personality traits are more environmentally determined: "Genes that irrevocably committed our ancestors to one personality type should in theory have lost out to genes that let the personality solidify gracefully." But their arguments are either-or. Traits, whether they are apparently more biologically based (such as sex drive) or apparently more environmentally based (such as sociability), are inevitably based on an interaction between genes and environment. Both nature and nurture play a part. Among the environmental factors that Neubauer and Neubauer (1990) identify as tending to have the most impact on personality development:

- Quality and quantity of language the child is exposed to

- Amount of play the child has

- Expressed affection
- Availability of toys
- Presence of parents
- Presence of other children
- Natural expression of emotion in the household
- Intellectual expectations (riddles, questions, problem solving, and so on)
- Control, limits, and discipline (deprivation and excess have a negative effect)

In summary, genetics would appear to be like a seed, with environment more like fertilizer, rain, or soil, in bringing forth the flower of personality. Or, as Neubauer and Neubauer say, genes appear to set limits for the range of development. They are not a blueprint that fully defines the final product; instead, they establish the range of possible variation. At birth, genetics accounts for practically 100 percent of who we are, environment for almost zero. Over time, as we become adults, genetics drops down to around 60 percent, with environment settling in around 40 percent. We simply cannot get rid of that 60 percent genetic basis of who we are, no matter how hard we might try. Prospero's frustration, and growing realization of its futility, at trying to change Caliban into a smooth, civilized mate for his daughter, Miranda, is captured by Shakespeare in *The Tempest* (IV, i, 188–190):

> Thirty years before Shakespeare's Caliban, Richard Mulcaster, British educator, wrote: "Nature makes the boy toward, nurture sees him forward."

> *A devil, a born devil, on whose nature*
>
> *Nurture can never stick, on whom my pains,*
>
> *Humanely taken, all, all lost, quite lost. . . .*

Applications

1 As a parent, you can only do what your informed judgment suggests is appropriate. Realize that some traits will emerge in your offspring that you do not share. To deny the validity of these traits can lead to guilt and frustration on both your part and your child's. Develop the habit of seeing your child's strengths and helping them develop. As Goethe wrote: "That which he has inherited has been made his own."

2 If you are a therapist, manager, coach, or other "people developer," you will find that the people you deal with will exhibit some traits that relate well to a job they are trying to do and some that do not. It is reasonable to hold people accountable for their relevant strengths, but it is unreasonable to browbeat them for their weaknesses. For example, if you coach a boy's basketball team and a player shoots well but shies away from the responsibility of calling plays, work on his shooting. Don't make him play point guard and browbeat him for not being more of a playmaker. If you must make him play point guard, praise his shooting and be knowingly supportive of his efforts to make plays. Say, "I know that playing you at point guard is not using your strengths to your advantage, but for now you're the best person for the job. I won't expect you to perform as well as you do as a shooting guard, but I will support you in every way I can to make the best of the circumstances."

3 In hiring or choosing someone to do a job, make the selection on the basis of the person's relevant strengths. Don't make the mistake of choosing employees because their credentials are generally impressive; hire them because their credentials are job-related. A common mistake is to hire a creative, innovative person for a routine job. This will lead to a higher-than-necessary error rate and eventual turnover. If you must hire a creative person to do a routine job, make sure you both know that the routine job is only temporary and that a better job fit will come soon. Then manage the employee with understanding and support in the routine job. Say, "We both need to be aware that much of the time you spend as a bank teller will be boring, and as a result you will be more error-prone than other tellers. Let's figure out what we can do to minimize error and keep you motivated during this rotation. When your next assignment comes along, your creativity will be more challenged. But for now, let's figure out a survival strategy."

4 As a rule, don't try to change people. Learn to build on who they are and compensate for who they are not. I'll never love the chore of managing family finances, but I've made it bearable by figuring out a way to make it more interesting. I've done this by learning a computer program. I know people who have entered into marriage with the confidence that they would ultimately be able to change the less desirable traits of their future spouse. This typically leads to frustration and resentment as the change strategies prove ineffectual.

⑤ Don't confuse personality traits with learnable skills. There are many bodies of knowledge and specific skills that I could learn if I wanted to. In that respect, you could "change" me by teaching me a skill or a body of knowledge. But that learning doesn't mean that a personality trait will change as a result. I have an architect friend who hated to make presentations before groups. He is an introverted, idea-focused person. He knew he would never love presentations, but he decided that he would at least become good at it. He took Ty Boyd's seminar on public speaking and learned the skills involved in making effective presentations. Now he gets good marks for his presentations, even though he still doesn't like doing them and prefers being creative in the privacy of his office. But he is less anxious about his presentations because he knows the tricks of the trade.

⑥ With respect to adopted children, Eysenck and Kamin (1981, p. 51) write, "At no time do adopted children and foster parents correlate more than .10, and adopted children do not grow to resemble their adopting parents." I have friends who have taken it hard when their incorrigible adopted children haven't developed the kind of loving, nurturing, thoughtful behaviors the adopting parents have shown them. This should not be seen as a personal failure. The parents should continue to provide support and encourage skill and social development, but they need to help their adopted children build on their strengths and limitations, rather than trying to force them into a path alien to their nature.

⑦ Nigel Nicholson (1998, p. 142) provides an excellent summary of the implications of evolutionary psychology for managers:

- Be aware that people always hear bad news loudest.
- Assign sensitive people, who can avoid communicating a sense of failure to people, to give performance appraisals.
- Remember that people resist change unless they are dissatisfied.
- Be aware that people think most creatively when they feel safe.
- People have a tendency to be overconfident, so check things out.
- Stereotyping strangers is natural, so build in opportunities to get beyond stereotypes.

- Rumors and gossip are natural. Don't eradicate them; just ensure that they are accurate.

- One-upmanship is natural. You can't get rid of it, but you don't have to take it seriously.

- Limit the size of the organizational entity with which one identifies to 150 people.

- Remember that people prefer identifying with one group at work, not two or more.

- Hierarchy building is innate and ineradicable. Accept it, but realize that it doesn't need fuel as an accelerant.

- The drive to lead is inborn. Know that encouraging reluctant leaders has little likelihood of payoff.

- Don't blame people for failing to exert leadership in a crisis when they haven't demonstrated it before; it's just not their nature.

❽ How environment interacts with inheritance is a mysterious process. However, Loehlin (1992) identified four circumstances that can lead to the expression of a particular trait:

- *Passive.* A predisposed individual is in an environment that supports the predisposed trait (a conscientious child attends a traditional school).

- *Active.* A predisposed individual is recognized by someone else (or by himself or herself) and thereafter is encouraged in the predisposed trait (a teacher asks an extraverted child, or the child volunteers, to lead the class line to lunch).

- *Interactive.* A moderately predisposed individual enters an environment supportive of the extreme form of the trait and then moves to the extreme (a moderately conscientious young adult enters the armed forces and excels).

- *Reactive.* A predisposed individual is in an environment that is opposite to the trait (a teacher suggests that a selfish child enter the candy-striper program, or a shy child is reared by pushy, gregarious parents).

In the first three cases, the trait develops naturally; the fourth case leads to unnatural expressions.

TOPIC 33.2   **The Big Five**

In this section, we define the five supertraits of the Five-Factor Model, or the Big Five. The terminology used here is based on two instruments developed at the Center for Applied Cognitive Studies: the WorkPlace Big Five ProFile (for working adults) and the SchoolPlace Big Five ProFile (for students ages 12–22).

Need for Stability (N)

The Need for Stability dimension of the Five-Factor Model relates to one's threshold of response to stressful stimuli. At one extreme we have the Resilient, who tends to experience life on a more rational level than most people and who sometimes appears rather impervious to his or her surroundings. I think, for example, of my choir director, who didn't miss a beat during a dress rehearsal when the podium on which he was standing collapsed forward. He simply placed his feet at an angle like a snowplow and kept his baton moving. Of course, all the singers and instrumentalists broke out laughing at this classic example of nonreactivity. He's unflappable. This extreme is also the foundation for many valuable social roles—from air traffic controllers and airline pilots to military snipers, financial managers, and engineers.

At the other extreme, we have the Reactive, who experiences more negative emotions and reports less satisfaction with life than most people do. This is not meant to place a value judgment on Reactives, however; a susceptibility to negative emotions and discontent with life provide the basis for filling extremely important roles in our society, such as social scientist, academician, and customer service professional.

Along the continuum from Reactive to Resilient is the Responsive, who has a mixture of the qualities of both the Resilient and the Reactive. Responsives are better able to turn behaviors from both extremes on and off, according to what seems appropriate to the situation. Typically, however, a Responsive cannot maintain the calmness of a Resilient for as long a time or sustain the nervous edge of alertness of a Reactive (as, for example, would be typical of a stock trader during a session).

Extraversion (E)

The Extraversion dimension is about the degree of one's preference for being actively engaged with other people. On one hand, the Extravert tends to exert more leadership, to be more physically and verbally active, and to be more friendly and outgoing around others than most people. This extraverted profile is the foundation of many important social roles, such as salesperson, politician, manager, and social scientist.

On the other hand, the Introvert tends to be more independent, reserved, steady, and comfortable alone than most people. This introverted profile is the basis of such varied and important social roles as production manager, physical or natural scientist, and computer programmer.

Between these two extremes is the Ambivert, who is able to move comfortably from outgoing social situations to the isolation of working alone. The stereotypical Ambivert is the player-coach, who moves easily from the leadership demands of a coach to the personal production demands of a player.

Originality (O)

The Originality dimension refers to the degree to which a person is curious about her inner and outer worlds. On one hand, the Explorer has broader interests, is fascinated by novelty and innovation, would generally be perceived as liberal, and reports more introspection and reflection. Explorers are not unprincipled, but they tend to be open to considering new approaches. The Explorer profile forms the basis for such important social roles as entrepreneur, architect, change agent, artist, and theoretical scientist.

The Preserver has narrower interests, is perceived as more conventional, and is more comfortable with the familiar. Preservers are thought to be more conservative but not necessarily more authoritarian. The Preserver profile is the basis for such important social roles as financial manager, performer, project manager, and applied scientist.

In the middle of the continuum lies the Moderate. Moderates can explore the novel with interest when necessary but consider too much novelty to be tiresome; on the other hand, they can focus on the familiar for extended periods but eventually develop a hunger for novelty.

This trait does not relate to intelligence; Explorers and Preservers both score well on traditional measures of intelligence. Instead, it helps to define creativity, since Originality to new experience is an important ingredient of creativity.

Accommodation (A)

The Accommodation dimension is a measure of altruism vs. egocentrism. At one end of the continuum, the Adapter tends to subordinate personal needs to the needs of the group and to accept the group's norms rather than insisting on his personal norms. Harmony is more important to the Adapter than, for example, broadcasting a personal notion of truth. Galileo, in recanting his Copernican views before the Inquisition, behaved as an Adapter. The Adapter profile is the core of such important social roles as teacher, social worker, and psychologist.

At the other end of the continuum, the Challenger is more focused on her personal norms and needs than on those of the group. The Challenger is more concerned with acquiring and exercising power. Challengers follow the beat of their own drum, rather than getting in step with the group. The Challenger profile is the foundation of such important social roles as advertising executive, manager, and military leader.

In the middle of the continuum is the Negotiator, who is able to move from leading to following as the situation demands. Psychoanalyst and author Karen Horney (1945) described the two extremes of this trait as "moving toward people" (Adapter) and "moving against people" (Challenger). In the extreme, tender-minded Adapters become dependent personalities who have a minimal sense of self; tough-minded Challengers can become narcissistic, antisocial, authoritarian, or paranoid personalities with a minimal sense of fellow feeling. This trait differentiates the dependence, or altruism, of the Adapter, the independence, or egocentrism, of the Challenger, and the interdependence, or situational response, of the Negotiator.

Consolidation (C)

The Consolidation dimension concerns self-control in the service of one's will to achieve. On one hand, the Focused person exhibits high self-control, resulting in a consistent focus on personal and occupational goals. In its normal state, this trait is characterized by academic and career achievement, but when it turns extreme, it results in workaholism. Focused people are difficult to distract. This profile is the basis for such important social roles as leader, executive, and, in general, high achiever.

On the other hand, the Flexible person is more easily distracted, less focused on goals, more hedonistic, and generally more lax with respect to goals. Flexibles are easily seduced from the task at hand by a passing idea, activity, or person; that is, they have weak control over their impulses. They do not necessarily work less than Focused people, but less of their total work effort is goal-directed. Flexibility facilitates creativity, inasmuch as people remain open to possibilities longer without feeling driven to achieve closure and move on. This profile is the core of such important social roles as researcher, detective, and consultant.

Toward the middle of this continuum is the Balanced person, who finds it easier to move from focus to laxity, from production to research. Balanced people would make ideal managers for either a group of Flexibles or a group of Focused people because they have some of both qualities. They can keep Flexibles reasonably on target without alienating them, and they can keep Focused people cautious enough to prevent them from jumping to conclusions and relaxed enough to prevent them from suffering a coronary.

Summary

The five dimensions fit onto a *bipolar continuum,* which is a progression with graduated changes between two extreme and contrasting characteristics. For example, temperature is a bipolar continuum that is defined by the two extremes of hot and cold. I generally report a person's profile by placing the five scores in one of three zones in each bipolar continuum: high, medium, and low. A Big Five feedback form is included as appendix F. Table 33.2 shows the Big Five traits with anchor words that describe extreme scorers. Midrange descriptors would consist of nearly equal anchors from each of the two extremes. For example, extreme Extraverts are usually talkative and sociable, extreme Introverts quiet and private; Ambiverts might see themselves as equally talkative and private. However, mid-range scores—those who are clearly neither high nor low, for whom neither of a complementary pair of traits is dominant—tend to come in two styles. Some mid-range scores are the result of preferring half and half—for example, gregarious half the time and solitary half the time. Other mid-range scores are the result of preferring neither extreme but rather a true medium—for example, neither large groups nor solitude but a small number of people around at all times.

The popularity of *sociobiology* (see E. O. Wilson, 1975) invites us to enjoy speculation about the evolutionary advantages of specific traits. The *sociobiologist,* or *evolutionary psychologist,* stipulates that in order to survive over the generations, a human personality trait (or animal trait, for that matter) must have clearly demonstrable survival value. Or, as D. M. Buss (1991) describes it, the survival values of the Big Five form a kind of *adaptive landscape.* Consider: High Need for Stability is helpful in a fight, low Need for Stability for patiently waiting through long periods of deprivation. High Extraversion is helpful in procuring mates, whereas low Extraversion is helpful in persevering in the solitary tasks of child rearing and being a hunter-gatherer. High Originality is helpful for innovating in the face of need; low Originality is helpful for reaping the benefits of steady, repetitive production activities. High Accommodation is helpful in nurturing relationships; low Accommodation is helpful in building empires. High Consolidation is helpful in achieving the discipline necessary for effective leadership, whereas low Consolidation is helpful in providing the flexibility necessary to accomplish the needs of the moment.

Table 33.2. The Big Five Personality Dimensions with Anchors for Extreme Scorers

Supertrait:	Need for Stability (N)	Extra-version (E)	Originality (O)	Accom-modation (A)	Consoli-dation (C)
High Score	**Resilient**	**Extravert**	**Explorer**	**Adapter**	**Focused**
High-Score Descriptors					
	Content	Sociable	Curious	Accepting	Productive
	Controlled	Taking charge	Liberal	Team player	Decisive
	Secure	Talker	Variety-seeking	Nurturing	Organized
	Stress-free	Happy	Dreamer	Agreeable	Dependable
Midscore	**Responsive**	**Ambivert**	**Moderate**	**Negotiator**	**Balanced**
Low-Score Descriptors					
	Tense	Reserved	Efficient	Assertive	Spontaneous
	Alert	Writing	Practical	Competitive	Multitasking
	Fast	Private	Conservative	Self-interested	Permissive
	Anxious	Inhibited	Habitual	Proud	Unfocused
Low Score	**Reactive**	**Introvert**	**Preserver**	**Challenger**	**Flexible**

If possession of each of these extremes is an adaptive behavior, then certainly possession of both extremes is also adaptive. Hence, none of us is characterized exclusively by any one extreme. Even Extraverts have to go it alone. In fact, the current definition of a *personality disorder* is what happens when an individual loses the flexibility to use each of these opposing behaviors (for example, trusting and questioning) and rigidly (and maladaptively) persists in only one of the extremes. For example, a person who engages only in trusting and never questions anyone would likely be described as having a *dependent personality disorder.*

Application

❶ The Center for Applied Cognitive Studies (*Cent*ACS, Charlotte, North Carolina) offers three Big Five inventories for use in three different contexts:

1. The WorkPlace Big Five ProFile (long form and short form; Howard and Howard, 2001) for use with working adults ages 18 and up

2. The SchoolPlace Big Five ProFile (long form and short form; Howard and Howard, 2005) for use with students ages 12–22

3. The NEO (long form and short form; Costa and McCrae, 1992)

In all three cases, the inventories may be used as self or rater versions (the NEO uses separate forms; the WorkPlace and the SchoolPlace use the same form for self or rater). The three long forms each contain subtraits, or facets, of each of the Big Five. For example, Extraversion includes subtraits of warmth, sociability, activity, and so forth. More information is available at **www.centacs.com**.

<hr>

TOPIC 33.3   **The Physical Basis of Personality**

Ongoing research is aimed at describing the biological, physiological, genetic, chemical, and—to sum it up in one word—physical basis of personality traits. I like to approach this subject by describing each of the Big Five dimensions as having its own "arousal system": a complex of physical factors that work together to determine the threshold at which an individual switches off a preference for behaviors at one end of the dimension and begins to prefer the opposite. For example, the threshold for Extraversion–Introversion would be associated with the point at which an individual has had enough of big, noisy, smelly crowds and begins craving quiet and solitude.

It also helps to think of this arousal system as comprising two "fuel cans" of opposing but complementary energy: solitude vs. society, skepticism vs. trust, stillness vs. activity, spontaneity vs. structure, and so forth. So, when one uses up all of one's "fuel" for one extreme behavior, say "sociability," then one actually feels as though one's fuel can for society is empty, running on fumes, and needs to switch to the complementary fuel can of "solitude." After a day of being around people, I need to go off by myself and stick my head into a book. Another example: I once visited New York City with my youngest sister—78 years young—along with my wife, our daughters, a husband, and a niece. The occasion was our older daughter's appearance in an off-Broadway play. Well, my O score is very high, and my sister's O score is also high, but not as high as mine. We both crave novelty. Beginning with our arrival on a Thursday evening, we tried all of the ethnic restaurants for which New York is famous: French for dinner, Polish for breakfast, Indian for lunch, Brazilian for dinner, and so forth. As we loaded into our van on Sunday morning to head back to North Carolina, my sister turned and queried me: "Little brother, could we have something Amurcan ["American"] for lunch?" She was saying that her fuel tank for novelty was empty and that she needed to switch to her tank for the familiar.

The arousal system for Need for Stability is based on the autonomic nervous system; its threshold is the point at which stressors take one out of a state of calm, known as *parasympathetic arousal* and associated with activity in the cerebral cortex, and into the *general adaptation syndrome,* or *sympathetic arousal,* associated with activity in the limbic system (see chapter 2). In fact, researchers in the United States and Germany, led by Klaus-Peter Lesch of the University of Würzburg, found a genetic marker for the negative emotions (*Science,* November 29, 1997). The gene in question comes in two forms, short and long, and is involved in the efficiency of serotonin transportation. Those in their sample of 505 people with one or two copies of the short form scored higher on self-report measures of anxiety, angry hostility, depression, harm avoidance, pessimism, fear of uncertainty, and fatigability. Having two copies of the short version does not appear to affect the level of negative emotions, as two-copy people scored roughly the same as those with one copy. In addition to serotonin levels, the negative emotions are associated with high levels of *monoamine oxydase* (MAO), *cortisol,* and *adenosine GMP* (guanine monophosphate). All three influence levels of central nervous system arousal.

The arousal system for Extraversion is associated with the peripheral nervous system (Heller, 1993), and the threshold is associated with the point at which a person has experienced so much stimulation that she or he retreats into isolation. Caffeine, dopamine, endorphins, and the general efficiency of transmissions within the afferent and efferent peripheral nervous system are all associated with determining one's threshold for sensory stimulation. Under the cerebral cortex is the area called the *basal ganglia,* which houses a structure called the *ventral tegmental area* (VTA). Among the most ancient of all brain structures, this is the staging area for the intense reward system that remembers past events that result in excitations (chocolate, touch, and so forth) and predicts that future repetitions of those events will result in the same excitations. The VTA is connected strongly with the *prefrontal cortex* and our sense of self (see appendix A). It is the VTA that is excited by addictive drugs. The VTA, when excited naturally or by drugs such as ecstasy (MDMA), causes increased levels of the neurotransmitter serotonin. Higher levels of serotonin are associated with increased sociability and more positive emotions—thus, increased extraversion (Quartz and Sejnowski, 2002; pp. 90 ff.). Studies also show that Extraversion is associated with increased activity in the right hemisphere and an accompanying tendency toward optimism and enhanced performance in the left visual field (Heller, 1993). Introversion, on the other hand, is associated with increased activity in the left hemisphere and an accompanying tendency toward pessimism and enhanced performance in the right visual field.

Moreover, Extraverts (who are also low in Need for Stability) show greater hypnotic susceptibility, which is related to the Extravert's faster path in habituating to physical stimuli. Introverts (who are higher in Need for Stability) show less hypnotic susceptibility and are slower to habituate. The speed of habituation is associated with the threshold of the peripheral nervous system. Because the Extravert has a higher threshold for sensory stimulation ("Sock it to me, baby!"), it makes sense that Extraverts would habituate, or get used to, increased levels and sources of sensation more quickly than Introverts. Interestingly, Extraverts can be visually identified by observing the tendency for their eyes to make quick, darting movements to the left, an indication of enhanced performance in the left visual field (and right hemisphere).

The opposite is true for Introverts; check out their quick, darting eye movements to the right.

The arousal system for Originality is associated with novelty seeking and activation of the associative area of the cerebral cortex; its threshold is the point at which a person has experienced a surfeit of novelty, rejecting the new and craving the familiar. The threshold is determined by, among other things, levels of acetylcholine, dopamine, and noradrenalin and the condition of the myelin sheath. Dopamine has been traditionally associated with movement, the reward system, and internal imagery—the capacity to fantasize, to see pictures in the mind's eye. Wolfram Schultz of the University of Fribourg has identified a more precise connection between this movement-imagery-reward pattern and the prefrontal cortex (see *Science*, 1997, Vol. 275, pp. 1593–1599). Namely, rather than being associated only with images, dopamine is associated with the prediction of rewards. In other words, the availability of dopamine permits one to imagine the possibilities of pleasure upon pursuing an imagined path. It is the presence or absence of dopamine that makes the difference in predicting new sources of pleasure: the chef sees jicama, goat cheese, oysters, garlic, apples, and soy sauce lying randomly around the kitchen, imagines combining them into a novel hors d'oeuvre, and predicts a novel taste sensation that will titillate the VTA. Upon confirmation of the expected reward, this pleasurable sensation migrates to the stored pleasure associations connected to the VTA and becomes standard repertoire. Apparently, it is dopamine that helps us build our pleasure menu by imagining new combinations, sensations, and events. Lower levels of dopamine (i.e., lower O) result in reliance on standard repertoire. Thus, dopamine influences decision making, with higher levels predicting pleasure from novel events and lower levels predicting pleasure from familiar events, based on past experience. (Note related discussion of dopamine's connection to O and C in the treatment of C below.)

The arousal system for Accommodation is associated with the sex hormones, whose effects result in a person's opposing cravings for dominance and nurture, for challenge and submission. The threshold is defined as the point at which the individual will submit to a challenge from someone else; it is associated with the sex hormones as well as with serotonin, MAO, and oxytocin. Men and women both have androgens as well as estrogens, so what determines one's level of Accommodation is the relative proportion of androgens to estrogens. Although I probably have more androgen than my wife, that does not necessarily make me lower on A (i.e., more aggressive). This depends on whether or not my ratio of androgen to estrogen is greater than hers; if my ratio is, say 3:1, then I will be more aggressive than someone whose ratio is 2:1, more nurturing than someone whose ratio is 4:1. Absolute levels of the sex hormones influence the intensity of the aggression or nurture, but not its dominance as a trait.

The A dimension is associated with a motley crew of brain chemicals, ranging from the bonding cement glue of oxytocin to the aggressive forces of testosterone. Quartz and Sejnowski (2002, pp. 164–166) write:

> Parent-child bonds, the pair bonds of romantic love, and the social bonds of friendship may all have a common root in the brain. They all activate brain systems that use the chemicals oxytocin and arginine vasopressin (AVP); endogenous opioids such as the endorphins . . . and dopamine. . . . We believe that the key to human bonds lies in the relation between these ancient bonding systems and the new capacities of your enlarged cortex. . . . The hypothalamus of the male brain contains more AVP than does the hypothalamus of the female brain. Under the influence of testosterone, AVP levels rise with the onset of puberty and are linked to both sexuality and aggressiveness. When AVP is injected directly into a male rat's brain, for example, the rat begins to patrol and mark his territory obsessively, and he also becomes particularly combative. Castration or damage to these AVP brain circuits, on the other hand, results in both reduced sexual interest and reduced aggressiveness. AVP isn't related to all aspects of male sexual behavior, but it appears to underlie male sexual craving and anticipation. . . . It is not AVP that appears to underlie female sexual desire, but rather hypothalamic oxytocin, which is present in higher levels in the female brain than in the male.

During both male and female orgasm, high levels of opioids and oxytocin flood one's system; this accounts for both the pleasure of orgasm and the pair-bonding that it encourages among humans. Estrogen, progesterone, oxytocin, and prolactin are associated with maternal, nurturing behaviors. "Blocking oxytocin interrupts the acquisition of maternal behavior. Once those maternal bonds have been established, however, blocking oxytocin doesn't stunt maternal behavior. This suggests that oxytocin is essential only to initiate maternal behavior and to support the learning phase. Once maternal behavior has been learned, other mechanisms maintain the behavior" (p. 176).

The arousal system for Consolidation is associated with the attentional focus system, with the threshold defined as the point at which an individual is distracted from the task at hand and engages in off-task behaviors. This threshold appears to be associated with levels of testosterone in both men and women, with higher levels associated with greater perseverance and ease in spending time automatizing new skills and behaviors (see topic 13.11 for information on automatization). Also, excessive levels of serotonin are associated with obsessiveness, including the anorexic's (who have high serotonin) obsession with perfection. Barry Richmond of NIMH has determined that the gene controlling the production of dopamine receptors is associated with procrastination and assiduousness. Turn the gene off, and monkeys will work seemingly nonstop. Turn the gene on, and the monkeys will procrastinate and laze around. Apparently dopamine's steady flow enables the monkey to sense when reward is coming. We know that dopamine is associated with curiosity and the capacity for envisioning things. So, apparently, this ability to "see" into the future associated with dopamine also enables one to see when rewards are distant, thus encouraging procrastination. This is interesting, as O and C show a slight negative correlation: the higher one's O, the lower one's C, to a small degree. This would be consistent with Richmond and his team's finding. To get the most work out of folks, lower the O—drop dopamine levels—and you should see a rise in effort.

The neurotransmitter noradrenaline is associated with mental activity leading to drive and motivation (Quartz and Sejnowski, 2002, p. 96). An allied chemical, adrenaline, prepares your system for intense physical activity (as in the fight-or-flight response—see chapter 36). This one-two punch combines with a third chemical, testosterone, which provides for sustained attention. These three, working together, lead to high achievement. When one or more is missing, we get different variations on C. Drive, action, and focus are the three chemically driven ingredients of C, and different levels of these chemicals are associated with different levels of C, from the flexible behavior of someone who is content, sedentary, and distractible up to behavior that is ambitious, energetic, and focused. Levels of noradrenaline can be maximized by the drug reboxetine (Edronax), which uses the same kind of reuptake prevention action present in Prozac.

Remember that of all the other animals, the chimpanzees are the only animal that demonstrates measurable C behavior. We have attributed that fact to the chimp's being our closest relative, having more of our DNA. C is the trait that is associated with building civilization—

the dream, energy, and discipline to achieve. Caltech's John Allman has identified a type of nerve cell in the anterior cingulate of the brain called the *spindle cell*. These cells are plentiful in humans but do not appear until the fourth month of life. They are less common in other primates, and missing from all other mammals. Allman's (and others') experiments suggest that these spindle cells are associated with one's capacity for focus in social situations, thereby being crucial for the development of social competence, mastering the norms of one's culture (see *Proceedings of the National Academy of Sciences USA,* Vol. 96, pp. 5268–5273).

Application

❶ Remember that each of us has a real threshold that influences how much of a behavior we can productively and effectively engage in. I am an Ambivert, and on a recent week-long writing retreat in the North Carolina mountains, I "hit the wall" after five straight days of writing, an introverted activity. My body wanted no more; I'd reached my threshold for isolation and was craving stimulation. Such moments can be addressed by experiences that refresh and restore us, such as walking in the fresh air. On this particular day, I'd had both enough isolation and enough high Originality, so I restored myself (along with my wife) by taking a two-mile walk and then watching the semifinals of the men's NCAA basketball tournament with red wine, French bread, and smoked trout with all the trimmings.

When your body seems to be saying "Enough!" (enough stimulation, enough stress, enough isolation, enough focused attention, enough submission, and so on), give it a break and engage in an opposite activity for a while. In other words, mentally switch "fuel cans" and engage in a complementary activity, thus allowing your empty can to replenish.

TOPIC 33.4   Personality Changes over Time

McCrae and Costa (1990), in their work with the Baltimore Longitudinal Study of Aging, have looked for changes in temperament over time. They found that up through the early 20s, the tendency is to score lower on Accommodation and Consolidation than on the other three factors. They attribute this to the preoccupation of young people with identity formation (people who are low on Accommodation are called Challengers) and to their low career commitment (those who are low on Consolidation are called Flexibles). By age 30, this difference has diminished as a result of increased Accommodation and Consolidation and reduced Need for Stability, Extraversion, and Originality. Another way of saying this is that as we enter adulthood and the world of work, we become more emotionally stable, somewhat less sociable, a little more conservative, a little easier to get along with, and a little more goal-oriented (see figure 33.4). From their 30s forward, most people's trait levels remain stable, with two exceptions. One subtrait of Extraversion—activity level—tends to decrease somewhat in one's 70s and 80s, as does one subtrait of Consolidation: ambition. In other words, in our seniority, we slow down a tad and set our sights a little lower. Makes sense. But not too much lower: When Hugh McColl, president of Bank of America, retired, within a year he'd already started up several new businesses.

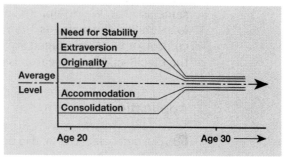

Figure 33.4. Development of Stability in the Adult Personality

In our research with the WorkPlace Big Five ProFile, which has been normed on 18- to 80-year-olds who are working full time, we found that in 19- to 20-year-olds who work full time *and* go to school (many of whom are also married and starting a family), the drop in N, E, and O and the concurrent rise in A and C are not gradual, as in normal maturation, but precipitous. It appears that working full time accelerates the developmental process—that is, they grow up faster.

Applications

❶ Be reasonably accepting of selfishness and impulsivity among youth, knowing that with understanding parents and societal nudging, people in their 20s tend to move toward a more cooperative and goal-focused adulthood.

❷ Conversely, be reasonably accepting of the higher emotionality, minimal time with self, and complaints of boredom of young people, for this too will change somewhat over time.

TOPIC 33.5 | **Sex Differences in the Big Five**

Virtually no differences exist between men and women on the Extraversion, Originality, Accommodation, and Consolidation dimensions. Costa and McCrae (1992) report some small differences on specific facets within these dimensions. Women do tend to score a bit higher on the Need for Stability dimension. On only one of the Need for Stability facets—anger—do women score the same as men. We do not know whether this difference on the Need for Stability dimension is the result of real differences in emotional control, or whether women are simply more forthcoming in reporting their feelings. More research is needed.

Application

❶ As a group, females tend to be more reactive—that is, they tend to make more overt responses to "good news, bad news" situations. This is not to say that males, who are less reactive, do not have internal reactions; they simply tend to show them less. Remember that this control can be either an asset (as in maintaining composure in stressful situations) or a liability (as in failing to show the intensity of a reaction to one's partner).

TOPIC 33.6 | **Relationships vs. Self-Development**

McCrae and Costa (1990) identify the second and fourth factors (Extraversion and Accommodation) as the two traits that are particularly important in developing relationships. The Extraversion dimension reflects the quantity of relationships, the Accommodation dimension their quality. The other three factors—Need for Stability, Originality, and Consolidation—refer more to the development of the self, regardless of the relationship context.

Application

❶ Understand that in building a relationship, it is important to continually communicate with one another, particularly on issues related to Extraversion and Accommodation. See Costa and McCrae (1992) and McCrae and Costa (1990) for further discussion and some examples.

TOPIC 33.7 **Can You Change Your Personality?**

For the most part, people are comfortable with the person they've become. Introverts like being introverted, Explorers like exploring, Balanced folk like being well-rounded, and Challengers seek challenges. However, situations may exist in which a person finds that his personality conflicts with his job, his co-workers, his spouse, his child, or other significant people. The reality is that one's personality as an adult is unlikely to change. Daniel Alkon writes movingly of this in *Memory's Voice* (1992), a testament to his lifelong search to find a cure for the effects of childhood abuse. He recommends "an attitude of humility toward the possibilities of change for people" (p. 163) and says that "the adult brain's networks . . . are to a significant degree hard-wired" (p. 162). For more from Alkon, see topic 17.1.

What can be done when we find our trait in conflict with our life situation? How can an Introvert improve, if not personally change, a relationship with an Extravert? Three kinds of strategies are available, identified as applications below. Each kind of strategy is supported by a list of specific suggestions in corresponding appendices.

Applications

❶ *Development strategy.* Attempt to learn some behaviors that offset the effect of your extreme trait. For example, extreme Extraverts could establish the habit of one hour of private reflection every day (through reading, writing, or some other solitary activity). See other suggestions in appendix G. But remember, you're not going to change yourself drastically; typically as much as 60 percent of your temperament is genetically based and consequently hard-wired, and, short of major surgery and pharmaceuticals, that 60 percent will not change.

❷ *Compensatory strategy.* Find a crutch, a "work-around," that relieves you of having to exercise a trait that is unnatural for you. For example, extreme Introverts who have responsibility for leading meetings could delegate the facilitation to a more extraverted colleague or team member. See other suggestions in appendix H.

❸ *Influence strategy.* Learn how people with opposite traits naturally act; then use that behavior selectively in situations where influencing them is particularly important. For example, if you are an extraverted salesperson who must establish rapport with an introverted purchasing agent, instead of dropping by and inviting the agent to lunch (both are extraverted strategies), send some written materials and make an appointment in advance (both are introverted strategies). See other suggestions in appendix I.

SUGGESTED RESOURCES

Alkon, D. L. (1992). *Memory's Voice: Deciphering the Brain-Mind Code.* New York: HarperCollins.

Costa, P. T. Jr., and R. R. McCrae (1992). *NEO PI-R Professional Manual.* Odessa, Fla.: Psychological Assessment Resources.

Howard, P. J., and J. M. Howard (1993). *The Big Five Workbook: A Roadmap for Individual and Team Interpretation for Scores on the Five-Factor Model of Personality.* Charlotte, N.C.: CentACS.

Howard, P. J., and J. M. Howard (2001). *The Owner's Manual for Personality at Work.* Austin: Bard Press.

Howard, P. J., and J. M. Howard (2005). *The Professional Manual for the WorkPlace Big Five ProFile 3.0.* Charlotte, N.C.: CentACS.

Howard, P. J., and J. M. Howard (2006). *The Professional Manual for the SchoolPlace Big Five ProFile.* Charlotte, N.C.: CentACS.

McCrae, R. M., and P. T. Costa (1990). *Personality in Adulthood.* New York: Guilford Press.

Website

Center for Applied Cognitive Studies website with Big Five information: www.centacs.com

34

Getting Smart about IQ

The Many Ways to Be Intelligent

66Can there be any doubt that walking on the street involves intelligence?99

—Robert J. Sternberg,
The Triarchic Mind

When people speak of IQ (intelligence quotient, or mental age divided by chronological age times 100), they typically are referring to a score on some test of verbal, spatial, and numerical reasoning. Those scoring above 100 are seen as having an above-average IQ; those scoring under 100, a below-average IQ. When reporting on matters of intelligence, it is usually this IQ score that the popular media focus their attention on.

For example, reporters write about the so-called "Flynn effect," named after the psychologist who has observed that across a dozen or so nations, IQ scores are increasing at a rate of three to seven points per decade (Flynn, 1999). The problem is that these test scores are not really based on any generally accepted theory of intelligence, nor do they help in predicting success in life (Epstein and Meier, 1989). In fact, the entire range of academic prediction tests (the SAT, GRE, ACT, LSAT, GMAT, MAT, and others) have been shown to predict only the first year of undergraduate or graduate school grades, when rote learning dominates the curriculum. These tests do not predict success in the later years of school, when more creative synthesis is required, nor do they predict work success (Robert Sternberg, 1997b, pp. 71 ff.); it remains to be determined whether the new essay component of the SAT will improve prediction of performance in the later years of school. In fact, Sternberg (1997b, p. 79) points out that traditional IQ (or ability) tests explain less than 10 percent of what society calls success. IQ tests originated in France as an academic screening device, and today, for the most part, they continue to be primarily an academic screening device.

At the beginning of *The Triarchic Mind,* Sternberg (1988) provides a stimulating history of IQ measurement. Among the problems with IQ measures that he has suggested are the following:

- Inappropriate use of the stopwatch

- Cultural bias

- Academic bias

- The assumption of a fixed quantity of IQ

- The lack of a generally accepted theory of intelligence

- The narrowness of verbal, spatial, and numerical reasoning as indicators of intelligence

- The assumption that verbally intelligent people read everything for detail

In addition to these concerns of Sternberg's, several others have emerged. Notably, in the work of Stephen Ceci (1990), we have learned that intelligence assessments attempt to measure abilities independent of specific contexts. Ceci has demonstrated that a person can score low on a context-free math test (such as the SAT-Math), yet act like a genius in the grocery store calculating per unit prices of products while doing comparative shopping for best values.

In another vein, Quartz and Sejnowski (2002) write: "Your mental life depends on interacting with intelligent artifacts, making intelligence much more akin to the pole vault than the 100-meter sprint. There's no doubt that individual differences still matter, but even these can be swamped by differences in the tools you have at your disposal, which can substantially alter your performance capacity" (p. 235). They are referring to the introduction of the fiberglass pole in 1963, with a resulting 23-centimeter boost in performance, and with other technological improvements, another 132 centimeters since 1963. In addition to the value of new tools and technology in improving individual ability, other contextual matters are in play: other traits, family influences (e.g., I couldn't have written this book before marrying Jane—her independence, her having her own "life," has freed me up to make time to write), historical necessities (writing my dissertation was advantageous to my employer), and so forth.

In fact, if traditional measures of IQ were adequate, then we could eliminate half our brain and still be plenty intelligent. Princeton's John Skoyles (in *Psycoloquy*, Vol. 10, 1999) points out that microcephalics and persons with half their brain surgically eliminated can have average and even above average IQ scores. Skoyles hypothesizes that the capacity to develop expertise in specific areas—that is, *talents* (Howard Gardner, 1983)—by extensive practice over time is related to brain size. To prove his point, Skoyles recommends research to determine whether or not persons with substantially diminished brain size show reduced ability to develop expertise.

In this chapter, we will discuss three different kinds of definitions of intelligence: content, process, and structure. A summary of these three aspects of intelligence is presented in table 34.1. The *content* definition is that of Gardner (1983), who maintains that different kinds of intelligence exist within an individual, and that an individual has differing degrees of ability in each kind of intelligence. The *process* definition is that of Sternberg (1988), who describes the various processes at work during intellectual activity. These two definitions complement each other: Gardner identifies several different unique domains, or playing fields, whereas Sternberg identifies the basic self-managing processes that operate regardless of domain. I like to call them *tools* and *talents*: Sternberg's tools that can be used in any of Gardner's talent areas. The tools are like the operating system of a computer (e.g., DOS); the talents are analogous to the many application programs (Word, Excel, Access, Draw). Consider the "resort" as an analogy. Gardner's content talents are rather like different kinds of resorts, such as golf or tennis resorts, theme parks, tropical hideaways, luxury hotels, beaches, arts centers, cruise ships, campgrounds, and sports camps. Continuing with this analogy, Sternberg's process tools are rather like the management principles that apply to all resorts regardless of content, such as those involved in information systems, sales and marketing, people management, long-range planning, financial systems, and research and development.

The third definition—*structure*—belongs to no one researcher but has been developed by such scientists as Hans Eysenck and Nathan Brody. Continuing with the resort management analogy, the structural definition of intelligence is much like the physical facility itself—its buildings, grounds, staff, equipment, supplies, and infrastructure—and the people who take care of it: construction workers, maintenance

Table 34.1. Three Approaches to Intelligence

Approaches: Common Name	Primary Names	Definition	Societal Relevance
Content Talents (knowledge and skills)	Gardner	One's ability to acquire and retain information in a given field of knowledge (talent)	Appropriate career choices Necessary for expert or professional status Cues for appropriate parenting and schooling
Process Tools (how we use the knowledge and skills)	Sternberg	One's capacity for mental self-management	Appropriate role within a career The difference between managers and doers The difference between achievers and average performers
Structure (the brain and associated systems)	Eysenck Zuckerman Brody	The combined effect of hereditary and environmental contributions to one's body and its component systems	The dependence of the speed, accuracy, and scope of one's intellectual efforts on the quality of one's physical body and the condition in which it is maintained

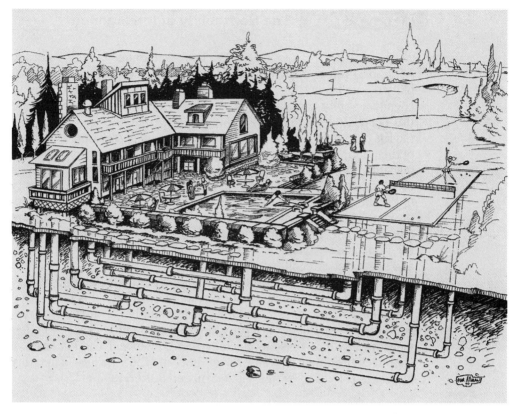

Figure 34.1. The Three Aspects of Intelligence as Illustrated by a Resort

crews, inspectors, groundskeeping crews, food service workers, and
sanitation workers. This description of the biological structure of intelligence applies regardless of content or process. It is molecular,
whereas Gardner's and Sternberg's descriptions are molar. Figure 34.1
shows the relation of the three definitions to each other. The domains
of intelligence (Gardner, 1983) are represented by the tennis court,
golf course, and swimming pool, three separate and distinct areas of
expertise; the structure of intelligence (Eysenck and others) is represented by the underground pipes and the structures with which they
communicate; and the process of intelligence (Sternberg, 1988) is represented by the administration building at the top left.

TOPIC 34.1 The Heritability of Intelligence

John DeFries, lead researcher for the Colorado Adoption Project, reports two strong findings concerning the heritability of intelligence (*APA Monitor,* May 1997). First, adopted children's cognitive ability correlates with the ability of their birth parents, and this correlation increases dramatically from age 3 to age 16. Second, the IQs of 16-year-old adopted children show no correlation with those of their adoptive parents. These two findings point strongly to the significant contribution of inheritance to intelligence. In a meta-analysis of 212 studies, Bernie Devlin, a psychiatry professor at the University of Pittsburgh School of Medicine, reports that genes account for approximately 48 percent of differences in IQ scores, with prenatal care (about 20 percent), environmental effects, and chance accounting for the remainder (*Nature,* March 1998). Specific ways in which prenatal and postnatal care influence IQ are listed in chapter 4.

In related work, researchers have identified over a thousand genetic causes of mental retardation in its many forms. It is hoped that the fruits of this research will result in effective strategies for prevention and treatment. As a rule, the basis of cognitive skills, whether measured by *g, s,* or school achievement, changes. The influence of shared environment decreases over time, and the influence of heredity increases (Plomin, DeFries, McClearn, and Rutter, 1997, ch. 9).

Application

❶ The brainpower of a child appears essentially to be set in his or her genetic endowment. Parents should provide a rich environment of love, toys, conversation, discipline, challenges, exercise, and nutrition to increase the likelihood that their children will use their potential to the fullest. Without the opportunity to be used, one's inborn talent may never get the chance to develop, as in a child with musical talent reared in a family that shuns music.

TOPIC 34.2 How Environment Shapes Intelligence

In 1994, Richard Herrnstein and Charles Murray caused a furor with the publication of their book, *The Bell Curve:*

Intelligence and Class Structure in American Life (Herrnstein and Murray, 1994). They presented research to support the conclusion that about a 15-point difference in measured, traditional IQ (math, verbal, and spatial reasoning) exists between the predominantly African American lower class and the predominantly Caucasian upper class. With that conclusion, most researchers agree. However, Herrnstein and Murray then claimed that the 15-point edge for Caucasians is accounted for by genetics, and that no environmental interventions can reduce the gap. In fact, they claimed, the gap is widening, with a dysgenic effect caused by the disproportionately higher birth rate among poorer African Americans. With that conclusion, a loud chorus rose in disagreement.

Robert Ornstein, in *The Roots of the Self: Unraveling the Mystery of Who We Are* (1993), recaps the dramatic impact that appropriate interventions have on the intelligence of lower-class children:

- *Vitamin and mineral deficiencies.* A three-month dose of 200 percent of the recommended daily allowance for vitamins and minerals increases traditional IQ scores by an average of 4 points.

- *Birth weight.* The average white infant weighs 3,286 grams at birth, the average black infant 3,069 grams. This is the result of cultural influences. Eradicating the difference in birth weight resulting from inadequate prenatal care increases the average black IQ score by 5 points.

- *Ascorbic acid levels.* Providing supplements for undernourished children who are deficient in ascorbic acid (vitamin C) increases their average IQ score by 3 points.

- *Head growth.* Malnutrition retards brain and head growth for an average effect of 5–6 points.

- *The mother's talking patterns.* If IQ were exclusively genetic, then it shouldn't matter from which parent a child gets its genes. In studies of interracial couples, children with white mothers and black fathers scored an average of 6–7 points higher than children of black mothers and white fathers. This effect is attributed to the observation that white mothers talk more with their children than black mothers do.

These five interventions alone could account for 23–25 points on a traditional measure of IQ.

In addition to Ornstein's summary of environmental factors, Sternberg (1997b) reports several additional significant factors:

- The degree of the primary caregiver's involvement with the child
- Avoidance of arbitrary punishment
- Organization of the child's schedule and environment
- Availability of play materials
- Variety in the child's daily opportunities

Citing the research of Bradley and Caldwell (1984), Sternberg states that these factors are better predictors of intelligence than is socioeconomic status.

Wendy Williams and Stephen Ceci (1997) address the issue of race and ability differences directly. After reviewing relevant trends over the last 30 years, they have formed three conclusions:

1. The gap between white and black students in ability and achievement has narrowed by between one-third and one-half. This is the result of increases in the test scores of black students.

2. The gap in intelligence scores between upper-class and lower-class families has decreased by about one-fourth.

3. The standard deviation of the Preliminary Scholastic Aptitude Test has remained stable, thereby mitigating the claims by dysgenic doomsayers that the gaps are widening.

In his review of Herrnstein's and Murray's book in *Scientific American* (February 1995, pp. 99–103), Leon Kamin concludes that "the book has nothing to do with science."

Application

❶ Do your part in leveling the playing field of life by lobbying for legislative guarantees for proper prenatal nutrition and postnatal child care with ample adult-child interaction (see topic 26.1, "How Language Grows Up").

TOPIC 34.3	**Process Tools: Sternberg's Triarchic Model of Intelligence**

Sternberg defines intelligence as the capacity for mental self-management. I suppose this is the sort of thing Jean Piaget had in mind when he defined intelligence as "what you use when you don't know what to do" (quoted in Calvin, 1996, p. 1). These definitions obviously include more than the traditional word, number, and space problems of current IQ tests. Sternberg sees three large, inclusive domains in which self-management is necessary: the *componential* (academic), *experiential* (creative), and *contextual* ("street-smart") domains. Figure 34.2 illustrates the relationship between these three

Figure 34.2. Sternberg's Components of Intelligence
Note: (1) goal formation, (2) research, (3) strategizing, (4) tactics, (5) creativity, (6) implementation.

domains. They take the form of six steps: (1) *goal formation,* (2) *research,* (3) *strategizing,* (4) *tactics,* (5) *creativity,* and (6) *implementation.*

I like to call the componential domain of intellect the *production* function: it researches, plans, and executes a mental effort. Two typical examples of the componential function at work are the college research paper and the corporate annual report. Pointing to the same kind of process, Gazzaniga (1985) describes the "Interpreter" as seated in the left hemisphere of the brain. Sternberg's componential and contextual functions would appear to be a more detailed analysis of the function of Gazzaniga's Interpreter.

Another name for the experiential domain might be the *creativity* function. This function engages in the quest for originality—novelty, uniqueness, innovation, insight, and so on. (See chapters 27 and 28 for further elaboration.) Sternberg identifies two aspects of dealing with novelty: how comfortable we are in dealing with new, unfamiliar experiences, and how readily we understand these experiences and are able to make them a part of our normal routine, or *routinize* them.

The contextual domain is the problem solver or, as Sternberg says, the *street-smart* function. Whereas the componential function deals with the efficiency of the mental effort and the experiential function deals with the originality of the effort, the contextual function deals with the rigidity of the effort. To the degree that a person always chooses the same strategy to solve problems, he is less intelligent than the person who calls upon different strategies appropriate to different occasions. The three main problem-solving strategy types are

1. *Altering yourself.* Maybe what I'm doing is causing the problem. Hence, if I change my behavior, I can solve the problem.

2. *Altering others.* Maybe what others (my spouse, boss, co-workers, friends) are doing is causing the problem. Hence, if I can change them, I can solve the problem.

3. *Altering the situation.* Maybe some features of the environment surrounding the problem (the workplace, home, organizational chart) are causing the problem. Hence, if I can change them, I can solve the problem.

To illustrate the three contextual problem-solving strategies, let's say that you experience a problem in your marriage. You could try changing your behavior (altering yourself), changing your spouse's behavior (altering others), or divorcing (altering the situation). The more intelligent (more mentally flexible) person will vary these three strategy types as problems arise. The less intelligent (more mentally rigid) person will tend to persist with the same strategy type. These highly patterned people become known as martyrs or doormats (always altering themselves), control freaks (always altering others), or quitters (always altering the situation). People with skill in this area maintain their flexibility by staying attuned to subtle verbal and nonverbal cues from their environment. Street-smart people are good at reading body language, for example. Figure 34.3 attempts to visualize how the mind manages itself according to Sternberg.

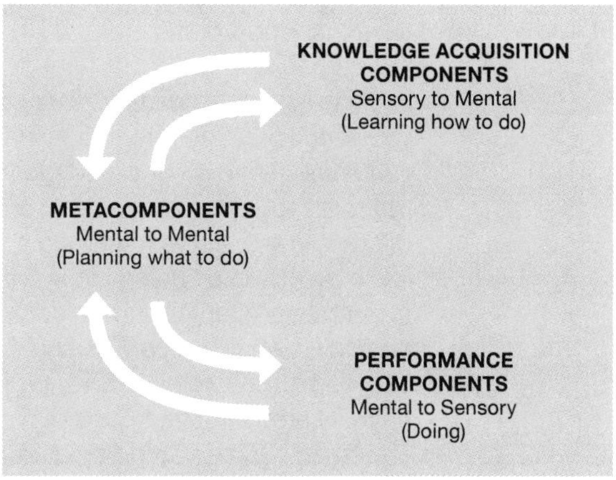

In a report to the 1997 meeting of the American Psychological Association in Chicago, Regina Colonia-Willner shared research on expert managers and how they reflected Sternberg's emphasis on situational flexibility. She tested 200 bank managers, 43 of whom were considered expert, with the rest simply ordinary. Sternberg's

KNOWLEDGE ACQUISITION COMPONENTS
Sensory to Mental
(Learning how to do)

METACOMPONENTS
Mental to Mental
(Planning what to do)

PERFORMANCE COMPONENTS
Mental to Sensory
(Doing)

Figure 34.3. How Sternberg's Three Componential Elements Relate to Each Other

measure of contextual or situational flexibility (street smarts), which Colonia-Willner referred to as *successful intelligence* to match the title of a book by Sternberg (1997a), was significantly better at identifying the expert managers than were traditional IQ measures.

An interesting footnote: Sternberg was not the first to observe these three features of intelligent behavior. In 1975, the Spanish physician Juan Huarte defined intelligence as the ability to learn, the ability to exercise judgment, and the ability to be creative (cited in Calvin, 1996, p. 13). Note the parallel of the first definition to Sternberg's componential (academic) element, the second to his contextual (street-smart) element, and the third to his experiential (creative) element.

Applications

❶ In figure 34.2, step 6 (implementation) is the aspect of intelligence usually referred to. The ability to use a great many words, numbers, and objects with masterful understanding, as measured by any of a myriad of IQ tests (Wunderlich, Schlosson, Wesman, California, Stanford-Binet, Wechsler, and so on), has served personnel and hiring managers, university admissions officers, counselors, and researchers for decades in their effort to distinguish the more intelligent from the less intelligent. In truth, all they have done is distinguish the more fluent in numbers, words, and object manipulation from the less fluent. And this is only the tip of the intellectual iceberg.

If you truly wish to identify more intelligent people, for whatever reason, you need to look for more than what we are here calling *fluency of execution.* Intelligence is not skin deep. You must look for the ability to establish goals for a complex project and administer it (step 1), find information relevant to the problem through appropriate research (step 2), be flexible in selecting a strategy to solve the problem (step 3), plan the steps of that strategy (step 4), and be appropriately creative in the design of the strategy (step 5). Steps 1, 2, and 4 are perhaps best measured through interviews and reference checks. Step 3, flexible strategy selection, can be measured directly by one of two tests: the Tacit Knowledge Inventory, published by The Psychological Corporation, San Antonio, Texas, under Sternberg's guidance, and AccuVision, a video-based metric distributed by Electronic Selection Systems Corp., Maitland, Florida. Flexible strategy selection can be measured indirectly through various authoritarianism scales such as the combination of scores for the Challenger and Preserver traits on the Five-Factor Model (see chapter 33). The various situational leadership instruments from Blanchard Training and Development, Escondido, California, also provide an indirect measure. Step 5, creativity, can be assessed by tests (see Amabile, 1983), portfolios, and interviews.

Appendix J is a guide to use in evaluating tests, interviews, references, portfolios, and so on as a way of assessing a person's overall intelligence.

❷ If you are trying to hire someone, you may decide that not all of the six components of intelligence are important, or at least not equally important. In that case, you may hire someone who has less overall intelligence but who can do a special job well. Generally, those who demonstrate mastery in all six areas rise to the positions of greatest responsibility.

❸ If you sense that you are lacking in one of these six areas, you can make up for that lack in one of two ways: either develop your ability through various educational opportunities or delegate tasks to others who excel in areas where you feel deficient. For example, if you tend to be rigid in selecting problem-solving strategies, then identify one or more co-workers with whom you can consult and who will be flexible in advising you to alter yourself, others, or the situation. Perhaps you are a person who consistently tries to alter the situation as a way of solving problems (spending money, reorganizing, rearranging, firing or transferring people, discontinuing products or services). Identify people who can advise you how to develop other, perhaps more effective, strategies, such as altering yourself (changing habits, increasing communication, learning or improving a skill or body of knowledge, changing an attitude, reordering priorities) or altering others (coaching and counseling, training, disciplining).

❹ Abandon the traditional management style that alters others, seeing employees as the root of all evil. Total Quality Management puts a heavy emphasis on altering the *situation;* it sees most errors as process-related, not people-related. *(Contributed by Rick Bradley)*

❺ Check yourself against the list of intelligent behaviors found in appendix K.

❻ Recruit individuals for management or leadership positions who exhibit flexibility in their problem-solving and a willingness to attack process issues. *(Contributed by Rick Bradley)*

❼ Provide training in problem-solving techniques. *(Contributed by Rick Bradley)*

❽ As a way of developing flexibility (street smarts), study Csikszentmihalyi's concept of flow. Two of his books provide insight: *Flow* (1990) and *Creativity* (1996). The concept is explained in topic 37.2.

❾ In the classroom, ensure that all three abilities are expected of students. Here is how the three might appear in two different subject areas:

Topic	Academic	Creative	Practical
Math	Find the error in this formula.	Create a formula that describes your theory.	How could this formula help traffic flow?
Business	Compare two types of reports.	Reengineer a process.	Find a problem and apply the process to it.

TOPIC 34.4   Content Talents: Gardner's Theory of
Multiple Intelligences (MI)

Howard Gardner (1983) established eight criteria for identifying a domain of intellectual content:

1. Isolation by brain damage

2. The existence of prodigies in that domain

3. A core set of operations

4. Developmental uniqueness

5. Evolutionary plausibility

6. Validation from experimental psychology

7. Validation from psychometrics

8. The existence of a unique symbol system to communicate its content

He proposed that eight domains of intellectual content (*talents*) satisfy these criteria, as outlined and justified in his book *Frames of Mind* (1983) and later writings. In his 1993 work, *Creating Minds,* Gardner provided in-depth biographies of individuals who illustrate the various talents (the category of "naturalist" was added after the book was printed, so no biography appears for it). I have summarized them as follows:

1. ***Linguistic.*** Isolated in the left hemisphere, the linguistic domain performs the primary operations of semantics, grammar, phonology, and rhetoric. Example: T. S. Eliot.

2. ***Musical.*** Isolated in the right hemisphere, the musical domain performs the primary operations of pitch, volume, rhythm, and timbre. Example: Igor Stravinsky.

3. ***Logical-mathematical.*** Located in the right hemisphere for males and both hemispheres for females, the logical-mathematical domain performs the primary operations of long chains of reasoning, the capacity for abstraction, and calculation. Example: Albert Einstein.

4. ***Spatial.*** Isolated in the posterior right hemisphere, the spatial domain performs the primary operations of correct perception of objects and the ability to transform and rotate objects in the mind. Example: Pablo Picasso.

5. ***Bodily-kinesthetic.*** This domain is isolated in the left hemisphere in right-brain-dominant people and the right hemisphere in left-brain-dominant people. It performs the primary operations of controlling the body and manipulating objects. Example: Martha Graham.

6. ***Intrapersonal.*** Isolated in the right frontal area for males and the bilateral frontal area for females, the intrapersonal domain performs the primary operation of intrapersonal understanding, or knowing one's own feelings. Example: Sigmund Freud.

7. ***Interpersonal.*** This talent involves interpersonal understanding, or knowing the moods, feelings, traits, abilities, and needs of others. Example: Mahatma Gandhi.

8. ***Naturalist.*** The naturalist domain involves skill in observing, understanding, and organizing patterns in the natural environment, as in the recognition and classification of plants and animals. Examples: George Washington Carver, Charles Darwin.

Gardner maintained that these eight domains are independent. High performance in one domain is not necessarily accompanied by high performance in another. Outstanding performance by one person in two or more domains is rare. Although William and Henry James are both known as great writers (linguistic domain), Henry's novels are said to read like psychology texts (logical-mathematical domain) and William's psychology texts like novels (intrapersonal domain). Gardner speculated that a ninth domain—existential—may emerge, but as yet he has been unable to localize a brain function associated with this talent for speculating about the nature of the universe and existence.

In a similar vein, Robert Ornstein (1986) developed the concept of the *multimind.* He identified 11 such talents: activating, informing, smelling, feeling, healing, moving, locating and identifying, calculating, talking, knowing, and governing. Notice the considerable overlap between Ornstein's list and Gardner's. Gardner's approach is certainly more widely known, and I suspect that efforts such as Ornstein's will ultimately be integrated into Gardner's model.

Gardner (1997) wrote of four ways in which each of the eight talents might appear. In a sense, what Gardner did was to write his own version of Sternberg's model. Gardner observed that extraordinary talent in any of the eight fields might take these four forms:

1. The *Master*, in which one achieves complete mastery of one or more of the eight domains. The work of the Master occurs within the scope of the practice of the time. For example, Rembrandt is a "master" of 17th century Dutch portrait painting—he took what was there and carried it through to its fullest expression, but was not particularly known as an innovator.

2. The *Maker*, in which one may or may not have achieved mastery, but whose efforts are directed toward creating a new paradigm in his field. For example, Darwin created the study of evolution, and Freud created psychoanalysis.

3. The *Influencer*, whose energy is directed toward developing domain mastery in others. Gardner's examples are Gandhi and Marx.

4. The *Introspector*, such as Virginia Woolf, who leaves us extensive records of her self-exploration.

The first three forms parallel Sternberg's academic smarts (Master), creative smarts (Maker), and street smarts (Influencer). Not only does the fourth form (Introspector) not parallel Sternberg's, it doesn't appear to be significantly different from Gardner's own Intrapersonal talent.

Applications

❶ School curricula should include all of the eight domains, and teachers should be prepared to help students develop their strongest domains. In the early school years, children should be encouraged in all domains so that their strengths and natural talents become apparent. Gardner's book *The Unschooled Mind* (1991) describes the curricular applications of his theory.

❷ Employers should expect high performance in only one domain and accept high performance in two or more domains as the exception. For example, to expect a human resources expert (interpersonal domain) to be a financial expert (logical-mathematical domain) is like expecting a starting quarterback (bodily-kinesthetic domain) to be a best-selling writer (linguistic domain).

❸ Parents should seek to recognize the domain of excellence in each child and encourage development in it. All too often, a parent will encourage development in one domain (say, musical) when the child has another domain of strength (e.g., bodily-kinesthetic). As in application 1, parents should encourage their young children in all eight domains, with the goal of identifying one or more for special encouragement. For a parent to expect a child to have strengths in a particular domain just because the parent does is to fail to acknowledge the role of genetics in human development (see chapter 1).

❹ Read Thomas Armstrong's *Multiple Intelligences in the Classroom* (2nd edition, 1994), which contains specific recommendations for identifying and developing the eight talents.

❺ Read Bruce Campbell's *Multiple Intelligences Handbook: Lesson Plans and More* (1994). He also coauthored with Linda Campbell and Dee Dickinson the 1996 book *Teaching and Learning Through Multiple Intelligences.*

❻ Visit the New Horizons website's special section on Gardner and multiple intelligences, including links to Harvard's Project Zero and related sites, at www.newhorizons.org.

❼ Howard Gardner (2004) recently updated his multiple intelligences model for the business community in an application-oriented work entitled *Changing Minds: The Art and Science of Changing Our Own and Other People's Minds.*

TOPIC 34.5 Structural Definitions of Intelligence

You Ming Lu and John Roder, neurobiologists at the University of Toronto, have discovered an enzyme closely tied to learning and memorization. Called *Src,* this neural chemical initiates the construction of neural pathways involved in the storage and processing of information. As reported in the February 27, 1998, issue of *Science,* Src stimulates phosphate in synaptic transmission and plays a significant role in keeping the synapse clear for future transmission. Referring to Src as a "smart" chemical, Lu and Roder predict that an "intelligence drug" is not far away.

In a direction of study that will proliferate in the 21st century, Hans Eysenck has explored the neurobiological correlates of intelligence. He has identified three correlates of traditional IQ: *reaction time, inspection time,* and *average evoked potential* (AEP) (Eysenck and Kamin, 1981; Eysenck and Eysenck, 1985). The first two, which are observed behaviors, are clearly less biological than the third, which is a description of brain waves, but they have a common thread in their effort to identify the biological basis of intelligence.

In both auditory and visual experiments, the reaction times of subjects with lower IQs—as measured by what Sternberg calls *performance measures,* such as the Wechsler and Stanford-Binet tests and Raven's matrices—increase as more stimuli are added. On the other hand, the more complex the stimulus, the faster the reaction of higher-IQ subjects (this is known as Hick's law). In other words, brighter people take progressively less time to react to progressively more complex stimuli. In addition, they show less variability in their reaction time. They are not only quicker, they are more consistent.

When asked to inspect a stimulus and provide a specific response, higher-IQ subjects take less time. An inspection test might have the following pattern: if you see a blue dot, press the button on the right; if you see a green dot, press the button in the center; if you see a red dot, press the button on the left.

The AEP is measured by the *amplitude* (height) of an electro-encephalogram (EEG) wave, the *frequency* of the wave (the inverse of the length of time in milliseconds between waves), and the *complexity* (irregularity) of the wave. According to AEP studies:

- The more intelligent the subject, the more complex the wave.

- The less intelligent the subject, the more variance there is across 100 tests.

- In studies of high- and low-income children, the AEP has been shown to be more culture-independent, with less difference between classes, than the Wechsler Adult Intelligence Scale.

- Facing familiar stimuli, higher-IQ brains fire fewer neurons. Richard Haier of the Brain Imaging Center at the University of California, Irvine, has found that positron emission tomography (PET) scans show higher brain activity while a subject is learning a game (for example, Tetris). Later, less activity is detected, with activity decreasing as scores increase. He also confirms that the higher the IQ, the less brain activity there is.

- Facing novel, unfamiliar stimuli, higher-IQ brains fire more neurons (that is, they bring more resources to bear).

Figure 34.4 shows the different patterns of higher-IQ and lower-IQ subjects while performing two tests of reaction time: an auditory test and a visual test. The graphs illustrate how, when faced with an unfamiliar task, the higher-IQ brains show more activity than lower-IQ brains. In similar tests conducted using familiar stimuli, the response (in terms of activity level) is typically reversed.

The weakness of these studies is that they relate speed to traditional performance measures of intelligence. To my knowledge, no studies have correlated speed with, say, creativity or street smarts, Sternberg's other two major dimensions, in addition to the more traditional performance, or academic, measures.

One of the significant physical components of intelligence is the quality of myelination. The thickness of the myelin sheath, its condition (brittle or flexible), and the effectiveness with which it grows are all associated with a variety of measures of intelligence. These relationships are summarized in an article by Edward Miller (1994). The quality of myelination is a function of diet, exercise, usage, and genetics.

In studying the preserved brain of Albert Einstein at McMaster University in Hamilton, Ontario, neuroscientist Sandra Witelson has identified two interesting characteristics. First, Einstein's brain was average in size, compared with the brains of "men on the street."

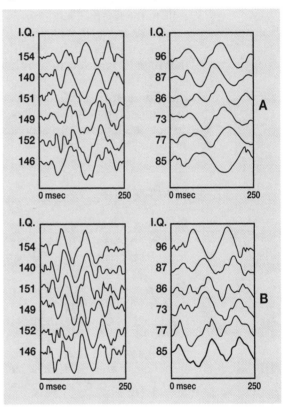

Figure 34.4. A Comparison of Evoked Potential Brain Waves in High- and Low-IQ Subjects
Source: H. J. Eysenck and M. W. Eysenck (1985), *Personality and Individual Differences: A Natural Science Approach*, New York: Plenum. Reprinted with permission of Plenum Publishing Corp. and the authors.
Note: (A) Auditory stimulation: Evoked potential waveforms for (left) six high-IQ and (right) six low-IQ subjects. (B) Visual stimulation: Evoked potential waveforms for (left) six high-IQ and (right) six low-IQ subjects.

Second, Einstein's parietal lobe (known to be associated with mathematical, spatial, and abstract ability) was 15 percent larger than average. Witelson also discovered that the fissure dividing the parietal from the temporal region was in a different position in Einstein's brain. These findings lend weight to the argument that ability is related to the size of particular areas of the brain. Anatomist Marian Diamond of the University of California, Berkeley, had already discovered that Einstein's brain showed a higher concentration of glial (or support) cells in the left parietal lobe.

Neuroscientist William Brooks of the University of New Mexico in Albuquerque, using magnetic resonance spectroscopy, discovered that high IQ is associated with lower levels of choline and higher levels of NAA (*n-acetylaspartate*). Further study is needed to determine whether dietary supplements of choline and NAA can improve cognitive functioning. Other studies have shown that choline supplements do not break down into acetylcholine, that only dietary sources (e.g., fat) result in increased acetylcholine.

Applications

❶ Where culture-free measures of IQ are critically important, consider using either a test of auditory reaction time with a supplementary test of visual reaction time (auditory tests are more reliable) or an EEG.

❷ IQ is less job-related when a worker is dealing with repetitive, familiar tasks. As tasks become more complex, IQ becomes more job-related. Don't look for bright candidates for routine work.

❸ Diet, exercise, sleep, and other factors can affect the purity of the synaptic gap and the durability and firing efficiency of neurons (see chapter 2). Don't let poor habits create a drag on your intellectual functioning.

❹ In your daily approach to life, consciously try to improve your reaction time and inspection time on the tasks that are of greatest relevance to your career and lifetime goals.

Table 34.2. An Application of Elliott Jaques's Model of Mental Processes

	Declarative (Disjunctive)	Cumulative (Conjunctive)	Serial (Conditional)	Parallel (Conditional and Simultaneous)
Level I Concrete Verbal				
Level II Symbolic Verbal	**Stratum I** 1 day–3 months Operator	**Stratum II** 3 months–1 year First-level supervisor	**Stratum III** 1–2 years Unit manager	**Stratum IV** 2–5 years General manager
Level III Abstract Conceptual	**Stratum V** 5–10 years Business unit president	**Stratum VI** 10–20 years Corporate executive vice president	**Stratum VII** 20–50 years Corporate CEO	
Level IV Universals				

TOPIC 34.6 | **Intelligence and the Time Span of Work**

Elliott Jaques has developed a specialized theory of intelligence as it applies to the management of work. Jaques (1994) has identified 16 levels, or phases, of mental functioning (summarized in table 34.2). The 16 phases encompass brain functioning that spreads from early childhood through advanced genius. Only seven of the phases are applicable to the world of work. It is these seven phases (he calls them *strata*) that constitute the core of his theory.

What makes Jaques's theory unique is that he has identified a *time span* associated with each stratum (phase or level)—the length of a task an individual can handle with no help from her manager. For example, a Stratum II manager can handle a task that spans anywhere from three months to one year, such as the orientation and training of a new employee. A Stratum III manager can handle a task that spans from one to two years, such as the identification, purchase, installation, and training relating to a significant piece of new equipment. Jaques's recommendations are listed below as applications.

Applications

❶ Remember that people who are engaged in work that exceeds their time-span capability tend to be frustrated.

❷ Be aware that people who are engaged in work that falls short of their time-span capability tend to be bored. (Notice the similarity to Csikszentmihalyi's *flow* concept in topic 37.2.)

❸ Ensure that no employee in your organization reports to a manager who is in the same time span. Managers, in order to be a resource for others, should be in the next higher time span, or stratum.

❹ People should be compensated according to their time-span capability.

❺ If you know a person's time span at one age—for example, at 25—you can accurately predict what his time span will be at a later age.

❻ The time span of a task is determined by interviewing people who are knowledgeable about the task, whereas the time-span capability of a person is determined by interviewing the person.

❼ For a catalog of resources related to Elliott Jaques, contact Cason Hall & Co., 872 Live Oak Lane, Green Cove Springs, Florida 32043, 904-284-8986, www.casonhall.com.

Some Final Thoughts on Intelligence

We humans are driven to find the simplest explanation for everything. Albert Einstein has cautioned us that "it is wise to express things as simply as possible, but not too simply." It appears that the 20th century witnessed an oversimplified understanding of intelligence. Early in this new century, let us usher in a model of intelligence that is more reflective of the marvelous array of individual differences in intelligence. My

Table 34.3. Thinking Metaphorically about the Three Approaches to Intelligence

METAPHOR	APPROACH		
	Content Talents	**Process Tools**	**Physical Structure**
Resort	Activities (golf, restaurant, swimming, tennis)	Management (advertising, planning, human resources)	Physical plant (computers, landscape, maintenance, construction)
Computer	Programs (word processing, spreadsheets)	Operating system (MS-DOS, MacOS, Unix)	Central processing unit, keyboard, printer
Church	Religion or sect (Christianity, Judaism, Islam, Hinduism)	Staff and volunteers	Buildings and grounds
Business	Line departments	Staff departments	Physical plant
Military	Branch (Army, Navy)	Support and command structure	Equipment, supplies, communications
Manufacturing	Manufacturing, research and development, engineering	Sales & marketing, materials management, planning, human resources	Maintenance, purchasing, construction management

friend John Kello, a psychology professor at Davidson College, commented to me, "One should treat one's A students well, because they will be one's colleagues. But one should also treat one's B students well, because they will be one's doctors and lawyers and other professionals. And, alas, one should treat one's C students well, because they will endow your chair." This politic observation pays attention to the reality that there is more than one way of being smart. Earlier in this chapter, we looked at the resort as a metaphor for the several aspects of intelligence. Listed in table 34.3 are several other frameworks and a description of how the various intelligences relate to them.

We at the Center for Applied Cognitive Studies have undertaken the long-term project of developing a single assessment package for use in both career counseling and personnel selection. This package would need to obtain scores in all of the 21 elements of intelligence portrayed in figure 34.5. In some personnel selection cases, one might want to obtain only measures that relate to a particular job in question. Table 34.4 shows how a variety of jobs fit into a matrix whose rows identify the Gardner talents and whose columns identify the Sternberg processes.

In closing this chapter on ability, allow me to loosely represent Stephen Ceci (1990) in identifying three important aspects of managing our ability:

1. To improve your ability:

   a. Increase your knowledge

   b. Practice

   c. Increase the complexity in how you use your talent

   d. Use your talent in new contexts

2. Be aware of three major factors that limit your ability:

   a. The constraints of your current context (family, work, and so forth)

   b. Personality traits (lack of discipline limits practice, for example)

   c. Mindlessness (failure to focus)

3. To manage your mental life:

   a. Match your personal resources to the demands made on you (see topic 37.2, "Flow")

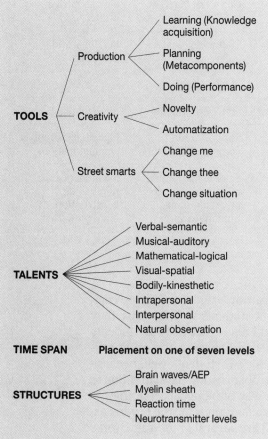

Figure 34.5. Intelligence

Table 34.4. A Gardner-Sternberg Job Matrix

Gardner Talents: / Sternberg Tools:	IA. Metacomponents (Planning Ability)	IB. Performance (Vocabulary and Verbal-Numerical Reasoning)	IC. Knowledge Acquisition (Learning Efficiency)	II. Experiential (Comfort with Novel Material and Experience)	III. Contextual (Situational Flexibility, or Street Smarts)
Linguistic-Verbal (Writing)	Book agent, publicist	Editor, speaker, actor, teacher	Critic, professor	Poet, novelist	Journalist
Musical-Auditory (Music)	Agent, arts management	Lyricist, singer, player	Musicologist, critic	Composer, jazz musician	Accompanist, teacher
Logical-Mathematical (Engineering)	Project manager	Systems analyst, technical writer	Purchasing agent, architect	Architect, design engineer	Project manager
Visual-Spatial (Art)	Museum administrator	Docent, trainer	Exhibit developer	Sculptor, painter	Director of development
Bodily-Kinesthetic (Sports)	Owner	Athlete	Sportswriter	Quarterback, point guard	Coach
Intrapersonal (Psychology)	Chief of staff	Therapist	Researcher	Writer	Social worker
Interpersonal (Management)	Production	Manufacturing	Quality	Research and development	Sales
Naturalist (Biology)	Department head	Editor	Researcher	Inventor	Environmentalist

SUGGESTED RESOURCES

Armstrong, T. (1993). *Seven Kinds of Smart: Identifying and Developing Your Many Intelligences.* New York: Plume.

Armstrong, T. (1994). *Multiple Intelligences in the Classroom.* Alexandria, Va.: Association for Supervision and Curriculum Development.

Brody, N. (1992). *Intelligence* (2nd ed.). Orlando: Academic Press.

Calvin, W. H. (1996). *How Brains Think: Evolving Intelligence, Then and Now.* New York: Basic Books.

Ceci, S. J. (1990). *On Intelligence . . . More or Less.* Englewood Cliffs, N.J.: Prentice-Hall.

Eysenck, H. J., and M. W. Eysenck (1985). *Personality and Individual Differences: A Natural Science Approach.* New York: Plenum.

Eysenck, H. J., and L. Kamin (1981). *The Intelligence Controversy.* New York: Wiley.

Gardner, H. (1983). *Frames of Mind: The Theory of Multiple Intelligences.* New York: Basic Books.

Gardner, H. (1993). *Creating Minds.* New York: Basic Books.

Gardner, H. (2004). *Changing Minds: The Art and Science of Changing Our Own and Other People's Minds.* Boston: Harvard Business School Press.

Jaques, E. (1994). *Human Capability.* Falls Church, Va.: Cason Hall.

Ornstein, R. (1986). *Multimind: A New Way of Looking at Human Behavior.* New York: Anchor Books.

Ornstein, R. (1993). *The Roots of the Self: Unraveling the Mystery of Who We Are.* San Francisco: Harper San Francisco.

Sternberg, R. J. (1988). *The Triarchic Mind: A New Theory of Human Intelligence.* New York: Viking Penguin.

Sternberg, R. J. (1997a). *Successful Intelligence.* New York: Plume.

35

EQ, Call Home

Getting Savvy about Your Emotional Side

> **Anger raiseth invention, but it overheateth the oven.**
>
> —George Savile,
> Marquess of Halifax

The word *emotion* comes from the Latin *motivus* and is thus a close semantic relative of *motivation*. Literally, emotion means to move around or to agitate. Both "motivation" and "emotion" suggest action, in the sense of a state that is the opposite of standing still or being calm and laid back. This action is related to an individual's goals: motivation is action in pursuit of a goal, whereas emotion is action resulting from situations that enhance or threaten a goal.

Hence, to the degree that I'm motivated, I'm pursuing a goal. To the degree that I'm emotional, I'm perceiving either a threat to my goal (negative emotion) or significant progress toward my goal (positive emotion). Or, I could experience conflicting emotions: joy that my grandson has come to visit, and stress (in this case, probably a combination of anger and sadness) that I'll have to stay up late in order to finish a project due early tomorrow.

Emotions weren't the subject of serious study by cognitive scientists until recently. This field of study is still young, and several theories compete for followers. I have included here the material that appears most compatible with the overall direction of cognitive research.

TOPIC 35.1   A Model for Emotions

A review of several major works on the theory of emotions (Lazarus, 1991a; Plutchik and Kellerman, 1989; J. G. Thompson, 1988) suggests a five-step model to describe what might happen to someone during an emotional situation:

1. *The event.* Something happens (a remark, a gesture, an accident) that potentially relates to one of the person's goals as either a threat or an enhancer.

2. *Perception of the event.* The individual becomes fully aware of the event (for example, through seeing, hearing, or reading).

3. *Appraisal of the perceived event.* The person determines whether or not the event relates to a goal. The value of the goal will directly affect the strength of the emotion.

4. *Filtering of the appraisal.* The status of the person's body (e.g., sleepy, alert) influences the intensity of his appraisal (for instance, very threatening or only mildly threatening). This filter can include past events with a strong emotional association. For example, the first funeral I attended was also my first introduction to the fragrance of gardenias. Now, for me, the scent of gardenias still gives any event an undertone of melancholy. Joseph LeDoux (1996) writes extensively of this memory-emotion relationship.

5. *Reaction to the appraisal.* The person channels her appraisal into some form of coping (from the Middle French *couper,* to

strike or cut). The strength of the reaction is a direct function of the value of the goal concerned and the degree of certainty that the event will thwart or enhance attainment of that goal.

Applications

1 Know that the reaction to the appraisal (step 5) can be either cognitive or emotional. Normally, when goals appear to be thwarted or enhanced by an event, emotions precede cognitions. These emotions can last for less than a second or for a lifetime, partly depending on whether we decide to will the cognitive part of the reaction to subdue the emotional part. See Seligman's ABCDE technique (topic 37.5) for ways to cognitively short-circuit a disturbing emotional event.

2 Analyze events and filters, and look past situations for patterns. *(Contributed by Rick Bradley)*

3 Put up these mottos:

> *We are disturbed not by things, but by the views we take of things.*
> **—Epictetus, *The Encheiridion***

> *There is nothing either good or bad, but thinking makes it so.*
> **—William Shakespeare, *Hamlet***

TOPIC 35.2 | **The Appraisal Filter: What Triggers Emotions**

The notion that the mind serves as a kind of gatekeeper for emotional behavior is at the core of the cognitive theory of emotions. The opposing theory, developed earlier in the last century, is that a person reacts automatically, without mental intervention, whenever certain emotion-evoking stimuli appear. A consensus is emerging that events with the potential to elicit emotional responses must first pass the appraisal activity of the mind. This appraisal activity is typically rapid. It may have several components and may be sequential or simultaneous, but researchers agree that it takes place between stimulus and response. When we receive "news" from our environment, it is neither good nor bad until our appraisal process has passed judgment.

Antonio Damasio (1994) has written an entire book exploring the appraisal process. The thrust of it is startlingly unexpected: he says that rational decision making and planning cannot occur without access to the emotions. In dozens of ways, Damasio illustrates the point that emotions are necessary for reasoning to occur. Studying patients with brain damage that had severed the frontal reasoning area from the amygdala's emotional resources, he found that these patients performed normally on traditional intelligence tests but were unable to plan and make rational decisions. They appeared to be locked into the present and past. Damasio explains it this way: People form *dispositional representations* (such as traits, values, opinions, and schemas) over time; these representations are linked to *somatic markers* that register pain or pleasure when the representations are activated. His brain-damaged patients who were unable to experience their somatic markers couldn't make decisions.

> "Reason generates the list of possibilities. Emotion chooses from that list."
>
> Wrangham and Peterson, *Demonic Males*

They were stymied, with no gut-level pointers to favor one alternative over another. They were unable to anticipate future pain or pleasure in connection with specific alternatives. With their decline in emotion came a concomitant decline in reasoning. Or, as Damasio put it, "The powers of reason and the experience of emotion decline together" (p. 77). Far from being an "unwelcome intrusion" or a "supernumerary mental faculty" (p. 75), the emotions are inextricably linked to rationality as the critical link in evaluating our perception of everyday events.

Lazarus (1991b, p. 827) has identified six ingredients that comprise the act of appraisal:

1. *Goal relevance.* Does this news relate to one of my goals or values?

2. *Goal congruence or incongruence.* Does this news serve to enhance or thwart my goal or value?

3. *Goal content.* How is my ego involved? (The answer helps to tap the relevant emotional response—for example, anger vs. guilt).

4. *Source of blame or credit.* Where does the responsibility lie, with me or thee?

5. *Coping potential.* Can I handle the consequences of this news or event?

6. *Future expectations.* Will things get better or worse?

Lazarus calls the first three elements *primary appraisal* and the last three *secondary appraisal.* Lazarus's secondary-appraisal elements resemble Seligman's three elements of learned optimism: *personalization, pervasiveness,* and *permanence* (see topic 37.5).

These six interventions control the gate that determines whether or not a perceived event leads to an emotional response. In reading the manuscript of this book, Rick Bradley commented that no one could use this appraisal process without a personal commitment to truth.

Applications

❶ Commit your goals to writing. Document situations that promote or thwart goal attainment. Analyze for patterns. *(Contributed by Rick Bradley)*

❷ Make a personal commitment to truth. *(Contributed by Rick Bradley)*

❸ Make a list of your personal hot buttons—the words, phrases, actions, or situations that cause you to become angry or emotional. Determine in advance what you will do to alter your normal response the next time one of your hot buttons is pushed.

TOPIC 35.3 **Emotions' Home: The Body as Catalyst**

J. G. Thompson (1988) identifies four ways in which biological mechanisms can influence emotion-related neurotransmitter levels. These mechanisms can influence the degree to which an emotion gets expressed, depending, of course, on the prior or simultaneous appraisal process. It's as though these four mechanisms served as a kind of catalyst, influencing the *degree* but probably not the *kind* of emotional response. They are

1. *Genetic vulnerability.* This is a very complex issue. See chapter 1 for a discussion of this topic.

2. *Diet.* Many of the chemicals that block or facilitate the development and transmission of emotion-related neurotransmitters can, at this point, be manufactured only within the body. See Kolata (1976, 1979) for more information.

3. *Hormone level.* In the complex interaction of hormones with neurotransmitters, hormone levels that are too high or too low can sometimes have a dramatic impact on the intensity of an emotional response. Research seems to be stuck at the chicken-and-egg stage here: do hormones control neurotransmitter levels or vice versa? Although it is not clear how the causal relationship works, it is evident that hormone levels are related to emotional response. As an example, we know that estrogen levels are directly related to left-brain activity (Kimura and Hampson, 1990).

4. *Circadian rhythm.* The degree to which we are able to satisfy the sleep-wake cycle and live with the 24-hour day can affect our hormone and neurotransmitter levels, intensifying our emotional response. That is why we may be more testy, tearful, or giggly during sleep deprivation, jet lag, or periods of low body temperature (typically between 3:00 and 5:00 in the morning or evening).

Applications

❶ The single most effective way to keep emotional responses comfortable is to stay in good physical condition, using the right diet (see chapter 7), aerobic exercise plan (chapter 10), sleep habits (chapter 9), and stress management program (topic 36.1).

❷ If application 1 doesn't work satisfactorily, consult appropriate cognitive scientists, such as neurosurgeons, psychiatrists, or neuropharmacologists.

❸ See the discussion of personality arousal systems in topic 33.3.

| TOPIC 35.4 | **Coping Mechanisms** |

Once we have appraised a situation as threatening or enhancing our well-being, we tend to follow one of four coping styles (J. G. Thompson, 1988):

1. *Verbal.* This left-hemisphere response suggests, for example, an individual who responds with vindictive thoughts but without any accompanying physiological arousal.

2. *Nonverbal.* This right-hemisphere response suggests, for example, an individual who feels upset but doesn't know why; that is, she doesn't relate the upset to an event or emotion but instead may think it's the flu.

3. *Both verbal and nonverbal.* This style is characterized by a high cognitive response (left hemisphere) and a high somatic response (right hemisphere), as when someone thinks, "I'm really letting my anger get me down."

4. *Neither verbal nor nonverbal.* With this style, a person chooses to see the event as neutral (neither threatening nor enhancing) with respect to his goals and values; therefore, no cognitive (mental) or somatic (physical) coping is required. This coping style is similar to the one in Seligman's ABCDE technique (see topic 37.5). With respect to this style, I like to recall Graham Greene's comment that hatred is a failure of the imagination.

Applications

❶ Understand that positive emotions are responses to events that are perceived as enhancing attainment of one or more of our goals. Positive emotions are healthy; they promote a feeling of satisfaction with life. We can increase the experience of positive emotions by changing our goals if not enough enhancing events happen, changing our environment (see Sternberg's three problem-solving strategies in topic 34.3), or changing our interpretation of events (we may be seeing events as threats when, in fact, they are enhancers, even if only weak enhancers).

2 The emotion of angry hostility places us in a double bind: both holding it in and venting it are bad for the heart (Ironson and others, 1992) and the immune system. The secret to dealing with anger is to express it calmly, without fury. Get it out, deal with it, and get over it.

3 Daniel Goleman (1995) presents a multitude of methods for considering alternative responses that could follow an appraisal of an event as threatening or enhancing. One example is "Red light, yellow light, green light," developed by Yale University psychologists as a part of the Social Competence Program for Troup Middle School, New Haven, Connecticut:

Red light: Stop and reflect when the emotion is first recognized.

Yellow light: Consider alternative interpretations and actions.

Green light: Pick the most satisfying ones and implement them.

4 Seligman's ABCDE model is an excellent approach to reconsidering how an event is appraised. See topic 37.5.

5 Bruce Arnow, an assistant professor in the Stanford University School of Medicine's Psychiatry and Behavioral Sciences Department, points out (1996) that many people with weight problems tend to eat as a way of assuaging emotions. Table 35.1 lists more constructive strategies for managing one's emotions.

TOPIC 35.5   The Behavioral Approach to Emotions

Most of the research on emotions has occurred at the *molar*, or *behavioral*, level. Many efforts have been directed toward listing the primary emotions. Various studies have worked with anywhere from 500 to several thousand words that describe emotions. Most of these studies have tended to accept two primary dimensions of emotion: *evaluation* or *valence* (pleasant vs. unpleasant) and *level of arousal* (alertness vs. sleepiness). Lazarus (1991a) points out that pleasure and pain, rather than being emotions, are some of emotions' raw materials. The *circumplex* model (see figure 35.1) locates each of the emotions on an *x-y* coordinate system based on these two dimensions. Anger, for example, would be located in the area suggesting unpleasant evaluation and high arousal. Sadness would be located in the

Table 35.1. Strategies for Emotional Management

Emotion	Anger	Frustration	Anxiety	Sadness	Boredom or Loneliness
The Task	Eliminate the cause of anger or release the anger itself.	Overcome a sense of failure or disappointment.	Relieve or get away from your worries.	Restore your enthusiasm and positive mood.	Find companionship.
Suggestions	Perform a productive physical task. Talk it out with a pet. Do aerobic exercise (walk or run around the block). Act it out with loud music, dance, shout. Play a physical game such as darts, have a pillow fight, use a punching bag. Meditate in your own way.	Write out your accomplilshments. Make a prioritized list and begin knocking off items in order. Put together a modest party. Read Jack Canfield's and Mark Hanson's *Chicken Soup for the Soul.* Read Seligman's *Learned Optimism* (1991). Read friends' comments in your old school annuals. Do a favor for someone.	Practice Benson's "relaxation response" (Benson with Klipper, 1990). Call an old friend. Engage in a repetitive activity such as crafts or weeding. Read a favorite writer. Meditate. Reminisce through old picture albums. Enjoy a good movie or TV comedy. Write to someone or in your journal.	Exercise. Act on the source of the sadness (visit it, write about it, or commemorate it). Plant or arrange some flowers. Immerse yourself in nature. Play music that touches your soul. Enjoy watching a romantic comedy like *Sleepless in Seattle.* Compare yourself to others with a greater loss.	Rent some movies and watch with a friend. Join a club with your interests in mind. Take a class or workshop. Visit others who are lonely (in hospitals, nursing homes). Get active on a committee for your children's school, your alma mater, or your office. Be a volunteer (a Big Brother or Sister, for example).

Source: Based on Bruce Arnow (1996), "Cognitive-Behavioral Therapy for Bulimia Nervosa," in J. Werne (Ed.), *Treating Eating Disorders,* San Francisco: Jossey-Bass.

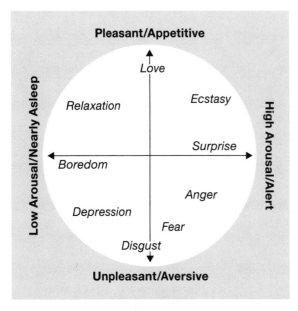

Figure 35.1. The Circumplex Model of Emotion
Note: Only a sampling of emotions has been placed on the circumplex.

area of unpleasant evaluation and low arousal, excitement in the area of pleasant evaluation and high arousal, and so on. A good discussion of the circumplex method of listing and differentiating emotions is available in Plutchik and Kellerman (1989).

A popular taxonomy of emotion (Baker, Zevon, and Rounds, 1994) maintains that positive emotions do not differ in quality, only in degree, and that negative emotions differ in kind as well as degree. Accordingly, love, surprise, delight, and ecstasy would all be similar in kind but different in degree, from less intense to more intense. Some have maintained that there are only three pure emotions—ecstasy,

Table 35.2. Emotional States and Parallels

Biological Regulatory Process	Behavioral Expression	Adaptive Function	Subjective State	Personality Trait Expression
Avoid	Withdraw	Protection	*Fear*	Timid
Approach	Attack	Destruction	*Anger*	Quarrelsome
Fuse	Mate	Reproduction	*Joy*	Affectionate
Separate	Distress signal	Reintegration	*Sadness*	Gloomy
Ingest	Eat	Incorporation	*Acceptance*	Trusting
Eject	Vomit	Rejection	*Disgust*	Hostile
Start	Examine	Exploration	*Expectation*	Demanding
Stop	Freeze	Orientation	*Surprise*	Indecisive

Source: R. Plutchik and H. Kellerman (Eds.) (1989), *The Measurement of Emotions,* Vol.4 of *Emotion: Theory, Research, and Experience,* Orlando: Academic Press. © 1989 by Academic Press, Inc., Orlando, Florida 32887. Reprinted by permission of the author and publisher.

terror, and despair—with all other emotions simply combinations of those three (see Schlosberg, 1954); however, most researchers seem to list somewhere between six and eight primary emotions. A popular model, for example, is the hexagon (see Rozin, 1997), which includes around the six points of the hexagon, in order, happiness, surprise, fear, sadness, disgust, and anger. The clearest listing of the emotions that I have found is that of Plutchik and Kellerman (1989). In table 35.2, I have italicized the column labeled "Subjective State," which contains the terms we commonly refer to as the emotions. But from glancing through the other columns, you can readily see that there are many ways of describing emotional activity.

Applications

❶ Use table 35.1 to become aware of your emotional patterns. If you find a pattern that is dysfunctional for you, make up your mind to deal with it either through learning a self-control skill on your own (such as Seligman's ABCDE model, described in topic 37.5) or through engaging in a therapeutic relationship with a counselor.

Diagnostic Extreme	Ego-Defense Regulatory Process	Coping Style	Social Control Institution
Anxious	Repression	Avoidance	Religion
Aggressive	Displacement	Substitution	Police, war, sports
Manic	Reaction	Reversal	Marriage, family
Depressed	Compensation	Replacement	Religion
Hysterical	Denial	Minimization	Psychiatry, shamanism
Paranoid	Projection	Blame	Medicine
Obsessive-compulsive	Intellectualization	Mapping	Science
Borderline	Regression	Help-seeking	Games, entertainment

② For serious emotional disorders that leave someone unable to hold a job or maintain a relationship, consult with a neurosurgeon, psychiatrist, or psychopharmacologist.

TOPIC 35.6   **The Biological Approach to Emotions**

Compared with other aspects of brain research, the emotions have suffered from inattention. Much of the research on emotion has been conducted at the behavioral level and has been centered on the researchers' play toy of choice: factor analysis. Factor analysis begins with a large amount of measurement data and attempts to find patterns (factors, clusters) within those data.

Beginning during the 1990s, researchers began to map the various emotions onto specific brain regions (see appendix A). One of the tests that is used to determine how many distinct emotions exist is isolation by brain area. Two emotions that have been so located are (1) fear, involved in a pathway terminating in the amygdala (LeDoux, 1996), and (2) disgust, whose primary activity is in the basal ganglia (Rozin, 1997). It is of interest to note that obsessive-compulsive disorder, which is associated with excessive reactions to conditions that cause disgust, also involves a disturbance in the basal ganglia.

At the time of this writing, few molecular, or microscopic, findings are etched in stone. For example, the amygdala has been strongly positioned as the "rage center"; however, the actual research findings have been inconsistent. Although surgical removal of the amygdala can eliminate rage, bizarre eating patterns and sexual behaviors sometimes follow. The inconsistency of the results is attributed to two factors: (1) the redundancy principle, which suggests that because of duplication of function it is impossible to pin any one function to a single location in the brain, and (2) the difficulty of absolute surgical precision, which makes it impossible to perform a procedure precisely the same way on two successive patients—that is, without invading a neighboring area that was previously left intact or leaving an area untouched if it was removed in a similar operation.

Nonetheless, some general principles are emerging (see Borod, 1999):

- A pleasure center seems to exist: the median forebrain bundle, which runs parallel to the pain center.

- A pain center seems to exist: the periventricular system, which runs from the hindbrain or medulla to the forebrain, parallel to both the median forebrain bundle and the RAS (see chapter 2).

- Frontal structures are associated with emotional expression, and right-hemisphere posterior cerebral structures are associated with emotional perception.

- Stimulation of the posterior hypothalamus excites the sympathetic nervous system (the fight-or-flight response).

- Stimulation of the anterior hypothalamus excites the parasympathetic nervous system (the relaxation response).

- Damage to the parietal, temporal, or occipital lobes results in no appreciable change in emotional activity.

- Damage to the frontal lobe can result in major increases or decreases in emotionality.

- The left frontal lobe houses both positive and negative emotional processes, the right frontal lobe only negative.

- If the same site in one human's brain is stimulated at different times, different emotions can be produced.

- Hormone levels influence the intensity of an emotional response.

- Levels of specific neurotransmitters affect one's propensity toward specific emotions; for example, high melatonin leads to depression, low melatonin to high sexual appetite, high epinephrine to elation, high prolactin to anxiety. For more on this topic, see Kolata (1976, 1979).

- Each emotion seems to have unique physiological responses; for example, anxiety leads to greater phasic increases in systolic blood pressure, anger to greater phasic increases in diastolic blood pressure, fear to vasoconstriction or narrowing of the blood vessels (which makes the skin pale), anger to vasodilation or widening of the blood vessels (which makes the skin flush). Progress is slow in describing these unique responses because of the difficulty of eliciting one single emotion and measuring its accompanying processes (J. G. Thompson, 1988).

- The physiological responses to emotion (cardiovascular, musculoskeletal, thermoregulatory, respiratory, gastrointestinal, urinary, and reproductive) can result in related disorders such as headache, stomach pain, blushing, sweating, Raynaud's disease (vasoconstriction in the digits of the hands and feet), muscular tightness, and diarrhea.

- These physiological disorders seem to be mutually exclusive: people who sweat don't blush and people who blush don't have chronic headaches.

- One emotion elicits different physical symptoms in different individuals: anger can elicit headache in one person, sweat in another.

- Physiological disorders are only partially connected to conscious awareness of one's emotional state.

Application

❶ Develop an appreciation for the fact that emotional responses, whether weak or strong, have complex origins. They may be attributed to brain structure, body chemistry, stress, habit, or personal cognitive intention. Do not assume that you know the cause of someone's emotionality. If knowing the cause is important, consult with a variety of specialists, such as neurosurgeons, neuropharmacologists, or psychiatrists. Never forget that although many emotions can be controlled by personal will, some people's emotions are held captive by aberrant biochemical forces.

TOPIC 35.7   EQ vs. IQ

Daniel Goleman legitimized research on emotions in one fell swoop with the publication of *Emotional Intelligence* in 1995. Again looms that word "intelligence." Sternberg (see topic 34.3) calls intelligence *mental self-management*. Extending that definition, then, *emotional intelligence* (EI) is a specific aspect of intelligence, namely, *emotional self-management*. Research clearly shows that emotional and mental intelligence are all part of the same bundle. Sternberg's definition of mental self-management, then, should include emotional components.

In fact, we can find all of the elements of Goleman's five-part model of EI (1995, pp. 43 ff.) covered in some aspect of chapter 33 (on personality) or chapter 34 (on intelligence) of this book. The five-part model of EI was actually developed by Yale University psychologist Peter Salovey (Salovey and Mayer, 1990). The five elements are presented in table 35.3.

The five elements of EI are closely related to the anatomy of emotions presented in the first four topics of this chapter. The five-step model of emotion presented in topic 35.1, for example, can be plugged

Table 35.3. The Salovey-Goleman Five-Part Model of Emotional Intelligence, with Its Analogs in the Big Five Personality Theory and in Sternberg's and Gardner's Theories of Intelligence

Element	Explanation	Analog in the Big Five	Analog in Sternberg	Analog in Gardner
Self-awareness	Ability to monitor one's own feelings	E1: Enthusiasm (*high*) O1: Imagination (*high*)	A part of contextual intelligence	Intrapersonal talent
Self-management	Ability to handle one's own feelings in such a way that they do not disrupt one's life	N: Need for Stability (*low*)	A part of contextual intelligence	Intrapersonal talent
Self-motivation	Ability to remain in Csikszentmihalyi's *flow* state	C: Consolidation (*high*)	A part of componential intelligence	None
Other-awareness	Awareness of emotions in others and an attendant empathy for them	E1: Enthusiasm (*high*) E6: Tact (*mid*) O1: Imagination (*high*) A1: Service (*high*)	A part of contextual intelligence	Interpersonal talent
Relationship management	Social competence that enables one to interact smoothly with others	N: Need for Stability (*low*) E: Extraversion (*high*) A: Accommodation (*high*)	A part of contextual intelligence	Interpersonal talent

Source: Adapted from D. Goleman (1995), *Emotional Intelligence*, New York: Bantam Books.

into the Salovey-Goleman model in several ways. Self-awareness relates to step 3, which is the point at which an individual consciously or unconsciously appraises the significance of an event. Self-management relates to step 5, which involves consciously planning how to cope. Self-motivation refers to the way in which an individual uses step 5—coping—to manipulate the events of step 1. By manipulating environmental demands and challenges with respect to his personal resources, a person can influence the degree to which he stays in the *flow* channel (see topic 37.2). Other-awareness relates to step 2 of the five-step model and how the individual perceives the behavior of others. Relationship management relates to step 5, coping strategies.

I prefer the five-step model presented in topic 35.1 because it presents emotion as a process that moves from an event through appraisal to coping. Whatever model is used, education in emotional self-management should be a high priority. In a study released in the November 1993 issue of the *Journal of the American Academy of Child and Adolescent Psychiatry,* researchers concluded that from 1976 to 1989, children aged 7 to 16 showed a significant worsening in 45 out of 118 specific emotion-related problems, with improvement coming in only one area. Whatever model we chose, it is clearly time to address the issue.

Newsome, Day, and Catano (2000) found no relationship between scores on the BarOn EQ Inventory and college grade point average. They did, however find a relation between the Wonderlic Personnel Test (a measure of verbal, numerical, and spatial reasoning) and measures of E- and C+ (Big Five terms; see chapter 33) using the 16-PF. This suggests two possibilities: personality measures may be a more sensitive measure of EQ than EQ measures, or EQ may not be a predictor of college grades. Probably the second: college is not the world of work and family, in which the kind of relational intelligence measured by EQ instruments is important. In college, one can be a social disaster yet make decent grades.

Applications

❶ A new area of school curriculum development called SEL, for Social and Emotional Learning, has sprung up around EI. For information on specific course material, write the Collaborative for the Advancement of Social and Emotional Learning (CASEL), University of Illinois at Chicago,

1007 West Harrison Street, Chicago, Illinois 60607-7137, 312-413-1008, www.casel.org.

② Read *How to Raise a Child with a High EQ,* by Lawrence Shapiro (1997), or *Playwise: 365 Fun-Filled Activities for Building Character, Conscience, and Emotional Intelligence in Children,* by Denise Chapman Weston and Mark S. Weston (1996).

③ Find hotlines and websites that provide good advice on children's emotional health. One example: call Beverly Mills's Child Life hotline at 800-827-1092 or e-mail her at **bevmills@aol.com**.

④ Review Reuven Bar-On's 133-item BarOn Emotional Quotient Inventory (EQ-i), published by Multi-Health Systems Inc. (Bar-On, 1996). Visit their website at **www.mhs.com**.

⑤ Review the 33-item EI inventory developed by Nicola Schutte and her associates at Nova Southeastern University, Fort Lauderdale, Florida (Schutte and others, 1998).

⑥ Read *Executive EQ* (Cooper and Sawaf, 1997).

⑦ Salovey, Caruso, and Mayer have developed a CD-based EI program. Find out more at **www.6seconds.org/training/msceit.html**.

TOPIC 35.8   **Emotions vs. Moods**

Robert Thayer (1996, p. 5) points out that emotions are caused by events, whereas a mood is a "background feeling that persists over time." Moods do not have a causal factor the way emotions do (see topic 35.1). Rather, moods reflect the state of one's body on two dimensions: relaxation and energy level. Hence, moods can be characterized as falling somewhere onto the kind of two-dimensional chart portrayed in figure 35.2. With relaxation on the vertical axis and energy on the horizontal axis, four qualitatively different mood states emerge: high energy/high relaxation (upbeat), high energy/low relaxation (edgy), low energy/high relaxation ("chillin'"), or low energy/low relaxation (down).

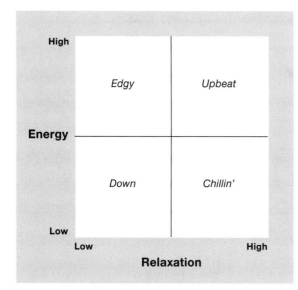

Figure 35.2. The Four Mood States, Based on Levels of Energy and Relaxation

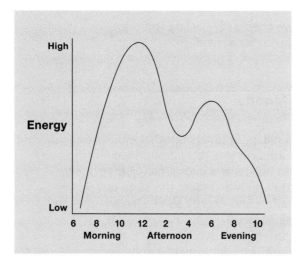

Figure 35.3. Natural Highs and Lows in Energy During Normal Waking Hours
Source: Adapted from Robert E. Thayer (1996), *The Origin of Everyday Moods: Managing Energy, Tension, and Stress*, New York: Oxford University Press.

Energy level is closely related to time of day (the circadian rhythm, as described in topic 9.3), with the highest energy typically in late morning and early evening (see figure 35.3). During the low-energy periods—morning, midafternoon, and late evening—people are most susceptible to increased tension. More introverted people exhibit high energy earlier in the day, more extraverted people later, so move the curve in the figure somewhat toward the left for Introverts, to the right for Extraverts.

Thayer finds that positive moods are associated with high energy levels, negative moods with tension. The most positive are high-energy, low-tension moods; the most negative are low-energy, high-tension moods. Depression is an example, according to Thayer, of an intense bad mood, with low energy and high tension. Mood is highly susceptible to personal control: we can alter our mood. Stress and exercise have the most profound effect on mood, as illustrated by figure 35.4. The various methods traditionally used to alter mood are presented in table 35.4. Note that most methods can potentially affect both tension and energy.

The final word is that events don't cause moods. Moods are the result of your body state, which is determined by the interaction of biorhythm, diet, exercise, atmosphere, sleep, stress level, and drugs. Moods affect how we interpret events. Hence, they are an important part of the filter that affects the appraisal of events described in topics 35.1 and 35.2.

Application

❶ The applications for this topic appear in table 35.4.

SUGGESTED RESOURCES

Damasio, A. R. (1994). *Descartes' Error: Emotion, Reason and the Human Brain.* New York: Grosset & Dunlap.

Damasio, A. R. (1999). *The Feeling of What Happens: Body and Emotion in the Making of Consciousness.* San Diego: Harcourt.

Ekman, P. (1985). *Telling Lies.* New York: Norton.

Goleman, D. (1995). *Emotional Intelligence.* New York: Bantam Books.

Goleman, D. (1998). *Working with Emotional Intelligence.* New York: Bantam Books.

Lazarus, R. S. (1991a). *Emotion and Adaptation.* New York: Oxford University Press.

LeDoux, J. (1996). *The Emotional Brain: The Mysterious Underpinnings of Emotional Life.* New York: Simon & Schuster.

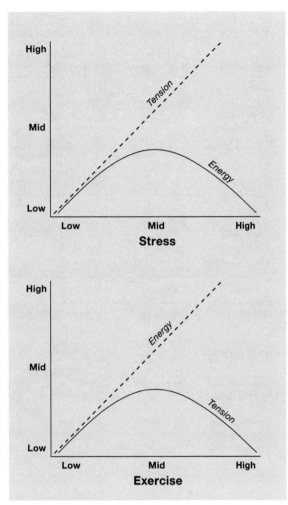

Figure 35.4. The Effects of Stress and Exercise on Energy and Tension

Table 35.4. Changing Mood: Effects of Various Interventions on Energy Level and Tension

Intervention	Effect on Energy Level	Effect on Tension level	Length of Effect
Yoga	Increase	Decrease	Varies
Ten-minute brisk walk	Increase	May decrease	Energy level enhanced for 30–90 minutes afterward; fatigue disappears first 1–2 minutes
Aerobic workout	Increase	More vigorous workouts more likely to reduce	Energy increase occurs about one hour later
Sugar snacks	Immediate increase	Increase	Energy level falls below pre-snack level one hour later
Good night's sleep (7–8 hr)	Increase	Decrease	Loss of sleep decreases energy and increases tension
Nicotine	Increase	Decrease	Lasts for only a few minutes
Alcohol	Increase	Lessens inhibitions, but not tension	Effect is temporary and only at the beginning of the episode
Caffeine	Increase	Increase	Depends on person and dose
Benzodiaz-epine (Valium)	Increase	Decrease	Few hours; drugs vary
Increase in negative ions (cleaner air)	Increase	Decrease	Ends when exposure ends

Plutchik, R., and H. Kellerman (Eds.) (1989). *The Measurement of Emotions. Vol. 4: Emotions: Theory, Research, and Experience.* Orlando: Academic Press.

Rogers, R. (Ed.) (1997). *Clinical Assessment of Malingering and Deception* (2nd ed.). New York: Guilford Press.

Thayer, R. E. (1996). *The Origin of Everyday Moods: Managing Energy, Tension, and Stress.* New York: Oxford University Press.

Thompson, J. G. (1988). *The Psychobiology of Emotions.* New York: Plenum.

36

Stress and Burnout

The Unrelenting Fire Alarm

66Emotion turning back on itself, and not leading on to thought or action, is the element of madness.99

—John Sterling

*E*motion, as we defined it in the last chapter, is "action resulting from situations that enhance or threaten a goal." When one's goal is substantially obstructed, the specific emotion that results is *stress.* The greater or more threatening the obstruction, the higher the stress. Stress that is sustained—either low-level stress over a long period or high-level stress over a shorter time—leads to burnout, which is, at its most extreme, the inability to feel any emotion at all, a total loss of motivation.

TOPIC 36.1   The Anatomy of Stress

When one senses that one's goal is being blocked, the "something" that serves as the obstacle is called a *stressor.* Put another way, stress occurs when the body's normal homeostasis has been disturbed (Sapolsky, 1994). Stressors can be anything from fear-arousing enemies to anxiety-arousing fantasies, from flat tires that prevent you from getting to your child's soccer game, to invitations to go on a much desired date or other social outing when you must complete an assignment with an imminent deadline. Stressors are not intrinsically good things or bad things—they simply get in the way of working toward your goal. The more important the goal and the more potent the stressor, the greater the felt stress. The stress itself is an emotion, or rather typically a blend of emotions. As you recall, earlier we defined emotions as feedback that we're proceeding on target toward our goal (positive emotions), or that we're being obstructed with respect to our goal (negative emotions). However, inasmuch as stressors can be joyful as well as saddening, the emotion of stress itself can include both positive and negative emotions in one blend. For example, the emotional stress you feel when your grandchild comes to visit when you've much work to do—joy mixed with resentment and dread. Events that normally are pleasing can be stressful—an invitation for sexual play from your partner when you must get a good night's sleep for an important early morning meeting.

One's *perception* of an event or situation as goal-deterring is crucial in determining its actual effect as a stressor. Woody Allen has said, "Eighty percent of success is showing up." Accordingly, 80 percent of the effect of a stressor is one's perception of it as goal-deterring. If I do not perceive an event as keeping me from pursuing and attaining my goals, I do not perceive it as stressful. Stress, then, is in the eye of the beholder. The critical test for a situation's having achieved major stressor status is whether the individual feels out of control. Stress is the point at which an event or circumstance makes the individual say, "I have lost control of my destiny." Or, as Chinua Achebe borrows from Yeats in the title of his novel, "Things fall apart." More fully:

Turning and turning in the widening gyre
The falcon cannot hear the falconer;
Things fall apart; the center cannot hold;
Mere anarchy is loosed upon the world.
—William Butler Yeats, "The Second Coming"

Just as the falconer feels the falcon slipping out of reach, so the stressed individual feels life's goals falling below the horizon, out of sight. There is no light at the end of the tunnel. There is no balm in Gilead. Things are out of control.

Stressors are not only negative and hostile, as when we are evicted from a home; they may also be positive and friendly, as when we move into a new home. In both cases, prolonged stress can be harmful, causing us to feel the need to get away from the stressor.

When stress occurs, our bodies mobilize for one of the three F's: freeze, fight, or flee (the fight-or-flight response). This reaction includes

- Dilation of the pupils, for maximum visual perception even in darkness

- Constriction of the arteries, for maximum pressure to pump blood to the heart and other muscles (the heart goes from one to five gallons pumped per minute)

- Activation of the adrenal gland to pump cortisol, which maintains pupil dilation and artery constriction by stimulating the formation of epinephrine and norepinephrine, sensitizing adrenergic receptors, and inhibiting the breakdown of epinephrine and norepinephrine

- Enlargement of the vessels to the heart to facilitate the return flow of blood

- Metabolism of fat (from fatty cells) and glucose (from the liver) for energy

- Constriction of vessels to the skin, kidneys, and digestive tract, shutting down digestion and maximizing readiness for the fight-or-flight response

Control of this process lies in the hypothalamus, which acts as a control console. Stimulation of the front part of the hypothalamus calms the emotions (the parasympathetic nervous system response); stimulation of the back section activates the mobilization processes (the sympathetic nervous system response). This is known as the *general adaptation syndrome* (GAS). The term originated with Hans Selye (1952); a complete and more technical, but highly readable, description of it can be found in R. Williams (1989).

Normally, stress comes and goes. Fears and anxieties, for most of us, subside shortly after their onset. Ira Black (1991) reports that a sympathetic nervous system stimulation of 30–90 minutes can result in a 200–300 percent increase in enzyme and impulse activity for 12 hours to three days and, in some cases, for up to two weeks. But what happens when fears and anxieties don't subside? What happens when stressors don't go away and the feelings of fear and anxiety persist over time? In a word, the high levels of cortisol become toxic. During this sustained period of GAS, when the posterior hypothalamus is active, the performance of the immune system (see topic 15.2) is seriously impaired. Minor results of this stress-related impairment include colds, flu, backaches, tight chest, migraine headaches, tension headaches, allergy outbreaks, and skin ailments. More chronic and life-threatening results can include hypertension, ulcers, accident-proneness, addictions, asthma, infertility, colon or bowel disorders, diabetes, kidney disease, rheumatoid arthritis, and mental illness. Killers that can result include heart disease, stroke, cancer, and suicide. In addition, chronic stress can result in energy depletion, depression, insecurity, impotence or frigidity, apathy, emotional withdrawal, insomnia, chronic fatigue, helplessness or hopelessness, anxiety, confusion, lack of concentration, and poor memory.

Thomas Kamarck, of the University of Pittsburgh, and his colleagues report that in a study of 901 Finnish men, those exhibiting the highest mental stress also showed blood vessel blockages similar to those associated with smoking and elevated cholesterol (*Circulation,* December 2, 1997, pp. 3842–3848). Further research is underway to determine the degree to which prolonged stress causes plaque buildup in the arteries, leading to higher risk for stroke and atherosclerosis. Sonya Lupien of Montreal's McGill University has found that prolonged high levels of cortisol shrink the hippocampus, causing memory impairment (*Nature Neuroscience,* May 1998). What this suggests is the following process:

1. Prolonged stress produces sustained high levels of cortisol.

2. As a result, the hippocampus shrinks.

3. The production of new neurons is significantly reduced.

4. Memory, mood, and other mental functions are affected.

John D. MacArthur ("Stress and Your Brain") summarizes the physical effects of stress in this manner:

- The sympathetic nervous system (SNS) is hierarchically dominant over the parasympathetic nervous system (PNS) and will not yield to the PNS until some resolution takes place (fight, run, meditate, etc.).

- At the first sign of a stressor, the adrenal gland releases adrenaline, only enough to get your attention (also associated with "flashback" memories).

- When the stressor persists (for a couple of minutes) and your evaluative system identifies it as the real thing, then the hypothalamus secretes *corticotropin-releasing factor* (CRF), which in turn triggers the pituitary gland to secrete corticotropin, which then triggers the adrenal gland to release glucocorticoids (especially cortisol). If this is not soon stopped, here's what happens:

  1. Energy (in the form of blood and glucose) is diverted from the brain (especially the hippocampus, one reason some persons have difficulty remembering traumatic events), the digestive system, and the immune system, in favor of supplying energy to the large muscle groups in anticipation of dealing with the stressor.

  2. The high levels of cortisol generally interfere with a variety of neurotransmitters.

  3. Cortisol triggers the release of excess calcium, which leads to the production of free radicals, which injure and destroy nerve cells. The hippocampus, seat of memory, is especially sensitive to cortisol levels, and autopsies of persons suffering excessive, continuing stress (as in untreated depression) show significant reduction in size of the hippocampus (up to 25 percent smaller).

  4. A high cortisol level reduces the effectiveness of the blood-brain barrier, allowing toxins to attack the brain.

  5. The hippocampus is the primary agent to trigger the PNS. So, as the hippocampus deteriorates over time, an individual becomes progressively less able to shut down SNS arousal.

  6. If one eats a meal while feeling stress, enzymes that digest carbohydrates are at lower levels. In one study, kids who meditated before eating cereal had 22 percent more of the

digestive enzyme *alpha-amylase* than kids who ate just after struggling with a math problem.

7. As cortisol levels rise, interleukin levels fall, increasing susceptibility to infection and disease and slowing healing.

8. Athletes experiencing stress are up to five times more likely to be injured than unstressed athletes.

9. Other sources of increased cortisol: caffeine, certain arthritis drugs that contain steroid hormones, and several nights in a row of insufficient sleep.

A visual overview of this process is available in figure 36.1. As you study this process, begin at the bottom left with the appearance of the stressor.

In a review of the literature on stress, McEwen and Schmeck (1996) summarize by identifying five clear markers for stress-related physical damage: blood pressure, blood sugar, cholesterol, cortisol, and abdominal fat. If one or more of these five have not been affected, then we may conclude that for the individual in question, stress-related damage has not been sustained.

The popularity of the word "stress" has resulted in its loss of meaning. Now it is fashionable to be "oh, so stressed." In 1988, Sterling and Eyer proposed a new term that more completely describes the process: allostasis. Others have followed suit (e.g., McEwen and Seeman, 1999; Ray, 2004). All too often, "stress" refers simply to having an imposing to-do list. The fullness of the term, however, refers to a period in a person's life when bodily arousal functions react over time to events that interfere with the person's goals. *Allostasis* literally means a change (*allo*) in behavior for the purpose of returning to equilibrium (*stasis*). We see the Bengal tiger, we get aroused (loss of equilibrium), we run like mad (change in behavior), and we rest under a distant shade tree out of harm's way (return to equilibrium). The entire process, from arousal to rest, is called allostasis. *Allostatic load* refers to the amount of arousal one experiences over time. McEwen and Seeman describe four kinds of allostatic load:

1. Repeated stressors, close together over time (bereavement, loss of job, house move, separation, childbirth, illness, etc.)

2. Single stressor, repeated over time, with inadequate adaptation or learning, with essentially the same long-term effect as above (getting teased, nagged, or blamed repeatedly and failing to come up with a satisfactory way of defusing the situation)

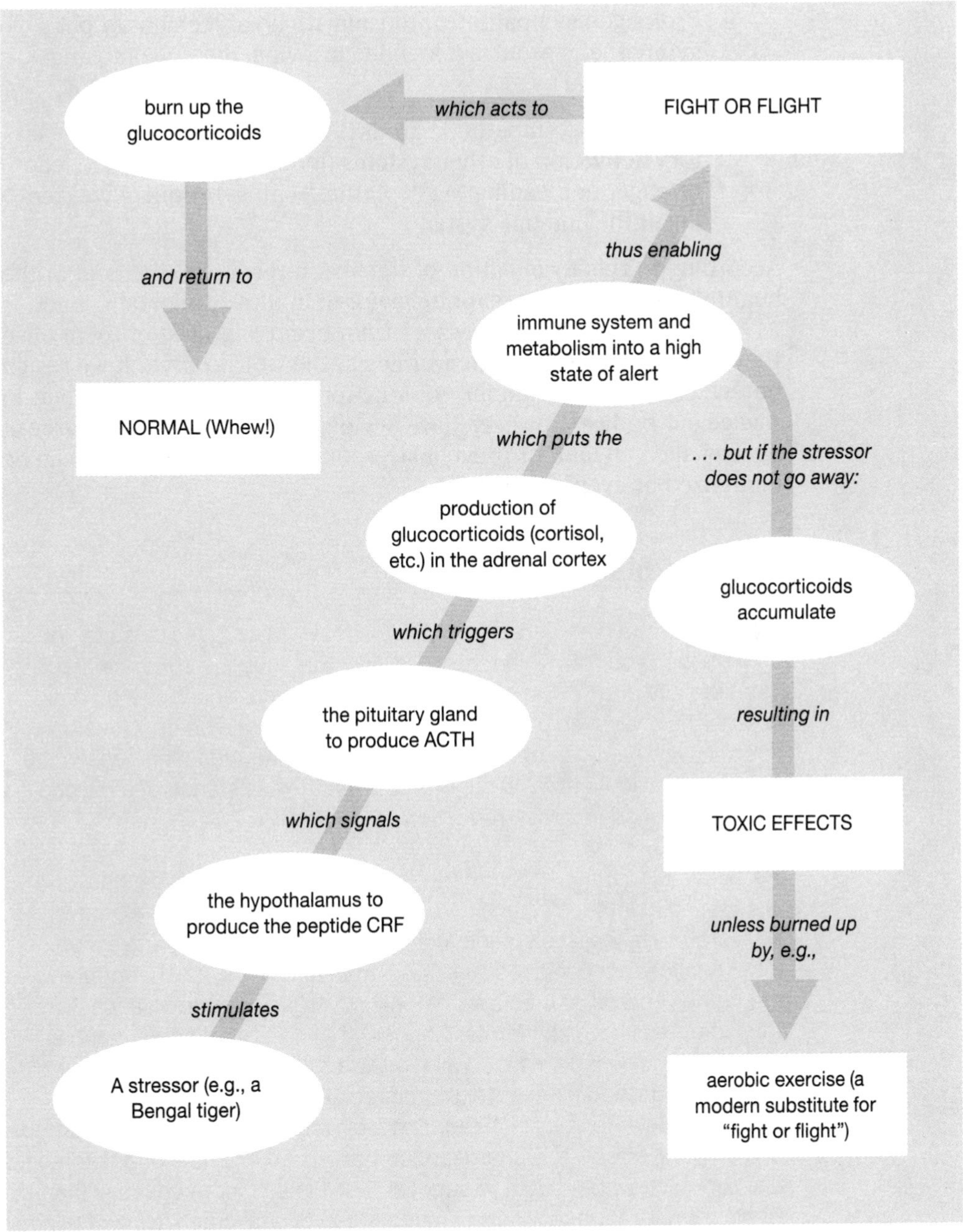

burn up the glucocorticoids

which acts to

FIGHT OR FLIGHT

thus enabling

and return to

immune system and metabolism into a high state of alert

NORMAL (Whew!)

which puts the

. . . but if the stressor does not go away:

production of glucocorticoids (cortisol, etc.) in the adrenal cortex

which triggers

glucocorticoids accumulate

the pituitary gland to produce ACTH

resulting in

which signals

TOXIC EFFECTS

the hypothalamus to produce the peptide CRF

unless burned up by, e.g.,

stimulates

A stressor (e.g., a Bengal tiger)

aerobic exercise (a modern substitute for "fight or flight")

Figure 36.1. The Chemistry of Stress

3. Prolonged sympathetic arousal with no abatement or para-sympathetic arousal (extended grieving, holding onto anger, living in fear)

4. Insufficient sympathetic arousal with subsequent compensatory activation of other systems (moderate resentment, fear, or anger not leading to adaptation, with subsequent weakening of the immune system)

According to this formulation of the stress response, the goal of the healthy individual is to adapt behavior to minimize allostatic load.

How do we prevent stressors from occurring or stop them once they begin? The simplest answer lies in the word *control.* If we resign ourselves to the inevitability of long-term stress, it will continue to ravage our bodies. However, if we decide that we have some degree of control and can limit or prevent stressors, the effects of stress can be minimized or even eliminated.

Applications

❶ If any of the disorders listed above affect you or those close to you, confirm with your physician the possibility that they are stress-related. Then identify and list the stressors that cause a continued feeling of tightness in the chest, rapid heartbeat, acid stomach, and so on. Consider specific ways you can control each stressor, using the techniques in the following applications. You might also seek the assistance of a psychotherapist trained in stress-reduction strategies.

❷ *Relax.* Meditation, hypnosis, deep breathing, napping, saunas, and just resting quietly—all these and other methods are equally effective. Research says that meditation techniques are no more effective than other relaxation techniques (see Druckman and Bjork, 1991). Popular magazines and other media commonly advertise or otherwise feature commercial "relaxation techniques" that consist of some mechanical, sensory, or meditative technique. As a rule, unless you really want to spend money to learn to relax, just read Herbert Benson's classic, *The Relaxation Response* (1990). The "Joy Touch," which can be learned only in workshops—at a charge, of course—is an example of a commercial approach with no data to suggest that it is any more effective than Benson's relaxation response. I'm reminded of a favorite saying of mine: "Meditation is not what you think."

The state of mind during hypnosis is no different from that of the normal, awake, alert mind. Hypnosis is a guided form of conscious selective attention and dissociation characterized by suggestibility. Even the best subjects do nothing under hypnosis that they wouldn't do otherwise. See an excellent summary of research on hypnosis in the *Harvard Health Letter,* April 1991, pp. 1–4. Daniel Goleman has written an account of the Dalai Lama's thoughts on meditation and its ability to reduce stress in his 2003 book, *Destruction Emotions*—recommended for students of various meditative disciplines.

❸ *Escape.* Do anything that "takes your mind off" the stressors, such as reading, watching television, listening to music, pursuing hobbies and crafts, or cooking. When our minds are filled with such activities, limbic arousal shuts down and cortical arousal takes over. As we take part in a totally absorbing pursuit, any activity in the posterior hypothalamus moves to its forward area and to subsequent parasympathetic arousal.

❹ *Exercise.* Although any exercise helps relieve stress, aerobic exercise is best. The simplest definition of *aerobic exercise* is any physical activity that keeps the heart pumping at elevated levels continuously for 12–30 minutes (see chapter 10). Jogging, swimming, and brisk walking are aerobic; tennis, golf, and basketball are not (unless played nonstop). See Covert Bailey's excellent book, *The New Fit or Fat* (1991).

❺ *Don't rely on sex.* Sexual orgasm releases the sympathetic nervous system's grip and leads to a parasympathetic response. But because sex drive and stress levels are inversely related, a person under extreme stress probably would not find sexual activity the release that others might. Instead, those who are experiencing extreme stress should probably try some other strategy, such as those in applications 2–4 and 6–15, before trying sex. When high stress levels have been reduced, sexual activity can arise more spontaneously.

❻ *Eat and drink moderately.* Moderate amounts of food or nonalcoholic beverages help dissipate stomach acids and return stress levels to normal.

❼ *Visualize.* Richard Restak (1991) relates an Eastern three-step technique for relieving "monkey mind," otherwise known as jumpiness or jitteriness. First, stare at an object, such as a plant. Then close your eyes and visualize that same object. Finally, open your eyes to confirm your visualization. This form of meditative observation, by focusing your attention, will calm you. (For more information on visualizing, see topic 37.5, application 5.)

8 *Laugh.* Cousins (1989) reports that 10 minutes of belly laughs can provide two hours of pain-free sleep. (See the extended treatment of humor and laughter in chapter 11.) Edward O'Brien of Marywood University in Scranton, Pennsylvania, found that college students who had to give impromptu speeches had heart rates of 100 beats per minute while they were speaking, but those who watched an episode of *Seinfeld* beforehand performed with heart rates of only 80–85 beats per minute.

> **"I had rather have a fool to make me merry than experience to make me sad."**
>
> —William Shakespeare, *As You Like It*

9 *Seek relief.* Make the necessary arrangements for getting away from stressors. Have lists of babysitters, substitute caregivers, and temporary help. Use your creativity and the creativity of others to develop ways to relieve stress, such as neighborhood dinner co-ops and babysitting co-ops. Research says that simply knowing that relief is available is relaxing in and of itself. Air traffic controllers are more relaxed if they know they can call on relief when they need it. Usually, when flextime is initiated in organizations, few people use it; just knowing that it is an option is comfort enough. In one experiment, subjects taking a test were randomly assigned to one of two conditions: both groups had noise outside their room, but only the members of one group were told they could shut the door if the noise became bothersome. The group given permission didn't close the door, yet its members scored higher than the members of the group without permission.

10 *Reframe the stressor.* Find a new way to explain your stressor so that it becomes less stressful. See Seligman (1991) and Bandler and Grinder (1982).

11 *Consider medication.* For severe, long-term stress, you might consult a physician for pharmaceutical relief when other measures prove to be ineffective. Medication could be aimed at

- Blocking alpha and beta receptors for adrenergic neurotransmitters to prevent sympathetic arousal

- Shutting down cortisol production in the adrenal gland (for example, by using alprazolam and ketoconazole)

- Inhibiting the release of epinephrine and norepinephrine (the neurotransmitter GABA inhibits production of epinephrine and norepinephrine; Valium is one of the catalysts for GABA)

- Increasing cholinergic neurotransmitters (for example, acetylcholine) and sensitizing muscarinic receptors, resulting in the release of cyclic guanosine monophosphate, which stimulates a parasympathetic response (the heart slows, pupils contract, and digestion is stimulated)

Drugs can help prevent or shut down a sympathetic response and bring on a parasympathetic response. One result of failure to shut down sympathetic arousal is Type A behavior (see topic 36.3).

⑫ *Get a pet.* Handling pets is a great stress reliever, which explains the popular practice of taking pets to rest-home patients. *(Contributed by Rick Bradley)*

⑬ *Develop a corporate policy.* Listed below are several corporate policies or practices that give employees a sense of having some control over the quality of their work life:

- Pay for performance
- Flextime
- Cafeteria benefits
- Two-way performance appraisals
- Negotiated rather than imposed goals
- Employee involvement programs
- Explicit management responses to employee suggestions
- Career development with visible, active support
- No boss for consistent performers
- Self-directed work teams
- An effective ethics code that contains a whistle-blowing policy
- Dual career paths
- A focus on team results

⑭ *Bust stress.* In the vein of more is better, here is a list of 18 "stress busters" by three researchers who suggest that extreme measures are not mandatory for stress reduction: look for smaller victories. Cardiologist Thomas Kottke of the Mayo Institute, cardiologist Robert S. Eliot of Scottsdale's Institute of Stress Medicine, and neuroscientist Robert Sapolsky of Stanford University suggest these modest measures:

- Every day, take 30 minutes to one hour to do something you really like to do, whether it's taking a bubble bath or playing with a child.

- Strengthen your ties with your family.

- Don't accept trouble in your marriage—do something about it.

- Recognize that people with some sort of religious belief experience less stress; consider giving religion a bigger role in your life.

- Stress is often a matter of one's point of view. Consider alternative interpretations of your situation; see difficult situations as challenging rather than enraging.

- Exercise as much as you can. Don't fail to exercise just because you can't get in 30 minutes; even small amounts have a positive effect on stress.

- Cut back at least a little on fats, sugars, smoking, and alcohol. Small changes will have some results, and you'll have the satisfaction of knowing that you're headed in the right direction.

- Don't spend time looking for the nearest parking space. Drive up to a distant space and enjoy the walk.

- Give or receive a massage.

- Make sleeping well a priority. (See chapter 9.)

- If your job is a major irritant and you can't leave it, try getting more control over the parts of the job that cause the most fear, anger, depression, or uncertainty. There is no job that can't be improved to some degree.

- Change what you can, and don't waste time trying to change what you can't.

- Delegate, train the delegatees, and trust them, whether at work or at home.

- Don't try to be perfect at everything. Identify two or three top priorities and do them very well; accept imperfect performance with the lower priorities.

- Avoid the FUD factor—fear, uncertainty, and doubt.

- Do whatever you can at home, work, or play to avoid the feeling that you're not in control of yourself.

- Be assertive: don't say yes when you mean no, no when you mean yes.

- Be clear on your goals; don't spend time, energy, and resources on activities that don't matter to you.

Now, don't go out and try to implement all these stress busters! Think of them as a cafeteria line, and take what seems appropriate for you.

15 *Rock!* No, not the music! Nancy Watson, of the Rochester (New York) School of Nursing, found that nursing home patients who used rocking chairs from ½ to 2½ hours per day over six weeks reported less emotional distress, fewer requests for pain medication, and improved balance.

16 *Problem-solve.* If solutions to the stressful situation are not apparent, solicit someone to assist you in going through a formal problem-solving process. More suggestions on creativity and problem solving appear in chapters 27–29. Most counselors and organizational consultants are trained in problem-solving processes. If you have no such budget, find free services (such as those provided by departments of social services and religious bodies) or teach yourself a problem-solving technique (or learn one with a friend or relative).

17 *Nurture.* Many individuals find that making time to nurture another living creature has the effect of soothing one's own stress. Some examples:

a. Listening to a friend's concerns over a latte.

b. Washing and brushing the family pet.

c. Combing/brushing out your daughter's hair.

d. Giving full attention to your child's interest of the moment (homework, model building, room arrangement, grooming, and so forth).

e. Babysitting, with gusto.

f. Volunteering in a service role.

Shelley Taylor, UCLA researcher, has pioneered work on the female stress response that she calls "Tend and Befriend," as an alternative to the male response of "Fight or Flight." See more in her 2002 book *The Tending Instinct.* Too much nurture as a stress reliever can be harmful to the nurturer, just as too much exercise, food, booze, and so forth, intended to relieve stress, can end up becoming toxic.

18 *APA tip sheets:* The American Psychological Association has developed a series of tip sheets for developing resilience in various groups of highly stressed citizens. Review their work at **www.apahelpcenter.org/featuredtopics/feature.php?id=6.**

⓳ *Prepare for mealtime:* Eating while feeling stressed results in inefficient digesting of carbohydrates and attendant fat storage. This is a good reason that parents should encourage kids, and each other, to "calm down" before eating. Simply saying a prayer or some such is not enough. Some form of physically shifting gears and shutting down the stress response is called for, whether it is meditation, story time, a walk around the block, or (as I like to do) playing favorite musical numbers (and singing along).

"A light heart lives long."

—William Shakespeare, *Love's Labour's Lost*

⓴ *Listen to chanting*: Dr Najeeb Alrefae sent an e-mail to me from Kuwait that related his efforts to help people reach the relaxing alpha brain wave state by listening to reciters chanting the Quran. It, like Gregorian and other forms of chanting, is mind-clearing and relaxing. Try listening to recitations from the Quran at **www.islamweb.net**.

TOPIC 36.2   Stress and Arousal

Although there is evidence of many kinds of arousal, including both limbic and cortical arousal, research over the years has proceeded as though there were only one general type. One of the more popular examples of this research has come to be known as the Yerkes-Dodson law (figure 36.2). It has two aspects:

1. There is an optimal level of arousal. Too low a state of arousal, as when you are sleepy, appears to result in errors of omission; too high a state of arousal, as when you are jittery from too much caffeine, results in errors of commission. In other words, when you are under-aroused, you may leave things out, skip things, and be forgetful; when you are over-aroused, you may hit the wrong key while typing, act impulsively, and lose proper restraint.

2. The optimal point of arousal for complex tasks is different from that for simple tasks. Higher arousal (for example, that extra cup of coffee) is more conducive to performing simpler tasks, lower arousal more conducive to performing more complex tasks (see topic 8.3).

Redford Williams (1989) has identified a hierarchical relationship between three different forms of arousal. The kind of arousal described here as the Yerkes-Dodson law might be described as normal cortical arousal. Williams describes two other forms of arousal that can suppress cortical arousal, regardless of whether an individual is under- or overaroused cortically. The first is what he calls "focused attention and aggression," such as the arousal exhibited in athletic competition or military observation duty. Focused attention and aggression is accompanied by higher-than-normal levels of testosterone and is characterized by partially suppressed cortical arousal; therefore, creativity and problem-solving ability are reduced. The other kind of arousal is what we have called the general adaptation syndrome (see topic 36.1) or the fight-or-flight response. During GAS, high cortisol levels are accompanied by virtually total suppression of cortical arousal. The three states, plus the sleep state, are shown in table 36.1, based on concepts developed by Redford Williams (1989).

Applications

❶ If you happen to let yourself get overstimulated—for example, by drinking too much of a caffeinated beverage—switch to a task that is simpler and more repetitive than the task at hand (for example, switch from writing to cleaning up). You will make fewer errors, and the increased

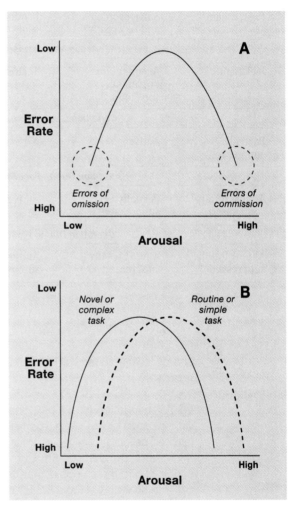

Figure 36.2. The Yerkes-Dodson Law
Note: (*A*) Normal optimal level of arousal. (*B*) Simple, routine tasks require a somewhat higher level of arousal than complex, novel ones.

Table 36.1. The Four States of Arousal

Sleep	Normal Arousal	Focused Attention and Aggression	Fight-or-Flight Syndrome
Typical Behaviors During This State			
Rest, dream	Solve problems and be creative	Productivity, routinized behavior	Automatic pilot survival mode
Active Neurotransmitters			
Melatonin	Acetylcholine, dopamine, serotonin	Testosterone	Epinephrine, norepinephrine, cortisol
Condition During Normal Arousal			
Partially suppressed	Active	Accessible	Accessible
Condition During Focused Attention			
Almost totally suppressed	Partially suppressed	Active	Accessible
Condition During Fight-or-Flight			
Almost totally suppressed	Almost totally suppressed	Almost totally suppressed	Active

Source: Based on ideas in *The Trusting Heart: Great News About Type A Behavior* by R. Williams, 1989, New York: Times Books.

energy level required will help to dissipate the high arousal. Otherwise, go exercise!

❷ If you must perform a particularly complex task, such as writing an involved report or reviewing a complex set of numbers, switch to a noncaffeinated beverage, limiting yourself to approximately one heavily caffeinated drink every six hours. (For me, one cup of strong, home-dripped coffee equals two to three cups of standard commercial brew, with respect to its caffeine effect.) See topic 8.3 for additional information on caffeine.

❸ If you are concerned that focused attention and aggression is or will be interfering with your mental self-management, try aerobic exercise to calm you down before the big presentation, meeting, or date. The exercise will lower your testosterone level and its accompanying aggression.

TOPIC 36.3   **Type A Research**

Redford Williams (1989) defines *Type A behavior* as a cyclical form of hostile behavior that originates with cynicism, progresses into anger, culminates in an outburst of aggression, and recycles whenever the original cause of the cynicism recurs. Williams defines the onset of Type A behavior as the fulfillment of negative expectations. He contrasts the cynicism of Type A with the trust of *Type B behavior*: cynicism expects the worst and has a toxic effect on the body; trust expects better and has a nontoxic effect. What makes Type A and Type B responses different is that although both types can be cynical and hostile at times, the Type A person has a physiological defect that prevents restoration of the parasympathetic response following sympathetic arousal.

In his research at Duke University Medical School and elsewhere, Williams has learned that Type A personalities' brain wave patterns take longer to return to normal after sympathetic arousal because their parasympathetic response is sluggish. This is also known as *parasympathetic antagonism.* It is directly related to their lower production within the neurons of *cyclic guanosine monophosphate,* which directly triggers parasympathetic responses. Williams accounts for about 50 percent of Type A cases by postulating a low-endorphin gene that results in prolonged sympathetic arousal. For the other 50 percent, Williams points to childhoods with low trust and low touch. Far less Type A behavior exists in Japan; Williams accounts for this by pointing to the reputation of the Japanese for unconditional love in child rearing. American kids take an average of 17.5 seconds to resume crawling toward a toy after an "angry mother" comment. Japanese children average 49 seconds; they are less accustomed to angry comments and as a result the comments have a stronger impact.

Williams suggests that Type A personalities can use three kinds of strategies to gain control over their uncontrolled sympathetic response: religion, behavior modification, and medicine.

Applications

❶ *Religion.* In Jerusalem's Hadassah Hospital, heart disease is four times higher among secular Jews. In Evans County, Georgia, churchgoers show lower blood pressure than nonchurchgoers. Williams suggests that religion typically encourages individuals to be less concerned with love of self, more with love of others. Such behavior, followed consistently, would short-circuit the whole Type A response by breeding trust rather than cynicism. An exception was seen in a study of 2,850 North Carolinians led by Keith Meador of the psychiatry department at Vanderbilt University Medical Center in Nashville, Tennessee. He found that Pentecostal Christians (Church of God and Assembly of God) exhibit an incidence of depression three times higher than that of other religious groups. The Fishers (1993, pp. 74–75) write about religious sects and the evidence that, in general, they provide a therapeutic effect for followers previously bothered by drugs, poor self-concept, psychological disturbance, vocational indifference, and medical complaints, with an overall effect of improved well-being, increased social and personal responsibility, and healthier habits. However, they observe that the nature of the research designs does not distinguish between the impact of the supportive nature of the sect as a group and the effect of the religious ideology and imagery.

❷ *Behavior modification.* In addition to books and workshops on communications skills such as assertiveness, conflict management, and negotiation, Williams suggests a 12-step approach:

1. Monitor your cynical thoughts.
2. Confess your hostility and seek support to change.
3. Stop cynical thoughts.
4. Reason with yourself.
5. Put yourself in the other person's shoes.
6. Laugh at yourself.
7. Practice the relaxation response.
8. Try trusting others.
9. Force yourself to listen more.
10. Substitute assertiveness for aggression.
11. Pretend that today is your last.
12. Practice forgiveness.

❸ *Medicine.* See topic 36.1, application 11.

❹ Williams and his wife, Virginia, wrote *Anger Kills* (1994) as a "how-to" approach to the issues surrounding Type A behavior. It includes a self-assessment tool and seven chapters of specific applications.

TOPIC 36.4 Burnout: Maximum Demotivation

What is burnout? Put simply, it is the result of unrelieved stress. Burnout occurs after one or more stressors continue their obstruction with unrelenting intensity and effectiveness; the individual feels out of control over an extended time and eventually gives up hope of eliminating or even reducing the effect of the stressor. Burnout can be reached through one of two routes: more intense, shorter-term stress or less intense, longer-term stress. Robert Golembiewski of the University of Georgia has developed a phase model for burnout (Golembiewski, 1988). The eight phases are defined by levels of depersonalization, sense of personal achievement, and emotional exhaustion (see table 36.2). Phase 1 exhibits little or no depersonalization, a reasonable sense of success and job worth, and little or no emotional fatigue, whereas phase 8 exhibits high depersonalization (people are seen as objects without innate value), absence of a personal sense of accomplishment or worth, and emotional exhaustion (a sense of being unable to cope anymore).

In a survey of more than 10,000 people, 43 percent scored in phases 1 to 3 (no burnout), 13 percent scored in phases 4 and 5 (borderline burnout), and 44 percent scored in phases 6 to 8 (from moderate to extreme burnout). Physical measures of cholesterol, uric acid, blood pressure, number of sick days used, weight, smoking, drinking, and so on appear to increase uniformly along this model. For example, phase 1 shows lower levels of cholesterol, with levels getting progressively higher through phase 8.

Earlier, we defined burnout as the result of prolonged stress. Golembiewski gets more specific by defining it as having a sense that we and others have no worth, with no energy to do anything about it. Notice the similarity of his definition of burnout to Seligman's (1991) definition of pessimism (personal, pervasive, and permanent helplessness). Seligman's research focuses on depression, Golembiewski's on burnout, but the working mechanisms appear similar. Burnout seems to be the organizational form of depression.

Golembiewski has two findings that are particularly important in dealing with the results of burnout. First, burnout does not occur randomly throughout organizations; instead, it seems to occur in clusters of workers with a common supervisor. His conclusion is that the quality of the supervisor is responsible for the lion's share of burnout in organizations. Second, people appear to use two different styles

Table 36.2. Golembiewski's Phase Model of Burnout

Factors of Burnout	Phases							
	1	2	3	4	5	6	7	8
Depersonalization	Low	High	Low	High	Low	High	Low	High
Personal achievement[a]	Low	Low	High	High	Low	Low	High	High
Emotional exhaustion	Low	Low	Low	Low	High	High	High	High

Source: From R. T. Golembiewski (1988), *Phases of Burnout,* New York: Praeger. Reprinted by permission of the author.
[a]Reversed: A low score equals a higher sense of personal achievement.

to deal with their stress: active and passive. When they reach the stage of burnout, passives have to take extended vacations or personal leave in order to restore their emotional resources and sense of worth, whereas actives might benefit more from workshops, self-help materials, and wellness programs.

Applications

1 If you are a human resources administrator, you should use employee surveys, Golembiewski's survey, or good common sense (sick-leave patterns, for example) to determine where the actual or potential pockets of burnout are in your organization. Then determine whether you need to train or replace the supervisors in those pockets. Some organizations are experimenting with eliminating the role of supervisor by developing self-directed work teams. For Golembiewski's survey, write to Dr. Robert Golembiewski, Department of Political Science, Baldwin Hall, University of Georgia, Athens, Georgia 30602, phone 404-542-2970, or e-mail rtgolem@arches.uga.edu.

2 Provide seminars, self-help materials, wellness programs, and employee counseling resources to help highly stressed employees learn ways to cope more effectively.

3 For people with more passive styles of dealing with burnout, the strategies in application 2 won't work. With passives, be prepared to offer extended leave, followed by transfer to a new work unit upon return.

| TOPIC 36.5 | **Trait Dissonance** |

Hans Selye observed that some of us approach life like a rabbit, running from place to place, nibbling when we can, shooting off in all directions; others more like a turtle, proceeding methodically from point to point with careful attention to detail, taking things one at a time. Neither extreme is necessarily unhealthy. What is unhealthy, or stressful, is trying to be different from one's nature. For example, the rabbit spouse says to her turtle companion, "You never want to go anywhere or do anything." The turtle, feeling guilty, decides to become rabbity for the night and go bar-hopping with his jumpy spouse. That, according to Selye, is what causes stress—being untrue to one's nature.

It is stressful to try to be someone different from who we are, to try to be solitary when our nature is to be gregarious. Being true to our nature is, in some ways, the ultimate goal (as in "to thine own self be true . . ."). Attempting to be something different is an obstacle to that goal. Along with Selye's work, a growing body of literature indicates that congruence between people's nature and the nature of their activities (whether at work, at play, or in their home life) is a crucial prerequisite for contentment with their pursuit of the goal. In order for them to be fully motivated, their personality traits, talents, special abilities, values, and beliefs should be compatible with their life tasks. Don't expect a recluse to be motivated to sell, a creative thinker to be a good proofreader day in and day out, or a sow's ear to be happy in the role of a silk purse. In chapter 37, we will demonstrate how this notion of being true to oneself—and, in fact, how to define one's true self—fits in with the larger theory of motivation. Topic 37.7 (human resource optimization) specifically explains the five different ways your personality might fit your personal context, and what to do about it.

Applications

❶ To what degree do you expect others to be like you—to use your vocabulary, to walk at your speed, to talk as fast or slowly as you do? Do you feel that people are inferior to you if they talk more slowly than you do (a classic source of misunderstanding between a New Englander and a Southerner)? Be aware of these judgments, and don't mistake such surface behaviors for indicators of ability. (Rick Bradley recalls a former manager whose perception of a co-worker was that he was "slow" because he had an unhurried gait.)

❷ When you feel pressured to change your personality to meet with a spouse's, friend's, or boss's approval, it's time to sit down with that person and talk it through. If you are unsuccessful, you may need to bring in a third party (counselor, consultant, friend) to help establish the necessity of maintaining your differences in personality and behavior. Don't ignore the conflict; that will only lead to resentment and may rupture the relationship.

❸ Know yourself; specifically, get a firm handle on where your strengths lie. In order to do this, it helps to have a template, or map, that covers all of the traits, abilities, and physical characteristics that constitute individual differences. Such a template is provided in appendix L.

TOPIC 36.6   Stress and Evolution

The popular and academic press is peppered with reports of high stress, depression, and unhappiness throughout civilization, this in spite of all-time high levels of material comfort. In a special issue of *American Psychologist* (January 2000) on the subject of positive psychology, David Buss (2000a) insightfully observed that a major explanation for the malaise of modern times finds its origins in a disjointed sense of evolutionary adaptability. The current genetic package we call *Homo sapiens* represents the level of natural selection attained during the time of hunter-gathers (Pleistocene epoch). We have advanced culturally since that time without a commensurate genetic refinement. We are, in essence, new wine in old skins. As a consequence, much of our "natural" behavior (such as "fight or flight," mating for maximum reproduction, and so forth) has no (or minimal) necessity in our contemporary environment. In a shrewd move, Buss recommends that we try to structure our lives for maximum happiness by recreating, as it were, characteristics of our hunter-gather ancestors. Here are a few of his suggestions:

Applications

❶ Being close to family typically makes us feel better, so in cases where our nuclear family has spread, Buss recommends using modern technology to reconnect with our kin: e-mail, frequent-flier points, strongly discounted travel prices such as "e-savers," telephone, videotape and audiotape exchanges, family websites with up-to-date digital photographs, family chat rooms, family news groups, video conferencing, and family reunions (including "mini-reunions"—I get together every year or so with two nephews I am close to).

② Hunter-gatherers lived a life characterized by close, deep, enduring friendships. Our life of travel, frequent moves, long hours, commuting time, and multiple community obligations related to career advancement all work to obstruct the time necessary to develop close friendships. As a result, when we need a friend, many of us fail to find one available, and we tough it out, essentially alone. Too often, we let the church, the police, or government agencies do for us what friends would have done in bygone days. Buss recommends that we place a conscious premium on developing and maintaining close friends. We need to make ourselves indispensable to our closest friends and committed to them for the long term.

③ In earlier days, we had little choice but to mate with someone who was similar to us in personality, intelligence, and cultural background. We did not have to look far. "You Tarzan, me Jane," and that was it. As a result, our genetic package has us attuned to find maximum long-term satisfaction from mates who are most similar to us. Our margin for error in mate selection has dramatically increased. In a hunter-gatherer's lifetime, only a couple of dozen potential mates were available (statistically this would be called "restriction of range"!), but today, the proximity of thousands of potential mates keeps our heads spinning. We need to encourage ourselves and those close to us to exert caution during courtship, and to be patient until we sense that we are in the presence of a mate with whom we resonate on most or all cylinders (see "My Shapers" profile, appendix L).

④ Having family members close by has been shown to be the best prevention for abuse, incest, infidelity, battering, and such wanton acts. Our ancestors had kin at hand to keep them in line, but today it is as though we have no accountability, with our family and the conscience they represent scattered to the four winds. Where possible, Buss recommends that we organize our life so that we may live near family members we love and respect, and who are willing to be interdependent with and accountable to us.

⑤ Our ancestors had communities marked by cooperation, because cooperation was necessary for survival. Many of us live under the illusion that cooperation is for wimps; the result of this attitude is a feeling of isolation and ultimate malaise. Buss recommends that we pursue cooperation as a culture, emphasizing reciprocity and equity in all our relationships. Make a commitment to be known as a reciprocator. Make long-term commitments (to church, to friends, to family, to work) that necessitate cooperation in order to be successful and satisfying.

SUGGESTED RESOURCES

Benson, H., with M. Z. Klipper (1990). *The Relaxation Response.* New York: Avon.

Caine, R. N., and G. Caine (1991). *Making Connections: Teaching and the Human Brain.* Alexandria, Va.: Association for Supervision and Curriculum Development.

Gazzaniga, M. S. (1985). *The Social Brain.* New York: Basic Books.

Golembiewski, R. T. (1988). *Phases of Burnout.* New York: Praeger.

Sapolsky, R. M. (1994). *Why Zebras Don't Get Ulcers: A Guide to Stress, Stress-Related Diseases, and Coping.* New York: Freeman.

Selye, H. (1952). *The Story of the Adaptation Syndrome.* Montreal: Acta.

Williams, R. (1989). *The Trusting Heart: Great News about Type A Behavior.* New York: Times Books.

Williams, R., and V. Williams (1994). *Anger Kills.* New York: HarperPerennial.

37

Happiness

The False God

> **66***Action may not always bring happiness; but there is no happiness without action.***99**
>
> —*Benjamin Disraeli*

*I*n the closing days of the 20th century, Mihalyi Csikszentmihalyi, a University of Chicago philosopher now at Claremont Graduate University in California, wrote an article in *American Psychologist* (1999) posing the following question: "If we're so rich, why aren't we happy?" Citing statistics that showed dramatic rises in standard of living in the U.S., he pointed out that surveys of "happiness" over the last half of the 20th century failed to show an accompanying increase. Well, the article went on to attempt to explain why increases in wealth failed to affect levels of "happiness," but I was unconvinced. The problem is with the way he asked the question.

Let's get it said from the very beginning: Happiness is not, should not, be a goal. The word comes from the Middle English *hap* and the Old Norse *happ,* both meaning "good luck"—the luck of the draw, an advantageous outcome from spinning the Wheel of Fortune. Currently psychologists define happiness as the sustained absence of negative emotions (anxiety, fear, depression) and the ongoing presence of positive emotions (joy and her many manifestations) (Costa and McCrae, 1992). Who are the folks who just happen to be "lucky" enough to be gifted with this combination of traits? Well, considering the Five-Factor Model of personality (see chapter 33), they comprise the folks who score low on Need for Stability and high on Extraversion. One in three scores low on N, and another one in three scores high on E, so the incidence of naturally happy folks in this world is statistically 1 in 9—the probability of scoring both low in N and high in E. That puts about 11 percent of the population in the category of "continually happy." You've met them: the cheerleader who is never down, always bubbly; the salesperson who bounces back quickly from rejection and moves on to the next prospect.

Happiness, then, is not a goal but rather a personality trait that is characteristic of about 11 percent of the population. Happiness is not something to achieve—it is a normally distributed matter of temperament. Our goal is not to increase happiness, but rather to insure that we enjoy our innate degree of happiness, and not more. To the extent that traits are genetically based, this incidence of happiness is immutable—and for good reason, evolutionarily speaking. What if the world were composed only of bubbly cheerleaders and effervescent salespeople? Who would worry about the details? Who would churn out the production in solitary silence? The world is built—evolution has assured us—out of differing gifts, a splendor of personality diversity. All the world may be a stage, but every stage needs set crew, light and sound booth, writers, producers, and, let's not forget, the essential audience. Oh, and critics!

In a December 2004 poll conducted by *Time,* 17 percent reported that they were "brimming with happiness just about all the time," with another 60 percent saying that they were "frequently" happy. Let's analyze that statistic. That distribution is roughly consistent with our earlier analysis. The 17 percent who report themselves brimming happily most of the time represents my 11 percent who are in a constant state of happiness, plus some borderline folks. The 60 percent who are frequently happy represent that middle two-thirds of the population who have proportionately more negative emotions that the brimming 11 percent, yet who are still happy with some frequency, and at other times anxious, angry, or depressed.

That leaves about ¼ of the population (60 percent plus 11–17 percent leaves about 25 percent) who do not report themselves as experiencing happiness. Those would be

"Happiness is good health and a bad memory."

—Ingrid Bergman

the people who score in the bottom third of E, plus the folks who score in the mid- to high ranges of N, thus having a predominance of negative emotion over positive emotion. The probability of scoring low on E *and* medium or high on N comes out around 22 percent.

Here's what this means to me:

1. Happiness is distributed in the population primarily according to our genetics, with (of course) some influence from our environment.

2. Happiness is not a unitary continuum from happiness to despair. Rather, it arises from two continua: one from positive emotionality to lack of positive emotions, and the other from negative emotionality to lack of negative emotionality.

3. Roughly 11 percent of the population tend to be happy pretty much all of the time, and little can happen to change that.

4. The rest of us are somewhere on those two continua: joyful and moderately worrying, joyful and extremely worrying, moderately joyful and worrying, nonjoyful and nonworrying (i.e., lacking either emotion), and so forth.

5. Happiness is not a goal for human development. Rather, it is a characteristic of a minority of the population.

6. Instead of *happiness,* we need to think in terms of *satisfaction,* which is what Csikszentmihalyi was studying when he discovered the flow concept (see topic 37.2). *Flow* is the state of being totally absorbed in what one is doing at the moment, neither bored because the activity is too easy nor frustrated because it's too difficult. According to Csikszentmihalyi, one can learn to manage circumstances to stay in this flow state.

7. Happiness is not intrinsically good. Permanent happiness could lead to taking things for granted, the end of progress.

It is through a variety of emotional configurations that we as a species have managed to evolve and survive, even prevail, over the constant efforts of nature to destroy us: the worriers seek improvement, the calm ones take the risks, the ebullient ones provide the leadership.

The Pursuit of PEG

Satisfaction is possible for all, regardless of typical mood state. In fact, the attainment of satisfaction displaces mood: a person experiencing satisfaction is unconcerned with her mood. To experience satisfaction is to displace mood from consciousness. According to Martin Seligman (2002) in *Authentic Happiness,* three roads lead to what we are calling *satisfaction*:

- *Pleasure.* The intense stimulation of the five senses, with the result of activating the "pleasure" system in the brain

- *Engagement.* Achieving total absorption in what one is doing, to the extent of losing one's sense of time, place, temperature, hunger, etc.

- *Gratification.* Being in relationships—at home, at work, at play—that call upon one's strengths and rely minimally on one's weaknesses

The strategy for achieving pleasure is to experience fullness of *flavor.* For engagement, the strategy is entering *flow.* To feel gratification in one's life situation, the strategy is to find the optimum *fit* between who you are and what your associates expect from you.

Pleasure through flavor, engagement through flow, and gratification through fit—these should be our goals in life. I consider them the overarching goals; by combining them in particular ways, we can achieve satisfaction. As we will see in the following discussion, all of life's goals—from minor goals (going to the store) to major ones (deciding on a career or mate)—have the potential of satisfying one or more of these three overarching goals. When we form a goal on the spur of the moment, we may not be consciously thinking through the PEG motifs, but they certainly influence our choices of goals: will X lead to pleasure, engagement, or gratification? The difference between a happy person and others is that continually happy people are in a positive mood state regardless of whether they are experiencing flavor, flow, or fit—it is simply their nature, much like the character Guido, played by Roberto Benigno in the movie *Life is Beautiful,* a memorably daring comedy set in a concentration camp. For individuals who experience flavor (e.g., Julia Child), flow (Thomas Edison), or fit (Mother Teresa), happiness is irrelevant—they may or may not describe themselves as "happy," depending on both their genetic temperament and their mood state of the moment. But the latter are satisfied with their lives, perhaps not in the sense of resting on their laurels, but content with the direction their life is taking and how their talents, traits, and other qualities are finding full expression.

What Is Motivation, and How Can We Increase It?

Much has been written about motivation, and the resulting mélange of viewpoints is more confusing than motivating. Suffice it to say that motivated people are satisfied people (in the sense of being content with how their life is playing out). To be motivated is to be satisfied, and to be satisfied is to be experiencing one or more of the PEG principles. Generally, motivation is described as goal-oriented behavior. The vast literature on the subject of motivation revolves around two aspects of goals: how an individual rates her chances of attaining a goal successfully, and how she rates the value of the goal itself. In the next section, we will explore three ways to accomplish that—to construct for ourselves a context, a way of living, that builds on who we are. For this purpose, we focus on the three overarching goals:

- Pleasure through fullness of flavor (topic 37.1)
- Engagement through finding flow (topic 37.2)
- Gratification through establishing fit (topic 37.3)

If we are not living a life that builds on who we are, and if we accept less than pleasure, engagement, and gratification (or, flavor, flow, and fit), then I suspect that we are the folks Abraham Lincoln had in mind when he opined that "most people are about as happy as they make up their minds to be."

TOPIC 37.1   Pleasure: Finding Flavor

In *Authentic Happiness* (2002), Martin Seligman describes sensual pleasures as the lowest of the sources of satisfaction, in the sense that they are the most transitory and the most difficult to experience independent of environmental context. The pleasures of the five senses, and the emotional states derived therefrom, are described in the English language by an avalanche of terms: blissful, ecstatic, rapturous, zestful, delighted, refreshing, rejuvenating, reinvigorating, energizing, hedonistic, luxuriating, indulging, gloating, erotic, filled with gusto, sated, merry-making, frolicking, gleeful, "in seventh heaven," ravishing, to name but a few. Our language is replete with names for sensory intensity, the kinds of pure pleasure represented by a virtual almanac of

- tastes
  - of wine, honey, cream, chili peppers, curries, cool pure water, eau de vie, properly mashed tea
  - of another's lips, of exotic herbs and woods, of dark chocolate, milk chocolate, licorice, fresh cut corn
- fragrances
  - of fresh cut grass, of honeysuckle and magnolia in May, of cedar wood and fermenting pine straw, of fresh roasted coffee
  - of a lover's body, of a baby's scalp, of the ocean, of the atmosphere before an electrical storm, of an open campfire
- visions
  - of a slow sunset over water with your partner in the periphery, of Andrea del Sarto's strikingly modern reds and greens and blues and purples
  - of impossibly huge cathedrals and palaces and great walls, of the sheer human beauty of face or body or manner, of the rain forest from within
- sounds
  - of a child's first babbling, of a Mozart serenade, of the Mullah's call, of Gregorian chant, of the King's College chorister at the last moment being chosen and launching into "Once in Royal David's City"
  - of groans from raw pleasures, of a gentle continuing rainfall, of the symphony of birds in a mountain cove, of the voice of someone you thought lost

- touches
  - of a baby's skin, of brushing delicately against someone you adore, of a flower petal, of immersion in cool water on a sweltering summer's day
  - of one's toes in the beach's sand and the ocean's waves, of holding close one you love, of fine velvet and silk, of a well-sanded tongue-in-groove joint that feels seamless
- and of the myriad combinations of the senses that make you stop in awe of the moment

I'm beginning to feel more like a poet than a brain science writer. But an important point is served thereby. These intense sensations vanish upon the arrival of the wicked witch of bodily pleasures—habituation (see topic 22.10). Take each of the sensory moments above and increase its frequency. You will soon find that the pleasure is gone. Having one chocolate cream from a candy sampler can be wickedly delicious, but having stuffed my face with morsel after morsel until I've finished the box, I find myself wondering why the last piece tasted nowhere near as good as the first. The reason: my sensory apparatus has habituated to the sensation, and the fullness of the flavor is now only a memory.

Seligman tells us how to avoid habituation: let time go by. Experience a given pleasure less often. Rather than one chocolate candy per minute for 15 minutes, settle for a couple of morsels to-night, a couple tomorrow night, and so forth. You could have the same 15 bonbons over the period of a week that you might otherwise have wolfed down in a quarter of an hour, but you would experience the same postprandial pleasure every night as the first. If you absolutely must experience another intense pleasure on the heels of the choco-late indulgence, switch to another neural pathway, such as touch or hearing; pet your dog or listen to Beethoven. You get the picture.

Seligman also teaches us that experiencing a sensation to the full is a function not only of avoiding habituation, but of savoring and mindfulness as well (which is why one is admonished never to forego foreplay). To the degree that you (1) savor the sensation (let the choco-late melt on the tongue and slowly, slowly descend; sip the cognac, and let it lie as a spring puddle on the tongue), (2) are mindful of the total context (be aware of all of your senses, not just the taste of chocolate; study the wrapper: where was the chocolate made? When? How long does it take to melt? How does it taste when accompanied by fruit? Cognac? Coffee? A kiss?), and (3) avoid repeating the experience right away, you will derive maximum pleasure.

Applications

❶ For your favorite sensory experiences:

 a. *Savor* (focus on the sensation itself).

   • *Share* after the fact with those around you (a way of keeping the memory alive).

   • *Create a memory* (press a flower from the scene, keep a pebble in your pocket).

   • *Take pride in it* (again, a way to keep the memory alive).

   • *Focus your perception* (by eliminating rival stimuli—close eyes while listening, don't precede sex with alcohol or other sense-altering agents).

   • *Surrender yourself to the moment* (by letting go of other things you could or should be doing).

 b. *Be mindful* (pay attention to the total context by slowing down and taking it all in, which is a tenet of Buddhism, as in "Be here now." This is the opposite of skimming; learn more from Marvin Levine's *The Positive Psychology of Buddhism and Yoga*, 2000).

 c. *Resist immediate repetition;* put space between episodes.

❷ Examples of savoring:

 a. *Sexual intercourse.* Avoid having sex when stuffed, under the influence, overly tired, and so forth, so that you can focus totally on the sensation itself.

 b. *Alcohol.* Put the glass, bottle, or goblet down between sips and enjoy the flavor, then alternate with another flavor (food, water), and let the new flavor subside, so that when you have your next sip your taste buds are refreshed and ready to return you to the intensity of the previous sip.

 c. *Reading.* Eliminate competing stimuli, such as radio, television, sun glare, and conversation, so you can read without distraction.

 d. *Candy.* Don't chew; let it melt slowly. If necessary, make a contest of it: see how long you can keep it on your tongue before it melts away.

 e. *Flowers.* Don't just glance at them or stuff them immediately into a vase. Sniff them; admire them from all angles; enjoy the subtleties of theirs color; taste them; feel the texture; look around you and choose the best place for this particular assortment of blooms.

❸ Examples of mindfulness:

a. *Romance.* Get to know all about your partner: look up the meaning and etymology of his or her name; select items as gifts or household decorations that reflect the meaning of the name; ask questions to find out new things about each other when walking, dining, etc.:

- What was your year in first grade like?
- What did you do in the summers when you were in middle school?
- How did you learn to cook?
- What were your hobbies as a kid?
- What was your best friend or worst enemy like in high school?
- What were the typical kinds of things to do on high school dates where you lived?
- What was the first paid job you ever held?
- What kinds of things give you the most pleasure?
- And so forth. In general, show genuine interest in knowing as much as possible about him or her.

b. *Music.* Take care of your instrument. Keep it clean and in peak operating condition; read books about its history; find websites about it; read biographies about famous people who've played it (or sung your voice part); learn how the instrument is constructed, perhaps even how to do repairs yourself.

c. *Coffee.* Know all about your favorite bean—where it comes from, how it is prepared, what the growers and connoisseurs recommend as the proper storage and brewing procedures; try experiments to bring out the optimum flavor; read one of the several good books about the history of caffeine.

❹ Putting space between episodes:

a. *Music.* In his Utopian novel *Walden Two,* B. F. Skinner (1948) suggests that a concert should feature only one work, such as a Mozart symphony, rather than the usual three or four pieces. The parallel at home would be, for example, rather than listening to one symphony after another on a leisurely Saturday afternoon, stop after one and let the melodies linger in the air, humming the more memorable parts, and just enjoy the memory of the piece for a while before chasing it away with another.

b. *Art.* In a museum, a common experience is to leave exhausted after frantically dashing from one masterpiece to the next. Rather than leave with an art overload (a form of habituation), focus on a few works by selected artists, or perhaps a group of works from a single art movement that interests you, and truly savor them, being mindful of the details surrounding their creation, by studying the signs and brochures. Relax, take your time, and pause to get coffee or fresh air before continuing.

c. *Food.* Put limits on yourself, and stick to them, such as no more than three pieces of chocolate after dinner, spaced at least five minutes apart. When dining, put your fork down between bites, and allow yourself to thoroughly chew and savor.

5 Draw up a poster to remind you of the "4-S Principle":

To Maximize Sensual Pleasure:

- Slow down
- Savor
- Study (be mindful of the context)
- Space things out

TOPIC 37.2 Engagement: Finding Flow

The goal of engagement is not sensory pleasure or emotional highs, but rather a total absorption in the moment that, in essence, results in a loss of self-consciousness. It is akin to Aristotle's *eudaimonia,* the "pleasure" in having done something well, whether a game of sport or the tutoring of a student. Csikszentmihalyi (1990) has identified a state of mind that he calls *flow,* in which the individual experiences intense satisfaction, losing all sense of time, place, and extraneous physical sensations. In such a state, the individual is so absorbed in the event that nothing else intrudes into awareness. He enumerates eight components of this flow state (pp. 49 ff.):

1. The individual feels she has a chance of successfully completing the event; this requires a sense of having sufficient energy, resources, and skill for the event.

2. The individual is able to concentrate and become one with the activity.

3. The individual's goals are clear.

4. The individual receives immediate feedback.

5. The individual engages in a deep, effortless involvement that pushes away everyday cares.

6. The individual has a sense of control over her actions.

7. The concern for self disappears, but the self feels stronger afterward.

8. Time is altered: minutes seem like hours and hours seem like minutes.

Mihalyi Csikszentmihalyi (pronounced "Mee-high Chick-sént-mee-high") has identified two factors that influence the flow state: (1) the level of proficiency of the individual, (2) the level of difficulty of the activity in which the individual is engaged. The chances of being in a flow state are optimum when the skill level and difficulty level are properly matched. The flow state is uncommon when skill exceeds or falls below the level of difficulty. Excess skill leads to boredom; deficient skill leads to frustration. Csikszentmihalyi (1990, p. 52) describes the relationship this way: "Enjoyment [flow] appears at the boundary between boredom and anxiety, when the challenges are just balanced with the person's capacity to act." This relationship is illustrated in figure 37.1. Over time, as one becomes stronger at the activity and the challenges become ever more demanding, one will tend to progress upward in the flow channel. The ultimate satisfaction of the flow process is not to stay at one level but to work upward, becoming more skilled and taking on greater challenges. Should skill or challenge level become fixed, one risks boredom and, hence, loss of flow.

But don't mistake flow for fun. Seligman (2002, p. 117) points out that studies of high-flow and low-flow adolescents show superior scores for the high-flow kids on all the self-esteem variables but one: they think the low-flow kids hanging out at the mall are having more fun and would like to be there. However, there is a long-term payoff of early high-flow experience. As we age and develop our strengths and virtues, simply hanging out becomes boring and unfun, and our longing for total engagement grows.

What it all boils down to is that lower-level pleasures are just not as satisfying as higher-level. Put another way, sensory pleasure (as in tasting the chocolate) is not as satisfying as engaging in a strength (as in making the chocolate). It is the old, familiar, active-vs.-passive experience: playing the game vs. watching the game, acting in the play vs. watching the play, cooking the gourmet meal vs. eating it, performing the music vs. listening to it, and so on. Not that all life should be active, for two reasons:

1. If we had to produce everything we experienced, we'd end up exhausted and have little time to make significant progress in our areas of strength (e.g., I couldn't finish the draft of this book if I had to grow the feed to feed the chickens that laid the eggs that I scrambled for breakfast this morning).

2. If everyone were 100 percent actively producing, and never passively receiving products, there'd be no reason to produce. The farmer actively produces food and passively experiences television, and the screenwriters actively create television dramas

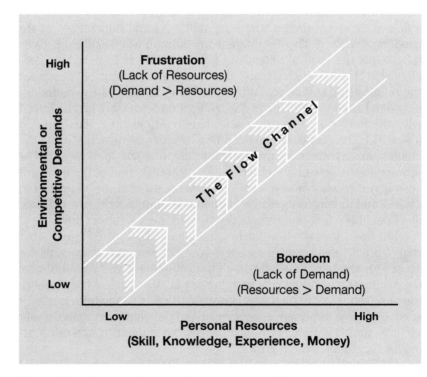

Figure 37.1. Csikszentmihalyi and the Ingredients of Flow

and passively experience their bagel and cream cheese. Clearly, this is how the concept of division of labor arose—so that individuals could spend more time actively engaged in their strengths, surrendering tasks depending on lesser abilities to neighbors with the complementary strengths.

The goal is some sort of balance, in which we seek to maximize active production and minimize passive experience, using the latter as reward for our labor. Seligman (2002, p. 118) identifies excessive use of shortcuts to happiness (i.e., passive experiences like buying a beer, buying a chocolate, indulging in a one-night stand, buying a music CD, watching television—the lower, bodily pleasures), especially when done without heed to habituation, savoring, and mindfulness, as the primary cause of increasing levels of depression.

In closing this discussion, consider this description of the flow state from Daniel Mason's novel *The Piano Tuner* (2002, pp. 272–273), where Edgar Drake (the piano tuner) is talking to his lady friend, Khin Myo:

> "I am sorry if I seem distracted," he said. "I'm always a bit slow to come out of the trance that I enter when I tune. It is another world. It's always a bit startling to be interrupted by . . . visitors. . . . It is hard to explain."
>
> "Perhaps like being awakened from a dream."
>
> "Perhaps. Perhaps. . . . But I am awake in a world of sounds. . . . "

Applications

❶ When an event bores you, reflect that your skill level probably exceeds the demands of the situation. One way to relieve the boredom is to reduce your skill, as in handicapping yourself. For example, I get bored folding clothes, so I time the event to match something of interest on television. Many a sock has found its mate during the news hour or a ball game. Another way to relieve the boredom is to increase the demands of the situation by raising the level of difficulty or competition. For example, if you are writing a long memorandum whose subject bores you, try putting high standards on your writing to create interest in the task: use only the active voice, sentences of fewer than 20 words, concrete figures of speech, or some other characteristics of fine writing that you might not normally use with such a piece.

➋ When an event frustrates you, realize that your skill level is probably too low for the situation. You can remedy this by either increasing your skill or reducing the level of difficulty. I remember that one day in the library I grew frustrated reading a research report. I realized that the frustration stemmed from a statistical term I didn't understand that was central to the report. I got out of my chair, found a statistics text, looked up the term, and returned to my chair. When I resumed my reading, the frustration was gone. Flow, and the possibilities for ensuing creativity and enjoyment, followed.

➌ Albert Bandura (in Sternberg and Kolligian, 1990) points out that one key to personal "happiness" (i.e., flow or satisfaction) is knowing when a specific ability is maxed out and not capable of taking on greater challenges. He recommends that, when one realizes one has done as much as one can with an ability, one should shift to another ability area in order to avoid the boredom of repeating the ability at the same level over time. A good example is Linus Pauling, who, after winning the Nobel in physics, recognized this phenomenon and switched to research on vitamin C.

TOPIC 37.3   Contentment: Finding Fit

The problem with motivation comes when individuals who have a good chance of success choose not to pursue a highly valued goal. It is my contention that people who are unmotivated, who have given up on their important goals, are people whose personal qualities are not able to find expression. The songbird must sing, the athlete must compete, the scholar must study, the servant must serve, the leader must lead. When our nature has no opportunity to express itself, it is just plain difficult to get up and go to work, to be responsible. So the first step in understanding our individual motivation is to understand who we are, what is our nature. That means getting a clear understanding of how we are similar to and different from other people in four areas:

1. Our behavioral traits (i.e., the Big Five—see chapter 33)

2. Our mental abilities (i.e., mental tools, such as logic and memory, and talents, such as verbal, math, and kinesthetic—see chapter 34)

3. Our physical characteristics (e.g., height, weight, speed, beauty, dexterity, gender)

4. Our memory (e.g., positively, neutrally, and negatively charged memories from childhood, school, community, jobs, sports teams, military service, religious activities)

In appendix L, I have provided an inventory that can help you identify how you are similar to and different from others. These four areas—traits, abilities, physical characteristics, and memory—form our core self. Certainly, this is only one of many ways of describing who we are, but it is comprehensive. You may ask questions such as "Where do our values come in?" Well, values are part of our memory—positively or negatively charged associations with a pattern of experiences, coupled with our traits, abilities, and physical characteristics in such a way as to form a clear pattern of what is important to us. For example, one of my strongest values is aesthetics—the importance of beauty in my life. Of course, what is beautiful to me may not be beautiful to you, so beauty becomes an intensely personal construct. For me, aesthetics builds on all four areas: traits (high originality), abilities (good auditory or musical skills), physical characteristics (auditory acuity, finger dexterity), and memory (sister an opera singer, mother a pianist who played every day for pleasure and stress reduction, brother a church organist and chamber musician, early experiences in church choir and school music programs, peers in high school who were seriously into chamber music). Put it all together, and it defines my strongly held value for aesthetics, particularly in the form of classical music. I have other strongly held values, such as learning and family. Similarly, I can trace the origins of these values to traits, abilities, physical characteristics, and memories.

In a major study of what makes us who we are, Quartz and Sejnowski (2002) write that there is not simply one core self independent of context: "The idea of a single, stable self is illusory. Instead, each of us has a repertoire of selves upon which to draw as we pass through the human drama"(p. 182). I maintain that, although we certainly adapt to the demands of varying contexts, we nonetheless have a core self. I may be naughty by nature, but I know not to be naughty around Aunt Sadie. To the degree that I am socially competent, I learn to vary my behavior by such contexts. However, although I vary my behavior, I have a core. That core consists of a series of complementary, or even opposing, capacities: solitary vs. sociable, trusting vs. skeptical, at ease vs. angry. Each of these pairs has a nature-given point of equilibrium that is defined by one's relative energy for engaging in each member of the pair. For example, I have nearly equal energy for solitude and society, and I call myself an ambivert. However, people who know me in certain contexts know me as an extravert, whereas people who know me in other contexts know me as an introvert. In order for my life to be consistent with this natural equilibrium, I need to make choices that permit a roughly equal balance of solitude and society. If I fail, and commit myself to more solitude than society, or vice versa, then my life will be unsatisfying—I'll be frequently running out of natural energy for the overused member of the pair. For example, if I choose to be a salesperson and to marry an outgoing wife and have a large family, then as an ambivert I am going to find myself exhausted at the end of every day and wishing for solitude. My life would be more satisfying if I chose a less social career or a less social partner.

With the Big Five, we use scores to express where one's equilibrium is set for each continuum. On a scale of 1 to 100, a higher score represents greater natural energy for, let's say, society, a lower score for its pair complement, solitude. The more extreme the score, either high or low, the more consistent one's behavior from context to context. The more mid-range one's score, the easier it is to vary one's behavior depending on context.

There is one sense in which Quartz and Sejnowski are right: we are composed of many traits, many talents, and so forth. But these all form part of a relatively stable core self, with different parts of that self being called upon at different times: sometimes our learning values are exercised, other times our aesthetic values, yet other times our family values. Imagine the thrill when all three would be satisfied, as in researching the musical literature (learning) in order to find material to use in a chamber music program (aesthetics) featuring me, my wife, my brother, my sister, three nephews, and a niece (family). In fact I did that recently in preparation for a family reunion—very satisfying.

We do have a core self, and we can define that core self by using the checklist, or template, in appendix L. When we draw upon our strengths, as reflected by the profile that emerges from this checklist, we are motivated. When we draw upon our weaknesses—as represented by trait scores opposite from what is required (e.g., a more introverted person being called upon to make sales calls), by low scores in a required ability (as in being required to critique a singer when we are tone deaf), by physical characteristics that are the opposite of what is required (being assigned lifting tasks when we have back problems), or by having memories that are inconsistent with what is required of us (being asked to travel extensively for work when we have a strong tradition of family activity)—that is demotivating. The challenge is to create for ourselves a life situation that builds on who we are.

Applications

❶ Make a copy of appendix L, "My Shapers," and create your own personal strengths profile. If you have difficulty completing your profile, invite the help of a family member, friend, psychologist, or teacher with whom you can frankly discuss each element and make an honest assessment of how each "shaper" expresses itself in you. Alternatively, you can take the WorkPlace Big Five ProFile (for adults) or the SchoolPlace Big Five ProFile (for students), available through the Center for Applied Cognitive Studies (*Cent*ACS: www.centacs.com) as a way of determining your trait levels. For the mental abilities, unfortunately there is no single test that you can take. I am working on such an instrument, but it will probably not be ready for several years. You might try asking a psychologist to help you assess your mental abilities. Otherwise, just make your best estimate.

❷ As you work on the far right column of "My Shapers," realize that there are many ways you can use a strength: at work, at home, as a volunteer, as a hobby, as an entrepreneur, and so forth. Don't limit yourself to thinking about work as the primary way to express your strengths. For example, I am very strong musically, but it has no expression at all in work; nevertheless, my work is satisfying, because it builds on other strengths. It is highly unlikely that all of any individual's strengths would be expressed in a single context.

❸ Be particularly concerned about weaknesses your current life situation overemphasizes, and find ways to minimize or avoid them. For example, if you're not a good detail person but your job calls for proofreading, see if there's some way you can get another person at work to do the proofreading while you take on a part of his job he doesn't care for but which builds on one of your strengths.

❹ For another approach to understanding who you are, how you're put together, and how you've come to be that way, I recommend *The Stories We Live By*, by Dan McAdams (1993).

TOPIC 37.4   A Goal-Centered Model of Motivation

Okay, let's take a deep breath. In this section, I will attempt to put it all together—goals, emotions, needs, values, traits, intelligence, perception, stress, and more—into one comprehensive model that purports to explain how an individual is motivated—in other words, what spurs him into action. For starters, scan figure 37.2. Notice two things: it comprises seven phases, and the *shapers* filter appears between the phases.

First, let's explain the shapers filter. You will see that I've made it resemble an old-fashioned, oversized, pill-shaped radio microphone. This device represents the cumulative sum of how we are put together as a person up through the current moment. I call this our personal *infrastructure,* the way we are wired and assembled, as opposed to our *superstructure,* which is the behavior that others see from us. Our infrastructure comprises all our traits, abilities, physical characteristics, and memories, as discussed earlier in topic 37.3. It represents our *core self,* which persists over time with only imperceptibly gradual change. Consider this description of the core self by Antonio Damasio (1999, p. 135):

> In all the kinds of self we can consider one notion always commands center stage: the notion of a bounded, single individual that changes ever so gently across time but, somehow, seems to stay the same. In highlighting stability I do not mean to suggest that self, in whatever version, is an immutable cognitive or neural entity, but rather that it must possess a remarkable degree of structural invariance so that it can dispense continuity of reference across long periods of time. Continuity of reference is in effect what the self needs to offer.

What Damasio is suggesting is that, although we may change our way of looking at things, we do not change our overall self to a significant degree. For example, when in graduate school, I scorned mystery novels, and before I met Jane, I scorned musical comedy. Now I enjoy them both and have even taken roles in Gilbert and Sullivan productions. But I'm no more a different person as the result of these two changes than my favorite beach would be different if two pebbles changed in color from tan to brown. Only as the result of major trauma (prolonged abuse, PTSD, major accident, or the like) would my core self change significantly—just as my beach would be changed by a tsunami or a massive oil spill.

It is this core self that makes up our shapers filter. And it is this filter that influences each phase of our motivation process. This process is, to put it succinctly, a series of goal formulations, from minor goals (such as deciding to mow the lawn) to major ones (such as deciding to write a book). Each day of our lives, we go through thousands of goal formulations, beginning with such goals as "Sleep more until the snooze alarm goes off," "Relieve my bladder," "Snuggle with Jane," "Make the coffee," "Fetch the morning newspaper," "Hmmm, today would be a good day to weed the garden," (a larger goal just crept in!), and so forth. Whether major or minor, the process is the same:

1. ***The moment.*** The sum of the qualities of the moment passes through our shapers filter and is perceived.

2. ***Perception.*** One or more characteristics of the moment resonates with some aspect of our filter or infrastructure and results in one or more clear images, thoughts, or feelings (e.g., fatigue, discomfort, hunger, curiosity).

3. ***Activation of salient state.*** Our perceptions pass through our shapers filter, with one emotional state emerging as dominant. This emotion—lust, fatigue, or whatever (see the explanatory text for step 3 of figure 37.2 for a longer list)—becomes the *activator,* which prompts us to form a goal.

4. ***Goal articulation.*** The activator emotional state checks in with our shapers filter, which influences the formation of the goal for this moment. In "consultation" with our core self (infrastructure, the shapers filter), we formulate—consciously or unconsciously—our goal of the moment according to three sets of criteria:

   a. The "overarching goal" category our goal will fit under—i.e., flavor (topic 37.1), flow (topic 37.2), or fit (topic 37.3)

   b. The value area we wish to express (wealth, spirituality, aesthetics, health, etc.)

   c. Our preferences at the moment, according to many different criteria:

      i. Specific vs. general

      ii. Close vs. distant

      iii. Selfish vs. altruistic

The Shapers Filter

The individual's personality infrastructure influences what emerges from each phase of the motivation process. This infrastructure comprises a fourfold database through which all processes are filtered:

1. *Traits:* N, E, O, A, and C, and all their subtraits (see chapter 33 for more detail)
2. *Abilities:* tools (Sternberg's triarchic model) and talents (Gardner's eight multiple intelligences) (see chapter 34 for more detail)
3. *Physical characteristics:* gender, ethnicity, age, allergies, metabolism, beauty, height, weight, sensual sensitivity, speed, strength, balance, histocompatibility, sleep requirements, dexterity, etc.)
4. *Memories,* each of which has some valence on a continuum from aversive to attracting

These four sets of *shapers* are represented by the capsule-shaped filters between phases.

Perception is the meaning we associate with what our senses are taking in. That meaning is influenced by the four sets of shapers: traits, abilities, physical characteristics, and memories. In a seamless blend of conscious and unconscious associations, we assign a positive, neutral, or negative valence to one or more aspects of the situation. We can amplify or reduce the actual elements of the moment based on our shapers—where there are 3–4 people assembled, we may see a party in the making, customers to be pitched, enemies to be assailed, or fellow beings to be avoided. How we assign value is strongly influenced by our capacities and our recent history—e.g., if we're moderately extraverted and have been around many people for most of the day, our "energy" or "fuel" for socializing is pretty much used up, and we're more likely to assign negative valence to a gathering of people. On the other hand, if we've been working in solitude most of the day, we would be more likely to see the gathering as welcome, as attracting.

The *moment* is just that—the point in time in which the individual finds herself: a romantic dinner, building a patio, in a meeting, meditating, in a concert, doing grunt work for someone else, in an argument, etc. Such moments could lead to insignificant goal formation (e.g., to cheer up a morose associate) or to major goal formation (e.g., to write a book).

Based on how we perceive the moment, in light of our shapers, one or more emotional states may become activated. These *activators* represent itches we need to scratch, by ultimately forming goals and pursuing them. Examples:

• Lust	• Curiosity	• Hunger
• Fatigue	• Envy	• Pride
• Greed	• Sloth	• Gluttony
• Despair	• Fear	• Anger
• Pain	• Disgust	• Impatience
• Surprise	• Relief	• Boredom
• Frustration	• Disgrace	• Shame
• Burnout	• Happiness	• Joy
• Ecstasy	• Bliss	• Satisfaction
• Comfort	• Satiety	• Love

To the extent that we want to satisfy one of these activators, we will then need to form a goal in such a way that maximizes our chances of satisfaction. The activator and the goal may appear unrelated. To satisfy lust, for example, we might form a goal around achievement.

1. The Moment (Context, Situation)	→	2. Perception	→	3. Activation of Salient State	

Figure 37.2. A Goal-Centered Model of Motivation

We make *goals* with one of three purposes in mind: gratification, engagement, or pleasure (defined in phase 7). The goal is formulated around one of many value areas (wealth, spiritual, aesthetic, health, power, escape, etc.). Goals are detailed according to many different criteria:

- Specific vs. general
- Close vs. distant
- Selfish vs. altruistic
- Easy vs. challenging
- Passive vs. active
- Physical vs. mental

Plus all the shapers: solitary vs. social (trait), kinesthetic vs. auditory (talent), etc.

Goals often involve current versions of past experiences, as in repeating, modifying, sharing, avoiding, offsetting, expanding, or combining them, or setting higher or lower standards. In addition, goals may be made in isolation, or in light of other conflicting or compatible goals which need to be kept in mind.

The actual *pursuit* of a goal, i.e., the effort expended to realize the goal, is one or a combination of three kinds of effort: mental, motor, or verbal.

Plans for goal attainment often run into unanticipated *promoters* (good luck, new resources, offers of assistance) as well as *obstructors,* which cause stress (we also call them "stressors"). Common obstructors and stressors:

- Unsupportive infrastructure
- Inappropriate autonomy
- Comparison to others
- Rival opportunities
- Inadequate resources
- Nature/"Acts of God"
- Goal conflict
- Competition
- Blockers
- Threats
- Scripts
- Illness
- Doubt
- Loss

For each of the three overarching goal purposes, our emotions tell us whether we are on or off target, and we must adapt accordingly:

Purpose	On Target	Off Target	To Fix
Gratification	Pride Joy Content	Resentment Aloofness Disgust	Adjust independence or dependence
Engagement (flow)	Detached from space, time, senses	Boredom	Increase challenge or decrease resources
		Frustration	Decrease challenge or increase resources
Pleasure	Blissful Ecstatic Sensory intensity	Habituation	Decrease frequency Increase spacing Increase savoring Increase mindfulness

4. Goal Articulation

5. Pursuit of Goal (Verbal, Motor, or Mental Effort)

6. Promoters (e.g., Luck) and Obstructors (e.g. Stress)

7. Feedback on Success or Failure via Emotions

Figure 37.3 illustrates these three sets of criteria for goal articulation. As a brief example of how the three areas work together, here is how my conscious and subconscious mind might form a goal when trying to satisfy the activator *curiosity* upon seeing a new book:

> Do I know enough about the subject to understand it, or do I know so much about it already that I'd be bored by it? (Flow as overarching goal.) Will this advance me toward getting the draft of my book finished, or is it a distraction? (Achievement vs. learning as primary values involved.) Have I read anything by this writer before, what did I think about it, and was it useful? (Memory valence as a criterion.)

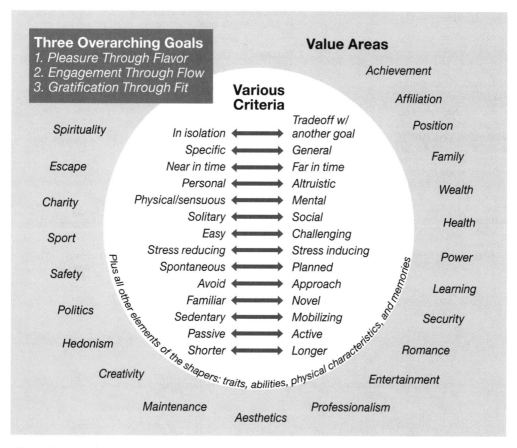

Figure 37.3. Criteria for Goal Articulation

5. ***Pursuit of goal.*** In attempting to achieve the goal, we must engage in some combination of mental, motor, and verbal effort. In deciding on how we will pursue our goal, we consciously or subconsciously let our shapers influence our decisions.

6. ***Promoters and obstructers.*** While in pursuit of our goal, whether a major or minor goal, we will experience promoters and obstructers. Promoters are anything that helps us move closer to goal achievement, such as good luck, availability of resources, offers of help, good weather, and so forth. In fact, one major promoter would be the absence of obstructers! An obstructer is anything that interferes with goal achievement. Obstructers are not necessarily unpleasant (as in Jane wanting to snuggle when I need to get to work). In essence, obstructers are stressors (see topic 36.1 and following), because anything that interferes with goal attainment has the potential to cause us stress. However, if the obstructer is minor, and if we feel we have control over it, it tends to cause little or no stress. Whether or not an obstructer is stressful depends on our shapers (e.g., whether we are high or low in N, whether we have sufficient ability, whether we are wide awake, or whether we have a positive memory of doing something like this before— traits, abilities, physical characteristics, and memories). See table 37.1 for a list of common obstructers, or sources of stress.

7. ***Feedback.*** As we continue our pursuit, we get emotional feedback on the nature of our progress, with positive emotions indicating the likelihood of success and negative emotions indicating the threat of failure or nonattainment. This continual emotional feedback ("Yes, I'm going to make it!" or "I'll never get there at this rate!") causes us to repeat the seven-phase goal formation process: the emotional feedback becomes a kind of *moment* (which is phase 1 of the process) in and of itself and sets the stage for either reaffirming the goal articulation, modifying it, or abandoning it.

Applications

❶ The clearer we are on our personal infrastructure, the easier it is to form our goals. Go through the self-study exercise of completing the worksheet "My Shapers" (appendix L), which is explained in the applications for topic 37.3.

Table 37.1. Common Sources of Stress (Sample Goal: Get Pregnant)

Type of Obstructer	How This Obstructer Might Interfere with This Sample Goal
Goal Conflict	Getting pregnant conflicts with finishing my graduate degree.
Inappropriate Autonomy	Having too much or too little autonomy with reference to the goal, as in concerns about genetic defects, timing of pregnancy.
Blockers	My partner is not ready for parenthood.
Threats	My partner's drinking or drug habits concern me.
Rival Opportunities or Distractions	There's an opportunity for a major promotion and reassignment coming up at work—should I wait. Or, I've met someone whom I think I would rather have as my co-parent.
Loss	Miscarriage.
Comparison/Competition	My best friend is already pregnant.
Inadequate Resources	We don't have enough health insurance. Our house is too small.
Nature/Acts of God	Drought. Crop Failure.
Illness	Influenza. Measles.
Doubt	Is this really the partner that I want to help raise my child? Am I really ready—have I done all I want to do before having a child?
Unsupportive Environment	My organization doesn't respect the needs of parents.
Scripts	I'm incapable of being a good parent.

❷ After you have completed your "My Shapers" worksheet, consider a major goal that you are trying to formulate, and use the content of the worksheet to help articulate your goal.

Maintaining Optimal Positive Mood

The preceding material was predicated on the assumption that we don't select happiness as a goal but instead experience something like satisfaction with life through flavor, flow, and fit. The reality is, however, that we occasionally find ourselves, or those close to us, in the throes of a bad mood. Current research suggests that flavor, flow, and fit result in optimal mood. However, when these three are operating, and our mood is still suboptimal, research suggests three corrective actions we can take to restore optimum mood. These three are treated in turn:

1. Optimistic explanatory style

2. Mood management techniques

3. Human resource optimization

TOPIC 37.5   Optimism vs. Helplessness

Martin Seligman, in his book *Learned Optimism* (1991), describes how rats and humans learn to be helpless. When they learn, in controlled experiments, that they have no control over their environment, they give up trying to exert control. Whether the bothersome stimuli are electroshocks or noise, unsuccessful attempts to stop them are followed by defeatist despair. Seligman has found three ingredients of this learned helplessness among humans, which he contrasts to learned optimism. The three ingredients are *personalization, permanence,* and *pervasiveness.* Depending on how we typically respond to success or adversity along these three dimensions, we are described as optimistic or pessimistic. In table 37.2, I have summarized the healthy, more motivated explanatory style and the less healthy, unmotivated explanatory style.

Seligman concludes from his research that the optimistic explanatory style is associated with high motivation, success, achievement, and physical and mental health, the pessimistic explanatory style with the opposite traits. He also finds that certain pessimistic people who constantly ruminate about their misfortune in life and brood about the pessimistic aspects of personalization, permanence, and pervasiveness are at high risk for depression.

Notice that the preferred explanatory styles are opposite in their response to success or adversity: the more healthy (optimistic) explanatory style for success (internal, permanent, and pervasive) is in fact unhealthy (pessimistic) as a way to explain adversity. Conversely, the more unhealthy (pessimistic) way to explain success (external, temporary, and limited) is in fact the healthy (optimistic) way to explain adversity. Figure 37.4 illustrates this model as a flowchart.

Neurophysiologist Benjamin Libet of the University of California, San Francisco, has demonstrated that brain activity precedes consciousness. Hence, he concludes, intentions are spontaneous and

Table 37.2. Seligman's Explanatory Styles

Explanation of Adversity	
Optimist	*Pessimist*
It's someone else's fault (external personalization).	It's my fault (internal personalization).
It's only temporary (not permanent).	It's gonna last forever (permanent).
It won't affect other areas of my life (limited pervasiveness).	It will affect every area of my life (universal pervasiveness).
Explanation of Success	
Optimist	*Pessimist*
I made it happen (internal personalization).	Someone else made it happen (external personalization).
This is one in a line of many successes (permanent).	It will never happen again (not permanent).
The effect will ripple throughout my life (universal pervasiveness).	It won't help me in any other areas of my life (limited pervasiveness).

actions are intentional. We choose our actions based on a spontaneous set of alternatives, so there is a point in time before an emotional reaction during which we can select a more optimistic response, as opposed to a more pessimistic one. (See Restak, 1991.)

A word of warning: The goal of understanding the explanatory style is not to create a world of Pollyannaish optimists. Too much optimism, like too much pessimism, is typically counterproductive. On the other hand, psychologists Katri Raikkonen and Karen Matthews of the University of Pittsburgh School of Medicine report that people with more pessimistic outlooks have an average blood pressure that is about five points higher (both systolic and diastolic) than that of optimists. Among people who have suffered one heart attack, pessimism predicts a second, more lethal heart attack more accurately than physical condition. And a University of Michigan research team headed by Christopher Peterson has reported that people (especially

> Mayo Clinic patients initially evaluated as more "optimistic" lived 19 percent longer than the pessimists.

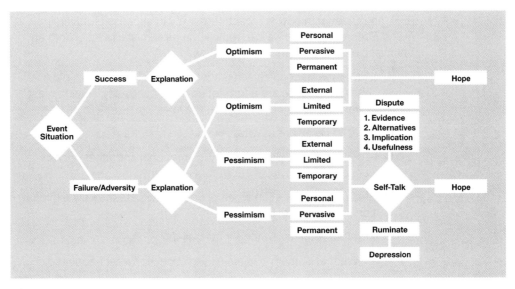

Figure 37.4. Optimism-Pessimism Flowchart
Source: Designed by the Center for Applied Cognitive Studies, based on the work of Martin E. P. Seligman (1991), *Learned Optimism,* New York: Knopf.

males) who "catastrophize" events, seeing them as part of a worldwide pattern of evil and pain, tend to die before age 65 and are more likely to die by suicide or accident (*Psychological Science,* March 1998).

Applications

❶ Seligman's *Learned Optimism* (1991) is an easy read, intended for the layperson. He provides both an adult's and a child's version of his "Explanatory Style Questionnaire," with which you can compare yourself with the rest of the population in terms of optimism and pessimism. The questionnaire also includes much research on the ability of the explanatory style to predict job or sports success, and it has a fascinating section on psychohistory—the ability of the explanatory style to predict the future (specifically, presidential elections). A computer-scored version of the Explanatory Style Questionnaire is available from Martin Seligman at 215-898-2748 in Philadelphia.

❷ Seligman has found success in teaching a form of learned optimism to people with a pessimistic explanatory style, using the *ABCDE* approach.

A, B, and *C* concern how we react negatively to success or adversity; *D* and *E* represent ways we can rethink the pessimistic reaction into an optimistic one. The letters are defined as follows:

A *(Adversity)* Recognize when adversity hits. For die-hard pessimists, successes are a form of adversity; they say, "It won't last," "I was just lucky," or "Too little, too late."

B *(Beliefs)* Be aware of what you believe about the adversity.

C *(Consequences)* Be aware of the emotional and other consequences of your belief about that adversity.

D *(Disputation)* Question whether your beliefs are the only explanation. For example, ask

- What is the evidence for my beliefs?

- What are other possible explanations for what happened?

- What are the implications of my believing this way, and do they make it worth holding onto my beliefs?

- How useful are my beliefs? Do I or others get any benefits from holding onto them, or would we get more benefits from holding other beliefs?

E *(Energization)* Be aware of the new consequences (feelings, behaviors, actions) that do or could follow from a different, more optimistic explanation or set of beliefs.

Here is an example of the ABCDE model as I applied it to a specific situation. My train of thought went like this:

1. I didn't finish this chapter by the end of the Thanksgiving holiday, as I promised my wife and myself I would do. *(Adversity)*

2. I'm an incurable procrastinator, and I will never meet my goals. *(Beliefs: a personal, pervasive, and permanent explanation, which is therefore pessimistic)*

3. I might as well abandon this project and settle for a life of less ambitious projects. That way, my wife won't be disappointed with me when I miss deadlines. *(Consequence)*

4. Wait a minute! Lots of writers set unrealistic deadlines. Besides, my wife and I did several things together and with her parents that

had a very positive impact on our relationship. And if sticking to my schedule were so all-fired important to her, she could have insisted on doing some of those things without me. *(Disputation)*

5. I'll talk about my schedule with her and get her input on whether the remainder of the schedule is important to her. If not, I'll push my deadlines back. If so, I'll ask her assistance and cooperation in finding ways to make more time for writing. I really don't want to give up this project. It's exciting, even if it is a little behind schedule. *(Energization)*

❸ If you or someone you know would like help in developing a more optimistic style, select a psychotherapist who practices cognitive therapy, a directive therapy aimed at changing the way a client perceives his environment, which is closely allied with Seligman's research.

❹ If you are a ruminator (someone who talks silently and continually to himself or herself in a negative vein, as in "I'm going to fail. I'm no good"), then you need to learn more than just a more optimistic explanatory style; you need to learn how to jerk away from the hold that pessimistic thoughts have on you. Seligman suggests several distracting techniques in his book, including wearing a rubber band on your wrist (snap it when you start ruminating) and creating physical distractions (such as slapping the wall or doing isometric exercises), as ways to pop the pessimistic preoccupation out of your mind.

❺ For some people, visualization techniques are effective both for removing pessimistic thoughts and for encouraging optimistic ones (Gawain, 1978). Here is an example. First, with your eyes closed, get a clear picture of the unpleasant thought in your mind. Then, as though you were turning a television control knob, make the image lighter and lighter until all you see is white light. Slowly bring it back into view, then continue to make it darker until all you see is blackness. When the unpleasant image reappears, take control of it and reduce it to whiteness or blackness, whichever you prefer. You can do the same with sounds in your head that are unpleasant and stressful, such as parental scripts: try turning up the imaginary volume knob until they are so loud that they sound like static, then gradually turn them down until they are inaudible.

❻ Seligman has developed a technique with which you can assess the attributional style of a public figure, such as your mayor or coach, by studiously watching television clips and reading newspaper and magazine accounts. If you send $3.00 (as of this writing), Seligman will send you the necessary instructions to conduct a CAVE (content analysis of verbatim explanations). Mail to Dr. Martin Seligman (or Peter Schulman), Department of Psychology, University of Pennsylvania, 3815 Walnut Street, Philadelphia, Pennsylvania 19104-6196.

7 Michael Lewis of the Robert Wood Johnson Medical School (formerly Rutgers University Medical School) in Piscataway, New Jersey, reports that most girls grow up with a pessimistic explanatory style. Parents and teachers tend to lavish more praise on boys. Be aware of this tendency, and be sure to encourage young girls to attribute their successes to their ability and their failures to bad luck.

8 Seligman has conducted extensive research on the benefits of teaching young children how to be in control of their explanatory style. Among 10-year-old children trained in optimistic explanatory style, Seligman found the incidence of depression during puberty to be half that of others. The results of this research, along with practical applications and exercises for young children, are presented in *The Optimistic Child* (Seligman, Reivich, Jaycox, and Gillham, 1995).

TOPIC 37.6   Mood Management

Ed Diener or the University of Illinois has identified two events that tend to derail most people from previously happy planes: losing a job and losing a spouse. Recovering from the former can last long after one has become re-employed, and recovering from the latter can take upwards of eight years. If these two events throw most of us for a loop, there are many other events that, though milder in impact, also manage to put us in a bad mood. Seligman (2002) writes about the "hedonic treadmill" effect (p. 49), the observation that particularly good or bad events (promotions, monetary windfalls, career setbacks, etc.) tend to lose their effect on mood in under three months and we return to our "set range." In this section, we list as applications a variety of mood enhancement techniques to help restore optimum mood, whether we've suffered a major or a minor setback. For a summary of the research justification for these techniques, see Seligman, Steen, Park, and Peterson (2005).

Applications

❶ Sonja Lyubomirsky of the University of California, Riverside, has grants to study effective mood boosters. She, along with Seligman, recommends a variety of simple activities that have been shown to improve mood. For example:

- Keeping a "gratitude journal"—writing down, at least once a week, things for which one is thankful

- Acts of kindness, generosity, or altruism; those who performed five a week showed marked improvement in mood, even more dramatic improvement when all five are done in the same day

- Gratitude visits, in which you write out a note of appreciation, then hand-deliver it, read it, and leave it with the teacher, rabbi, mentor, friend, vendor, or whomever you choose to show your appreciation

- Forgiving someone who has wronged you—for example, writing her a note in which you clear the air and say you're moving on and everything is forgiven and forgotten

- Putting in time with family and friends, especially when you can focus on activities that please them

- Getting and staying in shape

The catch: it's like brushing your teeth; you have to keep it up! When the effect wears off, you restore mood with new positive actions.

❷ Practice using the authentic smile, known among scholars as the "Duchenne" smile, named after Guillaume Duchenne (Seligman, 2002, p. 5):

> The corners of your mouth turn up and the skin around the corners of your eyes crinkles (like crow's feet). The muscles that do this, the orbicularis oculi and the zygomaticus, are exceedingly difficult to control voluntarily. The other smile, called the Pan American smile (after the flight attendants in television ads for the now-defunct airline), is inauthentic, with none of the Duchenne features. Indeed, it is probably more related to the rictus that lower primates display when frightened than it is to happiness.

Seligman relates a study in which female college seniors' smiles were evaluated and half were deemed to be smiling authentically. Thirty years after graduation, the Duchenne women were more likely to be married and to report a greater sense of well-being than the 21-year-old smilers without crows' feet beside their eyes. The Duchenne smilers also were no more likely to be judged prettier, on average, than the Pan American smilers.

❸ In a Princeton experiment, the regular colonoscopy was compared with one in which an extra minute was added to the regular exam, but with a different "twist"—the scope didn't move during the final minute. Because of their more pleasant final minute, the experimental group reported being more willing to undergo another colonoscopy, reinforcing other findings that the emotional tone at the end of an experience stays with us more strongly than the preceding tone. The point: to have participants recall the overall experience with optimal emotional overtones, design experiences that conclude with an unambiguously positive tone.

❹ Happiness can be increased (Seligman, 2002, p. 61) by

- living in a thriving democracy, as opposed to a poor dictatorship
- marrying
- avoiding negative events and shunning negative emotions
- developing a wide and satisfying social network
- getting involved in religious life

❺ Although you may pursue one or more of the following goals for other reasons, don't expect happiness to necessarily accompany their achievement:

- making more money and acquiring more material possessions
- pursuing improved physical health by means of surgery, drugs, doctor visits, and so forth, as opposed to subjectively feeling healthy
- increasing your perceived beauty (e.g., via cosmetic surgery)
- pursuing education for its own sake
- changing your apparent race
- living in a different climate (sunnier, cooler, drier, etc.)

❻ The emotional tone of our memories depends on how we hold onto anger and sadness. Both can be addressed through cognitive therapy, although a simpler approach has more recently been identified: gratitude and forgiveness. Seligman (2002, p. 70) recommends

- writing out a testimonial of gratitude to someone who has been important to you, but who has never been properly thanked, and delivering the written testimonial in person, reading it to him, and leaving it with him.

- making a nightly (or periodical) list of five things you are thankful for. Such gestures of gratitude, which are easily within one's willpower, have the effect of pushing out negative emotions.

- Using Everett Worthington's REACH model, which has been associated with significant reductions in anger and stress and attendant increases in health and optimism:

  1. Recall someone's hurt to you objectively, descriptively, without judging.

  2. Empathize by trying to understand the perpetrator's possible reasons for the act that caused injury.

  3. Altruistically forgive the person, beginning by recalling an incident in which someone forgave you for an injury you may have caused.

  4. Commit publicly by writing a note, poem, song, or other tangible or visible remembrance of your forgiving act.

  5. Hold onto this forgiving stance—reread your note, for example. No need to try forgetting the injury, but definitely remember the forgiving of it.

❼ Katherine Dahlsgaard led a group (including Martin Seligman) that read over 200 "catalogs" of virtues and strengths, from the Upanishads to Ben Franklin, resulting in a comprehensive taxonomy. The six large groupings are called the *six virtues,* each virtue containing its own unique family of *strengths,* for a total of 24 avenues that lead to attaining the overarching virtue (Seligman, 2002, pp. 140–141; Seligman, Steen, Park, and Peterson, 2005):

1. Wisdom and knowledge
   - Creativity/ingenuity/originality/practical intelligence/street smarts
   - Curiosity/interest in the world
   - Judgment/critical thinking/open-mindedness
   - Love of learning
   - Perspective

2. Courage
   - Authenticity/integrity/genuineness/honesty
   - Valor and bravery
   - Perseverance/industry/diligence
   - Zest/passion/enthusiasm

3. Love and humanity
   - Kindness and generosity
   - Loving and allowing oneself to be loved
   - Social intelligence/personal intelligence/emotional intelligence

4. Justice
   - Fairness and equity
   - Leadership
   - Citizenship/duty/teamwork/loyalty

5. Temperance
   - Forgiveness and mercy
   - Humility and modesty
   - Prudence/discretion/caution
   - Self-control/self-regulation

6. Spirituality and transcendence
   - Appreciation of beauty and excellence
   - Gratitude
   - Hope/optimism/future-mindedness
   - Playfulness and humor
   - Spirituality/sense of purpose/faith/religiousness

Seligman defines the goal for living as finding a way to use your top five (or so) strengths daily. Find out more about this list (and profile your strengths) by completing the self-scoring questionnaire on Seligman's website at **www.authentichappiness.org**. The survey is called the VIA Signature Strengths Survey. My personal top five are

- Love of learning
- Humor
- Appreciation of beauty
- Curiosity
- Perspective

I try to act on each of these daily.

Here is an exercise that you can do with your partner. Estimate what you see as your partner's five top strengths. Then think of something that he has done recently that illustrates that strength, and share it with him. If you have trouble thinking of an example, that becomes a good topic for dialogue, with a focus on finding time or opportunities for him to use strengths daily. Have him do the same for you.

❽ Quartz and Sejnowski (2002, p. 262) relate that Harvard political scientist Robert Putnam, in his book *Bowling Alone,* "presents a wealth of evidence from five hundred thousand interviews over the last twenty-five years to show a marked decline in activities that build social capital: We belong to fewer organizations that hold face-to-face meetings, know our neighbors less, and socialize with our friends less often." Community-based work centers are a way of overcoming isolation for those working at home. See P. Katz, *The New Urbanism: Toward an Architecture of Community* (1994). Related to the importance of being a part of "face-to-face" groups, Robin Dunbar argues for keeping our primary groups less than 150 in number.

❾ Starting in early childhood, encourage appropriate levels of make-believe and pretending—regular play, theatre, sociodrama, reading and writing fiction, dreaming, simulations, rehearsals, and so forth. The Fishers (1993, p. 10) quote Taylor (1983, p. 1171) on the role of illusion in happiness and adjustment:

> I maintain that illusions can have a dynamic force. They can simultaneously protect and prompt constructive thought and action. As the literature on depression and the self make clear, normal cognitive processing and behavior may depend on a substantial degree of illusion, whereas the ability to see things clearly can be associated with depression and inactivity. Thus, far from impeding adjustment, illusion may be essential for adequate coping.

Here are some of the purposes and benefits of the various forms of pretending and make-believe:

- To practice roles or skills
- To provide a temporary buffer from the real world's toxins (as in the film *Life is Beautiful*)
- To enhance relationships (as in the film *The Ya-Ya Sisterhood*)
- To escape routine
- To support problem solving, decision making, and planning (as in simulations; to help disentangle the requirements of his unwieldy estate, I once led a wealthy man and his lawyers and accountants in a simulation of his death)
- To facilitate humor

- To create necessary defense mechanisms (such as the "life lie" in Ibsen's *Wild Duck*)
- To increase optimism and a positive explanatory style
- To construct personal, familial, and cultural myths that are both self-enhancing and benign to others
- To assist in healing
- To establish routines that do not require effortful thought
- To form patterns of meaning and order in a complex, chaotic world, without which we feel lost, crushed by the immensity of the task of staying alive
- To enable quick responses in situations where careful analysis would slow you down ("He who hesitates is lost")
- To stimulate progress
- To promote risk taking
- To establish social norms, mores, taboos that promote ethical behavior ("Good men marry only virgins")
- To enable goal-setting
- To promote social cohesiveness ("chosen people")
- To counterbalance or subdue rival illusions that are more damaging (Heaven vs. Hell)
- To formulate and solidify a sense of self
- To encourage acceptance of diversity ("There is that of God in every person")
- To allow for hope and faith
- To enable us to accept contradictions
- To assist in helping children learn discipline (tooth fairy, Santa Claus)

Resist illusions, and approach truth through critical thinking, in the following circumstances:

- Evaluating candidates for hiring
- Making investment decisions
- Illusions that sustain hurtful behaviors or attitudes
- Quality inspection and testing
- Formulating business strategy
- Identifying market needs and preferences

- Unmasking malevolent fictions (Hitler and the superior race, al Qaeda and paradise as reward)

⑩ Finally, in addition to the above suggestions, consider the stress strategies in topic 36.1.

⑪ For self-study as well as possible research of your own, consider using the Steen Happiness Index (SHI), a 20-item survey that measures the three variables we have described here as PEG. More in Seligman, Steen, Park, and Peterson (2005).

⑫ Consider a career in positive psychology, or at least exposing yourself to the graduates and subject matter of such programs. The first graduate program of which I'm aware is the Master of Applied Positive Psychology at the University of Pennsylvania.

TOPIC 37.7 Human Resource Optimization

The third, and final, category of mood optimizers is one that relates specifically to the world of work. However, by extension, it also relates to our expectations of people in any role that requires certain levels of performance, whether at work, at home, or in the community.

In my 2001 book, *The Owner's Manual for Personality at Work* (with my wife, Jane), we presented the concept of *human resource optimization* (HRO). It appeared in chapter 16, "When Pigs Can't Fly." The HRO model is based on the following assumption: *there is an ideal set of personality traits that makes a particular performance area more or less natural.* For example, the performance area *proofreading* is easier or more natural for someone who is more introverted, less creative, and more disciplined, and is less natural for someone who is more extraverted, more creative, and less disciplined. In either case, one can be a good proofreader. It is just that, in the latter case—outgoing, creative, and spontaneous—proofreading is not as natural an activity, and therefore that kind of person is subject to greater effort, concentration, and subsequent fatigue than someone who has the more natural profile, or *infrastructure*. Such infrastructures for 54 different work competencies are presented in table 15.1 of Howard and Howard (2001). Another way of saying the same thing is that we are born with certain propensities. Pigs are not born with the propensity to fly, so further efforts to make them fly are risky. Similarly, I was born to be independent—efforts to turn me into a manager of others are doomed to failure. Pigs can't fly, and Pierce can't supervise. Flying isn't natural for pigs, and supervising isn't natural for me. Maybe a little bit I could handle, but not much!

The HRO process is used in conjunction with some kind of performance assessment that determines whether someone is performing higher or lower with respect to specific competencies. Once you have such performance assessment information (e.g., "performing below expectation in proofreading"), you can compare the person's performance level to the underlying trait infrastructure for that competency to see what kind of fit the person was expected to have to perform the competency. Your comparison can ultimately lead you to strategies from the HRO model. The model comprises five elements:

- If a person is performing a competency well and has a close or perfect match on the underlying personality traits for it, then we say that we need to *capitalize* on that competency and give the person even more opportunities to become better at performing it.

- If a person is performing a competency well and has a poor fit with the underlying traits for the competency, then we say that we need to *caution* the person that she may be creating stress for herself by working so hard to perform a competency that does not come naturally for her, like swimming against the river current.

- If a person is not performing a competency well but has a good fit with the underlying traits for the competency, then we say that we need to *develop* that competency for him and give him training, mentoring, books to read, tapes, etc.

- If a person is not performing a competency well and has a partial fit on the underlying traits for the competency, then we say that we need to *develop with support* that competency for her and give her training, mentoring, etc., plus plenty of regular follow-up feedback, an incentive bonus, and so forth.

- If a person is not performing a competency well and has a poor fit with the underlying traits for the competency, then we say that we need to *compensate* for that competency and come up with work-around strategies, such as delegation to another team member, job redesign, job reassignment, etc.

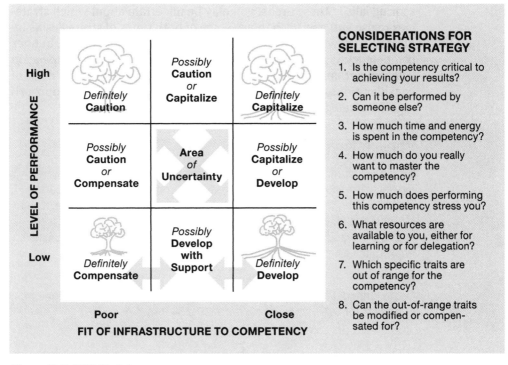

CONSIDERATIONS FOR SELECTING STRATEGY

1. Is the competency critical to achieving your results?

2. Can it be performed by someone else?

3. How much time and energy is spent in the competency?

4. How much do you really want to master the competency?

5. How much does performing this competency stress you?

6. What resources are available to you, either for learning or for delegation?

7. Which specific traits are out of range for the competency?

8. Can the out-of-range traits be modified or compensated for?

Figure 37.5. HRO Model

To enhance your understanding of HRO, refer to the visual representation of HRO in figure 37.5, showing *capitalize, caution, develop, support,* and *compensate.* The vertical axis represents the level of performance the person is demonstrating on the competency at work. Level of performance is also shown by the size of the tree above the ground, i.e., a small tree means low performance (*develop* and *compensate*), a large tree high performance (*caution* and *capitalize*).

The horizontal axis represents the level of fit (capacity) of the personality traits that underlie the competency. Closeness of fit between personality traits and competency is indicated by the size of the root system below ground. A small root system means a poorer match of personality traits to the competency (*compensate* and *caution*); a large root system means a closer match (*develop* and *capitalize*).

Scoring in the in-between areas on a competency indicates that the person may have some of the performance or some of the personality traits, but not all that you might wish for a specific competency. If scoring falls in these areas, you may be uncertain about which strategies to use and may wish to use some of both types of strategies as indicated. However, if an individual's performance is inadequate but her competency is needed, you may wish to undertake *support* (*develop with support*) strategies with her. To the right of the graph is a list of considerations you should think about before selecting the appropriate HRO strategy for your client on a specific competency.

Applications

❶ For yourself, or for someone for whom you feel some responsibility, determine a key competency area, then compare his level of performance in that competency to his trait infrastructure. Refer to table 15.1 in Howard and Howard (2001) for specific competencies and their associated trait infrastructures. Determine which of the five HRO strategies is appropriate for optimizing their fit.

❷ Supplement your own thinking about HRO strategies by obtaining the *OpTips* manual from *Cent*ACS. This manual contains about 10 pages of strategies for use with each of *Cent*ACS's 54 competencies.

A Reminder: Happiness Is Not a Goal

The University of Wisconsin's happiness researcher, Richard Davidson, (reported in *Time,* January 27, 2005) locates happiness in the left prefrontal lobe. There, electrical activity shows a sharp, sustained spike when a person is happy, as when a monk experiences bliss. This heightened left prefrontal activity is associated with elevated immune function and decreased death rates, both around 50 percent. Moreover, the evidence shows that one is born with the capacity for this activity. For example, infants with normally high left prefrontal activity are much less likely to cry when a parent leaves the room. Further, Davidson has found links of left prefrontal activity to levels of dopamine produced in the *nucleus accumbens* and the prevalence of highly effective dopamine receptors throughout the limbic region. Apparently, limbic excitement is associated only with pleasure (drugs, food, sex), whereas left prefrontal excitation *with* limbic excitement is associated with happiness. Here lies the difference between happiness and pleasure: happiness is pleasure *plus* meaning and mental engagement.

University of California's Dacher Keltner attributes heightened left prefrontal activity and the ensuing dopamine tidal wave with the sense of approaching attainment of a meaningful goal. This appears to be what Csikszentmihalyi means when he says that flow is attainable only when one perceives that one has at least a 50 percent chance of succeeding in a situation. Feeling on the path to goal attainment permits one to become totally absorbed in one's activity of the moment.

Related to happiness is laughter (see chapter 11 on humor), which is known to suppress the production of cortisol. Loma Linda University's biology professor Lee Berk studied two groups of cardiac patients. One group watched one half-hour of comedy daily but otherwise received the same medical treatment as the other group. After one year the "comedy" group showed lower blood pressure and cortisol levels, less arrhythmia, and fewer subsequent heart attacks.

Seligman (2002) suggests a formula to estimate our personal likely level of "happiness" (p. 45):

$H = S + C + V$

H = your enduring level of happiness (not of the moment, but over time)

S = set range (inherited—nature)

C = circumstances of your life (environmental—nurture)

V = factors under your voluntary control

In other words, *accept your nature* (as described in "My Shapers"), *accept your circumstances that you cannot change* (e.g., your local weather), and *take charge of the things you can (and want to) do something about* (e.g., open a savings account and start an automatic monthly payroll deduction into it).

SUGGESTED RESOURCES

Petri, H. L. (1991). *Motivation: Theory, Research, and Applications* (3rd ed.). Belmont, Calif.: Wadsworth.

Seligman, M. E. P. (1991). *Learned Optimism.* New York: Knopf.

Seligman, M. E. P. (2002). *Authentic Happiness.* New York: Free Press.

Seligman, M. E. P., K. Reivich, L. Jaycox, and J. Gillham (1995). *The Optimistic Child.* Boston: Houghton Mifflin.

Part Ten

Closing with a Prayer

*A Peek
at States of
Consciousness*

Part Ten. Closing with a Prayer
A Peek at States of Consciousness

38

States of Consciousness

Phases of the Mind

*O*n October 30, 1998, Vilayanur Ramachandran, a senior scientist at the Center for Brain and Cognition at the University of California, San Diego, addressed the first Learning Brain Expo in San Diego, California. In describing the many possible combinations of information substances and neural pathways, Ramachandran made the astounding comment that there are more possible brain states than there are particles in the universe. With that said, I now humbly attempt to execute a chapter on consciousness!

*66**Make me one with everything.** 99*

—Buddhist monk, to hot dog vendor

To begin: what is consciousness? David Chalmers, a faculty member of the philosophy department at the University of California, Santa Cruz, calls it "the subjective, inner life of the mind" (1995, p. 80). Gerald Edelman (1987), in elaborating his theory of neuronal group selection, talks of two kinds of consciousness: *primary consciousness,* which involves an awareness of the present, and *higher consciousness,* involving awareness of the past, projection into the future, and the ability to see patterns in the totality of one's behavior, past, present, and future. Francis Crick (1994), co-discoverer of DNA's structure, called it "no more than the behavior of a vast assembly of nerve cells" (cited in Horgan, 1994, p. 3). LeDoux (2002) describes the variety of neural circuits that form consciousness as similar to a number of computers, each working independently but each also connected to the others, so that what's happening on one computer can affect what's happening on others. (The IT world calls this *parallel processing.*) In a fairly readable summary, John Horgan reviewed these and other approaches to consciousness in the July 1994 issue of *Scientific American.* In a giant step toward pulling together all research on consciousness, Antonio Damasio compiled (1999) *The Feeling of What Happens,* in which he wrote (p. 4) both a dictionary and a "proper" definition of consciousness:

> *Dictionary:* An organism's awareness of its own self and surroundings.

> *Proper:* The feeling of what happens when your being is modified by the acts of apprehending something.

In this chapter, I will attempt to describe consciousness—first from a more comprehensive perspective, followed by several sections that look at particular aspects of consciousness, such as free will, hypnosis, and prayer.

TOPIC 38.1 What Is Consciousness?

In order to render the subject more manageable, I have toyed with the work of Harvard University's J. Allan Hobson. In *The Chemistry of Conscious States* (1994), he proposes three primary variables that underlie the many kinds of conscious states: *source, mode,* and *level of activation.*

Source

Consciousness is neural activity, and this activity can be initiated by an internal source (e.g., hunger) or an external source (a sunset). The source is not either-or in nature. In fact, much of the time we experience both internal and external sources. As I key in text at this moment, I am both referring to my written notes (external) and making connections to other ideas (internal). In fact, source is a continuum, ranging from the purely internal source of the dream state to the purely external source of a blaring rock band.

Francisco J. Varela, National Center for Scientific Research and the Hospital de la Salpetriere in Paris, led a research team that identified the brain pattern—called *gamma oscillation*—that fires when one recognizes or correctly interprets a previously ambiguous pattern, such as a "Mooney face" (February 4, 1999, *Nature*). The gamma oscillation is like a sudden linking of widespread brain resources that leads to correct interpretation. Where isolated patterns previously fired, the gamma oscillation occurs when the previously isolated patterns make the leap to each other and fire off in a high frequency ode to joy, celebrating their coming together as a team. For example, consider the excitement of thinking oneself totally alone, only to discover one or more other lone souls sequestered in remote corners of the library of a Saturday afternoon. The oscillation is a kind of arcing effect—perhaps what Candace Pert calls *metataxis,* ligands flying across intrabody spaces independent of neural wiring and forming connections between remote parts of the body. In essence, Varela here is describing one of the thresholds between external and internal sources of consciousness—the moment when simple perception of the present becomes connected to the remembrance of one's past and the hope for one's future.

Mode

Hobson sees two primary modes of chemical activity associated with neural activation: the *aminergic system* (including norepinephrine and serotonin) and the *cholinergic system* (including acetylcholine). The amines are associated with wakefulness and with managed, or controlled, neural activity subject to one's effort of will. Acetylcholine, on the other hand, is associated with unmanaged neural activity, the kind that occurs during REM sleep or delirium states. Volition inhibits acetylcholine and enhances the amines; absence of volition releases acetylcholine and suppresses the amines. During normal, non-REM sleep, these two systems are in balance. At other times, both are always operating, but one or the other tends to dominate.

Level of Activation

Level of activation is typically described in terms of the types of brain waves active at the time of reference. Chapter 2 covered the four types of brain waves, but for convenience, we'll recap here. These waves are ways of describing the electrical signals produced by the nervous system, from the fastest, beta (associated with normal alertness), through alpha (a twilight zone between alertness and light sleep, as in meditation), to theta (light sleep), and finally to delta (deep sleep). These four electrical impulses are called "waves" because of their appearance on an electroencephalograph.

States of consciousness can be described in terms of these three variables. For example, REM sleep has high activation, a cholinergic mode, and an internal source. To view how these three variables might interact to explain discrete states of consciousness, study the diagram in figure 38.1; its three dimensions delineate a cube that maps the functioning of the entire brain and nervous system. This is a conceptual diagram and is not intended to represent structure; do not attempt to see "left brain, right brain" or "cortex vs. limbic system" in it.

According to Allan Hobson, we can throw away all terms like *preconscious, subconscious, unconscious,* and their kith and kin. Only two terms are needed to describe this terrain: *conscious* and *nonconscious.* To the degree that the mind refers to the brain's collection of information, consciousness is one's awareness of the portion of it that is accessible at any one time; nonconsciousness is all of the information that is inaccessible at any particular time. Information moves from consciousness to nonconsciousness, and this movement is essentially ruled by chance, with the illusion of minimal guidance by something called the *will.*

Applications

❶ Understand that, to some degree, states of consciousness are subject to manipulation. By controlling internal sources of stimulation as opposed to external ones, by controlling stimulants such as caffeine, and

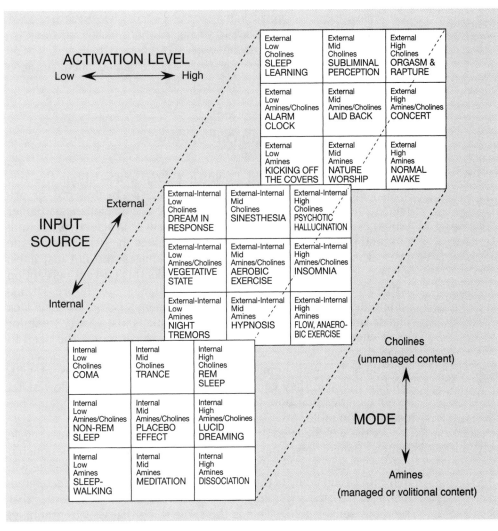

ACTIVATION LEVEL
Low ←————————→ High

External Low Cholines SLEEP LEARNING	External Mid Cholines SUBLIMINAL PERCEPTION	External High Cholines ORGASM & RAPTURE
External Low Amines/Cholines ALARM CLOCK	External Mid Amines/Cholines LAID BACK	External High Amines/Cholines CONCERT
External Low Amines KICKING OFF THE COVERS	External Mid Amines NATURE WORSHIP	External High Amines NORMAL AWAKE

External

**INPUT
SOURCE**

Internal

External-Internal Low Cholines DREAM IN RESPONSE	External-Internal Mid Cholines SINESTHESIA	External-Internal High Cholines PSYCHOTIC HALLUCINATION
External-Internal Low Amines/Cholines VEGETATIVE STATE	External-Internal Mid Amines/Cholines AEROBIC EXERCISE	External-Internal High Amines/Cholines INSOMNIA
External-Internal Low Amines NIGHT TREMORS	External-Internal Mid Amines HYPNOSIS	External-Internal High Amines FLOW, ANAERO- BIC EXERCISE

Cholines
(unmanaged content)
↑

Internal Low Cholines COMA	Internal Mid Cholines TRANCE	Internal High Cholines REM SLEEP
Internal Low Amines/Cholines NON-REM SLEEP	Internal Mid Amines/Cholines PLACEBO EFFECT	Internal High Amines/Cholines LUCID DREAMING
Internal Low Amines SLEEP- WALKING	Internal Mid Amines MEDITATION	Internal High Amines DISSOCIATION

MODE
↓
Amines
(managed or volitional content)

Figure 38.1. States of Consciousness
Source: Based on *The Chemistry of Conscious States* by J. A. Hobson (1994), New York: Little, Brown.

by controlling depressants such as alcohol, we can influence our states
of consciousness.

❷ Make peace with difficult philosophical terms. For example, how does
this definition jibe with religion and the concept of soul? If "neurons 'R' us,"

then what is the role of spirit? In the spirit of the times, we would not distinguish between body and soul. To the degree that soul outlasts body, we can understand the soul as the essence of a person that remains as a memory among others. We have eternal life to the degree that others keep our memory alive.

TOPIC 38.2 In and Out of Flow

Gerald Edelman (1992) writes about the two most common forms of waking consciousness—basic (core, or primary) consciousness and higher (secondary) consciousness. Hamer (2004) elaborates (pp. 92 ff.) that consciousness is selective, continuous, and personal. Core consciousness enables the perception of the present, so that we perceive meaningful images and not just lines, curves, dots, etc. Higher consciousness links this current perception both to our stored past experience and our anticipated future. The assumed difference between animals and humans is that animals lack higher consciousness. For a cat, a tin of tuna is just a tasty treat; for us, it engenders memories of past cats, past cat foods, the need to clean the bowl, tomorrow's dinner menu, and a myriad of other associations. Because animals are totally focused on the present, with no sense of self, they can be said to be in a permanent flow state, never experiencing boredom or frustration. These two systems are described in table 38.1.

As the will focuses, the self recedes, and vice versa, like a toggle switch. Hamer describes research documenting this relationship among Tibetan monks, whose meditation practices exercise the will and entail a subsiding of the self. He identifies this process as *deafferentation* (p. 125), the switching off of the afferent and efferent nerves that keep our senses going. This is the same thing that Csikszentmihalyi calls *flow*. (See more at topic 37.2.)

In short, the going back and forth between self and will is very much like listening to a lecture as your mind wanders from time to time. You can't wander *and* listen! Listening is will, and wandering is self. Or, as often happens with me, I'll be listening to others talk in a meeting, and from time to time my mind will drift to a concern other than the one being discussed, and I'll lose the drift of the conversation and have to ask for a recap. My will to listen to the present alternates on center stage with my self's connections to past and future. The relationship

Table 38.1. The Big Two: Contrasting Features of the Two Most Common States of Wakeful Consciousness

	Core Consciousness	**Higher Consciousness**
Biological location	Thalamocortical loop, comprising the cingulate gyrus, dorsolateral prefrontal cortices, inferior and orbital prefrontal cortices, sensorimotor cortex, and dorsomedial cortex pathway	Posterior superior parietal lobes
Features	• Also called *primary consciousness* (Edelman), *flow* (Csikszentmihalyi) • Seat of the will • Orients us to the present • Where our attention focuses through study, meditation, etc. • Damage here makes it difficult to make decisions and make connections among sets of information • We share this feature with animals	• Also called *secondary consciousness* (Edelman) • Seat of the self • Orients us to our past and future • Where our sense perception orients us to our immediate environment as we locate ourselves in space, time, and sensation • Damage here makes it difficult or impossible to know who we are—to connect the present to our past or future • Thought to be unique to humans

of these two processes is precisely the same as being in and out of Csikszentmihalyi's flow state (see topic 37.2), which he describes as the state of total absorption in the activity of the moment (= will), so much so that one loses one's sense of time and space (= self).

Application

❶ Will, or flow, is a more effortful state of consciousness than self, or pondering the past and future. Refer to the suggestions in topic 37.2 on how to maximize your time in the flow state. Although it takes effort and intention to enter flow, staying there is very satisfying, as in "Time sure flies when you're having fun!" Entering flow is easier, more natural, for some than for others (e.g., those with higher "C"). But, with proper understanding and use of the flow strategies in topic 37.2, anyone can enter.

TOPIC 38.3   Free Will

John Bargh and Tanya Chartrand, psychologists at New York University and Ohio State University, respectively, estimate (1999) that roughly 95 percent of all behavior is automatic, not consciously chosen. In fact, they have discovered in their research that consciously performed acts deplete a person of energy far more severely than automatic acts do. In a series of fascinating experiments, Bargh and Chartrand report that performing one act that requires conscious effort and control makes it more difficult to perform a second act, soon thereafter, that also requires conscious effort and control. For example, persons who first engaged in proofreading a manuscript were then subjected to watching a boring movie. Having depleted their "conscious, free will energy" in proofreading, they found it more difficult to take the necessary action to get up and leave the boring movie. However, persons who did not precede the boring movie with an act requiring conscious control had no trouble taking action in the face of a boring movie. Other paired, sequential activities included eating radishes instead of chocolates, followed by persisting in solving an unsolvable puzzle (persons persisted longer who had not been required to resist the chocolates). So the reason that we engage in consciously chosen and controlled activity so little is that it exhausts us.

They cite Alfred North Whitehead (p. 464):

> It is a profoundly erroneous truism, repeated by all copy-books and by eminent people making speeches, that we should cultivate the habit of thinking of what we are doing. The precise opposite is the case. Civilization advances by extending the number of operations which we can perform without thinking about them. Operations of thought are like cavalry charges in a battle—they are strictly limited in number, they require fresh horses, and must only be made at decisive moments.

In fact, Bargh and Chartrand have identified a typical pattern in which conscious activity is followed by extended periods of automatic activity, such as deciding to read a novel (free will, perhaps), then an extended period of reading (automatic). Further, the researchers report on dozens of experiments that suggest the powerful effect of *priming* such automatic behaviors. In lieu of an individual freely choosing an activity, one can prime that person into performing the activity by mentioning words or performing gestures that activate the person's schemas (see topic 21.4) or other psychological processes into action. For example, in one experiment, subjects were read a list of words that included a handful of words associated with old age, such as "slow," "gray," "retirement," "senior," and "nursing." Even though the subjects were told that the words were related to something else, the subjects who had heard the list with "senior citizen"–type words, when asked to walk across the room to perform another task, walked in a measurably slower manner than subjects who'd not heard the priming words. In other experiments, the experimenter could, for example, by casually rubbing his own forearm, get subjects—unaware they had been primed—rubbing their own forearms in turn! By mentioning achievement-related words such as "valedictorian," "president," and "successful," they found that subjects performing mental tasks got a higher percentage correct than did other subjects who did not hear the achievement words. Hearing the words and seeing the gestures has the effect of priming, or activating, psychological processes associated with the words.

Describing one special instance of automatic vs. intentional behavior, Laurence Gonzales (2003) wrote *Deep Survival,* a study of why some are able to survive in extreme situations (lost in the wilderness, extreme weather, other life-threatening emergencies) while others succumb. Gonzales writes that "only 10 to 20 percent of people can stay calm and think in the midst of a survival emergency. They are the ones who can perceive their situation clearly; they can plan and take correct action, all of which are key elements of survival. Confronted with a changing environment, they rapidly adapt" (p. 24). He adds later that these are the people who never lose their sense of humor, avoid taking themselves too seriously, and respect the forces of nature.

Applications

1 Find subtle or not-so-subtle ways to support behavior you desire in a particular group by placing wall posters or other media presenting words or themes you want to support. IBM posts posters declaring the value of the individual; counselors post declarations that "there is no failure except in no longer trying," thereby priming patients for optimism.

2 When speaking to a group for whom you wish to activate specific psychological processes (such as quality, initiative, or extra effort), you do not necessarily have to address the processes directly, but you can use words associated with these processes while talking about another subject.

❸ Review topic 21.5 on the two modes of information processing. Expository mode is like the conscious processes described here; narrative mode, the unconscious or automatic processes. Expository modes would appear to require more energy than narrative modes, allowing, of course, for exceptions based on individual differences.

❹ In a survival situation, Gonzales (2003, pp. 262–274) offers this advice:

- First, don't get yourself into situations for which you are unprepared. If you are hiking in the mountains, take proper equipment and have developed the proper skills. You never know when a storm will isolate you from civilization for an extended period.

- Second, don't do anything impulsive. Think and develop a plan based on a thorough review of the situation and your resources.

- Go for small victories; your plan should be incremental, aimed at brief, attainable objectives, allowing a small celebration after each segment is achieved.

- Be humble; respect the forces of nature, know when to wait or backtrack.

- Stay calm and exercise your sense of humor; just try to bury your fear.

- Count your blessings.

- Keep your mind active—puzzles, curiosity, counting, memory work, and recitations.

- Appreciate the beauty of the situation—it is calming.

- Never give up.

TOPIC 38.4 Hypnosis

In a review of the research on hypnosis, Irving Kirsch and Steven Jay Lynn (1995) endorse the definition of hypnosis proposed by the American Psychological Association's Division of Psychological Hypnosis as "a procedure wherein changes in sensations, perceptions, thoughts, feelings, or behavior are suggested" (p. 846). They propose the following known truths about hypnosis:

- The ability to experience hypnotic phenomena does not indicate gullibility or weakness.

- Hypnosis is not related to sleep.

- Hypnotic responsiveness depends more on the efforts and abilities of the person who is being hypnotized than on the skill of the hypnotist.

- Participants retain the ability to control their behavior during hypnosis; they are aware of their surroundings and can monitor events outside the framework of suggestions.

- Spontaneous posthypnotic amnesia is rare.

- Suggestions can be responded to with or without hypnosis; the function of a hypnotic induction is merely to increase suggestibility to a minor degree.

- Hypnosis is not a dangerous procedure when practiced by qualified clinicians and researchers.

- Most hypnotized people are neither faking nor merely complying with suggestions.

- Hypnosis does not increase the accuracy of memory.

- Hypnosis does not foster a literal reexperiencing of childhood events.

Applications

1 Psychologist Judy Lasher and surgeon Anne Ouellette of Jackson Memorial Hospital in Miami, Florida, team up to use hypnosis in lieu of general anesthesia for hand operations. Because they use only local painkillers and sedatives along with the hypnosis, the patient can move during the surgery, providing helpful feedback to the surgeon on the effectiveness of the operation. The hospital's staff have found significant reductions in postoperative complications and length of hospital stay as a result of the new practice.

2 Hypnosis has been found to be an effective supplement to other pain management therapies. Its effectiveness relies on the power of the hypnotic relationship to enable the subject to switch from external to internal sources of consciousness.

TOPIC 38.5   The God Module

Vilayanur Ramachandran of the Center for Brain and Cognition of the University of California, San Diego, presented findings at the October 1997 meeting of the Society for Neuroscience that couple temporal lobe activity with mystical religious experience. This so-called "God module" is common among people who suffer a unique kind of epilepsy that is typically accompanied by visions of God and feelings of being at one with the universe. There is apparently a region in the temporal or parietal area that is associated with both epilepsy and intense religious rapture. The area that fires just before the person experiences a temporal epileptic seizure also fires when people report a sense of the presence of God. Hamer (pp. 131 ff.) explains both the seizure and the religious rapture as a rapid firing back and forth between the two hemispheres with a resulting loss of sense of self and a feeling of being in the presence of something bigger. Michael Persinger (1983) has demonstrated that mystical, psychic, and paranormal experiences are associated with instability, or lability, in the temporal lobe. In fact, by introducing weak magnetic fields around the temporal lobes, he has been able to induce out-of-body sensations. Further pinpointing the nature and location of this phenomenon, Dean Hamer, a geneticist at the National Institutes of Health, wrote *The God Gene: How Faith Is Hardwired into Our Genes.* In order to investigate the nature of the God module, Hamer needed to identify subjects who qualified as godly. He used Robert Cloninger's *self-transcendence* scale, which measures the degree to which one sees all the elements of the world as somehow unified. Cloninger's scale is based on three constructs (p. 23):

- *Self-forgetfulness* (the same as Csikszentmihalhyi's *flow*—see topic 37.2)

- *Transpersonal identification* (feeling somehow connected to the world beyond yourself, having the desire to improve or preserve that world, and acting on the desire, as in working to eliminate or minimize war, poverty, abuse, racism, environmental degradation, and so forth—generally, the love of nature)

- *Mysticism* (valuing the irrational, miraculous, inexplicable, or supernatural vs. the rational, material, scientifically explainable, or natural)

Hamer points out that a high score would likely go to Mohandas Gandhi, a low score to Genghis Khan.

Collecting self-transcendence scores among the subjects of U.S. and Australian twins studies, Hamer determined that self-transcendence is significantly heritable, with shared environment having little effect on scores. Further comparing self-transcendence scores with DNA configurations, he identified one variant of the VMAT2 gene that is associated with the Cloninger score—more strongly with the self-forgetfulness scale than the other two, but strongly with all three nonetheless. This variant of the gene—often called the "spiritual allele" (p. 73)—controls monoamines, chemicals associated with levels of consciousness and interestingly with drugs that lead to mystical experiences. Monoamines comprise two subgroups: *catecholamines* (dopamine, adrenaline, noradrenaline) and *indoleamine* (serotonin). The psychoactive drug Ecstasy causes (1) a major release of serotonin, such that your mood is elevated and everyone is your closest friend, and (2) destruction of the serotonin-releasing cells, with the result that the long-term effects of serotonin depletion lead to depression and its attendant cast of symptoms. Prozac is in essence a more benign form of Ecstasy. Such variations in levels of serotonin occur naturally, due to genetic variation. With one allele, one gets less serotonin, hence lowered sociability and mood; with another, one experiences increased sociability and mood. This leads Hamer to conclude (p. 139):

> This is why feelings of spirituality are a matter of emotions rather than intellect. No book or sermon can teach one person to use a different monoamine transporter or another to ignore the signals emanating from his limbic system. It is our genetic makeup that helps to determine how spiritual we are. We do not know God; we feel him.

Hamer found (p. 78) a correlation between the VMAT2 gene and a measure of *persistence,* similar to the C scale (has to do with discipline, perfectionism, methodicalness, and ambition) of the Big Five (see chapter 33), which suggests that the ease with which one enters Cloninger's *self-transcendence* (Csikszentmihalyi's *flow* state; see topic 37.2), is probably related to one's C score, and that one's C score is related to the expression of one's VMAT2 gene. Persistence is the essence of flow; one tends to remain for long stretches in a state of self-forgetfulness, oblivious to temperature, time, hunger, and other input.

Further, Hamer points out (pp. 79 ff.) that people whose VMAT2 gene is activated score similarly on the Cloninger scale, and report self-transcendence experiences similar to other persons who take the psychoactive drug psilocybin (the active agent in the so-called "magic mushrooms"). Psilocybin activates the same pathways that the mono-amine serotonin does. So, it appears that some folks get their self-transcendence naturally from their genetic makeup, whereas others get there with a little help from the pharmacist or garden.

Neurologist James Austin (1998) describes a state of mind in which time, fear, and self-consciousness are unknown (sounds like flow or self-transcendence, huh?). The amygdala, seat of the emotions and the nervous system's threat messenger (see appendix A), must be still. Parietal lobe pathways, which orient one in space and define the border between self and the world, must be still. And the frontal and temporal lobe pathways that monitor time and support self-awareness must be still. Some of these self-transcendent persons report a "voice of God" experience. Apparently Broca's area, the seat of vocal production in the temporal lobe, is active when one hears voices. During meditation-type experiences, when incoming sensory stimuli are quieted, these internal voices can easily be falsely attributed to a source outside the body (see also Bentall, 2000).

In *Why God Won't Go Away* (2001), Andrew Newberg, who teaches in the Department of Radiology of the Medical Center of the University of Pennsylvania, describes the results of hooking up colleague and Tibetan Buddhist meditator Michael J. Baime to a SPECT (single photon emission computed tomography) machine, complete with an IV for tracking blood flow in the brain. Newberg's images of Baime during the height of meditation confirmed Austin's observation that the parietal orientation area showed absence of activity, but with high activity in the prefrontal cortex, indicating highly focused attention.

Other brain-imaging studies have shown how religious ceremonies with strong sensory input (drumming, dancing, and such) find a 180° path to stillness. In essence, during such ceremonial intensity, the emotional seat goes haywire, so much so that the hippocampus shuts off further input to the areas that become still during intense meditation. The result is a kind of meditative state in the midst of a strong sensory environment.

Finally, Hamer (p. 213) deals with the much-discussed relationship of the "spiritual" to the "religious," as in, "I'm not a very religious person, but I am rather a spiritual one." Or vice versa. Hamer:

> Spirituality is based in consciousness, religion in cognition. Spirituality is universal, whereas cultures have their own forms of religion. I would argue that the most important contrast is that spirituality is genetic, while religion is based on culture,

traditions, beliefs, and ideas. It is, in other words, mimetic. This is one reason why spirituality and religion have such differing impacts on individual lives and society.

Application

❶ Though the path of spirituality is relatively easily described, the effort required in walking that path is different depending on your inheritance. If you have the genes for self-transcendence, transpersonal identification, and mysticism, then enjoy them, appreciate that these behaviors and values come more easily and naturally to you, and be understanding of those who have not your genetic gift. If you sense you lack the natural tendency to walk the spiritual path effortlessly, I suggest that you follow the strategies in the previous chapter for achieving flavor, flow, and fit.

TOPIC 38.6 The Efficacy of Prayer

In 1988, physician and author Larry Dossey read about a computer-assisted review of 393 cardiology patients, half of whom were prayed for by home prayer groups and half of whom were not prayed for. It turned out that the prayed-for group were five times less likely to require antibiotics and three times less likely to develop fluid in the lungs (pulmonary edema). As a result of reading about this study, Dossey engaged in a five-year exploration of more than 130 scientific studies that resulted in the book *Healing Words* (1996). His conclusion: praying for someone's health makes a positive impact on that person's recovery in a significant number of the cases. Although skeptics abound, some impressive results have been reported, including one study in which 10 people focused their prayers on retarding the growth of a laboratory fungus while they were 15 miles from the cultures. Over 70 percent of the cultures showed retarded growth, with the same results occurring 16 times out of 16. (No mention was made of a control group.)

In the October 25, 2000, *Archives of Internal Medicine,* William Harris and colleagues at St. Luke's Hospital (Kansas City, Missouri) assigned 500 heart attack patients' first names to a prayer group, with another 500 patients unassigned. The prayed-for patients had no earthly idea that they were being prayed over daily for four weeks.

Result: the prayed-over group was doing about 10 percent better than the non-prayed-over, according to the staff's traditional measures of patient progress.

Application

1 Why not cover your bases and offer prayer for those who might benefit from it? Although I am not a prayerful person myself, I do have a strong belief in the power of positive personal regard. When my wife or a friend is making a presentation, I focus my positive attention on that person in a supportive manner. It can't hurt, and it seems to be well taken. A different sort of rationale for this kind of thoughtful, supportive behavior is offered in James Redfield's *The Celestine Prophecy* (1995).

SUGGESTED RESOURCES

Chalmers, D. J. (1995, December). "The Puzzle of Conscious Experience." *Scientific American,* pp. 80–86.

Crick, F. (1994). *The Astonishing Hypothesis: The Scientific Search for the Soul.* New York: Scribner.

Cytowic, R. E. (1993). *The Man Who Tasted Shapes.* Los Angeles: Tarcher.

Damasio, A. R. (1999). *The Feeling of What Happens: Body and Emotion in the Making of Consciousness.* New York: Harcourt Brace.

Dennett, D. C. (1996). *Kinds of Minds: Toward an Understanding of Consciousness.* New York: Basic Books.

Edelman, G. M. (1992). *Bright Air, Brilliant Fire: On the Matter of the Mind.* New York: Basic Books.

Hamer, D. (2004). *The God Gene.* New York: Doubleday.

Hobson, J. A. (1994). *The Chemistry of Conscious States.* New York: Little, Brown.

Kirsch, I., and S. J. Lynn (1995, October). "The Altered State of Hypnosis: Changes in the Theoretical Landscape." *American Psychologist,* 50(10), 846–858.

LeDoux, J. (2002). *Synaptic Self.* New York: Viking.

39

Updating Your Owner's Manual

The Continuing Search for New Mind-Body Applications

*66 **We should live for the future, and yet should find our life in the fidelities of the present; the last is the only method of the first.** 99*

—Henry Ward Beecher

66 I distrust summaries, any kind of gliding through time, any too great a claim that one is in control of what one recounts; I think someone who claims to understand but is obviously calm, someone who claims to write with emotion recollected in tranquility, is a fool and a liar. To understand is to tremble. To recollect is to re-enter and be riven. . . . I admire the authority of being on one's knees in front of the event."

It is in order at this point for me to offer an "apologia"—not necessarily an admission of wrongdoing, as in an apology, but rather a desire to explain my behavior, as in a defense. Harold Brodkey's strong condemnation of "summaries" above (in "Manipulations," quoted in Jon Krakauer's *Into Thin Air* (1997, p. 217) really hit home when I first came across it a month ago. After all, what is this book but hundreds of summaries? Does this make me a fool and a liar? Perhaps to Brodkey, yes. Perhaps to Brodkey, one should just leave well enough alone unless one can take the time to be "on one's knees in front of the event." However, the cost of that severe approach to learning would be great, for it takes significant time and resources to achieve such intimacy with a subject. But with respect for Brodkey's plea for in-depth knowledge and experience, I encourage you to consider this humble volume as an invitation for depth-diving. Of the many doors I've opened, select those most vital to your *joie de vivre* and explore to the point of trembling at the awesome beauty of deep understanding. Each topic in this volume, well over 300, could well be worth the equivalent of a college course or an independent study. So, don't stop here. The road map is laid. Continue your journey.

From the gaping head wounds of World War II to the drug-sizzled brains caused by poison-trafficking cartels, we try to learn from our misery. A recent television program described how doctors, noticing that the symptoms of crack cocaine addicts resemble those of patients with Parkinson's disease, have made advances in the treatment of the latter. But we do not have to wait for tragedy in order to make progress. Scientific exploration and discovery today make this an exciting time to be alive. And the more open we are to learning the work of others, the more exciting the 21st century will be.

While I was working on the first edition of this book, my wife and I overheard our daughter, Allegra, talking with a girlfriend who was lamenting her steady boyfriend's unwillingness to talk seriously about their relationship. Allegra told her friend that she had learned in her dad's book about females being wired to talk and males being wired to do, and that she had tried the suggestion of getting a boy to do something so that talking would become an accompaniment to the activity rather than an activity in and of itself. "And you know? It really worked! He talked while we were walking and didn't seem to mind it at all. Give it a try."

What I like about this story is that (1) it shows an experimental, evaluative approach in responding to research, and (2) it builds on differences rather than using differences to blame and justify resentments. I hope that this book will become something of a cafeteria for you. By that I mean that you can come to it for nourishment and ideas and take what appears to be helpful to you. Return to it when you are baffled by a concern that is covered by one of these chapters—for example, problems related to aging parents or friends; concerns about an unmotivated child, friend, or co-worker; or a gnawing dissatisfaction with your ability to memorize. This book should yield up to you a specific practical idea or at least suggest relevant resources.

In a sense, I have been sowing seeds, and I'm inviting you to reap from one or more of the many I have thrown out. My observation is that the Age of Research is alive and well. From the health and fitness enthusiasts to the corporate quality gurus, people are spreading the gospel of continuing improvement. But you can't continually improve without doing, following, and evaluating research and then implementing the findings appropriately in your own life. I emphasize, however, the need to be critical. Just as I included the Caveat Box in chapter 3, I urge you to keep your nonsense detector turned on whenever you encounter suggestions for improvement. On several occasions, while perusing futurist magazines, I see advertisements for pills "to make you more intelligent." Amused and alarmed, I call the telephone number provided and ask them to send me a copy of the research results of the product testing. They never have any. All they can send me is a somewhat longer version of the advertisements I have read. I'm still waiting for a get-smart pill with sound research behind it. I decline, incidentally, to accept various offers of a free 30-day supply.

This kind of irresponsible advertising will confront us with more frequency, more force, and more marketing savvy. We must all do what we can to be as informed as possible about what works, what's dangerous, and what's simply inert. In that spirit, I hope you will let me know what works, what doesn't, and what new ideas you'd like me to add (citing you as the source) in subsequent editions of this book. E-mail me at pjhoward@centacs.com.

The advances in brain research are breathtakingly rapid. As I write and you read, some piece of information in this book is being challenged or enhanced. Who knows where the next major advance will be and what difference it will make in our lives? Just this morning, I've read that, in fact, memory boosting drugs concocted from sea slug (*aplysia*) slurry may be forthcoming!

As research expands our sense of what is true and what is real, paradigms begin to shift, sometimes imperceptibly, sometimes earth-shakingly. In looking over the ways in which cognitive science affects our lives, I see 10 paradigms in the middle of major shifts:

Traditional Paradigm	Emerging Paradigm
1. Motivators are external.	Motivators are internal.
2. There are four personality traits.	The Five-Factor Model emerges.
3. Aging lowers ability.	Use it or lose it!
4. IQ is a single-faceted, academic concept.	IQ is a multifaceted, street-smart concept.
5. There are no sex differences.	The sexes are wired differently.
6. Nurture is the main factor.	Nature is the main factor.
7. Germs cause disease.	The mind controls disease.
8. Diet is unrelated to the brain.	Diet influences mental function.
9. The brain is seen as a computer.	The brain is seen as a pharmacy.
10. Memory is retrieval of complete episodes.	Memory is construction of episodes from pieces of information.

Perhaps one of these shifts is more significant to you than others. If so, grab onto it and learn all that you can about it, not settling for my leading you on a glide through time, but attempting to kneel at the event of complete understanding. Call me Ishmael, and become your own Ahab, diving the depths in pursuit of Moby Dick, at first seen only breaking the surface, but ultimately in totality. At first through a glass, darkly, then face to face. Now you know in part; then you will know fully.

Appendices

The Brain Illustrated
From Above

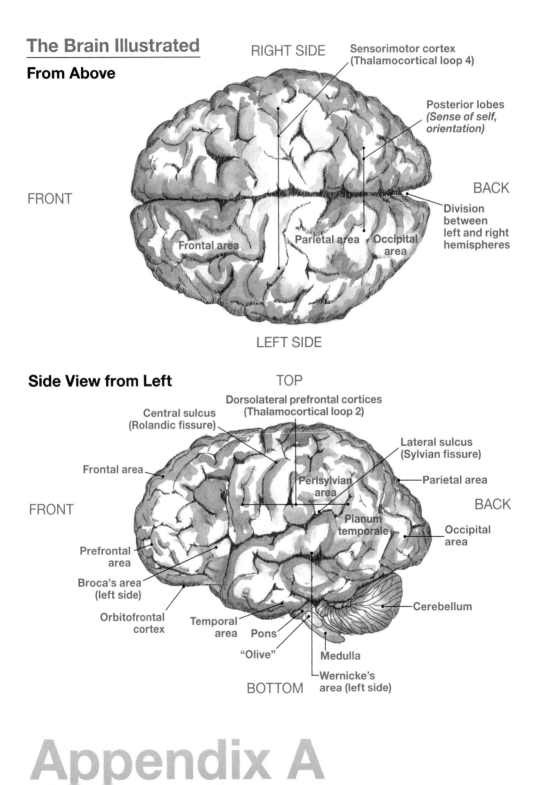

RIGHT SIDE

Sensorimotor cortex
(Thalamocortical loop 4)

Posterior lobes
*(Sense of self,
orientation)*

FRONT

BACK

Division
between
left and right
hemispheres

Frontal area

Parietal area

Occipital
area

LEFT SIDE

Side View from Left

TOP

Dorsolateral prefrontal cortices
(Thalamocortical loop 2)

Central sulcus
(Rolandic fissure)

Lateral sulcus
(Sylvian fissure)

Frontal area

Perisylvian
area

Parietal area

FRONT

BACK

Planum
temporale

Occipital
area

Prefrontal
area

Broca's area
(left side)

Orbitofrontal
cortex

Temporal
area

Pons

Cerebellum

"Olive"

Medulla

Wernicke's
area (left side)

BOTTOM

Appendix A

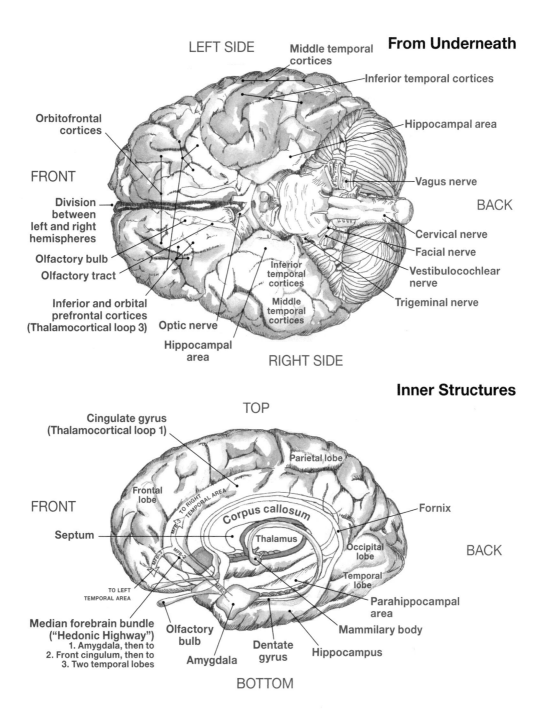

From Underneath

LEFT SIDE

Middle temporal cortices

Inferior temporal cortices

Hippocampal area

Orbitofrontal cortices

FRONT

Vagus nerve

BACK

Division between left and right hemispheres

Olfactory bulb

Olfactory tract

Cervical nerve

Facial nerve

Vestibulocochlear nerve

Inferior temporal cortices

Trigeminal nerve

Middle temporal cortices

Inferior and orbital prefrontal cortices (Thalamocortical loop 3)

Optic nerve

Hippocampal area

RIGHT SIDE

Inner Structures

TOP

Cingulate gyrus (Thalamocortical loop 1)

Parietal lobe

Frontal lobe

TO RIGHT TEMPORAL AREA

MFB-3

Corpus callosum

Fornix

FRONT

Septum

Thalamus

Occipital lobe

BACK

MFB-1

MFB-2

Temporal lobe

TO LEFT TEMPORAL AREA

MFB

Parahippocampal area

Median forebrain bundle ("Hedonic Highway")
1. Amygdala, then to
2. Front cingulum, then to
3. Two temporal lobes

Olfactory bulb

Amygdala

Dentate gyrus

Mammilary body

Hippocampus

BOTTOM

Cross Section (front to back)

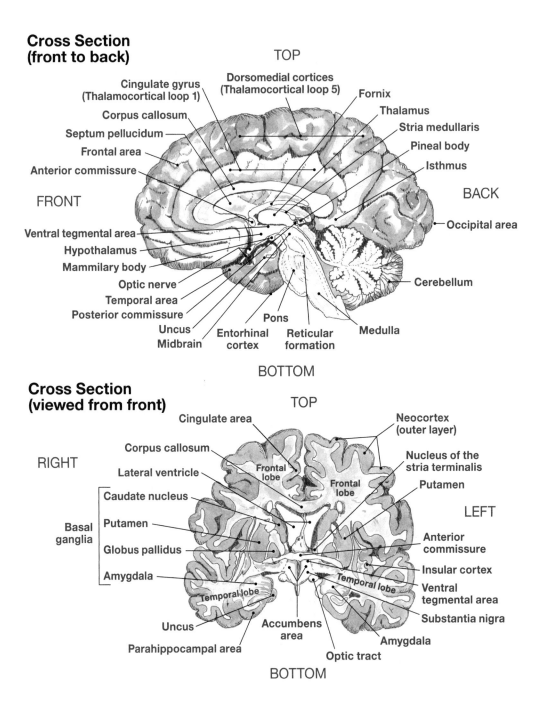

TOP

Cingulate gyrus (Thalamocortical loop 1)

Dorsomedial cortices (Thalamocortical loop 5)

Fornix

Thalamus

Corpus callosum

Stria medullaris

Septum pellucidum

Pineal body

Frontal area

Isthmus

Anterior commissure

FRONT

BACK

Occipital area

Ventral tegmental area

Hypothalamus

Mammilary body

Optic nerve

Temporal area

Cerebellum

Posterior commissure

Pons

Uncus

Entorhinal cortex

Reticular formation

Medulla

Midbrain

BOTTOM

Cross Section (viewed from front)

TOP

Cingulate area

Neocortex (outer layer)

Corpus callosum

Nucleus of the stria terminalis

RIGHT

Lateral ventricle

Frontal lobe

Frontal lobe

Putamen

Caudate nucleus

LEFT

Basal ganglia

Putamen

Anterior commissure

Globus pallidus

Insular cortex

Amygdala

Temporal lobe

Ventral tegmental area

Substantia nigra

Temporal lobe

Uncus

Accumbens area

Amygdala

Parahippocampal area

Optic tract

BOTTOM

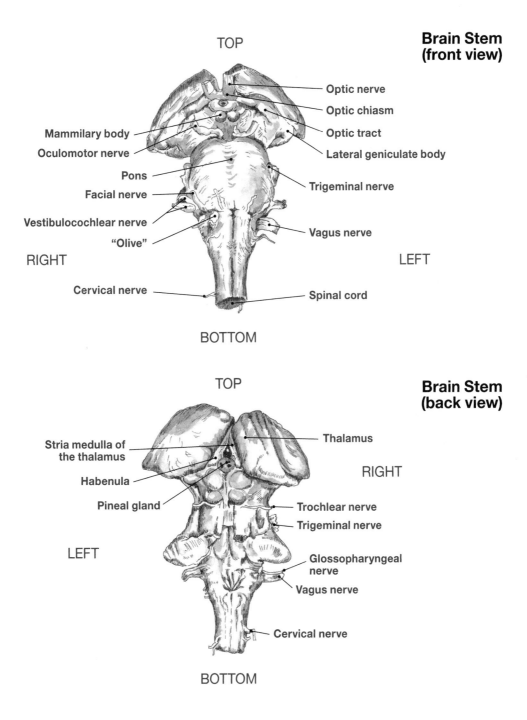

Brain Stem (front view)

TOP

Optic nerve

Optic chiasm

Mammilary body

Optic tract

Oculomotor nerve

Lateral geniculate body

Pons

Trigeminal nerve

Facial nerve

Vestibulocochlear nerve

"Olive"

Vagus nerve

RIGHT

LEFT

Cervical nerve

Spinal cord

BOTTOM

Brain Stem (back view)

TOP

Thalamus

Stria medulla of the thalamus

RIGHT

Habenula

Pineal gland

Trochlear nerve

Trigeminal nerve

LEFT

Glossopharyngeal nerve

Vagus nerve

Cervical nerve

BOTTOM

Sex and Gender Differences

Males	Females
Have better general math ability	Have better general verbal ability
Are better at spatial (3-D) reasoning	Are better in grammar and vocabulary
Are better at chess	Are better at foreign languages
Are better at reading maps	Have better fine-motor (hand-eye) coordination within personal space
Are better at reading blueprints	Have better sensory awareness
Have better vision in bright light (see less well in darkness)	Have better night vision (are more sensitive to bright light)
Have better perception in blue end of spectrum	Have better perception in red end of spectrum
Have more narrow vision (tunnel vision), but better depth and perspective	Have wide peripheral vision for "big picture"; have more receptor rods and cones
Have more stuttering and speech defects	Perceive sounds better
Enroll more in remedial reading (4:1)	Sing in tune more (6:1)
Take more interest in objects	Are more interested in people and faces
Talk and play more with inanimate objects	Read character and social cues better

Preschoolers:
- Average 36 seconds for goodbyes
- Occupy more play space
- Prefer blocks and building
- Build high structures
- Are indifferent to newcomers
- Accept others if they are useful
- Prefer stories of adventure
- Identify more with robbers
- Play more competitive games, such as tag
- Use dolls for "dive bombers"
- Are better visual-spatial learners

Preschoolers:
- Average 93 seconds for goodbyes
- Occupy less play space
- Prefer playing with living things
- Build long and low structures
- Greet newcomers
- Accept others if they are nice
- Prefer stories of romance
- Identify more with victims
- Play less competitive games, e.g., hopscotch
- Use dolls for family scenes
- Are better auditory learners

Males	Females
Require more space	Require less space
Have a better aural memory	Have a better visual memory
Are more easily angered	Are slower to anger
Talk later (usually by four years of age)	Talk earlier (99 percent are understandable by three years of age)
Are more sensitive to and prefer salty tastes	Are more sensitive to bitter tastes; prefer sweets and more subtle tastes
Have relatively insensitive skin	Have extremely sensitive skin

Appendix B

Males	Females
Have right hemisphere larger than left	Have left hemisphere larger than right
Favor right ear	Listen equally with both ears
Solve math problems nonverbally	Tend to talk while solving math problems
Handle multitasking more easily	Are less at ease with multitasking
Have better memory for relevant or organized information	Have better memory for names and faces and for random and irrelevant information
Use less eye contact	Use more eye contact
Have a shorter attention span	Have a longer attention span
Don't notice the smell of Exaltolide (a musklike odor)	Are especially sensitive to the smell of Exaltolide, especially before ovulation
Are more sensation-seeking	Are less sensation-seeking (but American females are more sensation-seeking than English females)
Are more frequently left-handed than females	Are more frequently right-handed than males
Use left hemisphere in spelling	Use both hemispheres in spelling
Have differentiated hemispheres: right for math and spatial skills, left for language	Have undifferentiated hemispheres
Have corpus callosum that shrinks about 20 percent by the age of 50 and is thinner relative to brain size	Have corpus callosum that is thicker relative to brain size and doesn't shrink over time
Have left hemisphere that shrinks with age	Have left hemisphere that shrinks symmetrically and minimally
Prefer greater distance from same-sex others	Are more comfortable than men are when they are physically close to same-sex others
Are three times more likely to be dyslexic or myopic	Are less likely to be dyslexic or myopic
React to pain slowly	React to pain more quickly; can tolerate long-term pain or discomfort better
Report feeling less pain	Report feeling more pain
Cope with pain less well	Cope with pain better
When left alone, tend to form organizations with hierarchical, dominant structures	When left alone, tend to form informal organizations with shifting power sources
Interrupt to introduce new topics or information	Interrupt to clarify or support

Source: Based on Anne Moir and David Jessel (1991), *Brain Sex: The Real Difference Between Men and Women,* New York: Carol Publishing/Lyle Stuart.

Evaluating Your Learning Practices

☐ 1. Do I design activities aimed at helping students remember what they are learning?

☐ 2. Do I periodically check with learners to see if they remember what they've learned in an earlier session?

☐ 3. Do I consciously assess my learning environment for stressors and attempt to keep it as stress-free as possible?

☐ 4. Do I provide learners with an opportunity to organize new learning into a form that is meaningful to them?

☐ 5. Do I provide learners with opportunities to rehearse or practice their newly acquired information as an aid in converting it to long-term memory?

☐ 6. Do I administer tests as a means to encourage learning?

☐ 7. Do I help learners to identify preexisting schemas that could help or hinder new learning?

☐ 8. Do I provide opportunities for learners to apply new learnings to situations that are meaningful to them?

☐ 9. Do I ensure that distractions are eliminated so learners can focus on the subject at hand?

☐ 10. Do I maintain appropriately high expectations for all my learners?

☐ 11. Do I expect and measure mastery on the part of all my learners?

☐ 12. Do I use a variety of methods and materials, resisting the temptation to use printed materials alone?

☐ 13. Do I communicate with learners ahead of time to prepare them for what they are about to learn?

☐ 14. Do I avoid trying to cover too many different lessons at one sitting by spacing lessons for maximum retention?

Appendix C

15. Do I allow and encourage both scheduled and spontaneous breaks?

16. Do I build follow-up for previous sessions into my lesson plans as well as pointing to follow-up for the current session?

17. Do I solicit learner feedback and respond appropriately?

18. Do I practice effective listening skills with learners?

19. Do I consciously do things to establish better rapport with learners?

20. Do I engage in specific activities at the beginning of each session that help learners feel at ease?

21. Do I vary my voice, posture, gestures, and location enough to prevent learners from habituating to me?

22. Do I consciously do things to enhance my prestige and respect with the learners?

23. Do I ensure that the learning environment has sufficient visual, tactile, and auditory stimulation to keep learners alert?

24. Do I provide opportunities for learners to get feedback from their peers?

25. Do I introduce new concepts with both an experiential-narrative approach and a rational-expository approach?

26. Do I assist my students in identifying how they can be more effective in their study strategies?

27. Do I allow students the opportunity to explain their answers?

28. After introducing new concepts or skills, do I allow time for them to settle in (with breaks, practice, review, and elaboration of familiar material) before introducing other new concepts or skills?

Brainstorming

Goals

1. To generate an extensive number of ideas or solutions to a problem by suspending criticism and evaluation

2. To develop skills in creative problem solving

Group Size

Any number of small groups composed of approximately six participants each

Materials

Newsprint and felt-tipped marker for each group

Procedure

1. The facilitator forms small groups of approximately six participants each. Each group selects a secretary.

2. The facilitator instructs each group to form a circle. He or she provides newsprint and a felt-tipped marker for each secretary and asks the secretary to record every idea generated by the group.

3. The facilitator states the following rules:

   a. There will be no criticism during the brainstorming phase.

   b. Farfetched ideas are encouraged because they may trigger more practical ideas.

   c. Many ideas are desirable. Go for quantity, not quality.

   d. Let others' ideas suggest new ideas to you; "piggyback" on their ideas.

4. The facilitator announces the topic, for example, "How could we reduce costs?" She or he tells the groups that they have five or ten minutes to generate ideas.

5. At the end of the generating phase, the facilitator tells the groups that the ban on criticism is over, then directs them to evaluate their ideas and to select the best ones.

Appendix D

Brainwriting

A procedure for generating ideas, brainwriting is a form of brainstorming. It is particularly useful in more introverted groups with less outward verbal energy.

Procedure

1. Each member of the group makes a list of ideas that address the issue at hand. The groups are directed to go for quantity, not quality, and to refrain from talking.

2. After five to ten minutes, the members pass their papers to the member on their left. They then read the items on their new list and allow these items to "suggest" new items, which are added to the list.

3. This continues until each member has had an opportunity to read and add ideas to each of the other lists.

4. The lists are circulated and some voting system is used to evaluate the ideas, for example, one to five stars. The scores are tallied and the top 10 or so ideas are written on the board for everyone to see. The group continues to evaluate the ideas, either by consensus or by a rational decision analysis process, such as the Five-Step Rational Decision Analysis (Plunkett and Hale, 1982; Kepner and Tregoe, 1981) or the Precedence Chart (Saaty, 1982).

Appendix E

Big Five Feedback Form

Name: Date:

Need for Stability (N) Scale	*Resilient*	*Responsive*	*Reactive*	Need for Stability (N) Scale
◄ 20 25 30 35 40	45 50 55		60 65 70 75 80 ►	

Positive descriptors: Secure, calm, Rock of Gibraltar, concentrating, steady, unflappable, stress-free

Negative descriptors: Lethargic, laid-back, unresponsive, unaware, insensitive, tunnel-visioned

Positive descriptors: Alert, aware, empathetic, expressive, energetic

Negative descriptors: Tense, high-strung, depressed, neurotic, restless

Extraversion (E) Scale	*Introvert*	*Ambivert*	*Extravert*	Extraversion (E) Scale
◄ 20 25 30 35 40	45 50 55		60 65 70 75 80 ►	

Positive descriptors: Private, reserved, serious, works alone, self-minimizing, prefers writing

Negative descriptors: Reclusive, fearful, submissive, retreating, eccentric, loner

Positive descriptors: Conversational, energetic, assertive, confident, happy, optimistic, sociable

Negative descriptors: Outspoken, talkative, overbearing, aggressive, exhibitionistic, heedless, shallow

Originality (O) Scale	*Preserver*	*Moderate*	*Explorer*	Originality (O) Scale
◄ 20 25 30 35 40	45 50 55		60 65 70 75 80 ►	

Positive descriptors: Seeks depth, practical, expert knowledge, down-to-earth, efficient, traditional, practice until perfect, conservative

Negative descriptors: Narrowness, no big picture, misses new opportunities, lacks perspective, set in ways, closed to new experiences, rigid

Positive descriptors: Broad interests, curious, likes novelty and variety, chases ideas and theory, imaginative, liberal, understands big picture

Negative descriptors: Dabbler, amateur, easily bored, impractical, head in clouds, lacks detail, lives in fantasy

Accommodation (A) Scale	*Challenger*	*Negotiator*	*Adapter*	Accommodation (A) Scale
◄ 20 25 30 35 40	45 50 55		60 65 70 75 80 ►	

Positive descriptors: Independent, skeptical, direct, self-interested, competitive, questioning

Negative descriptors: Rejecting, hostile, rude, self-centered, combative, argumentative

Positive descriptors: Friendly, tolerant, trusting, team player, considerate, accepting

Negative descriptors: Syrupy, spineless, gullible, dependent, doormat, unprincipled, conflict averse

Consolidation (C) Scale	*Flexible*	*Balanced*	*Focused*	Consolidation (C) Scale
◄ 20 25 30 35 40	45 50 55		60 65 70 75 80 ►	

Positive descriptors: Relaxed, spontaneous, open-ended, multitasking, experimental, roles not goals, accepts uncertainty

Negative descriptors: Lackadaisical, quitter, indecisive, chaotic, irresponsible, nonproductive, permissive, procrastinator

Positive descriptors: Industrious, dependable, will to achieve, productive, organized, decisive, persevering, driven

Negative descriptors: Overbearing, compulsive, workaholic, suppressed, meticulous, stubborn

Appendix F

Developing the Five Dimensions

Need for Stability (N)

To Increase	*To Decrease*
Use structured exercise (such as force-field analysis and itemized response) to communicate negative feelings.	Perform aerobic exercise within four hours of an event in which calmness is particularly important.
Engage in competitive sports or other competitive activities (such as chess) with someone you have a reasonable chance of beating (or use an appropriate handicap).	Take aerobic exercise soon after a stressful episode to trigger parasympathetic arousal.
When you are aware of your body beginning to react internally to your thoughts and feelings (rapid heart rate, queasy stomach, perspiration, and so on), communicate these changes to a significant other or partner and identify their cause and meaning, or write a note or journal entry about them.	Plan to consume your daily allowance of fats and simple carbohydrates after particularly stressful episodes.
	Refer to the list of stress relievers in topic 36.1.
	Read from the wide literature available on the subject of mental self-control, such as Epictetus's *Enchiridion* and works by the Stoic philosophers and Norman Cousins.
Use caffeine in some form as a way to increase general arousal.	If necessary, reduce or eliminate sources of stress by examining bad Big Five fits in your marriage or job.
Minimize the consumption of fats and simple carbohydrates for four hours before events in which the identification and expression of feelings is important.	Read Redford Williams's *Trusting Heart* (more technical) and *Anger Kills* (which he wrote with his wife, and which is more application-oriented, with specific suggestions on how to get a handle on your hostility). They also conduct a public workshop; he teaches at Duke University Medical School.
Read novels, biographies, or poetry that express negative emotion and emulate appropriate models.	
Join a drama or theater group.	
Participate in physical activities that emphasize expression, such as sports, music, dance, or landscaping.	Read chapter 35, which discusses the emotions.
	The combination of antidepressant drugs and psychotherapy works effectively to reduce depression.
Find and use support groups, either on the Internet or in the community, that explore a particular aspect of Need for Stability: how to express your anger, how to show your concern, and so on.	Katharina Dalton has found success in treating the mood swings of premenstrual tension by helping patients maintain optimum blood sugar levels by periodically snacking throughout the day.
Use a journal or diary as a means of identifying, describing, and exploring your internal feelings.	Try taking 10-minute "brief" walks as an antidote for various kinds of stress: sadness, anger, and anxiety.
Practice observing nonverbal behavior and other environmental cues to the negative emotions of others.	Try self-hypnosis or biofeedback.
Give explicit direction and permission to others so that they may encourage you to express feelings that they perceive you are holding back.	

Appendix G

Extraversion (E)

To Increase	To Decrease
Take a training seminar on assertiveness skills (broken-record technique, smoke screens, I-messages).	Keep a journal or diary as a means of developing your writing habit.
Read from the assertiveness-training literature.	Develop the habit of writing letters to your family or customers or letters of recognition to employees.
Read and digest Martin Seligman's *Learned Optimism* as a way to use explanatory style as a tool for developing more positive emotional responses.	Schedule a daily time for reading and writing.
Read Maureen Guirdham's *Interpersonal Skills at Work* (1995); it is a bit more academic than some approaches but provides some helpful models for the more thoughtful reader.	Schedule a few hours daily (for example, from 8:00 to 10:00 A.M.) during which you take no calls or visits and essentially work behind closed doors. Have a co-worker protect this time by fending off would-be invaders!
Read Stephen P. Robbins's *Training in Interpersonal Skills* (1996); it contains self-assessment exercises, key concepts, and skill development methods.	Get a laptop computer and start a computer-based project, such as writing a biography of a family member, developing a database on a particular topic, or organizing your memoirs.

Originality (O)

To Increase	To Decrease
Read chapters 27–29, which deal with the nature of creativity and how to develop it.	Develop a reward system that discourages unfocused exploration and encourages people to increase knowledge and expertise in a more restricted area.
Attend one of the many creativity workshops available, such as Charleen Swansea's "MindWorks."	Develop short-term lists.
Become familiar with the works of E. Paul Torrance (for example, Torrance, 1974).	Prepare a feedback system for short-term projects.
Learn the Synectics problem-solving technique.	Do volunteer work with groups—for example, Habitat for Humanity—that include people who are more practical and down-to-earth than you.
Practice brainstorming with two or three others.	
Join groups or activities that have values different from yours.	Attend Stephen Covey's seminars to bring reality into the planning.
Ask for special projects that focus on the future.	Limit the number of projects or interests you have so that you can prioritize them and begin to reach a sense of closure.
Develop the habit of playing "What If . . . ?"	

Accommodation (A)

To Increase	*To Decrease*
Read books on negotiation skills, such as *Getting to Yes: Negotiating Agreement Without Giving In* (R. Fisher and W. Ury, 1991).	Read *Women's Ways of Knowing* (Belenky, Clinchy, Goldberger, and Tarule, 1997).
Find a role model to serve as your coach or mentor and give ongoing feedback.	Take assertiveness training courses or read books on the subject.
Practice using neutral, open-ended questions rather than declarative statements.	Find a coach who is moderately less accommodating than you—that is, a negotiator.
Identify the more abrasive words that you use and practice substituting less abrasive ones.	Learn to recognize early on when you are losing control of the momentum, then reassert yourself and state what you need.
Resist shooting the messenger.	Practice assertive behaviors in nonthreatening, safe situations—for example, around children or strangers.
Pull back; redirect your energy by putting it in writing.	Read books such as R. Fisher and W. Ury's *Getting to Yes* (1991) or attend seminars on negotiation skills.
Develop the ability to read the body language of others; this will help you to detect when you've intimidated someone who is unable to respond verbally.	Read and discuss Sisela Bok's *Lying* (1979).
Find someone to give you feedback on how you affect others who are important to you.	Whenever you hear people tell you what's important to them, automatically think to yourself: "Well, what's important to me in this situation is. . . ." When what's important to you is clear, express it to the others.
Practice listening without interrupting until the speaker has clearly finished. Read Tony Hillerman's novel *Coyote Waits* for the importance of not interrupting in Navajo culture.	Intentionally select partners you can beat, whether at sports, cards, or business. Gradually increase your skill level and your competition.
Learn and practice the "talking stick" listening exercise. The talking stick is a Native American tradition in which some object, such as a feather or a pipe, is designated as the talking stick, and only the person holding the stick may talk. Others cannot talk until they have the stick in hand.	

Consolidation (C)

To Increase	*To Decrease*
Identify an appropriate time management system (also called a personal organizer), such as the Franklin or the Covey, and learn how to use it and adhere to it.	Read Bryan Robinson's *Work Addiction* (1989).
	Have your child call you at the office once a day and have a good chat.
Set attainable goals for yourself and establish a reward system for attaining those goals.	Call a friend and chat with no specific agenda in mind.
Read Stephen Covey's *Seven Habits of Highly Effective People* and implement the suggestions; attend one of his workshops.	Reprioritize your values and activities to provide for greater balance between work and leisure.
Engage in competitive activities or sports with someone you have a reasonable chance of beating.	Set a time to go home and make the next day's "to-do" list before going home.
	Perform relaxation exercises 14 minutes each day.
Ask a partner to regularly help you to set priorities and hold you accountable for sticking to them.	Increase the portion of your responsibilities that you can delegate both at home and at work.

Compensating for the Five Dimensions

Need for Stability (N)

If You Think You're Too High	*If You Think You're Too Low*
Invite significant others or co-workers to sit down with you after an outburst and rethink the outcome of the outburst.	Schedule a time to offer feedback to people whose relationship with you is particularly important, so that they'll know better where they stand in relation to you.
Negotiate with your team or partner to legitimize the value of your giving constructive criticism that comes naturally.	Invite members of your team or family who are high in Need for Stability to play the role of moderate opposer.
If you feel you are too self-conscious, try going in disguise to settings in which you would otherwise be uncomfortable.	Solicit the observations and feedback of more reactive people who can provide an insight into your blind side.

Extraversion (E)

If You Think You're Too High	*If You Think You're Too Low*
Use the round-robin technique and only say one thing per turn.	Delegate the responsibility for leading meetings to someone who is more extraverted than you.
Allow others to talk first.	Station yourself near food and drink.
Time yourself so that you talk no longer in a group than the total time divided by the number of people (for example, in a half-hour meeting of six people, talk no more than five minutes).	Think of specific things to say or questions to ask ahead of time.
	To get comfortable, find someone you know right away.
If it has been said, don't say it again.	Get with an Extravert, and keep the group small.
Don't expect everyone close to you to have your same need for stimulation; find appropriate partners.	Make it a point to speak with a minimum number of people.
	Don't speak first; get your thoughts organized and even prepare notes.
	Commit to having lunch with someone weekly.

Appendix H

Originality (O)

If You Think You're Too High	*If You Think You're Too Low*
Frequently ask others to evaluate your current "to-do" list as an aid in focusing on the areas with maximum benefit to your goals.	Bounce ideas off a person who is high in Originality.
	Delegate idea generation to those who are higher in Originality.

Accommodation (A)

If You Think You're Too High	*If You Think You're Too Low*
Avoid surrounding yourself with Challengers; you'll end up either a doormat or a second-class citizen.	Practice asking others something like "What are three things you don't like about this plan?"
Delegate the leader role to others.	Occasionally eliminate yourself from decision making and abide by the group's decision.
Invite others to raise questions.	Choose Negotiators as leaders.

Consolidation (C)

If You Think You're Too High	*If You Think You're Too Low*
Have a child call you at the office to remind you to go home.	Align yourself with a job or other setting that does not require ambition or responsibility.
Engage in planning to ensure maximum delegation: examine everything on your list and identify what others can or should do; then delegate tasks (or train or orient others and then delegate).	Find crutches for organizing, such as having a secretary, assistant, or computer remind you to focus on a schedule or other priorities.
Hire extra help for home or office.	Avoid being around too many people of either extreme in Consolidation.
Commit to regular (noncompetitive) aerobic exercise.	

Rapport and Influence Strategies

Trait	Most Effective Tactics for People with This Trait
Resilient (Low N)	Use a setting that is fresh, with appropriate background stimulation (for example, a park). Avoid excessive distances (for example, take the closer chair). Use logic and reasonableness. Make your limits clear. Do not interrupt Resilients. Use a problem-solving method or structure. Ask how Resilients see the alternatives; build on mutual ones.
Reactive (High N)	Minimize distractions (noise, music, activity). Maximize the distance between you; avoid the closer chair. Appeal to Reactives' pride in their organization or family. Take Reactives' stress seriously but not personally. Minimize your reliance on logic and reasonableness. Emphasize what's in it for them. Show the appropriate emotion to support your position. Illustrate that what you want will minimize their worry.
Introvert (Low E)	Rely on memos, letters, and e-mail. Try to match Introverts when their energy level is lower than yours. Don't rush Introverts; give them time to readjust. Allow or even initiate a move toward greater privacy. Resist your urge to draw other people in. Use ample visual cues. Use nonphysical rewards (for example, an honorary degree). Allow time for Introverts to read and have moments of silence. Don't get too close physically. Appeal to an Introvert's uniqueness as a person. Avoid sexual and aggressive humor; use subtlety. Remind Introverts of the names of things. Ensure that they don't become overstimulated. Give Introverts written material to review before meetings.
Extravert (High E)	Go out for a meal. Feel free to telephone. Meet with two or more people at a time. Don't assume that Extraverts want privacy (for example, don't assume that they would like to close their door during a conference). Hold frequent face-to-face meetings. Enjoy small talk if Extraverts initiate it. Try to match Extraverts' high energy in a genuine way (if they stand, you stand; if they walk, you walk). Appeal to an Extravert's sense of responsibility. Use the promise of physical rewards (sports tickets, dinner certificates).

Appendix I

Preserver *(Low O)*	Emphasize the tried-and-true. Walk Preservers through your proposal or idea step-by-step (use flowcharts). Play up to the Preserver's need to compete and win. Don't waste a Preserver's time; be specific and give examples. Emphasize the simple and easy-to-use aspects of your proposal or idea. Refer to established companies who have used your product, service, or idea. Emphasize the positive impact on efficiency.	Use mainstream humor, but in general be serious. Avoid appealing to novelty and curiosity. Avoid a complex vocabulary that is not common to a Preserver's specialty. Appeal to established, traditional values. Emphasize conformity with policies and procedures. Appeal to a Preserver's distrust of newfangled notions. Emphasize immediate returns and the payoff.
Explorer *(High O)*	Do not oversimplify. Refer to the individuals who developed the idea. Emphasize the uniqueness of the idea or product. Use metaphors to describe it. Let Explorers take credit where possible. Appreciate an Explorer's unusual sense of humor. Refer to the theory behind the application.	Appeal to an Explorer's need to innovate. Avoid concentrating on details (give the big picture first). Ask questions about an Explorer's opinions and ideas. Get agreement on specifics, yet be prepared for Explorers to change their mind. Appeal to their curiosity; use reason and logic. Take your time.
Challenger *(Low A)*	Push for closure on the basis of bottom-line results. Emphasize the logical tightness of your position. Be sure to do what you say you will. Have alternatives drawn up with plans for each.	Encourage Challengers' criticisms and build on their skepticism. Build on their need to win and to be right. Avoid references to consideration for others. Don't take apparent belligerence personally; be flexible.
Adapter *(High A)*	Emphasize how specific groups of people will react. Show how your agenda relates to human values. Push for closure on the basis of the impact on people. Inquire about an Adapter's family, hobbies, and so on. Emphasize your trustworthiness.	Emphasize the ethical rightness of your proposal. Take time to develop a relationship. Adapters tend to defer; hence, ask questions that draw them out. Emphasize how your proposal will help others. Elicit sympathy and empathy.

Flexible (Low C)	Help Flexibles identify what they need to make a decision. Emphasize your flexibility. Summarize the discussion frequently. Be patient if Flexibles make you wait or make you late. Permit yourself to be spontaneous; don't rush them.	Don't insist on your agenda when they want to veer from it. Help Flexibles manage their time and priorities. Be willing to wander off in new and different directions. Emphasize the pleasurable aspects of your position. Appeal to a Flexible's role as a consultant and adviser.
Focused (High C)	Be sure to arrive on time or somewhat early. Give plenty of advance warning about changes of plan. Relate to Focused people's good health and record of achievement; identify with their exercise of choice. To avoid a premature decision against your position, agree on steps for follow-up or future meeting dates.	Set goals and a point-by-point agenda for the meeting. Notify a Focused person if you're going to be late. Emphasize good work ethics. Be sensitive to Focused people's need and respect for structure. Use logic, with clearly identified priorities and goals. Emphasize that they are in control.

Evaluating the Intelligence of a Job Candidate

1. Does this person have the ability to administer a project from beginning to end in compliance with project requirements (cost, time, quality, and so on)?

   a. Interview evidence:

   b. Reference evidence:

2. Does this person have the ability to scan relevant resources and obtain accurate, current, relevant, and effective information to use in solving problems? Include habits and attitudes toward reading (using the library, periodicals, books, and so on), using Internet "search engines," and asking questions (particularly the habit of asking open-ended questions).

   a. Interview evidence:

   b. Reference evidence:

3. Does this person show flexibility in selecting problem-solving strategies? Through interviews or paper-and-pencil tests, determine the level of rigidity in choosing to alter self, others, or the situation in solving problems.

   a. Interview evidence:

   b. Reference evidence:

   c. Test evidence (Tacit Knowledge Inventory, Hersey-Blanchard Situational Leadership Inventory, or other measures of flexibility or rigidity found in multidimensional instruments):

4. Does this person have the ability to plan a sequence of events in a logical, effective manner?

   a. Interview evidence (ask about time management practices, use of tickle files, and use of various planning techniques; look at the individual's "calendars," such as daily agendas):

   b. Reference evidence:

   c. In-basket exercise (this shows the ability to prioritize a diverse set of documents):

5. Does this person have the ability to be appropriately creative?

   a. Interview evidence:

   b. Reference evidence:

   c. Test evidence (using multidimensional or single-dimension tests):

6. Does this person have the ability to execute through fluent use of words, numbers, and other tools?

   a. Test evidence (from the Wunderlich Personnel Test or some other similar test):

   b. Artifactual evidence (sample reports, drawings, and so on):

   c. Interview evidence (the ability to grasp complex patterns and concepts presented in organizational reports, charts, spreadsheets, and so on):

Appendix J

Personal Checklist for Intelligent Behaviors

This self-evaluation is based on Robert Sternberg's theory of intelligence presented in chapter 34. More intelligent people will answer affirmatively to many of the items in all of the sections. Consider increasing your "intelligent behavior" repertoire in any section in which you check few or no items.

1. Administrative Behaviors

☐ a. Do I keep a prioritized "to-do" list?

☐ b. Do I use a tickler file?

☐ c. Do I take time to evaluate my progress toward goals?

☐ d. Do I regularly solicit feedback from others on how I'm doing?

☐ e. Am I aware of my weaknesses, and do I delegate to compensate for them?

☐ f. Do I consciously devote resources to developing in areas that need improvement?

☐ g. Do I keep myself in good condition and full of energy?

2. Research Behaviors

☐ a. Do I regularly read periodicals that are relevant to my goals?

☐ b. Do I regularly read sections of the newspaper that are relevant to my goals?

☐ c. Do I scan the television schedules (especially of public or educational stations) for programs of value to my goals, and then either view them or tape them for future viewing?

☐ d. Do I visit and use one or more libraries regularly?

☐ e. Do I call reference librarians with my questions, and do I use the research capabilities of the Internet?

☐ f. Do I practice the art of asking open-ended questions to all the significant people in my life?

☐ g. Do I attend seminars and courses to update my knowledge and skills?

3. Problem-Solving Behaviors

Altering self

☐ a. Do I learn new skills or bodies of knowledge?

☐ b. Do I consciously try to improve old skills or bodies of knowledge?

☐ c. Do I discontinue ineffective habits?

☐ d. Do I consult a therapist or counselor when the need arises?

☐ e. Do I ask for feedback from the significant people in my life, then act on it by changing my behavior or habits when appropriate?

Altering others

☐ a. Am I a consistently good listener?

☐ b. Do I take the time to train others when they need training?

☐ c. Do I consciously make an effort to be a helper when others have problems?

☐ d. Do I offer sufficient praise and encouragement to others?

Appendix K

☐   e.   Do I take the time to give nonblameful, constructive criticism when it is needed? Do I allow time to discuss corrective measures?

☐   f.   When conflict arises, do I take the time to discuss its causes and to explore possible solutions?

Altering the situation

☐   a.   Do I know when to call it quits?

☐   b.   Can I let go of existing ways of doing things and explore new, improved designs or processes?

☐   c.   Do I regularly observe others' ways of accomplishing tasks similar to mine with an eye out for how I might change my situation for the better?

4. Planning Behaviors

☐   a.   Do I take the time to map out complex projects using tools such as timelines, PERT charts, or Gantt charts?

☐   b.   Do I take the time to test my project design or outline before actually implementing it by using potential problem analysis (Kepner and Tregoe, 1981), visualization techniques, simulations, modeling, and other tools?

☐   c.   Do I start a project with the end in mind and then determine the best way to get there?

5. Creativity Behaviors

☐   a.   Do I practice the habit of seeing old patterns in new ways (for example, seeing the half-empty glass as half-full, or letting go of old perceptual sets)?

☐   b.   Do I occasionally let go of old skills or ways of doing things and explore new, different, and possibly improved ways?

☐   c.   Do I ask W. Edwards Deming's question: "What can I do to improve, today?"

☐   d.   Do I tolerate ambiguity long enough to explore effective resolutions? (Or do I jump to find answers?)

☐   e.   Do I enjoy trying to understand complex situations?

☐   f.   Can I keep my options open long enough to find the best one?

☐   g.   Can I suspend judgment while exploring ideas?

☐   h.   Do I resist peer and social pressure to conform?

6. Execution Behaviors

☐   a.   Do I look up words when I don't know them?

☐   b.   Do I work puzzles such as crossword puzzles and math riddles?

☐   c.   Do I take pride in having my presentations show careful crafting?

☐   d.   Do I regularly edit my work for accuracy, completeness, and effectiveness?

☐   e.   Do I watch for feedback during my presentations and alter my behavior according to the feedback?

☐   f.   Do I ask for feedback after my presentations and incorporate suggestions into future presentations?

☐   g.   In general, am I genuinely interested in improving myself in most facets of my being?

My Shapers: A Personality Infrastructure Template

Elements	Concerns*	Actions
Traits: For each of the 24 pairs of opposite traits below, indicate whether you see yourself as more towards one or the other, or more balanced (in the middle). Then: • If you feel your level on the trait pair matches the current demands on you, both professionally and personally, simply check the box at the left. • If you feel your level on the trait pair is a source of concern for you, either professionally or personally, circle the trait pair, then enter an explanation in the "concerns" column according to the instructions at the top of the column.	For each trait pair that causes you concern (e.g., having an active nature but a sedentary job), write an "actual/ideal" statement that identifies the way things are and the way you'd like them to be.	For each concern, sketch out a possible action plan that would reduce or eliminate the concern (e.g., getting a "stand-up desk").
☐　　　　Calm • • • • • Worrying		
☐　　Controlled • • • • • Temper		
☐　　Optimistic • • • • • Pessimistic		
☐　　　Resilient • • • • • Stopped by stress		
☐　　　　Cool • • • • • Warm		
☐　　　Solitary • • • • • Gregarious		
☐　　Sedentary • • • • • Active		
☐　Independent • • • • • Taking charge		
☐　　Skeptical • • • • • Trusting		
☐　　　　Blunt • • • • • Tactful		
☐　　　Literal • • • • • Imaginative		
☐ Prefer simplicity • • • • • Prefer complexity		
☐ Prefer the familiar • • • • • Prefer the different		
☐　　　　Detail • • • • • Big picture		
☐　Serving self • • • • • Serving others		
☐　　Compete • • • • • Cooperate		
☐　　　Proud • • • • • Humble		
☐　　Assertive • • • • • Reserved		
☐　　Out front • • • • • Reticent		
☐ Casual standards • • • • • Perfectionist		
☐ Casually arrayed • • • • • Organized		
☐　　Content • • • • • Ambitious		
☐　Distractible • • • • • Concentrating		
☐ Spontaneous • • • • • Methodical		

* Traits may be a source of concern for you because of many factors. For example:
• If your job or private life requires you to use a trait more often than you feel comfortable using it, then you may feel stressed, worried, resentful, bored, or frustrated.
• If your job or personal life fails to take advantage of a trait that is particularly pleasing or natural for you, then you will probably feel a longing to exercise that trait.

Appendix L

Elements	Concerns*	Actions
Abilities: For each of the 15 mental abilities or talents listed below, indicate how you perceive your level of proficiency. Then: • If you feel your level on the ability matches the current demands on you, both professionally and personally, simply check the box at the left. • If you feel your level on the ability is a source of concern for you, either professionally or personally, circle the ability, then enter an explanation in the "concerns" column according to the instructions at the top of the column.	For each ability that causes you concern (e.g., having weak math skills in a job requiring numerical analysis), write an "actual/ideal" statement that identifies the way things are and the way you'd like them to be.	For each concern, sketch out a possible action plan that would reduce or eliminate the concern (e.g., find a math "help desk").
☐ Verbal Weak • • • • • Strong		
☐ Math/logic Weak • • • • • Strong		
☐ Visual/spatial Weak • • • • • Strong		
☐ Kinesthetic Weak • • • • • Strong		
☐ Auditory/musical Weak • • • • • Strong		
☐ Natural observer Weak • • • • • Strong		
☐ Interpersonal Weak • • • • • Strong		
☐ Intrapersonal Weak • • • • • Strong		
☐ Short-term memory Weak • • • • • Strong		
☐ Long-term memory Weak • • • • • Strong		
☐ Critical thinking Weak • • • • • Strong		
☐ Learning from context Weak • • • • • Strong		
☐ Learning curve Weak • • • • • Strong		
☐ Vocabulary Weak • • • • • Strong		
☐ Problem solving Weak • • • • • Strong		

* Abilities may be a source of concern for you because of many factors. For example:

• If your job or private life requires you to use an ability at a proficiency level greater than you currently possess, then you may feel stressed, worried, resentful, or frustrated.

• If your job or personal life fails to take advantage of an ability you are particularly strong at, then you will probably feel a longing to exercise that ability, or you may feel bored.

Elements	Concerns	Actions
Physical Attributes: For each of the 31 physical attributes listed below: • If you feel the attribute is benign and causes you no concern, simply check the box to the left. • If you feel the attribute is a cause of concern, either because your level of the attribute conflicts with current expectations of you or because your current situation fails to use the attribute in a way that is satisfying to you, circle the attribute, then enter an explanation in the "concerns" column according to the instructions at the top of the column.	For each physical attribute that causes you concern (e.g., having high blood pressure in a stressful job or relationship), write an "actual/ideal" statement that identifies the way things are and the way you'd like them to be.	For each concern, sketch out a possible action plan that would reduce or eliminate the concern (e.g., medication, exercise, diet change).
☐ Age		
☐ Allergies		
☐ Auditory sensitivity		
☐ Beauty		
☐ Blood pressure		
☐ Color blindness		
☐ Color sensitivity		
☐ Dehydration proneness		
☐ Digestion characteristics		
☐ Dizziness proneness		
☐ Ethnicity		
☐ Finger dexterity		
☐ Foot dexterity		
☐ Gender		
☐ Hand-eye coordination		
☐ Height		
☐ Joints (back, knees, wrist, elbow, etc.)		
☐ Metabolic rate		
☐ Odor sensitivity		
☐ Sense of balance		
☐ Sensitivity to motion (speed, swinging, etc.)		
☐ Sensitivity to sun		
☐ Sensitivity to temperature		
☐ Sexuality/libido		
☐ Sleep requirements		
☐ Strength		
☐ Tactile sensitivity		
☐ Taste sensitivity		
☐ Visual acuity		
☐ Visual sensitivity		
☐ Weight		

Elements	Concerns & Actions
Memories: For each of the 36 sources of memory below: • If you have a strong positive memory associated with the source, briefly summarize or identify the memory in the adjacent column; or • If you have a strong negative memory associated with the source, make notes that identify it. Circle each memory that reflects a feeling or experience you would like to recapture or in some way incorporate into your current life, as well as those you wish to take special precautions to avoid.	For each memory you would like to avoid or recapture (e.g., winning a national award, climbing Mt. Kilimanjaro, flubbing a major presentation), identify how you might avoid or recapture it (e.g., enter a national competition, descend Grand Canyon, take a presentation skills seminar).

Early childhood	
Kindergarten	
Elementary school	
Middle/junior high school	
High school	
Family life	
College years	
Graduate school	
Military service	
Religious experiences	
Summer activities	
Part-time jobs	
Extracurricular activities	
Early dating	
Awards and achievements	
Volunteer service	
Travel	
Vacation experiences	
Violent episodes	
Closest friends	
Enemies	
Sources of anger	
Most intense loves	
Biggest losses	
1st Job	
2nd Job	
3rd Job	
4th Job	
5th Job	
Other jobs	
Current job	
Unfulfilled goals	
Sources of pride	
Sources of envy	
Sources of shame	
Most admired persons	

Elements	Concerns & Actions
Values: For each of the 22 values listed below: • Indicate the values that are most important to you by checking the box to the far left. • Indicate your five most important values by checking the box to the near left. • In the first column to the right, indicate whether you have acted on that value recently to the degree you would have liked (e.g., "More one-on-one time with my kids," "More involvement with a nonprofit board").	For each value area in which you would like to increase your activity, indicate in the space below some specific actions you might take to accomplish that (e.g., "Take my older son on a camping trip," "Offer to raise funds for my nonprofit board").

☐ ☐	Achievement		
☐ ☐	Aesthetics		
☐ ☐	Affiliation		
☐ ☐	Charity		
☐ ☐	Creativity		
☐ ☐	Entertainment		
☐ ☐	Escape		
☐ ☐	Family		
☐ ☐	Health		
☐ ☐	Hedonism		
☐ ☐	Learning		
☐ ☐	Maintenance		
☐ ☐	Politics		
☐ ☐	Position/status		
☐ ☐	Power		
☐ ☐	Professional development		
☐ ☐	Romance		
☐ ☐	Safety		
☐ ☐	Security		
☐ ☐	Spirituality		
☐ ☐	Sports/exercise		
☐ ☐	Wealth		

Elements	Concerns & Actions
Roles: In each of our lives, we must fulfill many different roles and wear many different hats. Below we list some of the more common roles. After reviewing this list, add any other roles that you fulfill in your own life. Then: • Circle the roles that are most important to you. • In the first column to the right, indicate whether you would like to do more, less, or about the same amount of activity in that role in the future, compared with recent history (e.g., "More time as a parent," "Less time as a leader").	For each role you would like to increase or decrease your involvement with, suggest specific ways you might accomplish this (e.g., "Volunteer to help with sports team," "Delegate more work to subordinates").

Artist	
Babysitter	
Caregiver	
Clerk	
Counselor	
Entertainer	
Fixer/maintainer	
Flunky	
Follower	
Friend	
Grandparent	
Healer	
Host	
Learner	
Manager	
Neighbor	
Parent	
Peacemaker	
Presenter	
Producer	
Researcher	
Sibling	
Spouse/lover	
Teacher	
Technician	
Traveler	
Volunteer	
Writer	
Other Roles:	

Definitions

Acetylcholine. A neurotransmitter released in the neuron that is essential to the health of the neuronal membrane itself and to learning and memory; it is derived from fat in the diet.

ACTH (adrenocorticotropic hormone). Also known as corticotropin, ACTH stimulates the adrenal cortex to secrete glucocorticoids such as cortisol in times of stress. It is secreted by the pituitary gland in reaction to corticotropin-releasing hormone from the hypothalamus.

Action potential. An electrical charge in response to a stimulus that is strong enough to result in the release of neurotransmitters at the synapse; a basic measure of neural activity. See also Latency; Amplitude.

Adrenaline. See Epinephrine.

Adrenocorticotropic hormone. See ACTH.

Agonist. A drug that mimics (that is, can occupy the same receptor sites as and send the same signals as) a particular neurotransmitter (for example, sumatriptan is an agonist for serotonin); the opposite of an antagonist.

Amino acids. This family of 20 major compounds (each containing one carboxyl molecule BCOOH) comprises the alphabet of life. Various combinations of amino acids form "peptide chains." Chains of fewer than about one hundred amino acids are peptides. Chains of more than 100 but fewer than about 200 are polypeptides. Proteins are peptide chains comprised of some 200 or more amino acids. The amino acids are

Cystine	L-histidine	L-serine
DL-alanine	L-hydroxyprolin	L-tryptophan
Glycine	L-isoleucine	L-tyrosine
L-arginine	L-leucine	L-valine
L-asparagine	L-lysine	Methionine
L-aspartic acid	L-phenylalanine	Threonine
L-glutamic acid	L-proline	

Amplitude. The height of the wave resulting from measuring action potential; a measure of the amount of neural resources brought to bear on a particular stimulus. See also Latency.

Androgens. The family of male sex hormones (and drugs), the most familiar of which is testosterone; their level in the body is associated with degree of male gender characteristics, from body hair to aggression. It is present in both males and females but is usually higher in males.

Antagonist. A drug that blocks the receptor site for a particular neurotransmitter. The opposite of an agonist.

Antioxidant. A natural chemical with the capability for neutralizing free radicals, such as vitamins A, B-1, B-5, B-6, C, E, and beta-carotene; selenium and zinc; and uric acid.

Arousal. The level of activity of a bodily system: high limbic arousal indicates a rapid pulse, for example, and low limbic arousal suggests a far slower pulse. The absence of arousal is associated with sleep.

Astrocytes. Cells occupying space between neurons and non-neuronal matter; provide both a structural and functional purpose, and are suspected to have a more significant role in such disorders as Alzheimer's and Parkinson's than has traditionally been suspected. Though astrocytes are ten times more abundant than neurons, they have been less studied.

Attention. The capacity to focus the senses on a specific stimulus source; it is only possible to focus on one stimulus source at a time. When we appear to be focusing on two sources simultaneously (for example, using a car phone and driving), we are actually alternating attention. Attempting to focus on more than one stimulus source increases error proneness, unless one of the perceptual activities is completely routinized (we can suck a mint and drive at the same time).

Attributional style. The manner in which an individual attributes the causes of success or failure; it is usually described as either external (the causes are outside the individual, such as luck or sour grapes) or internal (the causes are inside the individual, such as hard work or talent). Also called explanatory style and locus of control.

Automatic behavior. See Automatization.

Automation. See Automatization.

Automatization. The process by which a new learning becomes automatic or routine; it refers to a skill or behavior that requires intense attentional focus when it is first learned but eventually demands little or no attentional focus, as in learning to tie one's shoes. Also called automation and automization.

Automatizer. Said of a person who can perform routine and repetitive activities for long periods with relatively little fatigue; associated with higher levels of testosterone. Also called automizer.

Automization. See Automatization.

Automizer. See Automatizer.

Average evoked potential (AEP). The printed wave that represents the average of many actual waves; it is described in terms of its amplitude and latency.

Axon. The connective branch of a neuron that conveys messages through the synapse to other neurons.

Behaviorism. A school of psychology popular through the 1960s that maintained a monistic view of the mind-brain, saying that humans display no mental activity between stimulus and response. Behaviorism is associated with B. F. Skinner and J. B. Watson; it is also called stimulus-response psychology. It has generally been replaced today by cognitive psychology.

Binding. The process in which a ligand leaves its axonic terminal, enters its dedicated receptor, and remains long enough to send its chemical message on its way. Candace Pert calls it "sex on a molecular level."

Biofeedback. Information about a bodily function; it is used in biofeedback training to gain personal control over that function.

Blocker. Generally speaking, any chemical that prevents passage of a neurotransmitter at the synapse.

Blood-brain barrier. A kind of membrane that surrounds the brain through which blood vessels feeding the brain must pass. At the point of entry, unwanted chemicals are turned back physically, electrically, or chemically. Only a select few chemicals, such as oxygen and sugar, may enter the brain.

Bovine spongiform encephalopathy (BSE, aka "mad cow disease"). Caused by prions and resulting in massive deterioration of brain matter, delirium and, ultimately, death; human version caused by eating prion-infected beef is called Creutzfeldt-Jakob disease.

Brain attack. Another (and more current) name for stroke.

Calorie. The amount of heat required to raise one gram of water by one degree Celsius at sea level.

Calpain. A neurotransmitter associated with efficiency of synaptic transmission. It is a calcium-activated intracellular proteinase.

Catecholamine. A family of neurotransmitters that includes dopamine, norepinephrine, and epinephrine.

Cerebral cortex. The part of the brain associated with rational thought; the most recent to appear, evolution-wise. Also called the cerebrum.

Chemotaxis. The capacity of a cell with, for example, receptor "X," to detect the presence of chemical "X" at some distance and then move itself (chemotax) toward the concentration of that chemical. Along with synaptic transmission, chemotaxis is the complementary process for intercellular communication.

Cholecystokinin (CCK). A neurotransmitter influential in controlling appetite. It is found at lower levels in bulimia cases.

Chunk. A single element of learning or memory; chunks are pieced together to create memories.

Classical conditioning. The learning procedure in which a neutral stimulus (a stimulus that does not elicit any particular response, such as a ringing bell) precedes an unconditioned stimulus (a stimulus that elicits a predictable response, as when red meat causes a dog to salivate) and thereby becomes a conditioned response (the dog starts salivating after hearing the bell and before seeing meat); the meat is said to have been "associated to" the bell.

Cognitive dissonance. The situation that occurs when a person's behavior (for example, eating snails and enjoying them) conflicts with his or her attitude toward that behavior (the person believes that snails are disgusting).

Cognitive psychology. The study of how the mind performs its operations, such as perception, judgment, memory, and problem solving; the term is typically used in opposition to the term behavioral psychology, which, in its purest form, denies that the mind performs any operations, but rather only hooks stimuli together with their responses. See also Behaviorism.

Cognitive therapy. The practice of changing the way a person thinks about the world for the purpose of improving his or her mental health.

Commissurotomy. A surgical procedure in which the corpus callosum is severed.

Comorbid, comorbidity. The situation that occurs when two diseases or disorders tend to occur together in the same person; for example, coronary heart disease is often comorbid with depression.

Corpus callosum. A bundle of neurons (mostly axons) that connects and permits communication between the two hemispheres of the brain.

Cortex. The outer layer of a bodily organ. From the Latin cortex, or bark (of a tree). See also Cerebral cortex.

Corticotropin-releasing factor, corticotropin-releasing hormone. See CRF/CRH.

Cortisol. A hormone produced by the adrenal gland that contributes to sympathetic arousal and the general adaptation syndrome. See also Hydrocortisol.

CREB. Cyclic AMP-response element binding protein, a molecule associated with long-term memory formation.

CRF/CRH (corticotropin-releasing factor/hormone). A hormone produced by the hypothalamus in response to stress. Stimulates the pituitary gland to produce ACTH.

Cyclic adenosine monophosphate (Cyclic AMP). A cyclic nucleotide of adenosine that acts at the cellular level to regulate various metabolic processes and mediate the effects of many hormones.

Dehydroepiandrosterone. See DHEA.

Dementia. A disease (also called senility) characterized by disinterest in life, disorientation, carelessness, and personality changes. It is often associated—wrongly—with aging, but it should be distinguished from age-related disorders.

Dendrite. The connective branching of the neuron that receives messages across the synapse from other neurons.

Deoxyribonucleic acid. See DNA.

DHEA (dehydroepiandrosterone). A steroid called the "mother steroid" because it metabolizes into estrogen, testosterone, and other steroids; the levels naturally produced at age 80 are about 10 percent of the levels at age 25.

DNA (deoxyribonucleic acid). The molecular basis of heredity found in cell nuclei.

Dopamine. One of the neurotransmitters associated with mood and movement.

DSM-IV. Diagnostic and Statistical Manual of Mental Disorders, 4th edition, the book that is the American Psychiatric Association's authority for the diagnosis of mental disorders.

Dualism. The theory that the mind and brain are two separate entities that act independent of one another.

Dvorak keyboard. A redesigned keyboard in which the most frequently used keys are assigned to the strongest fingers, to increase speed and accuracy and reduce fatigue. See also Qwerty keyboard.

Electroencephalograph (EEG). An instrument that places the business end of electrodes at various locations on the scalp, with the other end attached to a moving graph. Electrical impulses at each electrode location are recorded in real time on the graph paper.

Endorphins. Neurotransmitters that are triggered by aerobic exercise, pain, and laughter and that result in a noticeably pleasurable sensation, as in "runner's high."

Enzyme. A protein that actually performs work, as opposed to other proteins that merely structural.

Epinephrine. A hormone and neurotransmitter produced by the adrenal gland that is associated with sympathetic arousal. Also called adrenaline.

Epistemology. The branch of philosophy that studies the structure of knowledge.

ERT. Estrogen replacement therapy.

Estrogens. The family of female sex hormones (there are three: estrone, estradiol, and estriol) that is responsible for the development of female sexual characteristics, from reproduction to calmness.

Event-related potential (ERP). The brain's electrical response to sensations originating outside one's body. See P300.

Evoked potential. An electroencephalographic measure of a neural impulse in response to a controlled stimulus; it may take the form of a light flash or an audible beep.

Explanatory style. See Attributional style.

Extrinsic motivation. The condition in which an activity is performed in expectation of rewards that are controlled by someone other than oneself, such as a teacher, boss, or parent. See also Intrinsic motivation.

Fight-or-flight syndrome (or response). See General adaptation syndrome.

Free radicals. Molecules with an unpaired electron. They are unstable, seeking any other unpaired electron in their path, whether it is an element of DNA in the cell nucleus or antioxidants from your daily dose of broccoli. If an antioxidant is available, then the free radical will clutch it in an eternal embrace, leaving the DNA undisturbed.

GABA (gamma amino butyric acid). An inhibiting neurotransmitter; low levels are associated with proneness to violence. Valium is a catalyst for GABA. Among other things, this neurotransmitter serves as the primary inhibitory agent, slowing down and/or preventing the activation of particular connections. Opposed to Glutamate, the primary excitatory neurotransmitter.

Gamma aminobutyric acid. See GABA.

GAS. See General adaptation syndrome.

Gene. A section of DNA that contains instructions for making a protein.

General adaptation syndrome (GAS). The condition in which the body reacts to stress through activation of the sympathetic nervous system in preparation for having to fight, flee, or freeze. Also called the fight-or-flight syndrome.

Glial cells. Cells that support the networked structure of neurons; a kind of skeleton for the nervous system.

Glucosis. The conversion of carbohydrates (sugars/starches) into glucose.

Glutamate. Among other things, this neurotransmitter serves as the primary excitatory agent, increasing the speed and the activation of particular connections. Opposed to GABA, the primary inhibitory neurotransmitter.

Glycemic index (GI). A measure of how fast a carbohydrate converts into energy and thereby raising blood sugar levels, with glucose equaling 100; higher ratings are faster, while lower ratings are slower.

Gray matter. The outer covering of the brain; also, refers generally to brain cells, including nucleus and extensions.

Habituation. A loss of sensitivity resulting from a prolonged pattern of stimulation; for example, the steady blinking of a neon sign will soon become unnoticeable (we habituate to it), but a randomly blinking light will keep our attention.

Hard-wired. In computerese, said of a program that is built into the computer and can't be changed without major surgery. In brain lingo, the term refers to behaviors, traits, and instincts that we are born with.

Hemisphericity. The division of the cerebrum into two hemispheres, the right and the left. The right hemisphere is associated with more creative and holistic processes, such as painting and music; the left hemisphere is associated with more linear and rational processes, such as language and mathematics. See also Left-brained and Right-brained.

Histocompatility. Refers to the degree to which two persons' body tissues are compatible with one another. If they are, then one can accept a graft or transplant from the other (this is true of identical twins). The more different one's "Major Histocompatibility Complex" (MHC) is from someone else's, the more likely a transplant would result in rejection. MHC's emit an odor, and we are, for sound evolutionary reasons, attracted to person's with MHC's that are the most different from our own.

Homeostasis. A state that exists when all the body's elements and systems are present and operating in ideal amounts and balance. It is disturbed by stressors; chemicals such as glucocorticoids and adrenaline are released in order to permit restoration of homeostasis.

Hormones. Substances (typically peptides or steroids) made by one tissue that move to another tissue in order to perform a specific function.

Hydrocortisol. The pharmaceutical version of cortisol.

Hypothalamus. A part of the limbic system that is regarded as the body's main thermostat; it coordinates basic metabolism and related functions and the alternation between sympathetic and parasympathetic arousal.

Immunoglobulin-A (IgA). A protective antibody; the immune system's first line of defense against all diseases.

Intrinsic motivation. The condition in which an activity is performed for its own enjoyment, with no expectation of rewards from other people. See also Extrinsic motivation.

Ischemia. Technical term for stroke.

Latency. The width of the wave that measures action potential; a measure of the speed of response.

Left-brained. A figure of speech that refers to the more creative and holistic processes associated with the left cerebral hemisphere. Acknowledging the left brain means paying attention to one's creative needs. See also Hemisphericity.

Letter Navon. A large letter that is composed of small copies of another letter. See Object Navon.

Ligand. A substance (either natural or laboratory-produced) that binds—for a brief time—to specific receptors on the surface of a cell and thereby transfers information. The three types of ligands are neurotransmitters, steroids, and peptides.

Limbic system. The portion of the midbrain (including the hippocampus, amygdala, hypothalamus, and olfactory area) that is associated with activating the general adaptation syndrome, or preparing the body for fight or flight. It is the main housing of emotional functions and has the densest concentration of endorphin receptors.

Linkage study. In genetics, a study designed to find chromosomal patterns that are common to all family members who exhibit a particular trait across the generations.

Lipolysis. The conversion of stored fat into ketones for use as a body fuel; occurs when no other current fuel sources are available from recent food or beverage consumption.

Locus of control. See Attributional style.

MAO. See Monoamine oxidase.

Massed learning. An approach to learning in which a single topic of instruction is executed without significant interruptions (or "spaces") between modules; it is the opposite of spaced learning.

Melatonin. A neurotransmitter originating in the pineal gland (a metabolite of serotonin) whose production is suppressed by natural light. It plays a key role in setting the body clock and in sleep onset and is available in pill form.

Mental health. "The successful performance of mental function, resulting in productive activities, fulfilling relationships with other people, and the ability to adapt to change and to cope with adversity." U.S. Dept. of Health and Human Services (1999)

Mental illness. "Health conditions that are characterized by alterations in thinking, mood, or behavior (or some combination thereof) associated with distress and/or impaired functioning." U.S. Dept. of Health and Human Services (1999)

Mentation. A shorter expression than (but meaning the same thing as) mental activity.

Meta-analysis. A statistical technique in which a large number of separate studies on the same subject are analyzed for patterns.

Metabolite. In metabolism, something (the metabolite) that is the product of something else (the precursor). For example, serotonin is the precursor of melatonin and melatonin is the metabolite of serotonin. Serotonin comes first, then melatonin.

Microsleep. A brief period of loss of consciousness that is not restorative like a nap but is a signal of loss of control of consciousness; the result of sleep deprivation.

Modular perspective. See Molar perspective.

Molar perspective. A big-picture, or top-down, look at a subject, as in studying the behaviors associated with a personality trait; the opposite of molecular perspective. Also called modular perspective.

Molecular perspective. A microscopic, or bottom-up, look at a subject, as in studying the body chemistry associated with personality traits; the opposite of molar perspective.

Monism. The view that brain and mind are one and the same; that spirit cannot exist independent of matter.

Monoamine oxidase (MAO). An enzyme that breaks down some neurotransmitters, including serotonin, norepinephrine, and dopamine. Two variants of MAO exist: MAO-A is found in serotonin- and norepinephrine-secreting cells, and MAO-B is found in dopamine-secreting cells.

Monoamine oxidase inhibitor (MAO-I). A drug that prevents MAO from breaking down neurotransmitters, with the effect of raising levels of those neurotransmitters; used as an antidepressant.

Monozygotic twins. Twins that develop from one single fertilized egg and possess an identical genetic structure.

Myelin sheath. The coating of the neural fiber; the thicker it is, the more efficient the neural transmission. Poor nutrition prevents normal myelin development.

Myelination (also Myelinization). The process of forming the myelin sheath.

Negative feedback. In neurophysiology, the tendency of a system that has changed to return to a normal state, as when a fire is doused; this happens with the general adaptation syndrome. See also Positive feedback.

Nerve growth factor (NGF). One of many trophic agents; it is released as a result of neural transmission and supports the growth of neural processes.

Neurolinguistic programming (NLP). The theory that asserts that people are programmed to communicate through one or more of three channels—visual, auditory, or kinesthetic—and can communicate more effectively by matching another person's preferred channel.

Neuron. A nerve cell; its major parts are the nucleus, axon, and dendrite.

Neuropeptide. Any of a large group of peptides that act as neurotransmitters; they are involved particularly in emotions, hunger (for example, cholecystokinin), pain (for example, endorphins), and sleep (for example, melatonin).

Neuropharmacology. The study of the effect of pharmaceuticals on the nervous system.

Neuropil. The fibrillar substance comprising dendrites, axons, and synapses that facilitates interneuron communication.

Neurosteroid. Hormones that are synthesized in the brain itself (e.g., enzymes in the hippocampus make estradiol out of cholesterol).

Neurotransmitter. The smallest of the ligands. Neurotransmitters are often a modification of an amino acid; several are composed of just one amino acid (for example, glycine). These tiny chemical molecules send specific messages across the synapse. Different combinations of neurotransmitters, each of which can exhibit different states (such as weak vs. strong), result in different behaviors, thoughts, and emotions.

Neurotrophins. Chemicals (proteins such as BDNF, brain-derived neurotrophic factor) produced in the dendrite of the post-synaptic cell that are received by the pre-synaptic cell in order to encourage the sprouting of new axonal branches that will serve to strengthen the connection. Neurotrophins are essential to the growth, plasticity, and maintenance of the nervous system—fertilizers, as it were, for the brain.

Neutroceuticals. Same as phytochemicals, defined below.

NGF. See Nerve growth factor.

NLP. See Neurolinguistic programming.

NMDA (N-methyl-D-aspartate). A glutamate essential for neuronal transmission and growth.

N-methyl-D-aspartate. See NMDA.

Nootropics. A family of drugs that purportedly enhance brain structure and function.

Noradrenaline. See Norepinephrine.

Norepinephrine. Like epinephrine, a hormone and neurotransmitter from the adrenal gland that is associated with sympathetic arousal. Also called noradrenaline.

Nun Study, The. A longitudinal study of aging and Alzheimer's disease directed by David Snowdon involving some 700 nuns of the School of Sisters of Notre Dame; the largest known human brain-donor program; all were born between 1896 and 1916.

Object Navon. A large shape that is composed of small copies of another shape.

Ontogeny recapitulates phylogeny. This terse phrase states that the development of each individual organism (ontogeny) reproduces the development of its species (phylogeny) from its origins to the present. In other words, during a human embryo's time in the womb, one can trace the stages of development from lizard through ape to human: the reptilian brain is the first to be identified (hindbrain), followed by the mammalian brain (midbrain) and culminating with the human brain (forebrain).

P300. An aspect of the ERP, the P300 is a relatively large positive wave response at 300 milliseconds following a specific sensory stimulation; used to measure comparative strength of responses.

Paradigm. A set of assumptions in a defined area of knowledge that guides both research and applications in that area, such as the assumption in pre-Copernican cosmology that the Earth was at the center of the universe.

Paradigmatic shift. A fundamental change in one or more assumptions in a defined area of knowledge, such as Copernicus's assertion that the Sun, not the Earth, occupied the center of our solar system.

Parasympathetic arousal. See Sympathetic arousal.

Peptide. A compound formed by so-called head-to-tail linkups of two or more amino acids. When about 100 amino acids are linked, they are called polypeptides; chains of 200 or more are called proteins. As of 1996, eighty-eight peptides had been identified with from two to over 200 amino acid links; more await discovery.

Perisylvian region. The region of the brain surrounding the sylvian fissure. Language activity occurs in this area.

Pharmacotherapy. The treatment of disease, especially mental disease, with drugs.

Pheromone. In animals, a chemical secreted by one animal and detected by another through the vomeronasal organ (VNO), two tiny ducts in the nasal septum; supposedly detected by the smell organ, but without apparent odor. The jury is still out on whether or not humans have such secretions and detection organs, and the precise mechanism leading to sexual responses in animals remains a mystery.

Phylogeny. See Ontogeny recapitulates phylogeny.

Phytochemicals. Over 900 chemicals found in plants that, while they are not nutrients, contribute to disease prevention, as lycopene in tomatoes. Estimates put 100 or more phytochemicals in one typical serving of fresh vegetables.

Plasticity. (A) The capacity of brain cells to take on new functions, as opposed to being committed to a single function (or set of functions) over the lifespan. (B) The capacity of the brain to change its structure. (C) The capacity of an individual to learn new behaviors.

PNI. See Psychoneuroimmunology.

Polypeptide. A chain of 100–200 amino acids; a polypeptide is larger than a peptide and smaller than a protein.

Positive feedback. In neurophysiology, the tendency of a change in a system to continue increasing in intensity, as in fanning a fire. See also Negative feedback.

Prion. A disease-causing (e.g., BSE) protein that is virtually indistinguishable from normal proteins, hence protected from the immune system-normal treatments for infection, such as heat and acids, have no effect.

Proband. Subject of a research study.

Progestins. A family of female sex hormones (most famous is progesterone) that is associated with preparation of the woman's body to care for a fertilized egg; levels increase at ovulation and decrease at menses. During pregnancy, they perform a variety of health and nutrition functions, including breast development, increased blood volume, weight gain, and storage of nutrients.

Proteins. Complex molecules containing (at a minimum) carbon, hydrogen, nitrogen, oxygen, and a variety of amino acids that are connected by peptide bonds.

Proto-oncogenes. About 100 genes that, when activated in certain combinations, cause cancer.

Psychoneuroimmunology (PNI). The study of how the body's immune system is affected by changes in mental and physical states. Its premise is that negative emotions lower resistance to disease antigens and positive emotions increase resistance.

Qwerty keyboard. The traditional keyboard in which the second row from the top begins, from the left side, "q...w...e...r...t...y." See also Dvorak keyboard.

Rapid eye movement (REM). The phase of the sleep cycle that consists of dreaming and motor neuron activity (but without physical movement other than eye movement); it is also called paradoxical sleep, since the motor neuron activity makes it appear on a brain scan that the sleeper is awake.

RAS. See Reticular activating system.

Rational drugs. Drugs based on genetic information about a specific condition.

RDA. Recommended daily allowance for specific nutritional categories.

Receptor. A protein on a dendritic terminal that receives a ligand from the axon connected at its synaptic gap; it serves as a kind of lock into which the ligand fits like a key.

Relaxation response. The body's response to an activity, such as meditation or aerobic exercise, that helps to return a stressed or sympathetically aroused person to a more relaxed state (parasympathetic arousal). See also Sympathetic arousal.

REM. See Rapid eye movement.

Retardation. A term generally referring to mental ability below average. Specifically, an IQ of 50–70 is considered mild retardation, 35–50 moderate, 20–35 severe, and less than 20 profound.

Reticular activating system (RAS). An area of the brain that acts like a kind of toggle switch so that when the cerebral cortex is fully functional (relaxing, problem solving, planning, creating) the limbic system (stress response) is not, and vice versa. Under stress, the RAS shuts the cerebral cortex down; in the absence of stress it allows the cerebral cortex to be fully functional.

Reuptake inhibitor. Any chemical agent that prevents a neurotransmitter that has not reached the postsynaptic region from returning to the presynaptic region; it thus keeps the neurotransmitter from being retained for later use, leaving it available for maximum current use.

Ribonucleic acid. See RNA.

Ribosomes. Tiny manufacturing plants in the cell that produce peptides and proteins.

Right-brained. A figure of speech that refers to the more linear and rational processes associated with the right cerebral hemisphere. Acknowledging the left brain means paying attention to one's need for logic and reason. See also Hemisphericity.

RNA (ribonucleic acid). A copy of DNA in the cell nucleus made by the DNA. RNA migrates to the ribosomes and triggers the production of peptides and proteins. This is analogous to the process in which a computer operating system (like DOS) makes copies of its own key files (with human prompting, of course!).

Routinize. To practice a skill to the point of being able to do it without consciously thinking about it.

SD. See Standard deviation.

Serotonin. A neurotransmitter involved in depression (too little), relaxation and sleep (just right), and aggression (too much); it is associated with vasoconstriction and headache relief; when serotonin metabolizes, melatonin results.

Sinaesthesia. The tendency of one sensory system to become excited as a result of the excitation of another sensory system. A common example would be the elicitation of visual memories by listening to music.

Social capital. The capability of one's social contacts to assist in realizing mutual goals.

Somatosensory system. The neural process that conveys messages that deal with the bodily sensations of touch and movement.

Spaced learning. An approach to learning in which a single topic of instruction is broken up into modules and scheduled over time with breaks (or "spaces") between modules; it is the opposite of massed learning.

Standard deviation (SD). A measure of the distance from the mean of the scores of members of a group; roughly one-third of a group will score within 1 SD above the mean, another one-third will score within 1 SD below the mean, and the rest will score higher or lower than 1 SD from the mean.

Stem cells. Versatile cells that can make carbon copies of neighboring cells and continue to reproduce endlessly.

Steroid (also called steroidal hormone). A kind of ligand that starts out as cholesterol, then gets transformed (for example, by an enzyme) into a more specific kind of steroid, such as a hormone from the gonads or from the adrenal cortex. Unlike the other two kinds of ligands, steroids engage receptors inside the cell rather than on the cell's surface.

Stimulus-response psychology. See Behaviorism.

Stroke. A brain disorder brought on by reduction of the oxygen supply (from blood flow) to the brain; also called brain attack or ischemia.

Sylvian fissure. The deep indentation, or split, between the temporal lobe and the remainder of the brain.

Sympathetic arousal. Mobilization by the body of its vast energy resources to fight off threat; parasympathetic arousal is the body's return to a more normal, relaxed state. See also General adaptation syndrome; Relaxation response.

Synapse. The point of connection between two neurons. The synapse is the area where a branch of an axon of one neuron has established a connection (they don't actually touch!) with the branch of a dendrite of another neuron. The synapse is the basic unit of learning. Knowledge can be measured by the number of existing synapses; effective use of knowledge is a reflection of their physical condition. The actual space through which neurotransmitters pass from one neuron to another is called the synaptic gap. As with the gap in a spark plug, the adjacent membranes of the axon and dendrite that form the synapse must be clean and healthy.

Synaptic gap. See Synapse.

Talking therapy. The practice of talking with a therapist for relief of psychological distress; it may be used instead of, or in addition to, drug therapy.

Testosterone. See Androgens.

Trophic. Contributing to growth; nutritional.

Type I, II error. Terms used in research to describe two related cases: when a difference in means is claimed when in fact no difference exists (Type I error) and when an equality of means is claimed when in fact the means are different (Type II error); that is, in Type I, an effect is claimed and none is present, and in Type II, no effect is claimed when one is in fact present.

Vasoconstriction. Shrinkage of the walls of a blood vessel; it is thought to be associated with headache relief. See also Vasodilation.

Vasodilation. Stretching, dilation, or relaxation of the walls of a blood vessel; vasodilation of blood vessels in the brain is associated with the onset of headaches. See also Vasoconstriction.

Visualization. The process of using the mind to review a series of bodily movements such as a downhill ski run or to prepare for an activity such as delivering a speech by giving it without actually going through the bodily movements. Visualization may be accompanied by either a running verbal commentary, some limited physical movement (such as so-called body English), or both. It is usually performed with the eyes closed.

White matter. The inner portion of the brain, covered by the outer gray matter; also, the myelin sheath that covers the axon and thickens over time.

Working memory. The more current term that refers to what used to be known as *short-term memory*. Used now because the function includes much more than temporary. It is like the desktop of a computer, the area where the mind plays with various pieces of data for the purpose of making decisions, planning, comparing, etc.

Bibliography

Ackerman, D. (1990). *A Natural History of the Senses.* New York: Random House.

Adams, J. L. (1980). *Conceptual Blockbusting: A Guide to Better Ideas* (2nd ed.). New York: Norton.

Adams, J. L. (1986). *The Care and Feeding of Ideas: A Guide to Encouraging Creativity.* Reading, Mass.: Addison-Wesley.

Agor, W. E. (1989). *Intuition in Organizations: Leading and Managing Productively.* Thousand Oaks, Calif.: Sage.

Agor, W. H. (n.d.). "The Use of Hypnosis to Induce Creative Problem Solving." Unpublished manuscript, University of Texas at El Paso.

Ainsworth, M.D.S., Blehar, M., Waters, E., and Wall, S. (1978). *Patterns of Attachment.* Hillsdale, N.J.: Erlbaum.

Albrecht, K. (n.d.). *Mind Mapping: A Tool for Clear Thinking.* San Diego, Calif.: Shamrock. Videotape, 10 minutes.

Alkon, D. L. (1992). *Memory's Voice: Deciphering the Brain-Mind Code.* New York: HarperCollins.

Allison, M. (1991, October). "Stopping the Brain Drain." *Harvard Health Letter,* 16, 6 ff.

Allport, G. W., and Odbert, H. S. (1936). "Trait Names: A Psycho-Lexical Study." *Psychological Monographs,* 47(1, whole no. 211).

Amabile, T. M. (1983). *The Social Psychology of Creativity.* New York: Springer-Verlag.

American Psychiatric Association. (1994). *Diagnostic and Statistical Manual of Mental Disorders* (4th ed.). Washington, D.C.: American Psychiatric Association.

American Psychological Association. (1992). "Ethical Principles of Psychologists and Code of Conduct." *American Psychologist,* 47, 1597–1611.

American Psychological Association. (2002, December). "Ethical Principles of Psychologists and Code of Conduct." *American Psychologist,* 57(12), 1060–1073.

Anderson, J. R. (1993, January). "Problem Solving and Learning." *American Psychologist,* 48(1), 35–44.

Arkin, A. M., Antrobus, J. S., and Ellman, S. J. (Eds.). (1978). *The Mind in Sleep.* Hillsdale, N.J.: Erlbaum.

Armstrong, T. (1993). *Seven Kinds of Smart: Identifying and Developing Your Many Intelligences.* New York: Plume.

Armstrong, T. (1994). *Multiple Intelligences in the Classroom.* Alexandria, Va.: Association for Supervision and Curriculum Development.

Arnow, B. (1996). "Cognitive-Behavioral Therapy for Bulimia Nervosa." In J. Werne (Ed.), *Treating Eating Disorders.* San Francisco: Jossey-Bass.

Atkins, R. C. (2002). *Dr. Atkins' New Diet Revolution.* New York: Quill/HarperCollins.

Atkins, S. (1978). *LIFO Training: Discovery Workbook.* Beverly Hills, Calif.: Stuart Atkins.

Austin, J. H. (1998). *Zen and the Brain: Toward an Understanding of Meditation and Consciousness.* Cambridge, Mass.: MIT Press.

Axel, R. (1995, October). "The Molecular Logic of Smell." *Scientific American,* pp. 154–159.

Bagemihl, B. (1999). *Biological Exuberance: Animal Homosexuality and Natural Diversity.* New York: St. Martin's Press.

Bailey, C. (1991). *The New Fit or Fat.* Boston: Houghton Mifflin.

Baker, J. G., Zevon, M. A., and Rounds, J. B. (1994). "Differences in Positive and Negative Affect Dimensions: Latent Trait Analysis." *Personality and Individual Differences,* 17(2), 161–167.

Baldwin, T. T., and Ford, K. (1988). "Transfer of Training: A Review and Directions for Future Research." *Personnel Psychology,* 41, 63–105.

Bales, J. (1991, November). "Work Stress Grows, but Services Decline." *APA Monitor,* p. 32.

Bandler, R., and Grinder, J. (1982). *ReFraming: Neuro-Linguistic Programming and the Transformation of Meaning.* Moab, Utah: Real People Press.

Bargh, J. A., and Chartrand, T. L. (1999). "The Unbearable Automaticity of Being." *American Psychologist,* 54(7), 462–479.

Barker, J. (n.d.). *Discovering the Future.* Burnsville, Minn.: Charthouse International. Videotape.

Bar-On, R. (1996). *Bar-On Emotional Quotient Inventory.* North Tonawanda, N.Y.: Multi-Health Systems.

Barron, F., and Harrington, D. M. (1981). "Creativity, Intelligence, and Personality." *Annual Review of Psychology,* 32, 439–476.

Bartlett, F. C. (1932). *Remembering.* Cambridge: Cambridge University Press.

Basadur, M., Graen, G., and Wakabayashi, M. (1990). "Identifying Differences in Creative Problem Solving Style." *Journal of Creative Behavior,* 24(2), 111–131.

Becker, S. W., and Eagly, A. H. (2004). "The Heroism of Women and Men." *American Psychologist,* 59(3), 163–178.

Behn, R. D., and Vaupel, J. W. (1982). *Quick Analysis for Busy Decision Makers.* New York: Basic Books.

Belenky, M. F., Clinchy, B. M., Goldberger, N. R., and Tarule, J. M. (1997). *Women's Ways of Knowing: The Development of Self, Voice, and Mind* (10th anniv. ed.). New York: Basic Books.

Bem, D. J. (1996, April). "Exotic Becomes Erotic: A Developmental Theory of Sexual Orientation." *Psychological Review,* 103(2), 320–321.

Bem, S. L. (1993). *The Lenses of Gender: Transforming the Debate on Sexual Inequality.* New Haven: Yale University Press.

Bennett, W. (1991, October). "Obesity Is Not an Eating Disorder." *Harvard Mental Health Letter,* 8(4).

Benson, H., with Klipper, M. Z. (1990). *The Relaxation Response.* New York: Avon.

Biederman, J., and Faraone, S. (1996, Winter). "Attention Deficit Hyperactivity Disorder." *On the Brain* (Harvard Mahoney Neuroscience Institute Letter), pp. 4–7.

Birdwhistell, R. L. (1970). *Kinesics and Context: Essays on Body Motion Communication.* Philadelphia: University of Pennsylvania Press.

Birren, F. (1978a). *Color and Human Response.* New York: Van Nostrand Reinhold.

Birren, F. (1978b). *Color in Your World.* New York: Collier Books.

Bjork, R. (1994). "Memory and Metamemory Considerations in the Training of Human Beings." In J. Metcalfe and A. P. Shimamura (Eds.), *Metacognition: Knowing about Knowing* (pp. 185–206). Cambridge, Mass.: MIT Press.

Black, I. B. (1991). *Information in the Brain: A Molecular Perspective.* Cambridge, Mass.: MIT Press.

Blakeslee, S. (1991, September 15). "Study Ties Dyslexia to Brain Flaw Affecting Vision and Other Senses." *New York Times,* Current Events edition, p. 11.

Block, P. (1987). *The Empowered Manager: Positive Political Skills at Work.* San Francisco: Jossey-Bass.

Blum, D. (1997). *Sex on the Brain: The Biological Differences Between Men and Women.* New York: Viking.

Boden, M. A. (1990). *The Creative Mind: Myths and Mechanisms.* New York: Basic Books.

Bok, S. (1979). *Lying: Moral Choice in Public and Private Life.* New York: Vintage Books.

Bolles, E. B. (1988). *Remembering and Forgetting: An Inquiry into the Nature of Memory.* New York: Walker.

Bonanno, G. A. (2004, January). "Loss, Trauma, and Human Resilience: Have We Underestimated the Human Capacity to Thrive after Extremely Aversive Events?" *American Psychologist,* 59(1), 7–13.

Bond, J. T., Galinsky, E., and Swanberg, J. E. (1998). *The 1997 National Study of the Changing Workforce.* New York: Families and Work Institute.

Borod, J. (1999). *The Neuropsychology of Emotion.* Oxford: Oxford University Press.

Borysenko, J. (1987). *Minding the Body, Mending the Body.* Reading, Mass.: Addison-Wesley.

Bouchard, C., and Bray, G. A. (Eds.). (1996). *Regulation of Body Weight: Biological and Behavioral Mechanisms.* New York: Wiley.

Bowlby, J. (1965). *Child Care and the Growth of Love* (2nd ed.). London: Penguin Books.

Bradley, R. H., and Caldwell, B. M. (1984). "The Relation of Infants' Home Environment to Achievement Test Performance in First Grade: A Follow-Up Study." *Child Development,* 52, 708–710.

Bransford, J. D., and Stein, B. S. (1984). *The Ideal Problem Solver.* New York: Freeman.

Bransford, J. D., Brown, A., and Cocking, R. (Eds.). (2000). *How People Learn: Brain, Mind, Experience, and School.* Washington, D.C.: National Academy Press.

Bremner, J. D. (2005). *The Brain Imaging Handbook.* New York: W. W. Norton.

Brink, S. (1995, May 15). "Smart Moves." *U.S. News & World Report,* pp. 76–85.

Broad, M. L. (Ed.). (1997). *In Action: Transferring Learning to the Workplace.* Alexandria, Va.: American Society for Training and Development.

Broad, M. L., and Newstrom, J. W. (1992). *Transfer of Training: Action-Packed Strategies to Ensure High Payoff from Training Investments.* Reading, Mass.: Addison-Wesley.

Brody, N. (1992). *Intelligence* (2nd ed.). Orlando: Academic Press.

Brown, J. L., and Pollitt, E. (1996, February). "Malnutrition, Poverty and Intellectual Development." *Scientific American,* pp. 38–43.

Brown, W. A. (1998, January). "The Placebo Effect." *Scientific American,* pp. 90–95.

Brownlee, S. (1999, August 9). "Behavior Can Be Baffling When Young Minds Are Taking Shape." *U.S. News & World Report,* pp. 45–54.

Bruer, J. T. (1999). *The Myth of the First Three Years.* New York: The Free Press.

Brutus, S., Fleenor, J., and London, M. (1998). "Does 360-Degree Feedback Work in Different Industries? A Between-Industry Comparison of the Reliability and Validity of Multi-Source Ratings." *Journal of Management Development,* 17, 177–190.

Bush, B. J. (1986, June). *A Study of Innovative Training Techniques at the Defense Language Institute Foreign Language Center.* Research Report 1426. Alexandria, Va.: U.S. Army Research Institute for the Behavioral and Social Sciences.

Buss, A. H. (1989). "Personality as Traits." *American Psychologist,* 44(11), 1378–1388.

Buss, D. M. (1991). "Evolutionary Personality Psychology." *Annual Review of Psychology,* 42, 459–491.

Buss, D. M. (1992). "Mate Preference Mechanisms: Consequences for Partner Choice and Intrasexual Competition" (pp. 249–266). In J. H. Barkow, L. Cosmides, and J. Tooby (Eds.), *The Adapted Mind.* New York: Oxford University Press.

Buss, D. M. (1994). *The Evolution of Desire.* New York: Basic Books.

Buss, D. M. (2000a). "The Evolution of Happiness." *American Psychologist,* 55(1), 15–23.

Buss, D. M. (2000b). *The Dangerous Passion: Why Jealousy Is as Necessary as Love and Sex.* New York: Free Press.

Buss, D. M. (Ed.). (1990, March). "Biological Foundations of Personality: Evolution, Behavioral Genetics, and Psychophysiology" [Special Issue]. *Journal of Personality,* 58(1).

Buzan, T. (1991). *Use Your Perfect Memory* (3rd ed.). New York: Penguin Books.

Buzan, T. (1996). *The Mind Map Book.* New York: Plume.

Cacioppo, J. T., and Berntson, G. G. (1992, August). "Social Psychological Contributions to the Decade of the Brain: Doctrine of Multilevel Analysis." *American Psychologist,* 47(8), 1019–1028.

Cacioppo, J. T., and Tassinary, L. G. (Eds.). (1990). *Principles of Psychophysiology: Physical, Social, and Inferential Elements.* Cambridge: Cambridge University Press.

Cadoret, R. J. (1978). "Psychopathology in Adopted-away Offspring of Biological Parents with Antisocial Behavior." *Archives of General Psychiatry,* 35, 1171–1175.

Caine, R. N., and Caine, G. (1991). *Making Connections: Teaching and the Human Brain.* Alexandria, Va.: Association for Supervision and Curriculum Development.

Calvin, W. H. (1996). *How Brains Think: Evolving Intelligence, Then and Now.* New York: Basic Books.

Campbell, B. (1994). *The Multiple Intelligences Handbook: Lesson Plans and More.* Marysville, Wash.: Campbell and Associates.

Campbell, D. (1997). *The Mozart Effect.* New York: Avon.

Campbell, L., Campbell, B., and Dickinson, D. (1996). *Teaching and Learning Through Multiple Intelligences.* Needham Heights, Mass.: Allyn & Bacon.

Campbell, R. J. (1989). *Psychiatric Dictionary* (6th ed.). New York: Oxford University Press.

Caplan, P. J., Crawford, M., Hyde, J. S., and Richardson, J.T.E. (1997). *Gender Differences in Human Cognition.* New York: Oxford University Press.

Caplan, T., and Caplan, F. (1982). *The Second Twelve Months of Life.* New York: Bantam Books.

Caplan, T., and Caplan, F. (1984). *The Early Childhood Years: The Two to Six Year Old.* New York: Bantam Books.

Caplan, T., and Caplan, F. (1995). *The First Twelve Months of Life* (rev. ed.). New York: Bantam Books.

Cappon, D. (1994a). *Intuition and Management: Research and Application.* Westport, Conn.: Quorum Books.

Cappon, D. (1994b). "A New Approach to Intuition: IQ2." *Omni,* 16(12), 34 ff.

Capra, F. (1984). *The Tao of Physics* (2nd ed.). New York: Bantam Books.

Carter, R. (1998). *Mapping the Mind.* Berkeley: University of California Press.

Carver, R. (1990). *Reading Rate: A Review of Research and Theory.* Orlando: Academic Press.

Cassandro, V. (1998, October). "Explaining Premature Mortality Across Fields of Creative Endeavor." *Journal of Personality,* 66(5), 805–833.

Castle, L. R. (2003). *Bipolar Disorder Demystified.* New York: Marlowe.

Cavett, D. (1992, August 3). "Goodbye, Darkness." *People Weekly,* 38, 88 ff.

Ceci, S. J. (1990). *On Intelligence--More or Less: A Bio-ecological Treatise on Intellectual Development.* Englewood Cliffs, N.J.: Prentice Hall.

Chalmers, D. J. (1995, December). "The Puzzle of Conscious Experience." *Scientific American,* pp. 80–86.

Changeux, J. P. (1997). *Neuronal Man: The Biology of Mind.* (L. Garey, Trans.). Princeton, N.J.: Princeton University Press.

Chi, M., de Leeuw, N., Chiu, M. H., and LaVancher, C. (1994). "Eliciting Self-Explanations Improves Understanding." *Cognitive Science,* 18, 439–477.

Chisholm, J. S. (1999). *Death, Hope, and Sex: Steps to an Evolutionary Ecology of Mind and Morality.* New York: Cambridge University Press.

Clarke, W. V. (1956). "The Construction of an Industrial Selection Personality Test." *Journal of Psychology,* 41, 379–394.

Claude-Pierre, P. (1998). *The Secret Language of Eating Disorders: The Revolutionary New Approach to Understanding and Curing Anorexia and Bulimia.* New York: Vintage Books.

Clower, W. (2001). *The Fat Fallacy.* Pittsburgh: The Perusal Press.

Colangelo, N., Assouline, S. G., and Gross, M.U.M. *A Nation Deceived: How Schools Hold Back America's Brightest Students.* Iowa City, Iowa: University of Iowa.

Collin, F. (1992, May). "Sarah Leibowitz (Interview)." *Omni,* 14(8), 73 ff.

"Combatting Stress at Work" [Special Issue]. (1993, January). *Conditions of Work Digest,* 12(1).

Connellan, Thomas K. (2003). *Bringing Out the Best in Others! 3 Keys for Business Leaders, Educators, Coaches, and Parents.* Austin: Bard Press.

Coop, R. H. (1993). *Mind over Golf: Play Your Best by Thinking Smart.* Old Tappan, N.J.: Macmillan.

Cooper, K. (1968). *Aerobics.* New York: Evans.

Cooper, R. (1991). *The Performance Edge.* Boston: Houghton Mifflin.

Cooper, R., and Sawaf, A. (1997). *Executive EQ: Emotional Intelligence and Leadership in Organizations.* New York: Grosset & Dunlap.

Cooperrider, D. L., and Dutton, J. E. (1998). *Organizational Dimensions of Global Change.* Thousand Oaks, Calif.: Sage.

Coren, S. (1992). *The Left-Hander Syndrome: The Causes and Consequences of Left-Handedness.* New York: Free Press.

Coren, S. (1996). *Sleep Thieves.* New York: Free Press.

Costa, P. T. Jr., and McCrae, R. R. (1992). *NEO PI-R Professional Manual.* Odessa, Fla.: Psychological Assessment Resources.

Cousins, N. (1979). *Anatomy of an Illness.* New York: Norton.

Cousins, N. (1989). *Head First: The Biology of Hope.* New York: NAL/Dutton.

Covey, S. R. (1990). *The Seven Habits of Highly Effective People.* New York: Simon & Schuster.

Cramer, P. (1979). "Defense Mechanisms in Adolescence." *Developmental Psychology,* 15, 476–477.

Crawford, H. J., and Strapp, C. H. (1994, February). "Effects of Vocal and Instrumental Music on Visuospatial and Verbal Performance as Moderated by Studying Preference and Personality." *Personality and Individual Differences,* 16(2), 237–245.

Crawford, M. (1995). *Talking Difference: On Gender and Language.* Thousand Oaks, Calif.: Sage.

Crawford, M., and Gentry, M. (Eds.). (1989). *Gender and Thought.* New York: Springer-Verlag.

Crichton, M. (1990). *Jurassic Park.* New York: Knopf.

Crick, F. (1994). *The Astonishing Hypothesis: The Scientific Search for the Soul.* New York: Scribner.

Csikszentmihalyi, M. (1990). *Flow: The Psychology of Optimal Experience.* New York: HarperCollins.

Csikszentmihalyi, M. (1996). *Creativity: Flow and the Psychology of Discovery and Invention.* New York: HarperCollins.

Csikszentmihalyi, M. (1999). "If We Are So Rich, Why Aren't We Happy?" *American Psychologist,* 54(10), 821–827.

Cummings, T. G., and Worley, C. G. (1997). *Organization Development and Change* (6th ed.). Cincinnati: South-Western.

Cytowic, R. E. (1993). *The Man Who Tasted Shapes.* Los Angeles: Tarcher.

Dahlitz, M., et al. (1991, May 11). "Delayed Sleep Phase Syndrome Response to Melatonin." *The Lancet,* 337, 1121 ff.

Dalton, K. (1987). *Once a Month* (4th ed.). Glasgow, Scotland: Fontana Original.

Daly, M., and Wilson, M. (1988). *Homicide.* New York: Aldine de Gruyter.

Damasio, A. R. (1994). *Descartes' Error: Emotion, Reason and the Human Brain.* New York: Grosset & Dunlap.

Damasio, A. R. (1999). *The Feeling of What Happens: Body and Emotion in the Making of Consciousness.* New York: Harcourt Brace.

Davidson, J., and Davidson, B. (2004). *Genius Denied: How to Stop Wasting Our Brightest Young Minds.* New York: Simon & Schuster.

Dawkins, R. (1989). *The Selfish Gene* (2nd ed.). Oxford: Oxford University Press.

de Bono, E. (1967). *New Think.* New York: Basic Books.

de Bono, E. (1970). *Lateral Thinking: Creativity Step-by-Step.* New York: HarperCollins.

de Bono, E. (1994). *de Bono's Thinking Course.* New York: Facts on File.

de Groot, A. D. (1965). *Thought and Choice in Chess.* The Hague: Mouton.

Dean, W., and Morgenthaler, J. (1990). *Smart Drugs and Nutrients.* Santa Cruz, Calif.: B & J Publications.

DeAngelis, T. (1992, February). "Cutting Cholesterol: Feeling Feisty?" *APA Monitor,* pp. 8–9.

DeAngelis, T. (1995, April). "New Threat Associated with Child Abuse." *APA Monitor,* 26(4), 1, 38.

Deming, W. E. (1986). *Out of the Crisis.* Cambridge, Mass.: MIT Center for Advanced Engineering Study.

Dennett, D. C. (1995). *Darwin's Dangerous Idea: Evolution and the Meanings of Life.* New York: Simon & Schuster.

Dennett, D. C. (1996). *Kinds of Minds: Toward an Understanding of Consciousness.* New York: Basic Books.

Detterman, D. K., and Sternberg, R. J. (1993). *Transfer on Trial: Intelligence, Cognition, and Instruction.* Norwood, N.J.: Ablex.

Diamond, J. (1992). *The Third Chimpanzee: The Evolution and Future of the Human Animal.* New York: HarperCollins.

Diamond, J. (1997a). *Guns, Germs, and Steel: The Fates of Human Societies.* New York: Norton.

Diamond, J. (1997b). *Why Is Sex Fun? The Evolution of Human Sexuality.* New York: Basic Books.

Diamond, M. (1988). *Enriching Heredity: The Impact of the Environment on the Anatomy of the Brain.* New York: Free Press.

Digman, J. M., and Inouye, J. (1986). "Further Specification of the Five Robust Factors of Personality." *Journal of Personality and Social Psychology,* 50, 116–123.

Dinges, D. F., and Broughton, R. J. (1989). *Sleep and Alertness: Chronobiological, Behavioral, and Medical Aspects of Napping.* New York: Raven Press.

Dossey, L. (1996). *Healing Words: The Power of Prayer and the Power of Medicine.* San Francisco: Harper San Francisco.

Dotto, L. (1990). *Losing Sleep: How Your Sleeping Habits Affect Your Life.* New York: Morrow.

Dreikurs, R., and Cassel, P. (1972). *Discipline Without Tears* (rev. ed.). New York: Hawthorne Books.

Dreikurs, R., and Gray, L. (1993). *Logical Consequences.* New York: Meredith Press.

Druckman, D., and Bjork, R. A. (Eds.). (1991). *In the Mind's Eye: Enhancing Human Performance.* Washington, D.C.: National Academy Press.

Druckman, D., and Swets, J. A. (Eds.). (1988). *Enhancing Human Performance: Issues, Theories, and Techniques.* Washington, D.C.: National Academy Press.

Dunbar, R. (1997). *Grooming, Gossip, and the Evolution of Language.* Cambridge, Mass.: Harvard University Press.

Dunn, R., and Dunn, K. (1978). *Teaching Students Through Their Individual Learning Styles.* Englewood Cliffs, N.J.: Prentice Hall.

Dweck, C. S. (1989). "Motivation." In A. Lesgold and R. Glaser (Eds.), *Foundations for a Psychology of Education* (pp. 87–136). Hillsdale, N.J.: Erlbaum.

Eagly, A. (1995, March). "The Science and Politics of Comparing Women and Men." *American Psychologist,* 50(3), 145–158.

Eaves, L. J., Eysenck, H. J., and Martin, N. G. (1989). *Genes, Culture and Personality.* London: Academic Press.

Eckles, R. W., Carmichael, R. L., and Sarchet, B. R. (1981). *Supervisory Management.* New York: Wiley.

Edelman, G. M. (1987). *Neural Darwinism: The Theory of Neuronal Group Selection.* New York: Basic Books.

Edelman, G. M. (1992). *Bright Air, Brilliant Fire: On the Matter of the Mind.* New York: Basic Books.

Edmonds, D., and Eidinow, J. (2001). *Wittgenstein's Poker: The Story of a Ten-Minute Argument Between Two Great Philosophers.* New York: Ecco/HarperCollins.

Education Research. (1987). *Problem Solving.* New York: Education Research.

Education Research. (1988). *Decision Making.* New York: Education Research.

Edwards, B. (1989). *Drawing on the Right Side of the Brain* (rev. ed.). Los Angeles: Tarcher.

Eidelson, R. J., & Eidelson, J. I. (2003). "Dangerous Ideas: Five Beliefs That Propel Groups Toward Conflict." *American Psychologist,* 58(3), 182–192.

Eisenberg, A., Murkoff, H. E., and Hathaway, S. E. (1996). *What to Expect: The Toddler Years.* New York: Workman Publishing.

Eisenberger, R., and Cameron, J. (1996). "Detrimental Effects of Reward: Reality or Myth?" *American Psychologist,* 51(11), 1153–1166.

Ekman, P. (1985). *Telling Lies.* New York: Norton.

Elman, J. L., et al. (1996). *Rethinking Innateness: A Connectionist Perspective on Development.* Cambridge, Mass.: MIT Press.

Epstein, J. (2001). *School, Family, and Community Partnerships* (2nd ed.). Boulder, Colo.: Westview Press.

Epstein, R. (1996, July–August). "Capturing Creativity." *Psychology Today,* 29(4), 41 ff.

Epstein, Samuel (1994, August). "Integration of the Cognitive and the Psychodynamic Unconscious." *American Psychologist,* 49(8), 709–724.

Epstein, Samuel, and Meier, P. (1989). "Constructive Thinking: A Broad Coping Variable with Specific Components." *Journal of Personality and Social Psychology,* 57(2), 332–350.

Epstein, Samuel, and Steinman, D. (1995). *The Safe Shopper's Bible: A Consumer's Guide to Nontoxic Household Products, Cosmetics and Food.* New York: Wiley.

Epstein, Seymour (1997, March). "This I Have Learned from Over Forty Years of Personality Research." *Journal of Personality and Social Psychology,* 65(1), 3–32.

Erez, M., Kleinbeck, U., and Thierry, H. (Eds.) (2001). *Work Motivation in the Context of a Globalizing Economy.* Mahwah, N.J.: Lawrence Erlbaum.

Escher, M. C. (1983). *M. C. Escher: Twenty-Nine Master Prints.* New York: Abrams.

Eysenck, H. J. (1967). *The Biological Basis of Personality.* Springfield, Ill.: Thomas.

Eysenck, H. J. (1970). *The Structure of Human Personality* (rev. ed.). London: Methuen.

Eysenck, H. J. (Ed.). (1981). *A Model for Personality.* Berlin: Springer-Verlag.

Eysenck, H. J., and Eysenck, M. W. (1985). *Personality and Individual Differences: A Natural Science Approach.* New York: Plenum.

Eysenck, H. J., and Kamin, L. (1981). *The Intelligence Controversy.* New York: Wiley.

Ezzo, G., and Bucknam, R. (1998). *On Becoming Baby Wise.* Sisters, Ore.: Multnomah.

Falletta, N. (1983). *The Paradoxicon.* New York: Doubleday.

Fausto-Sterling, A. (1992). *Myths of Gender: Biological Theories about Women and Men* (2nd ed.). New York: Basic Books.

Fausto-Sterling, A. (1993, March–April). "The Five Sexes: Why Male and Female Are Not Enough." *The Sciences,* 33(2), 20–25.

Fausto-Sterling, A., and Rose, H. (1994). *Love, Power, and Knowledge.* Bloomington: Indiana University Press.

Fernald, R. D. (1993, July–August). "Cichlids in Love." *The Sciences,* 33(4), 27–31.

Festinger, L. (1953). *A Theory of Cognitive Dissonance.* Stanford, Calif.: Stanford University Press.

Field, T. (1998, December). "Massage Therapy Effects." *American Psychologist,* 53(12), 1270–1281.

Fisher, H. E. (1982). *The Sex Contract.* New York: Morrow.

Fisher, H. E. (1995). *Anatomy of Love: A Natural History of Mating, Marriage, and Why We Stray.* New York: Fawcett.

Fisher, H. E. (2004). *Why We Love: The Nature and Chemistry of Romantic Love.* New York: Henry Holt.

Fisher, M. (1981). *Intuition: How to Use It for Success and Happiness.* New York: NAL/Dutton.

Fisher, R., and Ury, W. (1991). *Getting to Yes: Negotiating Agreement Without Giving In* (2nd ed.). New York: Penguin Books.

Fisher, S., and Fisher, R. L. (1981). *Pretend the World Is Funny and Forever: A Psychological Analysis of Comedians, Clowns, and Actors.* Hillsdale, N.J.: Lawrence Erlbaum.

Fisher, S., and Fisher, R. L. (1993). *The Psychology of Adaptation to Absurdity: Tactics of Make-Believe.* Hillsdale, N.J.: Lawrence Erlbaum.

Flanders, N. A. (1970). *Analyzing Teacher Behavior.* Reading, Mass.: Addison-Wesley.

Fleenor, J., and Prince, J. (1997). *Using 360-Degree Feedback in Organizations: An Annotated Bibliography.* Greensboro, N.C.: Center for Creative Leadership.

Fluegelman, A. (Ed.). (1976). *The New Games Book.* New York: Dolphin/Doubleday.

Flynn, J. R. (1999). "Searching for Justice: The Discovery of IQ Gains over Time." *American Psychologist,* 54(1), 5–20.

Folkins, C. H., and Sime, W. E. (1981, April). "Physical Fitness Training and Mental Health." *American Psychologist,* 36(4), 373–389.

Forabosco, G., and Ruch, W. (1994). "Sensation Seeking, Social Attitudes and Humor Appreciation in Italy." *Personality and Individual Differences,* 16(4), 515–528.

Foreman, J. (1996, December 17). "Anxiety: It's Not Just a State of Mind." *Boston Globe,* p. C1.

Fossel, M. (1996). *Reversing Human Aging.* New York: Morrow.

Fowler, J. W. (1982). *Stages of Faith: The Psychology of Human Development and the Quest for Meaning.* New York: HarperCollins.

Fox, N. A. (1991). "If It's Not Left, It's Right: Electroencephalograph Asymmetry and the Development of Emotion." *American Psychologist,* 46, 863–872.

Franklin, J. (1987). *Molecules of the Mind: The Brave New Science of Molecular Psychology.* New York: Atheneum.

Friedan, B. (1993). *The Fountain of Age.* New York: Simon & Schuster.

Gallagher, R. M. (Ed.). (1990). *Drug Therapy for Headache.* New York: Dekker.

Gardner, H. (1983). *Frames of Mind: The Theory of Multiple Intelligences.* New York: Basic Books.

Gardner, H. (1985). *The Mind's New Science: A History of the Cognitive Revolution.* New York: Basic Books.

Gardner, H. (1991). *The Unschooled Mind: How Schools Should Teach.* New York: Basic Books.

Gardner, H. (1993). *Creating Minds.* New York: Basic Books.

Gardner, H. (1997). *Extraordinary Minds.* New York: Basic Books.

Gardner, H. (2004). *Changing Minds.* Boston: Harvard Business School Press.

Gardner, M. (1979). *The Ambidextrous Universe: Mirror Asymmetry and Time-Reversed Worlds* (2nd ed.). New York: Scribner.

Garfield, C. A. (1984). *Peak Performance: Mental Training Techniques of the World's Greatest Athletes.* Los Angeles: Tarcher.

Garfield, C., with Bennett, Z. (1984). *Peak Performance: Mental Training Techniques of the World's Greatest Athletes.* Los Angeles: Tarcher.

Gavin, J. (1992). *The Exercise Habit.* Champaign, Ill.: Human Kinetics.

Gawain, S. (1978). *Creative Visualization.* Berkeley, Calif.: New World Library.

Gazzaniga, M. S. (1985). *The Social Brain.* New York: Basic Books.

Gazzaniga, M. S. (1988). *Mind Matters: How Mind and Brain Interact to Create Our Conscious Lives.* Boston: Houghton Mifflin.

Gazzaniga, M. S. (1998). *The Mind's Past.* Berkeley, Calif.: University of California Press.

Geary, D. C. (1998). *Male, Female: The Evolution of Human Sex Differences.* Washington, D.C.: American Psychological Association.

Geen, R. G., Beatty, W. W., and Arkin, R. M. (1984). *Human Motivation: Physiological, Behavioral, and Social Approaches.* Needham Heights, Mass.: Allyn & Bacon.

Gibbs, W. W. (1996, August). "Gaining on Fat." *Scientific American,* pp. 88–94.

Gilligan, J. (1997). *Violence: Reflections on a National Epidemic.* New York: Vintage Books.

Gitlow, H., Gitlow, S., Oppenheim, A., and Oppenheim, R. (1989). *Tools and Methods for the Improvement of Quality.* Burr Ridge, Ill.: Irwin.

Gladwell, M. (2005). *Blink: The Power of Thinking Without Thinking.* New York: Little, Brown.

Glasser, W. (1990). *The Quality School: Managing Students Without Coercion.* New York: HarperCollins.

Gleick, J. (1987). *Chaos: Making a New Science.* New York: Viking Penguin.

Gogtay, N., et al. (2004, May 25). "Dynamic Mapping of Human Cortical Development During Childhood Through Early Adulthood." *Proceedings of the National Academy of Sciences,* 101(21), 8174–8179.

Gold, M. (1965). *Education of the Intellectually Gifted.* Columbus, Ohio: C. E. Merrill.

Goldberg, J. (1988). *Anatomy of a Scientific Discovery.* New York: Bantam Books.

Goldberg, L. R. (1993, January). "The Structure of Phenotypic Personality Traits." *American Psychologist,* 48(1), 26–34.

Goldberg, P. (1983). *The Intuitive Edge.* Los Angeles: Tarcher.

Goleman, D. (1995). *Emotional Intelligence.* New York: Bantam Books.

Goleman, D. (1996, August 13). "Brain Images of Addiction in Action Show Its Neural Basis." *The New York Times,* p. C1.

Goleman, D. (1998). *Working with Emotional Intelligence.* New York: Bantam Books.

Goleman, D. (2003). *Destructive Emotions: A Scientific Dialogue with the Dalai Lama.* New York: Bantam Books.

Goleman, D., Kaufman, P., and Ray, M. (1992). *The Creative Spirit.* New York: NAL/Dutton.

Golembiewski, R. T. (1988). *Phases of Burnout.* New York: Praeger.

Gollwitzer, P. M. (1999). "Implementation Intentions: Strong Effects of Simple Plans." *American Psychologist,* 54(7), 493–503.

Gonzales, L. (2003). *Deep Survival: Who Lives, Who Dies, and Why.* New York: W. W. Norton.

Gordon, B. (1995). *Memory: Remembering and Forgetting in Everyday Life.* New York: MasterMedia.

Gould, S. J. (1996). *Full House: The Spread of Excellence from Plato to Darwin.* New York: Three Rivers Press.

Gray, J. A. (1971). *The Psychology of Fear and Stress.* New York: McGraw-Hill.

Greenfield, S. A. (Ed.). (1996). *The Human Mind Explained.* New York: Henry Holt.

Gregorc, A. F. (1982). *Gregorc Style Delineator.* Maynard, Mass.: Gabriel Systems.

Gregory, R. L. (Ed.). (1987). *The Oxford Companion to the Mind.* New York: Oxford University Press.

Grossman, D. (1995). *On Killing: The Psychological Costs of Learning to Kill in War and Society.* Boston: Little, Brown.

Guirdham, M. (1995). *Interpersonal Skills at Work* (2nd ed.). Englewood Cliffs, N.J.: Prentice Hall.

Gzowski, P. (1981). *The Game of Our Lives.* Toronto: McClelland & Stewart.

Haas, R. (1994). *Eat Smart, Think Smart.* New York: HarperCollins.

Hafen, B. Q., Karren, K. J., Frandsen, K. J., and Smith, N. L. (1996). *Mind/Body Health: The Effects of Attitudes, Emotions, and Relationships.* Needham Heights, Mass.: Allyn & Bacon.

Hallowell, E. M. (1997). *Worry: Controlling It and Using It Wisely.* New York: Pantheon Books.

Halpern, D. F. (2000). *Sex Differences in Cognitive Abilities* (3rd ed.). Mahwah, N.J.: Lawrence Erlbaum.

Halverson, C. F. Jr., Kohnstamm, G. A., and Martin, R. P. (Eds.). (1994). *The Developing Structure of Temperament and Personality from Infancy to Adulthood.* Hillsdale, N.J.: Erlbaum.

Hamer, D. (2004). *The God Gene: How Faith Is Hardwired into Our Genes.* New York: Doubleday.

Hammond, S. A. (1996). *The Thin Book of Appreciative Inquiry.* Plano, Tex.: Thin Book Publishing Co.

Harris, J. R. (1998). *The Nurture Assumption: Why Children Turn Out the Way They Do.* New York: Free Press.

Hart, B., and Risley, T. (1995). *Meaningful Differences in the Everyday Experiences of Young American Children.* Baltimore: P. H. Brookes.

Hart, L. A. (1983). *Human Brain and Human Learning.* White Plains, N.Y.: Longman.

Hatfield, E., and Rapson, R. L. (1993). *Love, Sex, and Intimacy: Their Psychology, Biology, and History.* Reading, Mass.: Addison-Wesley.

Hayes, J. R. (1989). *The Complete Problem Solver* (2nd ed.). Hillsdale, N.J.: Erlbaum.

Healy, J. (1990). *Endangered Minds: Why Our Children Don't Think.* New York: Simon & Schuster.

Hedges, L. V., and Nowell, A. (1995, July 7). "Sex Differences in Mental Test Scores, Variability, and Numbers of High-Scoring Individuals." *Science,* 269(5220), 41.

Heisenberg, W. (1962). *Physics and Philosophy: The Revolution in Modern Science.* New York: HarperCollins.

Heller, W. (1993). "Neuropsychological Mechanism of Individual Differences in Emotion, Personality, and Arousal." *Neuropsychology,* 7(4), 476–489.

Henson, K. T., and Borthwick, P. (1984). "Matching Styles: A Historical Look." *Theory into Practice,* 23, 3–9.

Herber, H. (1978). *Teaching Reading in Content Areas* (2nd ed.). Englewood Cliffs, N.J.: Prentice Hall.

Herrmann, D. J. (1991). *Super Memory: A Quick-Action Program for Memory Improvement.* Emmaus, Pa.: Rodale.

Herrmann, N. (1989). *The Creative Brain.* Lake Lure, N.C.: Brain Books.

Herrnstein, R. J., and Murray, C. (1994). *The Bell Curve.* New York: Free Press.

Hersey, P., and Blanchard, K. H. (1976). *Management of Organization Behavior: Utilizing Human Resources* (3rd ed.). Englewood Cliffs, N.J.: Prentice Hall.

Hirsh, R. (1990). "Modulatory Integration: A Concept Capable of Explaining Cognitive Learning and Purposive Behavior in Physiological Terms." *Psychobiology,* 18(1), 3–15.

Hobson, J. A. (1988). *The Dreaming Brain.* New York: Basic Books.

Hobson, J. A. (1994). *The Chemistry of Conscious States.* New York: Little, Brown.

Hobson, J. A. (1995). *Sleep.* New York: Freeman.

Hoffmann, R. (1995). *The Same and Not the Same.* New York: Columbia University Press.

Hofstadter, D. R. (1979). *Gödel, Escher, Bach: An Eternal Golden Braid.* New York: Basic Books.

Holland, J. L. (1985). *Making Vocational Choices: A Theory of Vocational Personalities and Work Environments.* Englewood Cliffs, N.J.: Prentice Hall.

Holt, J. (1983). *How Children Fail.* Reading, Mass.: Perseus Books.

Honey, P., and Mumford, A. (1982). *The Manual of Learning Styles.* Maidenhead, England: Honey Press.

Hooper, J., and Teresi, D. (1986). *The Three-Pound Universe.* Old Tappan, N.J.: Macmillan.

Horgan, J. (1994, July). "Can Science Explain Consciousness?" *Scientific American,* pp. 88–94.

Horgan, J. (1996, December). "Why Freud Isn't Dead." *Scientific American,* pp. 106–111.

Horney, K. (1945). *Our Inner Conflicts.* New York: Norton.

Howard, P. J. (1972). "The Nonverbal Communication of Teacher Expectations." Unpublished doctoral dissertation, University of North Carolina at Chapel Hill.

Howard, P. J. (2000). *Visual Tools for Knowledge Workers: Aids for Critical Thinking.* Charlotte, N.C.: Center for Applied Cognitive Studies.

Howard, P. J., and Howard, J. M. (1993). *The Big Five Workbook: A Roadmap for Individual and Team Interpretation for Scores on the Five-Factor Model of Personality.* Charlotte, N.C.: Center for Applied Cognitive Studies.

Howard, P. J., and Howard, J. M. (2001). *The Owner's Manual for Personality at Work.* Austin: Bard Press.

Howard, P. J., and Howard, J. M. (2005). *The Learner: An Excel Workbook.* Charlotte, N.C.: Center for Applied Cognitive Studies.

Howard, P. J., and Howard, J. M. (2005). *The Professional Manual for the WorkPlace Big Five ProFile 3.0.* Charlotte, N.C.: Center for Applied and Cognitive Studies.

Howard, P. J., and Howard, J. M. (2006). *The Professional Manual for the SchoolPlace Big Five ProFile.* Charlotte, N.C.: Center for Applied and Cognitive Studies.

Hrushesky, W.J.M. (1994, July–August). "Timing Is Everything." *The Sciences,* pp. 32–37.

Huff, D. (1954). *How to Lie with Statistics.* New York: Norton.

Hughes, J. R., Daaboul, Y., Fino, J. J., and Shaw, G. L. (1998). "The 'Mozart Effect' on Epileptiform Activity." *Clinical Electroencephalography,* 29, 109–119.

Hunt, M. (1982). *The Universe Within: A New Science Explores the Human Mind.* New York: Simon & Schuster.

Hyerle, D. (1996). *Visual Tools for Constructing Knowledge.* Alexandria, Va.: Association for Supervision and Curriculum Development.

"Hypnosis." (1991). *Harvard Mental Health Letter,* 7(10), 1–4.

Ihilevich, D. and Gleser, G. C. (1986). *Defense Mechanisms: Their Classification, Correlates, and Measurement with the Defense Mechanism Inventory.* Owasco, Mich.: DMI Associates.

Ingelfinger, F. (1980). "Arrogance." *New England Journal of Medicine,* 303, 1506–1511.

Ironson, G., et al. (1992, August). "Effects of Anger on Left Ventricular Ejection Fraction in Coronary Artery Disease." *American Journal of Cardiology,* 70, 281–285.

Isaacowitz, D. M., and Seligman, M.E.P. "Is Pessimism a Risk Factor for Depressive Mood among Community-Dwelling Older Adults?" *Behaviour Research and Therapy.*

Izard, C. E., Kagan, J., and Zajonc, R. B. (Eds.). (1984). *Emotions, Cognition, and Behavior.* Cambridge: Cambridge University Press.

Jacobs, G. D. (1998). *Say Good Night to Insomnia.* New York: Henry Holt.

Jaffe, C. L. Jr. (1991). "Using 'Practical Knowledge' vs. Cognitive Ability to Predict Job Performance for Personnel in Customer Oriented Jobs." Unpublished doctoral dissertation, University of South Florida, Tampa.

Jaques, E. (1994). *Human Capability.* Falls Church, Va.: Cason Hall.

Jensen, E. (2000). *Music with the Brain in Mind.* San Diego: The Brain Store.

John, O. P., Angleitner, A., and Ostendorf, F. (1988). "The Lexical Approach to Personality: A Historical Review of Trait Taxonomic Research." *European Journal of Personality,* 2, 171–203.

Johnson-Laird, P. (1988). *The Computer and the Mind: An Introduction to Cognitive Science.* Cambridge, Mass.: Harvard University Press.

Jones, S. (1994). *The Language of Genes: Unraveling the Mysteries of Human Genetics.* New York: Anchor Books.

Jourdain, R. (1997). *Music, the Brain, and Ecstasy: How Music Captures Our Imagination.* New York: Morrow.

Joyce, B. R., and Hodges, R. E. (1966). "Instructional Flexibility Training." *Journal of Teacher Education,* 17, 409–416.

Jung, C. G. (1971). *Psychological Types.* Princeton, N.J.: Princeton University Press.

Kagan, J. (1966). "Reflection: Impulsivity and Reading Ability in Primary Grade Children." *Child Development,* 36, 609–628.

Kagan, J. (1998). *Three Seductive Ideas.* Cambridge, Mass.: Harvard University Press.

Kallan, C. (1991, October). "Probing the Power of Common Scents." *Prevention,* 43(10), 39–43.

Kassin, S. M., Tubb, V. A., Hosch, H. M., and Memon, A. (2001, May). "On the 'General Acceptance' of Eyewitness Testimony Research: A New Survey of the Experts." *American Psychologist,* 56(5), 405–416.

Kassirer, J. P., and Angell, M. (1998, January 1). "Losing Weight: An Ill-Fated New Year's Resolution." *New England Journal of Medicine,* 338(1), 52–56.

Katahn, M. (1991). *One Meal at a Time.* New York: Norton.

Katz, L. C., and Rubin, M. (1999). *Keep Your Brain Alive.* New York: Workman Publishing.

Katz, P. (1994). *The New Urbanism: Toward an Architecture of Community.* New York: McGraw-Hill.

Keeton, K. (1992). *Longevity: The Science of Staying Young.* New York: Viking Penguin.

Keirsey, D., and Bates, M. (1978). *Please Understand Me.* Del Mar, Calif.: Prometheus Nemesis.

Kelley, H. H., and Thibaut, J. W. (1978). *Interpersonal Relations: A Theory of Interdependence.* New York: Wiley.

Kepner, C. H., and Tregoe, B. B. (1981). *The New Rational Manager.* Princeton, N.J.: Princeton Research Press.

Kiecolt-Glaser, J. K., and Glaser, R. (1992). "Pschoneuroimmunology: Can Psychological Interventions Modulate Immunity?" *Journal of Counseling and Clinical Psychology,* 60(4), 569–575.

Kiesler, D. J. (1996). *Contemporary Interpersonal Theory and Research: Personality, Psychopathology, and Psychotherapy.* New York: Wiley.

Kimura, D. (1994). "Body Asymmetry and Intellectual Pattern." *Personality and Individual Differences,* 17(1), 53–60.

Kimura, D., and Carson, M. W. (1995). "Dermatoglyphic Asymmetry: Relation to Sex, Handedness and Cognitive Pattern." *Personality and Individual Differences,* 19(4), 471–478.

Kimura, D., and Hampson, E. (1990, April). *Neural and Hormonal Mechanisms Mediating Sex Differences in Cognition.* Research Bulletin No. 689. London, Ontario, Canada: Department of Psychology, University of Western Ontario.

Kinlaw, D. C. (1990). *Developing Superior Work Teams.* New York: Free Press.

Kintsch, W. (1994). "Text Comprehension, Memory, and Learning." *American Psychologist, 49*(4), 294–303.

Kirsch, I., and Lynn, S. J. (1995, October). "The Altered State of Hypnosis: Changes in the Theoretical Landscape." *American Psychologist, 50*(10), 846–858.

Kirton, M. J. (1977). *Research Edition: Kirton Adaption/Innovation Inventory.* London: National Federation for Educational Research.

Kline, M. (1953). *Mathematics in Western Culture.* New York: Oxford University Press.

Koestler, A. (1964). *The Act of Creation.* Old Tappan, N.J.: Macmillan.

Kogan, Z. (1956). *Essentials in Problem Solving.* New York: Arco.

Kohlberg, L. (1984). *The Psychology of Moral Development: The Nature and Validity of Moral Stages.* New York: HarperCollins.

Kolata, G. B. (1976). "Brain Biochemistry: Effects of Diet." *Science, 192,* 41–42.

Kolata, G. B. (1979). "Mental Disorders: A New Approach to Treatment?" *Science, 203,* 36–38.

Kolb, D. A. (1978). *Learning Styles Inventory Technical Manual.* Boston: McBer.

Kolbe, K. (1990). *The Conative Connection.* Reading, Mass.: Addison-Wesley.

Kolodnor, J. (1997, January). "Educational Implications of Analogy: A View from Case-Based Reasoning." *American Psychologist, 52*(1), 57–66.

Korzybski, A. (1948). *Science and Sanity: An Introduction to Non-Aristotelian Systems and General Semantics* (3rd ed.). Lakeville, Conn.: International Non-Aristotelian Library.

Kosslyn, S. M. (1994). *Image and Brain: The Resolution of the Imagery Debate.* Cambridge, Mass.: MIT Press.

Krakauer, J. (1997). *Into Thin Air.* New York: Anchor Books.

Kruger, J., and Dunning, D. (1999, December). "Unskilled and Unaware of It: How Difficulties in Recognizing One's Own Incompetence Lead to Inflated Self-Assessments." *Journal of Personality and Social Psychology, 77*(6), 1121–1134.

Kuhn, T. S. (1970). *The Structure of Scientific Revolutions* (2nd ed.). Chicago: University of Chicago Press.

Kurzban, R., and Leary, M. R. (2001). "Evolutionary Origins of Stigmatization: The Functions of Social Exclusion." *Psychological Bulletin, 127*(2), 187–208.

Lakoff, G. (1987). *Women, Fire, and Dangerous Things: What Categories Reveal about the Mind.* Chicago: University of Chicago Press.

Langer, E. (1989). *Mindfulness.* Reading, Mass.: Addison-Wesley.

Langer, E. (1997). *The Power of Mindful Learning.* Reading, Mass.: Addison-Wesley.

Latané, B., and Darley, J. (1970). *The Unresponsive Bystander: Why Doesn't He Help?* Englewood Cliffs, N.J.: Appleton-Century-Crofts.

Latham, G. P., and Yukl, G. A. (1975). "A Review of Research on the Application of Goal Setting in Organizations." *Academy of Management Journal, 18,* 824–845.

Lazarus, R. S. (1991a). *Emotion and Adaptation.* New York: Oxford University Press.

Lazarus, R. S. (1991b, August). "Progress on a Cognitive-Motivational-Relational Theory of Emotion." *American Psychologist, 46,* 819–834.

Leach, P. (1997). *Your Baby and Child: From Birth to Age Five* (rev. ed.). New York: Knopf.

Lecanuet, J. P. (1995). *Fetal Development: A Psychobiological Perspective.* Hillsdale, N.J.: Erlbaum.

LeDoux, J. (1996). *The Emotional Brain: The Mysterious Underpinnings of Emotional Life.* New York: Simon & Schuster.

LeDoux, J. (2002). *Synaptic Self.* New York: Viking.

Lee, C. (1987, September). "Mindmapping: Brainstorming on Paper." *Training, 24*(9), 71–76.

Lee, J. A. (1973). *The Colours of Love.* Toronto: New Press.

Lefton, R. E., Buzzotta, V., and Sherberg, M. (1985). *Improving Productivity Through People Skills.* New York: Ballinger.

Lemieux, M., and Bordage, G. (1992, April–June). "Propositional vs. Semantic Analysis of Medical Diagnostic Thinking." *Cognitive Science,* 16(2), 185–204.

LeShan, L. (1989). *Cancer as a Turning Point.* New York: NAL/Dutton.

Leslie, J., and Fleenor, J. (1998). *Feedback to Managers: A Review and Comparison of Multi-Rater Instruments for Management Development* (3rd ed.). Greensboro, N.C.: Center for Creative Leadership.

Lester, B. (1998, October 23). "Cocaine Exposure and Children: The Meaning of Subtle Effects." *Science,* 282(5389), 633–634.

LeVay, S. (1996). *Queer Science: The Use and Abuse of Research into Homosexuality.* Cambridge, Mass.: MIT Press.

Levine, M. (2000). *The Positive Psychology of Buddhism and Yoga.* Mahwah, N.J.: Lawrence Erlbaum.

Levine, M. (2002). *A Mind at a Time.* New York: Simon & Schuster.

Levine, M. (2003). *The Myth of Laziness.* New York: Simon & Schuster.

Livingstone, M. S., Rosen, G. D., Drislane, F. W., and Galaburda, A. M. (1991). "Physiological and Anatomical Evidence for a Magnocellular Defect in Developmental Dyslexia." *Proceedings of the National Academy of Sciences,* 88, 7943–7947.

Locke, E. A., and Latham, G. P. (2002). "Building a Practically Useful Theory of Goal Setting and Task Motivation: A 35-Year Odyssey." *American Psychologist,* 57(9), 705–717.

Loehlin, J. C. (1992). *Genes and Environment in Personality Development.* Thousand Oaks, Calif.: Sage.

Loftus, E. (1997, September). "Creating False Memories." *Scientific American,* 277(3), 70–75.

Loftus, E., and Ketcham, K. (1994). *The Myth of Repressed Memory.* New York: St. Martin's Press.

Long, M. E. (1987, December). "What Is This Thing Called Sleep?" *National Geographic,* 172(6), 787–821.

Lorayne, H., and Lucas, J. (1974). *The Memory Book.* New York: Stein & Day.

Louis, D. N. (1995, Spring). "The Brain's 'Other Cells' Go Awry." *On the Brain* (Harvard Mahoney Neuroscience Institute Letter), pp. 1–3, 7.

Maas, J. B. (1998). *Power Sleep.* New York: Villard Books.

Maccoby, E. (1998). *The Two Sexes: Growing Up Apart, Coming Together.* Cambridge, Mass.: Belknap.

MacLean, P. D. (1990). *The Triune Brain in Evolution.* New York: Plenum.

Maier, S. F., Watkins, L. R., and Fleshner, M. (1994). "Psychoneuroimmunology: The Interface Between Behavior, Brain, and Immunity." *American Psychologist,* 49(12), 1004–1017.

Maines, R. P. (1999). *The Technology of Orgasm.* Baltimore: Johns Hopkins University Press.

Mallandain, I., and Davies, M. F. (1994). "The Colours of Love: Personality Correlates of Love Styles." *PAID,* 17(4), 557–560.

Marston, W. M. (1987). *The Emotions of Normal People.* Minneapolis: Carlson Learning.

Martin, D. (August 1, 1999). "Late to Bed, Early to Rise Makes a Teen-ager . . . Tired." *New York Times,* 4A, 24–27.

Maslow, A. H. (1943). "A Theory of Human Motivation." *Psychological Review,* 50, 370–396.

Mason, D. (2002). *The Piano Tuner.* New York: Knopf.

Masten, A. S., and Coatsworth, J. D. (1998, February). "The Development of Competence in Favorable and Unfavorable Environments." *American Psychologist,* 53(2), 205–220. [Special Issue: "Applications of Developmental Science"].

Mayer, R. E. (January 2004). "Should There Be a Three-Strikes Rule Against Pure Discovery Learning? The Case for Guided Methods of Instruction." *American Psychologist,* 59(1), 7–13.

McAdams, D. P. (1993). *The Stories We Live By.* New York: Guilford Press.

McClelland, D. C. (1986). "Some Reflections on the Two Psychologies of Love." *Journal of Personality and Social Psychology,* 54, 334–353.

McClelland, D. C., and Kirshnit, C. (1988). "The Effect of Motivational Arousal Through Films on Immunoglobulin A." *Psychology and Health,* 2, 31–52.

McCrae, R. M., and Costa, P. T. (1989). "Reinterpreting the Myers-Briggs Type Indicator from the Perspective of the Five-Factor Model of Personality." *Journal of Personality and Social Psychology,* 57(1), 17–40.

McCrae, R. M., and Costa, P. T. (1990). *Personality in Adulthood.* New York: Guilford Press.

McDaniel, R. N. (1992). "The Relationship Between Personality and Perceived Success of Organizational Change." Doctoral dissertation, The Fielding Institute. *Dissertation Abstracts International,* 53(06), 3196B.

McEwen, B., and Seeman, T. (1999, August). "Allostatic Load and Allostasis." John D. and Catherine MacArthur Research on Network Socioeconomic Status and Health.

McEwen, B. S., and Schmeck, H. M. Jr. (1996). *The Hostage Brain.* New York: Rockefeller University Press.

McGuire, C. B., and Radner, R. (Eds.). (1972). *Decision and Organization.* Amsterdam: North-Holland.

McKay, M., Davis, M., and Fanning, P. (1995). *Messages: The Communication Skills Book* (2nd ed.). Oakland, Calif.: New Harbinger.

McNair, D. M., Lorr, M., and Droppleman, L. F. (1971). *Profile of Mood States Manual.* San Diego, Calif.: Educational and Industrial Testing Service.

McNamee, P., and Celona, J. (1987). *Decision Analysis for the Professional with Supertree.* Redwood City, Calif.: Scientific Press.

Medina, J. J. (1996). *The Clock of Ages.* New York: Cambridge University Press.

Medina, J. J. (2000). *The Genetic Inferno: Inside the Seven Deadly Sins.* New York: Cambridge University Press.

Mendosa, R. (2002, July). "Revised International Table of Glycemic Index (GI) and Glycemic Load (GL) Values." *The American Journal of Clinical Nutrition,* 76, 5–76.

"Mental Health: Does Therapy Help?" (1995, November). *Consumer Reports,* pp. 734–739.

Merrill, D. W., and Reid, H. H. (1981). *Personal Style and Effective Performance.* Radnor, Pa.: Chilton.

Merzbacher, C. F. (1979, April). "A Diet and Exercise Regimen: Its Effect upon Mental Acuity and Personality. A Pilot Study." *Perceptual and Motor Skills,* 48(2), 367–371.

Metcalfe, J., and Shimamura, A. P. (Eds.). (1994). *Metacognition: Knowing about Knowing.* Cambridge, Mass.: MIT Press.

Michalko, M. (1991). *Thinkertoys: A Handbook of Business Creativity for the '90s.* Berkeley, Calif.: Ten Speed Press.

Miller, E. M. (1994). "Intelligence and Brain Myelination: A Hypothesis." *Personality and Individual Differences,* 17(6), 803–832.

Miller, G. A. (1956). "The Magical Number Seven, Plus or Minus Two: Some Limits on Our Capacity for Processing Information." *Psychological Review,* 63, 81–97.

Miller, G. F., and Todd, P. M. (1998). "Mate Choice Turns Cognitive." *Trends in Cognitive Science,* 2(5), 190–198.

Miller, J. B., and Leeds, T. (1998). *The G.I. Factor: The Glycaemic Index Solution.* London: Hodder & Stoughton.

Mindell, J. (1997). *Sleeping Through the Night.* New York: HarperCollins.

Mindell, J. A., and Owens, J. A. (2003). *A Clinical Guide to Pediatric Sleep.* Philadelphia: Lippincott Williams & Wilkins.

Minninger, J. (1984). *Total Recall: How to Boost Your Memory Power.* Emmaus, Pa.: Rodale.

Mischel, W. (1968). *Personality and Assessment.* New York: Wiley.

Moir, A., and Jessel, D. (1991). *Brain Sex: The Real Difference Between Men and Women.* New York: Carol.

Moody, P. E. (1983). *Decision Making: Proven Methods for Better Decisions.* New York: McGraw-Hill.

Moore-Ede, M. (1993). *The Twenty-Four-Hour Society: Understanding Human Limits in a World That Never Stops.* Reading, Mass.: Addison-Wesley.

Morgan, W. P. (Ed.). (1997). *Physical Activity and Mental Health.* Washington, D.C.: Taylor & Francis.

Mukerjee, M. (1995, October). "Hidden Scars." *Scientific American,* pp. 14, 20.

Murray, H. A. (1938). *Explorations in Personality.* New York: Oxford University Press.

Myers, I. B., and McCaulley, M. H. (1985). *Manual: A Guide to the Development and Use of the Myers-Briggs Type Indicator.* Palo Alto, Calif.: Consulting Psychologists Press.

Nadler, G., and Hibino, S. (1990). *Breakthrough Thinking.* Rocklin, Calif.: Prima.

Nathanielsz, P. W. (1999). *Life in the Womb: The Origin of Health and Disease.* Ithaca, N.Y.: Promethean Press.

National Research Council, Committee on Diet and Health. (1989). *Diet and Health: Implications for Reducing Chronic Disease Risk.* Washington, D.C.: National Academy Press.

National Research Council. (1993–1994). *Understanding and Preventing Violence.* (4 vols.). Washington, D.C.: National Academy Press.

Neeper, S. A., Gomez-Pinilla, F., Choi, J., and Cotman, C. W. (1995, January 12). "Exercise Raises Brain Neurotrophins." *Nature,* 373, 109.

Nelson, H. D., Nevitt, M. C., and Scott, J. C. (1994). "Smoking, Alcohol, and Neuromuscular and Physical Function of Older Women." *Journal of the American Medical Association,* 272, 1825–1831.

Nemeroff, C. B. (1998, June). "The Neurobiology of Depression." *Scientific American,* pp. 42–49.

Neubauer, P. B., and Neubauer, A. (1990). *Nature's Thumbprint: The New Genetics of Personality.* Reading, Mass.: Addison-Wesley.

Newberg, A. B., d'Aquili, E. G., Rause, V. (2001). *Why God Won't Go Away.* New York: Ballantine.

Newsome, S., Day, A. L., & Catano, V. M. (2000, December). "Assessing the Predictive Validity of Emotional Intelligence." *Personality and Individual Differences,* 29(6), 1005–1016.

Nicholson, N. (1998, July–August). "How Hardwired Is Human Behavior?" *Harvard Business Review,* pp. 135–147.

Nicholson, N. (2001). "An Evolutionary Perspective on Change and Stability in Personality, Culture, and Organization." In M. Erez, U. Kleinbeck, and H. Thierry (Eds.), *Work Motivation in the Context of a Globalizing Economy* (pp. 381–394). Mahwah, N.J.: Lawrence Erlbaum.

Nierenberg, G. I. (1985). *The Idea Generator.* Berkeley, Calif.: Experience in Software.

Norman, D. A. (1993). *Things That Make Us Smart: Cognitive Artifacts as Tools for Thought.* Reading, Mass.: Perseus Books.

Norman, W. T. (1963). "Toward an Adequate Taxonomy of Personality Attributes: Replicated Factor Structure in Peer Nomination Personality Ratings." *Journal of Abnormal and Social Psychology,* 66, 574–583.

Northrop, F.S.C. (1946). *The Meeting of East and West: An Inquiry Concerning World Understanding.* Old Tappan, N.J.: Macmillan.

Northrop, F.S.C. (1947). *The Logic of the Sciences and the Humanities.* Cleveland: World.

Okogbaa, O. G., and Shell, R. L. (1986, December). "The Measurement of Knowledge Worker Fatigue." *IEEE Transactions,* 18(4), 335–342.

Ornstein, R. (1986). *Multimind: A New Way of Looking at Human Behavior.* New York: Anchor Books.

Ornstein, R. (1993). *The Roots of the Self: Unraveling the Mystery of Who We Are.* San Francisco: Harper San Francisco.

Ornstein, R., and Sobel, D. (1987). *The Healing Brain.* New York: Simon & Schuster.

Ortiz, J. M. (1997). *The Tao of Music: Sound Psychology.* York Beach, Maine: Samuel Weiser.

Ozonoff, S., Dawson, G., and McPartland, J. (2002). *A Parent's Guide to Asperger's Syndrome and High Functioning Austism.* New York: Guilford Publications.

Papolos, D., and Papolos, J. (2002). *The Bipolar Child.* New York: Broadway Books.

Peck, M. S. (1987). *The Different Drum: Community-Making and Peace.* New York: Simon & Schuster.

Pemberton, W. H. (1989). *Sanity for Survival: A Semantic Approach to Conflict Resolution.* San Francisco: Graphic Guides.

Pennington, B. F. (1991). *Diagnosing Learning Disorders: A Neuropsychological Framework.* New York: Guilford Press.

Perry, W. G. Jr. (1970). *Forms of Intellectual and Ethical Development in the College Years: A Scheme.* New York: Holt, Rinehart and Winston.

Persinger, M. A. (1995). "Out-of-Body-Like Experiences Are More Probable in People with Elevated Complex Partial Epileptic-Like Signs During Periods of Enhanced Geomagnetic Activity: A Nonlinear Effect." *Perceptual and Motor Skills,* 80, 563–569.

Pert, C. B. (1997). *Molecules of Emotion: Why You Feel the Way You Feel.* New York: Scribner.

Petri, H. L. (1991). *Motivation: Theory, Research, and Applications* (3rd ed.). Belmont, Calif.: Wadsworth.

Piaget, J. (1977). *The Essential Piaget.* (H. E. Guber and J. J. Vaneche, eds.). New York: Basic Books.

Pidikiti, R. D., et al. (1996, June). "A New Technique for Improving Rehabilitation of Movement after Stroke: A Pilot Study." *Journal of Rehabilitation Research and Development,* 33, 108 ff.

Pierpaoli, W., Regelson, W., and Coleman, C. (1996). *The Melatonin Miracle.* New York: G. K. Hall.

Pinker, S. (1994). *The Language Instinct.* New York: Morrow.

Pinker, S. (1997). *How the Mind Works.* New York: Norton.

Pirsig, R. M. (1974). *Zen and the Art of Motorcycle Maintenance: An Inquiry into Values.* New York: Morrow.

Plomin, R., & DeFries, J. C. (1985). *Origins of Individual Differences in Infancy.* Orlando, Fla.: Academic Press

Plomin, R., DeFries, J. C., McClearn, G. E., & Rutter, M. (1997). *Behavioral Genetics* (3rd ed.). New York: W. H. Freeman.

Plunkett, L. C., and Hale, G. A. (1982). *The Proactive Manager: The Complete Book of Problem Solving and Decision Making.* New York: Wiley.

Plutchik, R., and Kellerman, H. (Eds.). (1989). *The Measurement of Emotions. Vol. 4: Emotions: Theory, Research, and Experience.* Orlando: Academic Press.

Pollitt, E., Leibel, R. L., and Greenfield, D. (1981). "Brief Fasting, Stress, and Cognition in Children." *American Journal of Clinical Nutrition,* 34, 1526–1533.

Polya, G. C. (1971). *How to Solve It: A New Aspect of Mathematical Method (*2nd ed.). Princeton, N.J.: Princeton University Press.

Pope, K. S. (1996, September). "Memory, Abuse, and Science: Questioning Claims about the False Memory Syndrome Epidemic." *American Psychologist,* 51(9), 957–974.

Posner, M. I., and Raichle, M. E. (1994). *Images of Mind.* New York: Scientific American Library.

Potts, M., and Short, R. (1999). *Ever Since Adam and Eve: The Evolution of Human Sexuality.* New York: Cambridge University Press.

Poundstone, W. (1988*). Labyrinths of Reason: Paradox, Puzzles, and the Frailty of Knowledge.* New York: Anchor Books.

Prince, G. M. (1970). *The Practice of Creativity.* New York: Collier Books.

Putnam, R. D. (2000). *Bowling Alone: The Collapse and Revival of American Community.* New York: Simon & Schuster.

Quartz, S. R., and Sejnowski, R .J. (2002). *Liars, Lovers, and Heroes: What the New Brain Science Reveals about How We Become Who We Are.* New York: Quill/HarperCollins.

Raine, N. V. (1998). *After Silence: Rape & My Journey Back.* New York: Three Rivers Press.

Raloff, J. (1991, October 5). "Searching Out How a Severe Diet Slows Aging." *Science News,* 140(14), 215.

Ray, O. (2004, January). "How the Mind Hurts and Heals the Body." *American Psychologist,* 59(1), 7–13.

Real, T. (1997). *I Don't Want to Talk about It: Overcoming the Secret Legacy of Male Depression.* New York: Scribner.

Redfield, J. (1995). *The Celestine Prophecy.* New York: Warner Books.

Reichs, K. (1998). *Deja Dead.* Thorndike, Me.: Thorndike Press.

Reid, D. P. (1989). *The Tao of Health, Sex, and Longevity: A Modern Guide to the Ancient Way.* New York: Simon & Schuster.

Rein, G., Atkinson, M., & and McCraty, R. (1995). "The Physiological and Psychological Effects of Compassion and Anger" (Part 1 of 2). *Journal of Advancement in Medicine,* 8(2), 87–105.

Renzulli, J. S., and Smith, L. H. (1978). *The Learning Styles Inventory: A Measure of Student Preference for Instructional Techniques.* Mansfield Center, Conn.: Creative Learning Press.

Restak, R. M. (1984). *The Brain.* New York: Bantam Books.

Restak, R. M. (1988). *The Mind.* New York: Bantam Books.

Restak, R. M. (1991). *The Brain Has a Mind of Its Own.* New York: Harmony.

Restak, R. M. (1994). *Receptors.* New York: Bantam.

Restak, R. M. (1994). *The Modular Brain.* New York: Scribner.

Restak, R. M. (1997). *Older and Wiser.* New York: Simon & Schuster.

Rickards, T. (1974). *Problem-Solving Through Creative Analysis.* Epping, England: Gower.

Ricklefs, R. E., and Finch, C. E. (1995). *Aging: A Natural History.* New York: Scientific American Library.

Riskind, P. (1996, Fall). "Multiple Sclerosis: The Immune System's Terrible Mistake." *On the Brain* (Harvard Mahoney Neuroscience Institute Letter), 1–4.

Robbins, S. P. (1996). *Training in Interpersonal Skills: Tips for Managing People at Work* (2nd ed.). Englewood Cliffs, N.J.: Prentice Hall.

Roberts, R. D., and Kyllonen, P. C. (1999). "Morningness-Eveningness and Intelligence: Early to Bed, Early to Rise Will Likely Make You Anything but Wise!" *Personality and Individual Differences,* 27(6), 1123–1133.

Robinson, B. E. (1989). *Work Addiction: Hidden Legacies of Adult Children.* Deerfield Beach, Fla.: Health Communications.

Rogers, K. B. (1986). "Do the Gifted Think and Learn Differently? A Review of Recent Research and Its Implications for Instruction." *Journal for the Education of the Gifted,* 10, 17–39.

Rogers, R. (Ed.). (1997). *Clinical Assessment of Malingering and Deception* (2nd ed.). New York: Guilford Press.

Rose, R. J. (1998). "A Developmental Behavior–Genetic Perspective on Alcoholism Risk." *Alcohol Health and Research World,* 22(2), 131–143.

Rosenfield, I. (1988). *The Invention of Memory: A New View of the Brain.* New York: Basic Books.

Rosenthal, R., and Jacobson, L. (1968). *Pygmalion in the Classroom.* Austin: Holt, Rinehart and Winston.

Rosenthal, R., Hall, J. A., DiMatteo, M. R., and Rogers, P. L. (1979). *Sensitivity to Nonverbal Communication: The PONS Test.* Baltimore: Johns Hopkins University Press.

Rossi, E. L., and Nimmons, D. (1991). *The 20-Minute Break: Using the New Science of Ultradian Rhythms.* Los Angeles: Tarcher.

Rowan, R. (1986). *The Intuitive Manager.* New York: Little, Brown.

Rozin, P. (1997). "Disgust Faces, Basal Ganglia and Obsessive-Compulsive Disorder: Some Strange Brainfellows." *Trends in Cognitive Sciences,* 1(9), 321–325. (Includes response.)

Ruch, W. (1988). "Sensation Seeking and the Enjoyment of Structure and Content of Humour: Stability of Findings Across Four Samples." *Personality and Individual Differences,* 9, 861–871.

Saaty, T. L. (1982). *Decision Making for Leaders: The Analytical Hierarchy Process for Decisions in a Complex World.* Belmont, Calif.: Lifetime Learning.

Sackett, P., Hardison, C. M., and Cullen, J. J. (2004, January). "On Interpreting Stereotype Threat as Accounting for African American-White Differences on Cognitive Tests." *American Psychologist,* 59(1), 7–13.

Sacks, O. (2003, August 23). "Speed." *The New Yorker,* pp. 60–69.

Sagan, C. (1995). *The Demon-Haunted World.* New York: Random House.

Sahelian, R. (1997). *Melatonin: Nature's Sleeping Pill* (2nd ed.). Garden City Park, N.Y.: Avery Publishing Group.

Salovey, P., and Mayer, J. D. (1990). "Emotional Intelligence." *Imagination, Cognition, and Personality,* 9, 185–211.

Saper, C. (1996, Summer). "Why We Sleep (or Can't)." *On the Brain* (Harvard Mahoney Neuroscience Institute Letter), 5(3), 1–3.

Sapolsky, R. M. (1994). *Why Zebras Don't Get Ulcers: A Guide to Stress, Stress-Related Diseases, and Coping.* New York: W. H. Freeman.

Sapolsky, R. M. (1997). *The Trouble with Testosterone, and Other Essays on the Biology of the Human Predicament.* New York: Scribner.

Schachter, S., and Singer, J. E. (1962). "Cognitive, Social, and Physiological Determinants of Emotional States." *Psychological Review,* 69, 379–399.

Schacter, D. L. (1996). *Searching for Memory.* New York: Basic Books.

Schacter, D. L. (1999). "The Seven Sins of Memory: Insights from Psychology and Cognitive Neuroscience." *American Psychologist,* 54(3), 182–203.

Schaie, K. W. (1955). "A Test of Behavioral Rigidity." *Journal of Abnormal and Social Psychology,* 51, 604–610.

Schaie, K. W. (1994, April). "The Course of Adult Intellectual Development." *American Psychologist,* 49(4), 304–313.

Schaie, K. W. (1996). *Intellectual Development in Adulthood: The Seattle Longitudinal Study.* New York: Cambridge University Press.

Schaie, K. W., and Parham, I. A. (1975). *Manual for the Test of Behavioral Rigidity.* Palo Alto, Calif.: Consulting Psychologists Press.

Schaie, K. W., and Willis, S. L. (1996). *Adult Development and Aging* (4th ed.). New York: Addison-Wesley.

Schlosberg, H. S. (1954). "Three Dimensions of Emotion." *Psychological Review,* 61, 81–88.

Schmeck, R. R. (1983). "Learning Style of College Students." In R. F. Dillon and R. R. Schmeck (Eds.), *Individual Differences in Cognition* (Vol. 1, pp. 233–279). Orlando: Academic Press.

Schmidt, D. E., and Keating, J. P. (1979). "Human Crowding and Personal Control: An Integration of the Research." *Psychological Bulletin,* 86, 680–700.

Schoenthaler, S. (1983). "Diet and Crime: An Empirical Examination of the Value of Nutrition in the Control and Treatment of Incarcerated Juvenile Offenders." *International Journal of Biosocial Research,* 14, 25–39.

Schutte, N. S., et al. (1998, August). "Development and Validation of a Measure of Emotional Intelligence." *Personality and Individual Differences,* 25(2), 167–177.

Schwartz, J. M., and Begley, S. (2002). *The Mind and the Brain: Neuroplasticity and the Power of Mental Force.* New York: Regan Books/HarperCollins.

Searle, J. R. (Ed.). (1992). *The Rediscovery of the Mind.* Cambridge, Mass.: MIT Press.

Sears, W., and Sears, M. (1993). *The Baby Book.* New York: Little, Brown.

Segal, N. L. (1999). *Entwined Lives: Twins and What They Tell Us About Human Behavior.* New York: Dutton.

Seligman, M.E.P. (1984). *Seligman Attributional Style Questionnaire.* (Available by calling Martin Seligman or Peter Schulman at 215-898-2748).

Seligman, M.E.P. (1991). *Learned Optimism.* New York: Knopf.

Seligman, M.E.P. (1994). *What You Can Change and What You Can't.* New York: Knopf.

Seligman, M.E.P. (1996, October). "Science as an Ally of Practice." *American Psychologist,* 51(10), 1072–1079. [Special issue: "Outcome Assessment of Psychotherapy"].

Seligman, M.E.P. (2002). *Authentic Happiness.* New York: Free Press.

Seligman, M.E.P., Reivich, K., Jaycox, L., and Gillham, J. (1995). *The Optimistic Child.* Boston: Houghton Mifflin.

Seligman, M.E.P., Steen, T. A., Park, N., and Peterson, C. (2005). "Positive Psychology Progress: Empirical Validation of Interventions." *American Psychologist,* 60(5), 410–421.

Selye, H. (1952). *The Story of the Adaptation Syndrome.* Montreal: Acta.

Senge, P. (1990). *The Fifth Discipline.* New York: Doubleday/Currency.

Shapiro, L. (1997). *How to Raise a Child with a High EQ.* New York: HarperCollins.

Shaw, G. (2000). *Keeping Mozart in Mind.* San Diego: Academic Press.

Shaywitz, S. E. (1996, November). "Dyslexia." *Scientific American,* pp. 98–104.

Shaywitz, S. E., et al. (1992). "Evidence That Dyslexia May Represent the Lower Tail of a Normal Distribution of Reading Ability." *New England Journal of Medicine,* 326(3), 145–150.

Shebilske, W. L., Goettl, B. P., Corrington, K., and Day, E. A. (1999). "Interlesson Spacing and Task-Related Processing During Complex Skill Acquisition." *Journal of Experimental Psychology: Applied,* 5(4), 413–437.

Shelov, S. P. (1998). *Caring for Your Baby and Young Child* (rev. ed.). New York: Bantam Books.

Shermer, M. (2004). *The Science of Good and Evil.* New York: Times Books.

Shields, B. (2005). *Down Came the Rain.* New York: Hyperion.

Shorvon, S. D. (2005). *Handbook of Epilepsy Treatment* (2nd ed.). Malden, Mass.: Blackwell Publishing.

Shute, N. (1998, March 30). "The Ten-Minute Test for Strokes: New Breakthroughs in What MRIs Can See." *U.S. News & World Report,* pp. 69–72.

Siegel, B. (1987). *Love, Medicine and Miracles.* New York: HarperCollins.

Siegler, R. (1996). *Emerging Minds: The Process of Change in Children's Thinking.* New York: Oxford University Press.

Simon, H. (1969). *Sciences of the Artificial.* Cambridge, Mass.: MIT Press.

Simonton, O. C., Simonton, S., and Creighton, J. (1980). *Getting Well Again.* New York: Bantam Books.

Singer, R. B., Murphey, M., and Tennant, L. K. (Eds.). (1993). *Handbook of Research on Sport Psychology.* Old Tappan, N.J.: Macmillan.

Skinner, B. F. (1948). *Walden Two.* New York: Macmillan.

Slon, S. (1997, June). "Night Moves." *Prevention,* pp. 106–113.

Snowdon, D. (2001). *Aging with Grace: What the Nun Study Teaches Us about Leading Longer, Healthier, and More Meaningful Lives.* New York: Bantam Books.

Somer, E. (1995). *Food and Mood.* New York: Henry Holt.

"Spinal Cord Injury: Treatment and Outlook" [Special issue]. (1997, March–April). *BrainWork: The Neuroscience Newsletter* (Charles A. Dana Foundation), 7(2).

Staso, W. (1995). *What Stimulation Your Baby Needs to Become Smart.* Orcutt, Calif.: Great Beginnings Press.

Steele, C. M. (1997, June). "A Threat in the Air: How Stereotypes Shape Intellectual Identity and Performance." *American Psychologist,* 52(6), 613–629.

Steinberg, L. S. (2004). *The Ten Basic Principles of Good Parenting.* New York: Simon & Schuster.

Steinberg, L. S., and Lerner, R. (2004). *Handbook of Adolescent Psychology* (2nd ed.). New York: Wiley.

Steinberg, L. S., Reyome, N. D., and Bjornsen, C. A. (2005). *Adolescence* (7th ed.). New York: McGraw-Hill.

Sterling, P. and Eyer, J. (1988). "Allostasis: A New Paradigm to Explain Arousal Pathology." In S. Fisher and J. Reason (Eds.), *Handbook of Life Stress, Cognition and Health* (pp. 629–649). New York: Wiley.

Sternberg, R. J. (1986). *Intelligence Applied: Understanding and Increasing Your Intellectual Skills.* Orlando: Harcourt Brace.

Sternberg, R. J. (1988). *The Triarchic Mind: A New Theory of Human Intelligence.* New York: Viking Penguin.

Sternberg, R. J. (1997a). *Successful Intelligence.* New York: Plume.

Sternberg, R. J. (1997b). "Does the Graduate Record Examination Predict Meaningful Success in the Graduate Training of Psychologists? A Case Study." *American Psychologist,* 52(6), 630–641.

Sternberg, R. J. (1997c). *Thinking Styles.* New York: Cambridge University Press.

Sternberg, R. J., and Davidson, J. E. (Eds.). (1995). *The Nature of Insight.* Cambridge, Mass.: MIT Press.

Sternberg, R. J., and Grigorenko, E. L. (1997, July). "Are Cognitive Styles Still in Style?" *American Psychologist,* 52(7), 700–712.

Sternberg, R. J., and Kolligian, J. Jr. (1990). *Competence Considered.* New Haven: Yale University Press.

Sternberg, R. J., and Lubart, T. I. (1996, July). "Investing in Creativity." *American Psychologist,* 51(7), 677–688.

Sternberg, R. J., and Wagner, R. K. (1991). "MSG Thinking Styles Inventory Manual." Unpublished test manual, Yale University Department of Psychology, New Haven, Conn.

Stevens, W. (1967a). *The Collected Poems of Wallace Stevens.* New York: Knopf.

Stevens, W. (1967b). *The Necessary Angel.* New York: Knopf.

Stickgold, R. (1998). "Sleep: Off-Line Memory Reprocessing." *Trends in Cognitive Science,* 2(12), 484–492.

Stumpf, H., and Jackson, D. N. (1994). "Gender-Related Differences in Cognitive Abilities: Evidence from a Medical School Admissions Testing Program." *Personality and Individual Differences,* 17(3), 335–344.

Sylwester, R. (1995). *A Celebration of Neurons: An Educator's Guide to the Human Brain.* Alexandria, Va.: Association for Supervision and Curriculum Development.

Sylwester, R., and Hasegawa, C. (1989, January). "How to Explain Drugs to Your Students." *Middle School,* pp. 8–11.

Taylor, S. E. (2000). *The Tending Instinct.* New York: Times Books.

Tellagen, A., et al. (1988). "Personality Similarity in Twins Reared Apart and Together." *Journal of Personality and Social Psychology,* 54(6), 1031–1039.

Tesser, A., and Crelia, R. (1994). "Attitude Heritability and Attitude Reinforcement: A Test of the Niche Building Hypothesis." *Personality and Individual Differences,* 16(4), 571–577.

Thagard, P. (1992). "Adversarial Problem Solving: Modeling an Opponent Using Explanatory Coherence." *Cognitive Science,* 16, 123–149.

Tharp, T. (2003). *The Creative Habit.* New York: Simon and Schuster.

Thayer, R. E. (1989). *Biopsychology of Mood and Arousal.* New York: Oxford University Press.

Thayer, R. E. (1996). *The Origin of Everyday Moods: Managing Energy, Tension, and Stress.* New York: Oxford University Press.

Thomas, M. C., and Thomas, T. S. (1990). *Getting Commitment at Work: A Guide for Managers and Employees.* Chapel Hill, N.C.: Commitment Press.

Thomas, P. R. (Ed.). (1995). *Weighing the Options: Criteria for Evaluating Weight-Management Programs.* Washington, D.C.: National Academy of Sciences Press.

Thompson, C. (1992). *What a Great Idea! The Key Steps Creative People Take.* New York: HarperCollins.

Thompson, H. (1995, June). "Walk, Don't Run." *Texas Monthly,* pp. 114, 116–117, 136.

Thompson, J. G. (1988). *The Psychobiology of Emotions.* New York: Plenum.

Toates, F. (1986). *The Biological Foundations of Behavior.* Bristol, Pa.: Open University Press.

Tomatis, A. (1991). *The Conscious Ear.* Barrytown, N.Y.: Station Hill Press.

Tornow, W., and London, M. (Eds.). (1998). *Maximizing the Value of 360-Degree Feedback: A Process for Successful Individual and Organizational Development.* San Francisco: Jossey-Bass.

Torrance, E. P. (1974). *Torrance Tests of Creative Thinking.* Bensenville, Ill.: Scholastic Testing Service.

U.S. Department of Health and Human Services. (1999). *Mental Health: A Report of the Surgeon General.* Rockville, Md.: National Institute of Mental Health.

Veggeberg, S. K. (1997, September–October). "The Big Story in Depression: What Isn't Happening." *BrainWork: The Neuroscience Newsletter* (Charles A. Dana Foundation), 7(4), 1–3.

Vernon, P. A. (Ed.). (1987). *Speed of Information-Processing and Intelligence.* Norwood, N.J.: Ablex.

von Bertalanffy, L. (1967). *Robots, Men and Minds: Psychology in the Modern World.* New York: Braziller.

von Oech, R. (1983). *A Whack on the Side of the Head: How to Unlock Your Mind for Innovation.* New York: Warner Books.

Vroon, P. (1997). *Smell: The Secret Seducer.* New York: Farrar, Straus & Giroux.

Wagner, M. J., and Tilney, G. (1983, March 17). "The Effect of 'Superlearning' Techniques on the Vocabulary Acquisition and Alpha Brainwave Production of Language Learners." *TESOL Quarterly,* 7(1), 5–17.

Wall, P. D. (1999). *Pain: The Science of Suffering.* London: Weidenfeld and Nicolson.

Wallas, G. (1926). *The Art of Thought.* London: J. Cape.

Walsh, A. (1996). *The Science of Love: Understanding Love and Its Effects on Mind and Body.* Amherst, N.Y.: Prometheus.

Walsh, C. A. (1997, Winter). "Epilepsy: Genes May Build the Road to Treatment." *On the Brain* (Harvard Mahoney Neuroscience Institute Letter).

Walton, M. (1986). *The Deming Management Method.* New York: Dodd, Mead.

Watson, J. B. (1925). *Behaviorism.* New York: Norton.

Watzlawick, P., Weakland, J. H., and Fisch, R. (1974). *Change: Principles of Problem Formation and Problem Resolution.* New York: Norton.

Weatherall, D. (1987, September). "New Light on Light." *Management Services, 31*(9), 38–39.

Webb, W. B. (1992). *Sleep: The Gentle Tyrant* (2nd ed.). Bolton, Mass.: Anker.

Webb, W. B. (Ed.). (1982). *Biological Rhythms, Sleep, and Performance.* New York: Wiley.

Weinberg, B. A., and Bealer, B. K. (2001). *The World of Caffeine: The Science and Culture of the World's Most Popular Drug.* New York: Routledge.

Weiner, N. A., Zahn, M. A., Sagi, R. J., and Merton, R. K. (1990). *Violence: Patterns, Causes, Public Policy.* San Diego: Harcourt Brace Jovanovich.

Weingardt, K. R., Leonesio, R. J., and Loftus, E. F. (1994). "On Eyewitness Metacognition." In J. Metcalfe and A. P. Shimamura (Eds.), *Metacognition: Knowing about Knowing* (pp. 155–184). Cambridge, Mass.: MIT Press.

Weston, D. C., and Weston, M. S. (1996). *Playwise: 365 Fun-Filled Activities for Building Character, Conscience, and Emotional Intelligence in Children.* Los Angeles: Tarcher.

Wetter, D. W., et al. (1998, June). "The Agency for Health Care Policy and Research Smoking Cessation Clinical Practice Guideline: Findings and Implications for Psychologists." *American Psychologist, 53*(6), 657–669.

Whetten, D., and Cameron, K. (1984). *Developing Management Skills.* Glenview, Ill.: Scott, Foresman.

Whybrow, P. C. (1997). *A Mood Apart: Depression, Mania, and Other Afflictions of Self.* New York: Basic Books.

Wiertelak, E., Meier, S. F., and Watkins, L. R. (1992, May 8). "Cholecystokinin Antianalgesia: Safety Cues Abolish Morphine Analgesia." *Science, 256,* 830 ff.

Wilcox, S. M., Himmelstein, D. U., and Woolhandler, S. (1994, July 27). "Inappropriate Drug Prescribing for the Community-Dwelling Elderly." *Journal of the American Medical Association, 272*(4), 292–296.

Williams, C. L., et al. (1985). *The Negotiable Environment: People, White Collar Work, and the Office.* Ann Arbor, Mich.: Miller, Herman.

Williams, R. (1989). *The Trusting Heart: Great News about Type A Behavior.* New York: Times Books.

Williams, R., and Williams, V. (1994). *Anger Kills.* New York: HarperPerennial.

Williams, W., and Ceci, S. (1997, November). "Are Americans Becoming More or Less Alike?" *American Psychologist, 52*(11), 1226–1235.

Wilson, E. O. (1975). *Sociobiology: The New Synthesis.* Cambridge, Mass.: Harvard University Press.

Wilson, E. O. (1995). *On Human Nature.* London: Penguin Books.

Wilson, G. D. (1994). *Psychology for Performing Artists: Butterflies and Bouquets.* London: Jessica Kingsley.

Winner, E. (1996). *Gifted Children: Myths and Realities.* New York: Basic Books.

Winner, E. (1997, October). "Exceptionally High Intelligence and Schooling." *American Psychologist, 52*(10), 1070–1081.

Winner, E. (2000). "The Origins and Ends of Giftedness." *American Psychologist, 55*(1), 159–169.

Winter, A., and Winter, R. (1988). *Eat Right, Be Bright.* New York: St. Martin's Press.

Winter, R. (1995). *A Consumer's Guide to Medicines in Food.* New York: Crown Trade Paperbacks.

Witkin, H. A., and Goodenough, D. R. (1981). *Cognitive Styles: Essence and Origins.* Madison, Conn.: International Universities Press.

Wolfe, D. A., McMahon, R. J., and Peters, R. D. (1997). *Child Abuse: New Directions in Prevention and Treatment Across the Lifespan.* Thousand Oaks, Calif.: Sage.

Wrangham, R., and Peterson, D. (1996). *Demonic Males: Apes and the Origins of Human Violence.* Boston: Houghton Mifflin.

Wright, R. (1994). *The Moral Animal: The New Science of Evolutionary Psychology.* New York: Vintage Books.

Wright, W. (1998). *Born That Way: Genes, Behavior, Personality.* New York: Knopf.

Wyatt, R. J., and Henter, I. D. (1997, May–June). "Schizophrenia: An Introduction." *BrainWork: The Neuroscience Newsletter* (Charles A. Dana Foundation), 7(3), 1–3, 8.

Yepsen, R. B. Jr. (1987). *How to Boost Your Brain Power: Achieving Peak Intelligence, Memory and Creativity.* Emmaus, Pa.: Rodale.

Zatorre, R. J. (1998, March 17). "Functional Anatomy of Musical Processing in Listeners with Absolute Pitch and Relative Pitch." *Proceedings of the National Academy of Sciences of the United States of America,* 95(6), 3172–3177.

Zdenek, M. (1985). *The Right-Brain Experience.* New York: McGraw-Hill.

Zeskind, P. S., Marshall, T. R., and Goss, D. M. (1992). "Rhythmic Organization of Heart Rate in Breast Fed and Bottle Fed Newborn Infants." *Early Development and Parenting,* 1(2), 79–87.

Zuckerman, M. (1991). *The Psychobiology of Personality.* New York: Cambridge University Press.

Free Resources

The Brain in the News. Published by The Dana Alliance for Brain Initiatives; 1001 G. Street, NW, Suite 1025; Washington, DC 20001. A monthly collection of reprints from U.S. newspapers.

BrainWork: The Neuroscience Newsletter. Published by the Charles A. Dana Foundation; 745 Fifth Avenue, Suite 700; New York, NY 10151. A bimonthly newsletter with feature articles and brief news reports.

Mind-Body Health News. Newsletter of the Mind-Body Health Study Group Network; 444 North Capitol Street, NW, Suite 428; Washington, DC 20001; phone: 202-393-2210.

Resources with a Charge

The Brain Based Education/Learning Styles Networker. $15/year. Publisher: The Institute for Learning and Teaching; CARE; Rockhurst College; 1100 Rockhurst Road; Kansas City, MO 64110; phone: 703-599-9110.

Brain/Mind Bulletin. $45/year. Publisher: Marilyn Ferguson; Box 42211; Los Angeles, CA 90042; phone: 213-223-2500.

Consortium for Whole Brain Learning. $9/year. Publisher: Launa Ellison; 3348 47th Avenue South; Minneapolis, MN 55406.

Mental Medicine Update (The Mind/Body Health Newsletter). $9.95/year. Edited by David Sobel and Robert Ornstein. Published by The Center for Health Sciences; Cambridge, Massachusetts; phone: 800-222-4745.

Internet Resources

Websites

The following list includes every website mentioned in the text of this book, and possibly a few more. Addresses were accurate at the time of writing but may have changed by the time you try them. If they don't work, try a keyword search on the agency of interest and you should be able to get the current website address. Happy surfing!

General

American Academy of Child and Adolescent Psychiatry: www.psych.med.umich.edu/web/aacap

American Psychological Association's PsychNET site: www.apa.org

Brain Lab: www.newhorizons.org/blab.html

Cognitive and Linguistic Sciences Department of Brown University: www.cog.brown.edu/

Cognitive and Psychological Sciences Index (in Europe): dawww.essex.ac.uk/~roehl/PsycIndex

Cognitive and Psychological Sciences Index (in the United States): www-psych.stanford.edu/cogsci/

COGSCI discussion list: www.mailbase.ac.uk/lists/cogsci/

Evolutionary Psychology: A Primer (J. Tooby and L. Cosmides): www.clark.net/pub/ogas/evolution/EVPSYCH primer.htm

Hampshire College cognitive science program (oldest of its kind in North America): www.hampshire.edu/academics/cs/CS.shtml

Healthfinder (government-maintained, with links to over 500 documents and over 550 websites): www.healthfinder.gov

Healthgate (for-pay and free health information): www.healthgate.com

help! A Consumer's Guide to Mental Health Information: www.io.org/madmagic/help/help.html

Internet Mental Health: www.mentalhealth.com

Journal of the American Medical Association: www.ama-assn.org/public/journals/jama

Mediconsult (a "virtual medical clinic"): www.mediconsult.com

Medline medical database: www.nlm.nih.gov

Mental Health InfoSource: www.mhsource.com

Mental Health Library: melhlp.netusa.mntlhlth.htm

Mental Health Net (John Grohol): www.cmhc.com

Multiple intelligence theory (Howard Gardner's theory): education.twsu.edu/faculty/gladhart/mihtml

National Alliance for the Mentally Ill: www.cais.net/vikings/nami

National Institute of Mental Health: gopher.nimh.nih.gov

National Institutes of Health: www.nih.gov

National Mental Health Association: www.worldcorp.com/dc-online/nmha

New England Journal of Medicine: www.nejm.org

Online Psych: www.onlinepsych.com

PSYC SITE: www.unipissing.ca/psyc/info.htm

Psych Central (John Grohol's site with all on-line resources for mental health): www.coil.com/grohol

Scientific American magazine: www.sciam.com

Shape Up America (C. Everett Koop): www2.shapeup.org

Society for Applied Research in Memory and Cognition: www.atkinson.yorku.ca/~sarmac/index.htm

University of Arizona's Interdisciplinary Dialogues on Consciousness: www.consciousness.arizona.edu/dialogs

Virtual Psychology Lab: www.cardiff.ac.uk/uwcc/psych/stevensonwc/vp-lab

Part One: Forming a Foundation

National Center for Biotechnology Information (Human Genome Project information): www.ncbi.nlm.nih.gov

Part Two: Age
Part Three: Wellness

American Council for Drug Education referral service: www.drughelp.org

American Music Therapy Association home page: www.musictherapy.org

Associated Professional Sleep Societies home page: www.apss.org

Baby Center website, featuring Dr. Jodi Mindell's research on infants and sleep: www.babycenter.com/refcap/baby/babysleep/7526.html

Carnegie Corporation early childhood development site (*The Early Brain*): www.carnegie.org

Centers for Disease Control and Prevention, report on survey on vitamin and mineral supplements: www.cdc.gov

Environmental Protection Agency report on passive smoke: www.oehha.org

Humor profile based on Lee Berk's SMILE software: www.touchstarpro.com/smile-software.html

Mozart Effect Resource Center: www.mozarteffect.com

Music and mind site, with a variety of links, including the *International Journal of Arts Medicine* and the Mozart Effect Resource Center: www.mmbmusic.com

Music Intelligence Neural Development project: www.mindinst.org

National Association for Music Therapy home page: www.namt.com

National Clearinghouse for Alcohol and Drug Information, Research and Statistics page: www.health.org/survey.htm

National Council on Alcoholism and Drug Dependence: www.ncadd.com

National Sleep Foundation: www.sleepfoundation.org

National Sleep Foundation site on women and sleep: 206.215.227.10/nsf/publications/women.html

RxLaughter, the five-year study of the effect of laughter on the immune system: www.rxlaughter.org

School Start Time Study, Final Report Summary: www.coled.umn.edu/CAREIwww/General/sstbiblio.htm

Searle healthNet, sleep: www.searlehealthnet.com/sleep/dateline

Staleness and sports psychology information (John Raglin's site): www.indiana.edu/~kines/raglin.htm

USDA Center for Nutrition Policy and Promotion home page: www.usda.gov/fcs/cnpp

Part Four: Illness and Injury

Allied Products' site on EEG neurofeedback and ADHD: www.biof.com/neuroarticles.html

ALS site (Doug Jacobson's site): www.phoenix.net/~jacobson/beatals.html

Alzheimer's Disease: www.alzheimers.com

American Brain Tumor Association: neurosurgery.mgh.harvard.edu/abta/

Anorexia Nervosa and Related Eating Disorders, Inc.: www.anred.com

American Neurological Association neuro-oncology site: www.aneuroa.org/nlinkst97.html

Brain tumor site (Al Musella): www.lanminds.com/local/brain/trial.html

BrainWork: The Neuroscience Newsletter (full text copies): www.dana.org/dana/brainwrk.html

Brookhaven National Laboratories' GVG (gammavinyl-GABA) trials for cocaine addiction: www.pet.bnl.gov

Cerebral palsy site: www.familyinternet.com

Children's learning disabilities: www.ldonline.org

Dana Alliance for Brain Initiatives: www.dana.org

Eating disorders site: www.eating-disorder.com

Epilepsy Foundation of America: www.efa.org/index/htm

Huntington's disease site: www.interlog.com/~rlaycock/what.html

International Federation for Multiple Sclerosis: www.ifmss.org.uk/

Mental retardation site: www.healthanswers.com/database/ami/converted/001523.html

National Alliance for Research on Schizophrenia and Depression: www.mhsource.com/narsad.html

National Institute of Mental Health site on anxiety disorders: www.nimh.nih.gov/anxiety

National Institute of Neural Disorders and Stroke: www.ninds.nih.gov/healinfo/disorder

Obsessive-compulsive disorder site: www.ocdresource.com

Paralysis site for information and support: neurosurgery.mgh.harvard.edu/paral-r.htm

Parkinson's disease: www.santel.lu/SANTEL/diseases/parkins.html

Scientific Learning Principles, company with CD-ROM for working with dyslexia (Paula Tallal and Michael Merzenich's site): www.scilearn.com

Secret Language of Eating Disorders (Peggy Claude-Pierre): www.randomhouse.com

Trauma and Abuse Support Forum by OurPlace: ourworld.compuserve.com/homepages/Arael_Et_Al/TRMA-RX.htm

Traumatic brain injury site: www.tbidoc.com

U.S. Office of Disease Prevention and Health Promotion: www.healthfinder.gov

University of Alabama–Birmingham's "Comprehensive Stroke Center": www.uab.edu/neurol/stroke.htm

University of Washington's neuro-oncology site: weber.u.washington.edu/~chudler/disorders.html

Part Five: Being in Control

Bar-On Emotional Quotient Inventory (EQ-i), published by Multi-Health Systems Inc.: www.mhs.com

Executive EQ instrument (Salovey and Mayer): www.virtent.com/ei

Wounded Healer Journal: www.twhj.com

Part Six: Individual Differences

Big Five information: www.centacs.com

Center for Applied Cognitive Studies: www.centacs.com

New Horizons site on Gardner and multiple intelligences: www.newhorizons.org/trm_gardner.html

Part Seven: Learning

Critical Thinking presentation: www.centacs.com

Gifted Resources home page: www.eskimo.com/~user/kids.html

H & H Publishing Company's LASSI site: www.hhpublishing.com

Learning Styles site: www.geocities.com/CollegePark/Library/3543/learnstyle.html

Plain English law information (U.K.): www.wordcentre.co.uk

Plain English law information (U.S.): www.plainlanguage.gov

Part Eight: Creativity and Problem Solving

Brain Store (Eric and Diane Jensen's site): www.thebrainstore.com

Computer Assisted Qualitative Data Analysis Software site (Inspiration plus links to other tools and sites): www.soc.surrey.ac.uk/cagdas

de Bono site: www.edwdebono.com

Decision Explorer software: www.banxia.com

Part Nine: Working Smarter

Families and Work Institute *1997 National Study of the Changing Workforce:* www.familiesandwork.org

John D. and Catherine MacArthur Research on Network Socioeconomic Status and Health: www.macses.ucsf.edu/Research/Allostatic/notebook/allostatic.html.

Mediappraise online 360° feedback: www.workscape.com

Paradigm Mastery videotapes by StarThrower: www.starthrower.com

Thin Book Publishing Company (Sue Hammond): www.thinbook.com

Vita-Lite: www.backbenimble.com/office/vitalite.htm

Part Ten: Schemas, Reality, and Spirituality

allCLEAR 4.5 flowcharting software: www.clearsoft.com

Critical Thinking Presentation: www.centacs.com

Decide Right 1.2 for Windows 95: www.avantos.com

Institute for Professional Education problem-solving seminars: www.theIPE.com

Laban symbol system, software for notating movement: www.dance.ohio-state.edu/files/LabanWriter/index.html

Mind map software: www.mindman.com

STELLA system process flow software: www.hps-inc.com

SureFire Decisions for Windows 95, decision matrix: www.beaconrock.com

E-Mail Addresses

Ruediger Oehlmann (COGSCI editor, European address): oehlmann@essex.ac.uk

Ruediger Oehlmann (COGSCI editor, U.S. address): oehlmann@psych.stanford.edu

Newsgroups and Bulletin Boards

alt.bio.minority	alt.support.diet	comp.ai
alt.brain	alt.support.eating-disord	comp.ai.fuzzy
alt.drugs.caffeine	alt.support.epilepsy	comp.ai.genetic
alt.education.research	alt.support.ex-cult	comp.ai.neural-nets
alt.fan.hofstadter	alt.support.grief	comp.ai.philosophy
alt.handed	alt.support.learning-disab	comp.ai.vision
alt.human-brain	alt.support.menopause	misc.creativity
alt.left	alt.support.shyness	rec.org.mensa
alt.lefthanders	alt.support.sleep-disorder	sci.anthropology
alt.psychology.personality	alt.support.stuttering	sci.cognitive
alt.recovery.aa	bionet.neuroscience	sci.med.psychobiology
alt.support.attn-deficit	cbiz.ergonomic-sciences	sci.psychology.research
alt.support.cerebral-palsy	clari.news.aging	uw.neural-nets
alt.support.depression	clari.tw.health	
alt.support.dev-delays	clari.tw.science	

Listservers

Name	Address to Subscribe	Message
Cognitive Science	mailbase@mailbase.ac.uk	join COGSCI <firstname lastname>
de Bono	LISTSERV@SJUVM.STJOHNS.EDU	Subscribe DEBONO <firstname lastname>
Depression Forum	mailbase@mailbase.ac.uk	join depression <firstname lastname>
Tacit Knowledge	listproc@scu.edu.au	subscribe tacit-l <your E-mail address>

The Office of the Surgeon General of the U.S. Department of Health and Human Services maintains a website with abundant, up-to-date information on every physical and mental health topic imaginable, including links to other sites with even more in-depth information on specific health topics: www.surgeongeneral.gov

PubMed medical science database (with access to Medline): www.ncbi.nim.nih.gov/PubMed

Daniel Dennett's website with interesting materials related to the study of consciousness: ase.tufts.edu/cogstud/

Brain.com is a wide variety of resources on the general subject of the brain, from disorders to interesting facts; includes subscription to a free newsletter: www.brain.com

Center for Applied Research and Educational Improvement (CAREI) at the University of Minnesota (school-start time research is here): carei.coled.umn.edu

Community-based work centers (as well as their complete mission and activities) described at the Congress for the New Urbanism website: www.cnu.org

Neuroimaging of personality disorders is the special focus of The Mind Institute: www.themindinstitute.com

The James S. McDonnell Foundation in St. Louis, Missouri, sponsors research aimed at improving quality of life. Find out more at www.jsmf.org

Other Resources

National Public Radio: "What's On Your Mind?" Hosted by Dr. Linda Austin, M.D., on staff at the Eastern Maine Medical Center: "The anthropology of everyday life"

Index

Reader Participation Card

The Center for Applied Cognitive Studies continually scans the research literature to find new topics with practical applications. We plan to publish an updated edition of *The Owner's Manual for the Brain* every several years. If you know of topics you would like to see included in the next edition, or if you know of an application idea for one of the topics included in this edition, please list them below and mail or fax them to us for possible inclusion in the next edition. Of course, we will credit you as the contributor. Items that you send in may also be printed in our quarterly newsletter.

Topics I'd like to see included in the next edition:

_____

_____

_____

_____

Application ideas for topics in this edition:

Topic number _____ : _____

Topic number _____ : _____

Topic number _____ : _____

Topic number _____ : _____

Topic number _____ : _____

Other comments: _____

_____

Fax to 704-331-9408, send to e-mail address pjhoward@centacs.com, or send by regular mail to *Cent*ACS, 1100 Harding Place, Charlotte, NC 28204-2825.

Submitted by:

Name _____

Street address _____

City _____ State/Province_____ Country _____ Zip _____

Phone: Work ( )____-_____ Fax ( )____-_____ Home ( )____-_____

E-mail address _____

About
*Cent*ACS

The Center for Applied Cognitive Studies

The Center for Applied Cognitive Studies is a research-and-dissemination firm, headquartered in Charlotte, North Carolina, that is dedicated to providing assistance to clients in developing their people with the most current information on how the mind learns and performs.

The primary focus of *Cent*ACS is on the Five-Factor Model of personality, also known as the "Big Five." It provides certification programs for human resource professionals in the Big Five, plus specialized application workshops in which participants spend a day exploring how to apply the Big Five in a wide variety of human resource practices:

- Selection and validity studies

- Coaching and counseling

- Leadership development

- Team development

- Career development

- Partnership development

- Sales training

*Cent*ACS has trained thousands of professionals in the use of the Big Five. It now has business partners in Mexico, Brazil, Holland, England, France, Germany, Spain, Singapore, Indonesia, and Malaysia. This international cadre of master trainers provides Big Five certification training around the world.

In addition to Big Five certification, support, and annual learning conferences, *Cent*ACS offers a variety of presentations based on current brain research. Within the last several years, it has presented to educators in Canadian British Columbia and Arizona, to psychologists in Holland and Mexico, and to human resource professionals in Washington, D.C.; San Francisco; Atlanta; and Holland. Several excerpts from these presentations and a variety of informational material are available on the *Cent*ACS website, www.centacs.com.